The Bible Application Handbook

The Bible Application Handbook

Derek Williams
Dr J.I. Packer
Consultant Editor

Eagle
Guildford, Surrey

Photographic credits

The Image Bank, London, have supplied the majority of images used throughout this book. All other sources are listed below. The publisher wishes to thank them for their permission as follows:

Jon Arnold: pp 6-7, 37, 41, 46, 47, 60, 68, 88-89, 90, 91, 95, 106, 116, 128, 162-163, 170, 183, 200, 211, 218-219, 232, 242-243, 270-271, 294, 318, 320, 325, 334, 356-357, 374-375, 404, 406-407.

The Daily Telegraph Photographic Library: pp 113, 156, 168-169, 230-231, 252-253.

Eagle Publishing: pp 12, 13, 29, 50, 52-53, 80, 84, 112, 114-115, 156, 184-185, 194, 236, 258, 321, 327, 346, 361, 365, 370-371, 389, 401, 408.

Ronald Grant Archive: pp 48-49, 62, 64, 120-121, 128-129, 146-147, 224-225, 240, 285, 300-301, 329.

Sally Maltby: pp 36, 107, 241, 286, 397.

The Tate Gallery: pp 126-127,

Archive material: pp 8, 11, 14-15, 22, 25, 27, 31, 34, 38-39, 40, 44-45, 56-57, 66-67, 69, 70, 76, 78, 81, 82, 86-87, 102-103, 111, 118, 132, 134-135, 137, 141, 142, 143, 144-145, 146, 153, 166, 174, 175, 188-189, 190, 196-197, 212, 224, 226-227, 234, 234-235, 237, 261, 266, 268, 269, 290-291, 295, 296, 304-305, 316, 317, 318, 319, 328, 334-335, 347, 350-351, 353, 362, 368-369, 372-373, 379, 383, 396-397.

British Library Cataloguing in Publication Data. A catalogue record for this book is available from the British Library.

Published by Eagle, an imprint of Inter Publishing Service (IPS) Ltd,
PO Box 530, Guildford, Surrey GU2 5FH.

Typeset by Eagle Publishing

Page layout and design by Roger Judd

Printed in Indonesia

ISBN No: 0 86347 300 8

CONTENTS

Introduction
How to use this handbook

The Bible is a powerful book. It has influenced the lives of countless millions of people and through them has had a profound impact on the course of history and the shape of society for 2,000 years.

This book aims to open up the meaning and significance of the Bible for life today, using short articles and information boxes. It is intended especially for people who are relatively new to the Bible or others who want a practical guide to a passage they are reading.

It is arranged in alphabetical order of Bible books, rather than in Bible book order, for easy access. On the first spread for each Bible book you will find a short outline of the book and a brief summary of its message. Then over the next few pages its main themes or events are explained. Rather than retelling stories, we have asked 'What is being taught here and how may we apply it?' And rather than working verse by verse through passages, we have summarised the themes which emerge from them and asked, 'What are the main principles for life and belief here?'

Many parts of the Bible raise 'hard questions', perhaps concerning a peculiar event (such as Balaam's donkey talking to its rider) or an obscure piece of teaching (such as Paul's concept of 'the Man of

Lawlessness'). Where appropriate we have included a separate article to try to unravel in a simple way these often complex issues.

You will also find 'Where am I?' boxes which briefly locate the book in its biblical, historical and geographical setting. 'Fast fact' boxes summarise important background information about each book; further background information is put into separate boxes when appropriate. We do not spend long on academic questions and scholarly debates; our intention is primarily to unravel the Bible's meaning. But we do recognise that the meaning depends on our understanding of the origins of the text and the background of the writer and his subjects.

Each Bible book also has a 'cross-check' box so that you can follow up the themes elsewhere, and a concluding summary 'This book for today' which picks out the main applications for Christian living. Full Bible references are given throughout, and there is also a thematic index at the end.

In addition to the articles on each book of the Bible, there are also some feature pages which look at some themes in more detail. Most, but not all, are included in the introductory section. These either relate to how we approach the Bible (such as 'How to interpret different kinds of Bible writing') or to major doctrines (such as the return of Christ) which can only be understood when many passages are considered together.

This book is therefore a cross between a commentary and a Bible dictionary. It's companion volume *The Bible Chronicle*, which the story of the Bible in news magazine format and is written in chronological rather than Bible-book order for readers who want an overview of the narrative which spans numerous Bible books.

All Bible quotations are taken from the New International Version, unless otherwise stated. Readers are assumed to have a Bible to hand as they use this volume, something which was not necessary with *The Bible Chronicle*.

How to approach the Bible

The Bible has been called the world's best seller. At the end of the twentieth century the whole or part of the Bible had been translated into some 2,500 languages catering for almost 90 per cent of the world's population. (That still leaves some 4,000 mostly tribal languages with no part of the Bible available.)

Thousands of books have been written explaining it, and some condemning it. Despite the many versions in the English language (which are mostly produced for a specific readership and which have minor differences of nuance and emphasis through the vocabulary they use) it is not easy to get into. It is compiled in neither a chronological nor a strictly thematic order, and much of its teaching is to be deduced from historical narrative and poetic symbolism, rather than being given directly by its authors.

What the Bible is

- It consists of the Old and the New Testaments, with a total of 66 books written or originated by at least 40 different authors over a period of at least 1,500 years.
- It tells the story of the tribe of Israelites through whom God chose to reveal his character and purposes to the world.
- It shows how the Messiah, Jesus Christ, descended from the Israelites, fulfilled their God-taught expectations and founded the Christian church.
- It reveals truth about God, the world and humankind through a variety of literary genres so that readers can know God personally, serve him and live as he desires.

Different ways to read the Bible

We need to know how it fits together, so in this introductory section you will find an outline of the overall story to which each Bible book relates. All the Bible books meant something at the time they were written, so locating each one in a specific set of life-events helps us to understand what is going on. The companion volume, *The Bible Chronicle* does this in greater depth.

Most Bible reading plans and aids suggest reading small portions regularly. That is because it is a book to meditate on; it releases its wisdom and truth slowly. We need to come to it with open hearts and minds, ready to learn truths which may shock or challenge our lifestyles and our previous beliefs.

However, it is also helpful to read whole Bible books quickly in order to gain an overview of them. But whichever you happen to do at any given time, you will only glean God's truth from it if you ask the following questions as you read:

- What did this passage mean to the people who were its first intended readers?
- What timeless truths or principles about God, the world, human behaviour, etc. are embodied within it?
- What warnings, encouragements or commands are given?
- How might we translate biblical truths and principles into our different cultural world of today? (We are to measure our culture against the abiding principles of Scripture, not change those principles to fit our culture or contemporary ideologies.)
- How can we apply this teaching in practice day by day? (This may include our worship of and relationship with God personally, our attitudes towards others, and the way we live and act.)

And before you read, use the prayer which Eli the priest taught the boy Samuel: 'Speak, Lord, for your servant is listening' (1 Samuel 3:9,10). We will discover God himself through our reading of the Bible if we really want to, and if we are prepared to act on what we read whatever the cost may be to our pride and prejudice. If we do that, our lives will be challenged, changed, and enriched.

How to interpret the Bible

In order to glean what a passage means and how to apply it, we need to ask of it the following questions:

What sort of literature is it?

(History, law, teaching, poetry, letter, prophecy, parable.) It is wrong to interpret one sort as if it were another; poetry, for instance, is not meant to be read as prose.

What did the author intend to convey to his first readers? This will help us to glean the basic message.

What timeless truths are enshrined in the passage: about God, human nature, worship, etc?

If it is poetry (and some prophecy is also poetry), what was the natural meaning of the symbols in the author's historical context?

If it is prophecy, what social, political or religious situation did it refer to at the time?

This will show us the primary meaning; there may be 'spiritual' applications but these are secondary. For example, when Isaiah writes 'In repentance and rest is your salvation, in quietness and trust is your strength' (30:15) he is referring to a political situation in which the Israelite leadership was seeking military help from Egypt against the Assyrian invaders. Any application of these famous words today needs to take that into account and look for 'dynamic equivalent' situations rather than turn the statement into a blanket call to 'trust God and it'll be OK'.

What other Bible teaching can we compare this to?

The Bible does not contradict itself, and passages should be interpreted by other passages on the same or similar themes. We then avoid putting more theological weight on a passage than it can reasonably bear.

Some passages are hard to categorise and therefore hard to interpret. The early chapters of Genesis are a classic example. In such cases, we should look first for the timeless truths: what do we learn about God and people? The details then become secondary issues over which we can agree to differ while maintaining fellowship on the basic truths. In this case, what is basic is that God is the creator of all that exists, and humankind is endowed with the unique dignity of being made in his image.

How the Bible is 'inspired'

Christians often refer to the Bible as 'the word of God'. This is an accurate but potentially misleading term. It is not intended to imply that God dictated his 'word' to robotic scribes, nor that everything in it is literally true. There are stories which are intentionally fictitious (to make a point), such as Jesus' parables. And there is poetic symbolism used by prophets and psalmists to describe God's truth in figurative word-pictures: 'the mountains skipped like lambs' (Psalm 114:4–6).

Nor does 'inspiration' imply that every passage holds a specific message for me, today. Certainly regular reading can provide us with a 'thought for the day', but the gems scattered on the surface are but a fragment of the Bible's riches which are to be mined from its depths. It should not be treated like a horoscope.

Indeed, at first some parts seem to be completely irrelevant for today. However, instructions to the ancient Israelites about their religious sacrifices and dietary habits, for example, embody important truths about God and how we should approach him. In that sense, they are just as 'inspired' as Jesus' teaching, but they may not be quite so 'inspiring' until we grasp their wider implications.

The word 'inspired' is used by Paul in 2 Timothy 3:16 and literally means that Scripture was 'breathed out' (expired!) by God. 2 Peter 1:21 says something similar; authors were 'moved' or 'carried along' by God's Spirit. Not all authors were conscious of God telling them what to write (Moses and the ten commandments is a case of this, however, as is the bulk of the prophets recording sermons which were God's 'word' to a specific historical situation, person or group).

Much of the Bible is historical narrative which some authors acknowledge they compiled from a variety of sources. God's inspiration is in the selection of material and the specific truths which it highlights. 'Guidance' would be a better word, its effect seen after the event rather than during it. So for example, the overlap and repetition of stories in 2 Kings and 2 Chronicles (and in the Gospels) reflects specific authors' interests and perspectives. Together, they give different angles on the same events which under God give us a fuller understanding.

Belief in the inspiration of Scripture means that the books we have:

- tell us what God wants us to know about him (theology) and how to live for him (service and worship);
- are reliable and accurate in their teaching, and complement each other even when they differ in emphasis;
- are sufficient to lead us to a full knowledge of God through Jesus Christ.

The Old Testament story: *what happened, and when*

Prehistory

(not precisely dateable)
The first ten and a half chapters of Genesis act as a preface to the whole Bible story. They set out a pattern of events which is repeated frequently: God is the supreme Creator and Lord; humankind is made in his image to worship him but rejects his Lordship; God is patient with them, but finally shows his justice and Lordship by bringing their civilisation to an end.

However, he saves a remnant (Noah and his family) who begin a new community called to honour and serve him.

(Genesis 1–11:9)

The Patriarchs

(2000–1600 BC)
At a time when many peoples were migrating across the Near East, Abraham (a semi-nomad) moved from Babylonia to Haran (northern Syria) and then was led by God into Canaan, a land promised to his descendants.

When the childless Abraham was old his faith was vindicated and Isaac was born. From Isaac came Jacob, the trickster, who in turn fathered the founders of the twelve tribes of Israel. One of them, Joseph, was sold into slavery in Egypt. The rest of the family followed during a famine, and their descendants were enslaved.

(Genesis 11:10–50:26)

The exodus

(1300–1200 BC)
Moses was one of many Hebrew children threatened with death by a genocidal Egyptian king, but was rescued by the king's daughter and educated at the court. He murdered an Egyptian and fled to Midian. In old age God called him to rescue the Hebrews. After God had sent a series of signs (plagues) to an obstinate king, the Hebrews escaped into the Arabian desert.

Because of their lack of trust in God, they were sentenced to die there, but their children would enter the 'promised land'. During the next 40 years, the Israelites' religious and social practices were established.

(Exodus; Leviticus; Numbers; Deuteronomy)

Settlement in Canaan

(1200–1050 BC)

Under the leadership of Joshua the Israelites entered Canaan from the east across the Jordan. Slowly they spread, each tribe assisting the others in the conquest while also settling into the area Moses had allocated to each one. They were a confederation of tribes rather than a united nation, led by tribal elders and 'judges' who had both religious and social roles.

Then came a cycle of apostasies leading into pagan oppression. Each time one of the judges took on a national role, calling people to repentance and leading a combined army to victory.

(Joshua, Judges, Ruth)

The first kings

(1050–930 BC)

Frustrated by this ad hoc form of government, and afraid of continuing repression, tribal elders petitioned the outstanding judge Samuel for a permanent king. Interpreting it as the ultimate rejection of God as King, Samuel acceded to the request after warning them of the likely consequences. Saul was crowned, but he was unfaithful to God.

In his place came David, who (despite his own failures) became the epitome of a godly ruler. Through his leadership the Israelites secured their borders. Solomon his son brought in an unprecedented and unrepeated 'golden age' of peace and prosperity, erecting the temple and many public buildings and establishing major trade and political alliances. He did so, however, at the cost of heavy taxation and some religious compromise.

(1 & 2 Samuel, 1 Kings, 1 Chronicles)

The divided kingdom: Israel's fall

(930–722 BC)

After Solomon's death, his son Rehoboam was asked to lighten the people's load. He refused, and the kingdom split. The ten northern tribes seceded under the leadership of Jeroboam and from then on were known as Israel, ultimately with a capital at Samaria. The two southern tribes accepted Rehoboam and were from then on known as Judah.

The story then became one of steady religious decline and a running battle between kings and prophets. The record of 1 & 2 Kings flits between the two nations, that of 2 Chronicles focuses mostly on Judah. Israel's story was largely one of unmitigated polytheism and social evil, flouting Israelite law and customs.

The Assyrians, now the chief world power, harassed and eventually destroyed Samaria in 722 BC, deporting many of its inhabitants and replacing them with refugees from other areas. Israel ceased to exist from then on. Bible writers attribute the destruction to God's judgment for Israel's apostasy.

(1 & 2 Kings, 2 Chronicles, Amos, Hosea, Isaiah, Jonah, Micah)

The fall of Judah

(722–587 BC)

The decline was less rapid in the south, but the Assyrians harassed Jerusalem also in the time of King Hezekiah (and Isaiah). Judah, however, had some godly kings including Hezekiah and Josiah who reformed the temple worship (in Jeremiah's time).

When the Babylonian king Nebuchadnezzar took over the former Assyrian empire, most people in Jerusalem assumed they would be safe. Not so, said Jeremiah, warning them that the same fate as befell Israel would be theirs also, and for the same reasons. After several attacks beginning in 605, and a three- month siege, Jerusalem was finally destroyed in 587 and many people were deported to Babylon.

(2 Kings, 2 Chronicles, Habakkuk, Isaiah, Jeremiah, Lamentations, Nahum, Zephaniah)

The exile

(587–537 BC)

Jeremiah had warned the Judeans that they would be in exile for 70 years; they were, if the first (small) deportation in 605 is counted. He encouraged the people to settle there. Among the exiles were Daniel and Ezekiel.

During this period the foundations were laid for the religion we meet in the New Testament: the synagogue movement, and the rise of the scribes as (lay) teachers of the Law of Moses. The existing Old Testament may also have been edited into more of the form in which we know it during this time.

(Daniel, Ezekiel, Jeremiah, Obadiah)

The restoration

(537–440 BC)

The Babylonian empire was short-lived and the nearby Persians took over. One of the first acts of Cyrus was to grant an amnesty to all political prisoners. The Jews were allowed to return home, along with their temple treasures. There were high hopes for national revival with the first return in 537 but the desolation of Jerusalem and local opposition to the immigrants caused the temple rebuilding to cease.

After about 15 years it was restarted again under the inspiration of prophets Haggai and Zechariah, and was completed in 516. In 458 other Jews returned from Babylon including Ezra who was sent to enforce Jewish religious and cultural practice. In 445 Nehemiah, a Persian civil servant, heard the walls were not yet restored, and he returned and despite opposition refortified the city. At this point, the Old Testament record closes.

(Esther, Ezra, Daniel, Haggai, Malachi, Nehemiah, Zechariah)

HARD Question

What was God doing all this time?

The question why it took so long, and why the process was so tortuous, to get from Abraham's call to the coming of Christ, is one which puzzles many Christians. It gives rise to other hard questions, such as the purpose of blood sacrifices and the slaughter of innocent people by the Israelites, which we will deal with as they arise throughout this book.

We can begin to see that an explanation is possible (although ultimately it is hidden in the mystery of God himself) by thinking about what we know of God as revealed through both Testaments.

- His character is unchanging. He is both a God of love and a God of justice, and a God of wisdom and faithfulness.
- His purposes are eternal; they cover the whole sweep of history. The biblical concept of time and history is of a straight line moving from a specific beginning towards a definite climax. It is not an endlessly repeating cycle of events. In Scripture that climax is the new creation: the forming and perfecting of a renewed holy people, called the church, and the renovating of this whole disordered cosmos around his perfected people.
- God is never in a hurry.(Abraham and Moses waited decades for their calls to be fulfilled!)
- He takes people as they are. He changes them slowly, without violating their personalities, and works within the limitations of their culture and circumstances. (Are you perfect yet?) This is also true of people-groups, which develop very slowly indeed.
- The principle of starting where people are is seen supremely in the 'incarnation' of Jesus, when God the Son took on all the limitations of human life; he came alongside us to help. The incarnation also shows that sometimes God does step in to effect a major change.

Outline of Old Testament themes

Each one can be seen repeated on many occasions, but this simple outline also shows the overall purpose of God through history.

BIBLE BOOKS	PERIOD	MAIN THEMES
Early Genesis	Dawn of time	God creates
Genesis	The Patriarchs	God calls
Exodus–Deuteronomy	The exodus	God leads
Joshua–Ruth	Settlement in Canaan	God conquers
1/2 Samuel, 1 Kgs, 1 Chron	The first kings	God rules
2 Kings, 2 Chron, Prophets	The divided kingdom	God warns
2 Chron, Prophets	Fall of Judah	God judges
Jeremiah, Isaiah Ezekiel, Daniel	The exile	God cares
Ezra–Esther, Prophets	The restoration	God restores

- His sovereign purposes include working through 'secular' events and people to achieve his goals.

We need also to recognise three things about the authors of Scripture.

1 The Old Testament is not written from a New Testament (or later) world-view. We cannot blame the authors for not understanding what we understand; it had not been revealed to them.

2 The whole world in Old Testament times was highly religious. The gods were seen as fully involved in every detail of human life, and needing to be consulted or appeased constantly. It was against this background that God disclosed his distinctiveness to the recipients of his revelation.

3 The biblical way of thinking is very 'Eastern' and ours is very 'Western'. The Bible writers did not live in a world of abstract ideas but in a very earthy, black and white world of specific cause and effect. (Hence the Old Testament has a very hazy notion of life after death because it is not 'concrete' within that system.)

If we put these things together, we can begin to appreciate the possibility that in the Old Testament story God was working slowly with and through an imperfect group of people. They were conditioned by their culture to think of him in certain ways. So he revealed himself and his purposes in terms which they, at that time, could understand and respond to, while at the same time leading them slowly on towards a better and fuller knowledge of him and his purposes.

The question as to why God chose this way and not some other must wait until we get to heaven!

Consistent teaching from start to end

Perhaps the most remarkable thing about the Bible – and one which encourages Christians to accept that it is God's inspired word – is that despite the progressive revelation of God through the centuries, there is also a clear consistency in that revelation across the centuries.

For example, God appears on the surface to be seen as a stern judge in the early books of the Bible, and as a caring father in the teaching of Jesus. However, there are glimpses of God's love and patience right from the beginning. He expresses his love and compassion directly, and he waits patiently and coaxes people back to himself. When the time of judgment comes he still saves a remnant of people to continue with his purposes.

In the New Testament, Jesus' teaching is not all sweetness and light. He spent time teaching about hell and he warned constantly that God would judge those who self-righteously thought they knew better than Jesus. His teaching about God's love in fact appears in the context of a God who is also a judge.

What has happened is not that there has been a totally new revelation, but a new series of insights have been given on eternal truths. The progression of revelation has been to open up more clearly what was already there, and to set each aspect of God's character and purposes more firmly in the context of all the others.

When the time had fully come, God sent his Son, born of a woman, born under law, to redeem those under law, that we might receive adoption as God's children. Because you are his children, he sent the Spirit of his Son into our hearts, the Spirit who calls out, 'Abba, Father.'

Galatians 4:4–6

The covenant: *God's compact with his people*

The Bible has one consistent concern: how can people know God and have a right relationship with him? Central to that concern is the idea of 'the covenant', which lies behind both Old and New Testaments.

A covenant is an agreement between two people, with conditions attached to it. Biblical covenants are initiated by God and agreed to by his people who could not amend or alter the terms. There are three major covenants in the Bible.

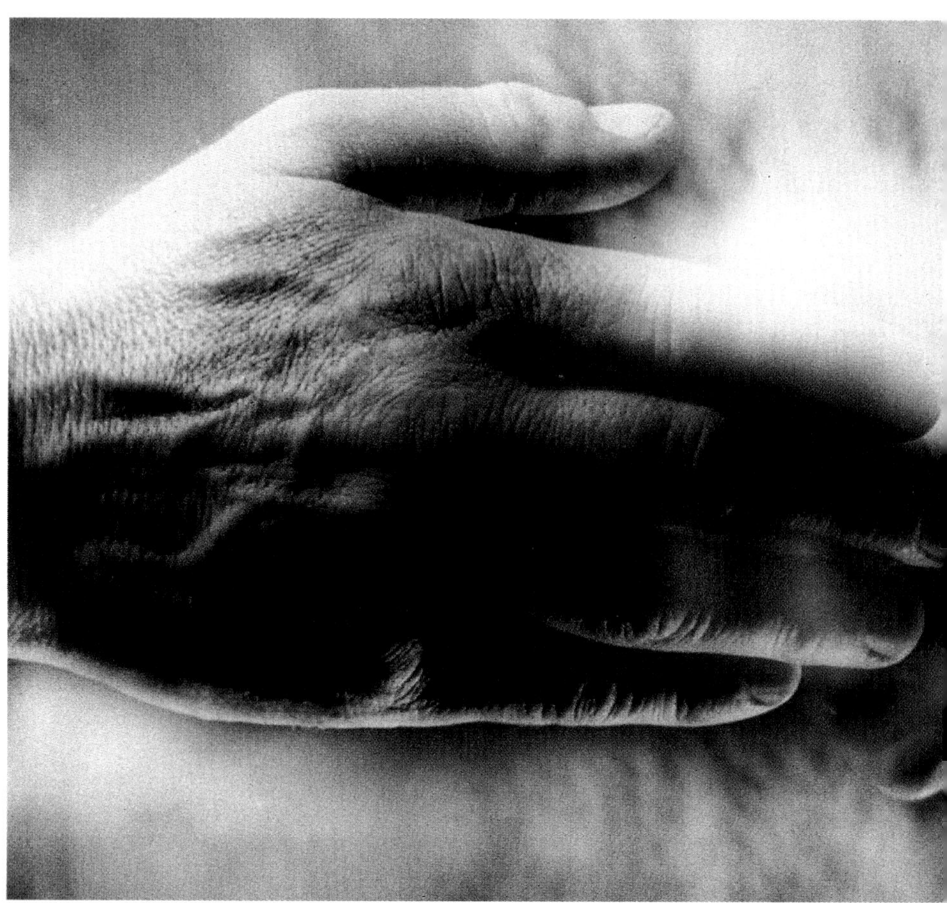

The covenant with Abraham

(Genesis 15, 17)

God promised that he would make a great nation from Abraham's descendants, and that he would give them the land of Canaan as their home.

When the promise was first made, Abraham consented to it by watching a supernatural 'ratification ceremony' (ch. 15). Later, he and his household were circumcised as a pledge that they accepted the terms and conditions of the covenant and would serve God alone.

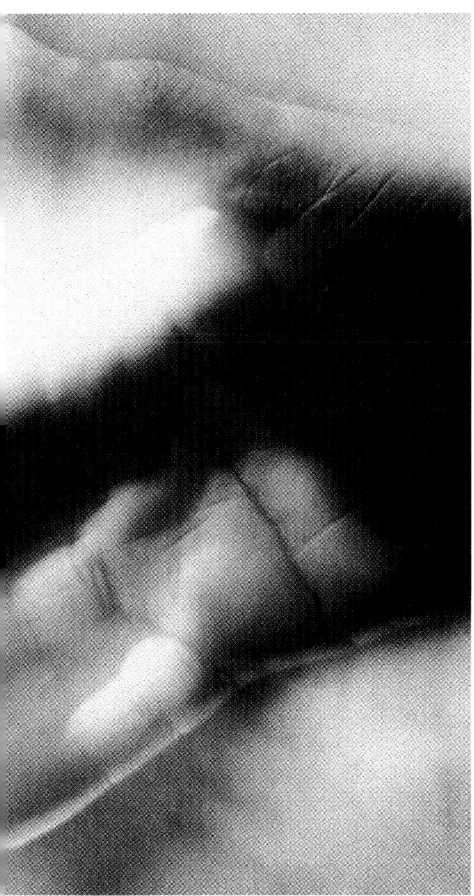

The covenant with Israel at Sinai

(Exodus 24)

The covenant with Jacob's descendants built on the one made with Abraham and looked forward to the new one made through Christ. The terms and conditions were set out in the ten commandments and other laws, which Moses read out and which the people affirmed (v. 3).

It was ratified by a ceremony which included setting up pillars (v. 4) as a memorial, and animal sacrifice (vv. 5–8). The shedding of blood indicated the seriousness of the agreement and was a sign of God's loving forgiveness.

The new covenant

(Matthew 26:28)

The terms and conditions of this covenant are that we accept by faith the offer of forgiveness through the atoning blood of Christ, and thereafter seek to live wholeheartedly for him. Hebrews 13:20 speaks of 'the blood of the eternal covenant', indicating that Christ's death implemented God's eternal purposes for his people.

The prophets looked forward to it as the start of a new era in which God would write his laws on his people's hearts so that they would be re-created to serve him. (Jeremiah 31:1, 31–34).

The New Testament, written from a Jewish context, sees 'the last supper' as a 'covenant meal'. In it, the terms of the covenant and the event which sealed it (the death of Jesus) are recalled. The apostles saw in Jesus' death a strong parallel between his shed blood and that which ratified the covenant with Israel at Sinai. Through his death, the curse of the old covenant was removed.

Other biblical covenant events

God made a covenant with Noah (Genesis 6:18; 9:8–17 promising never to destroy the earth completely by water again. The sign (or reminder) of it was to be the rainbow.

He also made (or renewed) his covenant with David (2 Samuel 7). The promise here links the Abraham and Moses covenants and looks forward to the new covenant; the 'line of David' will continue to lead God's people.

There are a number of re-affirmations of the covenant throughout the history of Israel. The most significant are when the Israelites crossed into Canaan (Joshua 24), and after the exiles had returned to Jerusalem and had become aware of their sins (Nehemiah 9).

When the 'book of the law' was rediscovered in the temple king Josiah was dismayed at how largely the Israelites had broken it. The covenant was renewed again in a solemn ceremony as the people turned back once again to God.(2 Kings 22–23)

Covenants in the ancient world

Israel was not unique in having covenants of some kind and many others are recorded in the Old Testament which are political treaties or business arrangements. For example, there are covenants between individuals (Genesis 21:27); tribes (1 Samuel 11:1); kings (1 Kings 20:34); and husband and wife (Malachi 2:14).

No other tribes had such a nagreement with a god, however. Yet the form of the covenant in Exodus is very similar to that of political treaties used by the Hittites. These followed a strict six-point pattern:

- Initiator's preamble
- Historical reasons for the treaty
- The terms and conditions
- How the treaty is to be recorded and remembered
- List of witnesses
- Consequences of keeping or breaking the treaty.

Although there is no reason to suppose that Moses composed a copy of an existing system, the parallels suggest that the Old Testament covenant pattern would not have been a complete novelty to the people. God was dealing with them in terms already familiar to them.

The abiding value of the covenant

Both old and new covenant relationships provide deep assurance for God's people:

- They know where they stand with God: he has pledged himself to them and he cannot go back on his word.
- They do not have to earn God's love and so are freed from uncertainty and fear.
- They know exactly how God requires them to behave.
- They have the confidence that God has selected (or 'elected') them to be a special group with a special purpose.
- They know that they cannot blame God if things go wrong when they break the covenant.
- They have the reassurance that God has built into the covenant a means by which they can be forgiven and make a fresh start.

A rather crude sign?

Abraham is told to circumcise his household as a sign that he accepts the covenant, and the sign is to be performed ever after on his descendants (Genesis 17:10). Male circumcision was common in the ancient world and the Philistines were thought barbaric because they did not practise it!

The Bible sees it as a sign of God's grace to his people, rather than a sign of their commitment to him, although that is also included as a secondary meaning and stresses the cost which discipleship incurs. The Jew carried a physical reminder that he had a special relationship with God.

Jeremiah reminded his hearers that their real calling was to 'inner circumcision'; in other words, God wanted them to live as the people of God, and not just carry the mark of being the people of God. Paul makes the same point in Romans 2:25–29 and Galatians 6:12–15.

Why circumcision was chosen is never stated in the Bible. Perhaps like the sign of the rainbow in Genesis 9, it is simply that God gives something familiar a special meaning. Throughout Scripture God makes the ordinary extraordinary.

The New Testament story: *what happened and when*

Between the Testaments

(c.400–4 BC)

After the book of Malachi, there is a gap of some 400 years in the biblical record. In this time most of the Apocryphal books were produced (see separate article). The Old Testament was formed into its present shape and translated into Greek (a version known as the Septuagint because it was translated by 70 Jewish scholars).

The Persian empire was replaced by the Greeks. During the mid-second century BC a Greek leader Antiochus Epiphanes invaded Judah and desecrated the Temple in Jerusalem by sacrificing a pig on the altar. Shortly afterwards, the Maccabean revolt broke out, in which the Jews succeeded in restoring their own independence. These events seem to be foreshadowed by some prophecies in the Book of Daniel.

The Greek empire declined, however, as Roman influence grew. In 63 BC the Roman General Pompey entered Jerusalem and the Roman occupation of Judea began which forms the political backdrop to the New Testament. The Romans and Jews lived in uneasy tension. The Jews enjoyed a measure of independence but generally resented the occupying soldiers and the tax demands.

The life of Christ

(c. 4 BC–AD 30)

Born into an ordinary (and for a while, a displaced and refugee) family, Jesus of Nazareth grew up as a carpenter. He began his public ministry without formal training when he was aged about 30. He gathered a band of twelve disciples together, who he trained to extend his mission.

His ministry lasted only for about three years during which he became famous as a teacher who stressed the caring fatherhood of God and who backed his teaching by miracles of compassion in which people were healed or fed. The crowds loved his homely stories (parables) which wrapped spiritual truths in everyday language.

He attracted hostility from the religious leadership of the day, however, and was betrayed by one of his own disciples. He was convicted of blasphemy by a Jewish court and of treason by the Roman governor Pontius Pilate, and was crucified. He rose from the dead after three days and for six weeks prepared his disciples for their future work before 'ascending' to heaven.

(Matthew, Mark, Luke, John)

The early church

(c. AD 30–90)

On the Day of Pentecost God the Holy Spirit empowered the apostles to fulfil their commission. Peter, who became the first spokesman and leader of the church, preached a sermon after which some 3,000 new believers joined the disciples.

Persecution soon dogged them. However, a chief persecutor, Saul of Tarsus, became a Christian, took his Roman name of Paul, and became the formative Christian church planter and theologian. He undertook three lengthy missionary journeys across the Roman Empire and wrote numerous letters to churches and their leaders, 13 of which are included in the New Testament. In them, he dealt with major issues of belief and practice which emerged in the young churches as Christians struggled to understand and apply their faith in a pagan world.

Others also travelled and wrote letters (some of which are in the Bible). The last book of the Bible, Revelation, is uniquely symbolic. It was written towards the end of the first century to encourage Christians, particularly those facing persecution.

(Acts; the letters (epistles); Revelation)

Introduction to the Gospels

One man - four lives

The four Gospels are essential to our understanding of who Jesus was and what he taught and did, and therefore they are fundamental to our understanding of Christianity.

They were not the first New Testament documents to be written and in the view of some scholars, Matthew and John may have been among the last. The first Christians did not consider texts on the life of Christ to be as important as texts on the theology and practice of being a Christian.

Paul himself hardly speaks of the life of Jesus at all, and then only of his death and resurrection. That is partly because the story of Jesus was still well-known, and Paul was troubleshooting (with the exception of his letter to the Romans) rather than writing systematic essays.

It was only as the first generation of believers began to die, and the gospel spread beyond Palestine and Asia Minor, that the need for authoritative accounts of the life of Jesus became apparent. People wanted to know what he had been like. Did his life really match the claims made for him? What sort of healings and miracles did he perform? And how did he fit into, and differ from, the Jewish religious environment?

Mark is usually considered the first Gospel to have been written (Matthew and Luke almost reprint it, and both add common material from an unknown source). Mark gives a breathless tourists' eye view of Jesus' ministry; Matthew wants Jewish readers to see how far Jesus matches their preconceptions of the Messiah; and Luke wants non-Palestinian readers to see the humanity and compassion of Jesus.

John, which probably (although not definitely) came last, picks up the symbolism and significance of Jesus' teaching and is almost a meditation on key moments in his life to encourage faith and devotion rather than a biography as such.

The four Gospels as we have them were, in God's providence, produced at exactly the right time. They were early enough to set the record straight while eyewitnesses and direct sources still existed, yet late enough to be tailored to the theological and practical needs of the second generation church which did not contain people who had met or heard Jesus personally. In that sense, we are in a similar position to them, hence the abiding value of the Gospels for us today.

Readers new to the life of Jesus are probably best advised to start with Luke, or possibly Mark. The differences you will encounter are much as you would expect when four reporters compile accounts of the same events from different perspectives and for different readers. But taken together, the Gospels provide a powerful testimony to the life and teaching of the man from whom our calendar is dated.

His teaching has often been admired but rarely practised in full. It has not been tried and found wanting, but as G.K. Chesterton said, found hard and not tried. These books will not provide you with a comfortable read if you are not also prepared to have your working philosophy of life radically challenged.

Put out of your mind the Sunday School image of a smiling Jesus carrying a lamb on his shoulders through a summer meadow. Imagine instead a kindly but forthright person surrounded by an angry mob in a narrow Near Eastern back street, telling them that they've had their religion all wrong for centuries and that he alone has got it right . . .

The story of Jesus

Because of the parallelism of the Gospels, we have generally covered the main incidents of Jesus' life only once. The following list shows you under which Gospel you will find an article about these main events. The list is not in chronological order, except for the approximate main divisions. Many attempts have been made to fit the Gospel accounts into a definite order, and all have floundered; we simply do not have all the data.

References below to John are only of the most well-known or 'common' events; see the articles themselves for the other events the book covers which are often difficult to fit accurately into the chronology of Jesus' life.

The early years

Birth of John the Baptist	Luke
Jesus' pre-existence	John
Jesus' ancestors	Matthew
Joseph his father	Matthew
Mary's song	Luke
The angels	Luke
The shepherds	Luke
The wise men	Matthew
Old Testament prophecies	Matthew
The virgin birth	Luke
Simeon and Anna	Luke
Jesus as a boy	Luke

The first months of ministry

Jesus is tempted	Luke
Jesus' baptism	John
Wedding at Cana	John
Call of the fishermen	Luke
Healing the paralysed man	Mark
Fasting and Sabbath observance	Mark
Cleansing the temple	John
Meeting with Nicodemus	John
Meeting the Samaritan woman	John

The second year of ministry

Gadarene demoniac	Mark
The sermon on the mount	Matthew
The sermon on the plain	Luke
Healing the centurion's servant	Matthew
Raising Jairus' daughter	Luke
Jesus is anointed	Luke
Call of Matthew	Matthew
Sending out of the twelve	Matthew
The unforgivable sin	Matthew
Parables about seeds	Mark
Kingdom parables	Matthew
Feeding the 5,000	John
Stilling the storm	Mark
Questions of Jesus' family	Mark
Doubts of John the Baptist	Luke
Cost of commitment	Luke

The final year of ministry

'Clean and unclean' debate	Mark
Death of John the Baptist	Mark
Sending out the seventy	Luke
The good Samaritan	Luke
Healing the Canaanite	Mark
Yeast parable	Mark
Peter 'the rock'	Matthew
The transfiguration	Mark
The 'Messianic secret'	Mark
The question of suffering	Luke
The 'lost' parables	Luke
The dishonest servant	Luke
Rich man and Lazarus	Luke
'Render to Caesar . . .'	Matthew
Teaching on prayer	Luke
Rich young ruler	Luke
Conditions of discipleship	Matthew
Attack on the Pharisees	Matthew
Parable of the tenants	Luke

The last week of Jesus' life, and after

Entry into Jerusalem	Mark
Teaching about his return	Mark
The last supper	Luke
The feet-washing	John
Betrayal of Judas	Matthew
The crucifixion	Mark; John
Signs at the cross and tomb	Matthew
Resurrection appearances	Luke
Peter's restoration	John
'Evidence' for the resurrection	John

More books in some Bibles

Some Bible versions (or some editions of them) include a section of 'deutero-canonical' books. Twelve of these are known as the 'Apocrypha' which are recognised as authoritative by the Roman Catholic Church and the Greek and Russian Orthodox Churches. They are recognised as of value for private study but are not included in public worship by most Protestant and Anglican churches. We do not include a commentary on them in this volume.

The twelve books of the Apocrypha

TOBIT: A story about a man blinded accidentally who is healed by a balm brought from Persia by his son. Probably dates from c. 550 BC.

JUDITH: A spy story of a woman who enticed Nebuchadnezzar's army chief and beheaded him, so that the attackers withdrew. Full of historical errors; probably from 200–150 BC.

ADDITIONS TO ESTHER: Six passages enlarging the biblical story, probably written before 100 BC.

WISDOM OF SOLOMON: A treatise on the virtue of wisdom life. Based on the Greek Old Testament and probably written in Alexandria c. 100 BC.

ECCLESIASTICUS (WISDOM OF JESUS BEN SIRACH; SIRACH): Not the biblical Ecclesiastes. Contains advice for wise living, from about 180 BC.

BARUCH: A short 'devotional' book allegedly by Jeremiah's scribe. Believed to be by several authors and of uncertain date.

LETTER OF JEREMIAH: Similar in tone to Jeremiah 29, it tells Jewish exiles in Babylon not to worship idols. Probably dates from after the exile.

THREE ADDITIONS TO DANIEL: These are usually printed as separate books. **The song of the three holy Jews** (the Benedicite of the 1662 Prayer Book) was allegedly sung in the fiery furnace; **Susanna** is falsely accused of adultery but Daniel proves her innocence; in **Bel and the Dragon** Daniel causes two idols in Babylon to be destroyed (for which he is thrown to the lions). All date from about 100 BC.

1 MACCABEES: An important historical book covering the Jewish revolt against Antiochus Epiphanes during the mid-second century BC. Probably written about 100 BC.

2 MACCABEES: Covers part of the history of 1 Maccabees but is considered less reliable and from a different source.

The other deutero-canonical books

Another collection (sometimes called the 'Pseudepigrapha') includes books variously recognised by some Orthodox Churches.

1 ESDRAS: Includes material from Chronicles, Ezra and Nehemiah plus the contest to determine what is the world's strongest power: wine, women or truth. (Women win!)

2 ESDRAS: A Christian development of a Jewish apocalyptic (end-time) book, with six visions.

PRAYER OF MANASSEH: Allegedly the Judean king's prayer of repentance (2 Chronicles 33). Probably from the second century AD.

PSALM 151: Allegedly a short psalm by David on his triumph over Goliath.

3 MACCABEES: A record of Jewish armed struggle during the period of Ptolemy IV (c. 220–200 BC).

4 MACCABEES: A celebration of reason over emotion.

During the first two centuries AD many pseudo-gospels and letters were written, some claiming apostolic authorship. The final 'canon' (authoritative list) of New Testament books was drawn up in the fourth century AD although debate continued over books such as the letter of James.

Action-packed story brings God down to earth

The Acts of the Apostles

- Tells the story of the first Christians after Jesus' resurrection
- Shows how the church spread across the Roman Empire
- Records the persecutions suffered by the first Christians
- Gives examples of how the Holy Spirit authenticated their message
- Gives summaries of the apostles' preaching
- Traces the story of Paul from his conversion to imprisonment in Rome

Adventure, drama, violence, injustice, miracles, human interest: Acts has all the ingredients of a fast-moving novel, except that this is fact, not fiction. Written by Luke, the Gospel author and a companion on some of Paul's journeys, it shows how the church expanded from Palestine across the Empire over some thirty years. It focuses on key moments such as the first year and the conversion of Saul (who became Paul), and it summarises his travels and trials.

Luke majors on the spectacular and summarises the rest. He wants readers to see that the Holy Spirit was active in the formation of the church just as he was in the formation of Israel after the exodus. God has set his new people on the road to a new kingdom.

He also wants readers to see that the gospel spread not just through the pioneer work of Peter and Paul but also through many others, often not named, who gossiped the gospel where they were. There are accounts of riots and disputes. Being a Christian, Luke is saying, is risky, but he shows that the troubles were not initiated by Christians but by jealous rivals.

What you won't find here is any systematic teaching. The speeches are summaries and we can't build much theology from the book. But we can see God at work in people's lives. Acts makes theology live.

While our established situation may be different from the apostles' pioneer situation, Acts reminds us that we too can and should expect to see God at work through the witness of the church. The Spirit did not retire after the apostolic period.

AT A GLANCE

ACTS

1	The disciples after the resurrection and ascension
2	The Holy Spirit comes to the disciples
3	A disabled beggar is healed by Peter
4	Peter and John arrested
5	Ananias and Sapphira lie, and die
6	Seven deacons elected
7	Stephen tried and killed
8	Philip evangelises in Samaria
9	The conversion of Saul
10	Gentile Pentecost at Caesarea
11	Jerusalem church welomes Gentile Christians
12	Peter released from prison
13	Paul and Barnabas begin to travel
14	Riots at Iconium and Lystra
15	The Council of Jerusalem
16	Paul goes to Greece
17	Paul in Thessalonica and Athens
18	Paul in Corinth
19	Paul in Ephesus
20	Eutychus raised; Paul's last meeting with Ephesian leaders
21-22	Paul arrested in Jerusalem
23	Paul before the Sanhedrin; threatened with death
24	Paul tried before Felix
25,26	Paul tried before Festus and Agrippa
27	Paul's shipwreck in Malta
28	Paul arrives in Rome

KEY QUOTE

When this became known to the Jews and Greeks . . . they were all seized with fear, and the name of the Lord Jesus was held in high honour . . .

Acts 19:17

Up, up and away

Acts 1

Renaissance pictures which show Jesus apparently levitating or being wafted away by swan-like angels do not help modern readers to grasp the significance of the ascension. We can be tempted to substitute our own prosaic images of hot air balloons, escalators or rocket launches. None of that, however, tells us what the event meant. Jesus' withdrawal into the cloud, which was his last resurrection appearance, was highly significant for the disciples.

- It showed that he had truly risen; the resurrection wasn't a hallucination, because such things do not stop so suddenly. But Jesus was never seen again after this incident. (Paul's vision of him in ch 9 was different.)
- It showed that Jesus was leaving the earth in his limited, bodily form. The ascension was a visual sign, an acted parable, which demonstrates that Jesus is going away, and that it is not possible to follow him yet.
- It spoke of his elevation to a higher plane of existence. The images of 'high table', 'promotion to higher things', 'being kicked upstairs' are common expressions of how we think of different levels of human life. This was elevation to the full life of heaven.
- It gave the disciples something to look forward to. They were promised that he would return in a similar way (i.e. visibly) and this was an important aspect of early Christian teaching.

Jesus' ascension means that he is at the 'right hand of God' (Hebrews 1:3). He sits in the place of authority. The ascension is not the end of his work on earth; it is more like his coronation as the world's King.

Wait for the green light then go for God!

Acts 1

Patience is a virtue which is spread thinly across the human race. We want 'it' now. The disciples, however, had to wait, and they didn't even know what they were waiting for. All they knew was that when 'it' happened, they would have no doubts that it was 'it'.

Luke does not imply that they were standing around aimlessly, however. Instead, they are more like racing drivers lined up with engines revving and raring to go. So while the disciples wait, they prepare, keep alert and pray regularly together. They appoint Matthias to replace Judas and maintain the symbolic number of twelve (parallel to the twelve tribes of Israel).

God often calls us to wait for answers to prayer, or for the right moment to launch a project. Having the vision is not the same as having the green light. We need to wait patiently and expectantly for his signal, which will usually be clear – unless we are so obsessed with 'achieving' that we make a false start, and hinder rather than help forward the task that he has set us.

This traditional view of the Ascension is by Mantegna.

FAST facts

Author: The same as that of Luke's Gospel, of which Acts is the second volume. Almost certainly Luke, physician and probably a Gentile native of Antioch (Syria).

Date of composition: Of two theories the most logical is to date it before AD 70 while Paul was in Rome. (He died, c. 67), which explains the 'incomplete' end. Some suggest the end reflects Luke's purpose of showing the spread of the gospel and that it fits better later (say 75–80) after the completion of the Gospels. This also assumes a late date for the Gospels.

Structure and purpose: Acts is written in a chronological order and its historical facts are accurate. It is not a comprehensive history, but probably intended to encourage Christians, and perhaps act as an 'apology' against charges sometimes levelled at them.

Sources: Some passages are clearly extracts from Luke's diaries (he uses 'we' in 16:10–17; 20:5–21:18; 27:1–28:16). Additional information would have been gathered from the apostles. No other source has been identified, but no other would be needed.

Where am I?

Date of events:
About AD 33–65

Location:
Begins in Palestine and spreads through Asia Minor to Italy

Place in Bible:
Follows John's Gospel; precedes Paul's letter to the Romans in the New Testament

Link to other books:
The second of Luke's two-part work which began with the Gospel of Luke; most of Paul's letters were written at various times during the period covered by the narrative

Story follows:
Luke and the other Gospels

Disciples fired up for mission after unmistakable sign

Acts 2

That Day of Pentecost (the Jewish harvest festival) dawned like any other day. The disciples were praying together as they had before. But this time the Holy Spirit came to them in such an unmistakable way that it just had to be what Jesus had promised. It was full of symbolism:

- The harvest celebrated God's physical provision; the Spirit brought his spiritual sustenance.
- Pentecost also celebrated the giving of the Law on Mount Sinai. The Spirit gave God's people the power to fulfil his requirements in a fresh way.
- The flames reminded them of God's purifying holiness which burns away sin, and prepared them for mission.
- The wind symbolised God's breath of life (the word 'Spirit' is used for both). God breathed new spiritual life into them, and blew them into the world as his witnesses.
- The languages (tongues) had a double symbolism. They emphasised that God would give his words for praise and proclamation (cf. Jesus' promise in Luke 12:11,12). They also showed that God's Word was for all nations. At Pentecost people who had been divided since Babel (Genesis 11:1-9) were reunited.
- Past prophecies of the Spirit showed that the church was building on what God had done before.

The disciples were never quite the same again. However he does it, whether quietly or spectacularly, God never leaves us as we were before. He is always blowing us by his Spirit into new avenues of service.

Costly – not cosy

Acts 2:42-47; 4:32-37

Probably the guiding philosophy of the latter half of the twentieth century has been 'independence'. We don't want to be herded in a crowd. Yet as a result we have lost a sense of belonging. The early church rediscovered it.

God created people to have 'fellowship' with each other. We are relational beings, not solitary individuals. If we try to be solitary, we miss or deny, aspects of our humanity.

But 'fellowship' (literally 'sharing') in the church is not the cosy comfort of gentle conversation. It is a costly matter of giving ourselves to people with whom, if it were not for our shared faith, we would never rub shoulders. These passages shows us that it is:

- Essentially spiritual. Fellowship with Jesus Christ (1 Corinthians 1:9) by his Spirit produces fellowship with each other (Philippians 2:1,2); it does not happen naturally.
- Expressed by sharing. There was no obligation to poverty (Mary still owned a house in Acts 12:12). But there was a willingness to share with those who had less. Fellowship is a sham if Christians do not care practically for each other (cf. James 2:14,15). We are to seek first God's kingdom, not our own comfort (Matthew 6:33).
- A basis for mission. The generous atmosphere was a conduit for God's Spirit to flow into the wider community, drawing people to Jesus (2:43,47; 4:33). Tight fists make for closed churches.

There is no hint in the New Testament that Christians' close fellowship was intrusive. It was a loving of people which respected their differences as members of Christ's body. It is a hard act to follow.

Work for unity

Acts 6:1-7

It is stretching political correctness too far to suggest that because human beings are of equal dignity (a fact endorsed by the Bible from page one) then it follows that cultural differences are unnatural accretions.

Paul recognised that God created cultural distinctions (Acts 17:26) as part of the great variety of God's creation which is also seen in the many types of animal and plant.

The early church quickly divided into cultural and racial groups: Jewish believers, non-Jews who were converts to Judaism and Gentiles with no previous contact with Judaism.

Many of the non-Jews spoke Greek rather than Aramaic as their first language, and would have been less punctilious about Jewish ceremonies. So it wasn't long before charges of favouritism began to circulate. The apostles' response is a model of wisdom which restored and deepened unity:

- They recognised that they were overworked and shared responsibility at once
- They appointed helpers who represented the aggrieved people
- They focused on their own calling and gifts, and by relinquishing other tasks enabled more people to use their gifts
- They looked for spiritual people to do what might have been regarded as 'mundane' tasks, hereby showing that any work in the church is essentially 'spiritual'.

These principles provide a foundation for harmonious ministry in any church. Cliques reflect pride and create tension.

Church dismayed by couples' fraud

Acts 5:1-11

Perjury – lying under oath to secure a conviction or release – is a punishable offence. This commonsense law owes its origin to the ninth commandment in Exodus 20:16. Lying destroys community.

Ananias and Sapphira have perjured themselves and damaged the church fellowship. No one would have raised an eyebrow if they had said that they were giving 50 per cent of the proceeds to the church.

Instead, they pretended to have given all the proceeds. Their chief concern was to create a good impression. And if they lied over this, what further claims might they make?

Both deaths were probably from shock-induced heart failure, even though Sapphira's had been predicted.

The harsh lesson is that any exaggeration for the sake of effect is sin, and the same as bare-faced lying. Honesty is the only policy if Christian fellowship is to flourish. Dishonesty destroys our relationship with God and distorts our relationships with others.

Fraud in financial circles always attracts media interest.

First martyr sows seeds of faith

Acts 6:8-7:60

'The blood of the martyrs is the seed of the church' according to second-century Christian apologist Tertullian. He meant that the church grew when Christians were executed. People saw their faith and believed in the Christ who inspired them.

The word 'martyr', used of someone who is killed for their faith, means 'witness'. Stephen's witness may have sown a seed of faith – or doubt – in Saul of Tarsus who watched the killing. Paul's later encounter with Jesus included the accusation that he was kicking against his conscience. Perhaps he saw in Stephen something that he knew was real.

In his defence, Stephen showed that the seeds of the church lay in the Old Testament.

- God built a nation from a childless nomad (vv 2-8)
- He turned a slave into a prime minister (vv 9-16)
- He allowed his people to be oppressed (vv 17-22)
- Moses was called as a leader after being an exile for 40 years (vv 23-34)
- The hardships of the exodus made the people doubt God's sending of Moses (vv 35-43)
- God remained faithful even when they misused the temple and rejected his prophets (vv 44-51)
- He sent Jesus as the fulfilment of his purposes (vv 52-53)

Several speeches in Acts look back to the Old Testament story. Yet Luke was a Gentile, writing for a predominantly non-Jewish audience for whom this was just poorly-known history. Luke wants us to see that God's purposes are like a continuous line, with a beginning, a middle, and – eventually – an end. There is no gulf between Malachi at the end of the Old Testament and Matthew at the start of the New.

New Testament terms for ministers

The system of full-time ministry and church structures which we take for granted was not known in New Testament times. Acts and the letters were written during the time in which methods of oversight were being developed.

The Jews had a structure of elders and priests, and it was natural for the first Christians to mirror the structure they knew, which they modelled on the synagogue (priests to make sacrifices were no longer needed because of the sacrificial death of Jesus).

In the church, deacons acted as administrators and practical helpers (Acts 6:1–6; 1 Timothy 3:8–13). The terms elders (presbyters) and overseers (bishops) seem to have been interchangeable at first. Their function was to teach the faith, pastor the church and chair the worship (Acts 20:28–31; 1 Timothy 3:1–10; 5:17–20).

Paul also refers to people with specific gifts or ministries, including the apostles who were the pioneer church planters and authoritative teachers. He stresses that ministry is a matter of each person using the gifts God has given to them (Romans 12:6–8; Ephesians 4:11,12; 1 Corinthians 12:7–11, 27–31).

Apostles refuse dirty money for ministry

Acts 8:1-25

Philip was forced into Samaria by persecution. Most Christians did not seek martyrdom, but sensibly did not take unnecessary risks. Having served as a deacon he has learned to be an evangelist. Philip is another example of how God grooms leaders.

He accepts the apostles 'confirming' ministry on those who have received Christ through his preaching; Philip works under authority within the church. But the three men then face a stern challenge. Temptations constantly come in the areas of money, sex or power. Here, it is money.

'Simony', taking money in return for spiritual power or ecclesiastical privilege, takes its name from this incident and became common among medieval popes. The apostles, who were not well off, are not open to bribery, however, because the gift they have is not theirs to bestow, but God's.

Simon wants something for himself; Peter wants nothing for himself. Peter's attitude, which Jesus expounded in Matthew 6:25 is probably the only sure defence against temptation in money matters.

Famous convert gets service contract

Acts 9:1-31; cf. 22:3-16; 26:9-18

Saul's dramatic conversion is clearly central to Luke's purpose in Acts, because he records it three times. The second and third accounts are in the context of Paul fulfilling his service contract, and it is this which Luke wants us to notice.

Paul was given a new status.

Paul believed he had right of entry into God's family (Philippians 3:4-7) but discovered that he needed adopting into it (cf. Romans 8:15,23). That alone made him 'God's chosen instrument' (v 15), saved by God's grace. All Christians enjoy the same privilege.

Paul was given a new service.

He had gone to Damascus carrying letters of condemnation of Christians. Now his new task was to carry Christ's name to Gentiles and kings (v 15). It was the biggest policy U-turn imaginable. His conversion was not simply to give him new life, but to commission him to serve God. We are saved in order to serve.

Paul was promised new suffering.

Suffering was built into his contract (v 16). It was not a punishment for persecuting Christians but part of the Christian life and of the devil's kick-back. The star convert wasn't spared ordinary problems; people (especially clergy) who actively serve God often experience many trials. It is part of the cost to be counted before signing up.

Saul came to faith without any illusions. He was given no promises of a wonderful, satisfying life. Instead, he was issued with a tough service contract which would probably kill him. He bought it. And after a lifetime of suffering he said that he was thoroughly satisfied (Philippians 4:11-13).

The night the wall came down

Acts 10:1–11:18

Peter's vision and subsequent actions was the equivalent of the demise of communism and the fall of the Berlin Wall. Jews refused to eat with Gentiles for fear of ceremonial contamination, and the Christians had unthinkingly accepted this as part of the gospel.

But it stemmed from racism rather than holiness. Peter discovered that people had equal status before God whatever their ethnic or cultural background, and that Jewish scruples over food were no longer matters of primary importance to God – although it took some time for the rest of the church to be convinced.

The account packs a double message for today. It condemns any form of social discrimination by Christians and it warns against elevating cultural behaviour patterns to the status of divine laws. Some Christians, for example, have made abstinence from alcohol a test of orthodoxy; it may be commendable as a discipline, but it is not essential for serving God.

Gospel invades Africa

Acts 8:26-40

Although there were visitors from Egypt in Jerusalem on the Day of Pentecost (Acts 2:10) the Ethiopian is the first known African convert. It is a classic example of how an alert Christian was able to turn a situation to God's advantage. Philip obeyed God and left a fruitful ministry for God's unspecified purpose (v 26)

- He listened to the Ethiopian before speaking (v 30)
- He started his message from the man's current understanding (v 35)
- He taught from the Bible (v 35)
- He led the man to commitment (v 36)

What he did not do was arrange for the treasurer's subsequent nurture. But as there was no church in Ethiopia, and no Bible correspondence courses, no doubt God cared for him! Traditionally, the treasurer founded the Ethiopian Coptic Church.

Paul disappears to train in obscurity

Acts 9:19-30; 11:19-30; cf. Galatians 1:11-2:2

Famous people who become Christians are often 'outed' by the church before they are ready to field questions about beliefs and to cope with the intense media gaze at their private lives. Saul lived in a more enlightened age and he was spared the limelight; in fact, the church shunned him until he had proved his genuineness.

When he did begin his recorded ministry he did not push himself; Barnabas had to encourage him (11:25). He was willing to start small, and his first travelling venture was more as a postman than a preacher (11:30).

There is an interval between Acts 9:30 and 11:25 of some ten years. What Paul – and – others, were doing in that time is unknown. Reading Acts may give the erroneous impression that the church grew from seed to maturity overnight like Jack's bean-stalk. Paul's story was probably as follows:

- Conversion near Damascus, c. AD 33 (9:1-19);
- Retreat into Arabian desert for up to three years (Galatians 1:17);
- Return to Damascus (Galatians 1:17; Acts 9:19) for a short while;
- Flees persecution there (in a basket, 2 Corinthians 11:32,33) and briefly visits Jerusalem (Acts 9:26-29);
- Death threat forces him to flee home to Tarsus (9:30) where he stays for some years;
- Barnabas takes him to work in Antioch c. AD 43 (11:25,26);
- From there, he takes famine relief to Jerusalem (11:27-30);
- Starts his first missionary journey c. AD 46 (13:1).

From then on, Acts focuses on Paul's ministry. The church in Jerusalem flourished without him (cf. ch 15) and Christians elsewhere were planting churches also (including in the capital city of Rome). Luke, however, did not chronicle those events, and these also are details now known only to God. Public awareness and 'fame' is not high on the scale by which God measures the significance of Christian activity.

A snapshot of Paul's missionary life

Acts 13-14

When Sir Winston Churchill was appointed Prime Minister of Britain in the Second World War he said: 'All my life has been a preparation for this hour.' Saul of Tarsus, now known by his Roman name of Paul, had been born a Roman citizen, schooled in Judaism, converted to Christianity and discipled in the church. Now it is God's time for him to launch out into his ministry, perhaps some 13 years after the encounter with Christ on the Damascus Road. Luke summarises Paul's life on the hoof, and most elements here occur on his other journeys. They are also a common feature of much Christian ministry and mission today.

Paul is led by the Spirit, but commissioned by the church (13:1-3). The church agreed with the prophetic word which came to someone or to several people during a period of worship and prayer. Paul always sought the backing and support of the church. Lone mission work is never envisaged in the Bible, and God's call is mediated through the church.

He faced spiritual opposition (13:4-12). The sorcerer is 'a servant of the devil' (v 10) and the temporary blindness probably reminds Luke's readers that there is a power of darkness who opposes all God's work.

It may be significant that as soon as Paul starts his travels, he is aware of satanic rather than merely human opposition. Many Christian leaders would testify to that kind of experience.

He began with the familiar (13:13-41). Paul always went to the Jews first, because Jesus fulfilled Jewish expectations. Paul, like Peter (2:14-40) and Stephen (7:2-53) recounts the Old Testament basis of the gospel. Paul's message is the same as that of others, Luke is stressing.

He coped with Christian casualties (13:13). Almost skated over, this significant verse excites some sympathy for Mark whom Paul refused to have on his team again (15:36-41), but to whom he was later reconciled (2 Timothy 4:11). Mark pulled out of the mission, but not out of his faith. The rigours of the harsh life proved too much for him, but he probably wrote the Gospel attributed to him, and was a helper of Peter and again of Paul. People who trip at one hurdle can still recover to run an effective race.

He faced human dissension (13:42-52; 14:6). It is specified as jealousy here. Paul attracted attention with his new message. But there was clearly disagreement with the message itself. Unregenerate human minds mixed with Middle-Eastern temperaments to create an explosive confrontation.

He healed as well as taught (14:8-10). Regular healing and a few spectacular miracles authenticated the message and demonstrated its truth. All Christian mission needs to be seen as well as heard, through the practical demonstration of God's love. That may include compassion ministries and occasional supernatural 'signs' which evade human explanation.

He was misinterpreted (14: 11-20). Paul refused the status of a pop idol and rejected any form of adulation. (According to a local legend the gods had visited the region before and not been recognised. The inhabitants did not want to make the same mistake twice!) Christians are not immune from the temptations of power and fame. Paul set an example of single-minded mission.

He nurtured the churches and reported back (14:21-28). Paul revisited churches because he was as anxious about nurture as he was about mission. He was no lightning evangelist, striking at random and never returning to the same place. He sought to leave a church, and not just a group of believers, with trained leaders and teachers. Still accountable to Antioch (and to encourage the church) he reported back on his return.

Fly away Peter!

Acts 12:1-18; cf. 5:17-40

Twice in Acts Peter is rescued from prison by an angel. The miracle obscures the more prosaic fact that he needed to be rescued from a potentially life-threatening situation as the authorities clamped down on the fledgling church.

Jesus had predicted persecution (John 15:20,21) and the apostles were not disappointed. Peter had already been flogged (5:40) which had all but killed his Lord (Matthew 27:26). Yet despite the suffering, the apostles apparently enjoyed the peace of God; Peter slept like a baby and Paul and Silas staged an impromptu 'Songs of Praise' (16:25).

Whether the angel was a sympathetic key-holder or a supernatural visitor (which is what Luke clearly believes because of the 'light' in 12:7) the effect was dramatic. Luke records these incidents because he wants to reassure his readers that while God does not prevent his people from suffering, he is there to support and rescue them in their suffering.

But as we rejoice in that truth, we should also spare a thought for the unfortunate guards (v 19). In a fallen world, even God's blessings to his people may be received at considerable cost to others. Luke reports the fact without comment, but by reporting it he is warning us not to lose our sensitivity.

Evidence forces the leaders to climb down

Acts 15:1-35

Messages which are alleged to have come from God find a ready market in every generation eager, like the Athenians, to hear something new. The gullible accept them as authentic, the curious make them talking points, and the sceptical dismiss them. In between, many are left confused, doubting if they will ever know what to believe.

Christians today generally appeal to the Scriptures and to the long tradition of scripturally-based understanding within the wider church, to judge new ideas of alleged 'revelations'. If something is consistent with revealed truth, then it is at least plausible.

In the first century, the only Scriptures available were the Old Testament writings. The apostles were recognised as having a unique teaching authority, but even they did not come with a pre-printed encyclopaedic knowledge of the entire Christian faith. They formulated it as they faced confusing questions.

Two major doctrinal issues challenged the apostles' inherited Jewish thought forms. One was the divinity of Jesus (and of the Holy Spirit) which led in later centuries to formulations about the Trinity. This, the apostles seem to have accepted without rationalising further than to stress the absolute unity of God and the absolute divinity of Father, Son and Holy Spirit.

The second question was the relationship of Gentiles to the old Jewish system through which Jesus

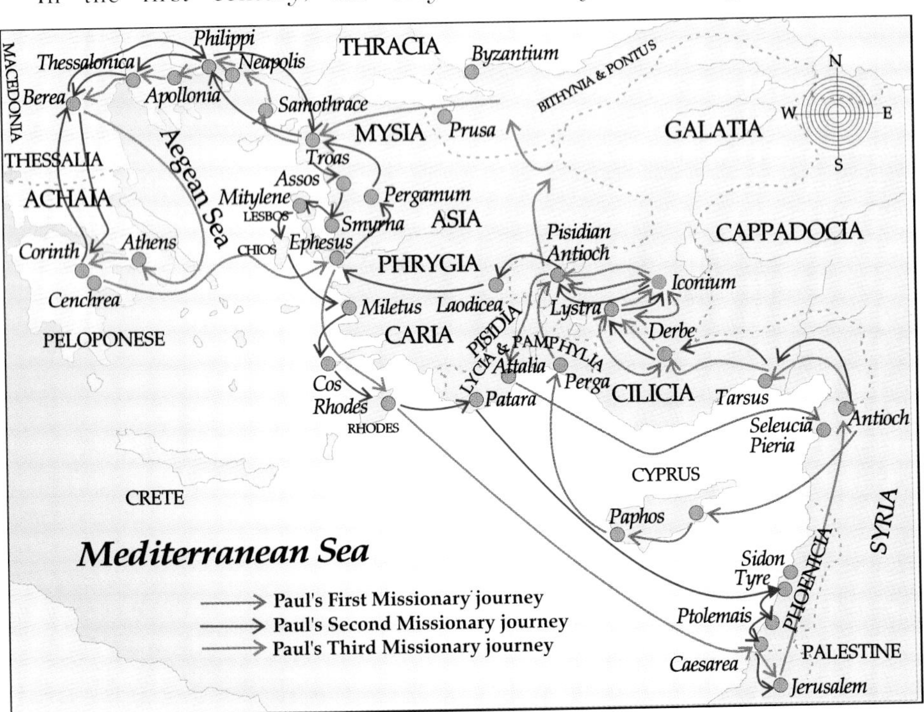

had come. It is addressed here as some nationalistic Jews insist on Gentiles being subject to the same rites as Jews in order to be kosher Christians.

(There is some debate about whether Acts 15 is the same incident as Galatians 2:1-10. It seems more likely that Galatians 2 is to be identified with Acts 11:30, although no one can be absolutely certain.)

The issue continued to trouble Christians for many decades, and the way it is handled here illustrates how beliefs were crystallised and leaves us with a model of how to deal with such questions.

- They were confronted with evidence that God was at work in a new way, which they could not dispute (vv 6-12)
- They reflected on the Old Testament teaching about the issue (vv 13-18)
- They reached an agreement which both recognised as new truth (God saved the Gentiles without the need for Jewish rites) and respected moral values and Jewish scruples which if not observed would divide the church hopelessly (vv 19-21)

The incident revealed that God is not static in his revelation any more than in his mission. His truth is living and dynamic, and he does things which require his people constantly to be seeking his wisdom and understanding. In so doing, they may discover new angles on his unchanging truths which hitherto have been hidden or only partially understood.

One of the few things God will not tolerate is the naive and proud assumption that we know all there is to know about him.

All things work for good

Acts 15:36-41

Paul comes out of this incident worse than Barnabas and it is to Luke's credit (as a companion of Paul) that he gives a frank, if brief, account of it.

In retrospect, within the wider context of God's purposes, we can conclude that both Paul and Barnabas were right. Their disagreement over method led to a more diverse mission in which a greater number heard the gospel and were nurtured as Christians.

Not all divisions in the church are disasters (although many are both needless and fruitless). God can use human differences for his greater purposes. Paul himself acknowledged that all things work together for good for those who love God and are called according to his purpose (Romans 8:28).

Good news begins where people are

Acts 17:16-33

The art of effective communication is to find ways in which the hearers can identify clearly with what is being said. It is of no value to begin with God as a good shepherd if the hearers have never seen sheep, or to suggest that Jesus is 'the lamb of God' if animal sacrifice is repugnant to them or they have no knowledge of sin.

Paul is sometimes accused of having made a mistake with the Athenians. This is the only occasion when he seems to have departed from his usual Old Testament-based approach and strayed into 'natural theology'. However, this is what the Athenians were interested in and what as polytheists they needed. In stating the gospel he got as far as Jesus' resurrection, after which they howled him down.

The fact that there is no record of an Athenian church being formed does not mean this visit was a failure. (1 Corinthians 16:15 states the Corinthians were the first in the region to convert to Christ in any numbers.)

Luke is showing us Paul's versatility and illustrating his claim that he 'became all things to all people' (1 Corinthians 9:19-21). He was a communicator who could build bridges with people from vastly different cultures and starting points. His mission thus became 'out-reach', and not an 'in-drag' based on a fixed formula.

HARD Question

Were they really Christians?

Acts 18:24-19:9

These two incidents have a thematic as well as a chronological link. Apollos and the dozen Ephesian 'believers' knew only of John the Baptist's ministry, although probably they had also heard of the Jesus to whom John had pointed. They were completely ignorant of the Holy Spirit.

Although they were in a similar situation, they required different ministries. Apollos' need is for instruction, which he receives gladly. The Ephesians' need is for a fresh experience of God in their lives, which they also receive. But the question as to where they would have gone eternally if they had fallen under the proverbial bus before their 'conversion' is never considered.

There are probably many people inside and on the fringes of the church whose knowledge of the Christian way is imperfect. It is the church's corporate responsibility to care for them and help them in their journey in a way which is appropriate to them. It is not the church's job to stand in judgment on them or to threaten them. Most of us have been in a similar position.

Aquila and Priscilla are the ancient equivalent of today's youth group or home group leaders who quietly nurture talented converts who go on to become great leaders (cf. 18:27-28). Their immense ministry is acknowledged in the New Testament and should not be overlooked.

Right message, wrong messenger

Acts 16:16-40

The early church may not have had its spin doctors, but it did recognise bad news. The slave girl Paul exorcised was telling the truth, but a medium employed by unscrupulous peddlers was not the sort of witness who would endear herself to most people. She would bring the gospel into disrepute.

Mission and evangelism is much more than ensuring people hear the 'right' words. The character of the messenger is also important. The New Testament suggests that those who share Christ's message publicly must also live his risen life and:

- speak from pure motives
- demonstrate the love of God by their actions
- be commissioned and supported by the local church.

Paul prepares for end

Acts 19-20

Paul spent almost three years in Ephesus (19:8-10), a fruitful ministry ended by the riot which was really an industrial dispute. Luke gives us a New Testament insight into the social structure of the Roman Empire; most trades were organised into guilds to protect workers' interests (19:25).

Luke focuses on the action, but is hazy about the preceding two years. Paul's ministry and the witness of the Christians had a powerful effect in the city and the region it governed (19:10). The apostles were not the only evangelists.

The Hall of Tyrannus seems to have become a teaching centre attended by Christians from a wide area. It is the only New Testament example of a building specifically hired for church meetings, but that does not mean it was unique.

In his farewell speech to the Ephesians, Paul gives specific instructions and examples to the leaders he has appointed. Mixed with his own aspirations, the speech tells us that:

- The leader's business is to be helpful to the church (20:20)
- The leader's goal must be to complete all that God has called him or her to do (20:24)
- The leader's lifestyle is to be exemplary, simple and peaceable (20:26,33)
- The leader's teaching must cover the whole gospel (20:27)
- The leader's task is to care for and protect the church members (20:28)
- False teachers will arise from within the ranks of the church (20:29-30)
- The leader's responsibility is to warn members of dangers they may not see (20:31).

Saved by grace – many times over

Acts 24–26

As someone has said, 'If you can keep your head when all around are losing theirs, you've probably misunderstood the situation!' No doubt some people might have thought Paul had done just that. The reasonableness of Festus and Agrippa suggests that he could have gone free had he not opened his mouth and appealed for a trial before the emperor (25:11; 26:32). But Paul knew he had to get to Rome somehow, and this was God's way.

Paul has been waiting in Caesarea for two years (24:27), and now gets two opportunities within a few days to speak again to secular leaders. He tells his story again to Agrippa (ch 26), with a few differences of detail. As he nears the end of his life, he shows his beliefs about God haven't changed.

It was God who chose and appointed him (26:16); he had not changed his religion because he liked the idea, or embarked on his ministry because it seemed a good way of earning a living. Like all of us, he was not just a mass-produced product of human genes but a purpose-made person with a unique place in God's story.

And in all his adventures, God had rescued Paul from danger and ensured that his task was completed (26:17). God had never abandoned him even though he had allowed him more than once almost to be killed. Paul's story is not of having been saved by God's grace at the outset, and then being left to fend for himself; he has been continually supported by that same grace. Such is God's way.

CROSS CHECK

The Holy Spirit: pp 30, 217, 135
Ministry in the church: pp 73, 400, 404
Jews and Gentiles: pp 134, 367, 373

For today

- We can only achieve God's purposes if we wait for God's timing
- Christian fellowship includes sharing material things as well as doing 'spiritual' things
- Everyone is called to share the load of Christian ministry, witness and service
- Mission may include suffering – be prepared for it
- Be willing for God to change your perceptions and presup-positions about others – or about himself
- Ensure that your life matches your message, and your message matches other people's lives

All riots lead Paul to ministry in Rome

Acts 21-28

The final, long section of Acts makes for exciting reading as it recounts a series of arrests, trials and Paul's shipwreck. Looking on it from afar, we see his inexorable journey towards Rome made in a manner which he probably would not have wished for.

Paul was not deterred by danger (21:10-14). He was determined to go where he believed God wanted him even though the dangers were predictable. His single-minded devotion to duty is an example few feel able to follow.

He was protected through sufferings (e.g. 23:12-35; 27:13-44). In all the horrors of prison and shipwreck, he still experienced God's protection. He was not spared trouble, but was assisted through it.

He made use of his citizenship status (e.g. 22:22-29; 25:10-12). Paul did not normally 'stand on his rights' to save his own skin. Here, however, he uses his Roman citizenship as a means of achieving what he believes to be God's specific calling, which is to preach before Caesar in Rome. Privileges in society are normally taken for granted; Paul used them for God's sake. Nothing, in Paul's experience, was ever wasted.

HARD Question

What happened after Acts 28?

The simple answer is that no one knows. There is a strong tradition that Paul was martyred by Nero after the great fire of Rome in about AD 67, but the period between his apparent release from house arrest in AD 63 and his eventual death is a mystery.

He had hoped to go to Spain (Romans 15:22-29) and early Christian traditions, including a comment by Clement of Rome dated about 95, suggest that he did.

However, the letters to Timothy and Titus suggest that he also made another journey eastwards to churches he had planted many years earlier. These may have included Crete, Miletus, Ephesus, Philippi and Nicopolis (all mentioned in 1 Timothy 1:3; 2 Timothy 4:20; Titus 1:5; 3:12), and possibly Colossae (cf. Philemon v 22, written from Rome c. AD 60).

Why Luke recorded no more is unclear. Perhaps he had completed his task as he saw it: recording the establishing of the church from Jerusalem to Rome. Maybe in the lull of Paul's imprisonment, he saw a good opportunity to complete and publish his book. What we do know is that Acts is not the end of the story; and neither are we. The task of evangelism and church planting is not yet complete.

Bumpy ride around the global village

It was never an easy life being a lonely goatherd and nurseryman tending a fig orchard. But it must have been a lot easier than laying down the milking bucket and pruning shears to go off as a missionary in a hostile nation (although with a shared language and common heritage) to preach a message no one wanted to hear.

But that was life for Amos. Like the tongue-tied Moses before him and the timid Jeremiah who would follow a century later, Amos was plucked by God from obscurity and sent on a seemingly impossible mission.

He had grown up in Judah (the southern kingdom) during the eighth century BC and was sent to call the northern kingdom of Israel to account. Being an outsider no doubt helped give him a clear vision of the state of the nation, but it did not endear its people to him. (They didn't take any notice of home-bred prophets such as Amos's near-contemporary Hosea, either.)

What makes Amos especially notable for today's readers is that he singled out a number of social evils for which we can find many parallels in any society and culture which has sidelined God or left him out of its reckoning altogether.

Amos reminds us that private faith and public conduct can never be divorced. God is far more interested in a just and righteous society than he is in a church offering orthodox worship while letting social evil go unchallenged. Worship is important, but only if it is backed by social harmony and justice.

In personal terms, this means that we cannot sing God's praises on Sunday and curse our fellow humans on Monday. We cannot pray to the Father in church and then ignore the cries of the needy outside. And above all, we cannot say that God is all we need, when we follow the crowd to amass every gadget, toy and comfort which it deems indispensable in order to get a life, whatever the cost to the environment and to the developing nations which contribute to or supply it.

Amos takes us out into the global village, and describes it to us not in the synthetic tones of a tour operator but in the harsh terms of an outraged journalist.

AMOS

1 God's judgment on the surrounding nations
2 God's judgment for Israel's sins
3 Destruction of Israel foretold
4 God's warnings through natural disasters
5 Religious and social sins will precipitate 'the day of the Lord'
6 Complacency and pride challenged
7 Visions of figs and plumb-line; persecution of Amos
8 Vision of ripe fruit ready for harvest
9 Destruction and restoration of Israel foretold

The Book of Amos

- Foretells the destruction of Israel (the northern kingdom)
- Condemns Israelites for social as well as religious sins
- Describes the ministry of a reluctant 'foreign' missionary
- Offers hope for the long-term future for generations unborn

But let justice roll on like a river, righteousness like a never-failing stream!

Amos 5:24

Date of events:
c. 760-750 BC

Location:
Most prophecies are directed at the northern kingdom of Israel and its capital Samaria

Place in Bible:
Amos is the third of the Minor Prophets placed towards the end of the Old Testament, after Hosea and Joel, before Obadiah and Jonah

Parallel books:
Amos worked roughly at the same time as Isaiah, Micah and Hosea.

God's parental care seen in judgment

Amos 1,2

In common with several biblical prophets, Amos does not direct God's words only to his own nation but to those around. This may seem unfair; these nations do not have the special relationship with God which Israel had (and which God himself initiated), so why should they be judged by the same exacting standards?

There is a natural judgment on those who reject or ignore God; they miss out on the benefits which come from serving him. But here the prophet describes God more as a protective parent of Israel than as an angry antagonist of all others. Amos is close to the picture Jesus painted.

All the nations described here had been specific enemies of Israel. Damascus (Aram or Syria) has 'threshed' Gilead (1:3), one of Israel's northern tribes: it has chopped it down. Gaza (Philistia) has ransacked southern Judah and sold its population into slavery (1:6).

Tyre (Phoenicia) has sold Israel into spiritual and economic slavery partly because of its alliance forged with Israel's Ahab a century earlier (1:9). Edom, a 'cousin' of Israel (founded by Esau, brother of the Jacob who fathered the twelve tribes of Israel) has continuously harassed it (1:11). The Ammonites frequently attacked Israel in its early days (1:13) as did the Moabites (2:1).

Therefore, however much God's people may drift from whole-hearted devotion to him, they are still the object of his care. He does not like to see them hurt, and those who cause that hurt will pay in some way at some point.

Today we may become aware of God's protection or even vindication as people actively discriminate against the church and its faith. But even when God seems to turn away from such attacks, his protective nature is unchanged. He is simply biding his time before acting on behalf of his people on the 'day of the Lord' when all inequities shall be judged.

FAST facts

Author: Amos was a southerner from Judah called to prophesy to northern Israel. He was a shepherd and a fig grower (7:14,15) rather than a priest or a professional prophet belonging to a religious community. Apart from his home (Tekoa, just south of Bethlehem) no more is known of him.

Date of prophecies: Amos dates his work during the reigns of Jeroboam II of Israel and Uzziah of Judah. His messages included here probably were given about 760-750 BC (see below).

Historical background: Israel was prosperous in Jeroboam II's reign, when Israel had taken advantage of the weakened state of Aram (Syria, and its capital Damascus) to the north. Israel had extended its borders and increased its income from trade. Aram had fallen to the Assyrians c. 800 BC, and remained a potential threat to Israel. Although not named by Amos, it was Assyria which eventually fulfilled his predictions of a northern nation destroying Israel and its capital, Samaria.

Privilege includes responsibility

Amos 2,3

Some of the younger members of the British Royal family appear to struggle with the conflict between public responsibility and personal desire. The tradition of putting duty before pleasure is not held strongly within society as a whole, and they have been severely tested.

Most people find the struggle difficult between doing what is expected of us and what we prefer. However privilege brings responsibility and people with power or wealth should use it wisely.

Israel, the northern kingdom, has failed where many individuals fail today. It has failed to live up to its privileged position, taken its status for granted and become lazy. Its chief privilege was belonging to the family of God (3:2), into which it was adopted when God redeemed the nation from slavery in Egypt (2:10). Instead of following the leaders God gave them, the people became self-indulgent bullies (2:6-8,11), silenced the prophets and dragged the more disciplined family members into their own dissipation. No royal or presidential scandal could match Israel's dereliction of duty.

So the house will fall, says Amos (2:13; 3:2,11,14-15). But far from being a popular uprising against the abuse of power as in the French or Russian Revolutions, this reversal will be the result of God himself bringing down the people who he once lovingly called into partnership (3:3). No one ends such a partnership without pain, and God's continuing love is shown in the promise of restoration (3:12).

Today's church is also a privileged family of God. It therefore has a responsibility to serve effectively at whatever personal cost to its members. If we do not accept our public responsibility to work with and for God, then we shall wither before him.

Shameless sins earn prophets' rebukes

Amos is very outspoken about the 'social' sins of his time, and uses immoderate language to condemn them. But he was not alone is seeing them. His near-contemporaries Isaiah and Hosea saw much the same thing.

Social sin	Isaiah	Amos	Hosea
Meaningless religious ritual	1:11-17; 29:13	4:4,5; 5:21-24	6:6; 8:13
Oppression of the poor	3:13-15; 10:2	2:7; 5:11,12; 8:4	
Pride of fashionable women	3:16-24; 32:9-13	4:1	
Ruthless property developers	5:8	5:11	
Complacent leisure seekers	5:11-12	6:1-7	
Reversal of values	5:20-21		
Legal injustice and bribery	5:22-23; 10:1,2	5:7,12	7:6
Drunkenness	5:11,22; 28:7,8		4:11
Slave trading		2:6; 8:5	
Sexual immorality		2:7	4:2,11-13; 7:4
Sabbath breaking		8:5	
Dishonest trading and theft		8:5	4:2; 12:7
Murder			4:2
Idolatry			8:4-6;13:1,2

Social temperature changes go unnoticed

Amos 4,5

It is said that if you put a lobster into boiling water it squeals, understandably. But if you put it in cold water and slowly heat it, the creature doesn't notice the temperature change until it is too late.

The same thing happens to people as the surrounding social climate changes. We get used to it and don't notice the enormity of the change until it is too late. It takes an outsider like Amos to point out the obvious. He does so with strong language (calling a woman a cow 4:1), and lists social sins which go unchecked and unchallenged (see chart on previous page).

Christians applying this passage should look beyond the evils mentioned (which may be repeated in any generation) to the social principles they represent (repeated in every generation). Complacency, indulgence, and disadvantaged people being exploited for other's profit and pleasure, are always common lapses. We can apply this principle also to the obsession with and flaunting of sexuality, child abuse, racism, verbal and physical violence and vandalism, and unremitting commercial pressure on poor developing nations to produce low priced produce for Western supermarkets.

This passage reminds us that righteousness and godliness is not a matter of having a private faith, of avoiding certain sins and doing certain charitable or religious acts. It is primarily living in and ordering God's world to reflect God's character.

Immersed in a decadent society we soak up attitudes and absorb lifestyles so that eventually we blend like chameleons into our cultural background. When we do denounce sins, they are often taken from a selective list (sex, lies and fraud) allowing the prevailing greed, injustice and idolatry to continue unchecked and even unnoticed.

Our prophetic role does not begin with shouting abuse at the world. Amos was speaking to the 'church' of his day. We need to repeat his uncomfortable message to ourselves, set our own lifestyles and attitudes in order, and then offer the world a new agenda which we are already practising.

Complacency kills

Amos 6

Lamenting the events which followed the Russian revolution, Alexander Solzhenitsyn wrote in *The Gulag Archipelago* that 'we didn't love freedom enough. And even more – we had no awareness of the real situation. We purely and simply deserved everything that happened afterward.' Complacency set in, leaving the door wide open to communist terror.

Complacency is the most dangerous of sins. It fiddles with its toys while Rome burns. It lives in an enclosed world of self-fulfilment, oblivious to the evils and threats to freedom and dignity which parade outside the window.

Complacency has one foot in the spiritual grave. It is afflicted with tunnel vision, over-confident of its standing before God, uncritical of its attitudes and actions, and unconcerned with life beyond its narrow interests.

The complacent Israelites, lying on their ivory beds, were comfortable. All seemed well with their world. But all was wrong with it. And they deserved what happened afterwards. When the terms of God's covenant are broken, he has no choice but to bring retribution upon his own people.

Today, our 'punishment' for complacency may be a spiritual 'exile' from the riches of God's blessing and from the place of influence in the world which marginalises us. But even that statement might be another form of complacency; such 'exile' itself is relatively comfortable.

As the twentieth century ended, the huge refugee crisis from Kosovo reminded us that war and sudden poverty is never far away. What would Amos say today?

It could be worse

Amos 7:1-9

When things go wrong and normal life is interrupted, nothing, it seems, could be worse. Without denying the real grief and pain which we encounter, we will never actually know if it could have been worse. In other words, to suffer does not mean that God's protective shield has been withdrawn; he could have saved us from something worse.

This is one of several Bible passages which indicate that divine protection does not always mean prevention of mishap.

The vision of Israel's ('Jacob's') destruction horrifies Amos. His prayer seems to stop God from carrying out his threat. Certainly prayer is a powerful element in our relationship with him. But this passage is not about prayer. It is about a covenant-keeping God who never loses faith with his people. If he did, then things would be a lot worse than they ever are.

God has already determined not to destroy Israel totally (cf. 3:12). So he shows the prophet what might have been, were it not for his love and restraint.

From Amos's human standpoint, the Lord 'relented'; from the Lord's divine standpoint this was a revelation of his character and purpose to a faithful prophet within the context of a spiritual relationship. In 3:7, this process is referred to explicitly.

God is taking Amos down an unknown path and teaching him something new. There is more behind the spiritual scenes than most of us are aware of.

A spiritual smear test

Amos 7:10-17

Prophets and politicians must have thick skins, because they are liable to be verbally abused or smeared when their message or policy does not meet with their opponents' approval.

God's word is not always easy to discern, however, and although we can see that Amos was right, at the time many good people must have thought him weird or misguided. To get rid of him Amaziah, of whom nothing else is known, tries to smear him (v 11 puts a spin on Amos's words to make him seem like an opportunist traitor).

When that fails, Amaziah appeals to Amos' lower nature. Today he would have tried a call girl or a bribe; then, he offered a secure living out of earshot of the northern kingdom implying that if the invitation is not accepted, the heavy mob might pay Amos an evening visit.

Amos has nothing of it, and Amaziah is promised ruin and bereavement for daring to oppose God's word. Amos is an example to pressured believers to stick to their principles and not to be side-tracked by opponents or temptations.

The fate of Amaziah suggests that those who oppose God's word will not find mercy on the day of judgment. That is awesome. We cannot wring our hands with glee that people like Amaziah will be punished. Rather, we should turn away sadly and pray that they will see the error of their ways and repent.

Amos for today

- God is protecting his people through difficulties, not from them
- Duty and responsibility shuld always come before pleasure and preference
- Beware that cultural norms in your society may be at odds with God's values and concerns
- The spiritual life includes acting justly and seeking the welfare of all within society
- Everyone will face judgment: be on your guard

Amos' Place in biblical history:

c. 850
the time of Elijah and Elisha (1-2 Kings)

c. 750
the time of the 'eighth century' prophets (Amos, Isaiah, Micah, Hosea)

c. 722
Assyria destroys Israel (the northern kingdom)

c. 605
Babylon begins to destroy Judah (the southern kingdom)

Grim harvest heralds a springtime of hope

Amos 8,9

Harvest in most societies, including ancient Israel, is a time for celebration and thanksgiving. There is a store of food for the winter; there is fresh fruit and grain to enjoy now.

But in the Bible, harvest is often used as a symbol for God's judgment. The grim reaper scythes down the errant peoples. So the vision of autumn fruit here is an ill omen; the time is ripe for the inescapable divine punishment.

Some past generations of Christians have over-stressed God's judgment and underplayed his love and forgiveness. The opposite is probably true today. Judgment is inconceivable on decent ordinary people; if it occurs at all, it is reserved for serial killers and mad dictators. So we think.

Couched in political and military terms (which will be fulfilled by the unnamed Assyrians about thirty years after Amos's message), this promise seems far removed from contemporary spirituality. We can never tell if a society in our time gets its just deserts in such a way; that is something hidden in God's diary to which even true prophets have only very limited access.

What we can know is that there will be a harvest at the end of time. And we do know that all actions have their inevitable consequences; those who live by the sword frequently die by the sword, and what is hidden is ultimately revealed to the embarrassment of many. There are signs or foretastes of judgment around us, but we often prefer not to notice them. We cannot rest on our laurels, nor trust our luck.

However, this dark cloud has a silver lining. Amos, like most TV news bulletins, ends on an up-note. After the war comes peace; after the invasion and destruction comes a time of rebuilding; after the earth is scorched by the angel of death, new life springs up from the charred remains.

Amos looks forward to the day when a remnant shall return, a hope shared by his even more dismal successor Jeremiah. That remnant will come from the southern kingdom of Judah rather than the northern kingdom of Israel, though.

God will start again, as he always does. There is hope for his world and for his people. Amos contents himself with this assurance, even though he knows that he will not live to see it personally. The gospel is a message of new beginnings, which encompass our lives but do not end with them. Amos's conclusion reminds us that we operate in the realm of world history and even eternity, and not just of our own lifetime on earth.

This is where you belong

Imagine yourself as a young Jew returning to Judea from Babylon in the fifth century BC. Jerusalem, about which you have heard so much, is still in chaos. You become disheartened by what you see and by the opposition you encounter as, with many others, you try to build a new life in a country which, though yours, in one sense is far from your big-city birthplace.

Occasionally, prophets like Haggai and Zechariah stir you to spiritual action. The scholarly teaching of people like Ezra helps you develop your distinctive Jewish lifestyle, and the zeal and skill of men like Nehemiah gives shape to civic life.

But over a frugal meal one dark evening, you wonder if the long trek 'home' from the green-banked canals and rich streets of Babylon was really worth it. You feel a rootless refugee. You set out with high hopes but where is the miracle-working God of your fathers? Life seems so hard.

Enter the Chronicler. He has written his books especially for you. He tells you how Israel under the great king David degenerated and became two kingdoms, Israel and Judah. Then he traces how your branch of the tree, Judah, degenerated further and was exiled to Babylon.

The story spans some 500 years, and as you skim over it you see the temple and what it stands for at the centre of your people's story. Chronicles focuses on the temple and Jerusalem, and reflects on the faith of God's people.

As you read, you discover that this is the start of your story. You are in the stream of God's purposes. And you begin to see how important it is for you to keep the law, to focus on the temple, and to honour God. He's not doing great miracles at the moment, but all the same he's a faithful God. So you go to bed inspired to be a loyal disciple once again.

AT A GLANCE

1 CHRONICLES

1-9	Genealogies of Israel's tribes, and David and Saul
10	Death of Saul
11	David becomes king
12	David's warriors
13	The ark is returned to Israel
14	David's family and conquests
15	The ark is brought to Jerusalem
16	David's praise to God
17	David accepts God's will for the building of temple
18	Battle victories and trophies
19-20	Defeat of the Ammonites
21	Census of the army
22	David plans the temple
23-26	Lists of priests, Levites and temple staff
27	List of army divisions and senior civil servants
28	Detailed plans for the temple
29	Gifts for the temple

(The story of David is paralleled in 2 Samuel; 2 Chronicles is outlined on p 51)

1 and 2 Chronicles tells us

- The stories of David and Solomon
- How the temple was planned and built
- How Israel was divided into two kingdoms
- A religious history of the southern kingdom (Judah)

If my people . . . humble themselves and pray and seek my face and turn from their wicked ways, then will I hear from heaven and will forgive their sin and will heal their land.

2 Chronicles 7:14

A long note of family descent

1 Chronicles 1-9

Modern mobility has caused family ties to slacken. Relations only meet for weddings and funerals, and maybe at Christmas. Many people have little sense of belonging to a family network, let alone a wider group of people.

Therefore we are less aware than previous generations of our family history. What our grandparents and great-grandparents did appears to have little relevance to us. Consequently, we have a sense of rootlessness; many feel themselves to be 'restless wanderers on the earth', like Cain (Genesis 4:14).

It was not so for the Jews in ancient times, nor, indeed, for many Jews today. Their family tree was and is an important pillar of support to individuals, with a solid base helping to hold the community together. Through it, relatives are linked to the past and are given a sense of mattering for the future. They can see how they fit into a larger group, through which God has worked and will work again.

Each person has a place, and hence a sense of belonging to something, Someone even, bigger than themselves. All is not lost when someone dies; the story goes on. And so the returning exiles needed these genealogies to stabilise them in their new life, as well as to settle the inevitable disputes over who was, and was not, a true Jew and heir of land in Judah.

This hotchpotch of lists covering many periods of time served an important purpose. They are not wasted space in the sacred record. Even if we do not read them word for word, our eyes should scan them to see behind the strange names hundreds of people who took their places in God's story and without whom the present would be far different.

We are not isolated individuals struggling to survive in a hostile world. Our past is written on our genes and engraved on the collective memory. To neglect that past is to lose a little of our humanity. Maybe the Chronicler could teach the world something about the art of belonging.

FAST facts

Name: 'Chronicles' was given by Jerome in the fourth century AD. The Hebrew book was called 'The events of the days' (or 'annals') and the Greek translators called it 'Things omitted' (from 2 Samuel and 1 & 2 Kings).

Structure: 1 & 2 Chronicles was originally one book and was split in the second century BC by the Greek translators of the Septuagint. It has been suggested in the past that Ezra-Nehemiah should also be linked to Chronicles to form an even longer book by the same editor/author, but this view has been strongly challenged in recent years.

Sources: The author uses numerous sources which are mentioned in the text (e.g. Samuel's records, 1.29:29; David's annals (1.27:24) and 'the book of the kings of Israel and Judah' (2.16:11). The author makes use of the biblical books of Samuel and Kings, re-writing or contextualising material to suit his own emphases.

Author: Traditionally Ezra (of the eponymous book) but this cannot be proved.

Date of compilation: Very uncertain. Somewhere in the fifth century BC (500-400) is most likely, but some have put it later.

Purpose: This is not clear, and the author seems to have several purposes in mind. He shows how in the history of Judah the covenant with God has been broken, while God himself has remained faithful. It is a religious history, with a focus on the temple. There are numerous prayers and prophecies, too. It contrasts with the more 'political' history of 1 & 2 Kings.

We'll always need a conquering hero

1 Chronicles 11,12

By comparing the way people in different ages use the same word, we can trace changes in culture. In 1000 BC, heroes are brave warriors who risk their lives to secure David's kingship. Less than 300 years later, the same society's heroes were those who could hold their drink (Isaiah 5:22).

The twentieth century saw the same process compressed into less time when wartime heroes such as the physically legless Douglas Bader gave way to sports and screen anti-heroes who became emotionally legless devotees of wine, women and narcotics.

In our more passive and indulgent age, we may have difficulty in identifying with the battle heroes of Chronicles. Today's role models may be the unsung heroes of the emergency services, or an intrepid conservationist.

To appreciate Chronicles we must enter the mindset of a different era. David was the Lord's anointed, and he (and the Lord) were worth dying for. These are the heroes who inspired Jewish readers in different walks of life. They lifted spirits and gave vision. The author may want to show that people from all the Israelite tribes were loyal to David and prepared to die for him. This would have been important in later years as people looked back over the tragic story of the divided kingdom. In fact, he plays down the role of Judah and Benjamin, which later formed the nation of Judah and took on the story of God's people.

David's apparently disdainful waste of the water brought to him at great risk by 'The Three' was actually an act of worship and thanksgiving. (Water was poured out 'before the Lord' in several rituals.) David, at this stage, was giving God all the glory and regarded anything done for himself as an act of service to the God who had chosen him.

God becomes the focus

1 Chronicles 15-16

If we want to do something for a person we love, we usually do it 'as they would like it'. In this passage David is making sure that everything will be as God would like it (15:13).

Once again the Bible is reminding us that worship demands the best and most professional effort we can make. Preparation involves both getting the logistics right, and also getting ourselves ready to meet with God afresh. The Chronicler shows that David rightly pays attention to detail.

The psalm in chapter 16 is almost certainly compiled by the author from several psalms ascribed to David (96,105,106). Many psalms would have been sung on this occasion, and the reader's attention is drawn to certain aspects of God's character. These include his faithfulness and everlasting care, for which all creation joins in praise.

The psalm says nothing about the ark of the covenant or of David's conquests; it focuses entirely on God. The 'official' opening of the ark's new home is the occasion of the celebration but the cause is God's unfailing goodness. These verses provide guidelines for worship at a time of thanksgiving when it is all too easy to focus on the the event, and not on the Creator.

The singing is accompanied by a fellowship meal (16:2-3; possibly 'dates' should read 'meat', a treat rarely eaten by ordinary people in the Old Testament). Worship is a corporate activity and eating together in God's presence can create a special bonding between believers and God.

1 Chronicles

Date of events:
From Saul's death c. 1010 BC to David's death c. 970 BC

Location:
Judah, centred on Jerusalem

Place in Bible:
After 2 Kings and before 2 Chronicles in the Old Testament

Fear was not awe

1 Chronicles 21

Once again David is frightened by God's holiness after he oversteps the mark, which is one biblical definition of sin. Previous occasions were the attempt to bring the ark to Jerusalem, thwarted by Uzzah's death (ch 13), and the affair with Bathsheba (2 Samuel 12).

His reaction is a good example of repentance. His act of penance left a hole in his pocket. Protestant Christians tend to avoid such gestures out of a fear that they are thinly-disguised attempts to earn forgiveness or to bribe God, but there can be spiritual and emotional benefits to the worshipper from actions of this kind.

Doing something can be cathartic, bringing home to sinners in a tangible way the full reality of the 'cost' of their error and the enormity and graciousness of the forgiveness which rationally the Scriptures assure them are theirs.

Prayer and action are two sides of the same coin. Just as praying for someone in need but doing nothing to help them is empty and vain (cf. James 2:14-17), so saying sorry to God and asking for his forgiveness without also finding some way of physically demonstrating one's sorrow can be a way of seeking 'cheap grace' which may not draw us closer to God.

Sadly, in David's case, the act was not followed by a renewed sense of 'peace with God'. He was so afraid of God that he dared not go back to the place, and preferred to meet with God in more comfortable surroundings. To have returned might have reinforced his spiritual resolve even more.

David's long-term view

1 Chronicles 22-26

Contemporary politicians tend to have a horizon which stretches no further than the next election. David takes a long-term view in the full knowledge that he will not live to see the outcome. He does this for two reasons.

Firstly, he developed the idea of having the temple and he naturally wants to bequeath its details to the next generation. He is being a good steward of his own gifts and insights. It is an act of humility; having been told he was not the man to build the temple he could have washed his hands of it.

Secondly, he knows that the next generation needs his experience (cf. 22:5) and that large tasks span generations. He had no guarantee that Solomon would take his advice, but he had a responsibility to prepare in such a way that Solomon could implement it.

From writing wills to setting out our vision for the future, we are closer to taking God's long-term view than if we leave matters to the next generation. Long-term planning is a real act of faith – and of faithfulness.

Solomon sets his sights high

2 Chronicles 1

There are several almost unbelievable promises in the New Testament. Jesus said we could ask for anything in his name, and he would do it (John 14:14; 16:24). Whoever asks, receives (Matthew 7:7) and those who seek God's kingdom get the earth too (Matthew 6:33).

Of course, the context of each statement contains assumptions about God, prayer and ourselves which rule out any possibility that our Heavenly Father is a soft touch for anyone brazen enough to ask for the moon. Riches are not a right for all believers; they are a responsibility for some.

Solomon is given an open promise and he chooses what he needs rather than what most of us would dream of (vv 8-12). He appears to be ruled by:

- A sense of responsibility; he is on earth to do an important job, and he wants to do it right.
- A sense of gratitude. God is good and has chosen him and his family; Solomon wants to acknowledge this fact and in some way honour his debt to God.
- A recognition that the people he leads are God's, not his. Solomon is a servant of God and hence wants to do God's work in God's way.
- A heart which reflects God's character. God rules the world by wisdom (cf. Proverbs 8:1,22,23), and Solomon asks for wisdom 'in God's name', that is, according to his character and will.
- An acceptance of potential discomfort and difficulty; he did not ask for the death of those who wanted to kill him. He put personal security low on his agenda in an age of political assassination, trusting God to sustain him, after the model of his father David.

Many Christians are afraid to take Jesus' promises seriously, often because we simply cannot believe they are true. But it may be that we are also unconsciously aware of the strings attached to them, and would prefer a less demanding discipleship. The bottom line is whether we prefer God's honour to our comfort. If we pray as Solomon did, the possibilities for world mission are great.

2 CHRONICLES

1	Solomon's prayer for wisdom
2	Preparations for the temple
3-4	The temple is built and furnished
5	The ark is taken to the temple
6-7	Dedication of the temple
8	Summary of Solomon's life and work
9	Queen of Sheba visits Solomon
10	The kingdom divides
11	Rehoboam king of Judah
12	Egypt attacks Jerusalem
13	Abijah's reign and civil war
14-16	Asa's reign and reforms
17	Jehoshaphat's reign and growth of Judah
18	Micaiah the prophet and Ahab's death
19-20	Jehoshaphat's reign and victories
21	Jehoram's reign and sin
22	Ahaziah's reign and sin
23	Jehoiada the priest reforms the nation
24	Joash's reforms and repairs to the temple
25	Amaziah's half-hearted reign
26	Uzziah's reign and prosperity of Judah
27	Jotham's reign
28	Ahaz's reign and sin
29	Hezekiah's reforms
30	Passover celebrated
31	Gifts for the temple
32	Assyria besieges Judah
33	Manasseh's evil reign
34	Josiah's reign and reforms
35	Passover celebrated
36	Four kings and the fall of Jerusalem

(The narrative is paralleled in 1 and 2 Kings)

Lay a good foundation

1 Chronicles 28–29

The detailed plans for the temple and its staff are important even to today's readers. They show again how important details are, and how significant individuals are. But here also we have a glimpse into David's heart at its best, as he lays the spiritual foundation for a godly life:

- Serve God; don't just take what he offers but give to him (28:9)
- Do so because you want to, not because you feel you must (28:9)
- Guard your thoughts and motives; God will know if you act for wrong reasons (28:9)
- Seek God actively and don't presume on his blessing (28:9)
- Persevere with the work he gives you despite inevitable setbacks (28:20)
- Trust God to provide the resources you need to do his work (28:20)
- Work closely with those whom God has appointed to assist you (28:21)
- In any work for him, however mundane, dedicate yourself and it to God (29:5-9)
- Remember that the resources you have for the work are themselves God's gifts (29:11,14)
- We are not perfect; what pleases God more than anything is integrity (29:17)

The plan of the temple is the same as that for Moses' tabernacle and for all subsequent temples. There are two rooms, the Holy Place and the Most Holy Place (Holy of Holies), and an outer courtyard where the sacrifices and most rituals take place.

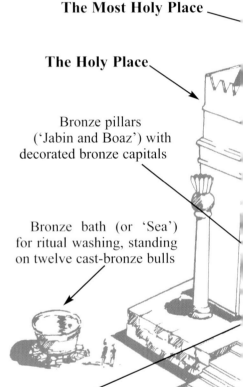

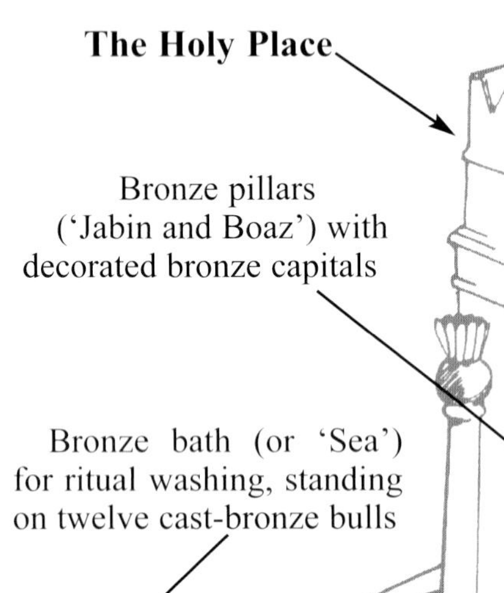

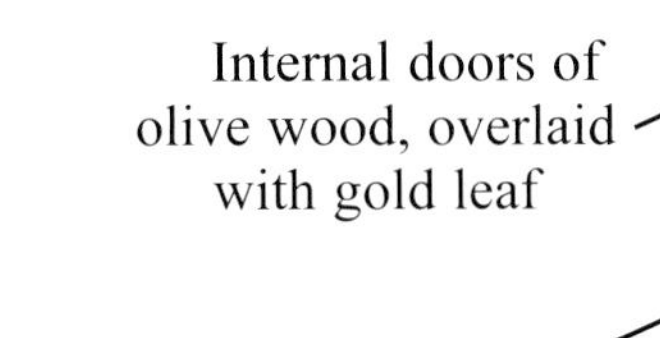

SOLOMON'S TEMPLE

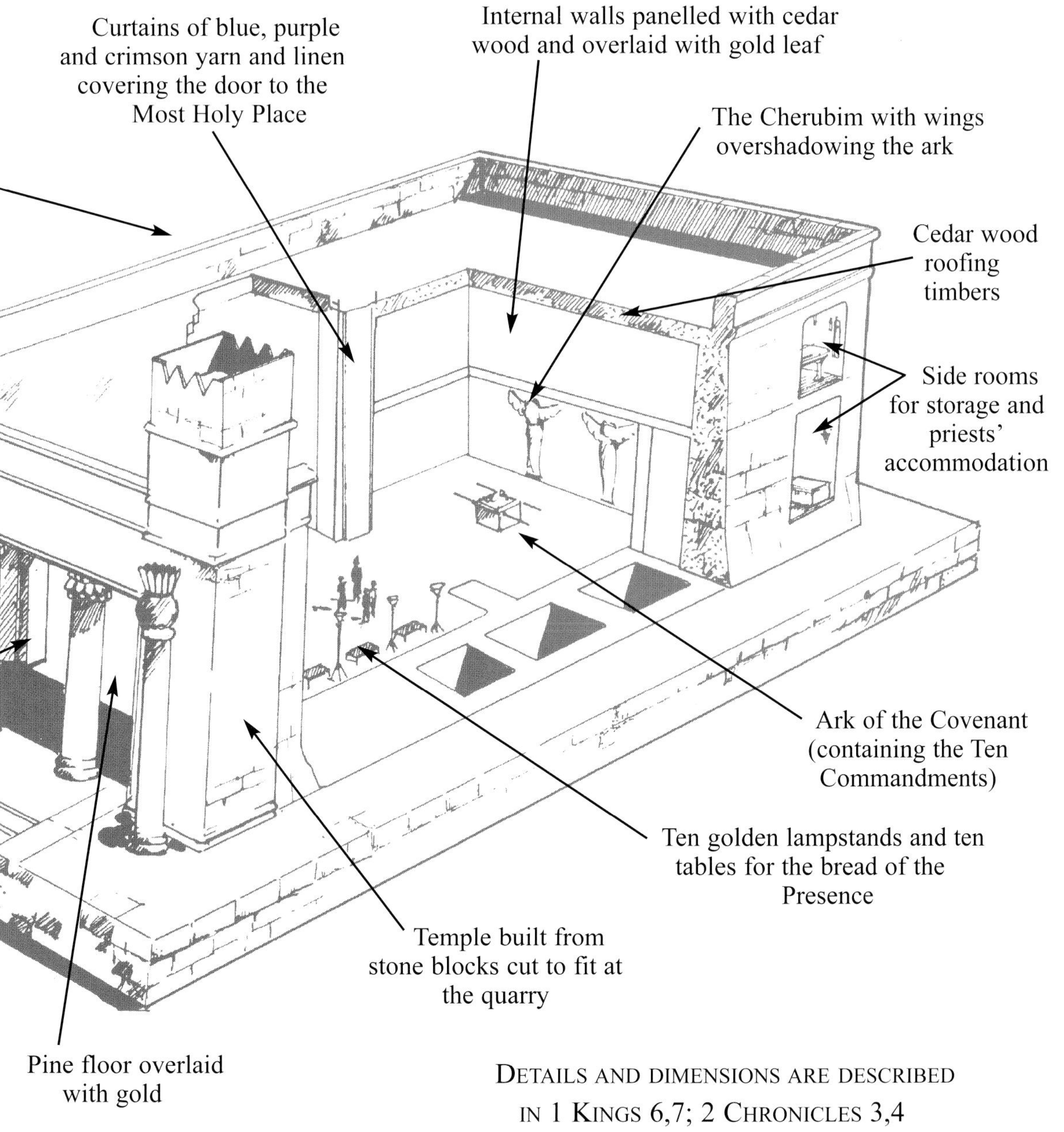

DETAILS AND DIMENSIONS ARE DESCRIBED IN 1 KINGS 6,7; 2 CHRONICLES 3,4

How to plan a building project and stay spiritual

2 Chronicles 2

There are two accounts of this planning which seem to contradict each other. In 1 Kings chapter 5 Hiram appears to take the initiative by sending envoys to Solomon, thus prompting the request for assistance. The Chronicler implies that Solomon approached Hiram (v 3).

The Chronicler is reporting everything from the point of view of Solomon and the temple; he is not as interested as the author of Kings in the niceties of political diplomacy. The two accounts fit comfortably together if we assume that Hiram sent his envoys as a natural gesture, just as ambassadors present themselves to new presidents and prime ministers today.

Solomon may have used the opportunity to send his request at once, or he may have sent it independently at a later date. He already had a relationship with Hiram, as had David before him (1 Chronicles 14:1; 22:4) and Solomon wisely used it:

- Both kings were powerful and would be a match for each other in a conflict. Working together on a prestigious building project was a good way of developing a peaceful relationship.
- Solomon was open in his witness to Hiram about the purpose of the building and the greatness of God (vv 5,6).
- He was willing to use 'secular' craftsmen for God's work. All human gifts originate from the Creator, whether those gifted recognise him or not. The organiser's intention in ordering the building, was more important than the lack of faith of those who physically erected it. Indeed, bringing unbelievers into such a project might stimulate their interest in the God to whom it is dedicated.
- And Solomon offered Hiram a fair deal. The payment would have fed an army. Solomon was not a mean businessman. (Although, as Chronicles makes clear later, it was the taxpayers who footed the bill, and the conscripted 'aliens' became virtual slaves.)

God's residence open

2 Chronicles 5-7

Many city-dwelling Russians have dachas – often no more than a wooden hut on a vegetable plot in the country – to which they retreat at weekends. In Western countries wealthier people sometimes have a holiday home. Solomon's prayer regards the temple as God's second residence.

He requests that God will hear his people 'from heaven' (e.g. 6:21) when they pray 'towards' the temple. This sets the Israelite faith apart from the cruder and more localised religions of other tribes and nations around them at the time; God doesn't live in houses.

The temple becomes an aid for the people's devotion to God, rather than something which God himself needs. It symbolises God's character and stands as a reminder of his existence.

At the end of the dedication the covenant is, in effect, renewed. God is pleased with his people's devotion and love, but he is not bribed by it. They are still to keep his commandments, whatever good things they have done so far. The temple, like any 'good work' is not a capital asset which they can use to offset any debts to God they may incur through their deals with the devil.

Solomon's thought here helps Christians today keep that difficult balance between treating church buildings with respect as 'God's house' on the one hand, and as functional tools no different from anywhere else on the other.

A place dedicated to God can be a channel for his ministry and grace, and therefore be holy in the biblical sense. The places where God makes his presence felt and his voice heard are rightly thought of as 'special' and not to be treated lightly.

Prophets rise through royal corruption

2 Chronicles 11,12

The first prophet to be named as a court adviser in the biblical narrative was Nathan, who confronted David. Now the nation has divided into two (Chronicles focuses entirely on Judah, the southern kingdom) we see prophets becoming more prominent. Kings no longer have the wisdom of Solomon and the piety of David. A new tier of spiritual leadership is required.

It is not a moment too soon. The kings of both countries embark on the pattern seen in the book of Judges. The best of them prosper, grow complacent, compromise their faith in some way causing themselves, and possibly the community as a whole, to suffer. The worst of them, to the Chronicler, are almost unspeakable.

Less than a decade after Solomon's death, Jerusalem has been ransacked by marauding pagans and the gold of its glorious temple looted (12:9-11). Thousands of people must have been heartbroken because there was 'still some good in Judah' (12:12). Had they and their parents served Solomon so faithfully just for this?

The world of unbelievers can be hostile and unfeeling; Christians must expect their setbacks too. Thieves do break in and steal, hence our true treasure is always to be in heaven, out of their reach (Matthew 6:19-21).

When opponents do attack, it is a good spiritual discipline to ask, 'Have we brought this on ourselves, as the Israelites so often did by pride, complacency or compromise?' We may not have; evil is not merely a repayment for error, but an enemy bent on destroying the good who do not merit its ministrations. But sometimes our error unlocks the door through which evil creeps.

Listen before you decide what to do

2 Chronicles 17-20

Conflicts sometimes arise because what one person thinks another is saying is not the case. We hear selectively what we want to hear. That was the problem with Ahab, Israel's king, whose court prophets were worse than court jesters; there was never a grain of truth in their zany predictions.

Jehoshaphat from Judah wisely discounted their views (they were probably prophets of Baal) and sought out a prophet of Yahweh who sarcastically imitates them at first (18:14,15). When he does speak the truth, Ahab doesn't believe a word of it (18:25) and Jehoshaphat apparently dismisses it as merely 'interesting' for which he is let off lightly with a later rebuke (19:2,3).

Judging what is right in a situation is always difficult. It requires listening to God (often through others) before we make detailed plans. Once an idea has begun to take shape in our minds, it is extremely difficult to change it.

HARD Question

How did kings shape the nation?

2 Chronicles 14-16

Throughout the Old Testament God acts for or against corporate groups, especially Israel and Judah. The fate of each country depends on the actions and attitudes of its king. The Bible holds together the principles of corporate solidarity and personal responsibility. In between, many ordinary people are caught up in the story.

The king has awesome responsibility as illustrated in the story of Asa. The narrative is stylistic with chapters 14-16 forming a 'chiasmus' in which opposite ideas lie either side of the central point (here it is Asa's covenant in 15:9-18).

Asa is God-fearing (14:2-6 summarise his best years as a preface to the story). His prayer in 14:11 captures a vital biblical truth: no one is stronger than when they are thrown helplessly on the mercy and grace of God.

He reforms worship under prophetic guidance (although not entirely, 15:17), which leads to stability (15:19). The country benefits from the leader's style, although many 'unfaithful' people remained using the 'high places' or pagan groves; a similar situation is reported in Jehoshaphat's reign (20:33).

But it doesn't last. Asa takes a humanly sensible approach, paying off one enemy in return for protection, which seems to succeed (16:1-6), but which is not God's preferred course. Wrong actions are not always doomed to failure, however. Boosted by the good results of his action, Asa rebukes the prophet (16:7-10), for which he later suffers (16:11-13), and there is further conflict (16:9).

This is a typical scenario from Kings and Chronicles, and leaves the reader in no doubt that the fortunes of many hang on the work of a few. To whom much is entrusted, much is required (cf. Luke 12:48). This does not however consign the majority to the status of short-sighted sheep! Yet modern management theory stresses that the leadership sets the tone from which all benefit, or suffer.

John Mott, an early twentieth-century American missions strategist once defined a leader as someone 'who knows the road, who can keep ahead, and who can pull others after him'. We may prefer to do our own thing and resist being told what to do, but history and Scripture both testify to the value of good leaders and the horror of bad ones. They have power, delegated by God and by the people, which they are to use wisely for the good of all.

Hence the requirement to pray for leaders and to encourage them, and for church leaders to exercise the prophetic role when necessary (and preferably in private in the first instance, according to Matthew 18:15-17 and the Old Testament precedents).

How the Bible books, kings and prophets fit together before the fall of Jerusalem

715 BC **Hezekiah**	697 BC **Manasseh**	640 BC **Josiah**	609 BC **Jehoiakim**	598 BC **Jehoiachin**	597 BC **Zedekiah**
2 Kings 18–25					
2 Chronicles	29–36				
Isaiah		Jeremiah			
Micah			Daniel		
			Zephaniah	Ezekiel	
			Habakkuk		
			Nahum		

We all need a pastor

2 Chronicles 22-24

Jehoiada and his wife Jehosheba are a model couple who shelter and nurture a future leader and then expose him at the right time.

They provide an example for church leaders to follow who find themselves entrusted with the pastoral care of talented young people or newly-converted celebrities. A time of secret, quiet nurture is essential before they are 'brought out' and given responsibility. And after that, they still need pastoral care and guidance.

Golden age tarnished

2 Chronicles 26

The 52-year reign of Uzziah had been a golden age marred only by his pride and illness. The borders of Judah were extended, and his building projects recalled Solomon's heyday. Significantly, Isaiah received his commission 'in the year that King Uzziah died' (Isaiah 6:1). He was a hard act to follow and there were social and spiritual signs that decline had already begun.

Uzziah himself had stumbled. Although the Bible prevents us taking a simplistic attitude to the relationship of sin and illness, the Chronicler's point is that sin affects both those who commit it, and those touched by it.

His skin disease picturing sin was unlikely to have been leprosy (the same word is used for numerous skin diseases). But its effect was the same: it separated the king from his people. Sin separates; it breaks relationships. Even golden ages can be tarnished by something which seems trivial. After all, Uzziah didn't cheat his wife, rifle the treasury or murder his rivals. But he could not complain that he was hard done by; sin is serious, in whatever form it is committed.

Corrupt religion grips the land

2 Chronicles 28

The precise nature of non-Israelite religion is not easy to establish. There are few records of what actually took place at the shrines and high places. The practice of Ahaz provides some details and shows why the prophets were so opposed to it:

- There were many gods, thus denying the sovereignty of the one true God, breaking the first commandment (v 2)
- They were worshipped as images, breaking the second commandment (v 2)
- Sacrifices were made to them, denying the sufficiency of those made to Yahweh. (The Ben Hinnom valley was a rubbish tip also known as Gehenna and an apt picture for the smouldering anguish of hell.)
- Fire rituals may have been initiation rites to the god Molech, or full child sacrifice, though this is only rarely attested by archaeologists (v 3)
- Rites included cult prostitution; the 'spreading tree' probably refers to shrines in groves associated with fertility rites (v 4; cf. 1 Kings 14:23,24)
- Superstition reigned; if a tribe or nation was defeated by another it adopted the apparently superior god of its victors as a talisman (v 23)
- The central Israelite shrine was abandoned, contrary to the law of Moses (vv 24,25)
- Spiritism and witchcraft may also have been practised (cf. 33:6).

The Chronicler notes two incidents which expose their spiritual bankruptcy. First, the Israelites (northern kingdom) feared God more than the Judeans and even possessed a true prophet (vv 9-15). Secondly, Ahaz was not given full honours in his death (v 27). Judah had sunk as low as it could.

CROSS CHECK

Solomon: pp 343-45
How the kingdom divided: pp 345-46
The fall of Samaria: pp 252, 254
Hezekiah: pp 168-69
The fall of Jerusalem: pp 186-87

Partial revival leaves many unmoved

2 Chronicles 29-31

Broad-canvas reports of any major event can imply that the situation is uniform when it is not. These chapters describe a spiritual restoration which sounds at first as if everyone was drawn into it. But the small print shows they were not.

The priests had been tardy in preparing themselves and were shamed by the zeal of their lay assistants, the Levites (29:34). The priesthood itself had become very run down (30:3) in the 16-year reign of Ahaz (cf. 28:1).

Public support was not overwhelming, either. The decimation of the northern tribes (Israel) in 722 might have caused the people not deported to Assyria to turn back to God, but many rebuffed the messengers (30:10,11). Judah was more faithful (30:12), but as the tardy priests came from there it is likely that the public response was still partial.

Such notes are important in our interpretation of Scripture. Biblical reporting is always selective and intended to illustrate certain truths, and its authors did not intend us to draw conclusions beyond this. When God moves in our midst, there will always be mixed responses. This is what Scripture teaches us to expect.

Hezekiah – a case study

2 Kings 18-20; 2 Chronicles 29-32; Isaiah 36-39

Hezekiah was another flawed leader, but one from whom there is a lot to learn:

- He trusted God (2 Kings 18:5)
- He reformed the nation and its worship (2 Chronicles 29:1-11
- He prepared practically for trouble when he saw it coming (2 Chronicles 32:1-8)
- He was granted an extension to his life to see his work through (2 Kings 20:1-11, probably out of chronological order in the story)
- He was hurt and frightened by those who ridiculed his faith (Isaiah 37:1-4)
- He faced a major threat he could not hope to defeat but he did buy himself time (2 Kings 18:13-16)
- He took his problem to God (2 Kings 19:14-19)
- He followed Isaiah's advice and trusted God (Isaiah 37:5-7)
- He grew proud in easier times (2 Chronicles 32:25,26).

Conversion story offers hope for all

2 Chronicles 33

People in trouble often turn to religion, giving sceptics a reason to dismiss faith as a prop for the desperate. Believers, however, see in that common reaction a sign that deep down human beings know they are accountable to the one true God.

Manasseh, who reigned longer than anyone in the Bible, made a dramatic U-turn when taken hostage at a turbulent period of Assyrian history. Several factions were rebelling, and subject states such as Judah and Egypt sought to take advantage of this fact by rebelling or withholding taxes.

As a hostage, the blasphemer became a worshipper, the polytheist became a monotheist, and he who consulted the spirits of the dead consults instead the Spirit of the Lord.

It happens. And because it happens, it forbids Christians to think dismissively about any human being, however evil and however negative they are towards God. Dramatic conversions are rare, but no nut is too hard for God to crack. Therefore, hope for such people should never be abandoned, and prayer for them should never cease.

Rolling reform based on Scripture

2 Chronicles 34-35

Having told us that Hezekiah's reforms were not universally accepted, the Chronicler here reminds us that even the best reforms took time to develop and to be completed.

Manasseh's reforms may have been undone by Amon (33:21-25) but he only lasted two years and the damage may have been slight. Josiah's reforms began 12 years after his accession and continued for some years (34:3,8).

The rediscovery of the 'Book of the Law' (ch 34) is a key event and it is generally thought that the book was Deuteronomy. It gave the reform movement a focal point. Josiah's awareness of God's righteous requirements had inspired the first part of the reform, but the Scriptures were needed to inspire the second wave.

Reforms within a church or an individual's life which accord with broad Christian principles may be the first stage in a more complete return to God. The spiritually-sensitive heart is then ready to receive the harder words of Scripture, like those which caused such consternation to Josiah.

Zealous reformers who go straight to the details may technically be right, but pastorally they may be moving too fast to expect instant conformity to a Christian lifestyle from people involved in un-Christian relationships and behaviour patterns. Shouting the scriptural commands at those who currently do not keep them is not always helpful.

God's word is sharper than a two-edged sword (Hebrews 4:12), but God is a surgeon not a butcher and applies his knife only when the patient has been prepared to receive it.

Judah's last days

2 Chronicles 36

The exodus from Egypt was the high point in Israel's history; the fall of Jerusalem and the exile of Judah to Babylon was its lowest. The Chronicler glosses over this period of anguish and suffering, which the prophet Jeremiah records in graphic detail. The sequence of events, gleaned from biblical and contemporary sources is as follows:

- 612 BC: Assyrian capital Nineveh is destroyed by the Babylonians
- 610 BC: Pharaoh Neco II takes control of Egypt
- 609 BC: Neco marches north to fight with Assyria against Babylon at Carchemish; Josiah attempts to stop him (35:20-25), is killed, and Egypt takes control of Judah having been defeated by Babylon in the battle
- 609 BC: Neco deposes Josiah's successor and replaces him with Eliakim (Jehoiakim; 36:2-4)
- 605 BC: Nebuchadnezzar of Babylon confirms his supremacy and makes Judah a subject state, deporting some citizens (including Daniel) and imposing heavy taxes (36:5-12; Daniel 1:1,2)
- 597 BC: Nebuchadnezzar places Zedekiah on the throne of Judah as a puppet ruler, having deported Jehoiachin (Jehoiakim's successor) and looted the temple (36:9-10)
- 588 BC: Zedekiah rebels against Nebuchadnezzar, who besieges Jerusalem
- 587 BC: Jerusalem's walls are breached, the city sacked and the temple destroyed. More people are deported (36:11-20; Jeremiah 52)
- 537 BC: Some 70 years after the first deportation, as prophesied by Jeremiah (Jeremiah 25:1-14) the Persians defeat Babylon and allow the descendants of all deportees to return to their homelands (36:21-23).

For today

1 & 2 Chronicles

- Each person has a place in the flowing stream of God's purposes
- Worship is to be offered in the way God would like it
- Prepare for the future and nurture future leaders carefully
- God's wisdom is of greater value than anything else
- Listen to God before you even start to plan, rather than asking him to bless your plan
- Pray for leaders and for people who are antagonistic to faith

A primer for faith and life

Paul's letter to the Colossians

- Rejoices in the faith of this young church
- Describes Jesus as the eternal creator, sustainer and redeemer
- Shows that Jesus is superior to all other objects of devotion
- Calls on readers to live out their new life in Christ in practical ways

Jesus was making headlines again in the last decades of the twentieth century. There were claims that his tomb had been found in France, that his family burial place was unearthed in Jerusalem, that he married, never died and was a Buddhist.

On top of that came the upsurge of interest in all things 'spiritual'. In what became a pick'n'mix religious market-place, Christ and crystals jostled for shelf space and credal faith made room for feng shui.

What has become true today in Colorado, Coleraine and Cologne was also true in similar ways in Colossae in the religious mish-mash world of the first century AD. All Paul's letters have contemporary significance, but perhaps Colossians is the most relevant. Its four brief chapters are packed with theological and practical truths which make it a superb introduction to Christian believing and behaving.

Here you will find a definite summary of who Jesus is and what he has done: the eternal God, incarnate as a human being, dying and rising in order to bring us to eternal life with himself. Here too is a classic exposition of Christian living using the image of taking off a grubby set of clothes and being vested in God's own righteousness (3:9-17).

And here is Paul's great assertion that Christ is all you need in the spiritual realm. Other religious systems and symbols can take us captive, he declares, but Christ sets us free from spiritual bondage.

COLOSSIANS

1:1-14	Paul's thanks and prayer for the Christians
1:15-2:5	Jesus, the church and Paul's labour
2:6-22	Christ frees us from slavery to superstition
3:1-4:1	The new Christian life in practice
4:2-18	Personal messages

Colossians is not to be read hurriedly. Ten verses at a time is probably more than enough for most people. You can linger in it for days, weeks even, allowing the precise language to seep into the depths of your being. Be prepared to be enlightened, amazed, challenged – and changed.

How to pray effectively for other Christians

Colossians 1:9-14

Many Christians find praying for others difficult. Apart from finding the time and remembering those who are out of sight (and therefore, in our busy world, often out of mind), there is the problem of knowing what to ask God for on their behalf.

Frequently our prayers are restricted to practical things: healing

Since, then, you have been raised with Christ, set your hearts on things above, where Christ is seated at the right hand of God. Set your minds on things above, not on earthly things.

Colossians 3:1,2

from illness, strength to cope with crises, wisdom to make the right decision. Paul sets his sights differently, and higher. Although this passage is not a model prayer in the sense that the 'Lord's Prayer' (Matthew 6:9-13) is, it provides a good template for intercessions.

- It reminds us that prayer should be regular and continuous irrespective of people's known 'needs' (v 9).
- Pray that people will know God's purpose in every part of their lives, including detailed responses and decisions for which we need an awareness of God's general purposes for his world (v 9).
- Pray that they may have wisdom and insight into God's truth and purposes, a growing awareness of his all-embracing concerns (v 9).
- Pray that they may live in ways which honour him (and which by implication 'speak' to others about him); pleasing him is more important than pleasing others (v 10).
- Pray for spiritual growth and 'fruitfulness' (becoming more Christ-like; cf. Galatians 5:22-26) in 'good works' (acts of self-giving which adorn our lives), v 10.
- Then (after all that) pray for inner strength to endure difficulty and suffering (not to escape from it), v 11.
- And because life is never easy, pray that the joy of knowing God may dominate people's consciousness and enable them to remain thankful that they are members of God's family (v 12).

Try some of that in your next prayer time, or in the intercessions on Sunday!

Big investment by man of small credit

Colossians 1:3-8; 4:12-13; cf Philemon 23

The pedantic minutes of the local church council are probably a better record of true church history than all the scholarly analyses put together. Because there, Mrs Jones is thanked for her years organising the cleaning rota and Mr Simpson is commended for chairing the outreach committee.

Historians have never heard of them, but they are logged in God's records. Epaphras is rather like them. He makes a small appearance in Paul's letters (along with numerous others who only get their name in print with no further details).

His name is a contraction of Epaphroditus (not to be confused with another of Paul's helpers by that name in Acts) which means he was a Gentile. The name derives from Aphrodite, the goddess of love.

He was also a Colossian (4:12) who, we assume, became a Christian under Paul's ministry in Ephesus and took the gospel back to Colossae (1:7). Later he became a delegate of Paul and was with him in prison (Philemon v 23). Epaphras also brought Paul news of the Colossian needs and trends (1:8).

He reminds us that most evangelism is undertaken by people who are not 'household names'. Paul was in the New Testament spotlight but people like Epaphras make up the backing which shaped the church.

Those with small tasks may yet have a big influence and an important role. We should neither despise them nor shrink from taking them as partners because they seem 'beneath' us. Even mention in the local minutes is more than many servants of God can expect; but there will be fanfares for all in heaven.

Location:
Colossae was a large city on the Lycus River in modern Turkey, built on two major trade routes

Date:
Between AD 55 and 60, depending on where it was written

Place in Bible:
Among Paul's letters in the New Testament, after Philippians and before 1 Thessalonians

Parallel books:
Colossians is very similar to Ephesians and was probably written alongside it. The letter to Philemon was sent to Colossae at the same time

He's the greatest!

Colossians 1:15-23

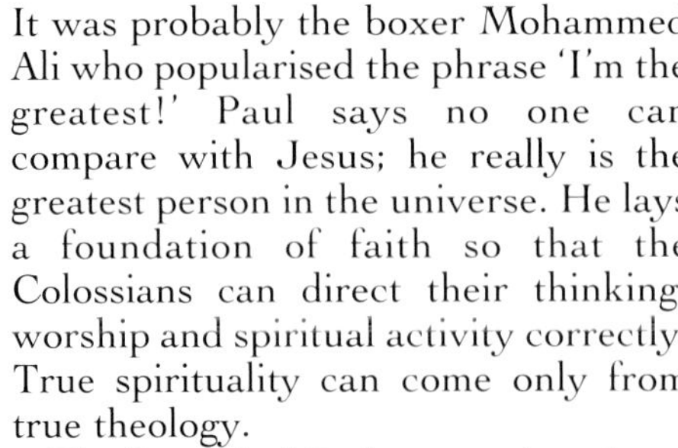

It was probably the boxer Mohammed Ali who popularised the phrase 'I'm the greatest!' Paul says no one can compare with Jesus; he really is the greatest person in the universe. He lays a foundation of faith so that the Colossians can direct their thinking, worship and spiritual activity correctly. True spirituality can come only from true theology.

- The 'image' of God means that Jesus is as divine as God the Father. He makes God seen and known in the world. For the equivalent of one millisecond in God's timeless story, he put on human clothes so that we could get a closer look.
- 'Firstborn' does not mean that Jesus was created. He is using the term in the Jewish sense of 'heir', the one to whom the family estate belongs.
- God's 'fullness' in Jesus is a term which means 'a full complement' as in a ship's company: nothing is missing. Jesus is God, completely, totally and eternally.
- Jesus was also the agent of creation, taking part in the Trinity's combined operation of forming matter out of Mind, and continued actively to sustain all from genes to galaxies.

Paul also describes Jesus as 'Lord of the church' (v 18). The church is central to God's purposes. God calls a corporate people to serve and worship him. So the church is Christ's 'body', the visible expression of his character and presence in the world.

In a fallen world of disunity, he brings people back to God, and joins enemies into the single body (cf. Ephesians 2:13-18). In a world crippled by the curse of death he has conquered the grave and opened up the possibility of endless new life.

Paul says Jesus is the greatest, so put nothing above him. He is Lord of your mind, your worship, your living, whether you acknowledge the fact or not. We cannot 'make' him Lord, but we can dethrone our other gods.

Author: The apostle Paul. A few modern scholars have disputed this because the heresy which he counters appears to include later (second-century) elements but its seeds probably existed much earlier.

Place and date of writing: Colossians is one of the four 'prison epistles' (with Ephesians, Philippians and Philemon). All were probably written at the same time and from the same place. Paul suffered three major imprisonments: Ephesus (c. AD 54), Caesarea (c. AD 59) and Rome (c. AD 60-62); there were others (such as an overnight stay at one in Philippi). Rome seems the most likely place of writing. Recently, N.T. Wright renewed the case for Ephesus as the most likely refuge for Onesimus (mentioned in Philemon) and closer to home for Epaphras. We cannot be certain.

How the church began: Paul never visited Colossae. While Paul was evangelising in Ephesus the Christian message was taken from there to Colossae by a new convert Epaphras (1:7; 4:12; cf. Acts 19:10). He then visited Paul in prison with news and questions about the church (1:4-8).

Purpose of letter and the 'heresy': False teaching was affecting new churches. Pagan and Jewish influences remained strong, and some new converts sought to combine elements of their old faith with the new one. The 'heresy' which Paul seems to counter in chapter 2 has never been identified and it may well be he is referring to a variety of dangers from several sources, rather than to one specific group or teaching.

Is salvation conditional on my faithfulness?

Colossians 1:21-23

The Old Testament Israelites broke their covenant with God and suffered for it. Christians seem to be able to get away with anything. That view can lead to 'antinomianism', which assumes that because we are saved eternally by God's grace we can do what we like now. However, Paul said it was a contradiction to have 'died' to sin yet still to live in it (Romans 6).

Some suggest that while salvation is a gracious and undeserved act of God we are thereafter responsible for maintaining that 'state of grace' through our worship, service and lifestyle. So 'salvation' becomes a matter of trusting that our Christian credit outweighs our sinful debts. But Paul insists that we cannot begin with grace and continue with 'works' (Galatians 3:2,3).

Another option is to agree that salvation is unconditional and irreversible; Jesus accepts us as we are and grants us eternal life. But having received his undeserved favour and love, we are called to demonstrate our gratitude by honouring God in daily life. We can never match his standards, but he delights in our attempts.

We will not be received into heaven because of what we have done, but we will be 'rewarded' in some way within heaven for our labours. Jesus implies this in the parable of the talents (Matthew 25:14-30).

Every true believer is assured of ultimate salvation. 'He who has the Son, has life' (1 John 5:12); nothing can rob them of it (John 6:39,40; 10:28). Paul's qualification in Colossians 1:23 therefore distinguishes between real and counterfeit faith.

A sign of genuine faith is seeking to remain faithful to God through life's trials, recognising our failures and repenting from them. If we are to forgive our brother '77 times' (Matthew 18:22) how much more will God forgive us? Failure will not disqualify us. With a hope like that, how can we dare to be careless?

Nothing's missing!

Colossians 1:15-23

Six times in this passage Paul uses the phrase 'all things' or 'everything'. It is completely inclusive. Physical matter, manufactured objects, mental process, principle for action, system of organisation, human institution: all things are embraced by God in creation, sustenance and redemption.

Therefore nothing in this life is beyond God's care, concern or redemption. Nothing is ultimately wasted. All human activity in its richness and diversity will somehow be swept up into the new creation. Even bad and foolish things can be redeemed in his purposes.

This world will be renewed, reshaped, retuned and resurrected, rescued from slavery to sin and death, in order for God to create for us what we vainly attempted and could never achieve: perfection, peace and purity. Your life and labour is not in vain; it is a small offering to an imaginative Lord who knows exactly what to do with it.

The person of Jesus, pp 205, 336
Work and leisure, pp 65, 341
Customs and Christianity, pp 71-3

Risk of Distortion

The Colossian heresies illustrate specific principles which may be repeated in any generation.

Confusion over concepts (v 8): We may reduce faith to 'sound' codes of conduct, specific definitions, and accept new ideas even when they contradict former beliefs. Truth never changes, even if our understanding of it does.

Confusion over customs (vv 16, 20-22): Religious practices may become in time the only acceptable expression of faith or test of orthodoxy, but customs can change with time zones, climate and the calendar. Christianity enhances human culture but does not abolish it.

Confusion over cosmic powers (v 18): Reports of 'near-death experiences' and stars consulting mediums, can confuse people over the powers of spiritual beings or saints. Christ is supreme; all other beings bow before him or serve him.

A model for ministry

Colossians 1:24-2:5

Being a church leader is a labour of love. Human approval is no indicator of spiritual effectiveness. Paul sets before us a model for ministers to follow, and something to pray for on their behalf.

- They are suffering servants (1:24,25). Paul does not mean that Christ's atoning death was insufficient, but that leaders suffer as they serve God, the world and their members, and thus finds a focus in the suffering of its leaders.
- They are commissioned by God (1:25). Paul had a spiritual calling (Acts 9:1-19) later confirmed by the church (Acts 13:1-3). The double recognition is especially important when minister and church argue!
- They are to teach the whole counsel of God, not just their pet emphases (1:25-27).
- They should admonish and teach wisely, so that the church may mature (1:28).
- Ministry continues behind the scenes (1:29; 2:1) in prayer and support of other leaders.
- Ministry aims to unite God's people (2:2), not to bulldoze their sensitivities.
- The centre and source of ministry is Christ, and he alone is honoured (2:2-4).

Shirley MacLaine

Old ideas return in 'new age' practices

Colossians 2:6-23

Ever since Shirley MacLaine lent new age spirituality her charms, everything from aromatherapy to yoga has been claimed to have 'spiritual' qualities. Some Christians have denounced it all as demonic. Others have dismissed it as worthless, like the placebo pill offered to volunteers in a clinical drugs trial.

Paul's denounciations here are against people who have elevated their ideas above Christ. It is Christ alone who is to captivate our hearts and minds. The 'written code' – the Jewish religious system and any methodology not centred on Christ – is ineffective as a way to God (v 13) although may hint at spiritual reality (v 17). It cannot 'restrain indulgence' and can lead to pride (vv 18-23).

But Paul did not abandon Jewish routines altogether. He took a vow in Corinth (Acts 18:18) and shared in the purification rites of others who had done the same (Acts 21:20-26). He did not dismiss all set disciplines as valueless.

There may be limited value in some so-called 'new age' disciplines and there may be food for thought in some of the linked ideas. But only Christ can bring you to God and impart the full riches of heaven, and only the Bible can enable us to discern what (and who) to believe. Beware of those who claim anything not harnessed to Christ has 'spiritual power'.

Faith into fashion

Colossians 3

The modern fashion industry sells images as much as clothes. But relatively few people buy new garments merely to hang them in the wardrobe. They want to be seen in them, and through them to make a 'fashion statement' to others.

Paul uses this idea in explaining the Christian life. He says it is like taking off one set of clothes that are dirty and unfashionable (that is, ungodly), and replacing them with a new, clean and attractive set which show we have a renewed nature (vv 9,10). We may or may not look different, but we are different. The make-over is permanent, as if we have died and been resurrected, as indeed in reality we have (v 3).

Now that you have been given these new 'clothes', Paul says, don't leave them hanging up but put them on (v 12). Being a Christian requires active co-operation with God in the life-changing process. This new 'image' comprises:

- A new status to celebrate (v 3). Our lives are infected by God's.
- A new society to join (vv 11,12,15). We belong to a universal community of believers which is expressed on earth in each local church.
- A new style of living to practise (vv 5-8,12-14). The list of evils puts greed alongside immorality. We cannot be culturally selective in our assessment of sin; the consumerism we tolerate is as spiritually destructive as the pornography we deplore. And in the place of common failings, we are to put such uncommon graces as caring and courtesy.
- A new speech to learn (vv 8-10,16). From innuendo to propaganda, from gossip to lies, the traffic in words has never been more dangerous. Character assassination and verbal violence are 'old clothes' to be incinerated. Our new wardrobe includes honesty, encouragement, and spiritual conversation.

We change by repenting of each path of vice that we become conscious of, which means that we renounce them and hand them over to Christ. Then we are to seek the aid of his Spirit to replace them with the virtues that are their opposite

Work is for people who know how to live

Colossians 3:17-4:6

A survey conducted by Berkeley University in California once suggested that up to a third of Americans would like to spend more time at work. They went there to escape the stresses of home. Other surveys have indicated the opposite, that people are tired of work-induced stress. The popular conception of work is that it is a necessary evil, but the Bible says it is a necessary good.

God invented it (Genesis 2:15) to be fulfilling (Ecclesiastes 2:24) although fallenness has introduced the drudge element (Genesis 3:17-19). Paul links it to teaching about relationships, implying that it is integral to society and not just something for our own benefit. But it was never meant to be all-consuming, so the sabbath principle was built in to human society (Exodus 20:8-10).

Here Paul says that work of all kinds is to be dedicated to God. Doing everything 'in his name' means to seek his honour in mundane and essential daily activities as much as in so-called spiritual activity.

For today

- Pray for people's spiritual growth, not just for immediate needs
- Think of Jesus as greater than all other people, ideas and priorities
- Focus on the essentials of the faith, and don't be side-tracked by human ideas
- Don't despise your daily work but see it as a service and ministry

Classic truth radiates from heated debate

Paul's two letters to the Corinthians

- Deal with a variety of problems which had arisen in the church
- Rebuke church members for their divisions, selfishness and indulgence
- Explore the concept of 'the body of Christ' and its application
- Describe Paul's working methods and sufferings
- Offer encouragement and comfort to hard-pressed Christians
- Advocate generous giving and personal restraint as marks of discipleship

Some people just seem to be problems waiting to happen. So do some churches, and Corinth was one. Paul tells the Corinthians about his mysterious 'thorn in the flesh' (II.12:1-10) but if we had not known that it was some personal ailment, we might have thought it was them.

These letters deal with a variety of teething problems which might confront a new church without the benefit of mature leadership and a library of books. They may not all be our problems but the principles Paul enunciates in dealing with them are permanently important in a variety of contexts.

They also let us see a little of Paul's personal emotions and ministry. At times he is desperately anxious, struggling to communicate and finally appeals to his apostolic authority. He tells us of the sufferings he endured for Christ and we are humbled by the great faith which kept his spirit afloat.

Written in the heat of the Corinthian troubles, these letters include teachings which have remained controversial. They include Paul's comments on women's ministry and on homosexual relationships. We shall need to remind ourselves of both the spiritual and cultural context in which he was writing as we seek to interpret them and compare his teachings with other New Testament passages.

AT A GLANCE

1 CORINTHIANS

1 A divided church and the wisdom of God
2 God's wisdom revealed by the Spirit
3 The church is united and should work together
4 Warning against pride and arrogance
5 Immorality within the church is to be rejected
6 Believers shouldn't take each other to court
7 Discussion about marriage and singleness
8 Discussion of food offered to idols
9 Paul's defence of his apostleship
10 The correct use of freedom is restraint, not licence
11 Instructions about propriety in worship
12 The body of Christ and gifts of the Spirit
13 What love is like
14 How to use prophecy and tongues in the church
15 Discussion of the resurrection of Christ and of believers
16 Personal greetings and comments

(NOTE: In the text when the two letters are considered together, they are distinguished in the references by Roman numerals I and II.)

Some writers claim that their best work is produced when they are under pressure. Paul might have said the same thing. For in the middle of his pleas and threats is his immortal prose poem about the nature of love. And much else that is memorable, instructive and uncontroversial is here too.

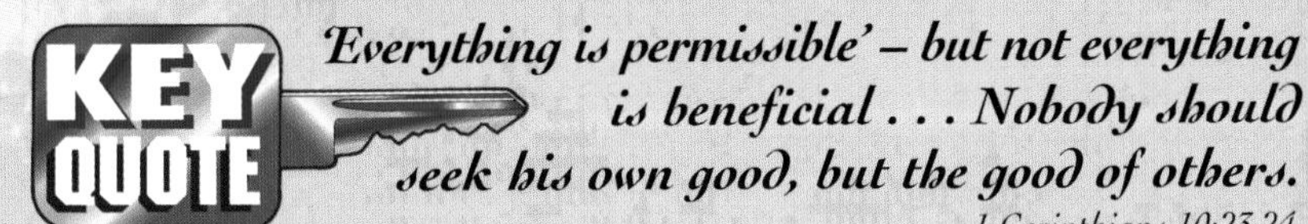

KEY
QUOTE
'Everything is permissible' – but not everything is beneficial . . . Nobody should seek his own good, but the good of others.
1 Corinthians 10:23,24.

Words of witness need wisdom of God

1 Corinthians 1:18 -2:16; 3:18-22

Some churches have as their motto, 'We preach Christ crucified' (1:23). Apart from the fact that this is only part of the gospel (the cross lacks its full meaning apart from the resurrection), it can become a coded message about the church's style of ministry.

It may mean 'we never employ "modern" methods of communication' such as drama or projected images. Paul, however, is not writing about preaching as a method, but about the approach he adopted: not that of philosophical argument (beloved of Greeks generally), but of a straight presentation of the historical facts and their practical relevance.

Indeed, to turn this text into a catch-phrase is to fall into the trap Paul was warning his readers against. It is a form of pride: we do this, believe that; others don't, therefore we are right and they are not. (The same charge can be levelled at churches which justify multi-media presentations!) Paul is stressing that reliance on any form of human 'wisdom' is unsafe. What counts is that we allow God the Holy Spirit to guide our ministry, inform our thinking and empower our evangelism.

He is not decrying 'apologetics' (reasoned argument for Christian truths) nor fresh methods (he sought to 'enculturate' the gospel in terms relevant to the different communities he visited, 9:19-22). But he does want the Corinthians humbly to depend on God and to seek his wisdom in all they do.

Above all he wants them, and us, to understand that the gospel can never be 'heard' by anyone unless the Holy Spirit takes the scales from their eyes and illuminates them. That is why neither preaching nor pictures can communicate anything unless God is at work in people's lives. That really does call for wisdom; our witness must be in the right place at the right time.

Unity in diversity

1 Corinthians 1:10-17; 3:1-19

In 1996, there were 243 Christian denominations recorded in the UK Christian Handbook, an almost threefold increase in 20 years.

In one sense the 'body of Christ' is divided today in a way that not even the Corinthians could imagine (1:10). Their divisions were caused by quarrelling and jealousy (3:3), yet another manifestation of the proud and competitive Corinthian mindset.

While it can be argued that the main historic denominations formed out of major theological rifts (such as the conflict over salvation by faith or works which spawned the Lutheran and Calvinist churches), sadly the 'quarrelling and jealousy' of leaders has caused the modern multiplication of church groups (cf. 1:12; 3:4).

Consumer choice has become society's holy grail, and independence its lowest common denominator. The disease also infects the church as we choose churches with subtly different spiritual flavours. To outsiders, Christianity is now many religions.

The New Testament urges leaders to sort out their differences. There is only one church, although it is not restricted to one denomination (the 'true' church is not an organisation but a fellowship of believers).

Today we can maintain the unity of our own group by learning to appreciate people's different approaches to spiritual life which reflect our diversity. We can also find ways to work with others to present a united front to society. This is harder work than sniping at each other, however.

Badly-built temples in danger of collapse

1 Corinthians 3:9-21

Temples were about as common in Corinth as churches are in Western cities. So Paul uses the metaphor of a temple (v 16) built on a foundation (v 10) to describe the nature and responsibility of the church. Often taken in an individual sense (the way I build my life), these verses apply primarily to the corporate life of the church as does most of the letter. The temple of verse 16 is 'you together', not 'you personally'.

The foundation of apostolic faith in the incarnate, crucified and risen Christ is profitless unless Christian living and service is built on it. Yet much 'church life' may be regarded as so much chaff, of no lasting benefit to saints or sinners.

The task of the church is to refine the 'gold' of its corporate gifts and scatter the 'precious stones' of its ministry in the spiritually impoverished community. So, Paul wants to know, is your church full of human hype or is it humming with holiness?

About 40 years later, the elderly apostle John will write at Jesus' behest a number of letters to churches in which they too are warned that by building the wrong kind of 'temple' they could fall into spiritual ruin. Today, we may be able to keep the shell standing for longer, but that is no guarantee that it has anything of value inside.

How the church began: Paul planted this church during his second missionary journey in about AD 51-52. He stayed in the city for some eighteen months, mostly in the home of a Gentile (Acts 18:1-17). He supported himself as a tentmaker for that time, taking every opportunity to preach and teach. It was here that he met Aquila and Priscilla, who were to become loyal friends and fellow-workers.

Date and circumstances: Although we have two letters to Corinth in our Bibles, and Acts records two visits there by Paul, there is every reason to believe that he wrote at least four letters and made three visits. The sequence of events seems to be:

1. Paul planted the church c. AD 51-52, then returned home to Antioch via a brief stop-over in Ephesus. After a break, he began his third missionary journey, spending three years in Ephesus (Acts 19).
2. While there, Paul received news from Corinth which disturbed him, and he wrote Letter 1 (not preserved) condemning sexual immorality (I.5:9). The Corinthians responded with questions about marriage, food offered to idols and spiritual gifts.
3. After visits 'from Chloe's household' and others (I.1:11,16,17) giving him more bad news, Paul wrote Letter 2 (1 Corinthians) answering the questions. He sent it by Timothy.
4. This did not have the desired effect so he interrupted his ministry in Ephesus to make a 'painful visit' to Corinth (II.2:1; 12:14; 13:1). This is not recorded in Acts.
5. Problems continued so he wrote a stinging Letter 3 via Titus (not preserved cf. II.2: 4; 7:8). Anxious for news, he hurried to meet Titus in Macedonia.
6. When they met, the news was much better, and Paul wrote from Macedonia Letter 4 (2 Corinthians). Halfway through he got more bad news and added a postscript (or wrote a separate letter), explaining the change of tone in II.10-13.
7. Finally he made his third visit (II.13:1; Acts 20:2,3) of which no details are recorded.

Sex mad saints shown the red light

1 Corinthians 5-7

In Victorian times any public reference to sex was treated with disgust or outrage. Today, attitudes have swung to the opposite extreme and sexual performance is, in some circles and much of the media, almost as common a topic of conversation as the weather or the football results.

Many people in our society would feel at home in Corinth. Aphrodite, the divine sex symbol, beamed down from temples and statues much as her living incarnations do from posters and screens today. Suggest modifying her sex appeal or clothing her more modestly and you will be regarded as emotionally deformed or psychologically perverted.

The Christian gospel therefore came as a shock and a challenge to the sex-mad city. And the new saints didn't know how to handle it. For some, Paul's preaching about spiritual liberty seemed to give them even greater freedom to have a good time. (That is why he quotes 'everything is permissible', 6:12; he is picking up a point from their letter and answering it diplomatically but firmly.)

For others, who heard more clearly the moral boundaries from Paul's discipleship classes, or who came from a Jewish background, the issue was not indulgence but abstinence. They advocated a kind of celibate monasticism as the highest form of sexuality (which is discussed in chapter 7).

Paul's teaching here is not the final word on the subject in the Bible, but relates specifically to the extremes he encountered. The principles he highlights are:

- Sexual relationships create a new and deep bond between people which is meant to be lasting; casual unions are therefore a denial of our human nature, and not a fulfilment of it (6:15-17).
- Sexual promiscuity is sinful, and will damage our spiritual health (6:18,19).
- Sex is to be 'stewarded' like any other gift or possession, for God's glory and not simply our own gratification (6:19,20).

Few people get sex completely right, and the church has sometimes failed its members by not recognising the sheer difficulty ordering this most powerful of human instincts. And because it clamours for so much attention, we may easily miss Paul's subtle aside.

He equates sexual sin with greed, slander and drunkenness (5:11; 6:10). Sexual failure is thus not to be elevated above sins which we rather easily overlook or forgive. And those sins ought to be treated with the same seriousness as we show towards sexual excess.

Destination of letter:
Corinth was a large city in southern Greece with a population exceeding 600,000 and many splendid buildings. Pagan religion was rife, and Aphrodite was its patron goddess. It was the 'pleasure city' of the Roman Empire, with a reputation much as Pattaya in Thailand. Romans with money went there for a good time.

Author:
The apostle Paul.

Date of writing:
AD 54-55. See 'Fast facts' box.

Place in Bible:
The two letters come after Romans and before Galatians in the New Testament.

Discipline matters, minor disputes don't

1 Corinthians 6:1-11

If you have a job you are protected from arbitrary dismissal by employment law. If you commit an offence you must be taken through a careful disciplinary procedure unless it is one of the few offences for which instant dismissal is allowed.

But you can't do that in church – at least not in most Western churches. Try and discipline a church member and you could have the world's media camped out in the churchyard within hours. Only a few churches have strict disciplinary rules for their members, not least because it is easy to become legalistic and cult-like. Differences over taste or temperament are reduced to tests of loyalty to God and the group.

Unlike secular social clubs, it is not possible for a church to specify what is or is not acceptable conduct. A ballroom dancing club could legitimately have a strict dress code, and a tennis club could decree that anyone who throws down their racket should be fined for unsporting behaviour.

But what would you do about a church member who is heard uttering a swear-word or seen breaking the road speed limit? Christianity is about living 24 hours a day in the real world and none of us is perfect in what we say or do.

Forgiveness of people who offend us in some way is part of the deal in church life (cf. Matthew 18:21-35), too. Sanctions sit uncomfortably on the same bench as forgiveness. So Paul's teaching here may seem anachronistic; it would be hard to apply it today and may seem a throwback to an Old Testament religion of law rather than a New Testament celebration of grace.

However, the passage does give some important, if uncomfortable, principles:

- Serious breaches of God's foundational laws (as in 5:1,2) should be disciplined. To welcome in fellowship someone who has fallen into such open sin is in effect to say that sin doesn't matter or that it is merely a 'private affair'. The Bible teaches that church life is damaged by sin.
- The person concerned was already a member, who then broke a basic moral law. Treatment would be different if an enquirer following such a lifestyle came to faith. He or she would need time, encouragement and support to change a probably complex set of relationships. But this is different.
- 'Delivering someone to Satan' (v 5) is almost certainly not some kind of curse. It means putting them out 'into the world' (Satan's domain) so that the seriousness of the sin is recognised by all; in practice this would mean a bar from Communion, and possibly from attendance of any kind.

But there is a limit to sanctions. All kinds of disputes can arise over nothing more serious than personality clashes and differences of opinion. The Corinthian Christians pre-dated today's litigation culture; they slapped a writ on anyone they disapproved of.

That, says Paul, is as wrong as letting people get away with serious misconduct. If discipline is required, it is the church leadership that must exercise it; church members are not to take the law (literally) into their own hands.

When such disputes do arise, we should seek reconciliation. Today, most people would let the situation fester. Indeed, says Paul, why not accept offence (which might arise from nothing more than human fallibility) rather than make a fuss? To stand on our own rights in church life is a sign of spiritual immaturity. There are more important things to get angry about.

Single-minded view of marriage

1 Corinthians 7

Single people often feel left out. Yet in Britain single people form over a quarter of all households (including the widowed). In one church survey, a third of all members were single.

Marriage is declining in popularity, divorce is relatively common and more people cohabit. In the first century, marriage was the norm. The Jews prized fidelity but among Romans infidelity was common. In Corinth, Christians were divided over whether marriage or singleness was more 'spiritual'.

Paul sympathised with those who advocated life-long singleness and sexual abstinence. He was himself unmarried (v 8). This was unusual among Pharisees and some conjecture that he was widowed.

He called on both married and single people to put God first. He either expected Christ to return soon (making procreative marriage unnecessary) or that persecution was about to break (adding stress for married people desiring to protect their families), vv 29-31.

Paul's concessions are not a veiled criticism of people with strong sexual drives. Paul is reacting against extremes: blatant immorality, and cult-like asceticism. Elsewhere, he uses marriage as a picture of spiritual union with Christ; he could hardly give it a higher honour.

Today's readers can gain from this passage important correctives to contemporary attitudes:

- Sex is not essential for personal fulfilment; sexuality is not to be over-stressed. Devotion to God's service is more important.
- Singleness is not a failure nor a sign of personal inadequacy. It can be a good choice; it may be an unfortunate consequence of living in a world of unequal opportunities.
- Single people face loneliness and pressure; families should build warm relationships with them.
- Proper stewardship of sexuality restricts its expression to a life-long partnership.

'Unsafe meat'

1 Corinthians 8:1-13; 10:23-11:1

The 1990's BSE cattle crisis was followed by debate about genetically modified crops. Food safety is a common talking point.

It was so in Corinth, too, only the alleged source of contamination there was spiritual. Butchers' shops were connected to pagan temples; animals were slaughtered according to ancient rites before being sold. Some Christians were afraid of being 'infected' by evil if they ate such food.

Today Christians may be concerned about 'guilt by association' with non-Christian activities or products, especially those which may orbit around the 'new age' system.

Products of any kind are not in themselves 'tainted' just because they have been handled by people with non-Christian religious beliefs.

Paul's robust view is to thank the Creator for food, remembering that no spiritual power can defeat him or harm those who trust him. However, Paul is sensitive to people who feel differently, so his advice appears contradictory.

There is a higher law: don't cause more sensitive Christians to act against their conscience. The self-pleasing Corinthians, needed to hear that. Don't just do what's right for you but think about its effect on others. People matter more than your enjoyment. We can certainly apply that today.

Train hard and overcome the opposition

1 Corinthians 9

Sports people usually train hard and play hard. That way, they win. Sometimes, though, they complain that the referee is biased against them or overlooks a blatant breach of the rules.

Paul has that kind of scenario in mind. The game is going against him. His opponents are fouling him. The onlookers are barracking him. He would be within his rights to protest at his unfair treatment. Instead, he just gets on with the job.

He had a right to be supported financially by the church he served. But he waived it so as not to burden them and, perhaps, so as not to be 'in the pockets' of a Corinthian faction.

In a strong post-match defence of his exemplary conduct, he says that it doesn't matter whether people recognise your worth or not; just get on with doing what God wants: play the game and leave the result to God.

He alludes to the Isthmian Games held in the city every three years, for which competitors trained hard for ten months beforehand. Like the athletes, he had a goal in sight: not the fading pine wreath (equivalent to a gold medal) of human acclaim but the unfading approval of God in the eternal glory of heaven.

That required the activity expressed by agonizomai (9:25) a Greek word for strict training, from which our word 'agony' comes! Spiritual 'training' includes keeping in tune with God, refusing all temptation, being keen to do good to others and willing to serve humbly. It's not easy; Jesus never promised it would be.

Ignatius Loyola captured Paul's meaning precisely in his famous prayer: 'Teach us, good Lord, to serve thee as thou deservest: to give and not to count the cost; to fight and not to heed the wounds; to toil and not to seek for rest; to labour and not to ask for any reward, save that of knowing that we do thy will; through Jesus Christ our Lord.'

Tempting times

1 Corinthians 10:11-13

Most of us are tempted every day to cut corners, tell white lies, or get something for nothing. The hard thing about temptation is that what we are supposed to say 'no' to is in fact 'tempting': it's attractive, desirable, like the fruit in the Garden of Eden (Genesis 3).

That is why we need a firm foundation of belief (so that we know what we should do) and a firm foundation of faith (so that we have the spiritual power to do it). If either is lacking, we are likely to fall.

Experiential faith is insufficient on its own because we may 'feel' something is right when it isn't, as the Corinthians so unfortunately discovered. Rational belief isn't enough on its own because it lacks the dynamic to say no and can degenerate into sterile legalism, as the Galatians discovered.

Paul's promise here is that nothing in the world is too hard for the Christian to be able to cope with. We have reserves of God's strength to draw on; we have resources of past examples to inspire us; and we have an escape route provided for us to run through, as Joseph did when confronted by a desirable and powerful temptation (Genesis 39:11,12).

But nothing will take away that feeling that we don't want to escape. One way to overcome it is to commit each day as it starts to God, and to remind ourselves of our commitment as the hours tick by.

HARD Question

What are the limits to women's ministry?

1 Corinthians 11:2-16; 14:33-35

During the 1990s the Church of England followed the example of many free churches, and admitted women to full ordination.

The decision went against the advice of the Roman Catholic Church, and a significant minority from both the evangelical and catholic camps left the church.

For many people (outside and inside) the debate was just another example of how archaic the institution had become. But when we encounter difficult scriptures and wish to remain faithful to them, the issue is not simply a matter of discrimination or chauvinism. We also have to grapple with complex theology.

Paul is clear here (and in 1 Timothy 2:8-15) that women are 'to keep silent' in church, 'not to teach' (and to be 'covered' that is, 'veiled', for which our equivalent is to wear hats). His words yield five possible interpretations (or combinations of them).

1. Some think that God has decreed that spiritual leadership is a male role, based on the male 'headship' of the creation order (11:7,8). Paul's teaching has the full force of a permanent commandment from God.
2. Others think that Paul was a misogynist, and did not reflect Jesus' acceptance and appreciation of women. His teaching is therefore invalid.
3. Others see Paul as a child of his age. On the evidence of God's calling of women to leadership (Philip's daughters in Acts 21:8,9) we should conclude that his teaching is culturally conditioned and not like the Ten Commandments.
4. As Paul did allow women to pray or prophesy (prophecy was related to teaching) in 11:5, yet tells them to keep quiet in 14:34, and also teaches the equality of the sexes in Galatians 3:28, he may have stated a general principle in chapter 11 (they are not barred from ministry) but made an exception for Corinth in chapter 14 because of local circumstances. Hence the command is of local expediency, and not 'from the Lord' and universally applicable (he makes that distinction also in 7:10-14).
5. His teaching may refer to the development of female-dominated mystery-religion tendencies.

As the debate has raged for a long time, and 'Bible-believing' Christians continue to disagree despite scholarly and popular pronouncements on the topic, each person has to settle the issue in their own minds and to recognise that others are genuine in their faith even if different in their practice.

It is an important issue for the church structure, but it is not a 'gospel' issue of the same order as the divinity of Christ or the effectiveness of his death and resurrection.

However, all involved should keep two points in mind. Those who believe in male 'headship' do not mean to imply a difference in status before God or in the church, only of role in the church community. This is not always appreciated by those who advocate womens ministry.

Alternatively, those who interpret Paul's teaching as universally mandatory need to state cogent reasons why, for example, women cannot teach but do not have to wear hats. By what criteria do we decide whether a rule is a 'creation' or 'cultural' ordinance?

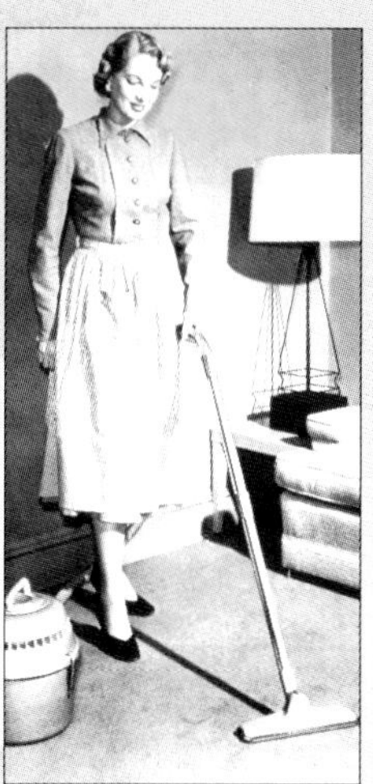

Women were not relegated to menial tasks by Paul

Bad manners corrupt worship

1 Corinthians 11:17-33; cf. 14:26-39

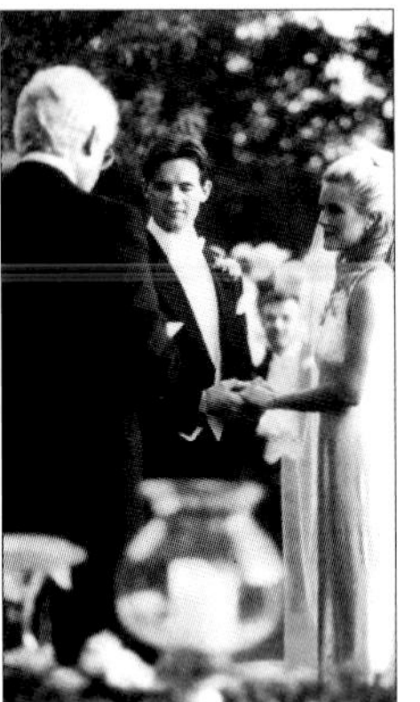

You have arranged a shared meal or pot-luck supper to which everyone brings food for a common table. But instead of handing over their contributions they all open their hampers and begin to eat. Visitors, and people with little to bring, are left out and hungry. Imagine their feelings.

That happened in Corinth. The shared meal was part of their Communion service. The special celebration of Christ's sacrificial death and resurrection was spoiled; the raucous party debased the symbolism and desecrated the sacrament.

Worship in Corinth was bad-mannered and insensitive. Despite the many spiritual gifts, it was unspiritual. 'Charismata' do not guarantee spiritual fruit. Corinthian worship dishonoured God and put off visitors (cf. 14:23).

Worship does not have to be dull to be orderly. Nor does it have to be rigidly led 'from the front'. Worship which welcomes spontaneous contributions can still be 'decent and in order', sensitive and helpful. Chaired by a mature person, it will ensure that certain people do not dominate or compete for honour and attention (14:27-33).

Paul assumes that people will prepare contributions in advance just as they come with prepared food (14:26). There is nothing especially spiritual (and possibly something very worldly) about waiting for on-the-spot 'inspiration'; ministry that has been prayed over beforehand has sieved out some of the human factors which may obscure God's word.

Bad worship carries a physical health warning (11:27-32). This supernatural 'discipline' of some members is the one rider to the regular New Testament assumption that suffering is not a punishment for sin.

Yet we still dare to attend church for 'what I can get out of it' or 'for what I contribute'. The only worthy reason for attending worship is to meet with God and honour him. Worship is a serious business; when we are ill a spiritual health check will do us no harm; none of us is perfect.

Church untied by missing love

1 Corinthians 12,13

Hasty typing often prints 'united' as 'untied'. The transposition of two letters reverses the word's meaning. When part of 'the body of Christ' slips the knot and loosens its connections with the rest of the church, the whole body is weakened and risks falling apart, like a climbing team originally roped together for safety and support.

Most congregations and clergy recognise at least verbally the importance of the 'laity' in the 'body life' and 'every member ministry' of the church and its witness to the community. Yet the force of this truth is sometimes missed. It is not simply that 'there is a place for you' (which there is). It is a challenge: take your part seriously and humbly. You have a job to do, which should neither be despised nor exalted but faithfully offered to God.

Paul's chief concern is to encourage unity. Selfishness and pride destroy the unity of the body. So he moves from teaching about gifts to his famous 'love poem' of chapter 13. For all its thought-provoking quality, its chief purpose is to inspire unity. 'Love' can be disuniting, if it is selective and cliquish. It is to be exercised by the whole body to the whole body.

A loving church can embrace a wide

variety of people, gifts and viewpoints, and weave them together into a model of what God intended community to be. For that to happen, there must be no loose ends: rope yourself in to the team (even if you are unsure about some of its members).

The gospel in a sound-bite

1 Corinthians 15

In a sound-bite culture, everyone wants simple statements which say everything and answer every question in a few words. We all know that life isn't like that, but we expect it just the same.

Christianity cannot escape the pressure: in thirty seconds, what is the irreducible minimum, the essential core, of the Christian faith? There have been many attempts at reducing the gospel to a few points believing which must inevitably make someone a Christian. But faith isn't like that, either.

Paul would have given a creditable performance in front of the Corinthian cameras, however. His thumbnail sketch of the essence of the faith (vv 3-5) has served the church well down the centuries. It's a useful yardstick to measure the gospel we believe and preach. Some presentations focus so heavily on the cross that the resurrection seems an afterthought, a bonus. Others so concentrate on the effects of resurrection or Holy Spirit life that the death of Jesus becomes a mere stepping-stone.

Paul holds cross and resurrection firmly together. Neither is fully meaningful without the other. In order to conquer death and sin Jesus had both to die and and to rise (cf. vv 54-57). Death and resurrection are both full of meaning; both were 'according to the scriptures'.

So when you are next put on the spot, don't put over a one-sided gospel. Even if you do only have a minute.

HARD Question

What does Paul mean by 'prophecy'?

1 Corinthians 12,14

The secular conception is foretelling the future, and there is an element of this in the New Testament as well as in the Old (e.g. Agabus in Acts 11:28). The 'charismatic' conception is a specific message from God to a church or an individual, delivered (potentially) through anyone who is open to God.

The 'liberal' notion includes preaching of any kind, and especially the denunciation of social or religious sins. The biblical definition is 'telling forth God's truth'. That may include any of the above.

In 1 Corinthians, Paul especially addresses the 'charismatic' conception. People delivered 'messages' during services. (This followed the Jewish synagogue pattern in which any male could speak after the reading of Scripture. It is still followed in some 'Brethren' Assemblies today.)

Such ministry is clearly open to abuse. People can claim to speak 'in the name of the Lord' just to have a go at someone. Or they can simply air their opinions. Discerning whether something is really from God is difficult, which is why Paul builds in some safeguards. Even those who genuinely believe God is speaking through them can be mistaken. The guidelines include:

- No prophecy can be contrary to Scripture or basic Christian belief (12:3);
- Prophecy is not to be delivered in a trance-like state, as in some of the mystery religions (14:32);
- No prophecy is to be accepted until it has been carefully considered by the church leadership (14:29).

There is nothing 'grand' or necessarily public about this kind of prophecy. A church member may receive in a prayer time a strong impression that God is saying something, and simply pass it on privately (and cautiously) to the minister. We may miss out if we do not encourage such sharing.

And if churches which major on it exercise due caution, few people will be hurt by erroneous or off-key messages. The ghost of Corinth still haunts some churches.

New matter for resurrection body

1 Corinthians 15:20-58

What will heaven be like? Will we recognise each other there? Most people have asked that especially when coming to terms with someone's death. Paul's teaching on the resurrection offers some clues, linked closely with the Gospel accounts of Jesus' resurrection appearances.

Resurrection – Jesus' or ours – used to be labelled impossible by people whose world-view was controlled by the strict 'cause and effect' laws of Newtonian physics. The story of Jesus walking unannounced into a locked room without using the door was explained away as what it seemed like to shocked disciples who failed to notice his entrance or exit.

However, since the advent of quantum physics – the science of sub-atomic particles – what seems impossible has become a little less strange. Among the particles which bombard the earth in solar radiation are neutrinos, which have a tiny mass but which do not behave like matter. They plunge through solid objects like a knife through warm butter.

Jesus' body appeared to have mass – he could be seen and touched, he ate – yet his body had properties unlike normal matter. He looked the same, yet was not recognised immediately (John 20:15; 21:4). He was the same, but different, like neutrinos. They do not 'prove' the resurrection but they make the idea of a different kind of 'matter' plausible.

Paul, without any knowledge of sub-atomic particles, figured out that as there are different kinds of body the resurrection body need be no more (or less) than another, if difficult to imagine, kind.

And if what was seen in Jesus was as Paul says, the prototype resurrection body, then we can be assured both that we will recognise one another and that life in heaven will be just as 'real' as life on earth. (C.S. Lewis' book *The Great Divorce* suggests that heaven is more real, and more 'solid', than this world.)

If God was good and powerful enough to arrange for the life and work of Christ on our behalf, and to conquer death through him, then we can face the unknown future with confidence: he has a big surprise waiting for us, that will not disappoint us.

New covenant is worth working for

2 Corinthians 1-3

When we are threatened or accused, we fend off our opponents by whatever means we can. We get a lot of practice in today's skirmish-filled world. Part of the reason is that we are constantly jostling for position in the pecking order.

Paul had a credibility problem in Corinth. He devotes considerable space in this second letter to defending his motives and methods (especially chs. 1,2,10,11). In the course of his defence, he contrasts the 'gospel' of Moses, the old covenant, with that of Jesus, the new covenant.

This covenant, in first its old and then its new form, is the cornerstone of biblical teaching. Everything hangs on it. It alone makes sense of the Old Testament and it alone explains the significance of Jesus' death and resurrection. A covenant is an agreement or compact between two parties, who in this case are unequal: God, and his people. He promised to be their protecting God; they promised to obey him.

God kept his side of the bargain;

they broke theirs, constantly. But because he kept his side, God always saved a 'remnant' of people with whom he could carry out his purposes, from Noah onwards.

The new covenant includes the promise of forgiveness and eternal partnership with God, through the Holy Spirit, assured because the death and resurrection of Jesus achieved what the old covenant could not: a permanent solution to humankind's tragic habit of sinning.

That, says Paul, is worth working for. The covenant kept him from becoming merely professional, working not for money but for the sheer truth, joy and reality of the gospel (2:17). He had embraced something more like a marriage certificate than a legal contract. The obligations were of love, not law.

The covenant provided him with a sense of security and a spur to service. God would never let him down; therefore he sought never to let God down. When we are tempted, as Paul must have been, to wonder if it's all worth it – when we are forced back on the defensive – knowing that we are people of the covenant could make all the difference between giving up and pressing on.

Halo, halo! God opens closed minds!

2 Corinthians 3,4

If you ever wondered why medieval painters crowned the saints with halos, here perhaps is a reason. Just as Moses radiated the reality of God, so Christians 'shine' for Jesus. Some non-Christians do notice that there is 'something different' about some Christians. We carry the presence of God with us, and he makes his presence felt through us.

2 CORINTHIANS

1	God's comfort and Paul's plans
2	Forgive the offending Christian
3	The new covenant
4	Current troubles do not hinder the gospel
5	Reconciliation and witness
6	What Paul has suffered
7	Paul's anxiety for the Corinthians
8,9	Teaching on giving generously
10	Paul defends his ministry
11	False apostles and Paul's sufferings
12	Paul's thorn in the flesh
13	Warning to Christians to examine their lives

That should give us confidence to witness boldly. But it does not guarantee that people will respond. Some just don't 'see' the gospel or its relevance for them. That is not because of our lack of persuasive skill (although we can help or hinder spiritual communication). It is because they are spiritually blindfolded (4:3-6).

That is why prayer for the uncommitted is vital. Evangelism can achieve nothing unless God alerts people to their need and illuminates their minds to understand. So don't get exasperated when people don't respond; just keep praying for them. At the same time, polish your halo; Jesus himself said that we are 'the light of the world' (Matthew 5:14-16).

Location:

Paul is writing from Macedonia (northern Greece; 2:13) to Corinth in southern Greece

Date and circumstances:

Written c. AD 54-55, three years after Paul planted the church in Corinth. This is his fourth letter to them. For details, see Fast Facts in 1 Corinthians

Place in Bible:

After 1 Corinthians, before Galatians, in the New Testament

KEY QUOTE

Therefore we do not lose heart. Though outwardly we are wasting away, yet inwardly we are being renewed day by day. For our light and momentary troubles are achieving for us an eternal glory that far outweighs them all.

2 Corinthians 4:16,17

Gandhi worked for human reconciliation

CROSS CHECK

'The body of Christ': p 375
The unity of the church: p 102
Wisdom: pp177, 339
The resurrection of Christ: pp 283, 296, 221
The return of Christ, pp 400-401

Reconciliation is always possible

2 Corinthians 5:11-6:2

People at odds with each other are liable to split up (if they are a couple or in a business) or fight (if they are two countries). They need to find common ground, a willingness to forgive, and the resolve to start again. It is not impossible, but it is difficult.

If reconciliation of human partners is difficult, how much more difficult is it when one of the partners is God. He will not and cannot compromise. His law has been broken, his covenant dishonoured, his person offended. The due consequences must be accepted.

On the other hand, he is the Great Lover. His yearning for his people never dies, his heartache when they offend him never disappears, and his efforts to bring them back never diminish. His capacity to forgive is infinite.

And that, of course, is what the Christian gospel is all about. 'Reconciliation' is a key word for Paul when he explains Christ's death and resurrection. He uses it in Romans 5:10,11; Ephesians 2:16 and Colossians 1:19-22 as well as here.

We have been reconciled to God through Christ without compromise on God's part. His reconciliation service is unequalled by any political mediators, industrial arbitrators or marriage guidance counsellors in the world.

Wonder at it; worship him for it. Then, says Paul, accept it humbly and live it wisely. If we are reconciled to God, then we have a dynamic whereby we can be reconciled to one another. Indeed, we cannot preach what we do not practise. A church split by division is a contradiction in terms.

This is not simply comfortable teaching about salvation, which we may note from afar on a Sunday morning. It is an uncomfortable challenge to go and be reconciled and reconciling on Monday morning.

God's people are called to high office

2 Corinthians 5:20

An ambassador may seem to have a glamorous life. The round of diplomatic functions and dinner parties, the access to high-level political and social leaders, is enough to give anyone a buzz of excitement and a feeling of importance. But with the glitz comes the grit; there is a hard job to do.

Ambassadors live in two countries. They are citizens of one and strangers in another. They retain their nationality but reside elsewhere. The Bible says we are citizens of God's kingdom called to serve in the world which does not accept his rule. Therefore we have a radically different outlook and purpose from people around us. In Ephesians 1:14 Paul speaks of the Holy Spirit as a guarantee of God's promises; he is like a passport authenticating our citizenship of heaven, while we work for God here on earth.

Ambassadors speak on behalf of their king or president. They are representatives, passing on to the host country the policies and concerns of their native country. Christians, led by the Holy Spirit, represent God to the world. We have the responsibility to speak up for his concerns in all walks of life. We cannot therefore restrict our ambassadorial duties to the 'embassy', the church; while we should be inviting people to visit us, we need to take our message into their world and institutions.

Give as good as you've been given

2 Corinthians 8,9

Money, said Anthony Sampson in The Midas Touch, 'like a religion binds together different parts of the world, providing the means by which people and nations judge each other. Like a religion it demands great faith, a huge priesthood with rituals and incantations which few ordinary people understand. Like missionaries, the bankers and brokers travel the still unconverted parts of the world . . . seeking to convert still more tribes to their own faith in credit, interest rates and the sacred bottom line.'

If you think that exaggerates, just note how swings on one stock exchange send market roundabouts spinning across the globe. Everything, however, including money belongs to God (cf. Psalm 24:1). Therefore Paul says:

- We are to be generous with it (8:3; 9:6)
- Giving and sharing is a privilege, not a duty (8:4)
- Generosity becomes real through our commitment to God and his people (8:5)
- It is based on the example of Jesus (8:9; cf. Luke 21:1-4)
- It should be based on, and proportional to, our means (8:12)
- We should share our resources fairly and not be greedy (8:13,14)
- Our giving is to be without compulsion (church 'dues' defeat the object; 9:6)
- And, as a result, we can expect (unspecified) spiritual returns (9:8; cf. Luke 6:37,38).

Many Christians believe that they should give one-tenth (the 'tithe'). It was the Jewish standard (Leviticus 27:30,31) and Malachi linked it with God's spiritual blessing (3:10, in the context of a wide range of law-breaking at the time), but no standard is given in the New Testament.

The stress there is always on giving freely and generously; some Christians believe therefore that the Old Testament standard should be a minimum guideline.

Grace is all you need

2 Corinthians 11,12

If anyone says to you that religion is an emotional prop, get them to read these chapters. No one goes through what Paul suffered because they need a prop! But he admits that he needed help through his sufferings: the all-sufficient 'grace' (loving-kindness) of God.

No one knows what his mysterious 'thorn' (12:7) was. There have been numerous suggestions: epilepsy, physical handicap, malaria, hypochondria, gout, gastritis, deafness, neurasthenia, a speech impediment, and short-sightedness (the favourite on the basis of Galatians 4:13-15 and 6:11).

His triple prayer to be rid of it (parallel, perhaps, to Jesus' triple prayer to escape the cross, Mark 14:32-42) suggests that it was no minor impediment. But his willingness to accept it is significant.

God does heal; Paul knew that. But healing is not always the best for the ministry God has called us to. It is the world, not the Bible, which says that perfect health is the greatest of all good things. God's grace is greater, and more productive.

Paul's 'delight' in his weakness is not masochism. He has realised that in order to serve God, he must rely on God. As a human being, he is not good at that; he prefers self-reliance. We can turn weaknesses to good use: they are a goad to prayer, a spur to trust, a reminder of priorities: I am not perfect or all-sufficient, but God is.

For today

- Celebrate diversity and preserve unity in your fellowship
- Keep human sexuality in its biblical perspective and framework as a servant, not a master
- Look for ways of healing disputes and reconciling differences in the church quickly
- Welcome the ministries and contributions of all people
- Be neither falsely humble nor proud about your gift: just use it
- This life is not all there is: keep your sights on the resurrection
- Suffering does not end human fulfilment or Christian service, but may be a means towards it.

Defiant stand defeats scholars

Daniel's three friends in the fiery furnace

The Book of Daniel

- Tells of the rise of Jewish exiles to power in Babylon
- Focuses on Daniel who is enabled by God to interpret dreams
- Encourages believers who are under pressure to keep the faith
- Contains a series of visions of the 'end times' in symbolic language

The book of Daniel is fascinating and irritating, illuminating and puzzling. It is so controversial that commentator Joyce Baldwin declares that 'opinions are divided on almost every issue'.

Yet the reader who takes it at face value will find that it conveys a simple message. God is in control of history, and the people who stay faithful to him may suffer, but never will be defeated. That's what the dreams of Nebuchadnezzar, and the writing which alarmed Belshazzar, really 'mean' for us. That too is the message of the stories of the fiery furnace and the lions' den.

The book also includes prophecies capable of diverse interpretations. They especially attract people who enjoy solving cryptic crosswords and mathematical conundrums and who assume, contrary to the Bible, that everything can be explained once you have the key. But reason is not God, and God is not a fiendish quiz master.

The prophecies also provide rich pickings for many cults, which often base teachings on them. That, and the fact that most interpretations differ markedly even when interpreters agree on other things, should caution us against reading a too hasty or assured exposition.

Daniel is unique in the Old Testament, and has some similarities with Revelation in the New Testament, but it is here for a purpose and its difficulties should not deter us from opening it and learning from it.

DANIEL

1	Daniel and friends taken to Babylon
2	Daniel interprets Nebuchadnezzar's dream
3	Three friends survive the furnace
4	Nebuchadnezzar's dream and insanity
5	Belshazzar's feast and the writing on the wall
6	Daniel survives the lions' den
7	Vision of four 'beasts' or empires
8	Vision of a ram and a goat
9	Daniel prays for rescue from exile
10,11	Heavenly being foretells future kings
12	Vision of the end of time

We can begin with the stories of Daniel and his friends, and discover in them spiritual truths to inspire anyone whose faith is tested. When we turn to the prophecies, we should look for general principles rather than press details into a mould which almost inevitably will be off-beam and unhelpful.

If God had intended us to have a clear view of the future, he would have used less confusing symbolism and provided clearer corroboration elsewhere in Scripture. Perhaps the genius of Daniel is to remind us that God is mysterious and his ways inscrutable. Daniel himself did not understand what he saw (12:8-13), and *he didn't try to*. Sometimes, agnosticism can be true faith.

KEY QUOTE

'If we are thrown into the blazing furnace, the God we serve is able to save us from it . . . But even if he does not, O king, we will not serve your gods.'

Daniel 3:17,18

Daniel dares to be different

Think about the day you left home, maybe for school or college, or to start a job in another town, or even to get married. You probably had mixed feelings. Exulting in your freedom and excited about new opportunities, there was also some apprehension about making new friends and coping with new challenges.

Imagine, though, that you are not going willingly but at gun-point. With a handful of friends you are being taken to a country with a different language and culture. Fear and anxiety become the dominant emotions. You are feeling what Daniel must have felt.

Talented as an Oxbridge or Harvard graduate, Daniel was spotted by Babylonian recruitment agents and shipped abroad during the first attack on Judah by Nebuchadnezzar in 605 BC. A devout Jew from an unsophisticated country, he found streets paved with marble, advanced banking and trade systems, and soaring ziggurat temples to strange gods.

He and his friends had big decisions to make. Either they melted into the Babylonian background and made the most of the opportunities, or they retained their Jewish identity and faced the possible consequences. They chose the latter, and their story is a testimony of faith withstanding pressure.

Daniel was disciplined as a person

- He was disciplined from the start (1:8). 'He resolved' to maintain his Jewish distinctiveness; initial compromise would have made a later stand more difficult.
- He disciplined himself physically. The food may not have been the healthiest on offer. The Bible encourages healthy living and care of the body (cf. 1 Corinthians 6:19,20; 9:24,25)
- He disciplined himself spiritually. The food was linked to pagan ritual and he wanted to avoid all impression of compromise.
- He was disciplined in his work (1:4, 20). He used his natural aptitude to become the best he could.

Daniel was disciplined as a prophet

- He was humble before God (10:12). He recognised that God alone could give him wisdom and insight (cf. 2:27,28), and so submitted to him.
- He was humble before people (5:16,17). He refused to 'perform' spiritual gifts for a reward. He was content with enough rather than excess. The temptation to seek gain (financial or status) in the church is always great (cf. Peter's reaction to 'simony' in Acts 8:18-24).
- He was bold in his witness. He showed no fear even when threatened (cf. ch 5) and did not mince his words (5:22-24).

Daniel was disciplined in his praying

- It had become a regular habit (6:10). His times of prayer sustained his faith and were the channel for God's wisdom to be revealed. Prayer is not a bandaid for emergencies, but bread for daily living.
- He continued even when it was dangerous (6:11-14). Although the expression of his relationship with God was forbidden, he persisted with it. For us, difficulty rather than danger may threaten prayer times, yet that is exactly when prayer becomes vital.
- As a result, he saw his prayers answered (10:12), he was protected in adversity (6:21,22), he received insight into God's will (9:22), and he was given patience even when things weren't clear (12:8,9,13).

Date of events:
Between 605 and 530 BC.

Location:
Babylonia, where the Jews were exiled.

Place in Bible:
The last of the 'major prophets', after Ezekiel and before Hosea and the other 'minor prophets' towards the end of the Old Testament.

Parallel books:
Revelation, the only other 'apocalytpic' book in the Bible. The period reported in Daniel is partially covered by Ezekiel and Jeremiah. Three books in the Apocrypha claim to be additions to Daniel: The song of the three holy children, Susanna, and Bel and the dragon.

HARD Question

Should Christians be vegetarians or not?

Daniel 1

Daniel and his friends have been offered as examples of the Bible's alleged preference for vegetarianism. By opting for a vegetarian diet, the four men were given 'knowledge and understanding' by God (v 17) and became 'ten times better than all the magicians and enchanters' (v 20).

However, the issue they faced was not simply whether or not to eat meat. The food of the royal household was suspect to loyal Jews for two reasons. The first was religious. The food was 'non-kosher', and may have been slaughtered as part of pagan religious rites. This was also faced by Christians in Corinth 500 years later (1 Corinthians 8,10). There were probably no secular or halal butchers available.

The second reason was social. To a Jew, eating someone's food was a sign of friendship and acceptance. To refuse was to distance oneself from the person. Daniel and company had no option but to work for the king, but they could display some independence by refusing to be drawn into his household of toadies.

A third factor is that Jews were not vegetarians. Meat was a luxury and so formed a lesser part of their regular diet than it does for many people today. But meat eating was central to their religion particularly when they shared in the Passover lamb each year.

The chief argument for 'biblical vegetarianism' comes from the early chapters of Genesis. Humans were given seed-bearing plants (grains) and fruit to eat (1:29). After the fall and especially the flood, meat was also included (9:3) and Abel, a shepherd and goatherd, offered a sacrifice from the flock (4:4).

In the New Testament, Jesus ate the Passover (Luke 22:7,8) and told a story about a celebration meal of a fatted calf (Luke 15:22-24). Paul instructed the Colossians not to let anyone pass judgment on what they ate (2:16) and told Timothy that God gave us everything to enjoy, including all foods (1 Timothy 6:17).

So there seems to be no explicit reason in the Bible why Christians should be either vegetarian or meat-eating. It is a matter of personal taste. But there is every reason in the Bible to suggest that Christians should not impose their preference on others or insist that theirs is the only or best way.

Author and date: Supposedly written by Daniel, a Jewish exile taken to Babylon in 605 BC. Since the 19th century many scholars claim the book was written during the mid-2nd century BC Maccabean rebellion. Although this has been questioned by more recent scholars in the light of later research. The book is problematic, but arguments for a late date can be answered. We have assumed an early date.

Historical background: Israel divided into two in 930 BC. By 722 BC the northern kingdom (known as Israel) had been destroyed by Assyria. Between 605 and 587 the Babylonians repeatedly attacked Judah (the southern kingdom) and took away prisoners of war, before finally destroying the capital and its temple. During the exile many Jews integrated themselves into Babylonian society, as it is claimed Daniel and his friends did. The exile ended in 538 BC when Cyrus declared a general amnesty, but by no means all Jewish families returned to Judah at that time.

Disturbing dreams, nightmare scenes

Daniel 2,4

Everybody dreams. Our minds are active even when we are unconscious. Dreams are analysed by psychiatrists treating patients and by therapists and counsellors at times of crisis.

Certain dream images such as falling or travelling seem to be common to many people, and there are books galore offering 'explanations' of what these and less common ones mean. Dream interpretation was big business in the ancient world, especially in Egypt, Babylon and Persia. So when Babylonian king Nebuchadnezzar had a disturbed night, he called in the interpreters.

Daniel succeeded where others failed, giving God the credit for the revelation in 2:19 when in effect he himself had the king's dream, and perceived its meaning.

This, and other revelatory passages in the Bible does not mean that all dreams are messages from heaven. They may teach us something about ourselves and our relationship with God and other people, but they may also be nothing more than the ramblings of a mind winding down after a long day.

God speaks in many ways, of which this may occasionally be one. Any apparent 'revelation' should be tested by comparing its content with Scripture, to see if it is in accord with basic Christian principles and theological precepts, and examined carefully through prayer and discussion. To do this is not to be faithless, but to take God seriously.

Learn from your dreams if you can, but don't build spiritual or personal dream castles on them without wider corroboration.

Great escapes

Daniel 3,6

Fairground escapologists make it look easy, wriggling out of ropes as fire or water threatens them. They will, however, be the first to admit that there are real dangers attached to their occupation. The difference between their stunts and the two great escapes recounted in Daniel is that the latter escapees did nothing to get themselves out of their predicament. These are really rescues rather than escapes.

Both punishments are probable. Biblical (Jeremiah 29:22) and secular records tell of Nebuchadnezzar burning people to death. Lions were kept captive and released for kings to hunt.

Surviving the lions is the less startling story; animal trainers spend hours with their charges without attack. The miracle here is that the unpredictable and presumably hungry creatures refused to eat the lean vegetarian. But fire is fire and flesh burns. There is no natural explanation for this escape. The presence of the angelic being suggested to ancient readers that this was a supernatural intervention of the highest order.

However, there is a point to these stories which both incredulous and believing readers should not overlook. The miracles are significant signs that God supports his people through ordeals. The heroes were unscathed, but they endured the ordeal first. You will suffer, the author is saying, but God is in there with you.

Secondly, God uses his people's faithfulness to bring about unlikely results. After the fire walk, Nebuchadnezzar declared Judaism legal (3:28,29). And after the lion taming, Darius publicly praised the Jews' God (6:25-27). The most compelling witnesses are those who remain faithful, against the odds.

Who biblical prophets were

There were three kinds. There were 'full-timers' like Isaiah who were court employees or members of religious communities.

There were also men like Amos who were 'freelance' in the sense that they were called to prophesy (possibly for a limited time) from another occupation.

And there were false prophets who deceived people but who could only be identified when their lives failed to match their message, or their message deviated from basic principles, or was simply unfulfilled.

They were certainly 'foretellers', seeing the future or (more often) predicting the likely outcome if a certain course of action was followed. They were also 'forth-tellers', speaking God's word on a variety of matters in a variety of circumstances. In this sense, they were like Bible teachers.

Daniel: background calendar

The narrative takes place in a complex period, and the prophecies refer to events at least down to the Romans. Here are the main relevant dates (BC) and the relevant Bible books in italics.

Date	Event	Bible Ref
612	Nineveh falls. Assyrian empire in decline; Babylonia taking over	
605	Battle of Carchemish: Babylon defeats Egypt and controls former Assyrian land	
605-4	Nebuchadnezzar becomes king of Babylon; invades Judah. Daniel among first exiles taken	
597	More Jews exiled including King Jehoiachin. Jerusalem captured.	2 Kings 2 Chron.
587	Jerusalem destroyed; end of Judah	Jeremiah
562	Nebuchadnezzar dies; Evil-Merodach becomes Babylonian king	
556	Nabonidus becomes king of Babylonian empire; Belshazzar regent in the city	Daniel
539	Fall of Babylon to Cyrus the Persian who declares general amnesty	Ezra Daniel
538	First return of exiles under Zerubbabel to Judah	Ezra
522	Darius I becomes king of Persia	Ezra Nehemiah
516	Jerusalem temple rebuilt and dedicated	Ezra Haggai Zechariah
486	Xerxes I (Ahasuerus) king of Persia	Esther
464	Artaxerxes I king of Persia	Nehemiah
458	Second major return of exiles, under Ezra	Ezra
334	Battle of River Granicus: Alexander the Great conquers Asia Minor	
331	Palestine comes under Greek control	
323	Alexander the Great dies; Greek empire divided among Ptolemies (Egypt and Palestine) and Seleucids (Syria and Asia Minor)	
198	Seleucids take control of Palestine	
169	Antiochus Epiphanes plunders Jerusalem temple	
167	Antiochus desecrates Jeruslaem temple and Maccabean revolt begins	
165	Temple rededicated	
129	Judah gains independence from Seleucids	
63	Roman general Pompey conquers Jerusalem; Judah made part of Roman province of Syria	

The writing's on the wall for you

Daniel 5

Of all the Bible stories to contribute to popular vocabulary, this is the most extraordinary. The phrase, 'the writing's on the wall' describes a predictable outcome that is often unpleasant.

You can interpret this either as a vision (it was all in Belshazzar's guilt-ridden mind), or as a 'materialisation' of a disembodied hand in a demonstration of God's judgment.

Another explanation is that the writing was by a human hand. Up in a servant's gallery orders and stock were chalked on the wall. Through a half open door in a gloomy, candle-lit banqueting chamber, the half-drunk Belshazzar saw a servant's arm writing up quantities of food and drink (which the words were normally used for).

However the words came to be written, they hit the king's conscience like an arrow. In a superstitious culture, this was an omen. And Daniel was able to give to an ordinary shopping list a divine spin. After all, people today sometimes 'hear' God in ordinary circumstances: God's Spirit can communicate through anything.

That is the point. God spoke. He first caught the attention of a complacent man. Then he spoke to a Gentile through a Jew. Finally he spoke of judgment, and showed himself to be the just Lord of history. Belshazzar was killed that night.

No one is beyond God's reach. Just as Saul of Tarsus was halted in front of God's warning light, so Belshazzar was shaken to pieces by a writer's hand. Pray for politicians and persecutors. God seems to have a closer eye on these wandering sheep than he does on the church safely tucked up in worship. And be ready to witness to them.

How to read Daniel's prophecies today

1. Approach them like any other biblical teaching

- Find out what they meant to, or how they were interpreted by, the people of the time. Most biblical prophecies had a current meaning even if they also looked ahead.
- Consider the overall message and theological teaching (e.g. that God is Lord of all the earth) before trying to interpret detail which can be done in the light of the overall theme.
- Ask what additional material in the Bible relates to, modifies or helps explain the principles and the details in the passage.
- Recognise that Daniel is 'apocalyptic', a rare form of biblical literature which symbolically and mysteriously gazes into the future. *It is intended for people to look back on to confirm God has been in control of events, rather than to look forward to 'planned' historical events and to be prepared for them (or even try to change or hasten them).*

2. Read the pictures as symbols and not photographs

- Ask what the pictures might have meant in the culture of the time. (Language and symbols change with time; today's meaning might not have been what the speaker intended.)
- Never press apparent parallels to current history or trends, especially in the political world. This kind of prophecy is only understood in retrospect.
- Remember symbols always point to something which cannot be fully expressed in any other way.
- Do not limit symbols which seem to relate to 'the end time' to terms or scenarios we are familiar with now. The picture is a broad-brush sketch, not a detailed blue print.
- Remember that the Bible warns us against constructing advance 'timetables' of history (cf. Matthew 24:36,42; Revelation 20:18)

3. Learn the lessons of the past

Prophetic interpretation is littered with horror stories which bring the Christian gospel into disrepute. Kind Christians have sometimes allowed the perpetrators to get away without rebuke when their 'prophecies' have failed; Paul would have verbally thrashed them.

A classic misinterpretation of Daniel was by the American preacher Leonard Sale-Harrison. He suggested that the rise of Mussolini in Italy fulfilled much of Daniel and that the Roman Empire was about to be revived. It did not happen.

Others saw the EEC as a revival of the Roman Empire and a fulfilment of the ten horns in chapter 7. But then its ten members increased and the idea was dropped. Our calling in the world is to proclaim Christ, not to check history against prophecy like pagans check their astrological charts.

Alternative names or false IDs?

Daniel 5,6

The title of Belshazzar and the name 'Darius the Mede' have caused some scholars to doubt the authenticity of Daniel, who assume they are historical mistakes.

Belshazzar was the son of Nabonidus, king of Babylon, who was frequently abroad. It is probable that he left the city governorship to his son, who assumed (or was given) the title 'king'. A 1990s parallel might be the 'rule' of Russia by others during President Boris Yeltsin's frequent illnesses, although they never assumed his title.

Darius the Mede is a more difficult problem – no one of that name is known. There are two possibilities. One, that King Cyrus was also known as Darius the Mede. The other is that it was another name for the city governor Gubaru. There is no reason why someone should not have used (or been given) different names by people from different cultures, but there is no firm evidence.

For today

- A disciplined life prepares you for opportunity and challenge
- Pray more, not less, when time and circumstance create pressure
- Learn from your dreams but don't get obsessive about them
- Accept that suffering may come but that God will always be there with you
- Rejoice that God is in charge of history: don't let current events get you down.
- Look forward to your hope of heaven

Kingdoms will always fail

Daniel 2:24-45; 7:1-28

In the late twentieth century the Soviet 'empire' collapsed, and the nation of Yugoslavia disintegrated into numerous tribal factions. History was repeating itself. Large empires never last for long. That is the message of these chapters. We can draw many parallels, although in our own time we should be cautious of *equating* these prophecies with specific events.

Both Nebuchadnezzar's dream and Daniel's vision refer to four empires which commentators generally agree are those of Babylonia, Medo-Persia, Greece and Rome. (Some suggest that in chapter 7 the Median and Persian empires should be considered separately, making the Greek Empire the fourth, which split rather more obviously than the Roman.)

The stone not cut by human hands, and the kingdom set up by God in 2:34,44,45, 7:13,14,27, refers to the coming of Christ and the inauguration of 'the kingdom of God', which Jesus announced (Mark 1:14,15).

The message to Nebuchadnezzar is almost flattering; his empire gets the gold medal and all others are inferior. It gave people at the time reassurance of God's long-term oversight of history. It reminds us that God's kingdom of love and truth will stand against all human power structures.

Cut down to size

Daniel 8

Pompous bullies, which is probably the most flattering description of dictators, are really very small people with small minds. They are to be despised rather than feared, despite the mayhem and anguish they cause. Before God they are puny. Such was Antiochus Epiphanes, the subject of this vision.

To the Jews, Antiochus Epiphanes was what Christians would dub 'antichrist'. He desecrated the Jerusalem temple in 167 BC, sacrificing a pig on the altar. The New Testament uses him to illustrate a parallel situation in the future (Matthew 24:15). The reference in verse 17 to 'the end' could refer to the end of time or the end of the Old Testament era; or even both.

But he is only a little horn growing out of the four horns, which are themselves the lesser successors to Alexander the Great in the declining Greek Empire. Antiochus' reign of terror was short-lived, if brutal. The maths of verse 14 probably refers to the period (1,300 days) between his entering the temple and its being cleansed. Once more, God's people are not spared the fire, but nor are they destroyed by it.

Our days are numbered

Daniel 9:24-27

You will hear people say that they will never do something in a thousand years. Your teenager could promise only to use the phone for two seconds. Both are exaggerated statements using symbolic periods of time to make a point. They are figures of speech.

Numerology is rare in the Bible (if you discount the similarly 'rounded' figures of the Israelites' '40 years' or Jesus' '40 days' in the desert). When it does occur, it is always intended to be symbolic, and therefore calculators are the last aid required in interpreting the figures. Seven (and its multiples) are a favourite for Bible authors, primarily standing for 'completion' or 'enough'.

Jeremiah's predicted 70-year exile

was more or less right (Daniel went in 605 with the first exiles, even though the city was sacked only in 587, and some exiles returned in 538). The '69 sevens' (483 years) is roughly from the restoration of Jerusalem to the coming of Christ.

This is one of those sums (like calculating the value of pi) which could go on and on and never be 'right'. Which is the point. God is checking off the days. Our days are numbered: keep going!

Conflict in high places

Daniel 10-12

We are never told Daniel's age, but like a number of the biblical saints he appears to have lived a long time. And like Moses especially, he's not allowed to go into retirement. Here, towards the end of his life, comes a fresh challenge which all but kills him.

Seen from another angle, it was only in his twilight years that he was ready to receive the vision which drained him so much. It was the grand finale to a lifetime of seeing visions and being the mouthpiece of God. Some might even describe this as a beatific vision or near-death experience.

Once again, the natural and contemporary relevance is to the rise of the Greek Empire after four Persian kings, the division of Alexander's empire between the Ptolemies and Seleucids, and the terror of Antiochus Epiphanes (the 'contemptible person' of 11:21).

There seems to be a transition at 11:36, because the circumstances of 11:40-45 differ from the historical reality of Antiochus' death. The vision moves towards the end of all time and the conflicts that will characterise the period before it.

It provides the chief Old Testament glimpse of what Paul describes as 'spiritual warfare' in Ephesians 6, and is paralleled in the book of Revelation. Once again, detail is lacking and the description is figurative but clear: Satan will be destroyed by God's cosmic 'forces'.

And there will be a resurrection (one of the rare occurrences of the idea in the Old Testament) of all people before the final judgment. Justice will not just be done, it will be seen to be done. People who appear to have got away with murder in this life will be faced with their sins in the next.

This, at the time, was 'revelation' (apocalyptic) indeed. Imagine what this meant to the Jews during the time of Antiochus' atrocities. They had reassurance that evil could not reign for ever. And so do we, from this book and from the fuller revelation which develops in the New Testament.

Daniel's son of man

Heavenly figures in Daniel's visions create problems for interpreters, but the 'one like a son of man' in 7:13,14 creates the most. Traditionally, Christians have taken this to mean Christ.

Seeing that Paul taught Christ's eternal pre-existence, there is no reason at all why the second person of the Trinity should not have been seen (even if not fully understood) by visionary people before his actual incarnation as a man. There also seems to be a glimpse of the final triumph of the church ('the saints' also receive the 'son's' kingdom in v 27).

Jesus, as reported in the Gospels, preferred the title 'son of man' to 'son of God' and he virtually quoted Daniel's description in his teaching about his return (Mark 13:26). However, it is important that we do not lean too heavily on this one reference. The title can carry other nuances, too and it is important that we hear Daniel say the figure was 'like' a son of man. To his readers, it could also have meant a human representative of the saints, or of the angels.

God is good but he can't be tamed

The Book of Deuteronomy:

- Spells out the main covenant requirements
- Reveals God as loving, faithful and just
- Recounts the obtuseness of the Israelites
- Summarises Moses' teaching to prepare the Israelites for Canaan

The book of Deuteronomy is the jewel in the crown of the Pentateuch. If ever a rebuttal was needed to those who accuse the God of the Old Testament of being vastly different from and inferior to the God of the New Testament, this is it.

Some of the laws of Exodus and Leviticus, with their strong language and strict penalties, are certainly repeated. But they are always contained within the context of a picture of God who loves his people warmly, who is constantly loyal to them, and will go to great lengths to assist and forgive them.

Deuteronomy is a book about God's covenant love. Like C.S. Lewis's Aslan, he is revealed as unbelievably good, but he cannot be tamed by any means. He can be gentle and patient, but when he roars, his people had better look out.

The scene is the borders of Canaan. The Israelites have gathered in Moab and are poised to enter 'the Promised Land'. Moses, forbidden to enter the land himself, prepares the people he has led for 40 years for their new life without him. He reminds them of their foolish faithlessness and warns them against repeating their mistakes in Canaan.

This was almost certainly the book which was rediscovered during the reign of King Josiah and which led to a national revival (2 Kings 22-23). Many of its passages have an equally challenging and heart-warming effect on present-day readers, even though the specific Israelite concerns are long past.

DEUTERONOMY

1,2	**Résumé of desert wanderings**
3	**Division of Canaan**
4	**Instructions to obey God**
5	**The ten commandments**
6	**Instructions to love God**
7	**Attitudes to other nations**
8	**Call to obey God**
9	**The golden calf**
10	**The great commandment**
11	**Call to love God**
12	**Principles for worship**
13	**Avoid foreign gods**
14	**Rules about food and tithes**
15	**Jubilee year**
16	**Summary of festivals**
17	**Instructions about civil government**
18	**Religious instructions**
19	**Cities of refuge**
20	**Conduct of war**
21-25	**Miscellaneous rules**
26	**Offerings of crops to God**
27	**Curses on disobedience**
28	**Blessings and curses**
29	**Renewal of the covenant**
30	**The choice Israel faces**
31	**Joshua commissioned**
32	**Moses' song**
33	**Moses' blessing on the tribes**
34	**Moses' death**

KEY QUOTE

Hear, O Israel: The LORD our God, the LORD, is one. Love the LORD your God with all your heart and with all your soul and with all your strength.

Deuteronomy 6:4,5

'It's all your fault!'

Deuteronomy 1; cf. 3:21-29; 4:21-24

Moses was a great man of God – perhaps the greatest in the Old Testament (see his obituary in 34:10-12). But he was no saint. In the desert he had lost his temper and performed a miracle that drew more attention to himself than to God (Numbers 20:1-13). The penalty for that one error was severe, and he found it hard to bear.

His reaction is so human that it has to be authentic. He blames the Israelites. Their refusal to trust God and constant complaints would have tested anyone's patience – even God's (9:13,14).

The incident demonstrates the huge power of a determined group over even a strong-minded leader; no wonder lesser leaders follow public opinion. But a good reason is not a good excuse. Moses was brought down by his own people but he was still personally responsible for his actions. It reminds us that we cannot blame others for our sinful actions.

Moses pleads with God to take the mitigating circumstances into account and to reduce his sentence. But although God can forgive sin, he cannot bend his own rules. Actions have consequences, and God does not often undo them. Moses gets no special treatment because of his good deeds in the past; and neither will we.

Look back in wonder, love and praise

Deuteronomy 2-4

We always see things more clearly when we look back. While a morbid hankering for the past is emotionally crippling, a right appreciation of the past is positively encouraging.

Moses pulls no punches in his catalogue of Israel's shortcomings. But his vision of times past is not the only thing he sees. He remembers some very good things which also happened:

- God's constant presence (2:7; 4:37)
- God's consistent provision (2:7)
- God's conquering power (2:31-3:10)
- God's commanding purity (4:3)
- God's covenant promises (4:10-14)

This is important for the Israelites. They stand on the verge of a new beginning. Ahead lies the uncertainty of invasion, so they need to recall who God is and what he has done.

The past could have been worse. They now must learn from their mistakes and vow not to make them again. Knowing God was faithful in the past reassures them that he will be faithful in the future. Every person regularly needs to go through this exercise to restore faith and renew commitment. 'You were shown these things that you might know that the LORD is God' (4:35).

Title: Hebrew 'The words' (from 1:1). Greek: 'The second law' (Deutero = second), from 17:18.

Author: Traditionally Moses. Much of the book is speeches made by him. His writing of the laws is referred to several times (e.g. 31:24). However, the account of his death must come from a different hand.

Date of original material: During Israel's period in the desert, c. 1230 BC.

Final compilation: Most scholars accept that Deuteronomy represents a summary of Moses' teaching and may have been edited into its existing form at one (or more) later dates, probably at key times in the nation's history perhaps during the lives of David or Solomon.

Structure: The book is divided into three 'sermons' by Moses (1-4, 5-28, 29-30) with an epilogue containing his last 'will and testament' and the account of his death (31-34); see box 'It looks real' (p 93).

Date of event:
Shortly before Israel enters Canaan, c. 1230 BC

Location:
The israelite camp in Moab (east of the Dead Sea)

Story follows:
Book of Numbers in the Old Testament set shortly after the events in ch 21

Story leads on to:
The book of Joshua

Teaching parallel to:
Exodus and Leviticus

Don't ease up when the going's easy

Deuteronomy 8

Everyone looks forward to a holiday, retirement or a new job. Anything where the grass is greener and life easier. Which was why the Israelites looked forward to Canaan after the desert.

But what they didn't know was that when things go well, guards begin to slip, disciplines begin to slacken, ambitions change and lifestyles alter. God's people can lose their distinctiveness and cutting edge as they merge with their cultural surroundings.

Moses tries to warn them of this natural human trait in advance. Their desire for comfort isn't wrong. Israelite religion was never ascetic. Nor is Christianity; monastic communities with minimal lifestyles serve a purpose, but the overall biblical conclusion is that God 'richly provides us with everything for our enjoyment' (1 Timothy 6:17).

When you are satisfied, Moses says:

- praise the Lord (v 10)
- keep observing his laws strictly (v 11)
- remember where you came from and how (vv 14-17).

That is also good advice for affluent Christians when persecution of the church is something we only read of in travel or history books.

What on earth is the church for?

Deuteronomy 4-6 (cf. 4:5-9; 6:7-9, 20-25)

You could picture King Solomon meditating on Deuteronomy 4 as he pondered that offer he couldn't refuse, to ask for anything he liked (1 Kings 3:1-15).

Israel was meant to be a wise and understanding nation radiating God's glory to the world (4:6). Solomon could hardly ask for any lesser qualities if he was to act responsibly and put country before personal interest.

The calling of God's people to be his witnesses – an example of true community, a moral light, a living testimony to God's presence and power – is slipped in here. It is stated infrequently in the Old Testament, but it underlies all else.

God did not call his people to become a holy huddle enjoying the exclusive benefits of his undivided attention. Some Israelites did think of him only as a tribal god, but they were taught that he was Lord of lords whose policies encompassed the whole world.

To fulfil their calling, the Israelites were to pass on their story and the obligations of the covenant to future generations. The strong Jewish sense of national identity is based on the constant family rehearsal of God's story. Their children still had to make up their own minds to follow the covenant. But they could only do so if they knew the story, the responsibilities of its acceptance and the implications of its rejection.

Deuteronomy not only reminds us of the value of good teaching and the regular telling of the old, old story, but it challenges those who love it to go and share it. Jesus also said his disciples must shine their light in the world desperate for wisdom (Matthew 5:14).

HARD Question

Were they really that wicked?

Deuteronomy 7; 9:1-6; 12:1-3

The Israelites were commanded by God to smash the inhabitants of Canaan (7:2) 'on account of their wickedness' (9:4). The author observes, however, that Israel does not get the land because of its comparative righteousness (9:3,5). So it is not simply the good supplanting the bad.

The term 'righteous' means 'measuring up to God's standard'. Israel may be 'God's people' but it's not perfect. In fact, it's 'stiff-necked' (9:6) – proud, arrogant and self-willed. Hardly 'righteous' behaviour.

The Canaanites may not have been much worse than any other people, although their religious practices are known to have included cult prostitution and child sacrifice at times.

Generally 'wicked' means 'not measuring up to God's standard'. It is a religious statement; the Canaanites were opposed to God and his ways and therefore subject to his judgment. The Bible is silent on the amount of prior warning and teaching they had.

We need to read this through thirteenth-century BC eyes rather than through twentieth-century AD eyes and remember that:

- the full purposes of God's love were not yet revealed
- they were discovering God slowly in the social context of many tribes fighting for living space.
- the Israelites saw God's activity in black and white terms (their success was his).

Christian theology would suggest that the Old Testament judgment on the nations is to be seen in the broader context of God's dealings with humankind as a whole. All who fail to measure up to God's standards are subject to judgment, in eternity if not in this life. Jesus' verdict and warning that 'unless you repent, you too will all perish' (Luke 13:3,5) confirms this.

Understanding brings growth

Deuteronomy 13

The nineteenth-century hymnwriter John Keble said that when there is no persecution, internal church disputes may be God's way of 'perfecting those whom he favours'. Belief is constantly being challenged.

Moses warned the Israelites not to listen to anyone who suggested anything which was already prohibited by the law. Historically, the church has taken the same line: what is explicitly forbidden, taught or sanctioned in Scripture is God's unchanging decree.

Credal and other primary beliefs can be legitimately discussed, of course. Thinking through why the Bible teaches something can be a useful spiritual exercise to strengthen our faith and broaden our understanding and appreciation of it. To accept without understanding is to remain in spiritual infancy, however, if not indeed in total darkness.

FAST facts

Baal(s): 'Baal' means 'Lord' or 'master' and he was seen as a storm god. He was given local names to associate him with particular tribes or cities. For example Baal Melkart was the Phoenician god brought to Israel by Jezebel (1 Kings 18).

An ancient hymn to Baal says he 'will send abundant rain, abundant moisture and snow; he will utter his voice in the clouds and send his light flashing to earth'.

Asherah: A goddess who was probably the consort of Baal. The name is also used in the Old Testament for the images of her which may have been wooden pillars (Deuteronomy 16:21); groves of trees may also have been dedicated to her.

Divination: All forms of fortune telling were banned by Moses (although they were practised by some Israelites later). People used the entrails of animals, cast sticks or stones, consulted spirits, and interpreted omens. No specific reasons for the ban are given except that all this was 'detestable' to God (Deuteronomy 18:9-13). It implied a lack of trust in his guidance and sovereignty and was an attempt to manipulate events.

Sun and moon gods: The sun was worshipped in Egypt especially, but planets were worshipped in Canaan also (Deuteronomy 17:2,3). An ancient hymn to Egypt's Aten describes him as 'Creator of seed in women, who makes fluid into man, who maintains the son in the womb of his mother . . . who gives breath to sustain all that he has made.'

DEUTERONOMY ELSEWHERE IN THE BIBLE

Josiah's reforms: 2 Kings 22,23
The great commandment: Mark 12:30
Jesus' quotations to combat Satan: Matthew 4:1-11

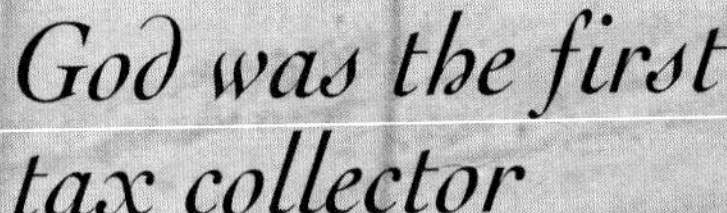

God was the first tax collector

Deuteronomy 14:22-29

A handful of European states including Germany support their churches from a tax, although there are ways of opting out of it. The Israelites' first taxes were to support the 'church', not the state.

The central shrine and its ministers, and the Levites who were scattered through the tribal areas, were to be supported by people's 'gifts'. The tax rate of ten per cent (tithing), was collected in kind rather than in cash (money as we know it was not in use at the time, although gold and silver were used by weight as units of exchange).

Tithing was not a new idea. Abraham gave a tithe to Melchizedek, the priest-king of Salem (Jerusalem) who served 'the Most High God' (Genesis 14:1-20). Much later it became a rigid requirement which blinded some Pharisees to 'the weightier matters' of righteousness, justice and compassion (Matthew 23:23). However, its neglect implied carelessness about God and his worship, and was seen by the eighth-century BC prophet Micah not simply as tax avoidance but as a cause of spiritual decline (Micah 3:10).

Part of the tithe was to be given to 'charity' (vv 28,29). This principle is continued in the New Testament in which Christians are encouraged to provide for the poor (2 Corinthians 8-9) as well as to support elders (1 Timothy 5:17,18).

The human tendency to avoid regular giving needs discipline to ensure that people do not suffer. Where churches rely on voluntary giving, a declared percentage provides that structure. The remaining tax system is also a structure which in part helps the poor, and is therefore also not [illegible]ded.

How to know when it's God who's speaking

Deuteronomy 18:14-22

The human brain is a complex super-highway of countless neural connections. They give us a unique 'eye-view' and personality which is different to everyone else's. Communication is therefore fraught with difficulty. Our mental filters divert streams of information into many different channels. What is clear to one person is obscure to another.

When someone claims to speak in the name of God the difficulties are compounded. How do we know they are 'hearing' God aright? To what extent are they giving us personal opinions couched in spiritual language? Might they, indeed, be giving no more than a 'flash of insight' from their subconscious that could be just the distorted combination of dream images?

Prophets have to be tested. There are three such tests in the Bible, two of them here. The first is 'wait and see'. A prediction can't be of God if it doesn't happen. (It might not be of God if it does, either; pre-cognition is not the sole prerogative of Christians, although it could be seen as a gift of God's providence). Therefore we should be careful how we respond before its fulfilment; our calling is to be found faithful, not foolish.

The second is that no true prophet can teach anything which goes against what God has already revealed. (Christians would add that no prophet can now bring 'new' truth in the way some biblical prophets did, although they might bring fresh insight into old truth.)

And the third, given by St Paul, is

that prophetic teaching should be 'weighed' carefully by the church leadership (1 Corinthians 14:29-32). God's truth and guidance are matters of community concern, not private judgment. Written long before modern neurological discoveries, the Bible has a healthy scepticism about wandering minds.

War is a damage limitation exercise

Deuteronomy 20

The concept of armed religious crusades is obnoxious to modern readers, not least because of the bloodshed caused by some religious militants. Deuteronomy introduces us to the war theme which will recur in the next book, and tells us that at least there are some limitations to be observed.

- Conscription is restricted (vv 7,8): people who have begun new relationships or embarked on long-term projects are exempt from military service. So too are those who don't have the heart for it; it's not compulsory.
- Peace treaties are to be offered (v 10): there is no excuse for wanton destruction of people who offer no resistance.
- The future is to be preserved (v 19): life goes on after wars, and fruit trees take a long time to grow; there must be no wanton destruction of plantations.

Later readers will see here glimpses of God's greater purposes than mere military victory. Yet even these modest restrictions are not always observed by nations which have signed the Geneva Convention.

Sex is for saving

Deuteronomy 22

The miscellany of rules, including concerns about female virginity, illustrate a biblical emphasis: sex is special and should be kept in its proper place.

That place is within the male/female bond of a recognised marital relationship. Sexual union creates relational responsibilities. Deuteronomy rules out:

- transvestism (v 5) because it violates the God-given gender distinctions
- pre-marital sexual relations (vv 13-21, 23-24) because they violate the principles of family structure and remove sexuality from its natural outcome of child-rearing in stable relationship
- adultery (v 22) because it is a sign of the breakdown of trust and stability in a marriage
- rape (vv 25-29) because it violates a person's freedom and treats them as a sexual object.

The principles are repeated throughout Scripture and reinforced by Jesus. The sanctity of sexuality removes it from the level of common bodily functions with which it is often bracketed.

It looks real!

Many Near-Eastern cultures about the time of Moses had law codes. There was a standard format in which they were presented and Deuteronomy conforms to it:

1. Title or prologue – who is involved (1:1,2)
2. The story so far – historical overview (1:3-4:49)
3. The laws in detail (4:1-26:19)
4. Recording of the laws for posterity (27:1-8)
5. Blessings and cursings (27:9-28:68)
6. A ceremony to adopt and ratify the code (29-30)
7. Reading the law to the people (31)

The order may vary slightly in other codes, but the basic pattern suggests that the book had its origins in the cultural milieu of the Near East before 1000 BC.

Money shouldn't be so interesting

Deuteronomy 23:19,20; 24:4; 10-15,17

Western interest rates are currently heavy enough on borrowers, but not nearly so crippling as in some poorer countries. In the ancient world, even in Moses' day, they could be as high as 50 per cent, so these rules are set firmly in a real-life context.

The concept of 'usury' has exercised the church for centuries. Such is the power of Mammon that Deuteronomy's rule that loans to believers should be interest-free has never seemed realistic. (There is some doubt as to whether it was ever widely practised.) The nearest some modern agencies come to it is to loan money to employees at rates pegged to inflation.

But this is a law like all the others, and we should look for principles behind it before dismissing it as not for our times. It poses a massive challenge to the whole Western way of life, which is built on the flimsy paper foundation of credit and the even flimsier paper foundation of huge institutions trading in money itself.

It reminds us that Christians with social concerns can attack soft targets such as violence and pornography, and like the Pharisees ignore 'weightier matters' of justice and righteousness in society. The ban on usury simply says we should not profit from each other's difficulties, which perhaps needs some prolonged and prayerful reflection.

The law on pledges is relevant too. It is so humane and so impractical: return a pledge when the owner needs it, when, of course, it ceases to be a 'pledge' and the agreement sinks to the level of trust. Deuteronomy tells us that people matter more than things.

The fact that Third World countries at the end of the twentieth century were paying eleven dollars in interest to the West for every one dollar they received in overseas aid is one graphic example of how the relatively rich can still 'rob' others of their livelihood in parallel ways to those listed here.

The covenant: pp 18-19
'Jubilee': p 265
Warfare in the Old Testament: pp 16-17, 227

Spiritual laws of cause and effect

Deuteronomy 27-30

God's purpose for his creation can be summed up by the Hebrew word shalom – wholeness, well-being. The biblical promise is that when God's laws are obeyed and his name is honoured, then even in a fallen world a measure of shalom will be enjoyed.

But God's laws are not obeyed. Even his people are selective in the ones they stress and those they let slip quietly by. Therefore, the opposite results. Instead of wholeness there is fragmentation, and instead of well-being there is trouble and strife.

These blessings and curses are not to be read as a quid pro quo reaction of a vindictive God. We have already seen plenty of evidence of his compassion and forgiveness.

Rather, they illustrate a spiritual law. When life is lived as God intended, society is relatively stable – and vice versa. A machine driven beyond its capabilities will blow up. So we see the snowball effect of the fall. As we float on the tide of godless ways, we drift further from the safe haven of shalom.

The teaching here is corporate, given to people as a whole. The promises and warnings are not individualistic; we are bound together into a web of social relationships in which we reap the results of each other's actions. Hence the need for Christians to work for 'kingdom values' in every area of human society.

Don't be afraid

Deuteronomy 31

Canaan is in sight. A new generation is about to go where its parents could not. Statesman to the end, Moses leaves them travelling instructions which God was to repeat later to Joshua.

Moses gives them three special words of assurance. He tells them that God will never leave or forsake them. Unlike the other gods they will meet on their journeys, Yahweh's loyalties would not change with the weather.

This unchanging God would go ahead of them to prepare the way (v 8) and they had a reminder of this when the 'shekinah' cloud, the visible manifestation of God's glory, descended on the tabernacle (v 15). The God who had brought them out from Egypt would be there to lead them on. His continued presence is promised; 'the Lord your God goes with you' (v 6).

For Christians facing new or threatening situations Moses' words are reassuring. But the passage has a sting in its tail. Along with the promise comes a prediction: the people won't keep their side of the bargain. Human nature will keep on falling away from God; and he will keep on calling them back. The stage is set for the next step in the Old Testament story.

What a way to die!

Deuteronomy 34

Few people want to die. The fear of the unknown - even with all the biblical promises of being with Christ for ever - is very strong. And the desire to achieve more in this life first is also powerful.

Moses has reached the end. He knows that he has accomplished the work God gave him, although he would dearly love to do more - to lead the Israelites right into Canaan itself. As we look with him across the great divide, we can see:

- There is no accidental death as far as God is concerned. However it may be seen from a human perspective, Moses has done what God wanted. Now it's someone else's turn on earth.
- A glimpse of 'the Promised Land'. Moses was allowed to see what lay ahead for the Israelites. As we lay foundations for others to build on, we can imagine what great things they might do. And we have through Christ a glimpse into heaven itself and the new life that awaits us.
- The prospect of reunion. Moses had a hazy but real hope that he would be united with his family (32:50). Life in heaven is something more, not something less, than life on earth.

For today

- God is patient, kind and loving
- God may not alter the outcome of our actions, but he still has good purposes for us
- Remember what God has done in the past, in good times and bad
- Be prepared to witness wisely and be involved in the church's mission
- Don't underestimate God's ultimate judgment of all people
- Use your money wisely and structure your giving
- God's laws were given for good reasons

Look at life another way

Generally, the Bible offers us God's view of human affairs, mediated through human writers inspired by the Holy Spirit. Ecclesiastes is an exception. It quite deliberately presents our perplexity about life, and yet at the same time can claim to be divinely inspired.

The author starts as the biblical equivalent of Eeyore, A.A. Milne's pessimistic donkey in his *Winnie the Pooh* books. He sees only the gloomy side of life and can hardly raise a smile on a sunny day or laugh at a joke. 'What's the point of it all?' he wails. 'Life's meaningless.'

Well, it is, of course, if death is the end and there is no God. Human life in all its richness – with its art and music, its creativity and complexity, its organisation and extravagance – is then a sick joke; full of promise, it amounts to nothing of significance.

Ecclesiastes looks at life through the eyes of a no-hoper, and offers us two positive thoughts. One is that the meaning of life, including its injustices, is known only to God. Christians who ignore that mystery and never face life's apparent contradictions squarely will appear gullible and shallow to non-believers.

Ecclesiastes helps us to think honestly and to admit that life's not so clear-cut as we wish and sometimes falsely make it out to be. It may be clear to God, but not to us.

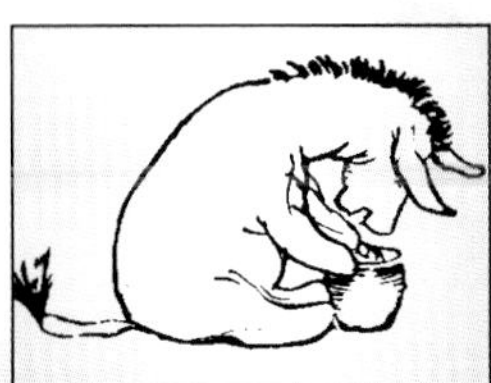

The Book of Ecclesiastes

- Looks at human life from the realist's viewpoint
- Suggests that life is meaningless without the spiritual dimension
- Tells us to be content with what we have
- Teaches us to keep everything in proper perspective

AT A GLANCE

ECCLESIASTES

1	We're never satisfied; what's the point?
2	Pleasure, wisdom and work all end at the grave
3	Be content and let everything have its place
4	Oppression, labour and loneliness add to human misery
5	Fear God and don't trust your riches
6	Why do we work so hard and never enjoy the fruits?
7	Walk in the way of wisdom; it'll cheer you up
8	The injustice of the world is incomprehensible
9	We'll all die, so eat, drink and enjoy what you have
10	Wisdom is better than war; fools should not become leaders
11	Plan ahead and do what is right
12	Remember God before you get too old

Secondly, Ecclesiastes encourages contentedness which accepts the puzzles of life philosophically, doesn't harbour impossible ambitions, and seeks to live 'wisely'. God is to be honoured, and life with all its imperfections and unanswered questions, is to be enjoyed.

Our enjoyment will be greater if we accept the limitations and know that life's delights are but short-lived and its pleasures temporary. Then we shall become wise.

KEY QUOTE

A man can do nothing better than to eat and drink and find satisfaction in his work. This too, I see, is from the hand of God, for without him, who can eat or find enjoyment?

Ecclesiastes 2:24,25

Trinkets are trivial

Ecclesiastes 1,2

Experts are predicting that so many people have 'everything' that Christmas presents will become 'experiences' – tickets for such things as hang gliding or bungee jumping. Most of us in the West have many possessions and few can detach themselves completely from them. House, car, furnishings, sentimental objects and clothes define who we are, and we hate to lose them.

But when life is laid bare on the autopsy table, these things look trivial. Who we were, the influence we exerted, the people we helped (or hurt) are what we will be remembered and missed. They will be a more powerful memorial than instructions in our will or words on our tombstone.

Ecclesiastes invites us to step back and look at our own silliness. We never think we have enough (1:8) and we keep on re-inventing the wheel (1:9). Knowledge is no good stored in our head and never used (1:16,17). Pleasure is an emotion that goes out like a light the moment its energy source is cut off (2:10,11). And we work our socks off for others to get the benefit (2:17-19).

The author poses a hard question: why on earth do we live like this? Why do we waste so much time and energy on trivial things and spend so little on lasting things like relationships with others and with God? Perhaps we all suffer from practical agnosticism, despite our protestations of faith. Wisdom starts when we look into the grave and reflect on our own mortality.

Take your time

Ecclesiastes 3

For the Hebrews and first Christians, time was essentially a progress from creation to consummation, rather than a recurring cycle of events. God was seen as the Lord of time, and certain moments had special significance.

Ecclesiastes offers that perspective in this famous passage. Certain actions are appropriate at certain times. Conversely, there are things which are inappropriate at other times. The passage is saying, with Paul in Ephesians 5:16, that we are to make the most of every opportunity (which the KJV rendered as 'redeeming the time').

The picture here is of someone who takes life in his stride, who is not fazed by its unexpected turns. Taken like this, life is less stressful. If we assume that life is to be filled with song and dance we shall be angry and frustrated when the music stops and we are faced with trouble and strife. And what's the point of getting like that?

For today

- Don't forget that life is temporary; without being morbid, keep death in your sights
- Don't go mad getting and spending; it doesn't satisfy and you'll just wear yourself out
- Enjoy what you have and be content with it; life will seem sweeter when you do

FAST facts

Title: 'Ecclesiastes' is the Greek rendering of a Hebrew word in 1:1: The teacher or preacher *(Qoheleth)*.

Author: Solomon, traditionally, although he is never named. The reason is found in such passages as 2:4-9 which reflect the kind of activity Solomon is renowned for. He is also referred to as 'son of David' (1:1) and there are allusions to royal functions (e.g. 8:2; 10:17). However, his claim to have been the 'greatest' king (1:16) is rather too grand since he was only the third. Most scholars keep an open mind on the subject.

Date of compilation: This depends entirely on the author. If it was written by Solomon, then it dates from c. 950 BC. The Hebrew seems to be of a later style, however, and many scholars suggest it is post-exilic (after say 550 BC), but there is little agreement on anything more specific.

Literary genre: Ecclesiastes is a wisdom book, and some chapters (e.g. 7) are similar in style to the book of Proverbs.

Stand in silent awe

Ecclesiastes 5:1-7

Suddenly in the middle of our doom-laden desert comes an oasis of spirituality worthy of the best psalms (vv 2,7).

To stand in awe of God in silent contemplation is an important element in spirituality. Silence should be built into worship; sometimes we cannot hear ourselves think for all the noise, still less hear the still small voice of God.

But Ecclesiastes tells us that we should be awe-struck all the time. Rash, hasty words are a symptom of self-centredness. We shout off our opinions but have little understanding of the wider context within which any issue or situations fits. Our ignorance may not be culpable, but our arrogance is remiss.

God is the unseen guest at every meal, the unnoticed listener to every conversation. Would we really want him to overhear some of the things we say to others? If we could see him standing there, we would be far more circumspect. The devil fools us into believing that God's invisibility is a sign of his absence or lack of interest. When tempers start to rise, look who's listening.

Enough is enough

Ecclesiastes 5:8-17

Occasionally, rich people are caught shoplifting. Once, when a British woman and her son were arrested the son immediately responded, 'It's no problem; we'll pay. We've got lots of money.'

But we never have enough (v 10). You can always think of more things to do if you had more money. Our eyes grow bigger with our bank balance.

How do you measure enough? Perhaps the place to start is where we are now. If we have food, clothes and shelter, that could be defined as enough (cf. Matthew 6:31). A little more might buy better or more things, but it will never satisfy the inner craving which most of us feel, because money can never fulfil our deepest human desires. Contentment begins when we learn to appreciate what we have already. We can do that by thanking God for it, treating it as a special gift, and being willing to share it.

You won't get wisdom from books!

Ecclesiastes 12:11,12

You could read these two verses as the height of arrogance; they seem to assume that the collected sayings of the wise Shepherd are the last word on everything. Christians might see a parallel here to the stark warning in Revelation 22:18 not to add to that prophecy.

However, the author is not claiming more than he should, nor is he making a statement about the rest of the Scriptures (which would not have been fully collected in his time anyway). Instead he is warning us against the habit of endlessly exploring matters at a theoretical level. Wisdom could (and did) become an academic pursuit rather than (instead of as well as) a way of living, often with unanswered questions.

The Bible does not tell us to empty our minds, nor to avoid reason. But study needs a purpose, and the purpose is to honour God and to live in his ways. Anything that does not contribute to that is indeed 'meaningless'.

Make the most of it

Ecclesiastes 9

The trouble with eating and drinking without a care in the world is that tomorrow we die, as the rich fool in Jesus' story found out (Luke 12:19).

Taken one way, the encouragement here in verse 7 is utterly self-centred, a statement of self-indulgent laziness and without a thought for God. That certainly was the attitude of the rich fool. But taken another way it recognises that life is unpredictable. Death can be sudden (v 11).

Part of our calling on earth is to appreciate and enjoy what the Creator has given us. All good things are to be received with thanksgiving (1 Timothy 4:3). Failing to do that is another way of using them carelessly and selfishly.

You're never too young to start

Ecclesiastes 11:7 - 12:8

As people get older, they may begin to regret the excesses of youth in which time, money, energy and opportunity are wasted. And as we grow older in faith, so we may become more aware of our lack of wisdom, more sensitive to the sin which so easily besets us. The spiritual path often becomes steeper, not easier, as the years roll by.

So it is commonsense not to leave setting things straight with our Maker until the eleventh hour. Besides, if we neglect him and his will in our younger days, we are missing out on some of his riches and possibly getting ourselves into difficulties which he would spare us, if he had not made us free to choose our own path.

Ecclesiastes concludes with a poetic description of old age which, charming in itself, is a stern warning that the twilight years bring failing powers so that we cannot any longer serve God and others as we might wish. The spirit may be willing, but the body cannot respond so well (v 1).

Among the facts of life we are asked to consider are: the loss of keen eyesight (v 2); trembling limbs, bent backs and rotting teeth (v 3); growing deafness (v 4); the nervousness which goes with frailty, the tell-tale greying of hair, and the funeral procession (v 5).

Yes, says the preacher, life may seem to be meaningless. But in this concluding chapter, he reminds us that God always has been close by, even though we may have chosen to ignore him, and it is his presence which offers to give us meaning and purpose. Wisdom, he says, includes God in our lifetime's equation.

Place in Bible:

- After Proverbs, before Song of Songs in the Old Testament
- **Similar books:** Proverbs; Ecclesiastes is linked with Job and the Song of Songs as well under the title of 'wisdom' literature
- **Easily confused with:** Ecclesiasticus, which belongs to the Apocryphas)

Spiritual health check for y'all

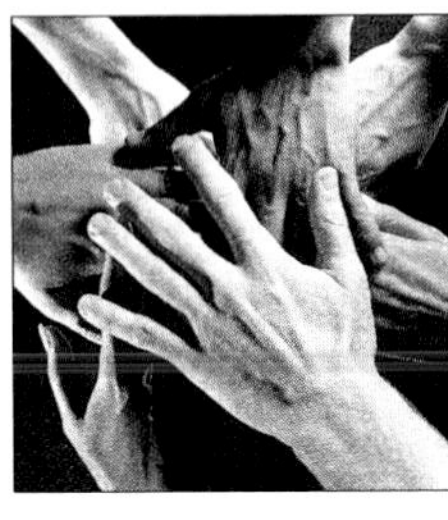

Paul's letter to the Ephesians

- Describes the eternal benefits of faith in Christ
- Explains Christian faith as a move from death to life
- Focuses on the unity which church members are given by faith in Christ
- Compares Christ's unity with the church with marital unity
- Tells readers to prepare for spiritual warfare

There's a Christian poster which reads 'God so loved the world that he didn't send a committee'. That is true, but he did send a church, which many might consider to be the next worst thing. As you open Paul's letter to the Ephesians, be prepared for a shock to your theological system.

The whole letter, including the teaching on salvation, is addressed to the church corporate. Paul never denies that faith is personal, but he stresses that it is not individual. Being a Christian is not about '*my* relationship with God' but about *our* relationship with God as believers together.

T.S. Eliot illustrated this perfectly when he wrote in *Choruses from 'The Rock'*:

> 'There is no life that is not in community,
> And no community not lived in praise of God.'

God's original purpose was to create humans in community ('It is not good for the man to be alone,' Genesis 2:18), and to call together a community of people who honoured him ('The LORD has chosen you out of all the peoples on the face of the earth to be his people' Deuteronomy 7:6).

So, mixing his metaphors, Paul writes: 'You are . . . fellow citizens with God's people and members of God's household . . . being built together to become a dwelling in which God lives by his Spirit' (2:19,22). It might be easier if you translated the letter into colloquial American-English, and substituted 'y'all' for 'you' whenever you see it. Or else read it in a French Bible, and see the plural *vous* where Western individualism would prefer to see the singular and more intimate *tu*.

Written more in the style of a tract than a letter, Ephesians sets out in memorable terms and vivid pictures the practical consequences of what God has done in Christ, and the essence of church life. Commentator William Barclay called it 'the Queen of the epistles'; it is probably unmatched in its combination of clear doctrine and practical advice.

EPHESIANS

1	**God's plan for our salvation**
2	**Christ has given us new life and reconciliation**
3	**Paul's apostolic ministry and his prayer for his readers**
4:1-16	**The church united, serving and growing**
4:17-32	**Principles of Christian living**
5	**Spirit-filled living: morality and marriage**
6	**Right relationships and spiritual warfare**

KEY QUOTE

[Christ] came and preached peace to you who were far away and peace to those who were near. For through him we both have access to the Father by one Spirit.

Ephesians 2:17,18

We're all special

Ephesians 1

However intimate the relationship between parent and child, there is usually something extra special in a parent's feelings for a child who is either conceived after fertility treatment, or is adopted. In both cases, there is no doubt that the child is 'wanted', 'chosen' and very 'special'.

Paul says that God feels the same about his people who he has chosen and adopted (vv 4,5). We might equate that with being 'rescued' (another biblical picture of salvation); as orphans are adopted from war zones, or babies from children's homes.

In Roman times, adoption was not generally out of pity. A rich family might adopt a talented young man, give him a new name, an education and a share of the inheritance in return for his service. Paul uses this parallel to show how Christians are 'special' to God.

- Christians are chosen (v 4). Paul does not say that others are not chosen or implies a crude selection process. He speaks of an attitude; God has set his love on his people, and they are privileged to know it.
- Christians have a new status (v 7). They are accepted and renewed, the equivalent of being given a new name and identity, a fresh start with God.
- Christians are specially educated (vv 9,10). The church is entrusted with the revelation of God's purposes for the world.
- Christians are given an inheritance (vv 3,13,14). All the wealth of heaven is made over to them; the Holy Spirit is a first instalment, or 'taster' of what is to come.

Dwelling on this, Paul bursts into thanksgiving and implies that this should be our response too. Knowing we are special to God provides us with a sense of spiritual security. But it is not to become a foundation for spiritual complacency. Thanksgiving leads to prayer for growth in knowledge and experience (vv 15-23).

That growth is to lead us into a fuller understanding of and involvement in the church for which Christ died (vv 22,23). Rejoice that you're special; remember that every other Christian is too. There are no misfits in the body of Christ; God chose others as much as you.

Date:
Written between AD 59 and 62.

Location:
Ephesus was a large city in Asia Minor, an inland port on major trade routes. It had grand architecture, including a theatre holding up to 25,000 people, and its temple to Diana (Artemis) was one of the seven wonders of the world

Place in Bible:
After Galatians and before Philippians in the New Testament

Parallel books:
Almost half of Ephesians is also included in Colossians, which was probably written at the same time

Author: The apostle Paul. This was challenged by nineteenth-century German theologians and some scholars still express doubt because the language and vocabulary differs from Paul's normal style and there is no personal greetings. However, early church writers accepted the letter as authentic as Paul did use different styles, (partly due to his secretaries).

Readers: The best manuscripts omit 'to the Ephesians'. An early heretic, Marcion, had a copy addressed to 'the Laodiceans'. This letter may have been a tract sent to several churches including Ephesus which would explain why the letter lacks personal greetings and does not address the specific problems of the congregations, as all Paul's other letters to churches do.

Date and place of origin: Ephesians is regarded as one of the 'prison epistles' probably written at the same time as Colossians, Philippians and Philemon. It is thought that Paul wrote them from Rome c. AD 60-62, although his remand in Caesarea (c. AD 59) would be another possibility.

How the church began: Paul visited the city briefly and later stayed for three year, ending when silversmiths objecting to his teaching rioted. The Christians regarded him highly and were deeply upset when he told them they would never see him again (Acts 20:13-38).

CROSS CHECK

'Choosing' and predestination: pp 101, 374
The Holy Spirit: pp 39, 217, 235
The role of women: pp 73

Faith is a matter of life and death

Ephesians 2:1-10

Advertisers claim their products are different from others. Some evangelists try to introduce the faith on the same basis: look at the difference Christ makes. Unfortunately, when you stand a Christian and a non-Christian next to each other, you may not see much difference.

That's because the real difference is under the skin. Paul says it's like that between life and death. There are seeds of death everywhere (v 3). They are evident today, as much as ever, in the way social relationships break up; in cut-throat competitiveness and insatiable demand for sensual stimulus; and in a passive torpor which afflicts many people.

All this stems, Paul suggests, from seeds of death inside us (v 1). 'Sin' (v 1) means 'missing the mark', not hitting God's target of righteousness. And 'disobedience' (v 2) means 'taking the wrong road'. We've sought fulfilment in the wrong place; we're digging for treasure on the wrong island; we're driving in the wrong direction.

Not to know God is to be dead to God, just as a child asleep is 'dead to the world'. And, like the child, most people are unaware of it. They only realise it when they wake up, and only Christ himself can rouse them (vv 5-9). Think about your faith like that, and you may realise what an amazing gift it is, and what enormous potential it has.

Which is why Paul says that faith should work (v 10). God's rule covers every part of our lives (v 6). We're to go into the world as his agents of re-creation. (The word 'workmanship' (v 10) is rare; it is used only in one other place and refers to the original creation.)

We do this by bringing the life he's given us into a dying world by our 'good deeds'. Think of the world as a wilting plant, and of the Spirit of God as life-giving water. You're a container filled with that life; your task is to pour it where it's needed.

Unity in community is good news today

Ephesians 2:11-22

Unionists and republicans in Northern Ireland do not have much time for each other. Nor do Serbs and Albanians. In fact, they often hate each other. And so did Jews and non-Jews in the first century. So when the Christian church started to bring warring factions together, the tension must have been uneasy for a while.

But there is no difference between people in God's eyes. A sinner is a sinner, a Christian is a Christian, whatever their colour, birth place, language or political allegiance. Stretched out on the cross, Jesus drew opposing sides to himself and made them one in him. The true counter-culture has begun; fragmented humanity is being glued back together.

This is so important today. Twenty-first-century people are not seeking ideas, forgiveness or even God, directly. They seek relationship and authentic human experience. They will be attracted to Christianity (and consequently find truth, forgiveness and God) if they see in Christians solid, unifying and caring relationships. They will reject it otherwise. Our community life is part of our witness: we are to be a 'building' radiating God's presence (vv 21,22).

Our unity here is based on faithfulness to our foundations (v 20). We are good at focusing on our differences. The need today is to focus on our similarities. There is only one foundation (the divinity of Christ and the effectiveness of his death and resurrection, vv 16,20) but the temple built on it has many rooms and a variety of decorations. God can and does live with those variations. We should too.

Fill up with fine fruit

Ephesians 5:1-21

The call to 'be filled with the Spirit' (v 18) was the focal point of the 'charismatic renewal' and provoked some bitter disputes. The argument has died down, but confusion remains. Is this a single or ongoing experience, and what does it look like? The term is fast becoming an empty cliché.

Paul contrasts it with being drunk. Therefore it is controllable (like prophecy, 1 Corinthians 14:32); it is not a trance. The fact that the first Spirit-filled apostles were accused of drunkenness (Acts 2:13) is irrelevant; that suggestion was made by people who assumed that song and praise in foreign languages was the over-spill of an all-night party of pilgrims.

The immediate context is what Christians do when they meet. In Corinth, they got drunk and partied, much to Paul's dismay (1 Corinthians 11:17-22). The model Paul sets forth here is not drowning in liquor but being immersed in the Spirit; instead of bawdy songs they are to sing praises to God.

The wider context is the life of the Spirit, which excludes immorality and bawdiness (vv 3-7) and is demonstrated by the 'fruit' of 'goodness, righteousness and truth' and whatever 'pleases the Lord' (vv 9,10). The tense of the original 'be filled' implies a continuous, not one-off, 'filling'. To be 'filled' with the Spirit is to be totally under the Spirit's control.

Every Christian has received the Holy Spirit (1:13,14) and is regularly to seek his fullness through worship and leading a life honouring to God. Individual experiences of the Holy Spirit's anointing may be perfectly valid but are not taught here.

Indeed, it is primarily *the church* which is filled and receives the 'gifts of the Spirit' distributed among its members (cf. 4:11,12; cf. 1 Corinthians 12:7,27). Paul's concern is not so much, 'Am I filled with the Spirit?' but 'Are *we* filled with the Spirit?' When we are, the body of Christ is more harmonious and effective

The art of church maintenance

Ephesians 4

Some churches are burdened by massive maintenance bills for preserving ancient fabric and heating cavernous roofs. Others are obsessed with maintaining their activities and keeping the rotas going. These have their place but the most important thing to maintain in a church, Paul says, is unity.

We cannot create it; it already exists (v 4). But we can either maintain it or destroy it (v 3). We maintain it by exercising the two most difficult human virtues: patience and humility (v 2). To this end we should remember that:

- Faith is worked out on a level playing field: we all relate to God in the same way (cf. 2:3-5)
- There is a unifying structure of belief and experience which holds us together (vv 4,5)
- Each person has a place in the body and a ministry to exercise (v 7)
- The teaching and evangelistic ministry of leaders provides a focus for united growth (vv 11-13)
- Discipleship requires us not to fall back into old ways of living (vv 17-24)
- We should not boast (which is falsehood) or otherwise assert ourselves over others (vv 25-27,29)
- We must learn to give to one another and lay aside bitterness, and above all accept each other (vv 28, 31-32).

How about putting that on the next church council agenda?

For today

- You are special to God: show your gratitude by the way you live
- You have been saved through faith, in order to do good works in the church and the world
- Work hard at relationships within the church; your own pride, envy, hatred and bitterness destroys the unity of the body of Christ
- 'Walk in the light' by honouring God in word and deed

Wedded bliss

Ephesians 5:21-6:9

To equate church life with married life might, in the present day, convey the wrong impression. Churches, like marriages, have a tendency to split up. That is the opposite of what Paul meant in verse 32. He is making three distinct points.

First, the church corporately has a 'union' with Christ so profound that the only suitable picture is the union of a man and a woman – not just sexual union but the unity of mind and heart which characterises a good relationship. This was as novel in the first century Roman empire as it may sound now; divorce was easy and adultery common.

Paul thus gives marriage a high status. And he gives the church a high status, too. God is wedded to it. So we are to nurture it, not regard it as a necessary evil or a temporary convenience.

Secondly, all church relationships are to be 'submissive'; verse 21 states a general principle. That does not mean that everyone should stand aside for everyone else so that no one goes through the door! Rather, our concerns are to be for others before ourselves – a common biblical theme. Our phrase 'at your service' expresses the attitude.

And thirdly, Paul advocates wifely submission and husbandly self-giving. In practice, these blend perfectly in the context of verse 21: it is another picture of unity. It is likely that some Christian women, enjoying their new freedom, were bossing their husbands around. Paul says no one should dominate anyone, in the family or in the church. Sadly, male abuse of the biblical idea of 'headship' has sometimes led to the disunity and dominance which Paul sought vehemently to avoid.

Standing room only in the battle

Ephesians 6:10-20

Round-the-world yachtsman Tony Bullimore, spectacularly rescued off Australia in 1997, wrote himself into the history books with the immortal quote, 'You're either a survivor or you're not a survivor'. As Paul gets to the end of his letter, he wants his readers to become survivors. Because even when they've done everything, they've still got to go on standing for Christ (v 13).

The principalities and powers which form the dishonourable opposition can be identified in institutional evils (which are no less personally-inspired for that). They lead to systems of unethical conduct, imbalanced priorities, short-term self-seeking motives and objectives, which just as effectively paralyse modern society.

Our glib talk about 'market forces' often obscures the fact that these forces have a life (and at times, it seems, a mind) of their own and cannot effectively be manipulated. They may not be directly controlled by super-demons, as if they were playthings on fiendish strings, but there is something dark and sinister about such systems which few have the courage to question or confront.

That is not to deny that evil spirits can afflict individual people and seek, in the mode of C.S. Lewis's *Screwtape Letters*, to trip up believers by foul means. But it would be wrong to limit Paul's concern to them. The battle, therefore, really is cosmic: evil is everywhere, and we should be on our guard against it. Don't let popular demonology (whether you agree with it or not) divert your attention from the bigger picture.

Great story for dark spiritual nights

Esther is a gripping story with tension, subterfuge, danger – and a happy ending. Why it is in the Bible has been long debated; it doesn't mention God, nor attempt to teach anything overtly. Yet it is a moral tale in which good eventually triumphs over evil. This is not a book for bit-by-bit study, revealing and its spiritual treasures best if you read it in one sitting.

Set in Susa, the capital of Persia during the reign of Ahasuerus (also known as Xerxes) about 480 BC, before Ezra returned to Jerusalem in 445 BC, it records an otherwise unknown incident. The pompous courtier Haman plots the destruction of the Jews (by tricking the king into signing a bogus decree) because Mordecai refuses to bow to him. Esther, Mordecai's cousin and surrogate daughter, groomed in the royal harem, catches Xerxes' eye after he expels his wife Vashti for insolence. In a second sub-plot, Mordecai saves the king's life.

Hearing of Haman's planned genocide, Mordecai and Esther conspire to tell the king the truth behind the decree he has just signed. Very annoyed, he issues another decree which annuls the first, executes Haman and promotes Mordecai.

Today, at the Jewish feast of Purim, the story is read and the audience boo every mention of Haman and cheer every mention of Mordecai.

ESTHER

1	**King Xerxes deposes Queen Vashti**
2	**Esther the Jew becomes Queen of Persia**
3	**Haman the proud targets the Jews**
4,5	**Esther and Mordecai plan a counter-plot**
6	**Mordecai is honoured by the king for another reason**
7	**Haman's plot is revealed and punished**
8	**Xerxes defends the Jews**
9	**The feast of Purim is celebrated**
10	**Mordecai is promoted**

Esther shows how God is sovereign in human affairs. The eye of faith can see him putting characters in place on the stage. They have no prophet to tell them God's word, and no priest to intercede for them. God is apparently silent and distant. There are just some coin-cidences which add up to a remarkable deliverance through the human agency of two people who risk all.

Esther is the ordinary Christian's book. Most of us live with problems for which solutions do not come easily. Yet looking back we see God's ordering of events which aid us through the troubles. Esther's message is, 'don't forget such signs', look back with thanks, and trust that God will show himself sovereign again.

The Book of Esther

- Tells how Esther the Jew became Queen of Persia
- Shows how with her cousin Mordecai she countered a genocide plot
- Records the origins of the Jewish Feast of Purim
- Reveals God's sovereignty working through circumstance and coincidence

Go, gather together all the Jews who are in Susa, and fast for me . . . When this is done I will go to the king, even though it is against the law. And if I perish, I perish.

Esther 4:16

A nation is born

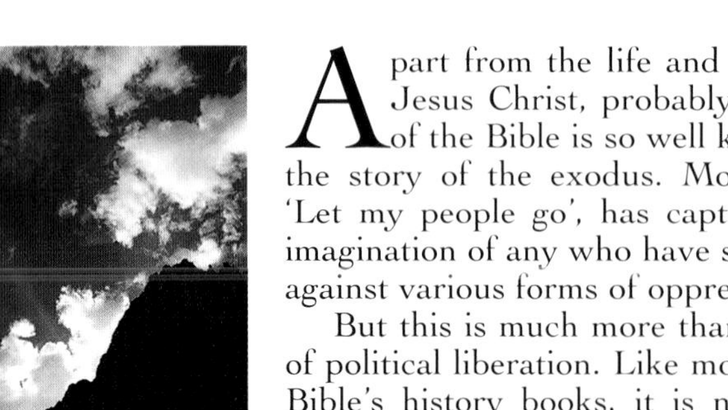

The Book of Exodus

- Traces the story of Israel's 'exodus' from Egypt
- Introduces the key character, Moses
- Summarises the unchanging laws of God
- Describes early Israelite worship

Apart from the life and death of Jesus Christ, probably no part of the Bible is so well known as the story of the exodus. Moses' cry, 'Let my people go', has captured the imagination of any who have struggled against various forms of oppression.

But this is much more than a story of political liberation. Like most of the Bible's history books, it is narrowly-focused and is concerned to teach rather than merely to inform. It begins the saga of the Israelite nation found in the Old Testament and vividly illustrates God's character as saviour.

Exodus concentrates on the traumatic events of the plagues in Egypt and the first few weeks of life in the desert. Central to it is the covenant between God and the Israelites, spelt out on its human side in the Ten Commandments and applied by numerous social and religious laws. It is expressed by the worship centred on the tabernacle, which is described in 12 of the book's 40 chapters.

It introduces later readers to a holy God whose character is expressed in his name, and who sets exacting standards for his people. He is seen to be Lord of history, a reliable guide and a righteous judge. He is not to be treated lightly but is to be worshipped with care. Above all, he is presented as a faithful God fully able and willing to keep the many promises he makes.

EXODUS

Narrative: light type
Laws: **bold type**
Tabernacle detail: *italics*

Chapter	Contents
1	Slaves in Egypt
2	Moses' early life
3	Moses' encounter with God
4	Moses returns to Egypt
5	Israelite slaves oppressed
6	Moses' genealogy
7	Aaron's stick; first plague
8	Plagues of frogs, gnats, flies
9	Cattle plague, boils and hail
10	Locusts and darkness
11	Warning of death
12	The Passover and exodus
13	Israel's first-born consecrated
14	Red Sea crossing
15	Moses and Miriam sing for joy
16	Food in the desert
17	Water in the desert
18	Moses delegates responsibility
19	Camp at Mount Sinai
20	**The Ten Commandments**
21	**Laws on injuries and servants**
22	**Laws on property and justice**
23	**Social and religious laws**
24	The covenant reaffirmed
25	*Design of tabernacle furniture*
26	*Design of tabernacle*
27	*Altar and courtyard*
28	*Aaron's robes*
29	*Consecration of priests*
30	*Other tabernacle details*
31	*Craftsmen;* **Sabbath observance**
32	Aaron and the golden calf
33	Moses and the tent of meeting
34	Fresh tablets of stone
35, 36	*Building the tabernacle*
37, 38	*Making the furniture*
39	*Making the robes*
40	Tabernacle set up

KEY QUOTE

The LORD, the compassionate and gracious God, slow to anger, abounding in love and faithfulness . . . Yet he does not leave the guilty unpunished; he punishes the children and their children for the sin of the fathers to the third and fourth generation.

Exodus 34:6,7

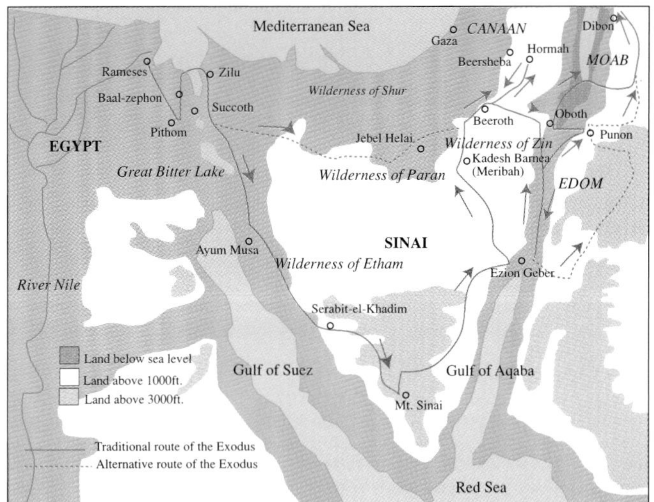

The exact route of the exodus cannot be traced. However, it is clear that the 'Red Sea' was the 'Sea of Reeds', a shallow, marshy area to the north of the Red Sea proper. Scholars differ over whether the Israelites took a northerly or southerly route through it. Once away from the marshes, they avoided the dangerous direct route to Canaan along the well-fortified Mediterranean coast, and struck south towards Sinai where Moses had first encountered God.

Light dawns at last

Exodus 1-3

The Bible contains a number of black holes – periods in which little is recorded. Exodus 1 reveals such a period, the 400 years between Joseph's arrival in Egypt and Moses' birth there. The Hebrews have multiplied and been enslaved. Of their religion, culture and lifestyle we know almost nothing. But one thing is certain: they had not been forgotten by God (3:7).

His ongoing kindness was evident in small ways, smiling through the pain and suffering (1:20,21). His care is seen in protecting the infant Moses and arranging his Egyptian education which prepared him for his confrontation with Pharaoh and his enunciation of Israelite law.

Another blank is the half-century (Acts 7:23 with Exodus 7:7 suggests 40 years) when Moses is a murderer on the run. He sees the plight of the Hebrews with strong emotion and perhaps he is already dimly aware of his calling to lead them. He leaps into action before God's appointed time, and has to seek asylum where he learns at first hand what it means to be an alien like his compatriots (2:11-22).

Exodus shows that God sometimes chooses people who have been written off by others. And that he makes his servants serve long and apparently pointless apprenticeships until they may consider that their opportunity to serve him is gone for ever.

Shorn of self-confidence, so timid that he pleads for a spokesman (4:13-17; 6:28-7:7), Moses was now ready to trust God completely and to receive a new revelation of him (3:1-6).

His story offers hope to those who think they have missed opportunities for God. It also warns those who grow impatient with God or question his call because of their limitations. Moses walks onto the Bible's stage as a spiritual giant, because he has been growing spiritually for 80 quiet years.

Date of events:
c.1280-70 BC

Location:
Egypt (Nile Delta) and Sinai Desert

Story follows:
Story of Joseph in later chapters of Genesis in the Old Testament

Story runs parallel to:
Narrative of Numbers, laws of Leviticus and Deuteronomy

Key people:
Moses, Aaron, the Pharaoh

How the plagues may inter-relate

The plagues are described as 'wonders' (3:20). The word implies God's use of the natural order to achieve his purposes, rather than his suspension of the natural order which is how we tend to define 'miracle'.

Hence there is no intrinsic reason why the plagues should not be seen as a series of natural phenomena. The wonder is in their prediction, their timing and their spiritual impact as they are seen as 'messages' from God.

They are likely to have been spread over about nine months, from July (when the Nile floods) until the following March, connected in this way:

- 'Blood': the word is used as a colour; excessive red earth and micro-organisms may have been brought down by an especially heavy flood, killing the fish
- Frogs: driven from the polluted river and infected by disease (possibly anthrax); Egyptians saw frogs as fertility symbols, so the plague has a double impact
- Gnats: the flood extended their breeding ground and warm, damp conditions increased their numbers
- Flies: attracted by the rotting corpses (flies symbolise Egypt's army in Isaiah 7:18)
- Livestock: probably caught anthrax off the frogs or some other disease spread by the flies
- Boils: skin infections caused by bites from the flies
- Hail: unusual but not unknown extreme weather conditions, possibly linked to the earlier heavy flood
- Locusts: like the flies, breeding in ideal conditions and blown into Egypt by the prevailing wind
- Darkness: dust storms brought by the spring 'hamsin' wind, whipping up the red soil brought by the flood and now dried out.

The final 'plague', the death of the first-born, has no 'natural' explanation. It should be noted that 'first-born' can also mean 'the best'. The cream of Egyptian society was suddenly swept away by an act of God.

Signs and wonders bring God to earth

Exodus 4-12

The Hebrews were unique among ancient peoples. They allowed no physical representation of God. It made life difficult. They were a very 'physical' people; they did not think in abstract philosophical terms. How could they believe in a God they couldn't see?

In Scripture, God is 'seen' by his acts. These include the big epoch-making events of the exodus, the conquest of Canaan, the later fall of Israel and the life, death and resurrection of Jesus Christ. They teach truths, as well as achieve results.

God is also seen through lesser signs, which reveal his presence and reinforce beliefs about his nature and purpose. The plagues were such signs (see box). Their impact was cumulative; Pharaoh was not impressed at first. Even the Israelites became discouraged at early setbacks (5:20; 6:19).

God normally reveals himself gradually; thunderbolts from heaven rarely have instant effect. Saul's experience (Acts 9) is an exception to the rule, and even that was the climax of a process.

It is said that average Westerners today need to hear the Christian gospel clearly at least seven times before they are ready to respond to it. It is the cumulative effect of faithful witness in word and deed which ultimately draws most people to God, not a stunning sermon or miraculous sign in itself.

Pharaoh's reaction reminds us that there are no short cuts to faith, no easy paths to victory over God's enemies and no quick-fix solutions to spiritual or other problems. And when we do see 'signs', they are always gracious encouragements and not the inevitable products of some formula of faith.

HARD Question

Could Pharaoh have said yes?

Exodus 4:21; 7:13; 8:15,19,32; 9:7,12,34,35; 10:20,27; 11:10

It seems unfair: God appears to be playing 'cat and mouse' with Pharaoh. He can't say 'yes' to Moses because God has hardened his heart. So does God predispose people to do certain things, thus robbing them of their free will? (The word 'predestination' is sometimes used in this context, although Paul gives it a specific meaning in Romans and Ephesians.)

In the verses referring to Pharaoh's hardness, the blame is sometimes laid at his own feet: he hardens his heart deliberately (8:15,32). Some passages refer to him simply as 'hard-hearted'.

The Hebrews thought of God as so bound up with life that everything happened because he was at work. (They would have approved of G.K. Chesterton's comment that the sun rose each morning not because of some natural law but because God told it to 'get up and do it again'.)

They saw no contradiction in ascribing something to God which later Christian thinkers might ascribe to Satan or to an individual. It was their way of saying, 'God was working out his purposes in a bad situation'. Exodus shows us that God is in charge of a series of setbacks in which his will appears to be thwarted. It is a message repeated often in Scripture and is at the heart of practical Christian faith.

Pharaoh could have said yes and the exodus would still have occurred. God timed the event to coincide with a particularly vindictive king.

It should also be noted that Pharaoh did not act alone. His advisers were equally hard (9:34), although Moses and the Israelites had won their respect (11:3). The dynamics of this situation were social as well as personal.

The Israelites were a source of cheap labour and were important to the Egyptian economy. The people as a whole wanted to contain them so the employers took a strong line against the union activists. In the end the whole country suffered for the leaders' tough line (11:5).

We will remember

Exodus 13

Celebration linked to commemoration is natural to human beings. Anniversaries are marked with parties or solemn services of remembrance. The Israelites were commanded to remember the exodus in two ways.

First, they were to celebrate the Passover annually. The Jews still do, and increasingly Christians also make Passover meals at Easter time to enact the events surrounding the last supper of Jesus and his disciples. Secondly, the Israelites were to consecrate their first-born sons and animals to God.

Memorials of this kind are reminders of seminal events which have moulded individuals or societies. Bastille Day in France, Independence Day in the United States and Remembrance Day in Britain set the present in the context of the past. They also help to define a group and to retain its corporate identity, a very necessary activity in an increasingly impersonal society.

For Christians, the Communion serves the same purpose, providing an interactive memorial of the central truths of their faith. It is a corporate event, drawing people into fellowship with each other and closer to God.

FAST facts

Title: Hebrew 'These are the names' from the opening words. 'Exodus' comes from the Greek translation (made c. 250 BC) and means 'going out'.
Authorship: Traditionally Moses, whose writing is referred to in 17:14; 24:4; 34:27.
Structure: The book majors on three key events: the exodus itself, the giving of the law, and the building of the tabernacle.
Final date of composition: Probably in Moses' lifetime, with subsequent minor editing of place names.

God is there when you're lost

Exodus 13:17-17:15

Probably few Israelites knew exactly where Canaan was, nor how long it would take to get there. The direct route along the Mediterranean coast would only take a few days. But when they turned south into the desert, their concerns were understandable. The rough scrubland could not sustain large numbers for long. Yet once again, in their extremity they discover more about God.

He is their guide. The cloudy and fiery pillars (13:21,22) were a sign of God's presence. The Israelites had no doubt that he knew where they should go. Had they relied only on Moses, they could have become convinced that he was a blind guide lost in the desert.

Later readers can see in this both the reassurance that God is always ready to lead his people, and the reminder that they should follow his lead even when it takes them down what seem to be wrong turns.

He is their provider. Manna, which defies any attempt at identification (the name means 'that stuff'!), the migratory quail and the hidden aquifer all reveal that when God leads his people, he also provides for the journey. He does not start an expedition of faith without also providing stores along the way. What the Israelites found, however, as countless others have since, was that the stores were not revealed until they were desperately needed.

Travelling by faith is also to travel blind and with very little baggage. Spiritual gifts are often not provided until the journey has begun and opportunities, or problems, are encountered.

He is their protector. Like the exhausted quail the Israelites looked easy pickings for the Amalekites (17:8-15). Aaron and Hur supporting Moses' hands is often used as an example of the effectiveness of intercessory prayer. The lesson for the Israelites, however, was focused on God. He achieved the impossible, and the instruments he used were both prayer and the courage of Joshua. God fights for his people *through* his people.

Another exodus: The Hyksos peoples migrated to Egypt about 2000 BC and by 1700 BC controlled much of the country. They were expelled in about 1570 BC by kings who had built a capital at Thebes. The Hyksos had introduced new methods of warfare including light two-wheeled chariots. Some of the invaders were also known as Habiru and have been identified with the Hebrews (Israelites), but this is unlikely.

Semitic slaves: The Hyksos were a Semitic people and would have favoured such people as Joseph.

Pyramids and kings: By the time of Joseph, the great pyramids had all been built. Cheops, with the sphinx 'guarding' it, had been built 1,000 years before the patriarch. The boy king Tutenkhamun died c. 1326 BC, about the time when Moses fled to Midian.

Religious beliefs: A little later (c. 1315 BC) the sun god Aten became the official Egyptian deity, displacing Amun. Other gods included Osiris, the guardian of the underworld. The Canaanite Baal was recognised, and some gods were worshipped in the form of bull-calves. The Israelites were familiar with polytheistic culture before they left Egypt and discovered it again in Canaan.

Education: Boys went to school from age four. The writing system was hieroglyphic (picture-symbols). Papyrus was used to make parchment. The Egyptians were among the first to record time and dates accurately.

Model leader shows the way

Exodus 18

Stress may be a modern epidemic but it has always been a human disease. Moses is wilting under the pressure of overwork. As a result he re-organises Israelite society along Midianite lines. He appoints trained judges.

This passage may be out of place chronologically. It presupposes that the Israelite laws are already known, yet it appears before they are given, only three months after Israel's departure from Egypt (19:1). It may anticipate what is recorded from a different angle in Numbers 11:16-30.

This passage reminds us that Moses, who is about to bring God's law, is not a dictator, but a mentor and model leader. He taught others carefully (cf. v 20) and shared responsibility with them.

Moses, known for his humility (Numbers 12:3) was also prepared to learn from his foreign father-in-law. He was neither so concerned about his status as a leader to consider himself an infallible oracle, nor afraid of admitting that he hadn't got it all right. Leaders are to be disciples – learners – all the time.

Holiness revealed on smoky mountain

Exodus 19

The spectacle of a thunderstorm in a range of mountains makes even the hardest climber or walker bow in respect. Humanity is dwarfed by creation and humbled by its power.

Such were the phenomena, perhaps accompanied by terrifying earth tremors or volcanic eruptions, which greeted the Israelites at Sinai. Beyond the visible signs they could sense the vast, weighty closeness of Almighty God himself. Accounts of past religious revivals refer to the almost tangible atmosphere of God's presence which causes people to collapse in shame.

The graphic description is not the Bible's first 'theophany' (visible appearance of God); Moses had seen his burning bush and the Israelites had followed the burning cloud. But the combination of images on Sinai reveals God's holiness as something:

- Never fully comprehensible. God comes in a dense cloud (v 9); evident yet still mysterious.
- To be approached carefully (vv 10,14). The symbolism of washing stresses the need to clean up our acts.
- Which infects places (vv 12,13). Wherever God is manifest, nothing remains the same; everything radiates his presence.
- To become a priority concern (v 15), human desires are to be laid aside. Fasting or abstinence of some kind, so as to concentrate on God, is a spiritual discipline in Scripture.
- To be feared (v 16). Fear in the sense of 'treating God with respect in the light of one's own sinfulness' is standard in the Old Testament and not denied in the New (cf. Hebrews 10:31; 12:28,29).

Because Christians often place God's strict holiness below his caring love, we should note that the theophany follows two crucial statements.

The first, reveals God's care: 'I carried you on eagles' wings (v 4).' The people are called to grow up spiritually and embrace the hard truths of holiness.

The second, in verse 6, is the commission given to every generation of God's people. As priests who know and serve him, they are his missionaries to bring the world to himself (cf. 1 Peter 2:9,10). They can only be a kingdom of priests when they are infected by the radiant, consuming holiness of God.

EXODUS ELSEWHERE IN THE BIBLE

The exodus recalled:
Psalm 106;
136:13-22;
1 Corinthians 10:1-5

Moses' life:
Acts 7:18-41

Jesus talks with Moses about his own 'exodus':
Luke 9:28-36

What God always wanted

Exodus 20

Imagine a walkway around the top of a tall building. It has a fence which serves two purposes. It prevents people from accidentally falling off the edge, and it gives sightseers a sense of security; they can lean against it and still be safe.

The Ten Commandments are like that. Within the confines of the fence we can explore what it means to be a human being made in the image of God. When observed, the commandments prevent us from falling into lifestyles which are injurious to human nature. They also provide us with the security of knowing what God requires.

The first three commands relate to God. To be truly human we are to worship our Creator (v 3); spirituality is a part of human nature. There are many modern equivalents to ancient idolatry (vv 4-6); anything which becomes the ultimate focus of attention qualifies.

How to tell the difference

It is difficult to tell when Old Testament laws have universal and timeless application, and when they relate specifically to the culture and times of the ancient Israelites. There are at least two distinct types of law:

- Categoric law, which is God's statute law focusing principles and limits (the Ten Commandments)
- Casuistic law, which is God's 'case law' relating to specific situations (often stated like: When or if X happens, you are to do Y)

This does not solve all the problems but it makes a start. Today's reader has to ask, 'What is the underlying principle behind this law?' For example, the command not to boil a goat in its mother's milk (23:19) suggests two things. One is a sensitivity to nature (it's just plain cruel). The other, and more important, is that Canaanite religious rituals included this; so the command is a call to avoid pagan ways of life and worship – a common Old Testament theme.

Blasphemy, including the simple matter of treating God lightly (v 7) belittles our Maker and exalts us above him. It is an expression of spiritual pride which easily leads to the anti-social behaviour legislated against in the next six commandments, which are basic social laws.

They show what is required if society is to function harmoniously as God intended. They can be stated as positive principles which help to explain why they are still important:

- The principle of rest (vv 8-11); essential to health and relationships, and to prevent economics becoming a god.
- The principle of family responsibility (v 12), i.e. supporting relatives, especially the elderly who do not become worthless when they become less productive.
- The principle of life's sanctity (v 13), giving everyone dignity and the right not to be disposed of by those who are stronger.
- The principle of faithful relationships (v 14); the intimate sharing in marriage builds trust which, once broken, has a domino effect on other relationships.
- The principle of private property (v 15); we need physical things in order to live effectively; stealing property is plucking out a piece of someone's life.
- The principle of public honesty (v 16); when truth gives way to convenience, greed or vengeful hatred, the social fabric wears thin.

The final commandment, requiring unenvious contentment under God's providence, takes us to the heart of the New Testament. It reminds us that what we think and feel is as important as what we do. Jesus takes this idea into the Sermon on the Mount (Matthew 5-7). He builds an even tougher set of standards on the foundation of the Ten Commandments.

HARD Question

Does God approve of capital punishment?

Exodus 21-22

Even in states which still use the death penalty, execution for cursing one's parents seems impossibly barbaric (21:17). Capital punishment is also imposed for witchcraft (22:18), bestiality (22:19) and taking part in non-Israelite religious rituals (22:20).

The problem is that the sentence appears to be sanctioned by God (21:1, cf. 20:22). It seems far from the ethics of Jesus who spoke of forgiving a brother seventy times seven (Matthew 18:22) and who reprieved a convicted adulterer (John 8:2-11). Three things may put these sanctions into context.

First, these laws proclaim the sacredness of life. To curse someone is in effect to wish them dead. Jesus said that is a crime against their humanity (Matthew 5:21,22).

Secondly, they fence the edge of Israel's religion which was still in its infancy. Babies need more protection than adults. The tough measures ensured that people knew that practices common elsewhere were forbidden by God. Later, they would be able still to condemn the sins but apply a less summary form of justice.

And finally, the penalty stressed the holiness of God the Judge. In the Bible, crimes are seen as primarily against him, and only then against people. One sin, however minor, is enough to estrange one from a perfect God (Genesis 3:17; James 2:10), just as one small spot on a Versace dress is enough to ruin it.

Jesus did not soften God's hatred of all sin. God has not changed by New Testament times, even if the application of his laws in social contexts has. Jesus warned that God still judges; people can get away with murder now, but not for ever. And then Jesus himself suffered the death penalty to atone for every human being's wrongdoing, major and minor.

Love your neighbour by what you do

Exodus 21-23

The Ten Commandments, known to Jewish commentators as the ten words, form the heart of the Jewish Torah, or law. The chapters which follow are a commentary on some of them, and relate mostly to social relationships.

They show that violence in any form is a grave matter (21:12-27). Compensation for victims is more appropriate in some cases than penal sentences (21:19; 22:3-6), an idea which modern jurisprudence is often poor and slow in enforcing. Reasonable care is to be exercised so that potential dangers do not become actual (21:28-35).

Vulnerable people deserve protection, not exploitation (22:16, 21-27). The prohibition on interest (22:25-27) was often broken but the selfless caring attitude it expresses is in sharp contrast to that of today's profit-motivated business world.

The ninth commandment is expanded in some detail in chapter 23, but the interjection of commonsense thoughtfulness (vv 4,5) brings us back to the simple care for humanity which underlies most of these laws.

Of course, there are problems (see box opposite), but these should not obscure the main principle: we are our brothers' keepers.

Tit for tat could be worse

Exodus 21:23-25

The famous *lex talionis* law (an eye for an eye) was not intended to be vindictive. It was meant to restrict punishment to fair proportions and prevent excessive retribution. A person who lost an eye might need to be restrained from doing something worse to his assailant.

Hell hath no fury like an aggrieved and frustrated human being. Without this restriction, violence would have snowballed in a society where there was no legal structure as we know it, and each family was responsible for securing some form of 'justice' or compensation.

True worship requires attention to detail

Exodus 25-31; 35-39

There is far more detail in the Bible about the size and structure of the tabernacle, which no longer exists, than there is about the created universe, which does still exist.

This reminds us that God pays attention to detail, even down to the design of the smallest clasps. A God who takes that kind of interest is also one for whom not a single sparrow dies without being noticed (Matthew 10:29,30) and who cares deeply about the details of human life.

We in turn should pay attention to detail in our service of God. The care with which the tabernacle is made implies that worship is not to be casual. Its place is important; any old room will not do (although any place can be consecrated to God) and there is something deeply satisfying in setting

THE TABERNACLE

This was a large but portable place of worship around which the Israelites camped. It, and especially the ark of the covenant within it, symbolised the presence of God among the people. It had a simple two-room design which formed the basis of all future Israelite temples.

OUTSIDE

Structure: A framework made of acacia wood overlaid with gold was draped with ten linen curtains dyed red, blue and purple. They were decorated with cherubim.

Covering: Eleven goat-hair curtains covered the linen curtains, and over these were ram and dugong (sea cow) hides. They were held in place with copper clasps.

Courtyard: This was like a stockade, with a wooden frame and curtained 'walls'.

Washing basin: A golden container of uncertain shape and size. It was used by the priests for their ceremonial washings

Altar of sacrifice: A hollow wooden box overlaid with copper stood on the east of the courtyard. It also had horns at each corner. It is uncertain if it was partially filled with stones to form a hearth.

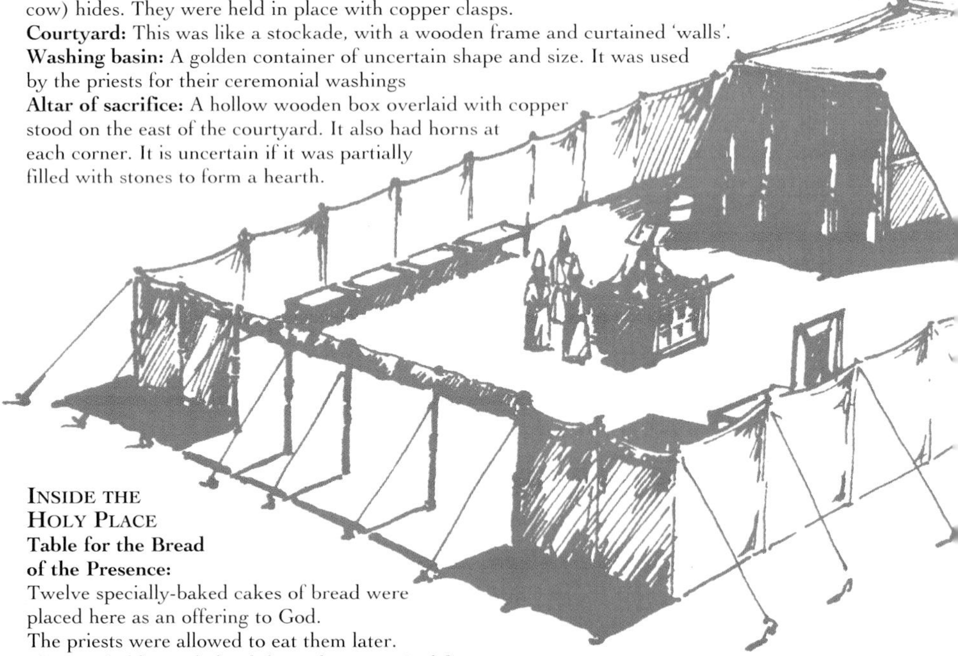

INSIDE THE HOLY PLACE

Table for the Bread of the Presence: Twelve specially-baked cakes of bread were placed here as an offering to God. The priests were allowed to eat them later. They probably symbolised dependence on God for all things. The table, overlaid with gold, was on the north side of the Holy Place.

Lampstand (menorah): This gold candelabra was on the south side of the Holy Place. It had a central stem and three branches either side. Its lampholders were shaped like flowers.

Incense altar: Placed in the Holy Place opposite the ark this acacia box was overlaid with gold. It had 'horns' at each corner.

aside special places for God. The early Christians, who could not afford the luxury, continued to use the traditional sacred places (the temple and the synagogues) until they were ejected.

Two people are singled out in Exodus: Bezalel and Oholiab (31:1-112; 35:30-36:5). They are the biblical patron saints of the arts. Gifted by the Spirit of God, their craftsmanship has worth in its own right.

In former generations, the church patronised artists but in modern times, utilitarianism is preferred. Some now look askance at the lavish gifts of artistic Marys (cf. Mark 14:3–10; John 12:1–8) but God appreciates their contributions.

INSIDE THE MOST HOLY PLACE

The ark of the covenant

This key piece of furniture was the only thing in the Holy of Holies. It was a wooden box overlaid with gold. Poles inserted into rings enabled it to be carried without being touched. On top was a gold slab and two golden cherubim. Inside were the stone slabs inscribed with the ten commandments, a piece of manna, and Aaron's budded staff.

Veil

The curtain dividing the two rooms. It was hung on gold hooks from simple wooden pillars.

VITAL STATISTICS

Dimensions: Length, 14m/45 ft; width, 4m/14 ft; height, 5m/16 ft

Gold used: Approx. 850 kg / 1,900 lbs (Tutenkhamun's tomb probably had 180 kg / 400 lbs)

THE TENT OF MEETING

The Bible also refers to 'the tent of meeting' which was a small, probably ordinary tent, pitched outside the Israelite camp. This was Moses' private prayer tent where he met with God. It may have served as a worship centre before the tabernacle proper was built (Exodus 33:7–11). Its physical distance from the camp reminded the Israelites of God's 'otherness'.

You have to laugh!

Exodus 32

The Jews are renowned for their religious humour, but Christians have sometimes been slow to see the wit of Bible writers. The narrative is often lightened by literary humour or dramatic irony which makes the message far more powerful than if it was stated as a simple theorem.

The incident of the golden calf is one example. The pathetic excuse of a guilt-laden Aaron that the calf 'just came out of the fire' (v 24) is meant to make us laugh. As we do, we see how foolish he was, and we learn more positively never to fall into such a silly trap ourselves.

The Israelites, with more wealth than they know what to do with (cf. 12:35,36) are like children left alone in a nursery who think that dinner has been forgotten. So they concoct something out of the unsuitable materials they have to hand. It shows how necessary a codified theology and law has become – and Moses is on his way with it.

Contemporary 'new age' spirituality needs that too. Having abandoned, or never consulted, the ancient theological structures of the Christian Scriptures, people mix their own beliefs and all kinds of strange things emerge from the religious production line.

Aaron should have known better. He is now the archetype of leaders who respond to public opinion rather than to divine revelation. Yet in mercy God forgave him and the Israelites. New agers are not yet beyond the pale

HARD Question

When did this happen?

The date of the exodus has been the subject of scholarly dispute. There are two main suggestions:

1. An early date: c. 1440 BC

According to 1 Kings 6:1, Solomon began the temple 480 years after the exodus. Solomon lived about 960 BC. However, some argue that this is an ideal number (not unusual in the Bible) derived from the twelve judges who each ruled for a generation (12 x 40 = 480).

A reference in Judges 11:26 can be dated to about 1100 BC. It claims that Israel had been in the land for 300 years, giving an exodus around 1400.

2. A later date: c. 1280 BC

The Hebrews had been in Egypt about 430 years according to Exodus 12:40 (this too could be a stylised figure). Ancient calendars were generally imprecise. Joseph is not likely to have been in Egypt until about 1750.

The cities of Pithom and Rameses, which the Israelite slaves worked on (1:11) in the Delta region are known from archaeological records not to have been earlier than Pharaoh Rameses II (c. 1290-1240 BC) after whom the latter was named. Interestingly, his son did not succeed him; did he die at the Passover? Later, there is evidence for the destruction of Lachish and Hazor in Canaan c. 1200 BC which would coincide with Joshua's invasion.

3. Making a choice

The majority of scholars today prefer the later date, which is followed here and in the companion volume *The Bible Chronicle*. However, absolute dogmatism is not possible, and the New International Version of the Bible (Study Bible edition), published in 1985, opted for the early date.

The message of the Bible is unaffected by the date of the exodus. Even the following chronology is hardly affected; the early date gives more time for the Judges while the later date reduces their time period. It is only when we reach the era of the kings that dates can be set with certainty.

CROSS CHECK

Israelite law: pp 260-5
Holiness: pp 155, 262
Tabernacle arrangements: pp 114-5
Later temples: pp 52-4, 127, 130, 320
Law and grace in the New Testament: pp 376-7
Israel in the desert: pp 89, 324-7

Moses' finest hour

Exodus 33

God is threatening divorce. You can achieve your ambitions, he says, but as your lover I'm not going to be part of them (v 2). Suddenly we are faced with a conundrum. We know sin separates people from God, so how can he prosper people he is punishing? The law of cause and effect falls apart.

The people are devastated. They want both God and their future dreams, so they strip off their jewellery in an act of remorse. Moses, however, only wants God. He doesn't want to achieve anything unless God is in the centre of it. He could gain the world, yet lose the essence of life (cf. Luke 9:24,25).

Moses desires God personally, for himself, and not for what God can do for him. Like a lover blind to all but the beloved, he wants to be with God even if he has to make do with the harsh life of the desert until he dies.

Moses wants others to know God too. This can only happen through the evidence of his presence among the people. Not through their conquests or their prosperity but through their community, their lifestyle, their words and deeds.

Success is not a witness to God. God is his own witness, by his presence cherished, enjoyed and radiated among his people who have no thought for their own well-being.

HARD Question

Did Moses write the Pentateuch?

Shakespeare did not write the plays attributed to him; the Jewish holocaust never happened; Elvis Presley did not die; and galactic aliens have been captured and hidden by the FBI in the Nevada Desert. There is no end to the questioning, criticising and challenging of accepted ideas.

So it is not surprising that the claimed authorship (as well as the authenticity) of Bible books has come under scholarly scrutiny. Few Bible issues have aroused as much controversy as the authorship of the Pentateuch (Genesis to Deuteronomy).

That Moses wrote it was accepted by all Jewish and Christian scholars until the eighteenth century. Parts of it are declared to have been written by Moses (Exodus 17:14). Later Old Testament figures assumed it was written by Moses (see Nehemiah 13:1). And Jesus himself accepted Moses' authorship (Mark 12:26).

This view was challenged by scholars who suggested that the five books of Moses were compiled by a later editor from at least four major sources. In the classic statement of the theory, these are known as J, D, E, and P. The sources were defined partly by linguistic variations, especially by the different names of God that are used in different places.

Those views have been modified during the twentieth century, and the debate has become less ferocious. The discoveries of archaeologists have shown that the books present a reasonably authentic picture of life in ancient times, as far as it can ever be unearthed.

And literary scholars have concluded that the date of compilation of material into its current form is not nearly so important as the date and authenticity of the content of the material – which is generally regarded as being very ancient.

For modern readers, the question of authorship need not affect the theology of the inspiration and authority of Scripture.

The occasional New Testament reference to Moses by Jesus could be taken as simply the standard shorthand title for the Pentateuch ('the Law of Moses') rather than as an infallible pronouncement about its authorship. In the contexts Jesus was not addressing that question but appealing to the Scriptures on other issues.

However, the very character of Moses and his Egyptian training lends great weight to the view that the Pentateuch contains at least a substantial amount of material from the hand of Moses. He was the sort of person who would have written down the laws he brought to the Israelites. He was a teacher who would have written down the story of their forefathers upon which their present experience was based.

How far what we now read is directly the work of Moses, and how far later hands (Samuel has been suggested, among others) have knocked it into its present shape, is uncertain. The fact that Moses is referred to throughout in the third person could be a mark of his humility, or the sign of a later editor. Most 'conservative' scholars are happy to maintain open minds on a subject which can never be decided finally.

For today

- Beware: God is holy, so approach him with awe
- Remember his laws are to keep us safe, not to stop our fun
- God is known in his past acts which encourage us to trust him now
- He deserves the best we can give in worship
- Look for timeless principles behind ancient customs and laws

Meet the 'Damian Hirst' of biblical art

Hieronymus Bosch was the medieval master of the macabre.

The Book of Ezekiel

- Covers the period of Babylon's attacks on Jerusalem
- Uses vivid symbolism to convey God's teaching
- Looks forward to the restoration of Jerusalem

Damian Hirst's 'sculptures' of dead animals preserved in formaldehyde evoked a storm of comment in the 1990s. Was it art or bad taste? Was it an ironic look at the art world, or perhaps a comment on society: we're dead?

Ezekiel is as shocking and as puzzling as that. Open this book and you'll be confronted by mythical creatures astride gyroscopic wheels made of eyes. You'll see a man cooking dinner on a fire fuelled by cow dung and be invited to caress, in your imagination, a beautiful woman who turns into a prostitute. That's before being given a tour of the cemetery. Ezekiel would be at home in the Tate Gallery.

It's all part of God's rich tapestry as he uses all means to drive his points home. If you bear in mind the principles of art appreciation, you'll get a lot out of this book.

The context is the decade between Nebuchadnezzar's first major incursion into Judah and the destruction of Jerusalem, c. 597-587 BC. Ezekiel was one of the first exiles to be transported like slaves across the Near East. There, he is called to prophesy to his fellow prisoners, and tells them what's happening back home. (He's psychic, too.)

A contemporary of Jeremiah (who stayed in Jerusalem), Ezekiel brings a similar message to explain why God has allowed the defeat, and a similar long-term hope that reconstruction will occur. Keep that as a theme for the exhibition, but take each canvas, story and performance on their own. They could enlarge your vision of God, and deepen your understanding of yourself.

AT A GLANCE

EZEKIEL

1	Vision of cherubim and wheels within wheels
2,3	Ezekiel's call to prophesy
4,5	'Performance art' of the siege of Jerusalem
6	Jerusalem will be ruined
7	The end of Jerusalem foreseen
8,9	Vision of Judah's idolatry
10	God's presence leaves the temple
11	Jerusalem's leaders die as punishment
12	More performance art: all Judah will be exiled
13,14	Prophecies against the false prophets
15	The untrue vine
16	The beautiful woman became a fallen woman
17	Parable of the eagles and the vine
18	We're responsible for our own sins
19	A lament for the exiled leaders
20	The story of Judah's rebellion against God
21	Babylon is God's sword of justice
22,23	Sins of Israel and Judah
24	Ezekiel's personal tragedy
25	Prophecies against various nations
26-28	Prophecy against Tyre
29-32	Prophecies against Egypt
33	The role of the watchman
34	The role of the shepherds
35	Prophecy against Edom
36	Judah will be restored
37	Vision of the valley of dead bones
38,39	Prophecies against 'Gog' and 'Magog'
40-48	The vision of the ideal temple

For every living soul belongs to me . . . The soul who sins is the one who will die

Ezekiel 18:4

Rapid response unit keeps eyes on the world

Ezekiel 1 (cf. ch 10)

The number of closed-circuit TV cameras in public places has mushroomed. Used for both crime deterrence and detection they create the impression of Big Brother watching us. We are always in view.

And so we are to God. That is what Ezekiel perceives in this vision of the cherubim and their wheels. For the prophet and his contemporaries this was not frightening, it was encouraging.

The exiles were in Babylonia, far from Jerusalem. God, in their understanding, was in Jerusalem if he was anywhere, but how could he hear them, let alone help them, from 600 miles (900 km) away as the crow flies?

The vision shows how. God's rapid response unit is not restricted by space or time. He does not have tunnel vision or short sight. He is everywhere at once, and nothing escapes his gaze.

When you go into a strange, hostile place, God is just as much there, and just as powerful, as he was the evening before in the church prayer meeting. When you travel miles (literally or metaphorically) from a church, where Christians are thin on the ground, God just blinks, shifts gear, and gets there ahead of you.

This vision also reminded the exiled Judeans of God's holiness (the light and fire of vv 4,13, and the sparkling gems of v 16), and of his strength and widom (the animal heads are of strong beasts and the human head speaks of understanding, v 10).

They would recall the cherubim from Isaiah's vision 200 years earlier (Isaiah 6), as we should from John's vision in Revelation 4:6-8. These angels, in their constant attendance on God, model for us the life of worship and service that we should always be living. God never changes; he is the same yesterday, today and for ever (cf. Hebrews 13:8). We need that reminder as we move into new places, new phases, during our 'exile' in a God-ignoring world.

PROPHETIC TIMETABLE

Date (BC)	King of Judah	Event or prophecy	Ezekiel
605	Jehoiachin	Babylon defeats Egypt, annexes Judah; hostages including Daniel taken into exile	(Living in Jerusalem)
597	Jehoiakim, then Zedekiah	Nebuchadnezzar attacks Jerusalem, takes more hostages including Ezekiel	(Exiled to Babylon)
593	Zedekiah	Prophecy of siege and destruction	chs 1-7
592	Zedekiah	Prophecy of temple being destroyed. Promise of restoration	chs 8-19
591	Zedekiah	Explanation of why it's happened	chs 20-23
588	Zedekiah	Prophecies against seven nations	chs 24-31
587	Zedekiah	Jerusalem destroyed, main exile to Babylon; prophecies of watchman, Egypt	chs 32,33
586/5	None	News arrives of Jerusalem's fall. Prophecy of shepherds, valley of bones	chs 33-39
573	None	Vision of the new temple	chs 40-48

FAST facts

Author: Ezekiel was a priest exiled from Jerusalem to Babylon in 597 BC (1:3; cf. 2 Kings 24:12-14). He was called to be a prophet in 592 BC when he was 30 years old (1:1,2). He was at one time happily married (24:15-18) and an influential leader (cf. 8:1; 20:11; 33:30-32).

Setting: The exiles lived in settlements on canals outside the city of Babylon but within its administrative district (1:1; 22,23). Communication with Jerusalem was possible although slow (33:21; cf. Jeremiah 29).

Book: Seven of his prophecies are dated (see chart) and the book is arranged in an orderly fashion.

Location:
Babylon, among the Jewish exiles
Date:
Between 597 and 573 BC
Place in Bible:
After Jeremiah, before Daniel, among the Old Testament prophets
Parallel books:
Daniel also belongs in the Babylonian exile. Jeremiah worked in Jerusalem at the same time and his message is like Ezekiel's in places

Tough guy weighs up the risks

Ezekiel 2,3

From John Wayne to James Bond, the tough guy who wins through is a familiar figure of fiction. We need heroes like that, even if they are make-believe. We all face challenges and we need the inspiration to overcome them.

Ezekiel is the biblical tough guy more than the strong man Samson (Judges 13-16). Ezekiel is the dogged, never-say-die guardian of truth who sticks to his spiritual guns. Samson was like a grunting Sumai wrestler performing tricks, but whose personal and spiritual life was a mess.

It seems from this passage that Ezekiel was temperamentally independent, not easily swayed by others. But he still needed to be prepared for his assignment. He is warned that it will be hard, that he will face opposition, and that he will be ostracised (2:4-6; 3:4-9). Ezekiel has to count the cost.

And so do we. People called to minister in the church are offering themselves for neither a sinecure nor an ego trip. It may be rewarding, but it is also tough. People called to witness in the secular world through ordinary jobs find it no less demanding. Ethical issues can be fudged easily when we do not wish to rock the boat. We should count the cost from the beginning.

Ezekiel is given God's word to sustain him in a vision and finds it 'sweet'. (So did John, but it turned his stomach because God's word is hard as well as nourishing; Revelation 10:9,10). Tough guys need the correct diet. We will not survive the battle without God's sustenance; giving time to his word can be as enjoyable and is certainly as essential as a good meal.

Performance art conveys powerful message

Ezekiel 4,5

One day, on your way to work, you see this odd character by the roadside. Beside him is a mud model of a city, with a frying pan propped against it. The 'artist' is lying on his side, his face against the pan. Nearby are his rations of lentils and cereal, a bottle of water and a heap of cow manure. You miss a step, and hurry on. Next day he's still there. Next week, he's still there. One day, you ask him what he's doing.

This is performance art, ancient style. And 1,500 years later, Ezekiel's crowd-stopping method is worth a thought. It was a prophecy without words. Not just a 'visual aid'; but a message in itself.

God communicates in many different ways. In the Bible, he teaches through actions, which speeches may interpret. The crossing of the Red Sea demonstrated who God was; Jesus was 'known' to the grieving disciples through the familiar action of breaking the bread (Luke 24:30-35).

We can so stress the words of the faith that we reduce it to a cerebral philosophy, and then wonder why the 'right' words don't connect with people. Many messages in the world are conveyed through dramatic and visual media (including TV commercials). People 'see' the point through them more immediately. There is a place for them in evangelism and teaching alongside the oral explanations.

But as you walk away from Ezekiel, don't get the wrong impression. When the sun goes down no doubt he'll pack up and go home for the night, returning in the morning (cf. 3:24)!

HARD Question

Did Ezekiel have psychic powers?

Ezekiel 8,11

Some commentators have doubted that Ezekiel could foresee the destruction of Jerusalem and suggest he simply commuted between the two cities. But the prophet gives the impression of being in a trance-like state, not merely dreaming. The explanation is therefore that they were 'paranormal' experiences.

Apart from the debate about whether such things happen at all, the possibility raises additional problems for Christians: all kinds of people seem to have paranormal and precognitive powers. Identical twins sometimes become instinctively 'aware' of something currently happening at a distance.

A spiritualist medium predicted the Harrods bomb blast in London in 1987 and was only 80 minutes and a short distance out. Ten years later, a Christian foresaw the nation mourning and 'filled with flowers', associated with the royal family. Three months later, Diana Princess of Wales was dead and a mountain of flowers covered the land. Greek lengend tells of Cassandra predicting disasters and Nostrodamus appears to have foretold a good deal of later history. These things happen.

Such experiences suggest that 'foreknowledge' is a human ability which a few people possess. Christians believe it should be harnessed for God and controlled by the Holy Spirit, but it can be taken over by other spiritual forces too.

The Bible shows that God can make things known in advance (cf Isaiah 42:9, 45:21), as can Satan (which is partly, no doubt, why Scripture declares occultism off limits). And, if spiritual communication with God is possible, then non-verbal, non-mechanical communication between people made in his image may be possible too.

The issue then is how unsought awareness should be used. The New Testament urges caution and common sense, prophecies of whatever sort are to be tested and weighed up (1 Corinthians 14). Paranormal intuitions are neither to be denied nor exploited. Neither excessive fear nor obsessive fascination is healthy or biblical; rather we are to have an open, prayerful mind framed by Scripture.

God walks out on a lover

Ezekiel 10

The divine promise 'I will be with you always' (Matthew 28:20) recurs in various forms throughout Scripture. But just occasionally, it is revoked. God is patient. God is love. Sometimes, however, his people become so insufferable that like an exasperated lover he walks out on his bride.

In Ezekiel's vision he leaves his 'house', the temple in Jerusalem, before it is destroyed. The symbolism is powerful. It says to the Judeans that God is leaving them to their own devices. His holiness cannot co-exist with their sinfulness.

It wasn't the first time he had walked out like that. When the ark of the covenant was captured by the Philistines in Samuel's day, it was said that the glory of the Lord had departed (1 Samuel 4:21,22).

It won't be the last time, either. Churches, like ancient castles, can become empty shells from which the Spirit of life has departed. Those that survive the invasion of property developers may echo with liturgy but do not vibrate with life. There were some like that even in New Testament times (cf. Revelation 3:1,2).

And people once zealous for God become shipwrecked on the reefs of materialism; no longer able to catch the wind of the Spirit they drift on the tide (1 Timothy 1:19; 2 Timothy 4:10) while God sails on without them. He will stay as long as you want him to, but he never outstays his welcome.

God likes his metaphors

Ezekiel 12

Most people know the frustration of trying to make a child 'see' something, or of failing to get through to an elderly person who is deaf or suffering from a stroke or dementia.

There is an echo of that in God's command here: 'perhaps they will understand' (v 3). The sign is extraordinary even for Ezekiel. Dressing up as a traveller, he digs his way out of his own house instead of using the front door.

God keeps on trying to get through to us. He uses all kinds of means. We probably don't recognise most of them. We gather like the townspeople around Ezekiel's home as spectators of incidents but we fail to ask what God is saying through them.

We could do far worse than ask that of anything which happens to us or attracts our attention. God likes his metaphors, and we could learn much about his character and purposes if we saw them as metaphors and not simply as 'events'.

Don't paper over the cracks

Ezekiel 13:1-14:11

'Spot the difference' puzzles can be very irritating. Two apparently identical pictures are placed side by side and you have to spot ten subtle differences. Two or three are obvious; the ninth and tenth are usually difficult to find.

It's the same with 'prophets'. It is all very well for Ezekiel (and for his colleague across the empire in Jeremiah 28) to call some of them 'liars', but how could people on the ground tell the difference? How could they know that those who said, 'The exile will be short' were wrong and those who said 'The exile will be long' were right?

Neither prophet tells us. But we can glean some guidance from them (and from elsewhere in the Bible; see side panel). The chief difference is that false prophets offered glowing hope but no explanation of present circumstances. They promised peace but did not say why peace had been interrupted. They never spoke of divine judgment.

Secondly, some of the false prophets were like fairground fortune-tellers (13:17-20). True prophets weren't paid and didn't parade their gifts. And thirdly, the false prophets lacked discernment. They colluded with people who sought 'wisdom' and told them what they wanted to hear, but did not point them to God.

So the false prophecies were like thin partition walls which couldn't bear any weight. They were papering over cracks in the religious fabric. But don't gloat; listen to the platitudes which form part of many Christian conversations and even convention addresses. 'It'll work out. Do this and God will intervene. She'll come to her senses. We'll get the money. This strategy will be blessed.'

And watch the speakers melt into the background when their puerile words fail to be fulfilled. False prophecy is not far from each one of us.

Tests for prophets

By their lives:
Are they selfless, loving, caring, consistent, giving, holy, prayerful, trustworthy? (cf. Matthew 7:15-20)

By their beliefs:
Do they teach the full New Testament gospel, hold to the incarnation, atonement and resurrection of Christ, and to the inspiration of Scripture?
Do they over-stress certain beliefs such as the second coming? (cf. 1 John 4:1-3)

By their submission:
Are they humble disciples themselves, willing to learn, or are they self-opinionated?
Do they submit to the discipline of the wider church?
Do they speak in love or harshness? (cf. 1 Corinthians 14:29,30; 1 Thessalonians 5:21; James 3:17)

A vine mess

Ezekiel 15

Readers familiar with the New Testament will recognise an immediate parallel with Jesus' teaching in John 15: 'I am the vine, you are the branches'. There, he reminds us that vines are pruned and fruitless branches burned.

The vine was the national symbol of Israel and dated back to Jacob's blessing of Joseph, 'a fruitful vine' in Genesis 49:22, and to the bunch of grapes brought by the spies in Numbers 13:23. Isaiah had portrayed Israel as a vine gone wrong (Isaiah 5), and now almost 200 years later Ezekiel says the Israelite vine is not even good enough to make a fire or a clothes peg.

Its understandable why people like Ezekiel were not popular. No one likes to examine their 'fruit' and 'growth' too closely. Fruit-bearing is the purpose of Christian living (see Matthew 7:20; John 15:8; Galatians 5:22,23). We may think we are in better shape than the Judeans, but few of us would receive any prizes at a spiritual fruit show.

My daughter sold her body

Ezekiel 16

Imagine the personal horror and shame; see the tabloid headlines. The adopted daughter you have lovingly rescued from poverty and degradation, nurtured and provided for, has gone on the streets and become a prostitute.

Sadly, it happens. And Ezekiel's analogy is meant to shock us. That, he says, is what Judah has done. The parent is God, the clients are false gods, pagan superstitions and unrighteous practices. It was a stock prophetic theme; Jeremiah used it, as had Hosea some years before.

But what is unique here is the tender, sensuous description of verses 1-14. Dwell on it. Feel the surge of affection. Then empathise with the sadness of verses 15-19. Now you know how affectionately God feels about you, and you can appreciate his horror when we turn our backs on him. The passage is meant to make us think twice about sin.

Don't sign deals with your fingers crossed

Ezekiel 17

Godly people stick to their deals, even if they later think they could get better ones, according to this allegory in which each figure represents something:

- The great eagle is Nebuchadnezzar, king of Babylon (vv 3,12)
- The cedar is Judah; its top is the elite people taken as exiles in 597 (vv 3,4,12)
- The seed is Zedekiah, the puppet king becoming a poor, low vine (vv 5,6,13)
- The second eagle is Egypt which Zedekiah allied with against Babylon (vv 7,15)
- Babylon will dig the vine up (vv. 9,10); Zedekiah died in Babylon five years after this prophecy (v 16; cf. Jeremiah 52:11).

At one level Ezekiel says simply, don't make the treaty with Egypt. But he also argues that the original submission to Nebuchadnezzar was the same as submission to God. The contract was morally as well as militarily binding; God regarded it as a covenant with himself (vv 16-21).

Believers who make agreements with people are making them with God too. No wonder we're told not to make rash vows (Matthew 5:33-37). Truth and trust are characteristics of God, and are to be ours also. It's better to stick to a deal than to break it; and never to sign it with our fingers crossed.

No rights without responsibility

Ezekiel 18

When things go well, responsibility gives us a sense of achievement. But when things go wrong we look for someone to blame. It's not my fault, it's:

- my genes; I was born this way
- my parents; they raised me badly
- my associates; they disobeyed me
- my suppliers; their materials were inferior
- the computer; it added some digits
- the government; they're useless.

In Ezekiel's time there was a popular saying: 'the fathers eat sour grapes, and the children's teeth are set on edge' (v 2; cf. Jeremiah 31:29). In other words, we're paying for someone else's mistake. And up to a point that was true. The destruction of Jerusalem ended centuries of national decline in which previous generations had not honoured God or heeded the prophets' warnings.

However, the present generation was no better. It was just as corporately guilty – although if they had turned back to God at the eleventh hour, like the thief on the cross, they would have known blessing (vv 10-18; cf. Luke 23:40-43).

The Bible never denies that some sins have an ongoing effect. But Ezekiel is anticipating what the New Testament takes for granted. There is a personal dimension to faith alongside the corporate solidarity of God's people.

Personally and corporately, faith is hedged by responsibility. We are loved and saved freely by God's grace. But grace has no practical effect until we respond to it. The response includes a willingness to live for him and not just 'believe' in him. We have the 'right' to become children of God (John 1:12) when we accept the responsibility of belonging to his family.

HARD Question

What 'life' is Ezekiel talking about?

Ezekiel 18 (cf. 16:6; 20:11)

'Get a life!' we say to someone whose existence seems dull. We mean they should seek fulfilment, achievement, pleasure and social interaction.

When the Bible uses the word 'life' (especially here and in John's Gospel) it often refers to 'knowing God' (who is the source of all life) actively in our experience.

Therefore, 'the soul that sins shall die' means 'be cut off from God's blessing', rather than being under the threat of premature demise. (In the historical context, this would have been taken to mean 'being cut off from God's land through the exile'.) The converse is true; obedience to God enables us to receive his 'life', his active presence in our experience.

That is what Jesus meant in his famous saying. 'I have come that they may have life, and have it to the full' (John 10:10). This is the 'eternal life' which Jesus defined as to 'know you, the only true God, and Jesus Christ, whom you have sent' (John 17:3).

In the New Testament this life is regarded as being separate from one's personal and physical circumstances. It could be enjoyed, even celebrated, by the imprisoned apostles (cf. Acts 16:25). It was a lesson which the exiles were beginning to learn, far from the centre of their traditional spiritual life.

Sometimes, God just doesn't listen

Ezekiel 20-23

A standard encouragement to enquirers by evangelists is that God accepts us as we are; we don't have to change first. Only he can give us the power to change. It's true, but Ezekiel points out two important caveats.

- Coming to God implies the desire for change; and
- it involves the abandonment of all other apparent sources of spiritual life.

The Judeans did not fulfil these requirements, as the long reprise of their sad history reveals. In 20:31, God says he will no longer listen (21:3). The sword of Babylon is about to descend (21:8,11,14).

We should never give the impression that God is soft. He doesn't turn on his love in response to a cute smile. Yet if we want him alone (not just what he can do or give) instead of those things which have failed to give spiritual life, he'll move heaven and hell for us.

But don't ask him to be one spiritual force for you among many. He'll close the door in your face. In that sense, he is a 'jealous' God (cf. Exodus 20:5).

Don't cry for me, Judea

Ezekiel 24

Ezekiel loved his wife; she was 'the delight of his eyes' (v 16). To be denied the chance to grieve, mourn, weep, to be alone with his thoughts and with his children, to be denied the traditional therapeutic customs which provided emotional support in bereavement – that must have been a double blow.

But the prophet obeyed. Draw aside and think about this extraordinary man. He had already been 'steeled' for a thankless task (3:8,9). But that would not have made experiences such as this easy.

He had two loves greater than his wife, however, which helped him to cope. One was God himself, and the other was God's people. Both lived longer than a beloved partner, and achieved more. That is not being unromantic, but realistic. To grieve is normal, but there is more to life than even a partner. When we forget that, our focus is unhealthily on ourselves rather than God.

Widen your horizons

Ezekiel 25-32

The Old Testament regularly reminds us that God's concerns embrace people beyond our horizons in preparation, perhaps, for the New Testament missionary mandate. This transported Ezekiel's readers from their immediate concerns and stressed that all the world was under the hand of the one and only God.

They show us how the world affairs, unknown to the players, revolve around God's purposes for his church and world. As you read the papers and watch the newscasts, remember that and lift the world in prayer to its Creator, Sustainer and Redeemer.

Who were the people of whom Ezekiel spoke?

- Ammon (25:1-7): a regular enemy of Israel, from east of the Jordan
- Moab (25:8-11) lay east of the Dead Sea and had tried to curse the emergent Israelites (Numbers 22-24)
- Edom (25:12-14) descended from Esau, Jacob's cheated twin and a constant thorn in Israel's side; sited south of the Dead Sea
- Philistia (25:15-17): also regular attackers, living along the Mediterranean coast
- Tyre and Sidon (Phoenicia, chs 26-28): Tyre was the chief maritime nation once allied with Solomon. Sidon was the home of Ahab's wicked queen Jezebel. Both were north of Israel.
- Egypt (chs 29-32) was a roller-coaster neighbour, sometimes ally, sometimes enemy, because Judah and Israel buffered it against nations to the east.

Pictures of God and heaven: pp 362-3
Prophets and prophecy: pp 75, 122, 164
Sheep and shepherds: pp 215, 410
Leaders' responsibilities: p 111

Watch out and speak up

Ezekiel 33

There was a radio commercial in which Robinson Crusoe told Man Friday to look out for passing ships. But Friday was so absorbed in his magazine that he was deaf to the sounds of cruise liners, launches and cargo vessels just off-shore.

We smile – but not if someone ignores a suspect parcel in a shop doorway and it explodes, killing and maiming scores of people. Nor if an air traffic controller sees two planes on a collision course but does nothing because it's his tea break. If you see someone in danger or need, the least you should do is call the emergency services, and not pass by on the other side (Luke 10:25-37).

Ezekiel applies this to a pastoral scenario. Church leaders especially (but also everyone in fellowship with others) has a watchman role. While we are not called to be intrusive, we are called to be our brothers' and sisters' keepers. If we see them taking a path away from God, or not seeing a potential spiritual danger looming before them, we should say so, gently and supportively.

Bar the black sheep

Ezekiel 34:1-10

Roderigo Borgia (Pope Alexander VI in the 1490s) was described as 'knowing neither shame nor sincerity, neither faith nor religion. He was possessed by an insatiable greed, an overwhelming ambition and a burning passion for the advancement of his many children.'

Ezekiel's picture of Judah's spiritual leaders paints a similarly black picture. We cannot serve God or the church for personal gain (v 3). Church workers deserve support, but are not to use religion to get rich or powerful (1 Timothy 5:18; 6:5).

We are also to be followers as well as leaders, sheep as well as shepherds: God is our shepherd, and we should not lead others where he has not led us. When appointing 'shepherds' we should beware of black sheep.

Model shepherd

Ezekiel 34:11-31

This is the Old Testament root of the familiar teaching of Jesus in John 10: 'I am the good shepherd'. It tells us both about God and about church life.

In biblical times, sheep grazed on open hillsides and wandered over large distances. Flocks could get split up, and mixed up with others. Rounding them up was not easy. Judah has been scattered, so God promises to 'round them up' and bring them home to Jerusalem from Babylon.

This is a promise for people who belong to God in any age but who drift from him. He organises a rescue mission to bring us back to himself. He may use our conscience, other people or circumstances. Thank him for his love and patience; but mourn that it is ever necessary.

Notice, too, that punishment is reserved for those who led the sheep astray (v 16). Jesus also warned us of the peril of being the cause of other people's spiritual divergences, whether by word or by example (Luke 17:1,2).

New life the dead receive

Ezekiel 36,37

The prison door has clanged shut. The bankruptcy has been filed. The diagnosis has been confirmed. Life has lost its meaning; the Judeans' religion and culture had been destroyed. So they hung up their harps and wept for lost days (Psalm 137:1).

Ezekiel does not gloat. Instead of 'I told you so', he offers a message of hope. The dead bones of Judah will live again. The nation will be resurrected. And eventually in 538 BC it happened. Cyrus, the Persian conqueror of Babylon, allowed the Jews to go home, taking their temple treasures from his imperial vaults (cf. Ezra 1).

Paul uses the image in Ephesians 2:1-10 to describe how a person who is 'dead to God' can become spiritually 'alive', and Jesus taught that literal resurrection was possible through him (John 11:21-44). But the contextual application is that when we reach the end of the road, God can create a new path, in his way and in his time.

The end of a perfect day

Ezekiel 40-48

Ezekiel's temple was never built. As it lacks the essential detail to make it an architectural blueprint, it is probably an illustration of something else. Again we enter the world of symbolism, and see:

- It was symmetrical. This is a picture of perfection.
- It was filled with God's glory (43:1-12). God's presence is restored and seen.
- It was the source of a river (47:1-12), a symbol of God's life (cf. Revelation 22:1-5).
- There is a place for everyone (45:1-12; 47:13 – 48:29; cf. John 14:2; Revelation 7:1-8).

We're meant to relax with this picture. It looks ahead to the final re-creation of all things. For the exiled Jews, the temple was the natural picture of God's forgiveness and restored presence with his people. For John in Revelation, the temple became a glorious city in which the presence of God and the Lamb (Christ) would be endlessly enjoyed (21:22-27). The image may change, but what it signifies does not.

We cannot think of heaven too much. It will enable us to put the world in perspective, and to live in it with faith, hope and love. There is a perfect holy day to follow.

HARD Question

Who or what are Gog and Magog?

Ezekiel 38,39

No one knows! Gog appears to be the name of a king, and grammatically Magog is his territory (but it is also a person's name in Genesis 10:2).

This section of Ezekiel it is more like 'apocalyptic' than normal prophecy: it uses highly figurative language to refer to God's eternal purposes and to the end of time. Indeed, Gog and Magog appear as opponents of the saints in Revelation 20:8 (their only other biblical reference).

The simplest explanation is to regard this as a figurative picture of the on-going battle between good and evil. The result is certain. No power can ultimately defeat God. But the battle is real, and should not be underestimated.

For today

- You can never go anywhere without God being there
- God 'speaks' in many ways; unusual methods may clarify the message for some people
- Don't be hasty in saying what you think God wants to say
- Keep your word even when it hurts
- Care for people in your group; we are responsible for each other
- Look ahead; the best is yet to be

Some relief from the pressures

The Book of Ezra

- Judean exiles returned to Jerusalem
- The second temple built
- Secular leaders became God's servants
- God's people struggle to fulfil their calling

Relatives of Jewish (and other) victims of the Nazi holocaust attempted throughout the second half of the twentieth century to recover property which had been confiscated or given to others. It proved a difficult, often fruitless, and always heart-breaking task.

Think, then, how the children and grandchildren of former residents of Jerusalem felt as they trekked 'home' to the old 'promised land'. It had been ravaged by invaders, resettled with foreigners and looted by those who had escaped exile. The settlers had a rightful claim to the land, but their official documents were treated with disdain by hostile residents.

That is the setting of the book of Ezra. It spans a century and the person after whom it is named appears when the story is almost over. He led the second of two returns recounted here, some 80 years after the first.

At first, the exiles arrived with high hopes, eager to rebuild the temple and put God back at the centre of national life. It was a second exodus (cf. Isaiah 43), complete with gifts from their former captors (1:6,7; cf. Exodus 12:35,36).

But the task was great and the opposition demoralised and hindered them. After the temple foundation was laid, the building remained a ruin for 20 years until the prophets Haggai and Zechariah rekindled spiritual zeal.

Meanwhile the law of God had been broken. Ezra put matters right, and was followed a decade later by Nehemiah who encouraged further reform.

The book is concerned with the temple and the law, but it also illustrates how God's people can have the best of intentions only to discover that serving God is like walking in lead boots through treacle. Ezra exhorts us to faithfulness in adversity, as God works out his purposes through it.

EZRA

1	Cyrus allows the exiles to go to Jerusalem
2	Names of the exiles who returned
3	Foundations of the temple laid
4	Temple rebuilding stopped by opposition
5,6	Darius allows rebuilding to continue
7	Ezra prepares to return to Jerusalem
8	Ezra arrives in Jerusalem
9	The problem of inter-marriage
10	Public confession of sin

. . . He has granted us new life to rebuild the house of our God and repair its ruins.

Ezra 9:9

HOW PERSIAN KINGS AND BIBLE BOOKS FIT TOGETHER

Cyrus (539-530)	**Cambyses** (530-522)	**Darius I** (522-486)	**Ahasuerus** (= Xerxes) (486-470)	**Artaxerxes** (464-423)
Daniel Ezra 1:1-4:5		Ezra 5,6	Ezra 4	Ezra 4; 7-10
	Haggai Zechariah			
			Esther	
				Nehemiah Malachi

Right person – but wrong faith

Ezra 1 (cf. Isaiah 45)

The British Prime Minister Winston Churchill said on taking office during the Second World War, 'All my life has been a preparation for this hour.' The Bible sees Cyrus, the Persian conqueror of Babylon, in similar vein. He has been prepared by God to be an agent of restoration for the Jews.

Isaiah calls Cyrus God's 'anointed' 'though you do not acknowledge me' (45:4,5). Although Ezra 1 shows Cyrus acknowledging his divine calling this should be read in the light of what Cyrus wrote on another occasion. It is likely that a Jewish scribe adapted a template edict to make it acceptable to the Jews, and other scribes did the same.

The astounding claim that God deliberately makes a servant of a king whose 'faith' is not kosher leaves us (readers) with an encouragement and an enigma. The encouragement is that behind the chaos of international politics, as ordinary people are shunted around like pawns on a giant chess board, God's guiding hand is at work for the long-term benefit of his people.

It is almost as if he is like a sheepdog, patiently moving the flock of nations towards the field he wishes them to enter. During the process, the sheep break rank, scatter, move in different directions, but gradually they are guided towards the goal.

The enigma is that if God calls and uses someone who doesn't acknowledge him as Yahweh but who sacrifices instead to Marduk, how will God treat him in the next life? Does he damn with faint praise?

In the New Testament, eternal life is granted only through the death and resurrection of Jesus Christ. But right belief about Christ does not guarantee salvation; only penitent trust in God's mercy does that. It is therefore possible to believe wrongly and still be saved. And perhaps God accepts penitent servants of unreal deities as if they actually served him.

There is nothing in the Bible to suggest that God plays with kings as kings play with human pawns, and everything to suggest that his judgments will be righteous. So we ought not to make God's judgments for him. His job is to judge; ours is to serve.

What Cyrus also said

'The gods who dwelt amongst them left their dwellings, in anger at having brought (them) into Babylon. Marduk . . . scoured all the lands for a friend, seeking for the upright prince whom it would have to take his hand. He called Cyrus king of Anshan . . .
The entire population of Babylon . . . bowed to him and kissed his feet. They were glad that he was king . . .
The gods of Sumer and Akkad whom Nabonidus had, to the anger of the lord of the gods, brought into Babylon, I at the bidding of Marduk, the great lord, made to dwell in peace in their habitations, delightful abodes. May all the gods whom I have placed within their sanctuaries address a daily prayer in my favour before Bel and Nabu, that my days may be long . . .'
(From the 'Cyrus Cylinder' in *Documents from Old Testament Times* by D. Winton, Thomas Nelson, 1958)

Author and composition: Ezra and Nehemiah were probably separate books combined by early editors. Both are thought to have been compiled by the same editor as 1-2 Chronicles, with which they clearly link up. He probably lived in the late 400s. The tradition that the author was Ezra himself has appeal but no proof.

The exile in Babylon: It lasted about 70 years from the first deportation in 605 to the return in 537, although Jerusalem fell and the main deportation took place only in 587 (cf. Jeremiah 25:11,12). During this period, Jewish religion was re-formed; the synagogue movement began, and scribes rose to prominence as teachers of the Scriptures. Despite the initial depression (cf. the sorrow of Psalm 137 and the dry bones of Ezekiel 37) many Jews settled into Babylon, became prosperous and did not return (cf. Jeremiah 29:4-7; Daniel 1:3-7).

The fall of Babylon: Its power waned after the death of Nebuchadnezzar in 562, with three kings in eight years. One, Nabonidus, was an absentee who left his profligate son Belshazzar in charge (cf. Daniel 5). In 539 Cyrus, who had ruled Persia for 20 years, finally captured the city after his army diverted the Euphrates River and used the dry bed as a means of entry. He encouraged all captive peoples to return to their homelands. (See side panel)

Date of events:
The first return led by Zerubbabel was in 537 BC, the second with Ezra was 458 BC

Location:
Exiled Jews return from Babylonia to Jerusalem

Place in Bible:
Follows 2 Chronicles, comes before Nehemiah

Story follows:
Fall of Jerusalem and beginning of exile in 2 Chronicles, Jeremiah and Lamentations, and the exile itself in Ezekiel and Daniel

Story overlaps with:
Nehemiah (in which Ezra appears) Haggai and Zechariah

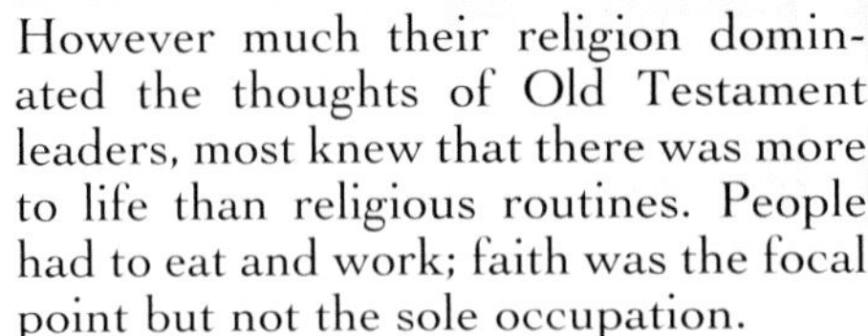

Not like the old days

Ezra 3

However much their religion dominated the thoughts of Old Testament leaders, most knew that there was more to life than religious routines. People had to eat and work; faith was the focal point but not the sole occupation.

There is a realism about the six-month settling-in period before the services began (v 1) which allowed people time to build houses, cultivate land, and set up trades and professions.

There is also realism about the order of events. Worship began in the ruins of the old temple (v 3) and only after another few months is the rebuilding planned (v 8). But there are mixed feelings once the foundations are laid. Joy is understandable, but why the tears (v 12)? There could be several reasons:

- Tears of relief: we've waited so long for this
- Tears of sorrow: we're dealing with the results of our fathers' sins
- Tears of disappointment: older people would see the new temple was not as splendid as the old.

Comparisons of that kind often occur in life, when we build new foundations on the ruins of a marriage, a career, a business, or even a church. The message of Ezra is that new life can spring from seeds of faith watered by the tears of repentance and trust.

Government policies affect the church

Ezra 4-7

Government policies change with the personalities in charge and with the tide of circumstance. These chapters show that such swings can affect the life of the church irrespective of its spiritual health. Chapter 4 is a summary of later opposition but is grouped with chapters 5 to 7 for the record. Together they highlight negative influences we should prepare to meet and give encouragement we should treasure.

- **The power of public opinion** (4:4,5). When we face a storm of ridicule or abuse we look for a hole to hide in. Thick skins and pastoral sensitivity do not go well together; Christians facing human scorn should look to God to change their accusers and for strength to maintain a loving witness.
- **The power of government advisers** (4:8-23). Artaxerxes' position was precarious and distant Judea was a strategic place on his south-eastern borders. So when his advisers spun him a slanted story he believed them and clamped down on the Jews. In our prayers for leaders, we should include the permanent advisers as well as the elected representatives.
- **The officiousness of local authorities** (5:3-17). Tattenai and friends were countered by a legitimate appeal to the former edict (which they did not believe existed). Like Paul in the New Testament, the Jews made use of their legal rights in order to continue God's work. We need to know where we stand and claim the protection of law.
- **The support of sympathetic rulers** (ch 6). Darius saw through the objections and was prepared to uphold the law, to compensate for the delay and punish opposition (vv 8-12). He brought to an end 17 frustrating years (537-520 BC) and the temple was completed in 516 (6:15).

Frustrations caused by unsympathetic people will always dog the church. The fact that the job was completed, eventually, testifies to the fact that God is never defeated, even when his victories seem dependent on the whims of secular leaders.

Ezra risks all in journey of faith

Ezra 7,8

Adventure holidays are popular and are not without their dangers. For example, not long ago a group of adventurers in Yemen was kidnapped and held hostage, and some died in a bungled rescue attempt.

Ezra is going on more than a holiday; he is emigrating on foot with others across 900 miles of potentially hostile country carrying expensive gifts and all their worldly possessions. The slow-moving group would be easy pickings for highwaymen or local resistance fighters.

Yet he prefers God's protection to an armed escort (8:22). One brand of Christian spirituality similarly refuses anything considered 'worldly'. Often this is biblically in error. God has given us minds to use, responsibility to exercise, and a world full of good things and people to work with. The realm of the 'spirit' is not exalted above any other part of creation; all are God's.

However, Ezra's example is to be seen, and followed, as a spiritual discipline of renunciation in specific circumstances, if not as a general rule. The priest throws himself on God's mercy (which all are to do) expressing his faith in this unusual manner, in order to make a point to Artaxerxes and the returning exiles (8:21-23).

A decade later his collaborator Nehemiah acted in just the opposite way. He armed his builders against threatened attack (Nehemiah 4:7-18). Both men honoured God. Both did the right thing at the right time. It just goes to show that the spiritual life is not simply a matter of thoughtlessly following rules!

Draconian remedy for complex failure

Ezra 9,10

Marriages between people of different religions can be a sensitive issue. Often, both partners give up their faith rather than fall out over which one should be followed in their family.

Today, many people believe that individual freedom of choice is sacred. If two people fall in love and wish to marry, they should be allowed to do so whatever their religious laws say.

However, the New Testament (2 Corinthians 6:14) also warns against 'unequal yoking' of believers and unbelievers with an analogy of an ox and an ass trying to pull the same plough.

In Ezra's time, God's law forbade intermarriage in order to preserve the national and spiritual integrity of Israel. In Paul's day, as in ours, the desire to avoid spiritual compromise and the tension of what to teach children about the spiritual basis for life would become relevant factors.

Sceptics point to mixed relationships with non-practising Christians which have 'worked'. What sometimes works is not the chief criterion for what is right, and Ezra's concern is that God's law has been broken however harmonious some of the marriages may have been. Although this law does not apply today, the wisdom which underlies it should not be overlooked; it is perennial.

But Ezra's draconian remedy could hardly be applied today! What happened to the women is not stated. Some may have been reduced to the status of concubine, others may have been freed to return to their own tribes and remarry.

Marriage is not essential to spiritual health or human happiness. Faithfulness to God is.

For today

- Be as broad minded as God is: recognise that he can use anyone for his purposes, so look for his activity everywhere, and not just in the church
- Come back to God when things fall apart, and allow him to rebuild your life.
- Be willing to go out on a limb and trust God for everything – but don't become super-spiritual and forget the commonsense he has given you.

The heart of the gospel is here

Martin Luther

Paul's letter to the Galatians

- Calls Christians back to personal faith in Christ
- Describes how people are 'justified' before God by faith alone
- Encourages Christians to use their freedom in Christ responsibly
- Contrasts the 'works of the flesh' with the 'fruit of the Spirit'

'Galatians,' the sixteenth-century theologian Martin Luther once said, 'is my Katie.' She was his wife and this letter was his love. He lavished his attention upon it. Galatians focused entirely on the central truth, forgotten by much of Christendom and which was then being rediscovered.

It asks the most important question a person can ever ask: what do I have to do, in practical terms, to gain a right relationship with God? Paul's answer is simple: nothing. Admitting there is nothing you can *do* and putting your faith in Christ, as the one who has already done for you everything that is necessary, is all you need.

Which is an answer few human beings except selfish spongers can accept easily. We value our independence and our ability to look after ourselves. When we become dependent on others we feel worthless.

The Galatians certainly found it hard to accept. They wanted to work their passage to the kingdom of God, to pay their entrance fee into heaven. On his visit Paul had explained that the price had been paid already; they just had to get on board. But as soon as he left they developed a set of regulations (including male circumcision) which they insisted must be kept by anyone wishing to remain right with God.

That, Paul claims, is 'another gospel', a denial of what Jesus had done and the apostles had taught. So after a lengthy résumé of his own credentials as a reliable teacher, he explains again what it means to be 'justified by faith'.

It is the heart of the New Testament gospel, whatever Christian tradition you come from or whatever emphasis of Christian living you espouse. By understanding it, rejoicing in it and applying it to your worship and daily living, you will be able to enjoy the privilege of developing a personal relationship with the living God.

That explains Paul's passion in Galatians. For him, as for Luther, this concept was his true love.

GALATIANS AND ACTS
PROBABLE ORDER OF EVENTS

Paul goes to Antioch (Syria) with Barnabas, *Acts 11:25,26*
Paul goes to Jerusalem with famine aid, and meets other apostles, *Acts 11:27-29; Galatians 2:1-10*
Peter visits Antioch, *Galatians 2:11-15*
Paul and Barnabas visit (south) Galatia, *Acts 13,14*
Judaisers follow them, *Galatians 1:6,7*
Paul writes Galatians from Antioch (Syria)
Paul and Peter go to Jerusalem council, *Acts 15*
Paul returns to the area later, *Acts 16:6, 18:23*

GALATIANS

1	Paul's credentials as an apostle
2	Paul and the other apostles
3	The difference between faith and law in God's purposes
4	Paul's plea to stop turning back to legalism
5	Freedom, the works of the flesh and the fruit of the Spirit
6	Warning to live carefully

KEY QUOTE

Clearly no-one is justified before God by the law, because 'The righteous will live by faith.'

Galatians 3:11

It doesn't matter what others think

Galatians 2

'There! I've done it again!' Our inherent weaknesses let us down more often than we care to admit. 'I wish I wouldn't keep doing that!' What makes Peter so human and appealing is he kept on making the same mistakes. Paul is hard to fault and seems austere but Peter was as flawed as a leaky bucket and we love him for it.

He blurts out, 'You are the Christ!' (Matthew 16:16); he's got it! Then he says, 'You'll never die, Lord,' (Matthew 16:22) and he's missed the point. When he denies Jesus (Matthew 26:74,75) we weep with him. When he preaches in Jerusalem at Pentecost (Acts 2:14) we know he's changed. Then we read this chapter, and see he hasn't changed as much as we thought.

Despite his boldness Peter was anxious about what others thought. So here, having been the first to accept Gentiles into the church (Acts 10), he now snubs them (v 12). He's denied Jesus, again.

This shows the power of peer pressure. We're likely to conform to a group, but groups can be wrong. Peter lacked the courage to contradict his friends.

So check your views and practices regularly against Scripture, not against groups. Ideally, do it as a group (as the apostolic church did on this question of Gentile inclusion in Acts 15). But follow the Bible, not the group, even if it loses you friends. Peter's frailty and fallibility is an encouragement, but not a model.

Paul is our model here. He was consistent and his rebuke of Peter was right. But be warned: there is no virtue is always making yourself the opposition. That, sadly, is more often a mark of pride than of fidelity.

Faith is all you need

Galatians 3

This is where the rubber of theology hits the road of life. Get this wrong and your Christianity will swerve dangerously if not crash altogether. Paul's argument is:

1. We're sinners separated from God and cannot match his righteousness (v 11).
2. This puts us in a double bind. The Old Testament law was given to enable us to please God, but we can't match its demands, either. So we're cursed (v 10).
3. Christ has redeemed us by fulfilling the law and shouldering the curse on our behalf (v 13).
4. Therefore, we can be acceptable to God through faith (trust) in Christ (v 14).
5. Then the entire Christian life is to be lived in dependence on Christ (v 3).

Paul does not teach 'only believism': tick the box if you agree and you're OK. People 'saved by faith' are to live by faith and not carry on as before (cf. 5:22-25; Ephesians 2:8-10), which is not exactly a picnic.

This faith is not undergoing certain experience (although it will be experienced), or practising a certain lifestyle (although it must result in a changed lifestyle), or embracing certain beliefs (although it does have a basis in rational beliefs).

Faith in Christ means trust in Christ. It is looking to the crucified and risen Son of God and saying, 'You died and rose so that I could be forgiven and know God. Thank you. I accept your gift of new life, and want you to direct my steps from here on.' It's simple. Which is why some people find it hard.

The Pharisees added rules, the Galatians ceremonies, the Colossians superstitions. But Christ's gospel has no artificial additatives; it is pure faith.

FAST facts

Author: Paul the apostle. No doubt has been raised about this.

Readers: There has been some debate over whether the letter was sent to native Galatians in the north of modern Turkey, where there is no record of Paul having visited, or to the Roman province of Galatia including the southern cities of Antioch, Lystra, Derbe and Iconium, which Paul did visit (Acts 13,14). The argument is complicated by the difficulty of relating Paul's itinerary in Galatians 2 to the Acts 11 and 15 accounts of his visits to Jerusalem. Most scholars opt for the 'south Galatian' theory.

Date and place of writing: If written to the southern cities, this is probably Paul's earliest letter written about AD 49 and probably from Syrian Antioch. If it was written to the north, it would date later, between 53 and 57, probably when Paul was in Ephesus.

Freedom is a relative value

Galatians 3:23-4:7; 5

Do you remember the day you left school? Freedom! No more petty rules; you felt grown-up. Paul says that the person who trusts Christ is like someone who has left school. ('Put in charge', 3:24, means literally a school teacher, or guardian.)

He also says it's like a Jewish boy who's come of age. There were no teenagers in the ancient world. You were either a child or a member of the adult Jewish community at the age of 13. Through faith in Christ, we have become spiritual adults. We can make God-honouring decisions without the discipline of the nursery.

Faith in Christ frees us from the prison of legalism (3:22,23), the impossible attempt to please (or bribe) God by keeping rules and regulations. John Wesley said of his conversion that he exchanged the faith of a slave for that of a son. He could serve God out of love, not out of fear.

The Galatian legalism had specific Jewish connotations, but we can become slaves too: to superstitions, fear of failure,and specific sins. Faith in Christ offers freedom and the dynamic to live wholeheartedly for God.

But there's another side to it. 'Freedom' was a watchword of the hippie sixties, when people tuned in and dropped out, abandoned taboos and did their own thing. Echoes of that lifestyle remain. While the pull back to 'slavery' is strong, so is the pull towards 'lawlessness'.

Freedom in Christ does not give us the right to please ourselves and ignore the wishes of God and other people (5:13-15). We should not impose our 'freedom' in such a way that makes others slaves to our whims and desires.

CROSS CHECK

Law and grace, and 'justification': pp 376-7
Faith and works: pp 102, 176
Paul's early life: pp 33-4
The conflict between the old and new natures: p 371

HARD Question

What does the Hagar analogy mean?

Galatians 4:21-31

This is an allegory. Paul takes an Old Testament story and uses it as a picture of the truth he is expressing. He is not saying the original story meant only this. It was a technique used by many Jewish teachers, and it is culturally alien to us.

His source is Genesis 16 and 21. Abraham was the revered father of the Jewish race. To be a real Jew, you needed to trace your ancestry back to him. But Abraham had two sons: Ishmael, born to Hagar his servant, and Isaac born to Sarah his wife. Isaac was the 'promised' son through whom the Israelites descended.

So, Paul says, which one do you really belong to: the slave or the son? If you pride yourself on being Abraham's (Isaac's) descendants (as the 'Judaisers' did who were troubling the church), then you should not live as if you were descendants of the slave Ishmael. (The bit about Sinai and Jerusalem simply highlights to a Jew the contrast between law, given on Sinai, and freedom represented by 'the city of God'.)

This is still relevant for modern, Western readers. We claim to be 'children of God' through faith in Christ, but can live as if we are still 'children of this world' caught up in its values, attitudes and ambitions. We can force our religion into a system, our lifestyle into a mould, which have more to do with law (neat and predictable) than faith (trust).

How to grow God's fruit

Galatians 5:16-26

You do not just pick berries off bushes and eat them. Some are poisonous. You need to distinguish between good and bad. Jesus used that analogy in Matthew 7:15-20, referring to the black berries of the Palestinian buckthorn which, when seen from a distance, looked like grapes. Paul tells us how to 'grow' good fruit: the genuine, visible product of our inner faith.

But first he warns us of what we know but which still surprises us: that we must expect a conflict (vv 16-18). Our imperfect human nature (some versions of the Bible use the word 'flesh') has been 'crucified' with Christ (v 24), but it won't lie down until we're dead! However, we do have the 'new nature' of the Holy Spirit to counter it and to conquer it.

Our task, Paul says, is actively to cultivate that new nature and weed out the old. Only God can make the fruit grow (another example of living by his grace through faith) but we have to prepare the soil by keeping 'in step with the Spirit' (v 25): allowing his holiness to penetrate our lives.

It is not an option but an obligation. Bishop J.C. Ryle said in his book *Holiness* that 'there is far more harm done by unholy and inconsistent Christians than we are aware of. Such people are among Satan's best allies . . . They supply the children of this world with a never-ending excuse for remaining as they are.'

Christians are under new management. They have been given a spiritual make-over. But sometimes we still look a mess. Moment by moment, ask: what fruit should sprout in this situation?

You only get what you pay for

Galatians 6

As a final warning, Paul uses a phrase sometimes used on posters: you reap what you sow (v 7). It's not true, of course, in one sense. Paul teaches that salvation is undeserved and unearned. We reap what Christ has sown. But in the the general Christian life, it is true.

We are used to the concept. Rubbish in, rubbish out is a basic computer principle. Often, low price means low quality. So don't be surprised if the fruit of the Spirit is slow appearing, if you are pursuing your own agenda still. Don't expect people to be kind to you if you are rude to them. And don't expect to be laden with spiritual gifts for ministry if you want to make your mark on the world. Worldly seed does not produce heavenly fruit.

For today

- Let the Bible be your guide
- Trust Christ, not your good works, for eternal salvation
- Enjoy your liberation in Christ but respect others' freedom too
- Don't live only the way you like; allow the Spirit to make you 'fruitful', that is, Christlike

Identify the fruit

Paul uses the singular 'fruit'. They all grow together – or not at all. Together, they define what a Christian 'looks like' to an outside observer.

Love: Self-giving. 'Knows no hunger to be filled, only generosity to give' (C.S. Lewis).

Joy: More than happiness, and not dependent on circumstance. Is delight in knowing God.

Peace: Outweighs any worldly comfort (cf. John 14:27). Is wholeness, not lack of conflict.

Patience: Means 'long-tempered', fortitude in the face of any challenge or set-back.

Kindness: Related to forgiveness; the compassion that recognises that others aren't perfect.

Goodness: The outworking of kindness; generous acts towards others.

Faithfulness: Loyalty, trustworthiness, ability to keep confidences, honesty.

Gentleness: Well balanced, considerate; 'sweet reasonableness' (Matthew Arnold).

Self-control: Not indulgent but disciplined; not carried away by passion; modest.

The roots of life, the universe and everything

The Book of Genesis

- Introduces the whole Bible story
- Shows God as Creator, Judge and Saviour
- Tells the story of God's promise to Abraham
- Catalogues the chequered lives of the Patriarchs

The emotional health of a human being depends partly on an awareness of one's roots. Persons who have been adopted usually want at some stage to rediscover their natural parents, just to satisfy a deep longing.

In the same way, the spiritual health of an individual, and even more of a group of people, depends partly on knowing their own story. Such knowledge puts the present into context and provides pointers for the future.

The book of Genesis provides people of all races, cultures and generations with a set of roots. Its first ten chapters address some of the deepest questions anyone can ask. Where did the world come from? Is it planned or just an accident? Why is there so much bad in the world now? What does God think about the wickedness?

Then in chapter 11 the story focuses on the family of one man, Abraham, which is to become the nation through which God promises to reveal himself to the world. The 'people of God' prove to be quite ordinary and extremely fallible. The 'Patriarchs' are not saints.

Genesis is a preface to the story of God's people. Christians who rank Genesis and the Old Testament below the New Testament Gospels and letters are ignoring their roots. The 'Christ event' springs from the opening chapters of the Bible.

Will not the Judge of all the earth do right?

Genesis 18:25

AT A GLANCE

GENESIS

1	Creation of the world
2	Adam and Eve created
3	Adam and Eve 'fall'
4	Cain and Abel
5	Early genealogies
6	Noah builds the ark
7	The flood
8	Dry land appears again
9	God's covenant with Noah
10	Table of Nations
11	Babel; Abram's family
12	Call of Abram
13	Abram and Lot separate
14	Abram rescues Lot
15	God's promise to Abram
16	Story of Ishmael
17	Covenant sealed by circumcision
18	Abraham and his visitors
19	Sodom and Gomorrah
20	Abraham's deal with Abimelech
21	Isaac born; Ishmael banished
22	A test of faith
23	Sarah dies
24	Isaac and Rebekah
25	Jacob and Esau
26	Isaac and Abimelech
27	Jacob steals the blessing
28	Jacob's ladder
29	Jacob's marriages
30	Jacob becomes wealthy
31	Jacob leaves Laban
32	Jacob wrestles with the angel
33	Jacob and Esau reunited
34	The rape of Dinah
35	Jacob returns home
36	Esau's descendants
37	Joseph as a boy
38	Judah and Tamar
39	Joseph accused
40	Joseph in prison
41	Joseph interprets Pharaoh's dreams
42	Joseph's brothers ask for corn
43,44	Joseph tricks his brothers
45	Joseph and his brothers reunited
46,47	The family goes to Egypt
48	Joseph's sons blessed
49	Jacob's final blessing
50	Joseph's last days

No chance for creation!

Genesis 1

The biblical account of creation is primarily theology. It answers the age-old questions, 'Why is there a world?' and 'Why is it the way it is?' in timeless terms from which people in every culture can gain insight.

For example, as the twenty-first century dawns people seek some unifying principle to hold together the vastly complex and apparently random systems of nature. Genesis reassures us by showing God weaving order out of chaos as part of his creative task.

It tells us that God is the one constant of the universe. He is uncreated and the reason for all that exists.

Christians may see in the passage a hint of God as a Trinity who uses the 'royal we' at the creation of people (1:26). There is also a reference to the Spirit of God (v 2). God is portrayed as a personal being, not simply as a 'force'.

We notice him to be a methodical Creator. He leaves nothing to chance but has an eye for detail. What he makes is good; it reflects his character and is pleasing to see. Built into it are the seeds of life reproducing itself at all levels. Creation is not a part of God but separate from him.

The ultimate purpose of his work is to make an environment fit for human beings. They are made in God's image, that is, they are capable of moral choice and of a willing relationship with him. They are not trapped in a body of instincts and desires but can transcend their physical limitations in a way that no other part of the animal creation can.

HARD Question

All in a day's work?

The chief conflict between science and Christian belief has centred on the interpretation of the 'days' of creation. Scholars have suggested that they are:

1. literal 24-hour days;
2. unspecified periods of time using 'day' poetically (as in Psalm 90:4; Isaiah 2:11);
3. markers in the stages in the revelation of creation to the author over a week;
4. part of a liturgical celebration pictured as a week's work.

If the author's purpose was theological rather than descriptive, then the issue of creation's mechanics must assume a secondary place. Indeed, the book of Job (chs 38,39) calls for humble agnosticism in the face of processes far beyond human understanding. (This applies as much to Christians anxious to maintain biblical integrity as to scientists anxious to explain everything!)

However, Christians also believe that the author chose his words carefully, and therefore 'day' must have some significance. For today's readers, perhaps the compactness of the story is a welcome balance to the mind-numbing statistics of the age and expanse of the universe.

From God's point of view, what is immense to us was really just a few days' work for him. The universe is not then such a frighteningly big place after all. There is Someone behind it so powerful that, as Isaiah says, he can hold the oceans in the palm of his hand and count the drops.

With that in mind, Christians do not need to fall out over the precise interpretation of 'day'. That God spoke everything into existence, when previously nothing was there, is the important truth to grasp.

GOD THE CREATOR ELSEWHERE IN THE BIBLE

Psalm 8 People are great!
Psalm 19:1-6 The glory of the universe
Psalm 24:1,2 The earth is the Lord's
Isaiah 40:12-31 Creation shows God's greatness
Acts 17:24-28 God gives life to all
Col 1:15-20 Christ the agent and sustainer of creation

People are a race apart

Genesis 2:4-25

The viewpoint suddenly changes. Having seen creation from God's standpoint, we now have our feet on the ground in Eden, and look at the creation of humanity from a fresh angle to see:

- Humans and animals share physical similarities (the same words are used for the creation of both, and both have 'the breath of life')
- People are given the responsibility of looking after God's creation (1:28; 2:15) and obeying God's rules (2:16,17)
- The gender difference is both a source of companionship and also a means of procreation (1:28; 2:18–24); both sexes are made in God's image and are therefore equal in status before him (1:27)
- God planned for people to live in harmony with him and each other, symbolised by the couple's innocent and unembarrassed nakedness (2:25).

The location of Eden is vague and only two of the rivers (Tigris and Euphrates) can be identified. However, it is perhaps significant that this area is known to be the site of some of the first evidences of *homo faber*, modern man building community, farming instead of gathering, and creating 'industry'. References to these things emerge briefly in Genesis 4.

All from one or one from all?

It's a classic chicken and egg question! Were Adam and Eve the first humans in any sense, and so the physical parents of the human race, or were they singled out for a special purpose from among other hominids who were already here?

Later Bible writers focus on the link between Adam, the rest of humanity and Jesus Christ. There is no biblical doubt that Adam and Eve, representing humanity, knew God's command and rejected it. Their sin was countered by Jesus who represented humanity in obeying God and so become the mediator of eternal life (Romans 5:12-21).

The author of Genesis wasn't interested in the existence and destiny of whatever other anthropoids may have existed. He writes from the narrow biblical definition of a human being as one who has been made capable of a personal relationship with God. He shows how God singled out the first couple to become the progenitors of the race of God – conscious people which God planned should live in this world to his honour.

All fall down before a holy God

Genesis 3

The talking snake is still distracting readers from the point of the story! God's revelation included a moral framework: certain things were right, others wrong. This framework is as essential to human society and spirituality as is the framework of a building. If it is broken, everything falls apart.

This narrative explains that it was broken because the first couple did not trust God's word. They could not foresee the purpose of what seemed like a silly little rule.

At this point in its introduction, the Bible shows us God's holiness which calls for perfect obedience. The deliberate espousal of what God calls 'wrong' is a disaster. Perfection and imperfection, holiness and sin, simply cannot coexist.

As a result, humankind is banished from the manifest presence of God. Their relationship is strained and must be continued at a distance. The rest of the Bible story shows what God does to redeem the situation.

And the snake? Religious people know that God, and Satan, 'speak' through a variety of means. For all we know, the snake could have been lunching on the fruit which Adam and

Eve were forbidden, immediately raising the question, why can't we?

There is no suggestion that the tree had magical properties; it was simply designated as one which, if touched, would have negative moral and spiritual consequences. The story stands as a salutary warning that what seems harmless is not always right.

God's patience runs out

Genesis 4:1-11:9

Perhaps most people take their sins lightly because God seems to be blind to them and infinitely forgiving. So having introduced him as Creator and holy Lawgiver, we now see him as Judge with the stirring message that sin does not go unpunished.

In the developing human society the religious instinct remains strong. To make offerings to God is as natural to people as breathing. Cain's offering, however, costs him nothing; he picks it off the ground. Abel's was expensive; animals were the equivalent of money to ancient peoples. The reader is reminded that worship should never be cheap and slapdash, even if it is cheerful.

When angry Cain murders innocent Abel, the results of the fall spread. People are now divided by suspicion and fear. Cain builds a walled city to protect himself (4:17), and is doomed to be a restless wanderer. He feels he doesn't 'belong' anywhere, what we call 'alienation' has ancient precedent.

God limits vengeance, lest the human race destroys itself in a frenzy of murder (4:15). People, however, live as they please. His patience is stretched. He is not a benign daddy who smiles at his children's wild and lawless antics: 'It's only human.'

He is incensed at the insult and cannot sit back and do nothing. People's self-centred actions are self-destructive and take them even further from him and his purposes. So he brings the flood.

Yet even now, his judgment is tempered by mercy. He does not destroy everyone. He saves a small group, who will form the core of his rebuilding programme. Another Bible theme has been introduced, that of redemption and a new start. There is a significant postscript. The story of Babel (11:1-9) reminds readers that society never seems to learn. As life was before Noah, so it continued after him. The gulfs between people widen still further. They are now separated by independent language and culture.

As successive generations survey the chaotic state of their worlds, these stories suggest that God may always be speaking his warnings, and even his judgments, in society's cataclysms.

HARD Question

What about life elsewhere?

The biblical narrative has a narrow focus. It is concerned only with this earth, and it recounts the story of only one very small group of people upon it. They just happened to be the ones through whom God chose to reveal his purposes to the rest (see Deuteronomy 7:6-11).

If rational and fully human life (as defined in the Bible) were to be found elsewhere, Christians can be assured of two things. First, that Christ's death and resurrection has cosmic scope and would be relevant to such people (Colossians 1:15-20). Secondly, that earthlings would immediately be responsible to share God with these 'aliens' just as they are responsible to take the gospel to every tribe on earth.

HARD Question

Does Noah's ark hold water?

The geological evidence for a global flood is disputed. Some scholars maintain there is some evidence of localised flooding in the Turkey/Syria region and as the Bible's 'world' focuses on one group of people in one place, this may be all the text requires.

Harder to imagine is a collection of creatures in a floating zoo not eating each other! But the text may only mean that Noah took on board pairs of cattle, birds and domestic animals from his locality.

The story of Noah is repeated in various forms in so many cultures (as is the story of Adam and Eve) that it must have some historical basis, printing it indelibly on popular memory.

The account is technically 'pre-history', that is, history in the style of legend. But that does not stop it being the vehicle for important truths about God and his errant people.

Growing faith in social turmoil

Genesis 12-20

The twentieth century BC would have looked as different to someone from Noah's day as the twentieth century AD would have looked to someone from medieval Europe.

When Abraham walks onto the biblical stage, the Egyptian pyramids have been built, and medicine, religion and culture have flowered along the Nile.

In Mesopotamia, Abraham's homeland and perhaps not far from the biblical Eden, the Sumerians and their exquisite art have flourished for over 1,500 years. They have pioneered the skill of writing, and have built huge ziggurats to their many gods, of which the 'Tower of Babel' (Genesis 11) was probably a prototype.

Life is stable and people are relatively wealthy. Trade between regions is growing. Suddenly, for no obvious reason, the calm sea of humanity begins to heave. People start to migrate, sometimes aggressively, across the whole ancient Near East. Abraham's family is among them (11:31,32).

How in that polytheistic culture he first heard the voice of the true God and began to follow him (12:1-5) is not revealed. He moved into Canaan maybe 200 years after a wave of tribal invaders had disrupted its culture and destroyed some settlements including Jericho.

Abraham's clan is a loose confederation of relatives who vie for the best land (ch 13) but help each other out of crises (ch 14). Their ethics have not developed far. Polygamy is common and Abraham, famous for his faith, practises 'situation ethics' when lies suit him more than truth (12:10-20; 20:1-17).

Yet God is at the centre of it all. The Abraham saga shows later readers that God is intricately involved in world events to fulfil his purposes for people caught up in them. It also shows him starting with people where they are, leading them slowly, almost imperceptibly, over long periods towards greater faith and understanding.

The view of God in Genesis 1-11

Creator: the reason for the universe (chs 1,2)

Holy: provides a moral framework (chs 2,3)

Judge: punishes wrong doing (chs 4–6)

Love: still cares even for a lawbreaker (ch 4)

Saviour: rescues a remnant to make a fresh start (chs 7–9)

Lord: oversees the nations and guides individuals (chs 10, 11)

HARD Question

Human dinosaurs

(e.g. Genesis 5; 11:10-32)

The Bible is not the only piece of ancient literature to suggest that people's lifespans in early times considerably exceeded the 70 years it assumes elsewhere as an average (Psalm 90:10). The Sumerians attributed even longer lives to some of their kings.

There is no easy solution to the problem. Ancient peoples did sometimes include subsequent generations in a person's 'life'. Their systems of counting lacked the mathematical precision which developed in Persian and Greek times, and they would sometimes use numbers to signify significance rather than formulate fact.

Some commentators suggest that we see here a slow fading of the Edenic influence. The curse of Genesis 3 took effect gradually. The ageing process accelerated slowly, and war and disease took an ever-increasing toll on human longevity.

Giant dinosaurs are inconceivable today, although we know they existed. Maybe these ancient peoples were the human equivalent.

No turning back

Genesis 18:10-19:38
Abraham might have been an ideal uncle. While still glowing over the good news that Sarah will have a baby, he pleads on behalf of his innocent nephew Lot, holed up in the doomed, wild city of Sodom where hedonism has sired moral bankruptcy.

'Innocent', however, is a relative term. Lot had taken the richest land and had already suffered for his greed (chs 13,14). And when confronted by a drunken mob intent on the homosexual rape of his guests, he offered his virgin daughters as substitutes, as if heterosexual rape of his own dependants was more acceptable.

Abraham's pleas for Lot are an example of effectual intercessory prayer. He does not ask God to save Lot. Rather, he asks God to act righteously, that is in accordance with his own rules and character.

In the New Testament Jesus promised that prayer 'in his name' (that is, according to his character) would always get an answer (John 14:14; 16:24). God will do what is right, not what we tell him.

As judgment rains down on Sodom, the author focuses on Lot's rescue more than on the city's destruction. The God who saved Noah at the end of his world rescues a fallible believer from a predicament he should never have got into. God is revealed as a gracious protector.

But the fateful pause by Lot's unnamed wife casts a further shadow over the tragic story. Almost certainly, and very naturally, she was mourning the loss of her family. Perhaps she was also pining for past security; grieving, even, over the trinkets she left behind.

Following God means leaving behind both the good and the bad. Pilgrims have to progress. They cannot afford to linger in a shady arbour. They cannot, in Jesus' graphic picture, plough a straight furrow while looking back over their shoulder (Luke 9:62).

'My kingdom for a son!'

Genisis 16; 18:1-15;21
Couples unable to have children suffer emotionally because of unfulfilled desire, because of a sense of failure or even guilt, and because everyone else has children.

In biblical times, other factors added to the pain. Male children ensured that remaining dependants (including widows) were cared for. There was no social security net to fall into. Children also provided 'hope' for life after death; people lived on in their families.

Then there was a sense of shame. Childless couples were thought to be cursed by the gods and inferior as people. The Abraham saga introduces a theme which recurs often in the Bible. A surprisingly high proportion of couples who feature in its pages were childless. They cried to God, their prayers were answered, and the resulting child was singled out for some special purpose.

The theme reveals a God who cares for the downcast. He is also a God who can do what seems impossible and who keeps his promises (for the covenant with Abraham, see page 19). And he brings into the world individuals chosen to be his special agents.

FAST facts

Title:
In Hebrew, 'In the beginning' from the first two words. 'Genesis' is a Greek word meaning 'story of origins' or 'birth'.

Structure:
There are two main sections. 1:1-11:9 gives a brief account of 'prehistory' and sets the scene for the whole biblical narrative. The rest tells the story of the Patriarchs, the founders of Israel. Scholars also see ten distinct sections, each starting with 'The account'.

Compiler:
Traditionally Moses, although there are signs of later updating. (e.g. Dan in 14:14 was not so named until about 1150 BC.)

Date of compilation:
Probably during Israel's period in the desert, c. 1280-1240 BC.

Does God have favourites

HARD Question

Two incidents in Genesis suggest God has favourites and deliberately rejects others, which makes him appear heartless and arbitrary.

The New Testament indicates that when Sarah pushed out Ishmael, Abraham's son by his servant Hagar, she was prompted by God (Galatians 4). Abraham, distressed by the idea, was assured that God had good plans for Ishmael too (Genesis 21:8-20).

Ishmael's descendants are the Arab nations, with whom Jews have struggled for millennia. The biblical story focuses only on God's purposes for Israel, so this passage warns Christians and Jews that God has not thereby condemned the Arab peoples. His purposes extend to all nations – even to rivals.

The case of Esau and Jacob is different (Genesis 25:23). The New Testament says bluntly, 'Jacob I loved but Esau I hated' (Romans 9:13 quoting Malachi 1:2,3). This story is about God choosing one person and rejecting another *for a specific task*.

There is no suggestion that Esau or his descendants (the Edomites) were hereby consigned to the pit. Jacob gets the job and Esau doesn't, but Esau is not therefore doomed to remain unemployed and unemployable in God's service for ever after. His shortcomings were matters of his own choice; they were not forced on him.

An important postscript occurs in the story of Leah, Jacob's first, unloved wife. When God saw her sadness, he blessed her in a special way (29:31); her offspring included the priestly line and that of Jesus. God's care for the underdog is a recurring theme of Scripture.

Date of Patriarchs:

c.2000-1600 BC

Location:

'Fertile Crescent' and then Canaan

Story leads to:

Israelite slavery in Egypt (Exodus)

Key people:

Adam, Noah, Abraham, Isaac, Jacob, Joseph

Trust God, not answers to prayer

Genesis 21,22

Faith, according to some cynics, is what Lewis Carroll's Queen of Hearts did. She 'believed as many as six impossible things before breakfast'. Faith according to Abraham, who sets the standard for the rest of Scripture, is taking God at his word. The picture emerges of a God who demonstrates his sovereignty by doing what people think is impossible, but which is not.

The promise of a child seemed crazy to the ageing patriarch, but he believed it anyway. He also tried to help it along. When Sarah bore no child he followed tradition and took a second wife who bore Ishmael (ch 16).

Abraham was very human. For him, faith was flavoured with a large pinch of realism. In the narrative God corrects him, but does not rebuke him.

His trust that God would do what he said was 'credited to him as righteousness' (15:6). It was this, rather than his character or actions, which enabled him to enjoy a personal relationship with God. The New Testament makes much of this verse as it encourages faith in Christ (e.g. Romans 4; Galatians 3:6-9; James 2:20-24).

When he heard God call him to sacrifice Isaac, he again trusted that 'God will provide the lamb' (22:8). (So, after the test, God did! See 22:11-14.) Child sacrifice was practised at the time, although not extensively. In terms Abraham could easily understand, God was challenging the root of his hope: would he love God without his son?

God's shock tactics were to ensure that Abraham's faith did not become focused on Isaac. Though answers to prayer remind us of God's love and bring us hope, they are not to be regarded as the ultimate expressions of that love or as the only source of that hope.

As Job was to say much later, 'The Lord gave, the Lord has taken away; may the name of the Lord be praised' (Job 1:21).

Families at war while God is at work

Genesis 24-50

The Bible is nothing if not frank. The stories of the Patriarchs (Abraham, Isaac, Jacob and Joseph) are like the script for a modern TV soap, full of intrigue and family feuds. They could even prompt a few theses in social psychology.

Look at the sequence. If ever there was a case of like parent, like child, this is it:

- Isaac, the probably spoiled favourite of an elderly couple, starts the rot
- He marries Rebekah, who is pushed into an arranged marriage and forced to emigrate
- They have twins. Isaac favours Esau, Rebekah favours Jacob. Result: sibling rivalry
- Jacob engineers supremacy over Esau (with lentil soup)
- Rebekah schemes (with venison stew) to ensure Jacob really does get the inheritance rights
- Jacob flees to his uncle Laban, who tricks him (serves him right!)
- But Jacob tricks him back, eventually leaving as a wealthy man
- He is reconciled to Esau (all credit to Esau) but Jacob still doesn't trust him
- Jacob settles and has twelve sons; he makes Joseph his favourite
- The jealous brothers sell Joseph into slavery and lie to their father
- Joseph gets tricked in Egypt and ends up in jail
- Eventually released and prospering, he tricks his brothers who don't recognise him
- Eventually, they all live happily together in Egypt – where their descendants are subsequently enslaved.

It has been said of Cecil Rhodes, the colonial leader in South Africa, that 'he was a man who tried to force the time to fit his vision'. That seems to sum up the patriarchal story. Each generation forgot Abraham's trusting faith and instead tried to force the pace to get what he wanted, or even what God had promised.

To the question, 'Where is God in all this?' comes a simple answer. He is everywhere. He meets with the key players at significant points and demonstrates his sovereignty over their affairs. He is way above their petty games and jealousies, and yet moulds them all so that his purposes are fulfilled.

Most people, including committed believers, have equally cloudy perceptions of God and his purposes, and operate in this world with equally mixed motives. The desire to serve God is often blended with human emotions, weakness, limited perception, and sometimes naked ambition. These stories show that God is not fazed by such perversity. On the contrary, it seems to be his raw material.

As Joseph said to his brothers, 'You intended to harm me, but God intended it for good to accomplish what is now being done, to the saving of many lives' (50:20). The patriarchal narratives bring a crumb of comfort to people of all ages who despair of messy relationships and twisted circumstances.

Genesis in the New Testament

Creation paralleled by the new creation: Revelation 21,22

Adam contrasted with Christ: Romans 5:12-19

Noah and the flood recalled: Matthew 24:37-41; 2 Peter 3:4,5

Abraham's example of faith: Romans 4; Hebrews 11:8-19

The story of Ishmael: Galatians 4:21-31

Isaac, Jacob and Joseph: Hebrews 11:20-22

Joseph in Egypt: Acts 7:9-16

Angels in disguise

Genesis 15-19, 22, 32

Today in the West, many people are wary of talking to strangers, still more of inviting them into their homes. In patriarchal times in the East, offering hospitality to strangers was considered normal and virtuous.

Both Abraham and Lot opened their homes to visitors and only afterwards discovered that they had 'entertained angels without knowing it' (Hebrews 13:2). Some of Abraham's other conversations with God are also recorded as if there was a visible person present (e.g. 17:1). Did an angel speak for God?

The phrase 'angel of the Lord' (16:7,9; cf. 18:1,17) is sometimes taken to signify the second person of the Trinity – the Son of God himself appearing in recognisable form – rather than one of God's senior messenger-angels.

All angelic messengers are identified with God, speak and act on his behalf and carry his authority. They are like ambassadors identified with their country, and speaking on behalf and with the authority of their rulers. It is no more than an interesting possibility that this figure is Christ in pre-incarnate form.

Angels appear regularly, although not frequently, in the Bible and they are generally associated with key events. Here, they appear at the foundation of two major people-groups one of which, Israel, is the subject of the rest of the biblical revelation.

Later, as Israel prepares to conquer the Promised Land, an angel appears to Joshua (Joshua 5:13-19). Angels also appear in connection with the birth, resurrection and ascension of Jesus (Luke 1:26; 2:9; 24:4; Acts 1:10).

The word angel simply means 'messenger' and some have suggested that on at least a few occasions the experience is simply of a person 'being an angel' (e.g. 1 Kings 19:5,6).

However, the existence of a supernatural order of beings living on God's plane of existence, which is normally inaccessible to humans is taken for granted by Bible authors.

Their appearance is often awesome, and they always point away from themselves to God (cf. Revelation 19:10).

They usually convey a specific message from God or work a specific 'act of God' which has long-term or strategic implications; they are not into trivia such as finding the equivalent of a spare parking place for a harassed traveller.

Jacob's angel (32:22-32) is very clearly in disguise and is only recognised as a result of the blessing he gives. This strange incident is the final humbling of a headstrong patriarch who has discovered at long last that he cannot manipulate God.

Jacob's strength of character is untouched, however, even if it is redirected. He wrestles for a blessing from his more-than-human assailant. He has discovered the faith of his grandfather. 'If you're this strong,' he is saying, 'then I need your strength to live by.'

He retires hurt, humbled and wiser. Encounters with angels are not always sweetness and light, even if they are ultimately profitable for the person concerned.

For today

- God is the reason and power behind the whole mysterious universe
- Human society is in a mess because people have left God out of their reckoning
- God is patient and forgiving, but he is also Judge of all disobedience
- Fallible human beings can be used by God to achieve his purposes
- Faith means trusting God alone and following him even when doing so seems crazy

When it's just one thing after another

Genesis 37, 39, 40

The story of Joseph only has a happy ending because he first struggles through a series of disasters. If the precocious boy brought the first one on himself, he could hardly be blamed for the others.

Anxious to live by his own moral code, he was falsely accused by his employer's wife and jailed on her say-so alone. Then, as a model prisoner, his favours were forgotten by the winetaster whose influence could have secured him an early release.

Once more, the story reveals a recurring biblical pattern. Moses, David and prophets such as Jeremiah will have similar experiences. The servant of God is not spared the slings and arrows of outrageous fortune.

Perhaps Joseph was sustained in his dark days by the bright dreams of his youth. But he would not be alone among the saints of God if he did not also succumb to doubt and despair at times in his Egyptian dungeon.

The observer can see God at work. The suffering subject can only see a series of inexplicable, undeserved, and seemingly endless troubles. One reason why these stories are included in the Bible at such length may be because they offer a simple encouragement when concepts and definitions about God and his character would leave sufferers cold.

Joseph and his dream world

Genesis 37, 40, 41

Dreams gained academic respectability in the late nineteenth century through the work of psychologists Sigmund Freud and Carl Jung. To Freud they contained personal messages from the unconscious; to Jung they were symbols of the great human themes of life and death.

Yet for centuries dreams had been taken seriously as portents of the future or as messages from the gods. In Egypt in Joseph's time, a class of magicians specialised in interpreting them, as did their later counterparts across in Babylonia.

The biblical treatment of dreams is far more conservative than that of other contemporary religious literature, however. Indeed, there is a strikingly modern insight in Ecclesiastes 5:3 (perhaps dating from as early as 950 BC), which links dreaming simply with the cares of the previous day.

Both academic literature and the tabloid press are familiar with predictive dreams or more broadly with people 'seeing' events in advance. So there is no need to doubt the authenticity of the stories; but the meaning of them is found only within the frame of the principles they enshrine:

- God knows the future (he is not trapped in time)
- God controls the future (he is not the victim of circumstance)
- God sometimes reveals the future (so that his people may be prepared).

These principles do not encourage intense speculation about future events. Biblical dreams and broader revelations of the future were neither sought nor induced. They were simply revealed by God when he chose. Nor do they encourage us to interpret every dream as some cryptic message from God.

They simply reassure later readers that God holds all things together, the future included. Indeed, detailed beliefs about the future are usually difficult to live with (e.g. John 21:18-19). They crowd out the present, which 'is the time of God's favour' (2 Corinthians 6:2).

CROSS CHECK

Moses' authorship: p 117
Existence and nature of Satan: p 271
God's covenants: pp 18-21
Other childless couples: p 383
Angels: pp 270-1

Thinking man's Thomas loses doubts

The Book of Habakkuk

- Asks why God seems to ignore wrongdoing
- Then questions why God uses godless people to punish wrongdoing
- And finally recognises that God's sovereignty and justice are finely balanced

Some people find it hard simply to believe. They are full of doubts and questions. They feel they cannot fully trust God when they cannot be sure what he is doing. They need to have ends tied up rather than left loose. So they tend to say awkward things. Especially when they see a mess and then hear someone say 'God's in charge.' But he isn't, apparently. So they make an issue of it.

We need those people and those questions. Without them 'faith' would be glib, a linctus to soothe away our fears without actually addressing the cause of the problem. Faith is nothing if it is not stretched and exercised intellectually as well as emotionally, practically as well as spiritually.

God knows what he is about, and he can handle hard questions about truth, even if some of us can't. Habakkuk, about whom we know nothing, provides the intellectual Christian's model in his beautiful little book. He is the Thomas of the Old Testament, unafraid to speak his doubts but very ready to listen to God's answers. He sought answers, and his genuinely open mind received them (cf. Matthew 7:7,8).

Looking around Judah in the early seventh century BC, he couldn't understand why God tolerated such sinfulness among his people. God told him he planned to do something about it by sending the Babylonians to destroy Judah.

Habakkuk was horrified; the plan seemed to deny God's holiness. How could God actually use godless people? He got an answer to which balanced God's sovereignty with his justice. And, as a result, Habakkuk found a real faith which satisfied his mind and warmed his heart. Don't be afraid to ask the questions; the answers will expand your vision and deepen your faith. (And when others ask them of you, remember that God's answers are never glib.)

HARD Question

Why doesn't God notice?

Habakkuk 1:1-4

The last year of the twentieth century saw

- Kosovans being 'ethnically cleansed' by Serbs
- Three nail bombs killing and maiming people in London
- TV presenter Jill Dando shot dead in cold blood on her doorstep
- Two teenagers gunning down thirteen fellow students in their American school
- A clergyman being found dead following accusations of sexual harassment.

Oh God, why? The list, of course, is endless and infinitely variable. The flow of evil never ceases. 'Violence, strife and conflict abound; the wicked hem in the righteous.' Those words could have been in today's leader in *The Times*, but they were penned by Habakkuk about 2,600 years ago.

Why doesn't God stop the carnage and suffering? Why do the innocent perish with the guilty? Please don't come up with knee-jerk pious talk about it 'being a result of the fall'. We know that. And please don't attempt to affirm that 'maybe it was God's special punishment of them'; read Luke 13:1-5 and see Jesus' response to that suggestion.

Instead, just stare at it. Let the question roll around in your mind. If God is good and powerful, why doesn't he act? God doesn't mind you asking – but you'll only appreciate his answer when you feel the real force of the dilemma.

Not what you'd expect from God

Habakkuk 1:5-11

When a man was arrested for setting off the London nail bombs, his family were aghast. It was not what they'd expected him to do.

God has a habit of shocking people, too. He shocked the orthodox leaders in Jesus' day when the person people claimed was the Messiah acted in ways which did not accord with the expected behaviour of the Messiah. So they rubbished the claims and plotted to get rid of him.

Here, God anticipates Habakkuk's reaction: 'You won't believe this' (v 5); God is right – the prophet doesn't.

We should never prescribe how God should act. God never acts in exactly the same way twice. Every situation and person is different. God tailors his acts to the needs.

So the moment you think you've got God taped is the moment you could begin to disbelieve him and then not to recognise what he really is doing. People who expect answers to prayer for revival to be given in one way should be prepared for them to come in another.

Long-term screen epic

Habakkuk 1:12-3:19

In asking how God can use ungodly people to fulfil his purposes, Habakkuk overlooks an important fact: he's not perfect either. God, however, graciously fails to point that out but instead provides a glimpse of divine sovereignty over history and a reminder that his concerns are global and corporate.

The Babylonians are responsible for their actions, and will suffer for them. Those who draw the sword will die by it (cf. Matthew 26:52). God may have used them as a teaching aid, but he did not manipulate them into doing anything they did not want to do.

However, there is no concession to Habakkuk's or our impatience. The answer will take time to appear (v 3) and therefore the prophecy must be written for the long-term record (v 2). Meanwhile, God's people must live by faith, trusting that the word will be fulfilled even if not in their own lifetimes (v 4).

This may not fit our concept of justice because we focus on the individuals involved. The debate here has nothing to do with individuals, but with nations – a common Old Testament perspective. The Bible story is an epic with a cast of millions and lasting for centuries.

Habakkuk enters into this long-term outlook in his final prayer. This alone can move him to rejoice even when the cupboard is bare (3:17,18) and receive strength to go on (3:19). He knows that the future promise will match God's past performance at the exodus andin the Israelite conquest of Canaan (3:8-15).

There are rarely instant solutions to pressing needs in the Bible. But there are ultimate solutions. Faith is often at its strongest when sight is weakest. To be true to God and grow in faith we need Habakkuk's long-term vision.

Date:
About 605 BC

Location:
Judah

Situation:
Babylonia has just defeated (or is about to defeat) Egypt and Assyria at Carchemish and take over the former Assyrian empire. It therefore threatens Judah

Place in Bible:
The eighth of the minor prophets at the end of the Old Testament, after Nahum and before Zephaniah

Parallel books:
Similar to Jeremiah, and from a similar time

Put God's house before yours

Moving home is never easy. There are new areas to discover, new people to meet, perhaps a new job to settle into, and the inevitable decorating and gardening.

The Judean exiles in Babylon have returned home to Jerusalem, courtesy of Persian king Cyrus who in 538 BC conquered Babylonia and issued an amnesty to political prisoners. Some accepted the offer, returned in 537, and laid the foundation of the temple which Nebuchadnezzar had destroyed (cf. Ezra 1-4). That was 17 years ago, and the temple is still in ruins.

Haggai says that God should have been their first thought, not their last. They have built their own houses, but not his. In modern terms, that means service and witness for God should be our first priority. Of course we need balanced diaries with home and work getting their fair share. But when something has to go, generally we should ask, how may I best honour God?

If we have gifts to use, it is a sin not to use them. Church is not a hobby horse to be ridden in spare moments. It is a vehicle which will take us further towards God himself.

Where am I?

Date: August-December 520 BC (the prophecies are dated specifically)
Location: Jerusalem
Place in Bible: The tenth of the twelve minor prophets at the end of the Old Testament
Parallel books: Zechariah. The story (including mention of Haggai) is told in detail in the book of Ezra 3-6

Your best is good enough

Haggai 2

It's a terrible put-down to be told that your predecessor was 'a hard act to follow'. The result of such a remark is either to make you quake at the prospect, or determine to be different for difference's sake in order to make your own mark.

Solomon's temple was an impossible act to follow. It had been spectacularly beautiful and richly decorated. The returned exiles couldn't hope to match it (v 2). Probably some of the older ones could remember it; most would have heard vivid descriptions from their parents.

Haggai says that it doesn't matter. The people had done their best with what they had. That pleased God and counted far more than architectural acclaim. When we work for God, we are simply to use our gifts and opportunities to the best of our ability and not compare them with others or with what we think 'might have been'. Perfectionism can be a sin.

If we try to be better than someone else, we risk becoming proud. If we aim to do better than others did before us we will create a competitiveness among organisers and activities will lose their spiritual vision and impact. Of course we can improve on mistakes made in the past, but 'bigger and better' is not a virtue in itself.

After the encouragement, however, comes a challenge. These people had done well, but were beginning to slip into sin again (v 14). They had accepted failed harvests as misfortunes, and not as God's warnings that all was not well (vv 15-18).

Yet God does not threaten them but promises to bless them (v 19). Instead of the stick, he uses the carrot. Having pointed out the sin, he immediately offers forgiveness.

The natural reaction to that kind of generosity is worship. The proper response to love is love. God makes that same offer to us through Christ, and we should be equally generous to one another. Sometimes love will have a more positive effect on someone than criticism.

Jesus fulfils another faith story

For most of us, memory, habit and accumulated knowledge and experience provide a framework for interpreting and assessing new things. But when it comes to Christian faith, it seems we're meant to throw out the past and take on a whole new set of beliefs. Or does it?

The Bible acknowledges that everyone has an innate (although often denied or suppressed) awareness of God and his requirements (cf. Romans 1:20). It's part of being made in his image. And Jesus was not a loner but taught within the context of Judaism, to correct and fulfil its emphases rather than to abolish them (Matthew 5:17).

Hebrews – which is more of an essay than an epistle, though it became a sermon before long – shows how Christianity is radically new while retaining a strong continuity with the past.

Readers from non-Jewish backgrounds may find some of its allusions puzzling but we can apply its thesis to contemporary questions. If Jesus fulfils the aspirations of one faith, it is not impossible that he could fulfil all aspirations – especially as Hebrews claims he is the final revelation of God and supreme ruler of the universe.

People who have been sincerely religious or hopefully superstitious in the past will find in Christ all that they looked for in the wrong place. Having found it in him, they may then understand how inadequate and misguided their former view really was, even though it seemed plausible at the time.

HEBREWS

1	Jesus is supreme above all others
2	Jesus is the author of salvation
3	Warning against becoming hardened
4:1-13	Keep going to enter God's 'rest'
4:14-5:10	Jesus is our great High Priest
5:11-6:12	Grow up and don't fall away
6:13-7:28	Jesus compared to Melchizedek
8	Jesus is the mediator of the new covenant
9:1-10:18	Jesus' sacrifice compared with tabernacle rituals
10:19-39	Press on despite persecution
11	Testimonies of faith
12	Accept God's discipline
13	Practical advice for discipleship

They may see too that in his gracious love God used that past belief to draw them towards the fullness of his truth.

Hebrews also reaffirms the Old Testament concepts of salvation and atonement. It explains why Christians stress such things as the 'sacrifice' of Jesus. It points to God's majesty and awesomeness which are important as today's interest in God's homeliness may shut out the counterpoint of his holiness.

Although Hebrews makes you think hard about ideas, it also offers plain practical advice, often coming unexpectedly in the middle of an argument. None of God's truth is impractical and the advice always follows directly from the truth that is being taught.

The letter to the Hebrews

- Shows how the Christian faith fulfils Jewish expectations
- Draws parallels between Old Testament rituals and the ministry of Jesus
- Describes why Jesus' eternal 'priesthood' is enough to reconcile God and humanity
- Urges faith and perseverance in the face of hardship

Christ is the mediator of a new covenant, that those who are called may receive the promised eternal inheritance.

Hebrews 9:15

Date:

Probably late 60s AD.

Place in Bible:

After the pastoral epistles (1 & 2 Timothy and Titus) and Philemon, and before James and other 'general epistles' in the New Testament.

The Force is with us

Hebrews 1

In today's egalitarian society we have difficulty believing that any one person or faith system is supreme. So did most people in the ancient world; there were many gods and religions so you chose what you liked. There were also people then, like many now, who believe in a life force but not of the force as 'personal'.

The Jews, by contrast, believed in the supremacy of a personal God but had trouble believing in his human incarnation, death and resurrection. Hebrews 1 sets out Jesus' credentials so that pagan and Jew could identify him.

- He is God's spokesperson. His words carry God's authority
- He is the owner ('heir') and creator of the universe
- He is the 'radiance' of God as light is the radiance of the sun: the two are inseparable
- He is the replica of God, as an impression in wax replicates the die: identical yet also distinct
- He keeps the universe and its entire life system going: nothing is outside his vital support.

Therefore, Jesus is not an angelic being (as early 'Gnostics' taught, and Jehovah's Witnesses teach today). As 'Son' he shares the same 'substance' as the Father. He is the human face of God.

This is important for daily life. If we believe in Jesus' supremacy then he can do anything for us and we can call confidently for his help at any time.

And since 'in him we live and move and have our being' (Acts 17:28) we should not live as if God is remote and the world mechanistic and in some way dependent on us. That sends out false signals. God is all-pervasive and personal. The force is with us, in Jesus.

Jesus helps – he doesn't hover

Hebrews 2

The hovercraft skims on a cushion of air just above the surface. Some visual and verbal images of Jesus seem to suggest that he 'hovered' above the earth, that he was only apparently human. Hebrews says that he had his feet planted firmly on our dirty soil.

Included in the Hebrew description of people as made 'a little lower than the angels' (vv 7,9; cf. Psalm 8:5) Jesus is assumed to be fully human. The author has an earthy reason for stressing this. Jesus knows what it is to be human, and to face the difficult ethical pressures of life. He too was tempted (cf. 4:15).

He coped because he was 'faithful in service to God' (v17); his mind was set on doing what God wanted at whatever cost and suffering to himself. He was able to say 'no' to the devil's wiles and when we draw on his power, we will be able to resist temptation too.

FAST facts

Author: Earliest manuscripts give no hint of the author (Paul always signed his letters). The content suggests that the author was an intellectual Christian from a Jewish background who was not an apostle (2:3 says he hadn't seen Jesus physically). Among the likely candidates are Barnabas (cf. Acts 4:36; 11:24); Apollos (Acts 18:24-28); Aquila and Priscilla (Acts 18:26,27); and Philip (Acts 8:4-7,26-40).

Date: Probably written before the fall of Jerusalem in AD 70 because the author refers to Jewish sacrifices as if they were continuing – they ceased when the temple was destroyed.

Readers: Unknown. Probably Jewish Christians tempted to return to Judaism, or who considered Christianity a sect of Judaism. Some suggest the readers are former Jewish priests.

HARD Question

What is the 'Sabbath rest'?

Hebrews 3,4

One writer has defined the 'Sabbath rest' as 'God's purposeful, creative activity and the satisfaction which belongs to it'. This helpfully prevents the concept from becoming 'quietist' or merely vague. It is not:

- a spiritual experience of 'blessedness'
- a state of inactivity
- a description of heaven in the future.

Jesus offered 'rest' to people willing to take his 'burden' of obedience and discipleship which is lighter than all attempts at self-fulfilment based on human work or leisure alone (Matthew 11:29). Lighter too than all forms of religion that prescribe labour to gain God's favour: these only generate anxiety. Rest here is like John's concept of 'eternal life', a relationship with God where we enjoy his renewing love.

The author's aim is to encourage perseverance, rather than describe an experience or state of faith. His readers are tempted to 'go back to Egypt' – their old ways of Judaism. He wants them to remain faithful to Christ as supreme Lord.

He uses Hebrew 'typology', taking an Old Testament incident as a model of something else. It is an illustration, not an exhaustive exposition of 'rest' as defined above. The Israelites' 'rest' in the promised land was incomplete; its full expression would be found in Christ.

Just as the Israelites disobeyed God and a generation died before the nation entered Canaan, so people today can say they follow Christ, yet disobey him and forfeit any claim to eternal life. They say 'Lord, Lord' but do not obey him (Matthew 7:21-23). Positively, God's 'rest' therefore becomes:

- believing his promises, obeying his truth and living his way;
- receiving and using his gifts in order to serve him;
- enjoying the assurance of his love and confidence in his sovereignty which is 'peace'.

Sin cancer gets radiation treatment

Hebrews 4:12,13

Nothing penetrates like radiation. A low dose of x-rays reveal your skeleton; a high dose can destroy internal organs. Used carefully, radiation can destroy harmful growths. If the author of Hebrews were alive today he could use this picture rather than the 'double-edged sword' Roman soldiers carried.

His message is simple: our thoughts are as visible to God as our bones are to a radiographer. His searching gaze penetrates to the deepest corners of our hearts to first expose, and then to purge out, all that is unworthy of him.

Therefore there is no point trying to hide anything from him, no point in shutting things out of our minds in an attempt to pretend they don't exist or never happened. But that is not necessarily threatening – although it will be if we are not ready to face up to our wrongdoing. It can be liberating to recognise that God knows us intimately.

We are free to say no to sin precisely because we live in the glare of God's spotlight. We are always on show and God's gaze is charged with the energy of radiation: acknowledging his presence can empower our reactions.

It is only those who wish to continue in 'the works of darkness' who refuse to stand in front of his x-ray machine (cf. John 1:5; 3:19-21).

Did Jesus have to win his spurs?

Hebrews 5:7-10 (cf. 2:10,11)
Knights of old had to earn their place at court by successfully completing a series of bold tasks. Hebrews has been thought to imply that Jesus similarly had to become perfect by overcoming temptation. Only then was he entitled to be called 'Son of God' and to become our eternal 'High Priest'.

The immediate context of Hebrews 1 flatly contradicts this suggestion. There, Jesus is described as the eternal Son of God. He was not adopted as God's Son because of his achievements.

During his human life, Jesus suffered horribly: in the desert after his baptism and of course on the cross (cf. Matthew 4:1-11 and Luke 22:39-46). Although never disobedient he 'discovered what it was really like', the full pain of obedience.

His prayer was heard, it was not for pain relief but for his Father's will to be done. His perfection was thus confirmed and his eternal ministry completed, rather than created, by his obedience. He was then exalted in triumph, his mission accomplished (cf. Philippians 2:8-11).

The unchanging reality of his eternal nature was unveiled to human observers during his lifetime. The author of Hebrews is looking at Jesus from that human angle, rather than down on him from the divine angle.

Can a believer forfeit eternal salvation?

Hebrews 5:11-6:12; 10:19-39
The possibility of throwing away our salvation in a surge of sin seems plausible and Hebrews continually warns us against doing so. This raises two intensely personal concerns. First, if we can lose our salvation by what we do, we depend ultimately on us and not on God. We entered the kingdom by faith in God's grace but now, it seems, it's up to us – which Paul vigorously denied (Galatians 3:1-5).

Secondly, the New Testament assures us that we cannot lose our salvation and are eternally safe in God's hands (see John 6:37-40; 10:28-30; Romans 8:37-39). Without that assurance we would be plagued by anxiety as to whether we'll make it to heaven.

Read Hebrews carefully. The author does not accuse anyone of having fallen away (6:9,10). He is stating a hypothesis, not a current reality. In positive and negative terms he assures that final salvation would be forfeit if faith failed, so Christians must stand steady. This letter urges active faithfulness; its readers are flagging and need encouraging.

The fatal sin in 6:5,6 and 10:26-29 is absolute rejection of Jesus Christ, as the Israelites rebelled against God in the desert, any who go this route can't 'be brought back to repentance' – they don't wish to be.

The writer is imagining those who for a time associated with God's people (6:5) but didn't produce fruit, i.e. true regeneration (6:7,8). These are not short-term 'backsliders' but absolute renegades; like an ordained minister joining the National Secular Society.

Whether a regenerate person can defect in this way is debatable. A natural reading of the New Testament suggests not. Paul says that even a fruitless Christian can be saved (1 Corinthians 3:11-15). We do not have to pass an exam before entering heaven. Through Christ's atoning sacrifice we are accepted by a loving Father even if we behave badly.

Therefore we have every incentive to live faithfully out of love for the Father and the Son. If we live carelessly, Hebrews says, we put ourselves in mortal spiritual danger.

Jesus takes over

Hebrews 6:13-8:13

Hebrews shows that Jesus has taken over the work of Levitical priests and made them spiritually redundant. (Church ministers, however, are not redundant; they are highly valued by the author, see chapter 13.)

The Jewish priests offered sacrifices, interceded for the people, and mediated God's blessing. Jesus' unique life, death and resurrection achieved all that permanently. To illustrate this the author author tells the story of Melchizedek (7:1-3; Genesis 14:13-20), a priest in Jerusalem before Judaism was formulated. With typical Hebrew 'logic' the author uses this aspect of the Genesis presentation as an picture of Jesus, not an assessment of Melchizedek.

For us, the important truth is that Abraham, father of the Israelite nation and recipient of God's covenant, was blessed by an unknown priest. In that sense Melchizadek was 'greater' than Abraham. The author milks the point to show that Jesus is greater than Abraham too. This returns us to the opening thesis of the essay: Jesus is greater than anyone so we should not put our faith in any merely human source.

Jesus' ministry is eternal. His sacrifice cannot be repeated (7:27). He pleads our cause for ever (7:25). He is 'the same yesterday, today and for ever' (13:8). His power is undiminished, and can be as effective for us now as it was for our forefathers, or our own earlier years of livelier faith.

No need for a blood bath

Hebrews 9:1 - 10:18

Generations of Christians have sung hymns that rejoiced in 'being washed in the blood'. That image contains important truths but which need to be understood afresh today.

The author shows how the rites and ceremonies of biblical Judaism are completed by Jesus, who supersedes them. Animal sacrifices were common in the ancient world and had special meaning for the Israelites. Sinners deserved to 'die', i.e. cut off from God. The animal's death, killed on the altar as God prescribed, showed that God alone could provide an alternative solution without ignoring the seriousness of the offence.

The permanent solution to sin, says Hebrews, is Jesus (cf. 9:15; 10:9). In his person (fully God and perfect man) he bridged the spiritual gulf between God and ourselves; in his death and resurrection he fulfilled the requirements of the Old Testament law. The 'sacrifice' of Christ makes sense in the Jewish culture from which Christianity sprang (9:8,9,23,24) for the Jews knew, as today's Western world does not, that unatoned and unforgiven sin is an abiding blockage to fellowship with God.

But the reality of Christ is greater than the illustration. Therefore, while the 'sacrifice' of Christ is central to Christian faith, the cross is more than *just* a replacement for animal sacrifices. In fulfilling the sacrificial pattern, Jesus transcended it.

The New Testament gives us many different 'pictures' of Christ's death, all however need to be explained. Therefore, in our evangelism, we would be unwise in Western contexts to focus without explanation on 'the blood'. Lurid blood-talk will disturb people without helping them to believe, and it is often hard to explain that 'blood' is shorthand for 'sacrificial death, understood in terms of Israel's God-given sacrificial system. Yet at some stage it is important to revisit this to enable us to present Christ crucified as the only way to God, forgiveness and new life.

An appreciation of Jesus' fulfilment of Old Testament imagery is a task for teaching ministry of today's church.

CROSS CHECK

Blood sacrifices: p 263
Assurance of salvation: pp 202, 209, 213
The unforgivable sin: p 307

Have faith, will travel

Hebrews 11

'I have no use for adventures,' declared Bilbo Baggins in J.R.R. Tolkien's *The Hobbit.* 'Nasty disturbing uncomfortable things! Make you late for dinner!'

Abraham and the other biblical heroes whose stories are recalled here would not have agreed. Faith to them was an adventure. Indeed, Abraham didn't even know where he was heading when he set out (v 8).

The faith which is applauded here is not 'saving faith', the initial trust in God for forgiveness and eternal life, but applied faith. If we are committed to God, then we are to go with him, wherever that takes us, knowing God has promised long-term blessings to those who continue to obey and endure.

The Bible suggests that 'saving faith' without such 'applied faith' is a contradiction in terms. You can have neither without the other. If we are saved, we shall be motivated to serve; if we want to serve, we must first be saved.

In *Cancer Ward* Alexander Solzhenitsyn commented, 'That small place in the breast which is faith's cramped quarters remains untenanted for years and decays.' If we don't exercise faith, one day in a crisis, perhaps, we may need it and find it's all dried up.

The people we meet in Hebrews 11 trusted God to provide for their needs, lead them, protect them, and overcome obstacles; they sacrificed in faith that God's purposes were greater, and his promises, sure. They weren't perfect: drunken Noah, cheating Jacob, immoral Rahab, mixed-up Samson and adulterer David. Yet each set us an example of faith going places with God.

We can begin to exercise faith in small ways in daily life, just as they did. The big tests come later. We must ensure we 'walk the walk'; as Bilbo discovered, it's better than staying at home.

Faith pays heavily for risking all

Hebrews 11

When C.S. Lewis's beloved wife Joy died, he wrote, 'Only a real risk tests the reality of a belief.' Faith involves risk. There is the risk that we might be proved wrong. We could mishear God, mistake his call, misapply his truth, misappropriate his promises. We could even mislead others.

Running through this chapter is a testimony to the biggest risk of all: that we will never see our faith justified. Twice the author says that they 'did not receive the things promised' (vv 13, 39). They were not wrong, but they never lived to see the fulfilment of their faith-dreams.

There is an everyday parallel to this. Parents do what they can to prepare their offspring for the future. They teach, they provide, they encourage. Yet it's often after the parents have died that 'children', older and wiser themselves, can look back at some achievement and think, 'They'd have liked to have seen this; they'd have been proud of me, now.'

Indeed, much of life, especially church life, is building for a future which we shall never see. Our calling is to be faithful to what God has revealed, to live as if he is fulfilling his purposes even when we can't see them, and to remember that we are but a small part of his very big enterprise.

In an age of impatience the real risk of faith is not to our well-being but to our pride; we want to be proved right. All that these saints were bothered about was proving God right for posterity. It took the stress out of waiting, because they knew God would sort things out in his own time.

Working hard at keeping the faith

Hebrews 12,13

Great entrepreneurs have frequently battled against the odds before they make the big time. Wealth and fame usually come only to people who have been prepared to work hard. Yet the idea of working hard at faith seems almost to be a contradiction in terms. Isn't faith a matter of trusting God? Eternal life cannot be earned; it is the gift of God's grace.

But New Testament writers regularly urge readers to 'work out their salvation with fear and trembling' (Philippians 2:12,13). In James's familiar words, 'faith without deeds is dead' (2:26). If God is at work, we can hardly be idle; we are his hands and feet in the 'body of Christ'.

The hard work of faith, according to Hebrews 12; is a 24-hour, 365-day occupation. It includes resisting temptation, enduring opposition and hardship (vv 2-4,7).

Chapter 13 goes into far greater detail. Applied faith is to include:

- Keeping an open home (v 2)
- Caring for prisoners and the disadvantaged (v 3)
- Replacing selfish ambition with contentment (v 5)
- Meeting regularly for corporate worship (v 15; cf. 10:25)
- Sharing our resources (v 16)
- Submitting to leaders (v 17).

The author sees the effort as 'discipline' or training. He does not mean in 12:1-12 that God is punishing us but that he is training us to serve him better and to improve our witness and discipleship.

Think about the time you spend on your job, your home or your hobby. Compare that with the time spent developing your faith through church worship, praise, prayer, Bible study and service. You might have a nasty surprise: the one which lasts the longest and counts for most may be getting the least attention.

Take time to be holy

Hebrews 12:14-29

In the haste of modern life, time to stand and stare is a rare luxury. We are activists, scurrying around like ants on their nest. Yet, for all the biblical stress on applying faith, we are called primarily to be holy. It is the Martha and Mary syndrome: the activist was rebuked for not also spending time with Jesus (Luke 10:38-42).

Hebrews returns to its overall theme to remind us that 'without holiness no-one will see the Lord' (v 14). It has shown us that we can only become accepted by God through faith in the crucified and risen Jesus, but in keeping with its emphasis on pressing on in the Christian life, it is now reminding us that holiness should characterise our conduct because God himself is holy (v 29).

Now, though, because of Jesus, we do not need to fear God's holiness, but can embrace it (vv 18-24). Yet it still remains awesome and therefore our worship and attitude to God should also be one of awe (v 28).

To achieve that, we need to remain quiet before him; to remember that he is greater than we are and that his purposes last longer than we do; and to recall that all that elaborate ceremony which the author has applied to Jesus was a physical demonstration of how careful we should be in all our dealings with God and people. And perhaps, therefore, to read Hebrews again . . .

For today

- Remember that Jesus is greater than any power or person you may confront
- Let God's truth soak deeply into you to inform every reaction
- Rejoice that Jesus' death and resurrection is sufficient to make you acceptable to God
- Don't worry about losing your salvation: just keep serving God
- Take part in the great adventure of faith and discover new dimensions of faithfulness!
- Dwell on the hope of future blessing: the best is yet to be.

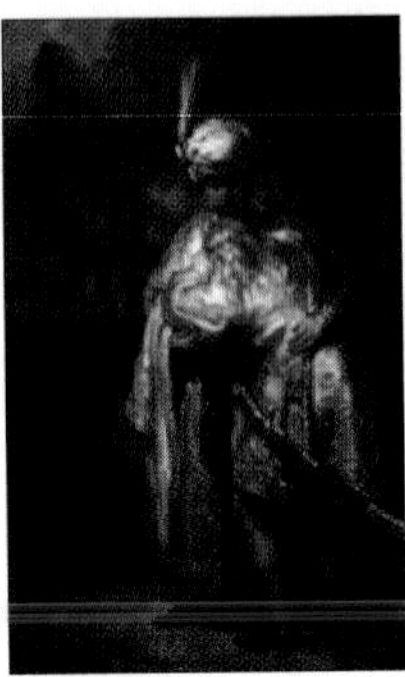

The Book of Hosea:

- Tells the story of Hosea's tragic personal life
- Draws a parallel with God's love for his people
- Describes the sins of Israel
- Warns of God's judgment and promises his forgiveness

God the lover pines for his partner

The book of Hosea equates to Jesus' parable of the prodigal son, who leaves home with his inheritance, wastes it and returns home penitent, only to be greeted by his father with open arms (Luke 15:11-24). We can identify with it; most of us have been prodigal somehow.

But we may also identify with the father, the real subject of the story. A child or close relative takes off on a road which we know will lead to disaster, and we can only watch and wait. How do you feel in such circumstances?

A few may forget and carry on as if nothing had happened. Most will shed a few tears and quietly carry the hurt. Some will wait with heavy heart hoping that one day they'll come home, ready to forgive just to have them back.

Hosea's story is a personal tragedy which God turns into a powerful message for the people of Israel (the northern kingdom). Hosea married – at God's direction – someone he knew would be unfaithful. Gomer bore him three children and then sold herself into prostitution. But Hosea loved her. He went and found her and paid a ransom to get her out of bondage. And she came home.

God's like that, Hosea said. He loves you wilful, prodigal Israelites to bits even though you've done your worst to him. Come back home to him, and he'll forgive you.

AT A GLANCE

HOSEA

1	Hosea's children given prophetic names
2	Israel's 'adultery' described and restoration promised
3	Hosea redeems his wife from prostitution
4	The sin of Israel described
5	The destruction of Israel foretold
6,7	Israel refuses to return to the Lord
8	Sowing the wind and reaping the whirlwind
9,10	The 'vineyard' of Israel will be overgrown
11	God is still compassionate
12	Israel relies wrongly on its wealth
13	Israel has forgotten God and will be punished
14	Promise of healing and restoration

But did they listen? No! That's the real tragedy of Hosea. Gomer humbled herself and returned but the Israelites didn't. Now God's pleading love is matched by his righteous anger – a combination we find hard to imagine because usually we experience one but not both at the same time. Hosea shows us two inseparable sides of God's character.

The doom of which Hosea warned happened and Israel was destroyed by Assyria in 722 BC. But as the people scattered, his words echoed after them: one day there would be a restoration. God's love never ends and that is true for everyone who belongs to God's family but runs off in wrong directions. His arms are open, still.

KEY QUOTE

Let us return to the LORD. He has torn us to pieces but he will heal us; he has injured us but he will bind up our wounds.

Hosea 6:1

Love so amazing, so divine

Hosea 1-3

Even before Gomer's unfaithfulness, Hosea's family was bearing God's message. His first son Jezreel bore a name that recalls Jehu's murder of two kings, over 100 of their relations, and numerous Baal worshippers (2 Kings 9,10).

It had been predicted as a punishment for Ahab and Jezebel's evil. But it was also literally an overkill. Jehu was bloodthirsty. On many occasions in the Old Testament God allows evil to be avenged, but he never condones the methods sometimes employed by the avengers.

This is another of the fine lines in God's character which Hosea reveals. We cannot understand how an act can be right and yet wrong at the same time. Only God's multi-dimensional view can throw it into the correct relief.

C.S. Lewis observed this in *The Problem of Pain*. He wrote: 'Love may forgive all infirmities and love still in spite of them: but Love cannot cease to will their removal . . . Of all powers he forgives most, but he condones least: he is pleased with little, but demands all.'

God now casts Israel, the spiritual prostitute, into spiritual darkness, to suffer hell on earth with God deaf to her cries. Yet he keeps his covenant even when she breaks hers. He rejects with heavy heart; it hurts God more than it hurt her. It is like a parent reluctantly grounding a child to teach it a much-needed lesson in acceptable behaviour. And like the parent's temporary banishment, the punishment will end when the lesson is learned.

Never take God's love for granted and indulge in whatever takes your fancy believing that his love will overlook your excess. You will pay for it, somehow. But when you feel and know that you have been wrong so to act, know and feel too that the enduring love of God has never gone away. It has been quietly weeping for you, and will welcome you back when you ask.

Which is why Isaac Watts could write, 'Love so amazing, so divine, demands my soul, my life, my all.'

KINGS AND PROPHETS 760-720 BC

	760 BC	750 BC	740 BC	730 BC	720 BC
ISRAEL'S KINGS	Jeroboam II 782-53	Zechariah 753 Shallum 752 Menahem 752-42	Pekahiah 742 Pekah 741-31	Hoshea 731-22	Fall of Samaria
BIBLE BOOKS	2 Kings 14	2 Kings 15		2 Kings 17	
	Amos	Hosea			
	Jonah				

JUDAH'S KINGS	Uzziah 767-40 (aka Azariah)	Jotham 740-32	Ahaz 732-16
BIBLE BOOKS	2 Kings 15		2 Kings 16
		Micha Isaiah	

FAST facts

Background: The united kingdom of Israel split into two in 930 BC after Solomon's death. Thereafter the Bible follows the story of both Israel (the ten northern tribes) and Judah (the two southern tribes). In Hosea's time (c. 750-720 BC) the state of the north is dire. Idolatry, immorality and injustice abound. Hosea brings God's final appeal. The Assyrians destroyed Israel in 722 BC.

Terms to note: *Covenant* (e.g. 6:7): the agreement between God and his people to be faithful to each other, made with Moses at Mount Sinai. *Ephraim* (e.g. 7:1): a synonym for Israel. *Samaria*: the capital of Israel.

Ecosystem suffers from our greed

Hosea 4,5

Half a century ago, Rachel Carson alerted the world to the growing ecological crisis in her book *Silent Spring*. Since then, we have seen among other things:

- An area the size of Bristol built on each year in the UK alone; an area the size of Wales has been built on since Carson's book was published;
- the UK population of countryside birds such as the song thrush has fallen by half since the 1970s;
- 60 per cent of the world's rain forests have been destroyed during the twentieth century.
- Cancers, allergies and other stress- and environmentally-related diseases have steadily increased, while millions in the Third World have inadequate diets and polluted water.

Christians believe the world was made and is sustained by the Christ who is our Saviour (Colossians 1:15-20). Human beings were given the task of caring for creation (Genesis 2:15). Yet they have triggered an ecological time bomb by selfish exploitation, partly based on a misreading of Genesis 1:28 and often unchallenged and unnoticed by God's people who should be among the keenest 'green' activists.

In his far less developed era, Hosea links fish dying in the sea with the sinfulness of God's people (4:3). His hearers were hardened to his message, however (5:4) and continued in their ways regardless of the environmental warning bells ringing on their shores.

We know more, but do little. If Hosea were alive today he would surely point to the dying planet and speak of God's sorrow and judgment, of human greed, and the urgent need for us to adopt a responsible lifestyle.

Creation and the environment: p 137
How kings and prophets relate: p 157

God's priorities

Hosea 6,7

Here's a semi-serious icebreaker for a Christian group. Ask each person to think of one thing they consider God wants more than anything else from his people. You will get a variety of answers, including love, worship and obedience, all of which are important.

Now read 6:6. The Israelites were going through the religious motions but they weren't being nice to each other. God's priority is mercy, not sacrifice; God-honouring conduct and not mere spiritual activity.

The Hebrew word for mercy is *chesed* which translates as 'loving kindness'. It implies loyalty (to God) out of a sense of love and gratitude, expressed by compassionate righteousness in our dealings with others.

The prophets loved the idea. Samuel used it in 1 Samuel 15:22; Isaiah in 1:12; Amos in 5:21-24 and Micah in 6:6-8. Jesus took it up in Matthew 9:13 and 12:7 in his disputes with the religious leaders who were set in their legalistic ways and who had begun to think God responded automatically to prescribed human actions.

So when you read the word 'mercy', forget the image of a cringing beggar seeking crumbs of comfort. This *chesed*, this loving kindness, is a bold, strong, positive, self-giving and kindly love.

Rubbish in, rubbish out

Hosea 7-9

Computer programmers will tell you that if you load rubbish data into a computer, you will get rubbish out of it. It happens also to be a more general fact of life. Hosea's familiar image of sowing the wind and reaping the whirlwind (8:7) has its application in every generation, and in most people's personal lives.

Israel's input into the divine memory was unchecked deceit and unchallenged crime (7:1); sexual licence (7:4); irresponsible pleasure seeking (7:5,6); naive international trade deals and political treaties; desertion of their traditional faith (7:14-16); breach of the covenant agreement (8:1-3); adoption of idol worship (8:4-6); and despising the prophets (9:7,8).

Life was just a load of hot air. It had no substance. So what they reaped was physical, emotional and spiritual emptiness and despair (8:7-10; 9:1-4,12-17).

A similar emptiness and despair today drives many people to drink, drugs and the addictive pursuit of pleasure in which fun ceases to be a by-product of creativity and relaxation and becomes an end in itself. Christians especially should be sad at the sight because they know there is an alternative: a God-centred enjoyment of the world which comes from responsibility and purposefulness.

However, they have to practise it as well as theorise about it, demonstrate it as well as believe it. To do that, we have to programme our lives with God's priorities, which is what the Israelites had failed to do.

Love is patient

Hosea 11,12

Raising a child requires patience. A toddler cannot learn every skill overnight. Even Jesus would have fallen while learning to walk, and smeared porridge on his hair while learning to feed himself.

The touching picture of God nurturing Israel as a mother nurtures her child unveils explicitly the tender side of God's character which we see circumstantially in the Old Testament story. He remained patient with an awkward and at times rebellious people unwilling to accept his tuition.

Patience never fails while love remains, says Paul (1 Corinthians 13:7). Henry Martyn proved that at the human level. Called to be a missionary, he loved a woman who felt unable to share in his work overseas.

In the early nineteenth century Martyn took his brilliant talents to three continents, translating the Scriptures into local languages. After a brief but fruitful ministry he died at the age of 31, unmarried and often lonely. He had loved Christ first, and had waited patiently for the wife who never came.

We can admire that dedication, and perhaps feel something of the pain. So perhaps we can begin to understand what God felt as he waited for Israel to return to him. And what, perhaps, he feels now.

He has rescued us from the slavery of sin through the life, death and resurrection of Christ who unleashed the power of God's Spirit into the world for all who believe. He has patiently brought us to where we are now, and waits for us to become what we should be. Thank him for his patience; don't try his patience by your obstinacy. And start practising his patience in your dealings with others.

For today

- If God holds together love and justice, so should we
- Find simple practical ways to consume less of the world's resources (and enjoy the challenge!)
- If you want to be fruitful for God, programme your mind with his priorities

A vision that soars above earth

The Book of Isaiah

- Contains majestic poems of God's greatness and supremacy
- Narrates the prophet's messages to Judah when the Assyrians conquered Israel
- Looks forward to the Judean exile and restoration
- Includes predictions of the Messiah as 'the suffering servant'

People who wait on the LORD shall 'soar on wings like eagles', Isaiah declares (40:31). His book does just that. In the second half especially, the poetry and thought rises above the petty concerns and trivial harassments of human life and transports us gracefully into the presence of God.

Isaiah looks down from a great height on Judah, Israel and the surrounding nations, and sees them all from God's vantage point. Then he looks upwards in paeans of praise and adoration that surpass even the best of the psalms.

Yet the book has been the subject of some of the bitterest wrangles among scholars. Although regarded by the Jewish community and the New Testament writers as a unity, Isaiah's authorship of chapters 40-66 has been doubted consistently over the past 150 years (see Fast Facts box).

Although such questions are important for our understanding of Scripture as a whole, they have only a mild influence on our interpretation. 'Second Isaiah' clearly relates to a specific historical situation (which, despite the often timeless character of its poetry, should inform the way we use its message), whether it was written in advance by Isaiah or closer to the time by someone else, prolonging the whole wide range of Isaiah's emphases.

Among Isaiah's great themes are the promises of God's refreshment and restoration after a time of trial, discipline and correction. Isaiah never minces his words but he is a prophet of hope even when he roundly condemns social injustice and religious apostasy.

He is at his greatest when he contrasts the power and resourcefulness of Israel's holy God with the poverty and impotence of idols which people create from what they can touch and see to give meaning and purpose to their lives. Our idols are different from those of his day, but they are aggressively marketed by image-makers in advertising and public relations agencies.

Music lovers will hear in the call to prepare the way (ch 40) and the catalogue of the servant's suffering in chapter 53 words immortalised in Handel's *Messiah*; readers familiar with the New Testament will recognise them as being fulfilled by John the Baptist and then Jesus' crucifixion.

If you come to the Old Testament with doubt and suspicion as to its relevance for today, and you want to retain your doubts and suspicions, avoid Isaiah!

KEY QUOTE

'To whom will you compare me? Or who is my equal?' says the Holy One. Lift your eyes and look to the heavens: Who created all these? He who brings out the starry host one by one, and calls them each by name. Because of his great power and mighty strength, not one of them is missing.

Isaiah 40:25,26

The heart of faith

Isaiah 1

The opening chapter introduces some important prophetic themes which will occur frequently throughout the book:

- Turning their backs on God and his laws resulted in political oppression of Israel and Judah as a sign of God's displeasure (vv 4-9);
- Turning to other religions is spiritual 'prostitution' (v 21). Some religions employed cult prostitutes to enable worshippers to 'unite' with the god, but any deference to other deities was regarded by the prophets as 'divorcing' God and committing spiritual adultery.

The chapter also confronts us with an important question concerning Jewish religious practice. If God first commanded the ritual system, why does he now abhor it (v 11)?

The answer is that the sacrifices have been stripped of their spiritual meaning. They have become empty rituals performed for their own sake rather than as signs of devotion to God. They were visual aids which showed that God hated sin but was gracious to forgive; the social and spiritual conduct condemned by Isaiah shows people at that time had no sense of sin or gratitude.

Every person, whether they worship with professional choirs in a Gothic cathedral or with an amateur rock band in a modern 'house church' can turn worship into feel-good ritual which does not connect with God. Isaiah reminds us that faith is a matter of the heart first, behaviour second and religious practice last.

ISAIAH

Key: Poetry normal type
Narrative in *italics*

Chapter	
1	**Judah's sins described**
2	**Visions of peace and judgment**
3	**Jerusalem will fall into chaos**
4	**The righteous branch will emerge**
5	**God laments his 'vineyard'; social injustices listed**
6	*Isaiah's vision and calling*
7	*The promise of 'Immanuel' to Ahaz*
8	**Prediction of Assyrian attacks**
9	**'Unto us a son is born'; God's judgment on Israel**
10	**God will punish Assyria**
11	**The shoot from the stump of Jesse: peace in the future**
12	**God has done wonderful things!**
13,14	**Babylon will be destroyed and Judah restored**
15,16	**Moab will be ruined**
17	**Damascus will be defeated**
18	**People of Cush will serve the Lord**
19	**Civil war and famine predicted for Egypt**
20	*Assyrian defeat of Egypt and Cush predicted*
21	**Prophecies against Babylon, Edom and Arabia**
22	**Jerusalem will be punished**
23	**The pride of Tyre will be smashed**
24	**The whole earth will mourn at the day of the Lord**
25,26	**Hymns of praise to God's greatness**
27	**Jerusalem will be restored**
28	**Israel will be brought down**
29	**Jerusalem will be besieged**
30	**People have not trusted God but he will forgive**
31	**Judah shouldn't trust Egyptian help**
32	**Justice will reign in the end**
33	**The Lord will save his people from distress**
34	**All nations shall be judged**
35	**The desert will become a garden**
36	*Sennacherib of Assyria attacks Jerusalem*
37	*Isaiah's message to Hezekiah*
38	*Hezekiah's illness and recovery*
39	*Hezekiah and the envoys from Babylon*
40	**Prepare the way of the Lord**
41	**God has chosen Judah**
42	**The first servant song; promise of restoration**
43	**God has called his people by name**
44,45	**The Lord is greater than idols**
46	**God's purposes will stand**
47	**Babylon will fall**
48	**Stubborn Judah will be refined and released from Babylon**
49	**The second servant song; Judah will be restored**
50	**The third servant song**
51,52	**The Lord will comfort his people**
53	**The fourth servant song: the suffering servant**
54	**Jerusalem will be restored**
55	**Let the thirsty drink from God's eternal stream**
56	**Those who keep God's law will be blessed**
57	**Those who reject God's law will be cursed**
58	**Real fasting is to help the oppressed and needy**
59	**Sin is everywhere**
60	**The Lord's glory will return to Jerusalem**
61	**Good news for the poor**
62	**Jerusalem will be safe for ever**
63,64	**A prayer that God will save his people**
65	**The promise of future restoration**
66	**Hope for the future**

Society drifting without a leader

Isaiah 3

The philosophy of leadership changed in the latter half of the twentieth century from 'command and control' to 'team building'. People who can inspire others are more likely to gain respect than those who shout orders, give few reasons and expect to be obeyed.

We need leaders at every level of society to hold the structure together. But sometimes people aspire to leadership simply to feed their own emotional or power-hungry needs. And the wrong people may be given leadership roles because other people can't be bothered to do the job.

The picture in this chapter is of a leaderless society, drifting like a rudderless ship. Instead of having mature, wise leaders with a steady hand on the tiller, Jerusalem is being piloted by inexperienced 'boys' prone to naive mistakes and laddish excesses.

It is a form of judgment on a degenerate society to have the leaders it deserves. As society drifts from God, it loses its bearings. When people in a church start to pull in different directions fellowship and outreach break up on the reefs of schism. Lack of leadership in such situations compound the misery of what is going on.

So we hear calls for 'strong leadership' to tug society or the church back to its moorings. But that sounds like a return to the command and control of a military dictatorship. Modern leadership theory is much more in line with Jesus' teaching. He said that leaders were to act as servants and lead by example (Matthew 20:24-28). When we feel ourselves to be drifting towards the rocks, don't pray for a tugboat; pray for a helmsman.

Author: Isaiah son of Amoz wrote at least part of the book (1:1). Jewish tradition says he was of royal birth with access to the corridors of power. He was married with at least two sons (7:3; 8:1-4) and lived in Jerusalem. An unreliable source claims he was murdered by being sawn in half during King Manasseh's reign (c. 687-642 BC).

Structure: The book can be divided into two sections (1-39; 40-66) or three (1-39; 40-55; 56-66). Literary similarities suggest they could have come from the same hand, and Jewish and New Testament traditions treat the book as a unity. However, the content of chapters 40-66 looks ahead to the capture of Jerusalem by the Babylonians, the Jewish exile, and the return allowed by the Persian king Cyrus II 44:28-45:1. Many scholars, dubious of the possibility of such detailed foresight, suggest that perhaps the second half comes from a later author. However, Cyrus I reigned in Isaiah's time (when Persia was relatively insignificant) so it is also possible that the prophet could 'see' what was likely to happen and thought of the king who was already known as the coming 'saviour' rather than his successor. Whatever the answer, the New Testament tells us that both halves point forward to Christ (John 12:38-41; 1 Peter 1:10-12).

Date of the prophet: Isaiah lived through the reigns of four kings of Judah c.740-687 BC. His call in 740 BC (ch 6) may not have been the start of his ministry but a new phase in it, as he claims to have worked before Uzziah died (1:1; cf. 6:1). See also the chronological table opposite.

Literary character: Isaiah is considered to be the greatest of the 'writing' prophets. The book's poetry is superb, put together in a roughly in chronological order, with some evidence of thematic ordering within that. But it does not flow smoothly in either time or thematic sequence.

Social sins show spiritual poverty

Isaiah 1,5

Heaven and earth are inextricably linked. Neither Judaism nor Christianity suggest that this world is unimportant or even subsidiary to the next, even if it is morally inferior. How we behave in this life reveals what we believe about the next, and what is the true state of our hearts (cf. Mark 7:14-23).

Therefore spiritual 'adultery' (1:21) is manifest not only by worshipping idols but also by such social sins as:

- Taking kick-backs (1:23; 5:23)
- Neglecting the needy (1:17,23)
- Rich people putting smallholders out of business (5:8)
- Maximising entertainment and minimising 'quality of life' issues (5:11,12)
- Grabbing what we can in a deceitful manner (5:18)
- Arrogant pundits overturning the wisdom and morality of the past (5:20,21)
- Turning socialites into heroes (5:22).

Therefore, says Isaiah, when God's law is ignored in these kinds of ways, a society will rot away (5:24). It is not difficult to see a similar pattern emerging in each generation. Incompetence, complacency, injustice and greed recur with tragic knock-on effects. It is always a sign of God's grace that things are no worse than they are.

Isaiah says that instead of resigning ourselves to this state of affairs, we should at least make it a matter for prayer. It is of concern to God as well as to us. Prayer today should be informed by news bulletins as well as the Bible. And prophets are needed in every age to shine light into the dark corners of society, where unfaithfulness to God and others abound.

CHRONOLOGICAL STRUCTURE

Isaiah is not compiled in either a strict chronological or thematic order. However, there is a general chronological development between sections, and some thematic grouping within them. Prophecies were given in a specific historical context although it cannot always be identified now.

CHAPTERS		DATES	
1-6; 9:8-10:4		c.740-735	
7:1-9:7		c. 734	
10-12		uncertain	
13-23		c. 732-715	
	[13-14		c. 729/8
	15-16		c. 715-3
	17		c. 732
	18-21		c. 715
	22		c. 701
	23		c. 715]
24-27		uncertain	
28-35		c. 705-701	
36-39		c. 701	

Vineyard's unpalatable vintage

Isaiah 5

The vine was a symbol for Israel, dating back to the giant bunch of grapes brought into the desert camp by the spies sent to survey the Promised Land (Numbers 13:23,24). Vineyards were central to the Israelite and Judean economies; wine was a standard drink throughout biblical times.

So this description of a fruitless plantation and its subsequent return to the wild was a powerful picture of the current depravity and forthcoming destruction of Judea. Jesus' parable of the tenants (Matthew 21:33-44) also speaks of God's rejection of his people entrusted with the vineyard, and his claim to be 'the true vine' (John 15:1) suggests a new people centred on him.

Judgment, says Peter, starts with the family of God (1 Peter 4:17). We cannot look back at these images with any complacency. What happened to them could happen to us.

T.S. Eliot's monument, in *Choruses from 'The Rock'*, to 'decent godless people' in a land 'where My Word is unspoken', was 'the asphalt road and a thousand lost golf balls' overlooked by 'the broken chimney, the peeled hull, a pile of rusty iron'.

Vandalised, abandoned inner city or rural churches in areas of dereliction and neglect 'where My Word is unspoken' provide a modern equivalent to Isaiah's grim image. They had once been fertile and productive. What went wrong?

Hot tips for real worship

Isaiah 6:1-8

No one is quite the same after an encounter with God – such an encounter cannot be engineered. However, there are some pre-conditions. Isaiah, we can assume, was already a man of prayer and insight. He was prophesying during Uzziah's reign (1:1) but received this vision after Uzziah died (6:1). He was already spiritually active.

Perhaps he received this vision as he contemplated the spiritual writing on the social wall. King Jotham, like his father Uzziah, was God-fearing although unable to stamp out the social and spiritual corruption (2 Chronicles 27:1-6). After a golden age of 50 years of peace and prosperity second only to Solomon's reign, Judah was crumbling.

The vision contains four elements to inform all our worship and prayer:

- God is king (v 1). We approach him as ruler of all.
- God is in community (v 2, and the 'we' of v 8). He does not live in splendid isolation, but rules over a true kingdom of which we are part. Worship joins us spiritually with the company of heaven.
- God is holy (vv 3-5). It is his worthiness, not his love, which is the true focus of worship. Worship which concentrates on his love is indirectly self-oriented; it thinks of what he has done for us, rather than who he is apart from us.
- God is merciful (vv 6,7). Isaiah became conscious of his own inadequacy and sin as he entered God's presence, even though he was 'committed'. Worship should include opportunity for confession.

We cannot tell whether Isaiah's response to the call was eager – 'Let's go, Lord! – or tentative like Andrew's at the feeding of the 5,000 (John 6:9) – 'If this is any use . . .' The latter is perhaps more likely. After such an awesome experience Isaiah was probably more humbled than fired up.

Indeed, it is those who come with empty hands, conscious of their shortcomings, saying, 'I'm here if it's any use to you' who God seems to choose for his service. Go-getters without the counter-balance of humility are likely to rush off on their own agenda rather than wait for God to set his.

HARD Question

Why did the prophets have a thankless task?

Isaiah 6:9-13

Isaiah (and other prophets) were given impossible jobs; to deliver a message which God knows will be rejected.

This passage, quoted by Jesus in Matthew 13, does not imply that God is vindictively hardening people so that they cannot turn to him. Rather, this is a description of what is inevitable, not what is determined, apart from, or against, people's own will. The people are so blind and prejudiced that they can't receive the truth when it is set before them.

Isaiah's clear message (people even despised it as simplistic, 28:9,10), hardened their hearts further because they had already decided to ignore it or reject it. They were not prepared to listen, so they were unable to 'hear'.

That was the fate of many prophets. People despised the message so they shot the messenger; but they could not accuse God of not having warned them of the coming tragedy that the prophets foresaw.

Christians face a similar scenario. Their message is not one which all people want to hear. But the task is to explain it clearly and faithfully and with as much cultural relevance as possible (Ezekiel used visual aids to enforce his message!). Some people will respond. There will be a harvest, and we should look for it. But we should not be surprised if some reject it scornfully and forcefully.

Double meanings in timely words

Isaiah 7,9

Prophecy in the sense of foretelling the future was a small part of the prophets' ministry. More often they forth-told – spoke out – God's word, describing his view of present situations and how as a covenant-keeping God he might respond.

But because these chapters include familiar predictive passages, we might assume that they only look forward to Jesus and that they had no other meaning at the time they were uttered.

The promise of Immanuel (7:14) was made specifically to King Ahaz and was fulfilled in his lifetime (8:3). The message was that by the time the unmarried woman (the meaning of 'virgin') had married, conceived and given birth – that is, in the space of a year or so – Assyria would destroy Aram and Ephraim (the northern kingdom of Israel) the communities which were conspiring against Judah (vv 2,4,5,16).

Also, Isaiah's words are so extravagant that 8:8 ('your land, O Immanuel') and the prediction the future king will be called 'Mighty God, Everlasting Father' (9:6) are clearly Messianic.

So the prophecy is double-edged. But while rejoicing in the Messianic message, we cannot ignore the historical part. God says to Ahaz: Even though you don't believe, my word will be fulfilled in a year's time. Ahaz panickd because he could only see threatening gestures. Isaiah remained calm, because he could 'see' God's rescuers (the Assyrians) in the distance.

Faith trusts that God will keep his word even when it seems impossible. We need people of Isaiah's long-sighted faith, pray for them. and for the calming insight which only God can give.

Future perfect

Isaiah 11

Children playing with smiling wild animals belong to the realm of fantasy fiction. Isaiah, however, uses the idea to suggest that the ultimate reign of God will be totally different from anything we can imagine.

The context is the Israelite longing for a Messianic king descended from David (the shoot from the stump of Jesse, David's father). Isaiah's description was fulfilled by Jesus:

- Led by God's Spirit (vv 1,2; cf. Jesus' own words quoting Isaiah 61 in Luke 4:16-21)
- Wise (v 2); Jesus was never fazed by trick questions (e.g. Matthew 22:21)
- Not judging by appearances (v 3; Jesus 'knew what was in people', John 2:24,25)
- Having God's authority to judge people's actions (v 4, claimed by Jesus in John 5:22).

The image is that wherever God rules, enemies become friends. Through reconciliation with God human adversaries can be reunited (cf. Ephesians 2:14-16). Then the strong and the weak can live in harmony without exploitation and with compassion.

That is not limited to the Messianic age to come. It has already begun with the resurrection of Jesus. Reconciliation and peace-making is a key element in New Testament Christianity, and central to the prophet's message.

Isaiah is looking forward to the reassembly of both Israel and Judah (vv 12,13) and the conquest of their traditional enemies (v 14). This expectation was partially fulfilled historically, which gives present-day readers hope that peace between factions in family, church and state is not a far-off dream but a practical possibility when God's rule is acknowledged by at least one party.

Grave concern buries stress

Isaiah 13,14

In theory, people who trust God should have such long-term vision that the natural desire for instant solutions is tempered if not removed. When we're frustrated at short-term events, we could do worse than read this chapter. Isaiah, predicting the rise and fall of Babylon, considers the ultimate fate of everyone: the grave. The word used is 'Sheol', the abode of the dead. In Old Testament thought this was a shadowy place of formles s existence, a ghostly realm of disembodied wraiths (14:9).

Sheol was where everyone was made equal. Gone were the pretensions of power and the swank of wealth (14:10,11). And Isaiah rejoices, because the oppressor has lost his glory.

When faced by an oppressor, unbelief can only simmer in the acidic juices of its own frustration, powerless to fight back. Faith, however, can take the eternal view. If things are not sorted out in this life, they will be in the next; we can wait, and God will not fail to fulfil our hope for justice.

There is a danger, certainly, that this view can lead to complacency about unrighteousness. The prophets however constantly urge us to join the fight against injustice, and not leave it until God breaks in at 'the end'. We are not to be glazed-eye dreamers oblivious to this world's ills.

How do we capture, or recapture this vision of justice being finally done? By focusing on the resurrection of Jesus and the promise of universal judgment which it guarantees (Acts 17:31). Then, patience will no longer be an unattainable virtue but a powerful antidote to the stress, anxiety and bitterness which constantly enslave those who have no such hope.

HARD Question

Did Isaiah portray Satan's primeval fall?

Isaiah 14:12-17

A popular belief that these verses relate to the pre-historic fall of Satan is fuelled partly by the Latin (Vulgate) translation of 'morning star' as 'Lucifer'. It has some justification because the Hebrew word is similar to that used for a Canaanite deity who, the myth suggests, attempted a coup in heaven.

However, the 'strong one' in the context refers explicitly to the king of Babylon (vv 4,22) and any parallel to other meanings is purely secondary. The word 'cast down' is more accurately rendered 'felled' (as with a tree, cf. v 8) and relates to the idea of death in vv 9-11; it is not the right word for 'eviction'.

Jesus spoke of Satan falling from heaven like lightning (Luke 10:18). This seems to be a figurative reference to the victory over him and the demonic legions which the 72 evangelists had witnessed, although the past tense could refer also to a cataclysmic heavenly event before time began.

Also, 'Babylon' in the New Testament is a figurative description of the principle of evil ruling the world without reference to God (e.g. Revelation 14:8; 17:1-6). It was also a code-name for Rome (1 Peter 5:13) which at the time was persecuting the church.

The Bible is vague about the origins of Satan and evil. It acknowledges his existence and notes his strategies but does not waste time detailing his story. Some things are best left unsaid, and unstudied. Evil has a hypnotic fascination for some people, but our focus should be the Almighty and all-conquering presence of God.

Global warning

Isaiah 13-23

This is the section everyone skips. Its prophecies about long-lost civilisations that will fall beneath the might of Assyria seem unrelated to the modern world. Yet because they were intimately related to Isaiah's world, and reflected God's verdict on real-time events, they offer some general truths which we should be the poorer without.

- **Babylon (chs 13,14,21)** is here synonymous with Assyria, being one of its leading cities and already ambitious. Assyria threatened the whole Near East and was in the process of destroying the northern kingdom of Israel at this time.
- **Moab (chs 15,16)** was the Australia or New Zealand of the day, famed for its sheep ranches (16:1). It had been an enemy of Israel since it refused the nomads right of passage (Judges 11:17,18) and hired Balaam to curse the emergent nation (Numbers 22-24). Friction had continued all through the monarchy. Moab's only saving grace was to produce Ruth, David's grandmother.
- **Damascus (ch 17)**, also called Aram or Syria, had waged continuous border conflicts with Israel and Judah since David's time. In Isaiah's time, Damascus's King Rezin attacked Judah's King Ahaz and took prisoners of war (2 Chronicles 28:5). As a result, Ahaz appealed to Assyria for help which was duly sent (Isaiah 8:4; 10:9,10; 17:1; 2 Kings 16:9).
- **Cush (chs 18,20)**, sometimes translated Ethiopia (from which the eunuch of Acts 8 came), was northern Sudan or Nubia. In Isaiah's time it was a strong country which took control of Egypt in 715 BC. It is always considered to be closely associated with Egypt
- **Egypt (chs 19,20)** was always a thorn in Israel's and Judah's sides. An ally when oppressors moved down from the north, Egypt was an adversary when northern nations were weak. Hoshea, Israel's last king, had appealed for Egyptian help against Assyria, and Hezekiah of Judah later did the same, against Isaiah's advice (2 Kings 19; Isaiah 37).
- **Edom (21:11,12; cf. 34:1-15)** like Moab had sporadic clashes with Judah and Israel.
- **Arabia (21:13-16)** may refer corporately to many tribes usually treated separately. The Assyrians had begun pushing into the Arabian peninsular, especially around the oasis of Dedan.
- **Jerusalem (ch 22)** is not excluded from God's global judgment. Its inclusion here is a reminder that when God's people went astray from God's plans, they became just like any other nation.
- **Tyre (ch 23)** was an important ally of the united kingdom and provided Solomon with his merchant ships and building timber. It had been annexed by Assyria in 841 BC and fell at the same time as Israel (722 BC).

For today's readers, this global survey should be heart-warming. The might of the nations is nothing to God; they conspire in vain (Psalm 2:1,2; cf. Isaiah 40:15-17). When the world seems out of control, it is not beyond God's understanding or reach. Indeed, he is guiding the heaving mass of rebellious humanity in ways hidden from our eyes.

Of special encouragement here is the claim that persecutors will be judged for their misdeeds. Opposition to Christians, condoned by some states, continues even today. Isaiah, like the book of Revelation, offers a long-term assurance that such groups will one day face severe consequences.

Date of events:
Chapters 1-39 cover the period c.750-690 BC; chapters 40-66 are less specifically focused but have special relevance to the period 587-537 BC.

Historical situation:
Isaiah speaks to the southern kingdom of Judah and refers to the situation in the northern kingdom of Israel which fell to Assyria in 722 BC

Place in Bible:
Follows the wisdom books (Proverbs, Ecclesiastes, Song of Songs) and comes before Jeremiah

Story parallels in:
Narrative of chapters 36-39 is covered in 2 Kings 18-20

Contemporary books:
Amos, Micah and Hosea (and possibly Jonah) were all working about the same time

A song and dance about nothing

Isaiah 24

Dwell long on this chapter. Isaiah is looking through his binoculars into the future yet is also describing what has been happening since the disgraced first couple were expelled from Eden. That is the genius of much biblical prophecy; it looks in several directions at once.

The carefree song of the godless is silenced by the collapse of the economy (v 7) but the song of the redeemed (or the remnant of God's people) is jubilant. God can be praised in all circumstances for who he is, even when righteousness is lacking in society and believers suffer along with the rest.

The key image is in verse 10. 'Ruined' is literally 'formless', the same word as is used for the shapeless matrix from which God precipitated water and solid matter (Genesis 1:2). It is the world un-created; it is Babel revisited.

Commentator Alec Motyer describes Isaiah's 'formless' city as 'without the ordering, life-giving hand of God, opting for a life on its own, within itself, depending on itself. Consequently, it is unstable and without purpose, spinning on the wheel but having dismissed the potter, its ever changing shapes and fashions not dictated by purpose but by whimsy. Life is simply one thing after another. Rejecting the moral absolutes of verse 5, everything is relative and ultimately individualistic. Humankind's great world city is "the city without meaning". . . where they thought they could find on earth and within themselves all they needed for secure community and a future, and they found only disorder, division and meaninglessness' (*The Prophecy of Isaiah*, IVP 1993, p 201).

You will recognise much that is familiar there. So when you next lift your voice in praise, lift your eyes also in sad reflection upon the world around you. The songs of the carefree may still echo through the streets, but the lights by which people walk keep going out.

The church is responsible to make the song of the redeemed heard above the unholy row, and to ensure that the light of the world shines brightly to guide to God those who can see it.

Faith plays the waiting game

Isaiah 30,31

As an aircraft prepares for take-off, the pilot pushes the engines to full power before releasing the brakes. The plane shudders as the two forces thrust against each other. Hezekiah is shuddering here; his officials are pushing him one way and Isaiah is holding him back.

The Assyrians had come within 20 miles of Jerusalem when Israel was destroyed. Now the nation threatens Judah and Hezekiah does not know what to do. He took the soft option and signed a treaty with Egypt (30:1-7; 31:1-3). On the surface it made sense; Judah needed a strong ally, and Egypt itself needed a stable Judah as a buffer to keep Assyria at bay.

Fools, said Isaiah; like a house infested by termites or undermined by subsidence, Judah would fall apart (30:12-14). His advice was to sit tight and wait (v 15).

Then God's guidance will come when necessary (vv 20-22). This promise assumes a steady onward journey of discipleship, walking in faith. It is only when we deviate from the path to the left (in crazy schemes) or to the right (sinking into the status quo) that we will hear the voice of God just as Hezekiah heard it through Isaiah.

Sometimes we should just ride out the storm, at other times we should act decisively. The guide calls us back when we deviate; when the path of wise and loyal discipleship is clear before us already, we should not expect him to speak to our consciences to dictate every step in advance. Isaiah's message was that God is to be trusted in all circumstances; Hezekiah's sin was to take matters in his own hands.

Hope endures when holiness is embraced

Isaiah 35

In another culture, Isaiah would have described trees and houses decked with yellow ribbons, ticker tape welcomes, popping champagne corks, tears of joy and hugs of relief. After years of oppression, Zion – Jerusalem – is free.

Quite when Isaiah envisaged this joyful scene taking place is not clear, but it doesn't matter. This superb poem is one of the Bible's glorious hymns of hope which has its fulfilment here and now in many ways and which awaits the grand finale of time for its last and greatest encore.

Water, in biblical times, was a symbol of life, and so the desert becoming a garden was the most powerful symbol of restoration and renewal which the Jews knew. It spoke of a covenant-keeping God who never abandoned his people and would restore them according to his promise. Hope never dies; God will come, for he takes no pleasure in his people's pain.

But good things come with strings attached. The new realm of hope is also a realm of holiness (v 8). The promise is not of indulgence but of plenty; it is a calm after the storm and a return to the senses.

When we relax, we can also relapse. The purpose of God's restoration was to return his people to the ways they should always have observed. The lessons of the past were for learning from, not for repeating. Restoration will only be temporary if discipleship is not more faithful than it was before.

How to pray in a tight spot

Isaiah 36-39

Having chased the wind in Egypt, Hezekiah redeems himself when confronted with the foul-mouthed and scornful Assyrian commander. Ruefully, no doubt, he recognises that the invader is right: Egypt is useless (36:6). But he disputes the suggestion that God is no use (36:7) and rightly appeals for prayer support from Isaiah (37:1-4) before getting on his knees himself (37:14-20).

It is not the most eloquent of Old Testament prayers but its simplicity is exemplary. Hezekiah knows there is only one God, and he throws himself unreservedly on his mercy. The king recognises God's greater sovereignty and prays that God will be honoured by delivering his people.

That is how we should pray in a tight spot. Often, such prayers are SOS: save our skin. Hezekiah's is SYN: save your name. He desperately wants to be safe, of course, but he recognises that there are greater issues at stake. God has been mocked; his name has been dragged through the mud. More important than Hezekiah's rescue, God must defend his own reputation.

God's honour may embrace the rescue of his people as a witness to his greatness. But it is his honour, not our rescue, which is to be uppermost. Discipleship makes some exacting demands!

Preparing the way so that people can meet with God

Isaiah 40:1-11

Picture two remote towns in a hilly area with only a footpath between them. Laying aside any conservation concerns, imagine the earth-movers carving a swathe through the hillside. You are building a road.

In ancient times there were only footpaths or sheep tracks outside the towns. The main caravan routes were only trodden-down earth. If a king or army wanted to get somewhere quickly, a battalion of engineers was sent ahead to clear the path of obstacles, bridge the worst ravines with rubble, lessen the steepest gradients, and tread down the path to reduce the risks of tripping.

The context of this prophecy is the return of the Jewish exiles from Babylon. They faced a 900-mile trek on foot. They could not build roads, but they still had to prepare for such an arduous journey. It provided the prophet with a timeless image.

It was applied in the New Testament to the ministry of John the Baptist (Matthew 3:1-3). It can be further applied to any Christian's witness. There are boulders of prejudice and stumbling-blocks of ignorance to clear away; there are rifts in relationships to bridge, and steep uphill paths we must travel to win people's confidence and respect.

Preparatory work is boring, as anyone who has wallpapered or painted a room will know. Stripping off the old layers is hard but essential work. If we want people to meet God, we have to prepare them to recognise and welcome him.

The 'Designer's' label

Isaiah 42-45

In life, you generally get what you pay for. Top brands of washers, freezers, cars and audio systems often show an increase in quality and reliability as they shift up the price scale.

God's people, says Isaiah, carry God's trade mark. They are crafted in his workshop and stamped with his image. It gives us a status bar none.

- **An exclusive mission** (42:5-7). Made by God, we are joined to him by his unbreakable covenant (guarantee) and sent on a mission that cannot fail.
- **A unique buy-back promise** (ch 43). The Maker will redeem his people when they fall into the wrong hands. The God who arranged the exodus will do new things to end the exile.
- **All other marques are fakes** (ch 44). The prophet says that however attractive the offers from other 'gods' may be, the gods are products of human inventiveness and they and their goods are guaranteed to go wrong.
- **The Maker provides full instructions and predicts all possible eventualities** (ch 45). He knows how we are to function and we should not question that. He has shown us how to live well and the consequences of not doing so.

When life is good we can acknowledge the Maker's help and recognise that what we enjoy and achieve is but a pale reflection of his purposes and capabilities. When trouble strikes, we can note the Maker's guarantee and trust him to sort out the difficulties.

And when we tear off his label, misuse the products of his creation or sell ourselves to some cheap idols, we know he has already paid the full market price to restore us to his ownership through Christ's death and resurrection. Our Maker's label is not just decoration; it is a badge of assurance.

The sad songs of the servant

These unique passages have been the subject of much debate, chiefly concerning the identity of the servant. There are three views:

- *an historical figure before the writer's time (e.g. Moses, a prophet or a king);*
- *a corporate term for the nation of Israel and its role in the world;*
- *the coming Messiah.*

It is possible to take the passages in all three ways. The writer may have been looking back at past models; he may well have been thinking of Israel's great mission. But it is certainly right to take them primarily as looking forward to God's promised deliverer, the Messiah, and to see them fulfilled in Jesus.

However, although they speak volumes about Jesus and his ministry, they also challenge and encourage our own.

We too serve the living God. And Jesus, who most perfectly fulfilled these prophecies, is our example, says Peter, quoting one of the songs (1 Peter 2:21-25).

The first song: The gentle servant (42:1-7)

Quoted in Matthew 12:15-21 where it explains the 'messianic secret', this passage reminds us that Jesus did not court publicity. Here is an example to follow. Endowed by the Spirit and encouraged by the fact that we are chosen by God in a profounder sense than that in which we have chosen him (cf. John 15:16) we can simply be ourselves and allow God to work through our ordinary lives.

Assertive, loud Christianity is often less honouring to God and less attractive to others than natural unassuming goodness. Jesus deals with the bruised and needy gently and kindly. Justice is a coin with mercy on one side, along with righteousness on the other.

The second song: The labouring servant (49:1-7)

Here is the first hint of setbacks. The servant, even Jesus the Son of God, is not guaranteed total success. His words fall on deaf ears. Yet those words are powerful (cf. Hebrews 4:12,13). They will remain on the record and be used in evidence against those who ignore them. Isaiah can say confidently that God's word achieves all it aims for (55:10,11).

Setbacks, in eternal terms, are temporary but also inevitable. We are to accept them, and to be grateful that the reward for faithful service is not dependent on numbers of conversions gained or needy people helped. God's statistical office measures motives. Besides, we shall never know exactly what 'results' come from our small pebbles of service thrown into the sea of history and sending ripples beyond our horizon.

The third song: The sustained servant (50:4-9)

The sense of opposition continues. Now the servant shows his true mettle. In need of support himself, and constantly looking Godward for it, he still has the presence of mind to pass on 'the word that sustains the weary'. Jesus had a word on the cross for the penitent thief (Luke 23:40-43) and his own grieving mother (John 19:26,27).

Here too is the model for turning the cheek when physically abused (Matthew 5:39). Only someone supremely confident in God's justice and the authenticity of his calling could ever behave like this. There could be no third song without the first.

The fourth song: The suffering servant (52:13-53:12)

Quoted often in relation to the crucifixion (e.g. Acts 8:26-40), this song describes virtually every form of suffering known to humankind. Jesus is thus able to identify with anything we experience (cf. Hebrews 4:15,16). This is a graphic and moving list of the horrors of crucifixion, pain and anguish beyond human imagining.

God's servant was disfigured and disabled (52:14); from an obscure and despised background (53:2); undesirable, unattractive and unwanted (53:2); despised, the butt of derision (53:3); rejected, discarded as useless (53:3); 'acquainted with grief', a companion to sorrow (53:3).

He was pierced by a sword, crushed by the weight of the cross, punished without cause, and wounded by a merciless flogging (53:5); oppressed by the forces of evil which nailed him to the tree (53:7); afflicted and downcast, as he agonised in Gethsemane and cried in dereliction on the cross (53:7). And finally, he was killed: murdered (53:8).

Yet it was all for a reason. And so is our pain and grief, even though that reason is originally hidden from us. Suffering, said Paul, is an inevitable part of being identified with Jesus (Colossians 1:24,25). Service of God is a privilege and a joy, but it also brings a cross.

Enlarge your vision and grow

Isaiah 54,55

Pioneer missionary William Carey used 54:2 as the text for a sermon in which his famous dictum was first used: 'Expect great things from God; attempt great things for God.' Isaiah's vision is expansionist, as he sees the exile coming to an end and the Jews getting ready for a restoration to the Promised Land.

In the last two decades of the twentieth century, many church leaders have been predicting a period of expansion if not revival. The growing interest of ordinary people in the broadly spiritual dimension to life, the sense of lostness and purposelessness which grips many and stimulates an ultimately unsatisfying race for possessions and experiences, fuel that idea.

The church growth movement has devised any number of potential strategies for taking advantage of this situation. Growth was never intended in the New Testament to be a private spiritual matter; it was intended also to be numerical as the disciples took the gospel into all the world and many were added to their number.

However, as many of its exponents would admit, this passage from Isaiah provides us with the only starting point for growth. Before anything can happen, even if revival and growth are promised in writing across the sky, God's people must first turn back to him and continue to depend on him.

In 55:1-7, the prophet describes first a necessary thirst for God himself, not just for what God can do or give. He is the source of all spiritual life (the waters). With that thirst comes an acknowledgement of our own spiritual bankruptcy in the call to 'seek him while he may be found'.

And following that, our dependence on him and not on our techniques and accumulated expertise, is to be absolute, for his ways are beyond our understanding and his strategies will not always follow our neat formulae (55:8,9).

CROSS CHECK

Parables and messages that people can't 'hear': pp 308-9
Satan and his cohorts: pp 192, 307
Hezekiah and the Assyrians: pp 254-6

The gospel is for all nations

Isaiah 56

The ancient Israelites had two major failings. One was that they persistently adopted the lifestyles and religious attitudes of the people around them, instead of maintaining their uniqueness and their identity as God's people with a mission. The other was that they forgot entirely what their mission was.

Those are two mistakes which Christians can quite easily repeat. The basic truths of the Christian message can be diluted by mixing it with politically correct and broadly religious views from the current generation.

At the turn of the twentieth century, dilution comes especially from an acknowledgement of Christianity as simply one religion among many rather than as a unique revelation from God (exactly like the Israelites). And many churches, burdened with heavy maintenance bills and dwindling numbers, have lost any sense of mission.

Isaiah, throughout his book, has scorned the idols and religious pluralism adopted by the Israelites. But as the last chapters approach, he reminds his readers of the vision for mission as well, and this chapter is another magnificent poem which heaps comfort and acceptance on people of all races.

For if Christianity is an exclusive religion in the sense that it renounces all other beliefs, it is an inclusive religion in that it knows no barriers of class, culture, race, gender or handicap. Here was good news indeed for the disabled, epitomised by the 'eunuch' who in the Law of Moses was barred from the priesthood.

Good news too for the 'foreigner', despised as a dog by pompous Jews. Anyone who seeks the Lord and wants to keep his laws is welcomed by the Lord, and therefore should be welcomed by the Lord's people.

Why can't we hear what God is saying?

Isaiah 58,59

The Judeans were seeking God and really wanting to hear his word (58:2), and they were fasting and humbling themselves before him (58:3). They were probably genuine and sincere in their devotion. Yet there was a barrier between them and God (cf. 59:2).

The same can happen to Christians who are faithful in their church attendance and participation in all the 'right' activities. Something is still missing. And Isaiah returns to the theme with which his book began to give the answer.

Their public life did not match up to their private spirituality. They were bad employers (58:3) and quarrelled with each other in church meetings (58:4). They were indifferent to the needs of the poor and blind to the injustice of society (58:6,7). They were also manipulating their religion for their own ends (58:13). These ideas are expanded in chapter 59.

Social justice, says Isaiah, is a hallmark of true spirituality. There is a big question mark against the profession of anyone who turns a blind eye to injustice and need, whose life is just as selfish as anyone else's but has the veneer of religion covering it. But as always there is a promise of restoration and healing (58:8-11). The covenant of God remains (59:21).

Isaiah applies the idea of 'the armour of God' (cf. Ephesians 6:10-18) to the battle for justice (59:16,17). The fight against evil begins in the world which stacks the odds against innocent people. 'Spiritual warfare' should include active involvement to change corrupt structures, as well as prayer-walking the locality.

Shine in the world

Isaiah 60,61

Once again Isaiah encourages God's people to get up and to go out. The time for mission has arrived, the light of the world is to shine in the darkness, and the Spirit of God will equip them.

There is a repetition here of several of Isaiah's favourite themes. People will seek out 'the church' when it shines (60:4-9). The people of God will unite all races (60:10-12). There will be peace and prosperity in the 'new Jerusalem' foreshadowing perhaps both the post-exilic period and the expected Messianic kingdom.

As you read these words, quoted by Jesus at the start of his own ministry (Luke 4:16-21), use 61:10,11 as a prayer of commitment. If such is true for each person who believes, how can we not move out into a world where the proportion of people who know Christ is falling in proportion to the growing population?

For today

- Care for the needy, oppose social injustice as part of your discipleship
- When you worship God, recall his holiness and his calling to be holy
- Fix your eyes on God's long-term agenda and live in hope of all he promises
- God is as fully in charge of world events today as he was in the past
- Find how to prepare the way in long-term personal witness
- Be prepared for suffering as God's servant

'Letter of straw' to resist storms of life

The Letter of James

- Is possibly one of the earliest New Testament documents
- Encourages practical application of Christian belief
- Tells readers to watch how they speak, and to pay their bills
- Encourages patience and prayer

The story of the three little pigs isn't quite as logical as is sometimes made out. The little pig who built a house of straw (which the wolf huffed and puffed down) almost got it right. For straw, when it is compacted, makes a strong, durable and even fire resistant building material.

Martin Luther, the sixteenth-century German reformer and theologian, described James as 'a letter of straw'. He meant that it was flimsy and fell down when you threw Paul's teaching at it. Mixing his metaphors he said it 'mangled scripture' and should never, in his opinion, have been included in the New Testament.

But he was wrong – proof that no Christian leader, however perceptive and helpful, is likely to be perfect in every judgment. James is more like compacted straw than chaff blowing in the wind. It provides a strong and firm framework for applied Christian truth; we would be the poorer without it.

James warns us about praying in doubt. He shows us how to keep going when the Christian way gets stormy. He shouts at us to get off the theological touchline and to start living out our theology. He has an acute social conscience and banishes all class distinctions from the church. And, perhaps from experience, reminds us to watch our tongues.

Far from contradicting Paul (as is sometimes supposed), it complements him and applies the common faith of the early church vigorously and even uncomfortably. James is to the New Testament what Proverbs and Ecclesiastes are to the Old Testament: full of sound wisdom, practical advice and startling earthiness.

Indeed, it's just the sort of book you would expect from a carpenter-builder's son (see Fast Facts). It's rough and ready like raw timber. James axes down pretentious piety. He saws through nebulous notions. He planes off the religious bark to reveal the smooth grain of truth beneath it.

But as you run your hand over the planks while he nails them together, don't be surprised if he hammers your fingers occasionally; James can be sharp and painful!

AT A GLANCE

JAMES

1 Face tests wisely and live the truth
2 Don't be prejudiced, do good deeds
3 Speak wisely and carefully
4 Submit to God, resist the devil
5 Don't be lazy, be patient, pray in faith

As the body without the spirit is dead, so faithwithout deeds is dead.
James 2:26

How to avoid sinking in rough seas

James 1:1-18

A disabled Christian wrote in the journal *Christianity Today*, 'In America Christians pray for the burden of suffering to be lifted from their backs. In the rest of the world Christians pray for stronger backs so they can bear their suffering.'

The path of life is an obstacle course. James recognises the fact and does not explain it away. He faces it squarely – the mark of a man who has 'got it all together'. 'Trials' (v 2) means any unexpected obstacle to progress, and the verb 'face' has the idea of a ship hitting a hidden reef.

But when he says 'count it all joy' he is not a beaming, bouncing extrovert belittling your problems. He is saying, approach it positively. However bad it seems, it's an opportunity to prove God's power, and to grow stronger in the faith. In the words of commentator Alec Motyer, any trial can be 'a stepping-stone to glory'.

For that, we need wisdom (v 5), knowing how to react faithfully to the unexpected. (James is not promising 'guidance' through alternative choices, although his promise is sometimes taken as if he were. He is thinking of conflicts, not career moves.)

'Temptations' (v 13) is the same word as 'trials' but used differently. Trials can breed temptations but while God does not shield us from trials, he never actively tempts us to sin.

In an imperfect world, God is the father of lights (v 17) but does not organise everything. Human freedom, satanic malice and our own human sinfulness have plenty of scope. The desire that comes from an imperfect perception of what is true and right causes us to stumble in that murky environment. We can't blame God.

Prison chaplains say that the criminals least likely to re-offend are those who admit that they are to blame. Those who pass the buck soon return. When you face trials and temptations, don't whinge at God (or even the devil) and pass the buck – it's the quickest way to fail the test. Rejoice instead at the challenge of proving God right and the devil wrong.

Place in Bible: The first of the 'general epistles' in the New Testament, after Hebrews and before 1 Peter.

Parallel books: There are some similarities with 1 Peter.

FAST facts

Author: Three James are mentioned in the New Testament: the son of Zebedee (martyred c. AD 44, Acts 12:2); the son of Alphaeus (numbered among the apostles but never mentioned again); and James the brother of Jesus. The latter received a personal resurrection appearance from Jesus (1 Corinthians 15:7) and headed the church in Jerusalem (Galatians 1:19; Acts 12:17; ch 15). He is the most likely author, although some commentators have suggested that the Greek of the letter is too sophisticated for the son of a Galilean carpenter. But he might have been good at languages.

Date: James was martyred in the early 60s according to non-biblical writers. The Jewishness of this letter suggests it was written very early, before Gentiles were a major force in the church (c. AD 49). Some suggest a date nearer 60 however, and there can be no certainty.

Readers: James reads more like a sermon (or extracts from several sermons). It is a compendium of teaching, maybe a kind of 'encyclical' rather than a letter as such. It is addressed to Jewish Christians (1:1) which fits James the brother of Jesus as author.

Acceptance: Because of the apparent conflict with Paul, the uncertain authorship and the lack of very early manuscripts, James was one of the last books to be accepted into the 'canon' of Scripture.

CROSS CHECK

Paul's teaching about
Faith: p 102, 133
Wisdom: p 339
The tongue: p 342
Wealth and riches: p 264

If you know it, do it

James 1:19-2:26

The English language does not always help our understanding of the Bible. To us, 'knowledge' is neutral data and 'faith' is credal belief. But to the Bible writers, knowledge was personal awareness of God's character and covenant and thus the foundation for right action. Faith was personal trust in God and the motive for right action. Both were practical concepts; theology was – and is – nothing if not applied.

James is not writing about 'saving faith' but the faith of the saved, and suggests two ways to express this:

- The poor are to be cared for (1:26,27; 2:14-17), which action reflects Christ's compassion on the needy;
- Partiality is to be avoided (2:1-13), which action reflects Christ's equal acceptance of outcasts and leaders.

Both are important expressions of faith today: we cannot have beliefs about life's big questions like a theological comfort blanket which has minimal impact on a our lives. James says beliefs are empty if they don't affect you radically. 'God is love' has major implications for my relationship with everyone I meet; 'Jesus is Lord' must rule both my work and leisure.

When James refers to correct but barren belief, such as demons have as 'faith': he is parroting the usage of some of his readers. To him, as to Paul, real faith is a life-transforming energy that goes beyond mere orthodoxy.

And when James speaks of persons being 'justified' by works, he does not mean, as Paul does, pardoned and accepted by God, but vindicated against doubts as to whether their professed faith was words without action.

What Paul said about faith and works

- We are brought into a right relationship with God by trust (faith) in God's grace: Ephesians 2:8,9.
- Abraham was 'justified' because he believed God's promise, not because he performed certain rites: Romans 4.
- Having begun with faith we are to continue to trust God for eternal salvation and not attempt to earn it: Galatians 3:1-14.
- We are to express our faith through good works: Ephesians 2:10; Philippians 1:12,13.
- Paul gave lots of advice on practical 'doing' of the faith: e.g. Romans 12:9-21; 13:8-14.
- We are to continuously 'put off' the old nature and apply our new life: Colossians 3.

Wagging tongues make Satan smile

James 3

Someone has worked out that the sentence 'watch the dark brown dog run down the street' has a total of 223,665,152,256 possible meanings, with each word (and combination) having many connotations.

No wonder our communication is often misunderstood! Relationships are like tender plants; easily bruised and even destroyed by clumsy handling. James says that the tongue can devestate a relationships, so take care!

Unfortunately we rarely choose our words carefully or consider their likely impact. Perhaps we should tell ourselves that God is recording every statement (he is, Matthew 12:36,37) or that every conversation is a sensitive diplomatic negotiation.

Above all, we are to be consistent. To truly praise God we cannot indulge in slander (cf. 4:11). Speech is meant to reflect God but slander proves malice and resentment rather than God's love ruling our hearts. Speech is an accurate external measure of our internal faith. Listen to yourself, and be ready for a shock.

Greed leads to conflicts

James 3:13 - 4:16

In 1993, top Italian businessman and racing yachtsman, Paul Gardini, shot himself. He was facing arrest for his part in a corruption scandal that implicated over 2,500 top people. He had pulled strings, made enemies and hurt people and justice had caught up with him.

In the same year there were no candidates for the Singapore Presidential election until four weeks before the ballot. Then one man put himself forward. To make it a proper election, someone else stood but the second candidate acknowledged the first was 'far superior' and hardly campaigned!

Sadly, consensus is less common than conflict. Greed and ambition plague us all, including the church.

The moment you say, 'I want' you trigger conflict: within yourself, with God and with others who may hinder your ambitions. You are shutting out self-giving love by focusing on yourself and obstructing God's purposes. So whenever you hear yourself saying, 'I want', listen to James's advice:

- Pray for God's wisdom in all things, and practise it (3:17)
- Ask God for what he wants (4:2)
- In all your prayers, seek his honour before your pleasure (4:3)
- Keep material things in their eternal perspective (4:4)
- Be content with God's grace (his undeserved favour for you, 4:6)
- Submit your entire life to God and resist temptation to greed (4:7)
- Learn to be a peacemaker not a conflict maker (3:18).

One day at a time

James 4:13-5:20

This section of miscellaneous teaching is held together by a thread of patience. James begins with the ambitious entrepreneur making grand plans and punctures his balloon before it's even got off the ground (4:13-17).

Of course we need to plan for the future but we don't know what tomorrow holds and we should make the most of the present opportunity for doing good (4:17; cf. Matthew 6:34).

The rich are among the most impatient of people and holding back payments is a regular expression of grasping immediate profit at the expense of others (5:1-6). The more we have, the more we want, and the sacred bottom line is guarded with religious zeal. Only patient people can be fair people, and only fair people can please God.

Patience in suffering was a major issue in the primitive church as persecution as well as poverty struck Christians down. When we are under pressure from outside, we tend to moan at people close to us (5:9). Patience refuses to take out its frustration on others.

Instead of complaining, we are to pray (5:13-18). The promise of healing in the context of confession echoes James's concern for humble righteousness, but does not imply that illness is punishment for sin. Rather, poor relationships are a hindrance both to personal healing and to corporate intercession; James wants us to be right with one another in order to receive God's grace. And we can only be right with one another if we are patient with one another.

The prayerful anointing of sick Christians that James directs probably reflects the then current belief in oil as medicine. The expectation of bodily healing that he encourages is a generalisation that will have exceptions. The 'prayer of faith' (5:15) is petition made in full confidence that our loving Father knows what is best for us.

For today

- Pray that God will give you a stronger back to bear life's difficulties
- Think of practical ways in which all your beliefs can be applied to daily life
- Say less and listen more – to God and to others
- Think of others before yourself

Jeremiah is arranged in an almost random manner. The approximate dates and kingships relating to each chapter may help to locate teaching in its original context. See also chart opposite.

Chap	*Main theme*	*Probable reign/date of prophecy*	
1	Call of Jeremiah	Josiah,	c. 626-609
2	Judah has forsaken God		
3	Judah's spiritual adultery		
4	Punishment coming from the north		
5	Everyone is corrupted		
6	Siege of Jerusalem predicted		
7	Call to repentance; warning of judgment		
8	Judah's indifference and Jeremiah's lament	Jehoiakim,	c. 609-598
9	Jerusalem will be ruined		
10	Idols are nothing compared to God		
11	Broken covenant; Jeremiah threatened	Josiah,	c. 609-598
12	Jeremiah argues with God		
13	Parable of the belt; call for humility	Jehoiachin,	c. 598
14	Drought as a punishment for sin	Jehoiakim,	c. 609-598
15	Destruction is inevitable; Jeremiah depressed		
16	God's favour is withdrawn		
17	Trust in the Lord and keep his laws		
18	Learn from the potter; Jeremiah attacked		
19	Parable of the broken jar		
20	Jeremiah locked up, and laments		
21	Message of gloom to Zedekiah	Zedekiah,	c. 589/8
22	Challenges to kings to be righteous	Several kings	
23	Righteous Branch promised; false prophets	Zedekiah,	c. 589/8
24	Parable of the fig baskets		
25	Seventy years' exile predicted	Jehoiakim,	c. 605
26	Death threat for Jeremiah		c. 607
27	Submit to the yoke of Babylon	Zedekiah,	c. 593-590
28	Hananiah breaks the yoke		
29	Letter of hope to the exiles		
30	Promise of restoration		
31	There will be a new covenant		
32	Jeremiah's field – sign of restoration		c. 598
33	Restoration and the Righteous Branch		
34	Zedekiah warned that Babylon will win		
35	Jeremiah tempts the Recabites	Jehoiakim,	c. 601
36	The king burns Jeremiah's scroll		c. 605/4
37	Jeremiah imprisoned	Zedekiah,	c. 588/7
38	Jeremiah thrown in the cistern		
39	Jerusalem falls to Babylon		
40,41	Jeremiah released; Gedaliah murdered	Babylonian occupation	c. 587/6
42	Warning to rebels not to go to Egypt		
43	The rebels go to Egypt		
44	Prophecy against rebels in Egypt		
45	A word of encouragement for Baruch	Jehoiakim, Zedekiah,	c. 609-593
46	Egypt will be laid waste		
47	Philistines will be destroyed		
48	Moab will be subdued		
49	Other nations will be destroyed		
50,51	Babylon will also be destroyed		
52:1-30	Fall of Jerusalem	Zedekiah,	587
52:31-34	Jehoiachin released	Babylonian occupation	c. 516

'Through your own fault you will lose the inheritance I gave you. I will enslave you to your enemies in a land you do not know . . . But blessed is the man who trusts in the LORD, whose confidence is in him. He will be like a tree planted by the water that sends out its roots by the stream.'

Jeremiah 17:4,7-8

Troublesome priest proved right

He is the sort of person who cannot sleep at night. He is racked with anxiety and self-doubt. He curses the day he was born. God has told him not to marry, he has few friends and many enemies. Meet Jeremiah, the troubled priest who won a reputation as a troubler of kings.

This is the longest book in the Bible and is arranged in an apparently arbitrary fashion (see the charts for the likely order of material). Its author has won a universal reputation for doom and gloom and his name is synonymous with pessimism. Yet once you open it, you will find inspiration and hope amid the predictions of judgment, all couched in colourful poetry.

The story spans the reigns of five kings (one, Jehoahaz or Shallum lasted only three months and is mostly ignored). Religious and political life in Judah (the southern kingdom) was deteriorating.

King Josiah reformed worship after the rediscovery of 'the Book of the Law' (probably a version of Deuteronomy) about four years after Jeremiah's call (2 Kings 22,23; Jeremiah 1:2). This reversed the policies of Josiah's evil grandfather Manasseh, but the revival was short-lived.

Crippled by 'spiritual adultery' and abortive attempts at political independence, Judah was slowly crushed first by the Egyptians and then by the Babylonians. The 'weeping prophet' brought a message no one wanted to hear.

The way of salvation, he said, was to submit to the yoke of Babylon. Such talk was treason and Jeremiah suffered imprisonment and death threats. Sensitive and introspective, he allows readers to enter his anguished heart as he asks God why he has to suffer for a message he cannot change.

But always there is a glimmer of light in the darkness. He looks beyond his own lifetime to when the Judeans will re-populate the hills of the promised land, and Jerusalem will be restored. His words came true. Wherever you dip into Jeremiah, you will find both challenge and encouragement.

The Book of Jeremiah

- Contains messages to Judah (the southern kingdom) in the 40 years before its destruction
- Predicts that Babylon will defeat Judah and exile its inhabitants
- Promises that after 70 years a remnant of people will return to start again
- Is an intensely personal book including heart-rending prayers by Jeremiah

Where am I?

JEREMIAH IN APPROXIMATE DATE ORDER

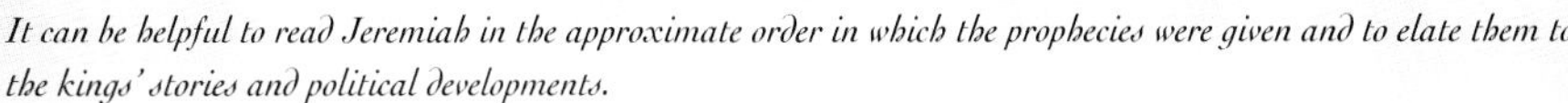

It can be helpful to read Jeremiah in the approximate order in which the prophecies were given and to elate them to the kings' stories and political developments.

King	Approx date of prophecies	Chapters in Jeremiah	Other biblical references
Josiah	c. 626-609	1-7, 11, 12	2 Kings 22,23; 2 Chronicles 34,35
Jehoiakim	c. 609-598	8-10, 14-20, (22) 25, 26, 35, 36, (45-51)	2 Kings 3:36 - 24:7; 2 Chronicles 36:5-8
Jehoiachin	c. 598	13, (22)	2 Kings 24:8-17; 2 Chronicles 36:9-10
Zedekiah	c. 598-587	21, (22), 23-4, 27-34, 37-39 (45-51), 52:1-30	2 Kings 24:18 - 25:26; 2 Chronicles 36:11-21
The exile period	c. 587-561	40-44, 52:31-34	2 Kings 25:27-30; cf. Lamentations; Ezekiel; Daniel

Date of events:
c. 626-580 BC
Place of events:
Jerusalem and surrounds; Jeremiah is forcibly taken to Egypt at one point
Book follows:
Isaiah
Book precedes:
Lamentations (also by Jeremiah) and Ezekiel

Age shall not hinder them

Jeremiah 1

Age is irrelevant to God. He called a pensioner to lead slaves out of Egypt. Jesus, much to his disciples' disapproval, welcomed children for a blessing. God delights in doing the unexpected. So he calls as his spokesman Jeremiah who, unusually for a young person, believes he is not experienced enough.

It was not the last time God would do something like this. Timothy in the New Testament was also young, timid and inexperienced. William Booth in the nineteenth century began to preach when he was 17, was challenged to become a full-time minister when he was 21 and went on to found the Salvation Army.

What is more important than age or experience is the divine anointing which bestows an unmistakable spiritual authority. Jeremiah received his commission in a vision (v 9). Isaiah had something similar (Isaiah 6:7) while Ezekiel was given a scroll to 'eat' (Ezekiel 3:3,4).

Enthusiasm and passion, often the attributes of youth, do not necessarily indicate a spiritual gift. Feeling strongly about a need does not of itself constitute a call to meet that need. It might be an urgent call to prayer.

Like Moses Jeremiah tried desperately to get out of God's call. But when he kept silent he burned up inside; he had to breathe out the fire he could not control (20:9). Some people are naturally shy, but that does not make them unsuitable for public office.

It is natural, too, to see Jeremiah as slow on his feet, someone who needed to write out his sermons carefully before delivering them. Certainly the poetry gives the appearance of being well-considered.

God would not take no for an answer; Jeremiah had to obey. His words became the sword of the Spirit because they were devoid of human pride and uttered with reluctance. There was nothing in Jeremiah to get in God's way. That makes him a model for all who seek to speak God's word to others.

Same product, different wrapper

Jeremiah 2-4

Chocolate bars are sometimes marketed under different names in the United States and Britain. Transatlantic travellers get used to the change of wrapper and are confident that the content is identical to what they are used to.

Similarly, biblical prophecy describes human faults six hundred years before Christ in a way they could not be described today. But the inner traits remain unchanged in the human race; only the wrapper has changed. These chapters illustrate this:

- Defilement of God's land (2:7); think of the ecological crises today
- Reliance of religious leaders on human ideas (2:8)
- Creation of 'gods' offering meaning and purpose in life (2:11)
- Attempts to assuage spiritual thirst in non-spiritual ways (2:13-19)
- Giving up on God when something more attractive comes along, which is like getting divorced and remarrying someone more 'attractive' (2:20-25; 3:6 - 4:2)
- The disintegration of social cohesion and the threat of being over-run by forces we cannot control (4:7-13).

There is much to learn from God's dealings with the Judeans 1,600 years ago. Their sins are our sins; their bitter fruits could be ours, too. Jeremiah provides an all-time warning.

Tarred by the same brush

Jeremiah 5,6

Searching vainly for someone in a crowd can be disheartening and alarming. Jeremiah knows the feeling. He has lost sight of anyone who follows God fully.

The theme occurs elsewhere in the Bible. Abraham gets God's agreement not to destroy Sodom if ten righteous people can be found there (Genesis 18). Isaiah 59:15,16 says that truth is 'nowhere to be found' and God can find 'no-one to intervene.'

Ezekiel, Jeremiah's contemporary, looked back at Jerusalem from exile in Babylon to find 'a man among them to build up the wall,' the moral and spiritual defences, 'but I found none' (22:30). And David described God looking down on earth to see 'there is no-one who does good, not even one' (Psalm 14:3).

We naturally want to question such a pessimistic verdict. In most people's experience, humanity is not that depraved. We see touches of goodness everywhere; the milk of human kindness still flows.

Only when we hear of the barbaric genocide of Rwandan Tutsis by rival gangs of machete-wielding Hutus, who could dispatch 1,000 souls to eternity in twenty minutes, are we inclined to agree with Jeremiah, Ezekiel, David – and God.

Jeremiah's Jerusalem in 600 BC was not like Rwanda in the 1990s. Bible writers measure righteousness against a different scale to ours. Faithfulness to God's covenant is more than human goodness; it honours God before all. By that standard, what we count as righteousness is 'like filthy rags' by comparison (Isaiah 64:6).

The New Testament reminds us that a loving heavenly Father delights in even the imperfect actions of his children done in response to him. But in rejoicing in that fact, we should not overlook another: we cannot please him by our own righteousness alone. We need the covering of Christ's new life. Jeremiah is seeing people naked before God.

Historical background: Assyria defeated the northern kingdom of Israel in 722 BC. Judah, the southern kingdom, was besieged but not attacked in 701 BC. The Babylonians began to expand, and Pharaoh Neco of Egypt successfully assisted Assyria against them at Carchemish in 609. (Judah's King Josiah died at the battle of Megiddo as he tried to stop Neco.) But Babylon's Nebuchadnezzar attacked Jerusalem in 605, taking some prisoners, and defeated it in 587.

The kings: See charts for dates. Jehoahaz, Josiah's son, was captured by Neco and replaced by Jehoiakim. He became a vassal of Nebuchadnezzar in 605 but rebelled in 602 (2 Kings 24:1), was taken prisoner and died (2 Chronicles 36:6). He was replaced by Jehoiachin (also called Jeconiah or Coniah) in 597 but in three months he too was exiled (2 Kings 24:8-12). Nebuchadnezzar replaced him with Mattaniah, changing his name to Zedekiah. He rebelled, was taken to Babylon and blinded (2 Kings 24:17-20; 25:1-7).

Author: Jeremiah was the son of a priest from Anathoth and unmarried. He dictated his messages to Baruch (cf. ch. 36) who may have arranged the book in its present form.

Main themes: Jeremiah says that Judah has rebelled against God in the same way as Israel and will be similarly punished by destruction of its capital and exile. He predicts that exile in Babylon will last for 70 years. He also predicted a remnant would return to Judah.

The truth about false religion

Jeremiah 7

Pluralism is a fact of life in Western society. No country is now a theocracy like ancient Israel, and therefore in welcoming people of other races to their shores nations cannot insist that they leave their gods behind. Interpretation of passages such as this must focus not on the nation but on the people of God, the church.

It is right to recognise that some other religions may have emphases which Christians should have but which they have lost sight of. The Eastern sense of unity with the rest of creation has been largely pushed aside by the utilitarianism of the West, for example.

God is certainly big enough to include a wide variety of understandings about his character and his ways. All human understanding is limited, imperfect and incomplete, and God can never be reduced to a formula. However there are limits between truth and un-truth; the mixing of worship with other religions is biblically unacceptable.

Christianity, like Jeremiah's Judaism, is monotheist, worshipping one supreme God. We cannot therefore acknowledge other deities. There are other supernatural beings, but they are either angels who hate being worshipped (Colossians 2:18; Revelation 22:8,9) or demons who should be avoided, who stand behind the unreal gods of human imagining in the world's assorted cults (1 Corinthians 10:19-21).

The distinction being made by Jeremiah is not like that between Roman Catholic and Protestant. It is between monotheism and polytheism. In modern terms, the people were mixing worship of God with worship of Wicca, and putting crystals and horoscopes on the same level as the Bible. Their spiritual decline was matched, as it often is, by social injustice (vv 6,10).

There is no need to picket the temples of other religions. There may be many proper opportunities to join with people of other religions in projects of mutual interest, such as seeking legislation to protect families or to clean up neighbourhoods.

We can be on good relations with them, as Christians in the early church were encouraged to be (Colossians 4:5). But to incorporate their worship into ours, or ours into theirs, is to deny the distinctive core of our faith.

HOW THE BIBLE BOOKS, KINGS AND PROPHETS FIT THE CENTURY BEFORE THE FALL OF JERUSALEM

Where am I?

715 BC	697 BC	640 BC	609 BC	598 BC	598 BC
Hezekiah	Manasseh	Josiah	Jehoiakim	Jehoiachin	Zedekiah

- 2 Kings 18-25
- 2 Chronicles 29-36
- ← Isaiah
- ← Micah
- Jeremiah →
- Daniel →
- Zephaniah
- Ezekiel →
- Habakkuk
- Nahum

Jeremiah feels the pain

Jeremiah 8:21-9:6

Jeremiah is a feelings person. Not for him the cool detachment of logic and the measured tones of a lecturer. He feels his message; it grips and moves him, and he surely must deliver it with passion. So he cannot pronounce God's judgment as if he were reading the weather forecast; he weeps at the truth he is forced to recite.

This is a rare but necessary gift. He identifies both with God in his righteous anger and with his contemporaries in their sad suffering. The temptation of social critics and Christian preachers is to coolly stand apart from the people and situations they denounce. Jeremiah suggests a better, but more costly, alternative.

Cold righteousness does not reflect God's loving passion and warm-blooded concern. More tears and fewer tirades might improve the effectiveness of ministry in pulpit and prayer meeting.

It's hard being so unpopular

Jeremiah 11:18-12:13; 18:18-23; 20.

On several occasions Jeremiah fell into an emotional pit as deep and as frightening as the physical one into which his enemies threw him (ch 38). He wished desperately that he had never been born (20:14-18). His words were unheeded and people were trying to kill him. Fear added to frustration creates volatile emotion.

Depression is not a new phenomenon. However, Jeremiah's condition was probably relatively rare in his times compared with its frequency today. Some researchers suggest that the incidence of clinical depression is doubling every ten years in many Western countries.

It may arise for all kinds of reasons, including the anger and frustration of unfulfilled desire. Jeremiah had been told to expect a negative response (cf. 5:21) but being human he probably hoped for something better. Today, we may set targets of career, relationships and status unrealistically, and fall victim to depression because we fail to make the grade or achieve an indefinable 'happiness'.

Jeremiah responded by praying for his enemies' downfall in typically Old Testament terms (18:21-23), while God assures him that the wicked will not prosper for ever (ch 12). He is still able to see that God is greater than his enemies and his problems, and therefore is able to praise him (20:11-13), which many would find difficult.

Those who do not experience these kinds of feelings should not hold them in contempt. Sensitive people do crumble under pressure. Realism, which recognises that this world is imperfect, a contentment which accepts that ideals can rarely be attained, and faith which acknowledges that God's ways are mysterious but his power infinite may go some way to protecting us from depression's worst assaults. We should not be ashamed if it doesn't; it is not a sin, just an illness.

Pearls of wisdom

Jeremiah 9:23,24; 10:6-13; 17:5-10

Jeremiah frequently offers positive thoughts for meditation, particularly the following:

- 9:23,24 is summarised by Paul in 1 Corinthians 1:31. It asks what, on judgment day, would be my greatest asset? How does that measure up to what I devote my time and attention to now?
- 10:6-13 contrasts the living God with manufactured objects (v 9). Surrounded by man-made objects we can forget God's eternal otherness which is not dependent on anything man-made. Look up, not around.
- 17:5-10 contains three distinct thoughts. The image of the flourishing bay tree shows that people who draw on the Spirit's refreshing presence have a unique resource to help cope with pressure and disappointment. Verse 9 reminds us of our humanity, which should be synonymous with humility and lead to inner discipline and outward conformity (v 10).

Drama plays on prophetic words

Jeremiah 13:1-11; 18:1-12; 19

Drama has been employed through the centuries to convey religious truth. Medieval mystery plays were a powerful teaching tool when few people could read. The prophets used, or were given, visual enactments to convey their verbal messages. These dramas were parables which had greater impact than mere pronouncements.

When Jeremiah first buried, then recovered his linen 'belt' (an underskirt) the sight spoke more loudly than all the criticism (13:1-11). It was an intimate garment; Judah had been close to and intimate with God. It was possibly a priestly garment, too; Jeremiah, a priest, wore linen (most others wore wool). That would have reminded people of their calling to be a 'nation of priests', a holy nation.

It was ruined and irreparable, a rag to be thrown away. God was about to discard his favourite people. There are New Testament warnings too that the church should not presume on God's love; some believers may be embarrassed on judgment day, and churches may die through lack of mission.

The parable of the potter (18:1-12) reveals that prophecies did not always come by words in the head. As Jeremiah watched the potter a message formed. The changing shape of the clay illustrated God's continual moulding of people. Our shape is not fixed. Personalities undergo, through the Holy Spirit, the re-mould of 'sanctification'. He gives us new gifts for new tasks, as a bowl can be moulded into a jug.

A fired pot, however, can only be used or broken (ch 19). God's people are shaped to serve God. In Jeremiah's time they had failed to fulfil that function and were smashed as a group. From the comfort of our New Testament faith, we dare not dismiss this image as being only for the Jews of old.

Believers can live useless lives (1 Corinthians 3:10-15). Apostasy, denying our faith, is also a distinct, if distant possibility (cf. Hebrews 6:4-6). These warnings fell on deaf ears; yet they have been preserved for us. As Jesus said, whoever has ears, let them hear.

King conned and Messiah praised

Jeremiah 23 (cf. 33:14-16)

Someone has said, misquoting Proverbs, that where there is no vision the people perish, but where there is a sham vision, they perish even faster. In a section denouncing kings of Judah, Jeremiah turns to Zedekiah (whose name means 'The Lord our vindicator') who has been led astray by false prophets and strong but godless advisers.

In a rare Messianic passage (accepted as such by Jewish commentators but doubted by some Christian ones), he looks into the future to see the ideal king leading his restored people to peace, piety and prosperity. The prophecy was fulfilled by Christ, but not socio-politically. Although Jeremiah's foresight is not clear it is accurate.

Christians can look on such passages and see that Jesus was more than a twinkle in God's eye centuries before he was born. And he comes for a nation, a people as a whole, and not just for the individuals who make it up.

The name given to him, The LORD Our Righteousness, takes Christian readers to the new nature bestowed and renewed by Christ (Colossians 3:5-11). He appeals to God the Father on our behalf; he expects us to live up to his name. The Righteous Branch has become the vine, of which we are now the branches (John 15).

Long-term signs of hope and forgiveness

Jeremiah 24:1-25:14

A parent who punishes a child for some wilful misbehaviour knows that the punishment will not last for ever, although the child may have other ideas. Love does not destroy; it disciplines.

And God is love (1 John 4:16). His righteous indignation at the way his children wilfully flout his spiritual health and safety regulations does not drive him to obliterate them from his memory. He looks instead for ways in which to coax them back, and creates opportunities for their rehabilitation.

This note of long-term hope is sounded all through Jeremiah. 'Return and I will have mercy on you' (3:12-18); 'reform your ways and I will let you live here' (7:3; cf. 15:19; 16:15); 'after I uproot them I will again have compassion and will bring them back' (12:15); 'I will gather the remnant of my flock' (23:3).

Here, however, Jeremiah is more specific. The tragedy for Zedekiah is that the king is such a bad fig that he is to be consigned to the compost heap of history through sheer weakness and incompetence.

The good news for people who accept God's word is that they, or in many cases their descendants, will return home after the inevitable exile in Babylon. Then, they will have a new start with God (24:6,7). Further, despite being God's instrument to teach Judah a lesson, the Babylonians will pay the price for enslaving it (25:12-14). No one touches God's holy people without ultimate sanction.

This is an important balance. God makes positive use of godless people acting on their own free and selfish choice. He withdraws his protection from Judah so that it collapses to 'my servant Nebuchadnezzar', but he does not guarantee the temporary victor immunity from prosecution.

God can make use of any and every person and situation to achieve his purposes without denying his holiness or their human freedom. Zedekiah couldn't accept that, so he opted for the pragmatic solution of making a defiant last stand instead of faithful and humble submission.

But God is not angry for ever (Psalm 103:9), even if the discipline is not commuted. Good will come from it, if not in our lifetime then in that of our children. There is more to life than our personal stay on earth.

Opposite reactions end in life and death

Jeremiah 26

This narrative should be read slowly in a quiet place. It displays the two faces of human nature which we may encounter at any time.

One is the face of good will. Jeremiah has some friends in unexpected places. There is a residue of respect for Judah's traditional faith among some members of Jehoiakim's court, and a belief in natural justice and free speech. So some secular officials countermand the religious leaders' call for Jeremiah's execution.

Not all is bad or corrupt in secular society. There are many people of goodwill who may, for whatever reasons, support what the church stands for and may even be wiser than its leaders.

But Jehoiakim is not pleased. This despotic king (see his sneering indifference even to common decency in ch 36) hounds a lesser prophet to his death. He cannot kill Jeremiah; the publicity would be adverse. But he can send a hit team to Egypt to take out a little back-street preacher with a small congregation whose message happens to be the same as Jeremiah's.

Uriah stands as a testimony to an ordinary man's faithfulness in dire times. He puts our frequent compromises to shame. Jeremiah must have been awed by this, too; someone died in his place.

Don't let the city go to seed

Jeremiah 29

Urban deprivation is a major issue in many Western countries. Some inner-city areas become no-go areas for the police. Politicians seem to lack the will to address the problems which keep people at the bottom of the pile; there are more vote-catching and money-making activities to occupy their time.

The exiles had the needs of the city of Babylon low on their agendas, too, especially when their captors tormented them with laddish gibes: 'Sing us one of your folk songs, stranger!' (Psalm 137). Thoughts in such situations turn to survival and escape, not to good citizenship.

Jeremiah, however, tells the exiles to put their roots down, to get a life in Babylon and, moreover, to contribute to its economy and well-being. They are to opt in to society, not opt out of it. They are to improve it, not undermine it. They are destined to be there for a long time; the city's welfare is therefore their welfare, too.

In New Testament imagery, Christians are also 'exiles', called to live exemplary lives seeking the welfare of a world which does not put God or righteousness at the top of its agenda (1 Peter 2:11, 12). Indeed, to do so is a commanded application of discipleship (Matthew 5:13; Romans 13:1-7).

We remain in our 'Babylon' for '70 years' – an average lifetime – just as the exiles did. We are called as they were, to make it a good place to live in for everyone; to build community and to care for the needy; to increase its (not just our) prosperity. It is part of building the kingdom of God, for all things that exist come within the scope of his redemption (Colossians 1:20).

Book of consolation opened for exiles of north and south

Jeremiah 30, 31

Sometimes called 'The book of consolation', these chapters look forward to the restoration of both Israel (the northern kingdom) and Judah in a new united kingdom.

There are several references to the former northern kingdom, which was destroyed by the Assyrians in 722, a century before Jeremiah. For example, 31:15, quoted in relation to Herod's infanticide in Matthew 2:18, refers to Jacob's wife Rachel's grandchildren Manasseh and Ephraim, the strongest of the northern tribes. Israel is often called 'Ephraim' by the prophets.

Many northerners had not been exiled and some went south for Jewish festivals organised by Hezekiah (2 Chronicles 30:1-31:1) and Josiah (2 Chronicles 35:17-19). Although some Israelites intermarried (for which the Samaritans were outcast), unity had been partly achieved by New Testament times.

During the exile, the scribes developed Jewish teaching, drew together the Scriptures and laid the foundations of the synagogue movement.

These chapters have Messianic implications (the new covenant of 31:31 was inaugurated by Christ's death and resurrection, Luke 22:20). So it is tempting for us to focus only on these and forget the historical fulfilment, but that would be to miss half the truth.

In contemplating their historic fulfilment, we may gain hope for ourselves. When we suffer for our sinfulness, we can also be assured that God will restore the penitent in due time. His love is everlasting, still (31:3).

The historical re-union and religious development reminds us that God keeps his word. His promises are fulfilled on a rolling basis from generation to generation. Christ comes to complete what has already begun and to bring a fresh dimension to it. When we appreciate this we can take the 'spiritual' teaching of these chapters and apply it to our personal and church lives today (see box).

Faith steps in where logic fears to tread

Jeremiah 32

The Babylonian army camped on the hills surrounding Jerusalem, harassing travellers, menacing the city dwellers looking anxiously from the ramparts, would have been a fearsome sight. Surely Hanamel wasn't alone in cashing in his capital assets! Silver he could carry; fields he risked losing.

Jeremiah's actions seemed madness. He was either a property speculator, hoping to make a profit when things got better, or he was a man of extreme faith. He was buying land which according to his own prophecy would fall into Babylonian hands.

It is of course another acted parable. It offered assurance that the exiles would return and that the Promised Land would be theirs again. Acts of faith which presuppose an unlikely outcome are hard to exercise.

Beginning a church development or expansion project when the resources are not yet pledged can be difficult. It is not always right, either. Some steps of 'faith' are foolhardiness that is not sanctioned by God; he does not always promise to bail out his people. His promises have to be validated locally by prayer and soul searching before being applied to our schemes.

But there does come a time when we have to make the first move. Faith ceases to be such if we always insist on waiting for sight.

Jeremiah's vision of the 'new Israel'

Jeremiah 30,31

A redeemed people (30:10,18-22; 31:10-12)
An exile is anyone who is separated from where they belong. Some Christians are exiled through sin or circumstance from effective Christian service and discipleship. There is a way back to God, says Jeremiah.

A remembered people (31:3)
God does not forget his people even when they are ineffective or sinful. Like the father of the prodigal son, his thoughts are always with them and he longs to draw them back into a fruitful relationship.

A refreshed people (30:17; 31:7-14)
The familiar Old Testament themes of joyful celebration, irrigated fields and material prosperity evoke feelings of relief, leisure and restoration. There is a time to relax, to enjoy the good things of God and his world.

A responsible people (31:27-34)
A new note enters the Old Testament revelation, repeated by Jeremiah's contemporary Ezekiel (ch 18; 33:1-20). Until now, the emphasis has been on corporate unity and responsibility. Here the biblical view focuses on the individual as a part of the united people of God, a perspective which will be amplified further in the New Testament.

For today

- Trust God to get his callings right
- The gods of this age are disguised by attractive wrappers
- False religion can damage your spiritual health
- Be prepared to stand out from the crowd, but do so graciously
- If you are called to preach or teach, find graphic ways to reinforce your message
- Remember that discipleship includes 'seeking the welfare of the (godless) city'
- Keep God's long-term agenda in your sights; it continues after you have gone

Epilogue to a sad but heroic life

Jeremiah 40-44

Jeremiah was spared exile in Babylon because of his constant message to submit. But in a deeply ironic twist, he was forcibly taken to exile in Egypt by rebels he had criticised. Defiant to the last, he repeats his message that Egypt is no place to be, and that the old ally cannot restore Judah's fortunes.

His capture might have broken a lesser man, especially after all he had suffered for upwards of 40 years. But he accepts it, and works through it. We assume he died in Tahpenes; nothing more is heard of him after these prophecies. His dogged faithfulness in the face of intense pressure and personal sensitivity made him a spiritual giant. He wasn't special; he was one of us. Therefore what he did, we could do, too.

Consistency is next to godliness

Jeremiah 34,35

In Jesus' parable of the talents, it was faithfulness over small things that qualified people for greater responsibility (Matthew 25:14-30). It has always been thus. Promotion is won on merit; experience equips us for greater challenges.

These chapters contain two opposite examples of trustworthiness. The slave owners who go back on their word (34:8-22) without rebuke from Zedekiah are the last straw for God. To obey the law, to be generous to others, and then to rescind the decision is worse than not having made it in the first place.

The slave owners had not counted the cost. But true discipleship accepts that there is a cost to obedience, and accepts it gracefully. We are not to give grudgingly.

The Recabites were just the opposite. They were faithful to a discipline which was not strictly necessary. Today they might even be regarded as a cult. But like many cults, while their extreme practices might not be biblically required, their faithfulness was exemplary and put others to shame.

People today look for churches and individuals who can demonstrate that they really believe what they say. If Christ is Lord, then there should be outward evidence of the fact. We should not return to a form of Pharisaism, a legalism which defines orthodoxy by customs. But discipline in consumption and in sharing, in putting other people's needs before our own, will be a powerful witness.

How not to be a leader

Jeremiah 37-39

Former British Foreign Secretary Douglas Hurd once said that 'good leadership is, 1) the ability to define an aim; 2) the persistence and courage to follow it; 3) the persuasiveness to bring others with you in the necessary 'coalition of the willing'. Zedekiah fails on all three counts.

The king cannot bring himself to define the aim Jeremiah suggests; kings fight, they do not submit. His secret meetings with the prophet suggest that he knows Jeremiah is right, but he doesn't have the courage to over-rule his advisers. 38:5 is the dismal epitaph of a weak king who could not lead.

He even had to beg Jeremiah to lie (38:24-27), which he did. Jeremiah had no mandate to provide ammunition to Zedekiah's wrong advisers, and he lived before the era of cheque-book journalism and strategic 'leaks'.

Zedekiah's last sight on earth, before being blinded, of his sons being butchered, must have haunted him until death. We cannot help feeling sorry for him. He was forced to be king by Nebuchadnezzar; had he remained a yes man to the conqueror he might have lived to see happier days. As it was, he did what many of us do: he tried to act a part he was not cast for, and he fouled it up. Better to obey the Lord, even when the instructions make us vulnerable.

Zedekiah even failed himself. His pathetic shrug in 38:5, consigning his spiritual adviser to probable death, is despicable. He hadn't even the decency of Judah who half-rescued Joseph (Genesis 37:26,27). Sadly, he was more willing to sacrifice a person than his pride.

Advice for when your boss is feeling low

Jeremiah 45

Boredom has reached epidemic proportions in the West. It is one of the factors which promote petty crime, mindless vandalism and recreational drug taking. Boredom is not being satisfied with what we have and who we are.

And Baruch is bored. He's fed up with being the writer of Jeremiah's gloomy predictions. He's tired of working for a boss whom nobody likes. He reckons he deserves better than this.

God's stern warning tells him not to consider his present role of service beneath him. Baruch is not to look for a better job, better pay and more exciting work for a less gloomy employer. He is to remain faithful and consistent.

There is a difficult balance to strike between stretching ourselves to make the best use of our gifts, perhaps by seeking promotion or applying for other jobs, and being content with doing a good job well but lacking the status and rewards which something higher up the scale would bring.

In some careers, teaching for example, people can even be looked down upon if they are not actively seeking promotion at certain stages. That someone can be content with doing the same thing is a mystery to others!

Baruch is to stay put. He does so with the touching reassurance that God will protect him. It's not a brilliant job, and the flak aimed at Jeremiah no doubt ricocheted onto him. His desire is understandable but wrong. As the wise man said, 'Better a little with the fear of the LORD than great wealth with turmoil' (Proverbs 15:16).

A long chapter closes

Jeremiah 46-51

There is little in these chapters to inspire modern readers. But don't turn over! Although full of destruction, they tie together some historical and theological ends.

This catalogue of prophecies against nations which at various times had been enemies of Israel and Judah told the original readers that God has acted, or was about to act, on their behalf.

In other words, God hadn't changed. The one who triumphed over the Egyptians at the exodus will triumph over later oppressors also. God is coming to rescue his people once again. Justice is being seen to be done.

From a Christian standpoint, it is not the way we expect justice to be seen. Ordinary people are killed for the sins of their leaders or their forefathers. But the Old Testament revelation focused on the corporate solidarity of nations and groups. So the conclusion of Jeremiah gives to Old Testament readers the conclusion of a chapter in their history.

From now on the plot changes. In chapter 31 Jeremiah introduces a note of personal responsibility into the drama. Religion is now set to become more directly personal, without losing its corporate dimension. (In the New Testament, personal faith and membership of the corporate 'body of Christ', the church, are inseparable.)

So we're ready to move on to the New Testament story. Yet it is still 500 years away! Progress continues to be slow, but the first steps of a giant leap of faith began when the Jews were exiled to Babylon.

God closes chapters for us, too. There are times when we must move forward. The past may be murky or memorable. The future beckons, every day.

Half truths double the trouble

The Book of Job
- Explores the problem of why good people suffer
- Tells of a respected man, Job, who suddenly loses everything
- Records discussions between him and others who assume it's all his fault
- Shows how God reveals himself as majestic and inscrutable, and how Job is restored

Few people get through life without at some stage suffering ill health or experiencing tragedy which is genuinely no fault of their own. It's just one of those things; they are afflicted by 'the slings and arrows of outrageous fortune'.

Yet invariably we ask, 'What have I done to deserve this? Why has God allowed it to happen to me?' The unfairness of it all is made worse when we see others whose indulgent lifestyles, immorality and even lawless behaviour seem part of a charmed life which brings them health, wealth and happiness.

Such is the setting of Job, but Bible readers devouring its magnificent poetry to discover an answer to the age-old question will emerge from it disappointed, although wiser. The book does not answer the question, 'Why?' It suggests, in fact, that this is not the right question to be asking.

Its chief point is nothing to do with Job, but his friends. Their often quotable speeches are full of half-truths. These men are neither heretics nor extremists. They live and speak within the limits of their own cultural and spiritual understanding. But they are spiritually blind, and unreliable guides.

Their half-truths only add to Job's misery because they neither point him towards a positive answer nor offer him sensitive pastoral support. Job is a book for anyone who knows a suffering person: learn how not to help your friend.

After his outpourings and their platitudes, helped along by the youthful but also misguided fourth debater, Elihu, the book turns to face God. In a superb broad canvas survey of creation, God is revealed as great, just and inscrutable.

Humbled by him, we see that our questions cannot be answered because we see things from the wrong perspective. Instead, we are encouraged to press on in faithful discipleship in a world which is harassed by Satan. Our exploration of God is not to be restricted to half-truths, but to trust that he is just and perfect, and that our suffering is not a sign of his personal displeasure of us.

Like the book of Esther, this is one to read in large chunks rather than in small portions.

I have heard many things like these; miserable comforters are you all!

Job 16:2

JOB: THE DEBATE AT A GLANCE

1,2	Prologue: Everything goes wrong for Job as Satan buffets him with God's permission
3	Job: I curse the day I was born!
4,5	Eliphaz: God corrects people for their wrong doing.
6,7	Job: You're no help; show me where I'm wrong. Why doesn't God forgive and let me be?
8	Bildad: You're talking nonsense. God doesn't afflict the righteous because he's just.
9,10	Job: How can a man be righteous before God? How can I question my creator? I need a mediator – and I wish I'd never been born.
11	Zophar: Put away your sin and you'll get better.
12-14	Job: I know all this; you're no help. Why can't I talk directly to God? Let me know my sin; people are so frail.
15	Eliphaz: You're denying what everyone knows: no one is perfect. People suffer most when they shake their fists at God.
16,17	Job: God tears my flesh; people tear my heart; I'm a broken man. What's the point of admitting what isn't true? Haven't you got a better answer?
18	Bildad: Don't treat us as stupid! Look at the facts: wicked people get snuffed out. Period.
19	Job: Shut up! If I sinned, that's my affair, not yours. I've been wronged, and now even my friends turn against me. One day, I'll be proved right by God himself.
20	Zophar: Your rebuke dishonours us. Ever since the world began proud people have perished.
21	Job: Then why do the wicked prosper? How often in fact do they actually get their just deserts?
22	Eliphaz: God doesn't rebuke people for being good, does he? Face up to your failings, man! Humble yourself before God and he'll restore you.
23,24	Job: If only I could find God and argue my case. He wouldn't convict me. I've done right, yet his oppression terrifies me while the wicked get away with murder.
25	Bildad: God is great; we're just maggots. You can't be righteous.
26	Job: (–31): A fat lot of good you are. Of course God is great.
27	I'll never deny my integrity. And we all know the wicked are hated by God.
28	There are mines for metal but where is wisdom to be dug from? Only from the fear of the Lord.
29,30	I long for the days when God was my close friend and people respected me. Now people scorn me and take advantage of me and God doesn't answer my prayers and treats me badly.
31	God sees all my ways. I've covenanted not to sin against him in thought or deed.
32,33	Elihu (–37): You oldies haven't refuted Job, so listen to me. God speaks in many ways to show up our errors.
34,35	God can do no wrong, and shows no partiality. He takes no notice of empty pleas.
36,37	However, God doesn't despise people either. If we listen to him we'll prosper, if we don't we'll perish. He's beyond understanding, so revere him.
38	God (–41): Where were you (all) when I made the earth? What do you know of how it is ordered?
39	Look at the animals: their strength and freedom. Can you match even that?
40	God: Did you accuse me of something? Job: How can I? I'll keep quiet.
40,41	God: Do you really think I'm unjust? Look at the monster creatures: you can't control them, but I can; I'm so much bigger than you imagine.
42	Job: Sorry. You are great. I know you now in a way I didn't before. Epilogue: Job is ordered to pray for his friends who had displeased God by their words, and then he finds his fortunes are restored.

Date of events:
Unknown but probably ancient (see Fast Facts)

Place in Bible:
After Esther, before Psalms in the Old Testament

Biblical parallels:
Associated with the 'wisdom' books of Proverbs, Ecclesiastes and Song of Songs, but is unique in biblical literature.

HARD Question

God and Satan: a gentleman's agreement?

Job 1,2

Readers new to Bible study could assume from this passage that God and Satan have regular board meetings for the governance of the world. There, the mischievous (or callous) Chairman plays devil's advocate by suggesting to his junior director that he should make a few social experiments which the Chairman knows will fail.

Readers familiar with ancient mythology might even think that this is no more than a sophisticated version of stories in which good and bad gods play games with men's lives.

Therefore we are thrown back at once onto two fundamental principles of biblical interpretation. One is that what is presented as reportage may be a picture intended to be read as figurative; the other is that scripture should be interpreted by scripture.

Exploring the wider biblical teaching about Satan, we find three basic ideas:

1. Satan is a fallen angel (sometimes described as a prince, as in Matthew 12:24). That is, he is a created being who is less powerful than God (not equal and opposite) who through pride or jealousy was ejected from God's presence (cf. Isaiah 14:12-15; Luke 10:18).

2. Satan is implacably opposed to God's work and people. He is an enemy who wishes to devour them (1 Peter 5:8; the word 'Satan' is used in the Old Testament for military adversaries as in 1 Kings 11:14,23); an accuser of sinners whom God has forgiven (Revelation 12:10); a compulsive liar (John 8:44) and a cunning deceiver (2 Corinthians 11:14); who has such a strong grip on those parts of human society which do not honour God that he is called 'the ruler of this world' (John 12:31; 2 Corinthians 4:4).

3. Satan's power is severely restricted by Jesus in this life (John 12:31) and he is already condemned (John 16:11). He was overthrown at Calvary (Colossians 2:15) and will be destroyed at the last judgment (Revelation 20:10). Meanwhile Christians face a spiritual battle against him for which they are equipped by God (Ephesians 6:10-18).

Therefore, the picture in Job 1 cannot be interpreted as jovial fraternity. There is no gentleman's agreement to have a little sport and Satan does not have access to God's counsel. Job's picture is figurative, and tells us two things about 'spiritual warfare':

- God protects his people from Satan's worst excesses. God is not testing Job for fun; he is stopping him from getting killed although not preventing him from having a bad time.
- In an imperfect world there are vagaries which God does not always prohibit. (See feature on suffering, page 196.)

However, the real point of these chapters is not to tell us anything about Satan at all! Their purpose is to pose a question which is crucial for any believer: do you trust and serve God because he gives you a good time, or do you trust and serve him solely because he is God even if life is hell?

Satan's accusation is that Job serves God because he feels he is on to a good thing. God's confidence is that Job's faith is real. The prologue figuratively launches us into a debate about a specific theological view held at the time of writing. But today we can empathise with Job's heartfelt agonies as his patience is stretched to its limits. Because although we now have a fuller theological perspective, the same old question just won't go away.

I wish I'd never been born!

Job 3,10

Job's tragedies plunge him, as they would plunge most people, into a pit of despair. We accept that life is not straightforward and has its setbacks. But when everything we have lived and worked for is smashed, then the question of whether life is worth living emerges.

Notice in these outpourings that the author does not offer any editorial platitudes. Platitudes are useless; Job is being real. He is in pain, and we are meant to hear his inner despair and grieve with him. We have no answers either: we cannot say, of course we know . . .

When tragedy strikes, Christians are sometimes forced into false piety. Occasionally people do receive supernatural grace to soar above their problems. But for most of us, the tragic situations are crushing, suffocating and meaningless. The sun goes out and a deep chill freezes the heart and paralyses the mind.

Even Paul experienced that; he survived, but only as one who was 'raised from the dead' (2 Corinthians 1:8-11).

If you have never been there, thank God for belonging to a fortunate minority. If you know someone who is there, Job may put into words what they are feeling just now better than they can themselves. Listen to him, then listen to them.

FAST facts

Literary genre: With the possible exception of some passages in the latter sections of Isaiah, Job includes by far the most eloquent poetry in the Bible. The book is carefully constructed as a narrative poem with a prose prologue and epilogue, and is not merely a report of a conversation among friends. It is categorised as wisdom literature but is unlike other biblical wisdom books which are mostly pithy observations or snippets of advice.

'The book of Job is an astonishing mix of almost every kind of literature to be found in the Old Testament. Many individual pieces can be isolated and identified as proverbs, riddles, hymns, laments, curses, lyrical nature poems' (F.I. Andersen, *Job,* Tyndale Old Testament Commentary).

Author and date: Although Jewish tradition ascribes this book to Moses, the author is unknown and the possible dates range from Moses' time (c. 1300 BC) to the Greek period between the Testaments (c. 200 BC). The Hebrew style is difficult and it is not possible to date the book by its vocabulary (Bible versions may vary considerably as they struggle to put obscure terms into meaningful language). Many scholars would guess that it was produced in the time of David or Solomon (i.e. after about 1000 BC).

Sources and parallels: Many cultures have stories about people who suffer as a test and explore the justice of it, but there the resemblances end. The literary debating style of Job is more common, however. No outside sources for the parts of the book can be identified, although it is suggested that the Elihu speeches were a separate section added later. Scholars differ over whether the book evolved over a long time through oral (and textual) transmission, or if it was compiled by one person substantially as we have it now.

Chief character and setting: The name 'Job' appears to have meant at one time 'Where is my father?' – an apt title for Job's spiritual distress. He is regarded as a historical person by Ezekiel (14:14,20) and James (5:11). The story appears to be set outside Israel, probably to the east.

Please don't prattle – you don't understand!'

Job 6,12,16,19

What many people today want more than anything is someone to listen to them. Loneliness fills doctors' surgeries, jams chat lines and keeps the Internet profitable. God made humans for community and we have isolated each other.

Job in his deep distress needs people to listen to him. He needs the comfort and support of knowing that there is someone beside him who cares about him. He needs a friend.

And, like long-awaited buses, three turn up at once. Job is a lucky man. They even do the right thing. They sit with him for a week and say nothing (2:11-13). They offer no glib explanations, no empty words of hope. They just offer themselves.

That is what he needed, and what countless others in similar circumstances need also. But then the friends spoiled it. They opened their mouths and prattled out of ignorance and perhaps insecurity. In effect, they tell him that his plight is his own fault.

Some Christians will do that. After initial empathy they will suggest that if you prayed more extensively and believed more fervently things would get better. They understand neither God nor man.

Job rebukes his 'friends' (miserable comforters, 16:2) and all who let their embarrassment or thoughtlessness rule their tongues. He doesn't find it merely of no help (6:21); it discourages him further, and drives him deeper into despair (12:2-6).

Why do we always want to solve other people's problems for them? It can be a sign of our pride. We may be given by God a word in season for

God can cope

Job 9,10,12,23,24

Many people react to suffering by shaking a fist at God to curse him for their misfortune. Job resists the urge (2:9,10), but he does make a list of questions for God. God, he feels, is too great to challenge (9:14-20, a passage with deep spiritual insight), and people cannot speak on his behalf (13:3-12).

Suffering Christians need not be afraid of having debates with God nor of hurling questions at him. After all, Jesus did on the cross (Matthew 27:46), and the man of sorrows is familiar with suffering (Isaiah 53:3).

It is natural to want explanations of what is happening, even if in our quieter moments we know that we could never fathom them anyway. Often, such 'debate' with God is the only form of prayer the sufferer is capable of other than the simple cry for help. It may even be therapeutic, part of the fighting that is essential to recovery.

Job, however, has another problem which faces many sufferers. Just when he needs God, the Almighty seems to be on holiday: 'If only I knew where to find him' (23:3).

The familiar truths of the gospel, the comfort of the sacraments and the inspiration of Scripture reading may lose their power to encourage, if we can focus on them at all. This is not a sign of spiritual 'backsliding'. Our vision has been clouded by external events; we cannot expect to see clearly. (We cannot see clearly even at the best of times; cf. 1 Corinthians 13:12.)

But God can see. He is there. And he cares. All the while you shout at him, you are keeping the communication channels open. Mayday calls never contain much information

A mind-blowing God

Job 38-41

'Despair is the price one pays for setting oneself an impossible aim,' Graham Greene writes in his novel *The Heart of the Matter*. Job's sin, if that is what it is, has been to set himself the impossible aim of understanding God's ways.

Image after image displays the magnificence of creation, the munificence of the Creator, and the minuteness of the creature called man. If you can't hold all that in your little brain, says God, how can you possibly understand the even more complex structures of mankind's affairs, including yours?

So there is no answer to poor Job's agonised questions, nor to ours. The Christian life is one of faith and trust, not sight and knowledge. But underneath this grand poem, there is a hint, a murmur of comfort.

For Job, for modern Moslems, and even for many Christians in practice although not in creed, whatever happens is God's imposed will. Such a fatalistic world view is not how the Bible writers see things.

God has made physical processes which operate in their own way under his overall management. He has endowed humans with freedom which they use for good and ill; they are not puppets on his string. God is gloriously free, and a master of what looks to us like improvisation. He can use anything to teach and assist his people and to bring others to faith.

Within his plans there is room for the variety which comes from the free use of human creativity and responsibility; within his purposes the vagaries of suffering, which may originate from malicious and ungodly sources, can be woven into some good outcome.

Rough and smooth, good and bad are swallowed up by something unimaginably splendid which at present is hidden from our eyes. We cannot begin to measure his wisdom, or to guess what he has in store for faithful souls like Job whom he loves. All we know now is that 'the best is yet to be' (Browning). In the final analysis, Job is not so much about the mystery of suffering as about the magnificence of God in whose light all mysteries will one day disappear like shadows.

I know I'm right – it's not fair

Job 21,27

Few Christians would dare tell God that they've done nothing to justify his displeasure. A Christian reaction to the contemporary cult of 'I'm OK, you're OK' is to say that theologically, we're not. We fall short of God's perfect standard.

Job seems very self-righteous when he asserts 'I will not deny my integrity' (27:5). The really wicked prosper while he falls apart (21:6-34).

Self-delusion can be a horrid thing. Believers know they have no call on God's mercy except through Christ's grace. Job is not 'humble', but neither is he deceived. He does have a clear conscience. He knows that before God he is nothing, yet he has also done what he should.

God does not have a downer on every believer; he loves and encourages us in our often faltering and imperfect steps. We fail, but not for want of trying, and he understands. Christian traditions which so wallow in human sinfulness that they heap guilt onto redeemed shoulders are in biblical terms false gospels.

Paul had a clear conscience (2 Corinthians 12:11-13,16-18) but he was never complacent (Philippians 3:13,14). Our sins are forgiven; we are to thank God for that and move forward in his strength.

Job's real problem is that life isn't fair. As in a game of cards good and faithful players get bad hands. It's just part of the deal.

A mystery investigated but unsolved

Why does a plane plunge from the sky, cancer devour a living person like a hungry werewolf, and rain fail in one place and flood another, causing famine in both? Why are children orphaned by bullets and pensioners robbed by thugs? And why did Judas betray justice, David divorce virtue, and Peter deny truth?

Suffering sneers at us, defying explanation and attacking indiscriminately. Usually, it's someone else's problem and therefore something to debate, but when it becomes our problem it really hurts.

Previous generations have been more philosophical about it, because they saw physical suffering as inevitable and without an answer. Today, however, with our ambulances, well-equipped hospitals and powerful drugs we expect not only answers to our questions but also quick solutions to our needs. And if we don't get better, we can always sue someone.

We neither expect to suffer at all nor to suffer long if the unthinkable happens. We are ill-equipped to deal with life's vagaries and tragedies.

The Bible, written and produced in a pre-modern society, is tantalisingly vague in its response to this issue. Apart from the book of Job (and to a lesser extent the prophets Habakkuk and Jeremiah) the subject is addressed only in passing.

But one truth rises above all others, and that is the denial of the initial idea of Job and his friends, that in this world the wicked always perish while the righteous always profit. (See the section on the Psalms for a discussion of this.) That belief was common in Old Testament times, and modern readers have to approach some passages (including many of the psalms) with a degree of caution.

For Jesus and Job suffering may be, but is not necessarily, a punishment for sin. Twice Jesus denied the simple equation that sin plus God's reaction equals human pain (see Luke 13:1-5 and John 9:1-3). At this point three realities emerge from the Scriptures.

1. An imperfect world

No one denies that the physical world is imperfect now. Matter decays; life dies. Machines wear out and break down, sometimes with disastrous consequences. The age-old formative processes of the earth, its earthquakes, winds and floods, continue like eternal sculptors to carve the terrain into varied shapes, and sometimes people fall victim to their unpredictable surges.

Insurers may label such events as 'acts of God' but there is nothing in the Bible to suggest that God is capricious or that the frequent victims of floods in Bangladesh are more wicked than the infrequent victims of floods in Belgium.

The Israelites did interpret some natural disasters and wars as God's interventions, both on their behalf and against them. But there is nothing to suggest that all such events should be thus interpreted. Prophetic insight made connections assisted by the guilty consciences of foolish sinners or the grateful hearts of hard-pressed believers who had been praying for a miracle.

Much suffering is human-inspired. The Bible is full of stories of people who wreak havoc. There are probably more murders in the Bible than would be reported in a supply of Western newspapers of comparable length.

The origin of suffering and evil is found in the story of Adam and Eve, suggesting that since mankind lost its perfect relationship with God everything it has touched has been tarnished and corrupted (cf. Genesis 3:16-24).

All have sinned, and hence deserve God's judgment (cf. Romans 3:23; 6:23). In that sense it is a wonder that we do not suffer more. It is a mark of God's grace that beauty, peace, love and pleasure still thrive so much that believers and unbelievers alike feel their loss acutely.

2. A caring God

From the moment Cain whines that his punishment for murder – becoming a rootless wanderer and a target for violence – is too great to bear, God has shown kindness to those who suffer even when (as in Cain's case) they may be deemed to deserve it (Genesis 4:13-16).

People at the bottom of the social pile (widows and orphans) are singled out for special concern (Deuteronomy 10:17,18). God is a God of compassion who understands human frailty and does not reward us according to our just deserts (Psalm 103:8-14).

Jesus offers rest to people who are burdened by life's cares and woes (Matthew 11:28-30). He reassures Paul that despite his unspecified physical disability God's work is not hindered and may indeed become more powerful, because the disability forces the apostle to lean harder on his Lord (2 Corinthians 12:7-10).

Time and again the promise of forgiveness and new life is made (e.g. 1 John 1:8-10) but never with any suggestion that the arrows of misfortune will now turn to paper darts. That would be to disturb the natural ordering of a fallen and imperfect world which God cares for but has not yet restored to its perfection. Such restoration will indeed be the end of the world as we know it.

Until that longed-for time, we are encouraged by one supreme fact: God himself has suffered horrendously. The catalogue of Jesus' sufferings in Isaiah 53 covers almost the whole of the human experience of pain. When we suffer, he feels it too, and offers special comfort (2 Corinthians 1:3-5).

3. A rough path

Living for God has its own problems. It is not always easy, and can bring upon disciples burdens in addition to those normally experienced by others. Jesus warned potential disciples to count the cost (Luke 14:15-25) and told them that they could expect troubles with their blessings (Mark 10:29,30; John 15:18-25; 16:33).

As we encourage people to walk in God's way and to submit to him in faith and trust, we are failing in our responsibility if we do not also point out that it is a narrow and difficult path (Matthew 7:13,14).

It is not impossible; the Holy Spirit is there to assist and empower. But it can feel hard. When we suffer in body or mind, we are to pray and call others to pray for healing (James 5:10-16). At the same time we are to accept all forms of suffering creatively as a means by which we can grow closer to God (Hebrews 12:5-13).

Furthermore, as Jesus had compassion on sufferers, so should we. Caring for one another up to the limit is a fundamental task of discipleship, because it reflects God's great love (see John 15:12,13; Romans 12:12,13; 15:1; 1 Thessalonians 5:14,15). Caring for others relieves one's own pain and being cared for cheers the heart.

Are natural disasters sent by God?

HARD Question

The Book of Joel

- Uses a real locust plauge as a warning of God's judgment
- Calls on readers to turn to God in their hearts, not just with rituals
- Promises the outpouring of the Holy Spirit

Joel 1:1-2:17

Swarms of locusts, possibly triggered by climatic changes, have regularly devastated the Near East. They consume every green shoot and leave nothing but famine. Joel says this is God's warning to the nation that something worse is to follow (2:2). He does not blame specific sins apart from allusions to drunkenness and materialism in 1:5 and sexual licence in 1:8.

In the Old Testament natural disasters and political oppression are seen as warnings or punishments from God on an errant Israel and Judah. But they were also part of everyday life. It is the prophetic function to interpret such historical events as conveying messages from God – which is not the same notion as the caricature of God disrupting his world by raining down vengeance.

Four things need to be held in balance. First, natural disasters are a fact of life in an imperfect world. Although phenomena as global warming contribute to destabilising the planet, natural disasters have afflicted people for centuries. Christians point additionally to 'the fall' (Genesis 3) which threw the created order out of perfect alignment (cf. Romans 8:22).

Secondly, Jesus explicitly ruled out the view that accidents of nature are punishments of those involved (Luke 13:1-5). Thirdly, Judah and Israel had a unique relationship with God; they formed a political, cultural and spiritual unit called to be his 'chosen people'. His dealings with them cannot be transposed directly to other nations. And finally, the Bible reminds us that God is a judge. Disasters alert us to our mortality and the certainty that we shall each appear before God for personal judgment.

In 1998, a hurricane in Honduras and earthquake in Afghanistan each killed 9,000. A cyclone in India killed 10,000. In 1999 a record wind speed of over 300 mph was registered above a tornado in the USA. Our proper reaction is not to look for 'reasons' but to turn to God, as there could be worse in store: an eternity excluded from his presence, which the Bible calls hell.

JOEL

This little book has an importance out of all proportion to its length. It takes a literal plague of locusts in Judah as a basis for prophecies about 'the day of the Lord'.

Some commentators see the swarm as an allegory for, or a literal forewarning of, the invasion of Judah by Babylon or other aggressors. However, the simplest interpretation is that Joel takes the literal disaster as a general warning of worse to come.

The second half offers a promise or renewal and restoration after repentance, and was quoted by Peter on the day of Pentecost (Acts 2).

Rend your heart and not your garments. Return to the LORD your God, for he is gracious and compassionate.

Joel 2:13

Religious structure has its place

Joel 1:13,14; 2:12-17

Joel calls for a return to the organised religious structures of the temple, while stressing the need for personal and heart-felt repentance by all. The formal structures of religion provided the Judeans with a framework for expressing their faith. Worship in the New Testament also has structure and order; the chaos of Corinth was not typical of most Christian churches, nor was it commended.

In our time, the law of entropy (everything tends towards disintegration) seems to grip both social and spiritual life. Structures are for breaking rather than preserving, except in the minds of those dismissed by the majority as 'reactionary'.

But the rhythm of the church year with its regular cycle of seasons and festivals can keep us mindful of the important truths of the faith and lend shape and awe to our lives.

Patterns of weekly worship which regularly include penitence, praise, adoration (and silence), declaration of faith, reading of Scripture, intercession, the teaching of God's Word and the memorial of the Lord's Supper can restore the balance of spiritual harmony which life in the community erases.

This need not be strongly 'liturgical', although many find familiar words helpful in times of stress. Flexibility unites structure and freedom; rigidity is being dominated by either. God brought order out of chaos (Genesis 1); and his church can testify to the value of order rather than mimic the chaotic world from which many look for escape.

Dark days forecast

Joel 1:15; 2:1,2

'The day of the Lord' was a common prophetic image. It refers to a cataclysmic manifestation of God and is generally portrayed as the day when Israel finally triumphs over its enemies. It is surrounded by figurative images of fires (Isaiah 10:16), storms (Isaiah (28:2) and cosmic collapse (Isaiah 2:10,19). It is the Old Testament equivalent of the New Testament's 'day of judgment'.

The Judeans in Joel's time did not consider that they too would be subject to judgment; the day of the Lord was to them simply the nemesis of the nations. Joel denies that; they too will be judged.

The New Testament agrees. Judgment begins with the household of God (1 Peter 4:17). Those who shelter under the umbrella of the church will not escape the storm. The outcome for Christians may be certain but many – if not all – will be saved only as 'escaping through the flames' (1 Corinthians 3:15).

Such teaching is not meant to frighten us into submission to God. It should encourage us to remain faithful and to warn us that careless lives contradict God's calling. Obedience may be joyful because it ultimately fulfils God's purposes and our potential.

Location:
Judah (the southern kingdom)
Date:
Uncertain; between 600 and 200 BC
Place in Bible:
The second of the minor prophets in the Old Testament, after Hosea and before Amos.

Author: Joel is unknown outside this book.

Date: Scholarly opinion varies greatly and strong cases have been made for dates ranging from 600 to 200 BC. There is no obvious clue in the book pointing to specific historical times, people or events. It is probably earlier rather than later if the locust invasion is to be taken literally rather than allegorically.

Authenticity: Despite the mystery surrounding its origins, there has never been any dispute over Joel's inclusion in the Hebrew 'canon' of Scripture from earliest times.

For today

- Remember that everyone will be judged: so keep going faithfully!
- Accept God's offer of a new start when you are aware of wasted time

CROSS CHECK

Suffering: pp 193, 196-7
Prophecy: pp 75, 164
Judgment: p 46

After the blight, fresh buds appear

Joel 2:18-27

'My years in the Unification Church have not blighted my life for ever,' Jacqui Williams wrote in her book *The Locust Years*, recounting her membership of the 'Moonies' sect. 'I do not live under a dark shadow. God has in truth given me back the years that the locust had eaten.'

Her experience is that of many people who find that a period of their life has been in effect eaten away. It is tempting to think of such times as a waste, and to continue to be eaten away by annoyance, anger and frustration. But God never wastes anything.

Sure, it might have been a time that we regret bitterly, when we threw away a great opportunity by some foolish action, entered some unwise relationship which left us washed up like debris on the shore, or squandered our best energies on some futile enterprise. In that sense, we reaped what we had sown, a famine of the spirit. That is what the Judeans were doing in Joel's time.

But when a person begins a new life with God, as Jacqui Williams did, Paul's words come glaringly true: 'The old has gone, the new has come!' (2 Corinthians 5:17). Where there was spiritual barrenness, buds of life appear. The locusts which devastated us do not return and fresh growth begins.

Joel's promise is that forgiveness is real, renewal is lasting, and in time there will be more to thank God for than there was before the sad story began.

HARD Question

Is Joel misquoted?

Joel 2:28-3:21 (cf. Acts 2:14-21)

Joel now portrays the day of the Lord in the image of the final triumph of God's people. He says it as the nations bowing before Israel which, in effect, is bowing before God (cf. 3:1-8,12-16).

Peter used this passage on the day of Pentecost to 'explain' the phenomenon of the outpoured Holy Spirit, and the tongues and prophecy spoken by ordinary church members to the bewilderment of onlookers (Acts 2:14-21).

But the sky did not fall in (2:31)! And Peter quoted the section about the Holy Spirit and prophecy but omitted armies being driven away (2:20) and the gathering of nations.

New Testament writers use Old Testament prophecy liberally. A specific event is not always the exact fulfilment of a prophecy but draws a parallel between the patterns seen in prophecies and in events. And Old Testament prophecies often have several applications.

Here Peter and Joel are both using the term 'day' in its regular biblical sense of 'era'. Joel is looking forward to God's uninterrupted rule. Peter claims that the 'day of the Lord' has arrived: his rule has begun and will continue until Christ returns; the Spirit has been poured out on the church for the blessing of the human race; we are already in the 'last days'.

Both speak of the completion of God's rule which the coming of the Holy Spirit foreshadows and guarantees (cf. Ephesians 1:14). Then the nations will gather at the gates of the new Jerusalem and acknowledge God's rule (cf. Revelation 21:2). So Peter was not misusing the passage, but neither did Pentecost fulfil it completely.

True knowledge is dynamic

Long before the explosion of information technology, T.S. Eliot lamented in *Choruses from 'The Rock'*

'Where is the wisdom we have lost in knowledge?

Where is the knowledge we have lost in information?'

The Bible regards wisdom as the practical application of knowledge, which is the personal apprehension of God's truth. Knowledge therefore is dynamic. But it is not only Christians who believe that; many sects do, too.

In John's day, as in ours, some groups offered a superior 'knowledge' into spiritual mysteries. They were the 'Gnostics' (from the Greek word for knowledge) and John's letters counter their influence and distortions.

Irenaeus, writing a century or so later, described the teaching of one Gnostic, Saturnius, as follows 'there is one Father, utterly unknown . . . the world and all things therein was made by certain angels . . . [Christ was] incorporeal and without form . . . a man in appearance only. The God of the Jews was one of the Angels and . . .Christ came to destroy [him] and to save them that believed on him, and these are they who are said to have a spark of his life.'

In response John says:

- Jesus was the Son of God and fully human. Gnostics believed flesh was evil, and either 'the Christ' was an angel inhabiting the man Jesus from his baptism and crucifixion, or Jesus only *seemed* to be a man: the truth of incarnation was intolerable to them.
- The Christian life involves obedience to God and avoidance of sin (e.g. 3:4-10; 5:1-5). Some Gnostics were 'antinomian' – in behaviour anything went.
- Knowledge of God focuses on the atonement and results in loving fellowship with God and fellow-Christians (1:5-2:6); Gnostics spoke of 'secret' knowledge of God obtained through rites , leading to loveless arrogance.

THE LETTERS OF JOHN

1 John	
1	God is light yet forgives our sin
2:1-17	Love God, love others, but don't love the world
2:18-29	Beware the false teachers
3	The nature of love
4	How to recognise false teachers
5	The nature of true faith
2 John	Don't welcome false teachers; keep the faith
3 John	Support missionaries and don't imitate evil

(Note: All references in the articles which follow are to 1 John unless otherwise stated.)

John focuses on Christian truth rather than on the error, to reassure his readers, who had been shaken by the exit of Gnostics from their fellowships (2:19). He refuses to slander the false teachers and his example is one to follow. He stresses that true Christian knowledge is dynamic and relational. Cults thrive when the church becomes too cerebral. Christianity combines understanding with experience in spiritual knowledge.

John's Letters

- Refute early heresies
- Stress the incarnation and atonement of Christ
- Encourage self-giving love

How great is the love the Father has lavished on us, that we should be called children of God! And that is what we are!

1 John 3:1

Where am I?

Date:
Late first century AD.

Place in Bible:
After the letters of Peter and before Jude and revelation in the New Testament.

Parallel books:
The Gospel of John and Revelation are probably by the same author

For today

- Make sure your head knowledge is felt and applied
- Find ways of loving others as Jesus loves you
- Thank God for the reassurance of your forgiveness

Life assured

The ultimate statistic is that one out of one dies. What happens next is less clear. Christians believe that the resurrection of Christ assures them that God has prepared an eternal place in his presence for them. The New Testament also declares that we can be confident of entering it (e.g. 3:1-2).

There is a difference between confidence and cockiness, however. The confident person knows limits; the cocksure person overlooks them. John's letters offer us true confidence bounded by conditions, so that his readers can be free from anxiety about their eternal destiny. They can *know* they are safe for the future because of:

- the historical life, death and resurrection of Jesus (1:1-3);
- the objective truth of the gospel preached by the apostles (4:2,6; 5:6);
- the complete forgiveness of sins offered through Jesus Christ (1:9; 2:2);
- the promise that we shall be made like Jesus when we die (3:2,3) even though we fall short of that perfection now (1:8);
- our personal relationship with and trust in Christ's atonement and love (5:10-12);
- the evidence of God's activity in our lives through answered prayer and the moral 'fruit' he induces (2:28,29).

If someone is unsure of salvation, we should not examine the ups and downs of their past experience or analyse their current feelings, but turn to 5:12. If we whole-heartedly trust Christ for forgiveness and eternal life now, then we have eternal life, whatever our feelings or experience.

However, people who are cocksure should also read John's reminders that those who have life obey God (3:7) and love each other (2:9). Consistent failing in these areas suggests that their profession of faith is unreal.

HARD Question

Are Christians perfect?

In the second century the theologian Tertullian advocated postponing baptism until the end of a person's life. He taught that 'The gate of forgiveness has been shut and fastened with the bar of baptism'. Perfection, he said, was essential for salvation and baptism achieved it.

Sixteen centuries later John Wesley taught that perfection (or 'sanctification') was a gift from God received after conversion. This led to a variety of 'second blessing' teachings in the holiness, Keswick and charismatic movements.

John expects believers to abstain from sin (e.g. 3:4-6). But he also said that we are to go on purifying ourselves in theassurance of eternal life (v 3). But no one is perfect (1:8). In other words a Christian does not carry on as if nothing has happened. Trusting Christ, one's sinful habits begin to die and the fruits of new life start to grow.

John says in 3:9, that the born-again do not and cannot sin (continue in anti-God ways). Regeneration, the implanting of God's 'seed' sees to that. The New Testament tells us that this change is gradual and challenges us to apply our faith in our everyday living.

The aim is to be flawless (Matthew 5:48). The theory is that we can always resist specific temptations (1 Corinthians 10:13). In reality we have to press on towards perfection (Philippians 3:12) because we do fall and are subject to the imperfect knowledge of being human (1 Corinthians 13:12). Full flawlessness will be ours in heaven, but not here.

God will forgive our sins when we confess them and he understands our weakness. However much grace we receive it will never make us sinless. Christians live by daily forgiveness.

Love is cross-shaped

1 John 3,4

One of the world's richest men, John Paul Getty III, once said, 'I'm very rude. I don't really like people very much. Most people don't like me, either. I don't trust anybody in the world.' Jesus taught that love was the essence of moral and spiritual law (Matthew 22:37-39) and Paul said it fulfilled the law (Romans 13:10). Love lubricates society; without it, we grab and fight.

Love is the very nature of God (4:8,16); everything he does is charged with love. This is expressed, not negated, by his justice (cf. v 17) and revealed through Jesus' death and resurrection (4:10). It therefore has shape to it; it is not a sentimental feeling but a righteous force for action.

Christian love is to reflect God's self-giving love (3:16; 4:21); enmity within the body of Christ is a contradiction in terms (1:9-11; 4:20). Just as God showed his love by giving his Son, so we are to show our love by sharing our possessions (3:17,18). That is humanly possible only when we experience God's love personally (4:19).

Love within the church enables God to reveal more of himself and his love to flow through us and make us effective in his service (4:12). His love banishes fear of other people, persecution and eternal punishment (4:18). It can purify our conscience and reassure us when we sin (3:16-24). You can't be rude to anyone when you've known love like that. And money can't buy it.

HARD Question

What is the 'witness of water and blood'?

1 John 5:6-8

John is using the terms figuratively although later commentators have also seen a sacramental allusion in them. Blood is a common New Testament shorthand for Jesus' death. John stresses that Jesus Christ, God's Son, really died as an atoning sacrifice (2:2; 4:10), because the Gnostics argued that a divine being could not die.

The 'water' could refer to two things. Most commentators take it to mean Jesus' baptism at which his status was confirmed by the heavenly voice and which Gnostics said was the moment of 'adoption' when 'the Christ' entered him. John means there was only one being, who also died: 'not just water, but water and blood' (v 6).

However, 'water' can also be a symbol of human birth. John could be arming his readers against those who claimed that Jesus was only the appearance of a man; he is stressing his full humanity. But in either case, John is teaching the dual nature of Christ – divine and human – which Christians in every age must hold together if their spirituality is to remain orthodox.

FAST facts

Author: The early church accepted it was John the Apostle who also wrote the Gospel of John. The style is similar (although, inevitably, there are also differences). Some scholars suggest that some of John's disciples or an otherwise unknown 'John the elder' (cf. 2 John 1) wrote the letters, but there is no proof of this.

Date: It is generally placed towards the end of the first century, because of John's 'elder statesman' style and because of the then prevalence of the heresy he is refuting in the letters.

Readers: John is associated with Ephesus, and it is likely that these letters were written to people in the province of Asia. The 'chosen lady' (2 John 1; some have suggested 'she' is a church) and Gaius (3 John 1) are unknown.

This way to life

John's Gospel

- Focuses on the meaning of Jesus' life and death for individuals
- Stresses the need to have faith in Jesus
- Promises eternal life to all who believe
- Contains a unique collection of well-known sayings and promises of Jesus

Right from the opening sentence, John's Gospel is clearly different to the other Gospels. It is dominated by one major theme: Jesus is the Son of God who came to bring eternal life into the world.

Everything in the Gospel illustrates it. Indeed, at the end John declares that 'Jesus did many other miraculous signs in the presence of his disciples which are not recorded in this book. But these are written that you may believe that Jesus is the Christ, the Son of God, and that by believing you may have life in his name' (20:30,31).

It is the only Gospel to give us the most explicit claims or hints of divinity which Jesus made, including the seven 'I am' sayings. Missing are many familiar incidents and when Jesus encounters the scribes and Pharisees it is not over Sabbath or ritual laws, but over the vexed question as to who he is. Bystanders are overheard whispering, 'Could this be the Christ?' and John wants us to answer, 'Yes.'

Here, though, are some of the best-known stories and teachings of Jesus: the conversion of water into wine, the encounter with the Samaritan woman and the raising of Lazarus; the good shepherd and the vine and its branches. John alone of the evangelists gives us Jesus' teaching about the nature and work of the Holy Spirit.

If Luke is the historian's Gospel, John is the worshipper's. The entire book is littered with memorable quotations, from its majestic opening, 'In the beginning was the Word' to Thomas's accolade towards the end, 'My Lord and My God'. Weak on narrative (it seems to assume that readers are familiar with Jesus' story) but forthright and strong on teaching, it lifts the heart and mind to the personal relationship with God which is at the heart of Christian faith.

JOHN

1	Prologue; Jesus' baptism; first disciples
2	Water into wine; cleansing of the temple
3	Jesus and Nicodemus
4	Jesus and the Samaritan woman
5	Healing at Bethesda; teaching about life
6	Feeding the 5,000; walking on water
7	Jesus at the Feast of Tabernacles; debate over his identity
8	The adulterous woman; whose son is Jesus?
9	Healing the man born blind
10	The good shepherd
11	Raising of Lazarus
12	Anointing at Bethany; triumphal entry into Jerusalem
13	Jesus washes the disciples' feet
14	Teaching about the promised Holy Spirit
15	The vine and the branches
16	Jesus warns the disciples about his departure
17	Jesus prays for his disciples and the world
18	Jesus is arrested; Peter's denials
19	Trial before Pilate, and crucifixion
20	Resurrection appearances
21	More appearances, and the restoration of Peter

KEY QUOTE

'I tell you the truth, whoever hears my word and believes him who sent me has eternal life and will not be condemned; he has crossed over from death to life.'

John 5:24

There's a mystery behind history

John 1:1-18

'Words,' the American poet and essayist Ralph Waldo Emerson once wrote, 'are also actions, and actions are a kind of words.' With God, word and deed are synonymous throughout Scripture. Creation occurred when God spoke (Genesis 1:3-26; cf. Hebrews 1:3).

The word is God's revelation of his character and purpose and is itself as powerful as he is (Isaiah 55:11). His words give life (Deuteronomy 32:46) and light (Psalm 119:105), both of which are strong Johannine themes. Later in the Old Testament period God's 'Wisdom' came to be almost personified (Proverbs 8:22-30).

John uses 'word' in a way which was familiar to Hellenistic (Greek cultural) thought, which still dominated much philosophy and non-Jewish religion even in Roman times. Philo, a near-contemporary of Jesus and a Jew steeped in Greek thought, personified the Word (Logos) and regarded it as an intermediary between God and man. The idea of the Logos as that which gives the universe life dates from the sixth century BC.

So John is expressing the meaning of Jesus' incarnation in terms which Hellenistic Jews could readily understand. He reminds us that Jesus is:

- pre-existent before creation (vv 1,2)
- the creator himself (v 3)
- the author of life (v 4)
- the giver of revelation and truth (vv 4,5,14,17)
- to be widely rejected (v 11)
- the author of eternal life (v 12)
- a divine being incarnated as a fully human being (v 14).

These eighteen verses form the 'Prologue' of John, and are very different to the rest of the Gospel.

HARD Question

Does John say that Jesus is God?

John 1:1

Jehovah's Witnesses are fond of pointing out that the statement 'the Word was God' is slightly ambiguous. They note that there is no definite article in front of 'God', and urge that John is telling us Jesus was a god but not The God: a more-than-human being, on the level of a senior angel, but not equal with God.

Neither the Greek nor the rest of John's Gospel will support this view, however. The Greek order of words is not as it is in English; it reads literally, 'God was the Word', which, if translated that way, might have been less ambiguous!

But this is a matter of style only. John intends 'the Word' to be taken as the subject of the sentence (and indeed the subject of the whole section). To make this unambiguously clear, 'Word' (as subject) is given the definite article while 'God' (as predicate) is not. This is standard Greek usage. Greek readers will grasp at once that John means the Word is fully divine in every sense.

The rest of the prologue implies Jesus' equality with God; he is the Creator, for example, and the giver of life and salvation. Elsewhere, John leaves us in no doubt that Jesus and the Father are one in essence as well as in purpose and desire, and that he wants us to worship Jesus, with Thomas, as 'My Lord and my God'.

Where am I?

Date of events:
c. AD 29-33

Location:
Palestine

Account supplemented by:
Matthew, Mark, Luke

Events followed by:
Acts of the Apostles

By the same author:
1,2,3 John; Revelation

Place in the Bible:
After Luke, before Acts, in the New Testament

Lamb bred for the butchers

John 1:19-39

Following the prologue, in which John has stated his thesis rather formally, he begins his story not with Jesus' birth, but with the beginning of his ministry. He ignores John the Baptist's detailed call to repentance (cf. Luke 3:7-14) and focuses instead on his role of pointing people to Jesus (see 3:30 for his classic statement of self-effacement).

This Jesus, the Baptist informs his disciples, is 'the Lamb of God' (vv 29,35). The concept was familiar to the Jews. Isaac's life was saved by a substitute lamb (Genesis 22:8,13); the Israelites were saved from the angel of death by the Passover lamb (Exodus 12); and every day in the temple a lamb was offered to God.

Jesus has been born in order to die for human sins, the Gospel is saying. (Matthew 1:21 says the same thing.) His crucifixion, although tragic and unjust, was also inevitable and Jesus knew it. It is hard to imagine what that must have meant for his incarnate outlook to have hanging over him this constant intimation of his own mortality. It makes his love seem all the more remarkable.

One shall tell another

John 1:35-51

The 'success' of evangelistic campaigns in which people are invited to a meeting to hear an address explaining how to become a Christian, depends largely on 'Operation Andrew' – the personal prayer and witness of Christians before the meeting. Lasting effects generally come from this 'personal evangelism on a large scale' more than from the much parodied 'mass evangelism'.

Jesus' first disciples doubled in number because Andrew and Philip told others that Jesus was worth

Author: Second-century testimony points to John the Apostle, the son of Zebedee and brother of James. The author refers to himself only as 'the one who Jesus loved', but he is associated closely with Peter and James (as John was in the other Gospels). He seems to have been an eyewitness (he knows how many pots there were at Cana). However, this has been doubted, mostly because the Greek text seems too sophisticated for a Galilean fisherman. But he could have learned the Greek, or dictated to someone who polished it. John lived much of his later life in a Hellenistic area.

Place of composition: Traditionally, the Gospel has been associated with Ephesus, where John lived. Polycrates, Bishop of Ephesus (189-198) said John had taught and was buried there.

Date of composition: Fragments are known to have existed by 150. Some suggest a second-century date and a disciple of John as author, because the Gospel and the letters of John seem to be aware of the second-century Gnostic heresy. However, if it was written by John Zebedee, then a date approximately around 65 and 85 is the most likely.

Sources: The author appears to know Mark's Gospel, and possibly Luke, although he does not seem to draw on either. He may simply have referred to sources which the others used. John Zebedee was the one Gospel author closer to the action than any of the others.

Readers: It is generally thought that John was written for Jews outside Palestine, who would have been familiar with the sort of Hellenistic thought forms which Philo had embraced (see article on John 1:1-18 p 205).

listening to. Once in his presence, Peter and Nathanael were dealt with according to their individual personalities.

Peter received a new identity and opportunity of service, important for one who was a blunderer. (It is stressed at the end of the Gospel, too.) Nathanael was sceptical, secure in a comfortable life. ('Under the fig tree' was a common Jewish expression for well-being.) He needed to know that Jesus was a caring and secure guide. The insight confirmed that he was.

The witnesses were different from the people they brought, too. Quiet and sensitive Andrew brought the brash Peter to Jesus. Philip seems even more cautious; when some Greeks wanted to see Jesus, he asked Andrew to go with him to tell Jesus (12:20-22)! A person does not need to be 'upfront' to be a useful servant of God.

Nathanael is probably to be identified with the Bartholomew of the other Gospels. Bartholomew is a patronymic ('son of . . .') so he would have had another name. In the Synoptic Gospels, Bartholomew is always closely associated with Philip. Nothing is known of either of them after the death of Jesus.

Angry outburst reveals God's priorities

John 2:12-25

Some things always get up your nose. You've only got to think about them and you feel your blood beginning to boil. When you're confronted by them directly – well, it's better if you're not.

Jesus was angered beyond words by the commercialisation of the temple precincts. The poor were being ripped off, and the bankers (who changed Roman coins into Jewish coins, legal tender in the temple area but nowhere else) were making a fat profit. The whole place resembled a chaotic bazaar. Where was anyone supposed to pray?

In 'cleansing' the temple, Jesus is not just protesting at the misuse of it. He is also indicating that his mission is not to reform it but in a sense to destroy it. As the Lamb of God (1:29) his ministry will abolish the need for a centre of sacrificial worship (v 19).

Righteous anger is not always out of place. Our anger, however, is often mixed up with temperamental factors, and our knowledge of the situations which cause it is often limited. Therefore it needs to be let loose with great caution.

Jesus equated human anger with murder (Matthew 5:21,22) and James says that 'man's anger does not bring about the righteous life that God desires' (1:20). Those who justify outbursts by quoting 'In your anger do not sin' should be very sensitive to how the Bible defines sin; anger is an opportunity to 'give the devil a foothold' (Psalm 4:4; Ephesians 4:26,27).

Anger is best channelled into positive action on behalf of people affected by the injustice. Verbal explosions rarely achieve anything, they just foul the air. Jesus' action is not so much an example to follow as a reminder of God's priorities and of his character as a judge.

The incident also challenges those who currently are custodians of historic tourist-attraction churches and cathedrals, incurring high maintenance costs. They need to balance a visitor-friendly and economic approach with maintaining an atmosphere which helps people to seek and find God. Calls to silence and prayer might help still the crowds and silence the tills sufficiently to remind visitors that the ground they walk on is dedicated to God.

All change when Jesus takes over

John 2:1-11

This short story is shot through with both implicit humour and explicit theology. Imagine dirty, unpaved Palestinian streets along which animals wandered and people walked in open sandals. Then imagine the herringbone banqueting formation, with people lying on low cushions with their faces close to their neighbour's feet.

Footwashing was not just a courtesy, but a necessity. The water in the jars on this occasion was fresh (v 7) but there was possibly some sediment in the bottom from when towels had been wrung out over them. The trepidation of the cup-bearer as he approached the MC with a sample of the liquid must have been considerable indeed!

From that graphic image, we can glean numerous theological truths:

- We can take 'ordinary' needs to Jesus (v 3)
- He is under no obligation to respond exactly to our requests on demand (v 4; however, any situation taken faithfully to him cannot remain unaffected)
- Faith is simply obeying him (v 5)
- Jesus can achieve extraordinary results from the ordinary things of life (vv 7,8)
- He changes that which is bad into something which is superbly good (vv 8-10)
- And he does so with great generosity and lavishness (v 6).

John tells us this was the first of Jesus' 'signs' (v 11). It reveals the kind of Messiah he is. It pictures the new life he came to bring to people who are contaminated by sin, a life that is as intoxicating as new wine and as different from the old life as wine is different from ditchwater.

Get a new life!

John 3:1-21

'I used to think that faith was a head trip, a kind of intellectual assent to the truths and doctrines of our religion,' missionary to Africa, Vincent O'Donovan, wrote in *Christianity Rediscovered*. 'I know better now. When my faith began to be shattered, I did not hurt in my head. I hurt all over.'

Massai warriors told him his description of faith was like a hunter killing his prey from a safe distance. A better way of describing it, they said, was to think of a lion which embraces its prey 'and makes it part of himself'. In other words we need a personal encounter with the target.

That is what Nicodemus had to learn. He knew the Scriptures backwards and taught them to others. He was sincere and sought a private audience with Jesus rather than heckling from the crowd.

Jesus' link between water and spirit (v 5) perhaps refers to Christian baptism as an outward sign of an inner change (cf. Matthew 28:19). Or it might refer to John's baptism of repentance (a change of mind and behaviour) to show a changed spirit or heart is needed.

Or 'water' might parallel 'flesh' in v 6 and refer to natural birth in v 4, with 'water' representing the fluid in which a foetus is contained and breaks at birth. (Some suggest it refers to semen.) The meaning of the passage is that each person needs two 'births', natural and spiritual. Any allusion to baptism becomes secondary. The same is true if 'water-and-Spirit' is taken as two aspects of one inner change, in echo of Ezekiel 36:25-27 or Psalm 51:7-12.

John is exposing the root of faith while the Synoptic Gospels focus more on the shoot. The ethics of the Sermon on the Mount (Matthew 5-7) are impossible to people who have not undergone an inner transformation.

Free drink for life

John 4:1-26; cf. 7:37-39

Water is a precious commodity throughout the Near East, and today some Arab countries survive only because of desalination plants which pour life into the parched desert. Bible readers in temperate climates take water for granted and may miss the impact of the biblical imagery.

The 'water of life' is used in both Testaments as an image of God's renewing, life-giving presence. It is like a stream in the desert, transforming barren terrain into lush forest where animals can play and people can find food (Isaiah 35:1-7). Therefore the spiritually 'dry' can find satisfying refreshment from God's bottomless spring of life (Isaiah 55:1-3).

John uses the wordplay between Jesus and the woman at Sychar to show what is this new life that God offers. For the woman, 'living water' was a running stream which never stopped flowing, unlike many of the wadis near her home which flowed only in the rainy season.

To Jesus, it was the life of the Spirit (cf. 7:37-39), always present, always flowing on (just as the wind of the Spirit is always blowing, 3:8). The thirst it quenches is the human desire for 'something more' than material life and relationships can bring – the innate thirst for God himself.

However, it is not true to say the thirst ceases when a person becomes a Christian. There is always more of God to discover and so the 'stream' keeps flowing and never stops to become a stagnant pool.

Once again, John is complementing the other Gospels. The lifestyle of the Sermon on the Mount, when practised spontaneously, is the visible emergence of the bubbling stream from God's people.

What is being 'born again'?

The term 'born again' is used only four times in the New Testament: here, by Paul in Titus 3:5 and by Peter in 1 Peter 1:3 and 23. It never features in the apostolic preaching.

It is not unique to Christianity. The first-century mystery religions offered 'new birth' into a higher life, often through bizarre rituals. The rabbis thought of the baptised proselyte (convert from another race) as a new-born child, too.

The idea of a fresh start runs through the New Testament, usually described by theologians as 'regeneration'. It is a description of the injection of God's living presence into a person's daily life. It is illustrated by images such as passing from death into life (Ephesians 2:4,5) and from darkness into light (Ephesians 5:8-11). Christians are already 'raised with Christ' (Ephesians 2:6) and the life of the kingdom to come is available to them (Romans 8:11).

However, the new nature isn't yet second nature. We have to 'put it on' (and take off the old) constantly, Paul says in Ephesians 4:22-24 and Colossians 3:5-10. The 'sanctification' which follows 'regeneration' is a life-long process.

God is not a machine, operating in our lives according to set formulae which we can define. He deals with people individually, so there is no biblical justification for claiming a decisive 'moment of commitment' or a certain kind of 'conversion' experience. Nicodemus's lack was not so much 'experience' as 'insight'; he couldn't see how to relate to God in a personal rather than a mechanical way.

The New Testament test of faith which brings eternal life is not, 'Have you said or done certain things?', but 'Are you trusting Jesus Christ now?' (1 John 5:12.) The past process is not important; the present reality is.

However, it is possible to believe the truth of Christianity and to serve in the church, and yet to lack the transforming dynamic of Christ's energy in one's inner life. Whether that is a lack of 'new birth' or of the fullness of the Holy Spirit, or the 'dark night of the soul', and what effect this has on a person's eternal destiny, is never speculated upon. Human beings cannot judge the state of someone else's heart.

What is required of each individual is to ask, am I firing from a distance, or am I embracing the target? If the former, an acknowledgement of guilt and a request to know and trust Christ personally will initiate a closer encounter. But even if the answer points to the latter there is no room for complacency. New birth is not an insurance policy but the launch pad for an often bumpy journey into inner space.

Desperate to believe

John 4:43-54

Faith becomes real only when we act on what we believe; until then, it's simply theory. The official who worked for Herod Antipas, the puppet ruler of Galilee, has what T.S. Eliot described as 'the faith that issues from despair' as he pleads with Jesus for help. Jesus makes him do the hardest thing imaginable: go home without evidence that his request has been granted. Imagine his feelings as he leaves with only a promise from a teacher who had apparently questioned his motives (v 48). It is only when he sees the evidence that he 'believes' in the full sense (v 53), which in John means to acknowledge Jesus as the Son of God. Faith that issues from desperation is not ignored by God, but it is of value only if it goes on to become a lifelong trust in better times as well as bad.

Fortunately, no one asked who she was!

John 4:27

The return of the disciples to Jesus is noted by this telling verse which illustrates the gulf between their viewpoint and Jesus'. They were surprised that Jesus was talking to a woman. Women were not taught by rabbis, and lone interviews with strange females were frowned upon. And this one was a Samaritan: a heretic and a foreigner.

It was probably just as well that they knew nothing of this woman's series of affairs and marriages. At least they had the presence of mind not to voice their surprise!

Having introduced us to the concept of new life, John is also reminding us that it is available for everyone. He does not quote Jesus stating his mission 'to call sinners to repentance' (Luke 5:32); instead, he shows it happening. Jesus accepts the woman as she is without being judgmental (as in 8:1-11); instead of sternly calling her to repent, he offers her something better than her current life and gives preachers and evangelists an example to follow.

Health spa healing

John 5:1-15

Jerusalem's Pool of Bethesda, fed by a natural spring, was a place of pilgrimage for the sick. Legend had it that an angel occasionally stirred the water and that the first person in would be healed (v 4, omitted in most modern versions, and v 7).

On this occasion, Jesus detects some inner need as well as the outer problem; the man seems to have become rather comfortable with his ailment (v 6). To be healed would be demanding; he would have to work! When God effects change in our lives, he also presents us with new responsibilities which we might prefer to be without.

In telling the man to 'stop sinning' (v 14) Jesus is not implying that his suffering was a punishment for sin. It is possible he had a sinful attitude, but that was not the cause of his problem. Rather, Jesus is reminding him that there is a fate worse than pain: eternal separation from God, which is death indeed. A life of sin renders a person liable to it. John's Gospel never strays far from its central theme.

Family secrets exposed

John 5:16-47

The relationship between God the Father and God the Son are of course shrouded in mystery, not least because the truth of the Trinity is ultimately beyond human comprehension. But in his limited, incarnate form, the Son of God had a relationship with his Father which reveals something of God, and of how we also can relate to him. It was a relationship of:

- dependence (vv 19,30): as the Son 'copies' and obeys the Father, so should we copy Jesus as a model of conduct
- devotion (v 20a): theirs is not a merely formal relationship, but one of love and warmth; we too are called to love God, and not merely obey him;
- development (v 20b): Jesus seems to have 'grown' even in his ministry; he did not raise the dead in the first week;
- delegation (vv 22,27): Jesus did not lay aside all his authority, and the Father gave him the responsibility of judgment. Christians also are given the responsibility to represent God in his world.

This passage also uses two titles for Jesus which are important in the Gospels: Son of God (v 25) and Son of Man (v 27). The former, as used in John's Gospel, expresses Jesus' divine identity. Commoner however, on Jesus' lips (79 occurrences in the Gospels all told) is Son of Man – The Man, to use an English phrase of comparable force.

Jews would have been familiar with the exalted 'one like a son of man' who takes the kingdom for keeps in the vision of Daniel 7:13, so although the title stresses Jesus' humanity, there is little doubt that it was one of his hints at his own divinity. It both links him to God and also identifies him with the human race; it is the perfect description of the incarnate Son of God.

You can't live without it

John 6

Bread has been the staple ingredient of the world's diet since earliest times. Jesus has already offered the 'water of life' and now he offers the 'bread of life'. The symbolism is obvious: Jesus offers humankind something which is basic to their existence as human, that is spiritual, beings.

The feeding of the 5,000 is the only incident in Jesus' life prior to the final 'passion week' which is recorded in all four Gospels. John alone picks out the teaching associated with it, although the others do include a later warning about 'the yeast of the Pharisees'.

The quantity and value of the food was considerable (a working man received a denarius a day, and the 'eight months' wages' thus came to 200 denarii) and the impact was immense. It was this incident which encouraged some in the crowd to try to make Jesus a king (v 15), setting him up to be quizzed over the nature of his 'kingship' and the request for a definitive 'sign' of it (v 30).

The essence of Jesus' teaching, as he told the devil in the desert, is that 'people do not live on [physical] bread alone' (Luke 4:4). Instead:

- We are to trust God for everything, because he is the ultimate provider of everything
- Eternal life is more precious even than temporal life and should be our prime concern
- A relationship with God (pictured as feeding on him) can satisfy our deepest human needs.

The stress on consuming his flesh and blood (vv 53-58) has naturally been assumed to refer to the sacramental use of bread and wine in the Communion rite. While the parallel is easily drawn and can be helpful, it is unlikely that the whole passage is intended to be taken sacramentally. The word 'flesh' is never used elsewhere in reference to the Lord's Supper.

Jesus' concern is to present himself as the heavenly Saviour who is the source of true (God's) life. His life is mediated to us in a variety of ways, of which the right use of the sacraments is one.

No room for doubt

John 6:32-40

There are two kinds of doubt. One is related more to basic beliefs: Is God really as they say he is? The other is more concerned with our standing before God: I'm not sure if he'll have me.

The former was the kind which Thomas experienced (20:24-29), the latter is dealt with in this passage. There is nothing equivocal about Jesus' assurances:

- spiritual hunger and thirst are satisfied (v 35)
- all who trust God are never rejected by him (v 37)
- he will hold firmly those who trust him and include them in the final resurrection (vv 39,40).

Jesus does not say that eternal life is assured so long as we keep the rules. He says that it is assured come what may. This may seem to encourage 'easy believism', which treats faith in Christ's death and resurrection as an insurance policy that has little bearing on daily life.

However, true believing (trusting, 'feeding') is a whole-person activity which results in personal growth and transformation. It cannot be undertaken without a commitment to the lifestyle which is the outworking of salvation in daily life. Someone who has truly encountered God can never be the same again – although they may be far from perfect.

The assurance here is especially for those who have grown weary in well-doing, or who are conscious of having failed (yet again) in the Christian life. Doubt added to tiredness or guilt is a recipe for spiritual depression, and Jesus offers an alternative: keep feeding on him, because he is always there to sustain us.

Claims for divinity

The Jewish reaction: On three occasions they recognised Jesus' claim to be God or equal to God (which was the same thing): 5:17-18; 8:59; 10:33. It also formed part of the charge before Pilate, 19:7.

Jesus' other claims: He frequently alluded to God as his Father in deeply personal terms. He claimed specific equality in 10:30. In 8:58 he took on his lips the sacred Name and apparently referred it to himself (although he might have been saying, 'Before Abraham was, God was,' but in the context that would make less sense than claiming himself to have been the pre-existent 'I am').

The seven 'I am' sayings: Apart from 8:58, Jesus claimed to do or be what only God could do or be. Bread of life (6:35); light of the world (8:12); gate for the sheep (10:7); the good shepherd (10:11); the resurrection and the life (11:25); the way, truth and life (14:6); the true vine (15:1).

Will the real messiah stand up

John 7,8

Images of Jesus have varied immensely, from the halo-covered figures of Renaissance paintings to the fallible and unmystical revolutionary cult leader depicted by the so-called 'Jesus seminar' of contemporary radical theologians. The on-going debate prompted *Time* magazine to conclude in 1994: 'It is impossible for ordinary churchgoers to follow the action, much less determine which of the competing Jesuses will win.'

That is perhaps an exaggeration, as the orthodox view of Jesus is accepted by all but a small minority of vociferous teachers, but the debate attracts media interest as it challenges accepted views. However, it does lead back to similar debates occurring while Jesus was on earth. Then, the opinion polls came up with numerous suggestions:

- A good man (7:12)
- A deceiver (7:13)
- Clever but not taught in the right seminary, therefore suspect (7:15)
- Mad and demonic (7:20; 8:48,52)
- Of unknown origin, therefore disqualified from being Messiah (7:27,41-42)
- If he's not the Christ, he's his twin brother (7:31)
- A mystery (7:35,36)
- The prophet whom everyone expected to come (7:40)
- Definitely the Christ (7:41)
- A remarkable teacher (7:46)
- Illegitimate and therefore barred from high office (8:41)

Interestingly, the one thing he was not accused of was being a rebel leader! That did figure in the case against him before Pilate, however.

His own comments were both very clear and very confusing. We can have some sympathy with his family who told him to declare himself openly if he wanted to be a religious leader (7:2-5) and with the people who simply couldn't work out the true meaning of his veiled allusions (7:36).

However, Jesus did leave some very strong statements. In these two chapters alone, he claimed

- to be sent from God (7:16,28; 8:14,23,42)
- to speak on God's behalf (7:17)
- that he knows God personally 7:29; 8:55)
- that he will return to God, having come from him, and then reappear (7:33)
- to be the one who brings God's Holy Spirit to the world (7:38,39)
- to be able to forgive sins (8:11)
- to bring God's truth to light (8:12)
- to be the Son of the Heavenly Father (8:18,34-38)
- to have existed before Abraham was born c. 2000 BC (8:58).

These were not the only times in John's Gospel that Jesus makes claims to divinity (see opposite) but it was the apostle Paul who spelt this out in detail. C.S. Lewis, in his book *Mere Christianity*, expressed the classic Christian position in some memorable words, focusing on the Gospels, not on Paul's letters:

> 'A man who was merely a man and said the sort of things Jesus said would not be a great moral teacher. He would either be a lunatic – on a level with the man who says he is a poached egg – or else he would be the Devil of Hell. You must make your choice. Either this man was, and is, the Son of God: or else a madman or something worse. You can shut Him up for a fool, you can spit at Him and kill Him as a demon; or you can fall at His feet and call Him Lord and God. But let us not come up with any patronising nonsense about His being a great human teacher. He has not left that open to us. He did not intend to.'

Don't throw stones in glass houses

John 8:1-11

The proverb that runs 'people who live in glass houses should not throw stones' dates at least from the time of Chaucer (14th century AD) but could easily have come from Jesus. He does not condone the woman's action – he tells her to stop sinning, v 11– but his greater concern is with her accusers.

They were self-righteous. They were pointing the finger at her but overlooking their own sins. Jesus frequently said or implied that there could be no league table of sins. Adultery is not worse than pride in God's sight; it's just different. And pride is as deadly and inexcusable as any other sin.

We all live in glass houses: our lives are partially open to the stare of others, and fully open to the scrutiny of God. If we do need to expose publicly the sins of others (and that is often questionable, and 'public interest' is often merely a synonym for morbid, self-righteous public curiosity), we should do so with great sensitivity and sadness. Indeed, we are all sentenced to another sort of 'glasshouse' – the detention centre – because we are guilty of sin and need God's forgiveness. The woman and her accusers were on a level playing field before God.

Although some important early manuscripts omit this incident (see the margin notes in your Bible) it has all the marks of authenticity. Jesus' writing in the sand is probably not out of boredom but an interviewer's technique of using silence to get people to incriminate themselves! The suggestion that he was writing out the Pharisees' sins is ingenious but purely speculative.

Blind man sees the light of Christ

John 9

Most people experience the occasional 'Eureka!' or 'Aha!' moment when something 'clicks', and we 'see' it for the first time. Usually it's understanding how something works or how to do a job; it may be a concept or an idea which never 'made sense' before.

Invariably, after a miracle in John there is a debate, and the healing of the blind man leads to a discussion about spiritual blindness (vv 35-41). The Pharisees claimed to see spiritual truth more clearly than others, but in failing to recognise Jesus for who he was showed themselves in fact to be 'blind guides' (cf. Matthew 23:16,17).

Paul wrote of the 'god of this world' blinding people to God's truth (2 Corinthians 4:4). Christian faith is not merely something which is obvious once the basic facts are explained. It is not so rational as a railway timetable. For that reason, prayer for God to open people's inner eyes is a vital part of sharing the faith with them. A vivid example of the need for this new 'sight' is given in Elisha's experience in 2 Kings 6:17.

It was God's grace – his undeserved love – which enabled former slave trader John Newton to exclaim

Amazing grace, how sweet the sound –
that saved a wretch like me!
I once was lost, but now am found,
was blind, but now I see.

It is not enough for us to devise impressive presentations of the faith for unbelievers; we need to pray that their spiritual sight will be healed.

CROSS CHECK

John's thought continued: pp 201-3
Christian assurance: pp 154, 202, 209, 213
The Holy Spirit: pp 30, 135, 217
The resurrection: pp 76, 221, 283, 296

God cares for his needy people

John 10

Sheep are very short-sighted and prone to following the crowd. It is not the most flattering of analogies for human beings made in the image of God, but one which the Bible frequently finds appropriate for its purposes.

That is partly because the Bible is set in largely rural communities where sheep were a unit of wealth and a source of food, drink (milk) and clothes. So the psalmist called God his shepherd (Psalm 23:1) and the prophets used sheep to draw various analogies (e.g. Isaiah 53:6; Ezekiel 34).

Several differences between sheep-rearing in first-century Palestine and twenty-first-century Western Europe and North America should be noted if we are to understand the full impact of Jesus' teaching. Sheep in the East were led, not driven, by the shepherd. They followed him not by seeing him but by hearing his distinctive call; whole flocks merged at a well can be separated as the shepherds walk away uttering their call-signs.

Out on the common grazing lands (there were no fenced fields) wolves roamed (and, in Old Testament times, lions too) looking for a tasty meal. Hungry omnivorous bears would take a stray sheep or lamb, and human rustlers were all too common. So at night sheep were herded into dry-stone enclosures, and the shepherd might lie at the entrance, acting as a human gate, to prevent animals escaping or intruders entering.

With that in mind, the picture of God's care is fairly obvious. For Christians today, the passage especially offers to its readers the reassurance that:

- God knows us personally by name (which means he knows all about us)
- He leads us through life (often by going ahead into difficult situations)
- He rescues and saves us (both eternally and, at times, temporally).

Dismissed by some as sentimental, this picture of God's care provides a necessary counter to the observed harshness of life in which the law of the jungle seems to prevail. God is not like the wolves, and is against them.

Life in all its fullness

Life is a central theme in John's Gospel. It is defined in 17:3 as 'knowing God and his Son'. It is dynamic, something to be experienced and not merely to be discussed (10:10). It is also something which only God can give, and does not spring from within us (5:26).

Its main characteristics in John are:

- It is received only by those willing to obey Jesus (3:36)
- It lasts for ever (5:29)
- It requires constant dependence on God (6:53)
- It is related to acceptance of Jesus' teaching (6:63)
- It provides the greatest fulfilment possible of our human potential (10:10)
- It assumes constant trust in and acceptance of Jesus' atoning death and resurrection (20:31)

At our period of 'post-modern' history, when cerebral rationalism is being increasingly rejected in favour of feel-good experience and relationships, this teaching is an important access point into Christianity for many people. Christianity is an experience, but one which goes hand in hand with study and knowledge of biblical events and concepts in order to remain authentic.

Anger and grief at cruel obscenity

John 11

Horror films with corpses and ghostly encounters are two a penny. They play on our fear of death and the unknown, but the reassuring knowledge that the world outside the cinema is vibrant with normality enables us to accept them as entertaining fantasies. The scene in this chapter makes the nightmare a reality.

It doesn't take much imagination to see that Mary, the 'spiritual' sister who sat at Jesus' feet (Luke 10:38-42) is devastated by an unexpected death. She was too upset to meet Jesus (v 20), too angry with him for not saving Lazarus. Martha and the neighbours were angry, too; Jesus is greeted with rebukes, not relief (vv 21,32,37).

The women had lost their beloved brother and a means of support. Neither appears to have been married, and single or widowed women without supportive families were defined as beggars.

Then to be confronted with a mummified corpse walking out of a cave tomb, and being told to unbind it, must have been mind-blowing. Was this a trick? Were they hallucinating? What state would the decaying flesh be in? As Martha knew, in the heat corpses decayed very quickly (v 39).

There are so many human and authentic element to this story, extraordinary as it is to modern ears. It is a major event for John as it brings together the great themes of his Gospel and sets the stage for the final scenes of Jesus' life.

He uses it to stress three things. First, that Jesus bestows life beyond the grave (v 25). Secondly, that his new life begins before the grave, symbolised by his bringing Lazarus back. This counters the pessimism among some Christians that this life is a largely worthless necessity to pass through before the real business of heaven starts.

But thirdly, and most importantly, John shows what a perverse obscenity death is. It is an intruder into God's world, a thief snatching away the life that rightly belongs to us. That is why Jesus wept (v 35). In the original Greek his deep feelings (v 34) are more of anger at death itself than grief.

The theologian B.B. Warfield put it thus: 'It is death that is the object of his wrath, and behind death him who has the power of death, and whom he has come into the world to destroy. Tears of sympathy may fill his eyes, but this is incidental. His soul is held by rage: and he advances to the tomb, in Calvin's words, "as a champion who prepares for conflict". Not in cold unconcern, but in flaming wrath against the foe, Jesus smites in our behalf.'

To the bereaved, the comfort Jesus offers is more than compassion. The raising of Lazarus tells us that he is doing something to overcome what most people instinctively recognise, and which Scripture confirms, to be nothing less than an unmitigated evil.

We want to see Jesus

John 12:20-26

The Greeks were Jewish proselytes (converts) from a Gentile background. This small incident reminds us that:

- People still seek Jesus; the natural spiritual quest, however, often leads them to look in the wrong place for what only he can do and give
- Faith includes sacrifice. The old in us must die before the new can blossom (vv 24,25)
- Jesus still draws people to himself. His name and reputation inspire interest; his Spirit creates hunger in people's hearts. The evangelistic task is neither fulfilled as yet, nor is it ever futile.

Ram Sharan Nepal was brought up a Hindu. 'For me, Hinduism was an external religion,' he said. 'I was looking for a religion of the heart.' He found it in Christ, and became pastor of a growing church in Nepal at a time when Christianity was barely tolerated.

Put your feet up!

John 13

Many churches today mark Maundy Thursday (the day before Good Friday) with either a Passover meal or a Communion service, which may include a symbolic foot-washing ceremony.

Foot-washing was a courtesy offered to guests at a Near Eastern dinner party, usually performed by a servant. Jesus and his disciples celebrated the meal in a borrowed room (Luke 22:7-14) with no servant present, so Jesus performed an acted parable.

The incident is not recorded in the other Gospels (but alluded to in Luke 22:27) and John does not include the Last Supper as such. He implies that it was the day before the Passover, v 1, posing a problem about the chronology of Jesus' last 36 hours. (It seems that the Jews used two calendars for fixing the date of Passover, differing from each other by one day; John refers to one, the Synoptic Gospels, to the other.

The action introduces the New Testament concept that **leadership is service**. Clergy and lay leaders should not be egotists and exert power. Leadership is a gift of the Holy Spirit (Romans 12:8) and requires a balance between being decisive and domineering. Their role is to help people grow spiritually and serve each other (cf. Ephesians 4:11,12).

This episode also shows that **discipleship is self-sacrificial**. The so-called eleventh commandment (vv 34,35) is the hallmark of Christian living. It is a different love from fraternity or friendship; it is caring for people with whom we might otherwise have no natural contact or rapport. The common denominator is our faith in Christ.

Therefore, Christians need to 'have their feet washed' regularly. Jesus is saying that by living in the world that does not know God we pick up its attitudes from which we need cleansing.

'I'll always be there for you'

John 14-16

Parting is always difficult, especially if the person leaving is someone who has contributed to our lives in a positive way. Jesus, knowing this, prepares his followers for his departure, but puzzles them by his ambiguous message that although he was going away he would come to them again.

The Holy Spirit, he said, would remain their constant companion. His return to the Father would mean the end of his bodily presence with them, but through the Spirit's action his personal presence would continue in a new and richer way.

The term variously translated Counsellor, Advocate, Helper or Comforter (Paraclete in the Greek) can mean an adviser, a legal advocate who pleads on our behalf, or a prosecuting counsel who seeks to convict.

In John's context, all three are implied, although the first two are uppermost. (Conviction is a work of the Spirit in those who do not yet believe, 16:7-11.) The Paraclete, then, is someone who is called alongside to help in time of need whose character and functions include:

- being ever-present (14:16)
- embodying and mediating God's truth (14:17; 15:26)
- indwelling believers (14:17)
- coming from both the Father and the Son, 14:26; 15:26; 16:7; the interpretation of this 'procession' of the Spirit from within the Trinity is a contributory factor to the major split between Eastern (Orthodox) and Western (Catholic and Protestant) churches
- being holy as God is (14:26)
- teaching the disciples what accords with God's truth and Jesus' words (14:26; 15:26)
- pointing to Jesus and not to himself (15:26)
- convicting the ungodly of their sin (16:7-11).

There is more teaching about the Holy Spirit in John, and in the rest of the New Testament, which must be placed alongside this in order to build up a complete theology of the Spirit. The picture here, however, is important in that it stresses what some extreme views of the Spirit have overlooked: that he is holy, cannot contradict God's truth revealed elsewhere, and does not draw attention to himself.

HARD Question

Is there only one way to heaven?

John 14:6

The attitude of many Christians to people of other faiths changed during the twentieth century from believing that other religions were the devil's delusions to believing that Jesus is one among many ways to God. The change coincided with greater exposure to other faiths through travel and migration.

In this famous verse, Jesus claims to be the exclusive way to God. He also spoke of being a 'narrow gate' in Matthew 7:13,14. In saying that he had sheep of another fold (John 10:7,16), the context implies they are Gentiles who would believe in him through the church's mission. The apostles continued his exclusive claims (Acts 4:12).

Paul says that God has revealed something of himself to all people (Romans 1:19,20) and that any who have been faithful to what they know of God will be treated justly (Romans 2:12-16). Might this include people of other faiths who have never understood Christian teaching? Views differ.

In fact Christians have very vague ideas about other faiths and similarly adherents of those faiths have vague ideas about Christianity. The founder of Islam rejected Christianity not on the basis of its true teaching but on a caricature of the Trinity.

However, Paul was a tireless missionary to many cultures. He taught that Christ was and is the only sure way to know God in this life and the next and that before knowing him people who had followed other (Roman and Greek) religions were 'alienated from God' (Colossians 1:19-21).

The solution to the issue seems to be:

- Accept that Christianity is exclusive
- and Jesus is the incarnation and therefore most complete revelation of God
- and that the only certain way to enter 'eternal life' (which is a dynamic encounter with God before and after death) is through faith in Christ
- in missionary work to be sensitive to peoples' cultures and cause no unnecessary offence, remembering that the gospel is true for all but may be expressed in culturally diverse ways;
- and to leave to a just God the question of the destiny of those who have never heard of Christ or whose hearing of him has been defective.

On that basis it is possible for Christians to under-emphasise elements of God-revealed universal truth but which other faiths stress. The lifestyle of some devout Hindus, with very little regard for material things, may embarrass Western Christians when they read passages such as Matthew 6:25-34!

Love has its limits

John 14:15-24

St Augustine is often misquoted as saying 'Love and do what you will'. He said it, but he did not intend to sanction the post-modern view that anything goes so long as it's loving. Three times in this passage Jesus stresses that love and obedience are not incompatible but inseparable.

John uses the word *agape* for love, meaning self-giving, sacrificial love. It is never out to please itself, but only to please God and others. Such love cannot break God's commandments because they set out the limits for human conduct. To stray beyond them is not loving but damaging – even if it feels 'good' or 'right'.

Theoretical ethicists pose questions about the relationship between love and law (such as a starving person stealing bread from a rich miser), but in the normal course of life the basic law of God defines what is and is not loving conduct. Christians are not released from its strictures, and Paul's discussions about 'law' (e.g. Romans 3) concern a quite different Jewish religious issue.

Peace is not a dream

John 14:27

The thunder ceases, the wind dies down; the shelling stops and the guns are silent; the argument rages no more and the tide of anger ebbs. Peace reigns. Most people know the feeling; most would like to feel it more often.

Jesus, the Prince of Peace (Isaiah 9:6) offers the disciples 'peace which the world cannot give' (v 27). Generally in the Bible 'peace' means more than the absence of conflict. It is a positive quality of wholeness in which anxiety is replaced by trust in God's unfailing love and care.

Jesus suggests that this peace can even exist within conflict and stems from what Paul describes as 'peace with God' (Romans 5:1). Jesus united a holy God with a sinful people, bringing a peace which nothing else achieved.

But Jesus implies it is more than a received status; it is a felt experience. His first word to the terrified disciples after the resurrection was, 'Peace!' (20:21). It is not the peace of drink or drugs, but an abiding inner reassurance of our security in God (cf. 6:39,40).

American poet John Whittier wrote the familiar lines:

Drop thy still dews of quietness,
Till all our strivings cease;
Take from our souls the strain and stress,
And let our ordered lives confess
The beauty of thy peace.

What is less familiar is that the hymn *Dear Lord and Father of mankind,* from which these lines come, occurs in the middle of a narrative poem called *The brewing of soma.* It describes the attempt of Indian mystics to brew the elixir of the gods, ending in 'A storm of drunken joy' as 'From tent to tent Soma's sacred madness went'. Written in 1872, it captures the spirit of every age which seeks to discover the peace which only Christ can give.

A prune a day helps you work, rest and pray

John 15

The English have a rose, the Scots a thistle, the Welsh a leek and the Irish a shamrock. The Israelites had a vine as their national symbol. It was sculpted on Solomon's temple and engraved on the Maccabees' coins. It dated back to the grapes the spies seized in Canaan (Numbers 13:23) and was a frequent prophetic image (Isaiah 5:1-7).

So Jesus, 'the true vine', is the embodiment of the true Israel. His teaching is not just about an individual's relationship with himself as Lord, but with himself *as the head of the church*: it has corporate as well as personal overtones. It is the Johannine equivalent of Paul's 'body of Christ' image of Christ as the inseparable 'head' (Romans 12; 1 Corinthians 12).

Palestinian vines were drastically pruned for the first three years, and regularly thereafter, otherwise their fruit would be useless. So 'pruning' is making strong, fruitful disciples within the church, as well as being divine discipline of individuals' sins.

In the early church, the 'catechumenate' (training and instruction of converts) was taken seriously. Today, while we accept training in every other walk of life, we tend not to stress its importance in the Christian life.

But it is essential, says Jesus, suggesting two things. That it should be a normal part of church life, and that individuals should seek and welcome it.

'Abiding' or 'remaining' in the vine then becomes second nature, because we accept that the Christian life is a corporate affair in which we are all learning together and dependent on each other and Christ. That may not make pruning easier, but it makes it more natural – and understandable.

For today

- Jesus is God's final and most complete revelation of his character to the world
- The purpose of faith is to encounter the living God in this life and the next
- Jesus comes into ordinary experience and transforms it when we let him
- Trust God in all circumstances to care for you
- Serve each other, don't dominate each other
- Be willing to learn, and to change, under God's 'pruning' hand
- Don't criticise people for their failings; welcome and trust the repentant sinner

Only we can answer Jesus' prayer

John 17

Jamaica has 2.7m people and over 300 Christian denominations. That is probably one of the world's higher proportions, but is not atypical. As non-Christians walk through any town or city they get the impression that Christianity is not one religion but many.

The general public can neither see the spiritual similarity nor understand the theological distinctions. The 'ecumenical movement' which sprang up in the early twentieth century to encourage Christians back together had limited success.

Some theological disagreements are considerable, and most systems of church government are incompatible. However, inter-church activity has increased as Christians have discovered a common faith beneath what are often (but not always) secondary differences of emphasis.

The New Testament does not think in institutional terms (although it does envisage some church structures), and the apostles fought to minimise needless divisions (1 Corinthians 1:10-17). Much of Jesus' prayer is for protection against evil and error (vv 15-19). They destroy the natural Christian unity that reflects the Godhead and offers the world the hope of harmonious relationships (vv 21-23).

Christians are one when they share the same basic faith in the divine, crucified and risen Christ (Ephesians 4:4-6). Hence co-operation in evangelism and compassion ministry is not only possible but essential if we are to be obedient to him. Refusal to 'compromise' is sometimes (but not always) an excuse to maintain an ungodly superiority.

'How can we work with others?' should be the first question asked when activity is contemplated, not an item under 'any other business' once the action has been planned. In that sense, we are the only people who can answer the prayer 'that they may be one'.

The world is a messy place to be in

John 17:16

Jesus' assertion that his people are 'in' but not 'of' the world has led to some extreme applications. John Wesley forbade children to play games in his schools because he believed that 'he who plays as a boy plays as a man'. Successive generations (and different cultures) have blacklisted alcohol, tobacco (or cigarettes but not pipes), make-up, the cinema, theatre, television, dancing, mixed bathing, classical music and pop music, as 'worldly'.

In the New Testament, 'world' normally means 'human society organised without reference to God'. (It can on occasions also mean the physical earth.) Never does Scripture call on Christians to attempt to separate themselves from it (cf. 1 Corinthians 5:9,10), and it condemns the pharisaism which imposes needless petty restrictions on others (Colossians 2:20-23).

Instead, it calls us to lives of love in which the spiritual matters more than the material. We are to have a different 'mindset' (cf. Romans 12:2) with God at the centre of our 'world'. Sadly, our attitudes often remain 'worldly'. Personal gain may figure higher on our agendas than global justice; maintenance of church life may take precedence over mission. Such self-seeking is 'worldly' and in marked distinction to Jesus' attitude of self-sacrifice.

Failure is an opportunity to serve

John 18:15-27; 21:1-19

The deflating knowledge that we've blown it can paralyse any further action. If it involved letting others down, we can't face seeing them again. We feel awful. Peter must have shared that experience after he denied Jesus.

Jesus' treatment of him is deeply encouraging. He doesn't simply offer forgiveness (it is implicit) but does something far better. First, he comes to Peter in a familiar way: on the lake, where Peter is. What had first convinced Peter of Jesus' divinity? A miraculous catch of fish (Luke 5:1-11). So Jesus says, in effect, 'Peter, I'm still the same, and I'm still with you.'

And then Jesus re-commissions him, the triple charge surely being a deliberate reference to Peter's threefold denial: the restitution was complete, the slate was wiped clean. He was forgiven, he could begin again, and he had a ministry to fulfil.

Having failed himself, he could 'feed the lambs' – the new believers who would join the church – with greater sensitivity. Peter, who comes over as rather hard, thoughtless and insensitive, wouldn't be quite the same again after this; he would be more compassionate.

Christians fail like Peter because they are human. Jesus' example shows that we cannot hold their confessed sins against them. Compassion, forgiveness and restoration are to be complete, not partial. We are to have short memories for failings and long memories for achievements – not the other way round.

God's love is unchanging, so we can be reassured that failure in serving Christ does not mean the end of our service for Christ.

Finished!

John 19:30

There is nothing so satisfying as seeing a hard job completed. In his agony on the cross, Jesus' cry 'It is finished' is not one of relief – it's all over – but of triumph. He has accomplished his task. The cruel death at the end of an unblemished life was not an accident but part of the Father's purpose.

The Greek word *tetelestai* was sometimes written on a discharged bill. It meant 'paid in full'. Christians see in that the assurance that in his death, Jesus Christ paid the full price of their reconciliation to God. Nothing remains but to accept gratefully his vicarious payment of a debt we could never afford.

How do we know Jesus rose?

The evidence of the New Testament points strongly to a real bodily resurrection and not just to a 'spiritual experience' as has been suggested. (Such things as the Nazi holocaust have also been vigorously denied.) The chief reasons are:

- The Jewish leaders could never produce the body and they bribed the soldiers to say it was stolen (Matthew 28:11-13)
- There was no doubt over the location of the tomb
- The graveclothes remained but were unwound and the turban was laid to one side
- The blood and water (John 19:34) suggests Jesus was really dead, not merely in a coma
- Had the disciples lied, would they have faced death and persecution without someone confessing the facts
- The appearances ended suddenly
- The disciples were transformed from being timid and fearful to bold and fearless
- The disciples had not been expecting Jesus to rise despite his repeated predictions that he would.

None of this conclusively 'proves' it happened, but the spiritual experience of those who have based their lives on it is undeniable. If it is true, then the only logical response is that of Thomas: to bow before Jesus and say, 'My Lord and my God!' (John 20:28).

Is it a whale of a tale?

HARD Question

The real question raised by Jonah is not did he get swallowed by a big fish (the Bible uses a different word than 'whale'), but what sort of book is it meant to be? Is it history, theology, parable, a moral tale for children, satire or a combination of these?

There are secondary points also. Firstly, the book is not about Israel (or Judah) but about Assyria (of which Nineveh was the capital at one time) and no reference is made to 'God's people'. Secondly, Nineveh was never as big as Jonah claims in 3:3 (unless he means a wider administrative district outside the city wall). And thirdly, there is no other evidence for this incident. Certainly, God's initial prediction was not then fulfilled; Nineveh did not fall at this time although it did later. But the story shows that the prediction of doom had assumed impenitence, and Nineveh's humbling brought a stay of execution.

In favour of the book's historicity, we should note that Jesus quoted Jonah as a parallel to his own resurrection (Matthew 12:39,40; Luke 11:30,32). This could imply that Jesus accepted the historical reality of Jonah, but even if he did his allusion is still primarily to Jonah as a figurative 'type'.

To focus too closely on the historical likelihood (which can never be either verified or discounted) can distract today's reader from the timeless messages of this small but important book. For our purposes we shall assume that it has a historical basis and note that the references to the fish (which cause most problems) are slight and incidental.

The author says little of the method of rescue but a lot about the fact of rescue. So focus on what the book intended to say to its original readers and what God can say through it to us now. And next time you are in a public library, get out a book or video on the remarkable and peculiar creatures that do lurk in the murky depths of oceans . . .

For today

- Don't be surprised if God's plans differ from yours
- Be willing to do hard things God asks
- Remember that God cares for the world, and not just for the church

JONAH

1 Jonah refuses God's call and is thrown to the waves
2 Jonah prays in repentance and praise
3 Jonah gets to Nineveh and preaches there
4 Nineveh repents but Jonah is angry

FAST facts

Author: Jonah is mentioned in 2 Kings 14:25 as a prophet working during the reign of King Jeroboam II of Israel the northern kingdom, c. 793-753 BC. He foretold the extension of Israel's borders during this time of relative prosperity and peace when the Assyrian threat was reduced. However, the book is anonymous and claims only to be about him and not by him.

Date: Linguistic scholars suggest that the book's language comes from a date later than that of the prophet Jonah. This, however, could be due to the final revision and editing of an earlier work and does not of itself prove that the story is not authentic. The late date would be during the Judean exile in Babylon, c. 550 BC; an early date would place the narrative in Jeroboam's reign two centuries earlier.

Hooked by God's line

Jonah 1:17-2:10

You are a respected adviser and consultant in the corridors of power. You are a loyal servant of God and a nationalist. One day a voice whispers, 'Go abroad and work for your enemies.' The Assyrians were potential military conquerors. They worshipped other gods.

Well, would you? You'd tell the devil to go away. Only you know it's not the devil but the authentic voice of God, and it does not make sense.

Challenge of that kind disturbs us. Yet in the church, we evangelise or die spiritually. The wind of the Spirit never entirely drops and sometimes blows a gale. We are to always go with the wind.

The Old Testament people of God saw themselves as preservers rather than proclaimers of the faith. Israel was a conservation area to protect the endangered species of believers. Some churches today are like that, too.

Jonah's message is that the church of God should be a multinational enterprise with a mission to the world. The global village has been Coca-Colonised but it hasn't been Christianised. There are sub-cultures even in our own countries who have not heard the message of Christ in terms they can understand and respond to. So spreading the gospel is our constant business. But like Jonah, we shrink from this and other calls from God. 'Not me, Lord; send them!' We keep our heads down and hope he won't notice. But he does, and sets his rescue plan in operation.

He has already rescued us from 'death' and 'darkness' through Christ. When we try to escape some other responsibility or calling he'll hook us back with his love; when we drift from him he will redirect the current. If he has a special task for you, he won't rest until you've done it. Because no one else can do it.

God doesn't like fireworks

Jonah 4

People who have been hurt by injustice and evil have a Bible-based assurance that God will rectify it at the last day. Some may even look forward to that – but they could be in for a shock. Thieves on the cross can be forgiven (Luke 23:40-43). We just don't know what happens in a person's dying moments. We do know that God is 'slow to anger' and 'relents from sending calamity' (v 2).

Jonah has come to see the fireworks of judgment and the bonfires of Hades lit by the anger of the Lord. He finds instead that they've been cancelled; the shops are closed, the party's over and the government has declared a national day of mourning.

So don't rub your hands in eager expectation that horrible people will be forced to swallow an unending draught of their own bitter medicine. God does not delight in the spiritual death of a soul; Solomon was commended for not praying for the death of his enemies (2 Chronicles 1:11).

Instead, we are to pray for our enemies and do good to them (Matthew 5:44; Luke 6:35; Romans 12:20), because our heart is to be as compassionate as God's who observes even bad people as spiritual babes lost in the world's wood.

KEY QUOTE

I knew that you are a gracious and compassionate God, slow to anger and abounding in love, a God who relents from sending calamity.

Jonah 4:2

Place in Bible:

The fifth of the minor prophets at the end of the Old Testament, after Amos and Obadiah and before Micah and Nahum.

Parallel books:

Nahum is also about Nineveh, but probably from the seventh rather than eighth century.

Working with God achieves the impossible

The Book of Joshua

- Describes Israel's entry into, and conquest of, Canaan
- Gives examples of God's power and justice
- Tells the story of Israel's greatest military hero
- Details how Canaan was divided between the tribes

The book of Joshua has inspired many sermons, usually when its tales of battlefield exploits are recast in New Testament terms of spiritual warfare and the struggle between flesh and spirit.

But discerning readers feel uncomfortable with that without also asking searching questions about the events Joshua records. Western Christians can hardly condemn Islamic *jihads* (holy wars) while they exult in the bloody massacres of Joshua executed in God's name.

However, when these questions are answered within the context of the historical period, the book can become inspiring and challenging.

As the book traces Israel's first steps into a nd across the Jordan to the point years later when the tribes have settled into their allocated regions, it illustrates the working partnership between God and his people.

It is dynamic on both sides. Joshua is to 'be strong' because the Lord is with him (1:6-9). He must fight, and also listen to God and follow his sometimes surprising lead. Marching in silence round Jericho needed courage just for its peculiarity. And while God is both directing operations and intervening in order to give the land to his people (1:2), yet he also requires them to follow his orders and work for it.

Much later, Paul was to write that 'we are God's fellow-workers' (1 Corinthians 3:9). Look for the partnership as you read, and consider how it may be developed as you face your 'battles' in an alien culture which has little respect for God.

AT A GLANCE

JOSHUA

1	**Joshua commissioned**
2	**Rahab hides the spies**
3	**Israel crosses the Jordan**
4	**Memorial set up**
5	**Circumcision and Passover**
6	**Capture of Jericho**
7	**Achan pays for his greed**
8	**Capture of Ai**
9	**Gibeonites deceive Israel**
10	**Long day's fight**
11	**The land subdued**
12	**Lists of conquests**
13	**Tribal lands east of Jordan**
14	**Tribal lands west of Jordan**
15	**Land for Judah**
16,17	**Land for Manasseh and Ephraim**
18,19	**Other tribal lands**
20	**Cities of refuge allocated**
21	**Towns for the Levites**
22	**An altar for the eastern tribes**
23	**Joshua's farewell speech**
24	**Renewal of the covenant**

Do not let this Book of the Law depart from your mouth; meditate on it day and night . . . Then you will be prosperous and successful . . . Be strong and courageous. Do not be terrified; do not be discouraged, for the LORD your God will be with you wherever you go.

Joshua 1:8,9

Sex and lies save the God squad

Joshua 2

God isn't as fussy about the company he keeps as are some of his followers. He is more interested in what people will become than what they are like when they first encounter him. So Rahab the prostitute (some suggest she was simply a hotel keeper, as the Hebrew is less specific than the translations) was accursed in Israelite law – but the spies went to her, and God used her, none the less.

Whereupon she deliberately deceived her own people, which fuels ethics debates: is it ever right to lie in order to defend God's cause? Some twentieth-century 'Bible smugglers' have said yes; others, fearing this is the thin end of the wedge which leads to all kinds of cover-ups, have said no.

As truth-telling is highly prized in Scripture, this suggests that God is using, without condoning, a person whose own ethic at the time is limited. Rahab does not yet honour God, even though she acknowledges him.

She was a shrewd woman. Her 'faith' was a seed planted through market-place gossip; a reminder that any talk about God can awaken an interest in him. But her chief interest was self-preservation. People turn to God for many reasons, and only slowly move to a mature faith.

The story is full of irony. The spies' expedition contributed nothing to the capture of Jericho. It was a waste of time – except that one family was saved. And Rahab is one of only two women apart from his mother listed in Christ's genealogy (Matthew 1). The other is Ruth, also a foreigner. You never know what may become of that unlikely encounter.

Travelling blind into an unknown future

Joshua 3

Finding your way in a strange place, or starting a new activity, can be difficult. The Israelites 'have never been this way before' (v 4). So they are given reassurance to help them face an unknown future. They walked:

- The way of God's promise (v 5): the Lord had promised to act powerfully
- The way of God's presence (v 11): the ark would go with and ahead of them
- The way of God's power (v 10): he would defeat their enemies as he had done before
- The way of God's provision (v 16): when they obeyed, God provided an answer.

The incident is theologically parallel to the exodus. God was supernaturally present in the parting of the Red Sea, and the Jordan. The generation born in the desert sees that he is the same God and that the promised new beginning is happening after a 40-year hiccup.

The text implies a natural explanation (a landslide) for the phenomenon (v 16). It was a miracle of God's timing; the crossing was in April–May, when the flooded Jordan cannot be forded.

Later readers may underestimate the apprehension of Joshua (who had received his own personal reassurance in ch 1) and the Israelites. William Williams' great Welsh hymn links this event with the greatest, and in some respects most fearsome, journey into the unknown that anyone can make:

When I tread the verge of Jordan,
Bid my anxious fears subside;
Death of death and hell's destruction,
Land me safe on Canaan's side;
Songs of praises
I will ever give to Thee.

Date:
About 1220 BC
Location:
Canaan
Story follows:
immediately after the end of Deuteronomy in the Old Testament
Story leads to:
the history of Judges

Pause for thought at the green light

Joshua 5:1-12

When the lights turn green, the natural impulse is to accelerate away quickly. The Israelites, having crossed the Jordan, are raring to go. And God turns the lights back to red. For at least a couple of weeks, they cannot continue with the invasion.

Despite the attention to worship detail in the desert, with the building of the tabernacle, for some reason the covenant sign of circumcision has not been applied to the new generation. But if they are to do God's work, they must first be signed up as God's committed people.

Logic would have said, do it before crossing the Jordan. Spiritual dynamics operate differently. The imagery of circumcision and the Passover celebration is all the greater now they are actually in the land. They are starting out as they mean to go on: reaffirming their identity as God's people, partly in response to what God has done in leading them across the Jordan.

In a more frantic age when everything must be done yesterday, such pauses may have important places in church and personal life. They teach us to rely on God just when we might rush ahead on our own.

God is on no one's side

Joshua 5:13-6:5

This is a crucial preface for our understanding of the battles which are to follow. Joshua is confronted by an angelic figure whose interests are greater than which side will win the forthcoming fight. He is emphatically not on Israel's side just because it is God's chosen people (v 14).

He does have a battle plan but it is the most unlikely scenario any commander could conceive (vv 3-5). God seems to be making two points:

- He is not a 'God of war' like a mascot to bring good luck. His purposes may embrace human battles, but they are neither restricted to them nor, ultimately, dependent on them.
- In such times when war was a normal human activity (e.g. during widespread tribal migration) God may act differently and supernaturally in order to demonstrate his sovereignty.

Today, this means that Christians cannot assume God is automatically on the side of military might to smash whatever is the 'free world's' current *bête noir*. Nor can they embark on any project in God's name and assume he will automatically sanction their use of the world's methods to complete it.

Yahweh is his own person, independent even of his people. He is a God of surprising alternatives.

Title: From the name of the chief character which means 'The Lord saves'.
Author: Joshua wrote some things down (18:8; 24:25), and the book includes some first person accounts (5:1). However, scholars generally believe that the frequent use of 'until this day' (e.g. 7:26) implies that the present book was compiled from earlier records by an unknown editor. Samuel has been suggested as a possibility.
Date of final compilation: Possibly in the time of Samuel or the early kings, c. 1100-900 BC.
Structure: There are three parts: the conquest of Canaan (1-12); the division of Canaan (13-21:42); the renewal of the covenant (21:43-24:33).
Position in the Bible: The first book of the 'Former Prophets' section of the Hebrew Bible, which continues until 2 Kings.

HARD Question

Does God condone the slaughter of innocents?

e.g. 6:1-24; 10:29-39

The sixth commandment is 'You shall not kill', normally translated as 'murder' because of the other biblical sanctions on slaughter in war (Exodus 20:13). The distinction seems unreasonable to modern minds.

The 'just war' theory, which is frequently espoused by Christians to justify military action, legitimises only the killing of combatants and only in self-defence. It cannot sanction 'saturation bombing', least of all genocide, which in effect is what Joshua is ordered to do.

Several points of both history and overall biblical revelation need to be held together in what is clearly an uneasy, but not impossible, tension:

- We are at an early stage of Israel's discovery of God's character. He is revealing himself to them in a cultural and social milieu which is dominated by inter-tribal rivalry, and several invasions (the Philistines are also moving in around this time; the gypsy-like Habiru are marauding). They discover God in the everyday life of their own time, which he uses as a building block for the revelation of his greater purposes over succeeding centuries.
- God imposes limitations on Israel. He is not primarily a God of war (Joshua 5:13,14); he restricts the Israelite armoury to infantry (they are not to use captured chariots, 11:6, which is like guerrillas not using captured tanks or helicopters but sticking to their rifles).
- The ethnic cleansing of Canaan is portrayed as a giant visual aid of God's greater purpose, which is the building of his kingdom in the world, and his judgment on those who reject him.
- The genocide is not to be continued beyond the borders of Canaan; Israel is not called to be a superpower, and never attempted to build an empire like Assyria or Babylonia.

The crunch issue relates to the slaughter of prisoners of war and the destruction of their property. It is called 'the ban', a term usually rendered as 'devoting the city to the Lord'.

It was not peculiar to Israel; it was common at the time. It reinforced the Israelite awareness that they had to obey God fully; that they were not to be greedy; and that the land was God's, not theirs, and must be cleansed of all traces of religion and culture which denied God's character. A modern equivalent sometimes noted is the pastoral and spiritual need for Christian converts from occult sects to burn their artefacts.

The difficulty modern readers have is primarily with the long-term timescale in which the wider and 'spiritual' purposes of God are revealed. It appears to imply that God is inconsistent. However, his love and faithfulness, and his concern for the sanctity of life is also apparent even in the early books of the Bible. And his righteous judgment is apparent in the teaching of Jesus.

It is one of those questions which can never have a complete answer because we cannot see things from God's perspective. What we can be certain of is that God is consistent and that he would have been as just and righteous in his eternal dealings with the people who were slaughtered as he would have been had they died in some other way.

CROSS CHECK

Were they *that* wicked? p 91
God is on no one's side: opposite page

Some Bible resources for further study

The sanctity of life and origin of war
Genesis 1:26,27; 4:3-16; 9:5,6; Psalm 139:13-16; Matthew 5:21,22; 26:50-54; James 4:1-3

God the eternal judge
Leviticus 11:44; 20:23; Matthew 11:20-24; 24:50,51; Luke 12:49-53; Acts 5:1-11; Romans 2:5-11; Revelation 16:1-14; 20:11-15

God's purposes for his people and the world
Exodus 19:6; Isaiah 2:3-5; Zechariah 4:6; 9:9-10; Matthew 5:9,38-44; Luke 9:51-56; Romans 12:17-21; 13:1-7; 2 Corinthians 10:1-6; Revelation 21:1-15

Conditions imposed on Israelite warfare
Exodus 21:22-27; Joshua 5:13-15; 6:17,24; 11:6-9; 24:11-18; Judges 7:2-8,19-22; Hosea 10:12-15

One hole can sink a ship

Joshua 7,8

One man commits a foul, is sent off the field, his team loses and a whole country vilifies the culprit. One man scores a winning goal and his whole country erupts in wild excitement and adulation.

We are familiar with the concept of 'corporate solidarity' at this level. One person or team doesn't merely represent 'us', but in a real sense is us. However, we mostly operate on the different level of individual accountability. In biblical terms, 'the soul who sins shall die' (Ezekiel 18:4).

The Bible holds both truths in creative tension. We are personally responsible for our *actions*; we can't blame our genes, environment, other people or even Satan. But we are also bound together in an intricate web of relationships in which each person's action *affects* others.

Paul speaks of the 'body of Christ', the church, being a single entity so that 'if one part suffers, every part suffers with it' (1 Corinthians 12:26). Achan's greed brought the whole nation down. When Joshua mourns, he is told to stop (v 10). There is no point in crying over spilt milk, the mess has to be cleaned up.

By methods which are not detailed, Achan is exposed and confesses – but he is not then restored to fellowship. He is punished. The draconian, exemplary sentence makes God's verdict clear. A holy God cannot dwell among an unholy people. But the damage has been done. The defeat at Ai has shown the Canaanites that Israel is not invincible and their awe turns to spite (ch 9).

One person's sin weakens the whole church. We may not see the effect so dramatically, but the pain it causes, the faith it damages, the witness it destroys is often cumulative. The consequences can be beyond imagining; realising that should put a brake on personal indulgence.

Too long in the sun?

Joshua 10

This account seems to come from someone suffering from sunstroke. The solar day cannot be lengthened without major cosmic consequences. Most nature miracles do not go against God's creation, just as God cannot deny his own character. Several possibilities have been suggested. The two most likely are that

1. Joshua, tired after a night march, prayed to get a potentially two-day job done in one 'before sundown' – and did; and/or
2. he prayed that the sun would remain covered by cloud so that the heat would not sap the army's already low strength and enable them to keep fighting without a midday break (which was normal at the time).

A promise is a promise

Joshua 8,9

The renewal of the covenant at Mt. Ebal was intended to put Israel back on course and help prevent another Achan situation arising. In keeping with its insidious and beguiling nature, temptation quickly turned up in a fresh disguise. Or rather, a tatty one.

Gibeon was a major settlement of the Hivite tribe north of Jerusalem. Not relishing a fight, their elaborate deception works and makes Israel look stupid. Natural human instincts call for immediate revenge. But natural human instincts are not in accordance with a covenant-keeping God.

If he keeps his word, so must the Israelites, even though they had not asked him first (v 14) and so had made a wrong decision. Keeping faith with people is the practical expression of keeping faith with God – who keeps his covenant.

Claim the gift – then share it

Joshua 13-19

The extensive list of unpronounceable place names rivals the lists of personal names in Numbers and Chronicles for potential boredom. But they are there for a purpose. To the Jewish nation, they presented a permanent and authoritative record of God's gift of the land to them.

Later readers can see several principles at work. The whole book of Joshua is based on the premise that the land is God's gift, and has to be claimed by faithful obedience to him. It is an exact parallel to the New Testament assertion that a new relationship with God not based on land is his gift and must be claimed by faith.

The boundary details remind us that God gives to his people what they need, but sets limits on what each can have. Each has a different 'gift' apportioned by the sovereign Lord (cf. 1 Corinthians 12:11). Within those limits, we are called to be content, not covetous (Exodus 20:17; Philippians 4:12; Colossians 3:5).

And the gift was corporate and hereditary. It was to families, not to individuals, and therefore to be shared and then passed on. A clearer parallel to New Testament Christian fellowship can hardly be imagined.

Turning over the ancient stones

Archaeologists have unearthed many sites referred to in Joshua. While not providing conclusive evidence of Israel's invasion, they do corroborate the picture in Joshua of life at the time. It is important to note that 'city' may mean any fortified settlement and is not a term which implies a certain size. And 'king' does not mean the ruler of a country, but of a small city-state.

Mt. Ebal (8:30-35)
The remains of what seems to have been an altar of unhewn stones was found on one of the peaks, with ash and animal bones and dating from the thirteenth century BC.

Jericho (ch 6)
A problematic site because although well-excavated there is no evidence that it was a large or well-defended city in Joshua's time. It had been, centuries before, and was again later. However, popular imagination has exaggerated the biblical account and a smaller settlement, perhaps with a 'wall' of terraced houses (including Rahab's) could well be meant.

Gibeon (ch 9)
Little has been excavated, but there are tombs from the thirteenth century.

Hazor (11:10)
Its alleged headship is not surprising; a huge site of 26 acres reveals a city which may have accommodated 40,000 people. There is evidence of burning at a thirteenth-century layer. A Canaanite temple has been found there.

Ai (chs 7,8)
The word means 'ruin' and no evidence of occupation has been found from 1500 to 1200. However, it is possible that because it was a ruin with substantial walls, people from neighbouring Bethel used it as a first line of defence against the Israelites.

Safe houses and priest holes

Joshua 20,21

Justice was rough in Old Testament times. Although there was a basic civil and religious law, there was no police force and only a rudimentary system of circuit judges, even in later periods.

It was the duty of a family to avenge crimes committed against its members, a tradition which survives in certain aspects of Islamic law today. (See Leviticus 24:17; Numbers 35:16-28.)

So the provision of a safe place to run was essential for those unfortunate enough to have killed someone accidentally. There, he or she could be assured of a fair trial before impartial judges, and if acquitted could live there. This set-up demonstrated that vengeance is God's, and anger should be regulated.

The time limit on vengeance – until the death of the high priest (20:6) – has led some commentators to see a link with the death of Christ as 'High Priest', bringing forgiveness and new life.

The Levites, the ministers of religion, had their bolt-holes, too (ch 21). Their cities and lands were gifts from the people, a kind of visible and permanent tithe which reminded them that having received a gift from God they were to show their gratitude through giving something back to him.

Perhaps also, far from the central shrine, and with nearby tribes worshipping idols of wood and stone, the Israelites needed the physical reminder of God's law and presence in the person of the Levites. Even today, a personal encounter with a minister in the street or a casual visit to a church on the corner provides some people with spiritual support at times of need. We should not underestimate the value of simple visual witness and Christian presence in the community.

CROSS CHECK

Israel's enemies: p 328
The covenant: pp 18-21
Circumcision : pp 19, 21
Priests and Levites: p 263

Two important documents date from the time of Joshua. These are:

Ras Shamra texts: Ras Shamra is another name for Ugarit, an important archaeological site in northern Syria. Shortly before the time of Joshua it was a rich and flourishing city, but was sacked by another group of invaders, probably the Philistines.

Apart from a massive palace and many beautiful carvings, there was a big library of documents in several languages, chief of which was Babylonian (cf. the link with Babylonia in Joshua 7:21). The local Ugaritic language is closely related to Hebrew. The documents included religious epics of creation and the flood, a story like the biblical Job, and hymns to Baal and other gods. There are also treaties which bear structural similarities to the Old Testament covenant.

The Amarna letters: Amarna is well south of modern Cairo in Egypt. Almost 400 letters from diplomats were found there, dating from c. 1385-60 which is probably before the exodus, but they shed light on the state of life in Canaan at that time.

Settlements such as Shechem, Gezer and Jerusalem are mentioned, as are the marauding Habiru gypsies who are causing mayhem. (These were once thought to be the Israelites, but the connection is now considered unlikely, not least because the Habiru used chariots, banned in Joshua 11:6.) The documents show there were alliances between Babylon and Egypt, and there is a reference to a Semitic leader in Egypt who some have suggested was Joseph.

'Take my bones home with you'

Joshua 24:32

There are no strong theological reasons why human bodies should be disposed of in one way rather than another. However, although there may be good environmental reasons for cremation, burial has the added value of providing a physical place where family members can remember their forebears.

Going to a grave to grieve, to reflect or even to pray, can help minister to a person's deepest emotions and keep alive treasured memories.

This seemingly insignificant verse is not one to gloss over.

- It fulfilled a charge (Genesis 50:25) which Jacob had laid on his descendants; fulfilling a person's last wishes is an important sign of human respect
- It continued a family tradition, linking past and present with a special place (Genesis 33:19); it expressed the strong bond which should exist, but which is often broken, between generations.

Converted flock to altar call

Joshua 24

Joshua has done his job; soon he will die. One task is left; like Moses before him he must prepare the people for a new life.

From now on Israel is not a single entity but a federation of semi-autonomous tribes. It is united not by one charismatic leader but by common worship and aims. The new relationships are given public affirmation, and the age-old covenant is renewed.

Although often used as an evangelistic text, verse 15 is a call to God's people to reaffirm their faith. The evangelists' 'altar call' bears repeating; public acts of rededication can help unite members of a church in a common task and reinforce their sense of identity as God's people.

Symbols don't clash with simple faith

Joshua 22

Human beings have short memories; anniversaries are easily forgotten. Most societies erect monuments as a witness to ideas, people or events they consider significant. The presence of war memorials in many communities ensures that the cost of conflict is not forgotten by successive generations.

The Bible is fond of memorials. Jacob set up several (Genesis 28:18; 31:45), as did Joshua to mark the crossing of the Jordan and the renewal of the covenant (Joshua 4:6-9; 24:27). As the Israelites disperse, the eastern tribes set up what appears to be an altar for sacrifice, but which they claim is a memorial. Israel was allowed only one central sacrificial altar (Deuteronomy 12:5-7).

Their explanation is accepted; the memorial was altar-shaped and open to misuse, but that made it a significant reminder that the eastern tribes belonged to Israel.

Religious symbols are always open to abuse, but that does not mean that they should be avoided altogether. The fear of 'idolatry' has robbed some groups of potential spiritual enrichment which can come from the right and thoughtful use of symbols and memorials.

For today

- We are workers with God and not just for God
- God will ultimately destroy all that is opposed to him
- He supports his people when they obey him
- Action is to be accompanied by prayer

Keep the fences mended

As any pet owner or farmer knows, it is a chief purpose of animal life to get through fences. Rabbits will burrow under them, sheep will squeeze through them, and goats will eat them.

Jude wanted to write a letter or tract about the delights of the spiritual meadow in which the church grazed, but instead he spends his strength telling his readers to stay within the fences which surround it: the doctrines 'once for all entrusted to the saints' (v 3). The reason for his change is that some church members have torn down the barriers and others are in danger of falling.

They have impure motives and bad intentions. They have 'secretly slipped in' like enemy agents in a government department, like wolves in sheeps' clothing (Matthew 7:15). They look right, and sound right, but subtly undermine faith. They also encourage immoral conduct.

To counter them, Jude says we are to stay within the boundaries of faith previously laid down. Today, these are encapsulated for us in the creeds which are based on Scripture, and in the broad but definite boundaries of conduct outlined in the historic Ten Commandments.

In an age of moral relativism, there are many voices advocating practices and beliefs which are not genuine interpretations or fresh applications of unchanging truths, but denials or distortions of those truths. We are to resist them as Jude's readers were to resist the false teachers of their time.

G.K. Chesterton once wrote that the breaking of barriers could be the breaking of everything. The fence of faith is not a prison wall to restrict our freedom but a guard rail for our benefit and safety. And human beings are not meant to behave like animals searching for greener grass.

JUDE

Jude is one of the shortest New Testament books (only one chapter) but, as the early church writer Origen said, 'it is full of mighty words'.

Jude tells his readers in no uncertain terms to withstand false teachers and to hold fast to the apostolic faith.

Place in Bible: The penultimate book of the New Testament, after the letters of John and before Revelation.

Parallel books: Almost all of Jude is quoted in 2 Peter. In the scholars' debate over which was first, Jude wins by a short head.

FAST facts

Author: usually taken to be Judas (Judah, a common name) the brother or half-brother of Jesus (cf. Mark 6:3), and hence the brother of James (v 1) the leader of the church in Jerusalem (Acts 15:13; Galatians 1:19). The chosen description 'servant of Jesus Christ' shows Jude's humility in light of the family link; the same self-description was used by James also (James 1:1). A less likely contender is Judas (not Iscariot), the apostle, but verse 17 suggests that the author was not one of the twelve.

Date: Thought to be in the second half of the first century AD because of the apparently established faith (v 3) and the refuted heresy refuted. Probably AD 65-75.

Readers: Jewish Christians troubled by false teachers, but no location can be identified from the letter.

Authenticity: Jude was accepted as authentic from the later second century, although his quotations from apocryphal books gave rise to some perplexity.

HARD Question

Are unbiblical sources vehicles of God's truth?

Jude was rejected by some early church leaders because he used books not recognised as authoritative Scripture and considered to be 'unsound'.

He quotes from *The Assumption of Moses* (v 9); draws from *The Book of Enoch* (vv 6,8,13-15), a bizarre work full of extravagant symbolism, and possibly from *The Testament of Naphtali* (v 6) and *The Testament of Asher* (v 8). These were all items of Jewish fiction.

Other biblical books quote dubious sources: Paul used Greek and Cretan writers (Acts 17:28; 1 Corinthians 15:33; Titus 1:12). Old Testament authors acknowledged outside sources (e.g. Numbers 21:14; 1 Kings 14:19,29) and Luke says there were many records of Jesus' life (1:1-4). Jesus himself quoted an old wives tale (Matthew 16:3)!

Jude's use of the Michael legend does not imply that it is true; all we can say is that he uses a familiar story to make a point about the false teachers.

This encourages us to take a robust view of biblical authority and inspiration. God draws on surprising sources. Many of the people whose story is told in the Bible and who were used by God were far from being 'saints'. They were, in fact, pretty sinful!

So the sources used for and quoted by the Scriptures were far from perfect too. But woven together under the direction of God's Spirit the overall message of the scriptural writings became his. Use of other authors does not imply that all they wrote was right, inspired, or even helpful; only that what is quoted is now, in its context, the vehicle of God's message.

Don't slander the devil

It is the habit of groups of all ages to heap abuse on their current *bête noir*. Mocking superiority and malicious scorn spew from mouths like lava vomited from a volcano. The verbiage kills spiritual life and hardens into an emotionally barren crust when it cools.

False teachers love to scorn the orthodox, preferening to argue rationally against their beliefs. Christians are called, by contrast, to love their enemies and to oppose error with grace, and Jude's vitriolic language needs to be copied with some caution in only extreme circumstances! We should realise, however, that critical speech in Bible times was regularly more forethright than is usual today.

These false teachers were even scorning 'celestial beings' (v 8). Nothing and no one was sacred. This is close to outright blasphemy. But notice that Jude cautions against slandering the devil, a fallen 'prince' of heaven (v 9).

He says that the archangel Michael recognised Satan's former position in heaven's hierarchy. One so high-born should be treated with respect, however far he may have fallen, both for his past status (like an impeached President) and for his present power.

We should not underestimate Satan. The devil likes being laughed at because that prevents us from taking his subtle stratagems seriously. So mind your language as you maintain your 'spiritual warfare'. The enemy should not be mocked, even though he is already being destroyed. All good soldiers respect the enemy general, even when they are winning the war.

CROSS CHECK

Angels: pp 270-1
The devil (Satan): pp 192, 166, 271, 307
Inspiration of Scripture: p 11
False teachers in the church: p 135

KEY QUOTE

Keep yourselves in God's love as you wait for the mercy of our Lord Jesus Christ to bring you to eternal life.

Jude v 21

The time when God's record got stuck

The Book of Judges

- Describes how the tribes of Israel continued to conquer Canaan
- Shows how they compromised their faith and brought suffering on themselves
- Tells of twelve leaders (judges) called by God to rescue them from oppression
- Describes the raw nature of life and warfare in a society where anarchy was rife

Probably more problems for modern readers are raised by the book of Judges than by any other biblical writing. Readers vaguely aware of Deborah's maternal leadership, Gideon's timidity and heroics, and Samson's tragic affair with Delilah which left him 'eyeless in Gaza' are likely to be shocked by crude killings, grisly rape and revenge, and general licence.

The author, who is working like a senior editor on *Time* magazine, compiling a selective essay from a number of reports, answers the ethical questions with one sentence: 'In those days Israel had no king; everyone did as he saw fit.' It was anarchy, so what sort of behaviour would you expect?

Carefully constructed, the thesis is summarised in chapter 2. This is the only biblical book to speak of a 'cycle of history'. Normally the Bible regards history as a continuous line from creation to heaven. But here, as poet Steve Turner has aptly put it,

History repeats itself.
Has to.
Nobody listens.

Judges reads as if God's record has got stuck. But in fact it is God's people who are stuck in a cycle of faith degenerating into indulgence, followed by crisis which prompts repentance. We've all done it, although maybe not quite so brazenly.

JUDGES

1	Israel conquers Canaan
2	The cycle of disobedience
3	Othniel and Ehud
4	Deborah and Barak
5	Deborah's song of praise
6	Gideon called by God
7	Gideon's small army conquers Midian
8	Gideon pursues the Midianites
9	Abimelech made king
10-11	Jephthah's victory and vow
12	The Shibboleth test
13	Samson is born
14	Samson's marriage and early exploits
15	Samson's vengeance on the Philistines
16	Samson and Delilah
17	Micah and his priest
18	The priest defects to Dan
19	Rape of the Levite's mistress
20	Benjamites punished en masse
21	Benjamite survivors found wives

And the glory of Judges is that God doesn't give up on his people. He does rescue them, eventually. He keeps his covenant even though they break theirs. It's not savoury reading, but it's salutary. Our sins may be different to those of the time of Judges, but they are no less real. Christians today can sacrifice to the three related idols of greed, envy and avarice at the altar of consumerism without even realising they are doing it. Maybe there's a message for us here, too.

Whenever the LORD raised up a judge for them, he was with the judge and saved them out of the hands of their enemies as long as the judge lived . . . But when the judge died, the people returned to ways even more corrupt than those of their fathers . . .

Judges 2:18,19

A long way to go

Judges 1:1-2:5

The Israelites, in common with many tribes of their time, intended to drive out the inhabitants of Canaan to preserve the purity of their own social and spiritual life (cf. Deuteronomy 18:12; 31:3). They had not completed this task by the death of Joshua.

There could have been a good reason for this. Palestine was geographically difficult. Much of the land was craggy hills pitted with ravines. The fertile parts 'flowing with milk and honey' were scattered. So too were Israel's enemies. They were small tribes in isolated city-states or clumps of villages.

Israel had no unified leadership once Joshua had sent the tribes into their designated territories; communications were slow and difficult and there was no centralised standing army. And, after a generation tramping through Sinai and another forcing their way into Canaan, the people probably looked forward to a time of peace and quiet.

But whatever the reasons, the author of Judges wants readers to know that the incomplete task was a snare to the Israelites. It involved them in compromise. Many tasks remain uncompleted by the church today, too, such as the evangelisation of the world; and the task of forging the genuine unity and understanding between different Christian groups for which Jesus prayed. Any let-up is likely to lead to compromise with the world around us and failure to fulfil God's purposes.

Gauche loner murders gross ruler

Judges 3:12-30

Left-handedness has been derided in most cultures, and their languages testify to it. The French *gauche* can mean crooked or ugly; Italian *mancino* can mean deceitful and dishonest; and the Russian *levja* may be a racketeer. The Romany *bongo* has come into English as a card trick, a sleight of hand. In medieval times, left-handedness was seen as a mark of the devil.

In Israel, being left-handed was regarded as being disabled. It is hardly referred to in the Bible except here and in references to the Benjamites who seem to have had a higher than average incidence of it than today's ten per cent (Judges 20:16; cf. 1 Chronicles 12:2).

Ehud, therefore, is an outsider. He operates alone and is not a judge in the sense of legal adviser or military leader. He is discounted by others, but is perfect for this one task. The security at the Moabite court was lax; no one thought of body-searching the right hand side for concealed weapons.

The grisly details of the obese king's intestinal rupture are probably intended to convey the depth that the knife sank into his many layers of fat. They are also the sort of things people like to gossip about.

The author is saying (and will say it again, in different ways) that allegedly awkward or 'gauche' people have a place in God's purposes alongside everyone else. When all others were wringing their hands in anguish, this man just saw what needed to be done and quietly got on with it. That, and not the method he used, is what we are intended to remember.

Date of events:
About 1200-1000 BC (assuming the Exodus was about 1275 BC)

Location:
Various parts of Palestine

Place in Bible:
Follows Joshua, precedes Ruth and 1 Samuel in the Old Testament

Story follows:
Directly after the conquest of Canaan by Joshua

Story leads to:
The account of Samuel, the last judge who held Israel together until King Saul

Parallel book:
The story of Ruth takes place at this time

HARD Question

Does the Bible condone political assassination?

The question has been on the public agenda at least twice in the twentieth century. Christian pastor Dietrich Bonhoeffer was executed shortly before the end of the Second World War for his involvement in a plot to kill Hitler.

More recently, the possibility of killing Iraqi dictator Saddam Hussein was discussed. And in a different realm, but similar vein, has been the bombing of abortion clinics and murder of doctors in north America by groups who claim to be doing God's work.

We cannot take passages such as Judges 3 as precedents for modern times. So much has changed. The 'theocracy' (a nation-state chosen by God for a specific purpose, governed by his laws with no discrimination between 'church' and 'state', secular and sacred) no longer exists. But that was Ehud's environment and it gave the judges their broad mandate.

Further, we have the fuller revelation from Jesus Christ that under the new covenant (Ehud operated under the old covenant) Christians are to love their enemies and do good to them. (It is a matter of debate as to whether this prohibits Christians from joining the armed services, and if secular governments should ever use force against other countries.)

The judges acted within their own understanding of God's purposes, and God accommodated his activity to the developing culture of the people he had called at their time in history. We cannot turn the clock back and mimic them because we are in a different time and have a fuller revelation. What we can do is draw unchanging theological principles from these incidents.

However, few people will feel no sympathy for the Bonhoeffers of this world who considered that exceptional means were needed in an exceptionally evil case. Yet to reason so is to open the door for the abortion bombers to push their way through and blaspheme the name of Christ.

FAST facts

Title: Judges takes its name from the title given to the leaders described in it. In the Hebrew Bible, it is included among the 'Former Prophets', not among the historical books as in Christian Bibles, stressing the view of the judges as God's appointed agents of change.

Structure: The book has three main divisions: 1:1-3:6 (introduction and over-view); 3:7-16:31 (stories of the judges); 17:1-21:25 (concluding stories about the tribes of Benjamin and Dan). It recounts incidents from the lives of twelve judges (which is probably symbolic and they may each come from different tribes) who represent specific 'types' of people (loners like Ehud and Samson, outcasts like Deborah (a woman) and Jephthah, with Gideon as the archetypal small-town boy who made good). Although it has a historical base, Judges is illustrating a theological thesis and is not intending to give us a comprehensive account of the period.

Purpose: It shows that God remains faithful to his people despite their unfaithfulness to him. As a result, he periodically raises up deliverers for them. A repeated refrain (see 17:6) may indicate that the author wants us to compare the bad old days of the judges with the good new days of (possibly David's) kingship.

Author and date: Unknown, except that clearly it was written in the time of the early kings (c. 1050-950 BC). Some have suggested Samuel compiled it.

Girl power beats army

Judges 4,5

Israel was a largely patriarchal society dominated by men. Women did rise to leadership, however, as Deborah indicates. Her prophetic gifts (4:4) were not derided because of her gender, but she was not a military leader like Joan of Arc.

Barak, the army commander, probably wanted her to go with him as a gilt-edged insurance policy. Her presence would indicate her utter faith in her own prediction, and as a woman of God she would have been akin to a lucky charm; Barak would have considered God less likely to let his prophet be killed in the battle she witnessed.

Jael's cold-blooded murder is rather un-ladylike. It's not exactly fair, either; she fooled Sisera with her charms. Had she been Samson's Delilah, we would have booed; as it is, we cheer. She's on our side. The disgrace for Barak is not in the deed but in the hand; as a man, he should have had the supposed 'pleasure' of executing his enemy.

The point is that Deborah and Jael are the last people who in their culture would have been expected to achieve such things. If we turn away from the blood-stained sand beneath Jael's tent, we can see an abiding principle that God does not require his servants to have a certain human or social status.

Many players, but the same tune

Judges 3-6

Along with its catalogue of unlikely judges the book is also giving us a list of different enemies. The Moabites (defeated by Ehud) were bullies who occupied the land. The Canaanites confronted by Deborah were conquerors bent on genocide. And Gideon faced the Midianites (Moses' in-laws) who were hit-and-run vandals determined to smash up Israel's domain (6:6). Later, we shall meet the Philistines who exercised an economic stranglehold through their monopoly on iron products.

The effect, however, was always the same. Eventually oppression drove the Israelites back to God. They cried for the help they had been too proud to seek earlier and confessed the sins they had enjoyed.

The church also faces varied opponents at different times. Direct persecution, indifference, theological division, or subtle derision have all presented themselves to Christians.

Man of doubt given unbelievable role

Judges 6

Gideon is one of the Bible's doubters. As such, he offers much encouragement!

- He questioned basic truths (v 13). Current theology did not match his experience. God did not seem to be in control. Gideon's call alerts him to facts he has not thought about before.
- He doubted his own hearing (v 17). Rightly afraid of being deluded, he sought a sign which would authenticate the messenger, and the holy fire with which God honoured his request was not a sop to mere curiosity.
- He was afraid to be open (v 27). Doing the job at night didn't negate it but reveals how scared he was. He started with a small task – which seemed big enough.
- He hid behind his family (v 31). He let his dad defend him, and huddled behind the curtains!
- He sought double confirmation of his guidance (vv 36-40). There are two kinds of dew in Palestine. One comes from the air and soaks into the grass, but would leave the fleece wet. One comes up from the ground, wetting the grass, but not penetrating the fleece.

After that, he did what he was told. God is patient with genuine. But he put Gideon to the test in what can only have been one of God's big jokes. Read on . . .

There's danger in numbers

Judges 7

If the news had leaked out that General Gideon was planning a night raid on tens of thousands with 300 men, armed with trumpets and candles, he would have been immediately relieved of his duties, certified insane and relegated to the annals of military incompetence along with the leader of the charge of the Light Brigade.

There are two 'spiritual' applications of this familiar story. God can use a small minority to achieve great things, so the church should not complain about its relative proportion in society. Also, he may use strange tactics that only real faith can cope with.

Every age has worshipped numbers. Big is beautiful and mega churches are rated highly while mini churches are reckoned to be spiritual failures. Or at least, their ministers are, who are regularly overlooked by the head hunters who see only balance sheets and not the godly faithfulness for which God never guarantees 'success'.

We also pin our hopes on methods. It used to be the 'Four spiritual laws' as an infallible guide to leading people to Christ. Now it is Alpha courses. Soon, it will be something else. God hates being pinned down; so the really visionary will be looking already for God's surprise tactics. And woe to those who package them as a method.

However, these are probably secondary considerations to the author's main message for the Israelites. He is anxious that they do not fall into national pride (v 2). 'We've done this!' they would cry, and God would be lucky to get a mention. He does not share his glory with another and we bask in his reflected glory at our peril. It can lead to cancer of the soul.

We also see an alternative way of waging war. The story hints that there is a better way of national life, under God, than blood-letting. Inducing panic was the tactic here, followed, of course, by a lot of blood-letting. It took many centuries before people were ready to hear Jesus' message that there was a kingdom greater than the nation, and a weapon better than the sword.

Don't blame dad!

Judges 8-9

When the child of Christian parents 'goes wrong' – from giving up church to getting into drugs – the parents often receive criticism. Some Christian preachers declare that most of today's problems are due to bad parenting.

The Bible will not allow such blanket judgments. It has several examples of children who rebel from godly upbringings. We can't judge how good a father Gideon was. With 70 sons and a harem of wives he was hardly a model for New Testament monogamy and modern 'new father' bonding. But the author does not consider this worthy of comment.

Gideon's only recorded sin was to make a shrine which stimulated (but doesn't seem to have been intended for) idol worship (8:24-27). And to his credit he resolutely refused to disobey God by becoming, or allowing his sons to become, king of Israel (8:22-23).

Abimelech (who was semi-legitimate, 9:18, and perhaps felt marginalised in the family) lusted for power and (probably falsely) implied that his brothers were about to set up a power-sharing dynasty. Armed with a dubious mandate, he liquidated his potential rivals (9:1-6). Only Jotham appears to have inherited something of Gideon's spirit. He hid too (9:21)!

Biblically, Gideon cannot be held responsible for the actions of his adult son. Children rebel usually for a complex mass of reasons. The incident is treated by the author of Judges as a stand-alone sin and is an early example of the sense of individual responsibility which balances the more frequent biblical stress on corporate solidarity.

Rash vows lead to long regrets

Judges 10-11

It was natural to Jephthah to 'devote' to God (that is kill) a creature as a thank offering for good success. We might promise a cheque.

He evidently never considered that a returning warrior was more likely to be met at the gate by a relieved member of his family than by a sniffling dog or scratching hen ('whatever', not 'whoever', v 31). That was his undoing; in the heat of the moment, he just did not think.

Jephthah is another 'rejected' person by an accident of birth (11:1-3; Tob was outside Israelite territory on the Ammonite border). It is only when people need his skills that they ask him back. It is an ancient example of the modern vice of valuing people only for what they can do.

But God has looked after him. Jephthah understands the Scriptures (11:14-27), and is open to God's Spirit (11:29). He's not too proud to accept the task – having made sure first that he'll be paid for it (11:9-11) – when some people would have refused.

His daughter's appearance devastates him. He's not a hard man; he's a caring father. But he feels he can't break a vow to God (11:35). It's an impossible dilemma. Perhaps Jesus had this in mind when he told his disciples not to take rash oaths (Matthew 5:33-37).

Vows used as bargaining tools ('get me home and you'll get this') should not be part of our lives at all; bribing God will entangle us as it entangled Jephthah. Once the heat of the moment has cooled, we'll probably find we can't keep the vows. And then what will we do?

On display: the weakest man on earth!

Judges 13–16

If Judges was written by the equivalent of a *Time* editor his source for the Samson saga must have been the local tabloids. Salacious, farcical, trivial – and tragic. That's Samson, and he's given as much space as Gideon.

This is not the Israelite equivalent of a Hercules myth. Any novelist could have thought up more effective adventures than telling riddles at a party and setting light to foxes' tails. This has all the marks of authentic tribal memory.

Samson is pathetic. Over-sized and over-sexed he's a bear of a man with very little brain. But God chooses him and uses him. What must his peers have been like, one wonders? The author wants us to notice:

- Samson is a comic hero. He serves a purpose; his bizarre antics lighten the spirit and inspire faith and hope: the Philistines are not unbeatable, even if by unconventional methods.
- He was a child of promise (ch 13), one of several biblical children singled out and born to otherwise sterile parents.
- He was dedicated to God. His Nazirite vow (which included the long hair, but not celibacy) was like a monastic vow. He kept the letter but not the spirit.
- He provides a warning. In a woman's arms the strong man became soft as putty. Recent history has reminded us of the sexual vulnerability of public figures.
- He fell through his own fault and couldn't blame genetic weakness. John Milton in *Samson Agonistes* makes him acknowledge that 'swoll'n with pride, into the snare I fell' and admit 'All wickedness is weakness: that plea therefore / With God or man will gain thee no remission.'
- God was able to work through his stupidity rather than in spite of it. That is the genius of God, and probably what the author most wants us to remember. He can work through our stupidity, too – but that's no excuse for it.

For today

- Don't give up when God's work isn't completed
- Remember that apparently 'odd' people have a ministry too
- Doubt is not a sin; deal gently with those who have it
- Don't get carried away by size and numbers
- Beware the area of your vulnerability
- When it's everyone for themselves – you're probably included.

CROSS CHECK

Battles sanctioned by God: p 227

Right in their own eyes, wrong in God's

Judges 17-21

If the Samson saga was tasteless, this last section of the book is absolutely disgusting. God gets a mere bit part (see Hard Question) and the picture of Israelite society is one which most would want to hide from public gaze. But the Bible never does that. The author is being frank. This is anarchic Israel at its worst (17:6).

Micah was corrupt: he robbed his own mother (17:1-6); allowed his Levite guest to make a forbidden local shrine (Israel was to have only one, central shrine), thereby abusing his calling and compounds the sin by accepting idols into his 'ministry'. Later he is tempted by offers of preferment and power (18:19) from the neighbouring bully boys (18:25 could be straight out of a gangster movie).

Yet there remains a glimmer of decency. The horrific rape of the (different) Levite's concubine penetrates the corporate conscience when her grisly remains turn people's hearts as well as their stomachs (ch 19). The touching provision of wives for surviving Benjamites following the bloody massacre of rather more than had perpetrated the original crime shows that community spirit was not quite dead (ch 20).

We are not so barbaric. Except those who abuse children. Rob cars and houses. Vandalise estates. Arrange contract murders. Ruin relationships by greed and selfishness. Cut up drivers on the highway. Drive workers to breakdowns by threats of financial and employment loss. Not us, of course, but others. But when it's everyone for themselves (17:6), everyone's guilty.

HARD Question

How did people 'enquire of the Lord'?

Judges 20: 27-28

The phrase occurs quite often in the Old Testament but the method is uncertain. This passage (chronologically before the main events of Judges if Phinehas is the one in Joshua 22:13 and not the one in 1 Samuel 2:34) emphasises the role of the ark of the covenant and the high priest.

The ark represented God's presence, and so they came (prayerfully) to God. The high priest had the Urim and Thummin (Deuteronomy 33:8-10) which were used for determining God's answers to specific prayers. These were most likely dice or stones, which were cast or drawn to represent 'yes' and 'no'.

Modern mathematicians would work out the odds on either and conclude that the outcome was a matter of luck, equivalent to tossing a coin after saying a prayer. At the time, it was a God-ordained method, and respected as such (cf. Proverbs 16:33). If God ordained it, presumably he controlled it.

However, those who might be tempted to use such methods today should note that the Urim and Thummin have disappeared and that there is no sanction in the New Testament for seeking guidance in this way. Rather, the combination of prayer, Bible reading, consultation with others, personal conviction, prophetic ministry rightly tested, and circumstantial events seem to be the most suitable way for Christians to 'enquire of the Lord'.

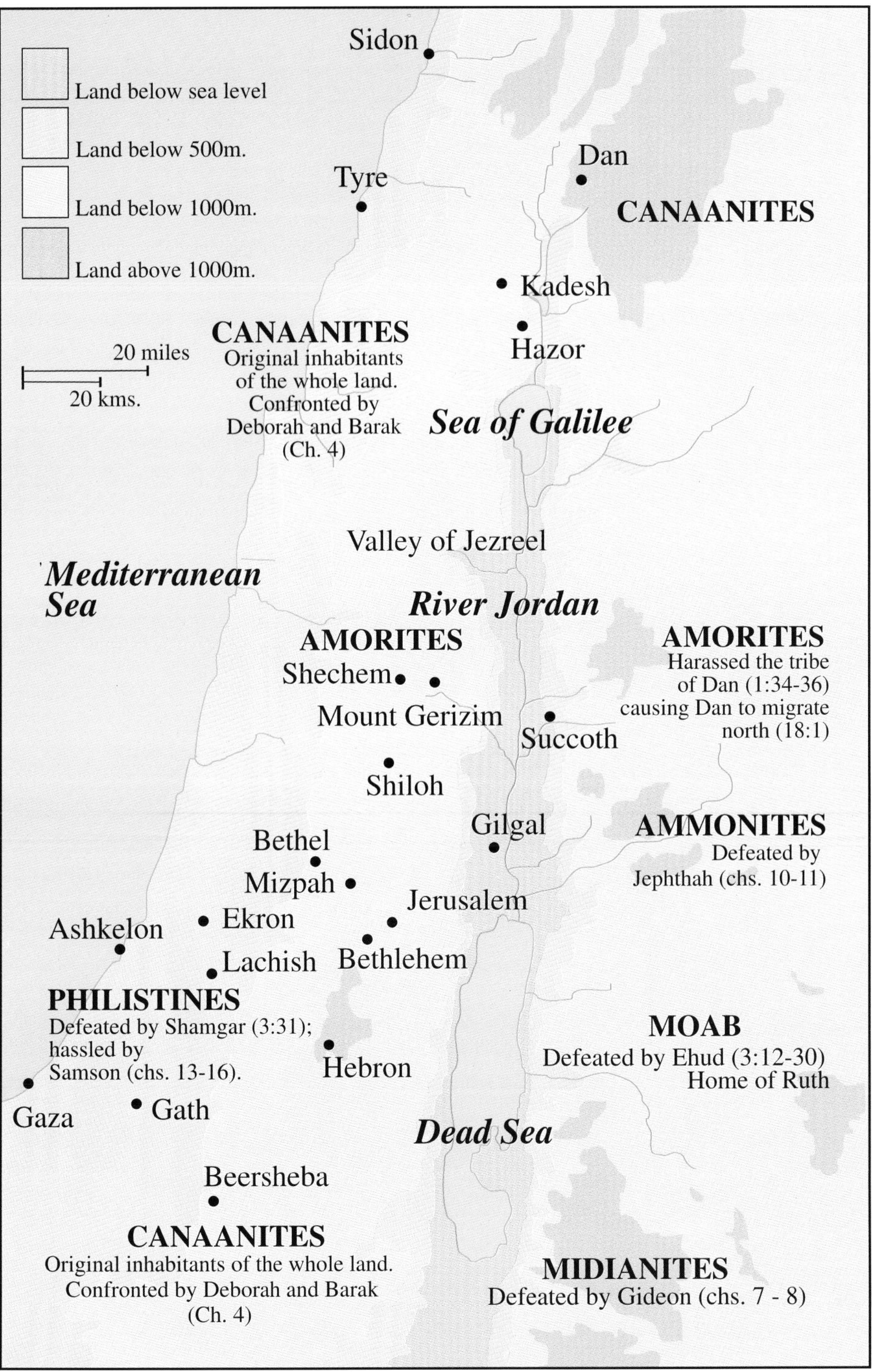
Sidon
Land below sea level
Land below 500m.
Land below 1000m.
Land above 1000m.
Dan
Tyre
CANAANITES
Kadesh
Hazor
CANAANITES
Original inhabitants
of the whole land.
Confronted by
Deborah and Barak
(Ch. 4)
20 miles
20 kms.
Sea of Galilee
Valley of Jezreel
Mediterranean
Sea
River Jordan
AMORITES
AMORITES
Harassed the tribe
of Dan (1:34-36)
causing Dan to migrate
north (18:1)
Shechem
Mount Gerizim
Succoth
Shiloh
Gilgal
AMMONITES
Defeated by
Jephthah (chs. 10-11)
Bethel
Mizpah
Jerusalem
Ashkelon
Ekron
Lachish
Bethlehem
PHILISTINES
Defeated by Shamgar (3:31);
hassled by
Samson (chs. 13-16).
MOAB
Defeated by Ehud (3:12-30)
Home of Ruth
Hebron
Gaza
Gath
Dead Sea
Beersheba
CANAANITES
Original inhabitants of the whole land.
Confronted by Deborah and Barak
(Ch. 4)
MIDIANITES
Defeated by Gideon (chs. 7 - 8)

A skeleton from the cupboard

The Books of 1 & 2 Kings

- Tell how Israel divided into Judah and Israel
- Summarise the story of both kingdoms until their destruction
- Introduce the prophets Elijah, Elisha and Isaiah
- Describe the extent to which successive kings obeyed God's covenant
- Show how world events were used by God to teach his people lessons

Apart from jellyfish and worms, most animals have a skeleton which provides a solid framework for their flesh and vital organs. The book of Kings (the two were originally one) provides a historical skeleton which holds the heart of the Old Testament story together.

That story also encompasses most of the prophets and many of the psalms and wisdom books. It is partly paralleled in Chronicles and in the historical sections of Isaiah and Jeremiah. The links are summarised in the Where am I? charts and the composite story told in detail in the companion volume *Bible Chronicle*.

When Solomon died, the kingdom split. The ten northern tribes, eventually centred on Samaria, became known as Israel and were led initially by a rebellious member of Solomon's civil service, Jeroboam. The two southern tribes of Judah and Benjamin, known together as Judah, were led initially by Solomon's heir, Rehoboam.

The narrative of Kings moves between the two. It shows that despite the prophets and occasional national revivals, the kings and their people constantly compromised the covenant. After many warnings, the world superpower Assyria fell like an axe on Israel, destroyed Samaria, scattered its population and re-settled refugees from other campaigns in their place. In 722 BC, Israel ceased to exist.

Tiny Judah was threatened by the Assyrians but spared defeat. However, the prophets' warnings went unheeded and about a century later, when Babylon overran the Assyrian empire, Jerusalem was besieged and sacked. Solomon's beautiful temple was destroyed and many people were exiled to Babylon in several waves, ending in 587 BC.

The story continues in the books of Jeremiah, Ezekiel and Ezra. But you will appreciate their human poignancy and spiritual message better if you set aside any impatience with accounts of kings, dates and battles and listen first to the historian whose main purpose is not to tell us in detail *what* happened (he doesn't), but *why* it happened. This skeleton needs to come out of the cupboard in order to enable us to dissect the spiritual anatomy of God's people which, like the human body, never changes.

AT A GLANCE

1 KINGS

1	Adonijah's attempted coup
2	Solomon becomes king
3	Solomon's prayer for wisdom
4	List of civil servants
5	Solomon starts to build the temple
6	The temple is built
7	Solomon's palace; temple furniture
8	Temple and ark dedicated to God
9	God's promise to Solomon
10	The visit of the Queen of Sheba
11	Solomon's wives and enemies
12	The kingdom divides
13	A tale of two prophets
14	Bad news for Jeroboam
15	Abijah, Asa (Judah); Nadab, Baasha (Israel)
16	More kings of Israel
17	Elijah sustained in the famine
18	Elijah and the priests of Baal
19	Elijah flees for his life
20	Ahab fights Ben-Hadad
21	Ahab and Naboth's vineyard
22	Ahab condemned by Micaiah

(Some incidents in 1 Kings have parallel accounts in 1 Chronicles)

FAST facts

Author: Hebrew tradition suggests that it was Jeremiah, but there is little evidence for this and it is not generally accepted today. No other biblical names are obvious candidates, and it is best to conclude that one person compiled the book from a number of existing sources. Some scholars have suggested that the original compilation was heavily edited a century or so later, to account for some dating problems raised by the occasional phrase 'to this day' or 'later' names put in an earlier context.

Date of compilation: This depends to some extent on the authorship question. As the book seems to have been written to explain to the exiles in Babylon (see introduction opposite) why they had got into such a state, it seems likely that Kings was written not long after the fall of Jerusalem in 587 BC.

Structure and style: Originally one book, it was divided by the Greek translators of the Septuagint. It was linked to 1 & 2 Samuel to form four 'Books of kingdoms'. The author uses distinctive formulae to start and conclude his summaries of the reigns which he includes and notes the king's relationship to the covenant, and whether he obeyed or rejected it.

Sources: Several source documents are referred to (e.g. 14:19,29) and no doubt others were used as well, both official state records and the annals of prophets. Kings itself appears to have been used as a major source for the next book in the Bible, Chronicles.

Don't swim against the tide of God's will

1 Kings 1-2

Trying to divert the purposes of God into personally profitable channels is like standing in front of a tidal wave and hoping to brush it into a storm drain. Four people discover that in this passage, to their cost.

For a long time Joab, David's loyal but unprincipled commander, had pushed his luck. Now he goes too far and gets his just deserts (cf. 2:5,6). Adonijah, another of David's spoiled brats (cf. 1:6), Abiathar, a previously loyal priest who seems to have had a brainstorm, and Joab, all knew that Solomon was both David's and God's choice as successor to the ailing king.

Even after the initial failure of the coup, Adonijah made a second and thinly-disguised attempt to get in the throne-room by the back door when he requested Abishag, David's last companion, as a wife (2:13-25).

Solomon's conduct in this messy start to his reign is exemplary, which is why the author tells the story. Solomon is the golden boy of Kings, the model who most others fail to emulate. He gave Adonijah a second chance; he placed a curfew on David's tormentor, Shimei (cf. 2 Samuel 16:5-14); and he banished the disgraced priest, but let him live for wholly noble reasons.

However, even kindly Solomon could hardly countenance a conspiratorial commander-in-chief, although he executed Joab for murder, not rebellion. Joab's luck ran out when, clinging to the altar as a traditional way of pleading for clemency, he discovered that the law allowed his execution nonetheless because his crimes were pre-meditated.

The author has set out his thesis and bequeathed an unchanging message. All four learned too late that it is better to go with the tide of God's will, even if that is not to our greatest material and social profit, than to swim against it.

In an age when the pressure to succeed is increasing, the temptation is to manipulate events to our advantage. God is interested in other things, and his view of our advantage may be different to ours.

KEY QUOTE

Ahab sent word throughout all Israel and assembled the prophets on Mount Carmel. Elijah went before the people and said, 'How long will you waver between two opinions? If the LORD is God, follow him; but if Baal is God, follow him.'

1 Kings 18:20-21

Date of events:
970 (Solomon) – 587 BC (fall of Jerusalem)

Location:
Palestine, with incursions from Egypt, Assyria, Aramea (Syria) and Babylon

Place in Bible:
After 2 Samuel, before Chronicles in the Old Testament

Story follows:
Death of David

Story leads to:
The return of exiles

Parallel Bible books:
2 Chronicles, Amos, Hosea, Isaiah, Micah, Jeremiah, Zephaniah, Nahum; possibly Jonah and Joel

Picture of happiness fetches high price

1 Kings 4

If ever there was a golden age for the Israelites, this was it; 4:25 is the classic biblical description of peace, security and contentment – what we all dream of.

But there's no such thing as a free lunch; someone has to pay for it. Samuel's warning of what a king would do to his own people (1 Samuel 8:10-18) is already being fulfilled by Solomon's lavish lifestyle, civic and military expansion, and growing bureaucracy. National taxation is introduced.

For a while, harvests are good, international trade is lucrative, and the nation prospers. It can pay its bills and still enjoy the change. Soon, the pinch will be felt and the public will grow discontented (12:4), but until then we can rejoice with the author at Solomon's achievements (which continue in chapters 5-7) and assume that, in common with his contemporary monarchs, he created garden cities where he could observe at his leisure the wildlife which gave colour to his proverbs (cf. v 33).

The good old days were founded on wisdom, the author is telling us. And wisdom in the Bible begins with 'the fear of the Lord' (Proverbs 1:7). Peace and contentment exist at the start of this long narrative because God and his kingdom are sought by Solomon above all else.

It is a classic example of Jesus' teaching to seek God's Kingdom first if we are to enjoy the peace and blessing of God.

Shalom is a by-product of spiritual faithfulness and not something which can be gained by human endeavour alone. Later we shall see kings try to buy it or kill for it and like millions in our own day fail to find it. Instead they heap up trouble for themselves and those around them. That is not a price worth paying.

Temple eclipsed by king's huge palace

1 Kings 7:1-12

Solomon's splendid temple was knocked into the shade by his even more splendid palace, part of which was longer by a third and twice as wide (6:2; 7:2). It also appears to have been built on three floors, highly unusual in days when upper storeys were often no more than flat roofs with awnings. And these were not Solomon's private quarters; they are described later (v 8).

The author makes no comment on the relative splendour and size apart from the wry aside that the temple took seven years to build and the palace thirteen (6:38-7:1). For the time being we are allowed to marvel at this God-given prosperity, but also, perhaps, to note where Solomon's human aspirations may lie; he enjoys the trappings of power.

He was a man of his kind; sumptuous palaces are often the mark of success or symbols of power for rulers and tycoons. The wise reader rejoices with Solomon in his good fortune, but also prays for others in similar circumstances that they may maintain their grip on the God who gave it and who can take it away.

Good King Solomon was not invincible

1 Kings 10-11

The account of Solomon's riches and power reaches its climax with the visit of the Queen of Sheba (probably modern Yemen). Her polite words of praise to God (10:9) do not imply that she became a believer, but echo the polytheistic view that a person's god is responsible for their success.

The Chronicler's parallel account adds the theological observation that God placed Solomon on his (God's) throne to rule on his behalf (2 Chronicles 9:8).

Pride in a job well done is natural and is commended by the Preacher, (sometimes thought to be Solomon) in Ecclesiastes 2:24. To dismiss it and say, 'It wasn't me, it was the Lord' is often a needlessly false humility (and even spiritual pride: 'Look what God was able to do through me').

Solomon's success, and ours, comes from a complex interplay between our God-given talents as such and our voluntary harnessing, careful development and responsible deployment of them. Solomon worked hard and co-operated with God, which is the example we are to follow.

The example we are not to follow is his habit of using his talents to arrange numerous marriages of convenience to secure deals, which eventually led to him worshipping other gods (ch 11). Today, other 'marriages of convenience', in the work place or community, may eventually lead us to compromise with the principles of this world without our realising the risk at first.

The author is preparing us for what is to come. The detailed account of the splendour contrasts with the brief and often uncomplimentary accounts of later kings. Solomon stands at the head of the league as an example of what should be; many of his successors are examples of the opposite.

But Solomon believed that he was invincible, and so strayed; and any follower of God who believes the same is almost certainly standing on the edge of a spiritual precipice. Solomon personally got away with it, but he sowed the seeds for his own empire's decline.

Solomon: p 51
Solomon's temple: pp 52-3
Overlap of kings and prophets: p 56

Youthful agenda based on greed

1 Kings 12

Most people who take 'recreational' drugs stop doing so when they reach their mid-30s when perhaps family responsibilities modify the rash behaviour of youth.

In general terms, young people tend to be more idealistic and extreme; older people tend to be more tolerant and balanced. Society and the church need both energetic idealism and balanced realism, and so should be led by groups reflecting both.

Israel was not so led after Solomon's death. Rehoboam had grown selfish in his privileged upbringing. Some modern tycoons do not allow their offspring to live off parental success but send them into the market-place to fend for themselves. Solomon had not done this, so now Rehoboam has all the arrogant assertiveness of the footloose high-born yuppie. Although he was 41 when he became king, he was still a spoiled brat at heart.

Jeroboam may not have been any older, but he was more cunning. He had tasted the bitter fruits of hasty action by trying to force God's timing (11:26-40). So he raised popular support by offering lower taxes. But like his rival his wanted control, not the people's welfare.

The resulting split was tragic. Rehoboam kept the throne of the southern kingdom of Judah and his father's sumptuous palaces. But the national economy dived because 80 per cent of its tax districts defected to the north. The ten northern tribes got their lower taxes, and with them religious compromise. Jeroboam, knowing a spiritual focus was needed, created bull calves to represent Yahweh, but which later came to represent anything.

The lusts and ambitions of youth brought the kingdom to its knees and launched a 200-year period of hatred and even civil war. The divided kingdom had been prophesied, but it was not inevitable. The human factors which led to it were avoidable. Yet still we make the same mistakes.

Claiming prophecy doesn't make it true

1 Kings 13

The opinion polls suggest that people in the West are highly sceptical about the truthfulness of politicians and journ-alists. Yet at the same time, they believe what they see and hear to the extent that even if an alleged scandal is sub-sequently found to be false, belief in its truth remains.

Christians can be as gullible as anyone else. Rumours about leaders or organisations are seized on and circulated with vigour and often persist for years despite regular denials.

Anyone hearing anything about anyone ought perhaps, as a spiritual discipline, read this chapter of the Bible before passing the information on. It is a tragic story of a well-meaning, earnest believer who is duped by an apparently well-meaning and earnest believer, and as a result loses his life.

The tragedy is greater because the first prophet correctly heard God's word, and boldly confronted Jero-boam. He was brave, obedient and faithful. But then he failed to discern the lie (v 18) from the old man who was also a genuine prophet at times. Like most people, however, the older man was not above misusing his gifts.

Today, millions of messages flash around the earth at the speed of light. There was never a time when discern-ment was more needed. If the prophet could be deceived by one message, we could be deceived by hundreds. The moral of the tale is that we are to listen carefully for the devil's suggestion that God may have changed his mind.

Prophecy, or any alleged 'word' from God is to be tested not only by leaders (1 Corinthians 14:29) but also by Scripture. It should be taken so seriously that it is never believed until it has been checked, and should never be removed from its original context.

Mentor takes protégé to task

1 Kings 14

There is nothing more satisfying for a mentor than to set a protégé on the road to success and to assist them at various stages in the journey. And there is nothing more saddening than to see them start right and end wrong.

Ahijah has this experience. He was part of the prophetic school (community) at Shiloh, which had been Samuel's base and remained an important religious centre. He may have been new to his job (he was wearing a new cloak, perhaps the badge of office, 11:29) when he prophesied Jeroboam's leadership. But he is old in experience as well as in years when Jeroboam's desperate wife comes to him in 14:2 and he has no words of comfort for her.

Instead, he piles on the bad news. Ahijah has been consistent in his devotion to the Lord, a necessity for any spiritual leader. Jeroboam, his protégé, has not been so faithful and the old prophet does not spare his criticism.

Friendship and patronage sometimes prevent pastors, advisers and mentors from saying the hard thing to an individual they have previously encouraged. Ahijah stands as a model, opting for higher considerations than keeping in the glamorous king's good books.

There is a postscript to his story in 2 Chronicles 9:29, where Ahijah is described as a chronicler of Solomon's (presumably last) years. He was a man of stature whose reputation was untarnished, unlike that of his protégé.

Butcher gets the chop

1 Kings 15-16

This catalogue of bit-part kings (as far as the author is concerned) reminds today's readers of God's complex way of seeing that justice is done. It rules out simplistic human assessments of crime and punishment.

Jeroboam (of Israel) has been promised the ultimate sanction within the customs and culture of his time: the end of his family line (14:10-16). In parallel Christian terms this was like being condemned to hell; Old Testament belief at this time conceived of 'eternal life' in terms more of a continuing family name than of personal survival in another life.

However, when the sentence was carried out by Baasha, who assassinated the rightful heir and his family (15:25-30) he was not complimented on the deed. He was not a better king, and butchery, even when it was apparently deserved and prophetically predicted, is not an act of which God approves. Baasha was himself condemned for his reign and 'because he destroyed' Jeroboam's household (16:7).

This helps us to see that some predictive prophecy is not expressing God's will as if he himself was a summary executioner who will reward his henchmen. Rather, it is foreseeing the spiritual and human consequences of certain forms of action.

Those consequences are indeed punishment, but they are also self-inflicted; they are like the gangrene which sets in after the initial needless wound has been made. That is how God in his sovereign goodness has made the world to operate. We cannot complain if bad consequences follow deliberate sins.

God's character seen in extreme times

1 Kings 17

Jesus pointed out that there were many widows in Israel but God chose one in Sidon – the region from which wicked Queen Jezebel originated – to look after Elijah (Luke 4:24,25; cf. 1 Kings 16:31; 17:9). Jezebel was responsible for the disaster which had befallen Israel, by importing her god, Baal Melkart, and Baal's prophets (16:30-33; 17:1).

Jesus used the incident to make the point that prophets are not honoured in their own land. Yet there were faithful people in Israel (cf. 19:18). And the woman was not initially, if ever, a believer in Yahweh alone (she refers to him as 'your God' in v 12).

The story is not intended to teach us about God's provision for ordinary people, nor how faithful people in Israel shared in the suffering. It does show that when God calls someone to a special task he will provide what they need to see them through, possibly in a surprising manner.

But most of all, the narrative demonstrates Yahweh's supremacy even in the homeland of Baal. It is about who God is, not about how Elijah fared.

Message in capitals

1 Kings 16:21-28

The reign of King Omri is glossed over by the author although historically he made an important mark. Omri moved the Israelite capital from Tirzah to Samaria (v 24) which he and his son Ahab built up almost to rival Solomon's Jerusalem for grandeur, except that instead of gold they used ivory.

Although the author of Kings has told us a lot about Jerusalem, he is not interested in buildings as such. He is only interested in the builders. Solomon's achievements are given extended coverage because Solomon obeyed God; Omri's achievements get little coverage because he did not.

It is an example of how we tend to judge people by their measurable achievements. The Bible reflects God's assessment, which is on entirely other grounds. Omri, sadly, achieved nothing for God even though some of his buried buildings remained to be excavated in the twentieth century.

Secret believer commended

1 Kings 18:1-15

Jesus said that his followers were to let their light shine (Matthew 5:16), and that they were not to be ashamed of owning him (Mark 8:38). That is usually interpreted as a command to be open and upfront about faith, making no secret of church attendance and personal religious beliefs.

The story of Obadiah suggests that shining for Jesus may sometimes be achieved by a less overt testimony. Obadiah could not have served God and his people if he had worn his faith like a badge; he would have been executed in Jezebel's purge.

Christians in countries hostile to their faith may also find that the Western encouragement of 'public witness' is not always appropriate. God is not dishonoured by careful stewardship of one's life which in extreme circumstances may restrict verbal witness and even public worship.

However, Obadiah does not present us with an excuse for blending into the surroundings just because it is more convenient to do so; his was an exceptional situation.

Elijah – a case study

Elijah is the archetype of the prophets. He met with Jesus and Moses on the Mount of Transfiguration (Mark 9:2-8). Popular spirituality based on Malachi 4:5 expected him to be reincarnated before the Messiah came (cf. John 1:21), and Jesus said he was represented by John the Baptist (Matthew 11:14; Mark 9:11-13). He offers an example of total dedication to God.

- He was close to God. 'Whom I serve' (17:1) means 'before whom I stand' implying that he was always conscious of being in God's presence. James 5:17,18 says he was a model for prayer.
- He obeyed God and accepted material deprivation (17:1-6). This period was also lived in obscurity; he did not court publicity.
- He lived in a period of spiritual compromise (18:21). Belief in Yahweh was mixed with other religions in a similar way to modern 'pick and mix' religion.
- He was prone to exaggeration. Like many single-minded people, he suffered from tunnel vision; he thought he was alone when he wasn't (18:4,22; 19:10,18). He was more of a loner than was good for him.
- He trained up his successor (19:16-21). Elisha, even more than his mentor, started as most do, at the bottom.

High flyer falls flat

1 Kings 19

Many Western people today claim to have suffered from some form of depression. Elijah's experience comes as an encouragement; the great man of God has a weakness and his emotions really were just like ours (cf. James 5:17). Several causes of his collapse can be traced:

- He was physically tired. He had been standing in the heat all day and then had travelled a long distance. The angel's hospitality enabled him to recover some strength. Our physical condition affects our feelings and spiritual perception.
- He was emotionally and spiritually drained after the conflict with the priests of Baal. He had been running on adrenaline for too long; once the high of the contest was over, he crashed.
- He felt lonely. He wrongly believed that he alone was left, and he had little faith in the people's response. He needed company at this point, not seclusion, to revive him.
- He was afraid. Jezebel's death threat was the last straw. He had been in danger before, but this time it weakened his faith. Fear is natural; in the past Elijah would have trusted God with it but now he collapses under it.

God did not abandon him, of course; being given a fresh task to do helped Elijah understand that. God went with him, ensured his needs were met, and spoke to him again in a different and less spectacular manner than the prophet had been used to. Elijah had to learn more of God.

God ministered to him as a whole person, body, mind and spirit. He was practical and gentle, yet also firm. We could hardly ask for a better model in dealing with people we know who also crash under the weight of life.

Twisted rulers don't measure up

1 Kings 21

The incident of Naboth's vineyard provides a study in contrasts. On the one hand are Ahab and Jezebel, rich and greedy. On the other is Naboth, relatively poor, but principled.

Israelite law forbade compulsory purchase of property for any reason, hence Ahab's sulks. Jezebel, however, does not recognise Israelite law as anything but an obstacle to be overcome.

In so doing she provides evidence of the vestigial conscience which is part of God's image stamped on humankind. Everyone knows that a framework of law is necessary, so we keep up the appearances of abiding by it. But Jezebel is like the human-rights abuser who twists the law to achieve morally unlawful ends.

Yet even if we would not go so far as those who frame 'laws' to curtail people's basic freedoms and rights (and then condemn outside activists for interfering in 'domestic matters'), most people are guilty of justifying dubious actions by twisted argument to give the action an appearance of legitimacy.

The commonest form is to claim that as no one is likely to be hurt by a given action, 'it doesn't matter'. But all stones thrown into a pond cause ripples, however small; no one is unaffected, least of all the initiator of the action.

Naboth has a quite different spirit. If he sells, he will profit, but his children and grandchildren will lose their livelihood, so he opts for long-term security rather than for short-term gain. In so doing he becomes an example of godly living.

The story is here, no doubt, because the long-term view was what Israel's leaders lacked most at this time. It is what most of us lack, most of the time, and which only a genuine trust in God can restore.

2 KINGS

1	Elijah and Ahaziah
2	Elisha begins his ministry
3	Elisha advises Israel
4	Elisha's miracles
5	Naaman is healed
6	Elisha and the Arameans
7	Samaria beseiged
8	Elisha's foresight of Hazael's regime
9	Jehu king of Israel
10	Jehu wipes out Ahab's family
11	Joash hidden
12	The temple repaired
13	Jehoahaz, Jehoash, kings of Israel
14	Azariah (Judah); Jeroboam II (Israel)
15	Amaziah, Jotham (Judah); five kings of Israel
16	Ahaz and the Assyrians
17	The fall of Samaria
18	Hezekiah and Sennacherib
19	Hezekiah advised by Isaiah
20	Hezekiah and the Babylonian envoys
21	Manasseh's evil reign
22	Josiah's reforms
23	The covenant reaffirmed
24	Jerusalem besieged
25	The fall of Jerusalem

(Some of the events in 2 Kings are also reported in 2 Chronicles, Isaiah and Jeremiah)

Acts of Vengeance

HARD Question

2 Kings 1,2

In these chapters, we return to the question of miracles and summary judgments.

The fire-eaten soldiers (1:1-17)

Ahaziah has embarked on a wrong course of action – seeking healing from a non-Israelite deity (v 2) and God intervenes to stop him (v 3). But Ahaziah is not to be stopped. He sends soldiers to Elijah to force him to change his pronouncement, otherwise to kill him; either way the curse would be lifted, according to popular religious thought.

The fire shows Ahaziah that God's mind cannot be changed by human will. The sinner is judged, but his action has brought tragedy to others. Ahaziah is responsible for the soldiers' deaths. He sent them to hell as it were in an attempt to stop himself going there.

Elisha and the bear bait (2:23-25)

Prophets were to be taken seriously, by order of the law (Deuteronomy 18:19). Those who belittled God's word belittled God, which was a capital offence (Leviticus 24:15,16). These ancient equivalents of today's drunks at a soccer match, chanting senseless jeers from the safety of numbers, are probably challenging Elisha's claim to be a prophet. They want him to perform a miracle or are wishing him dead. 'Go up' could refer to Elijah's reported mode of death and they wish Elisha to follow quickly. The curse may be seen as an apt punishment for wild animal-like behaviour.

God is not mocked

The point of both incidents is that God is demonstrating that his law is to be upheld and his word respected at a time of widespread disrespect. However, it would be wrong to suppose that Elijah and Elisha were constantly pronouncing curses and killing people. Both saved life, too (1 Kings 17; 2 Kings 4). These exceptional incidents gave later readers pause for thought: in their situation, they are not to trifle with God either.

In the New Testament, Jesus forbade his disciples to call down fire on an unwelcoming village (Luke 9:54,55) and Paul stresses that vengeance is to be left to God's own timing (Romans 12:19-21). Christians are not called to curse, but to bless; the prophets are exceptional people called to give special revelation of God's character in specific one-off incidents and utterances.

But we should also note that the New Testament teaches that everyone will have to face the consequence of loose words and false deeds. Getting away with them now does not guarantee future immunity from divine prosecution.

Inspiring overture creates vivid picture

2 Kings 3

Music is a well-known stimulus for artistic creativity and a balm for troubled hearts (cf. 1 Samuel 16:14-23). Here it cools Elisha's annoyance, calms his spirit and makes him receptive to God. This is a rare insight into the spiritual disciplines of biblical prophets.

As a result of Elisha's intervention, the superstitious Moabites see a picture in an unexpected and, to some eyes, beautiful, change in the natural landscape. A flash flood reflecting the sunrise is, to them, a portent, and they rush like the Light Brigade to their doom.

God is thus shown as the master of improvisation. He is capable of infinite variety in the way he works. Jehoshaphat comes out of this in a better light than in a similar incident (2 Chronicles 18-19), but once again he only consults a prophet as a last resort. The author has no need to press the point.

Whirlwind exit for fiery prophet

2 Kings 2:1-18

There are four biblical accounts of people dying and their bodies disappearing. Enoch was simply 'no more' (Genesis 5:24). Moses was 'buried by God' and his grave never found (Deuteronomy 34:5,6). Jesus was raised from the dead with a transformed body as the 'firstfruits' of the life to come (1 Corinthians 15:20-44).

Elijah was taken to heaven in a whirlwind, surrounded by chariots of fire. It is more than a coincidence that while the report of Enoch's death could be interpreted merely as a euphemism and not a statement about his body, the other three appeared together on the Mount of Transfiguration (Mark 9:4) – representing the law, the prophets, and the new covenant.

We have something here of theological significance, which we should not pass by. Elijah and Elisha were men of special insight (cf. 6:16,17). To them, as to later readers, their vision of the whirlwind spoke of God's Spirit, and the fire pointed to God's purity. Elijah's death was timed by God and he was taken into God's nearer presence – a rare Old Testament insight.

For Elisha, the significance of seeing Elijah thus taken was a test of commitment. He had to be with Elijah all the time, and only on the basis of similar spiritual commitment could he expect to receive God's power in abundance.

Modern stories of near death experiences, and the final words of believers as they hover between consciousness and death often draw on the divine chariot imagery as the best vehicle for describing the most momentous journey any of us will ever take.

Miracle a minute

2 Kings 4; 6:1-7

One genre of Christian literature strings together remarkable stories to create the impression that dynamic Christianity is just one miracle after another. It can be quite depressing for the ordinary faithful believer for whom life is more grey than colourful.

The author of Kings (and he is not alone among Bible writers) seems to have used such a source for this section of his account. Elisha comes across as the star of a Steven Spielberg spectacular, numbing the senses with a series of special effects.

Yet the prophet had a life apart from these high points; they may have been the only high points in an otherwise less eventful life. Elisha, neither a city dweller nor a great homemaker, seems to be unmarried and peripatetic (4:8,25,38). Rather aloof, he expects people to visit him (rather than go to them) yet may refuse doorstep interviews when they arrive (5:8-10).

References to the company of prophets suggest that he often followed a semi-monastic discipline of prayer, worship and teaching his junior disciples. Although ministering to kings on occasion, he seems semi-detached from political and social life. All that is assumed and hinted at by the author, creating a context for the miracles which he may have selected because they each brought a message from God to the exiles, for whom he was writing 300 years after Elisha.

God is the provider in hard times (4:1-7); the giver of life (4:8-37); the healer (4:38-41) who blesses the law-abiding worship and gifts of his people (multiplying the harvest offering in 4:42-44). Also, he rescues his people from slavery, as at the Exodus. The prophet who lost the borrowed axe-head (6:1-7) would have faced bonded labour to repay the debt; the exiles were prisoners of war away from home.

To the original readers of this book, the stories were an encouraging call to praise and trust God at a time when change for the better seemed impossible. You don't have to be an exile in Babylon in 550 BC to appreciate that. We can look back to God's character seen in these incidents to receive encouragement that he can see us through the difficulties we face.

Wholeness restored

2 Kings 5

Damascus was the Paris of the ancient Near East. It was the commercial capital of a wide area (Aram), and a city of great beauty, aptly named 'the Pearl'. It was also a frequent enemy of Israel. But a faithful Israelite slave girl there never forgot her God, and her witness to a needy military officer ensured a story that would be preserved for ever.

In a way, the honours belong to her, one of the Bible's anonymous saints who were indispensable yet are only briefly mentioned in the account. Simple witness of the 'I know a man who can' variety can have far-reaching effects.

Naaman, at the peak of his career, had all the trappings of success, but his skin problem made him a social outcast and the only way from now on was down. He is one of the Bible's classic examples of a person with a surface-level problem masking something deeper.

Naaman's real problem is pride, and Elisha knows it, which is why he refuses to meet him personally. (How many Western church leaders would not give the red carpet treatment to the commander-in-chief of China's forces if he came seeking their counsel, laden with a fat cheque book and a container full of top-of-the-range products from his finest manufacturers?)

It didn't help when the prescription ordered not one but seven dips in the muddy and unattractive Jordan which bears no resemblance to the clear waters of rivers in Naaman's native Syria. And there was no noticeable change in his condition until after the seventh. The faith must have been as hard to exercise as the humility.

But he did it, and it turned him into a believer (v 17) and a challenge to the readers: if a non-church member can exercise such faith and humility, why can't you?

At which point the real villain of the piece enters: Gehazi. Elisha's refusal to accept a fee for the occasional office he has performed seemed to Gehazi incomprehensible: why shouldn't the world contribute to the church if it makes use of its services?

Maybe it should sometimes, but not now when God has demonstrated his power in this compassionate and strategic manner (v 26). Naaman's new and fragile faith must not be allowed to assume that he has somehow earned his reprieve. Elisha's refusal of the gift is a witness to the graciousness of grace. Yet Gehazi, one of the custodians of the message of grace, fails to see that. Even believers can be spiritually blind. But such blindness is a guilty thing, and calls for chastening, as Gehazi found out.

Vision of hope

2 Kings 6,7

We are only a couple of generations on from Solomon's death, yet the writing is already on the wall for the northern kingdom: Samaria its capital is threatened. But God has not abandoned it yet and Elisha's second sight protects its people (6:9-10).

The vision of divine protection was granted to Gehazi (Elisha's servant) while blindness from God incapacitated the attackers (6:16-20), and the author's message to his readers is simple: open your eyes. God knows what's going on; his spiritual forces are more than a match for the forces of darkness and can lead them captive like tame animals.

So in the darkest of times (when cannibalism is the only means of survival, 6:28,29) there was hope for those who could see it. And as so often happens in Scripture, it is outcasts who first discover the good news that light has overtaken the darkness (7:3-11). To the exiles the story brought encouragement that hope was not dead, and a warning that only the poor in spirit would ever inherit the divine kingdom. Those principles do not change with the political, cultural and spiritual scenery.

Bad spirit, bad blood

2 Kings 9-10

Hidden in this unpleasant record of blood-letting on an enormous scale – but typical of Middle-Eastern war lords for centuries either side of the birth of Christ – is an author's footnote which puts it in perspective.

Jehu fulfilled the prophecies but he did not wholly follow the Lord (10:31). He approached his reign from a political angle, securing his power base and using the name of Yahweh as a convenient banner to fight under. And, like many military dictators, he does not seem to have made a good community leader.

The author's concern is to show that when God does pronounce judgment, he will ensure it is executed. That execution may not come until later generations, however, and the relatively innocent descendants of lawless families will then reap the effects of their forbears' crimes.

While not stressed and unfamiliar today, the undeniable truth is that we are bound together in families and communities, and the evil that people do lives on after them and affects their descendants. We are to think long-term before we act; we may think we will escape unharmed from some wrong course of action, but it may well cause pain and suffering to countless others.

Lifestyles cemented while the church's stonework crumbles

2 Kings 12

Anti-clericalism has thrived at several points in history, usually when the church is perceived to be a self-interested power structure, removed from the people.

The author of Kings hardly disguises his contempt for the priests who maintained their own income and lifestyle rather than the fabric of the temple (vv 5-8). The ordinary craftsmen and their overseers, by contrast, are portrayed as honest and hardworking (vv 13-16).

Spiritual life at this time had descended to the level of formality. The religious machine ticked over but leaders and people seem to have lost their way. Lack of spiritual vision can create tiredness and indifference which is reflected in the careless treatment of church property and the insularity of church leaders.

The author shows without comment that good as Joash's reforms had been, they did not restore the nation's stability (vv 17,18). In repairing the building, important as that was, Joash and Jehoiada failed at the same time to rekindle the nation's devotion to God. Faith can be expressed in stone, but stone of itself cannot create faith.

Defeated by low confidence

2 Kings 13:10-24

We often achieve difficult things when we believe we can or should, and fail in lesser things when our confidence is drained. Sports people are especially sensitive to changes in confidence levels, which can enable an average player to beat a superstar, and cause a superstar to become mediocre.

That may be part of the human feeling behind Jehoash's failure to fire only a few of the arrows in his quiver into the ground. He may have been mystified by Elisha's command, and not seeing the point of it, felt self-conscious. His lack of confidence then became a lack of faith.

But God had spoken to him (through the prophet, as God's mouthpiece) and he should have gone on shooting until told to stop. Jehoash was half-hearted, and no one can serve God or achieve anything for him in that frame of mind.

For today

1 & 2 Kings

- Don't try and make God change his mind
- Be careful that success does not bring a false sense of spiritual security
- Remember that the contributions of old and young are equally important
- Keep the balance between physical, emotional and spiritual well-being
- Simple witness for God may have far-reaching effects

God's pain

2 Kings 13:1-9; 14:23-28

Asides by the author suggest an important truth about God in 13:4 and 14:26. God does not view his people's suffering with anything other than concern.

The severe oppression of Israel by the Arameans hurt him as much as it hurt the people with whom he was closely identified. But to be true to his character he could not deliver them until they returned to living his way.

In this case, the agent of deliverance was from outside Israel. The Assyrians, now becoming a major threat to the region, subdued Aramea c. 806-804 BC and again in the 770s BC. They did not at that time march further south, so Israel was safe. God, the Lord of history, is not indifferent to our needs and is able to deal with them through the ordering of apparently unrelated events.

Failure blamed on the illegitimate gods

2 Kings 15,17

The northern kingdom is beyond the pale as the mighty Assyrians now plough south from Aram and oppress the ten tribes. Israel's kings with monotonous regularity 'did not turn away from the sins of Jeroboam son of Nebat, which he had caused Israel to commit' (15:9,18,24,28). By the time of the more moderate Hoshea (17:2) the end was in sight.

The last 30 years of Israel's existence (from Jeroboam II c. 753 to the fall of Samaria in 722) are skated over here, because the author is now more interested in telling the meaning than in showing the facts.

In so doing he provides us with a detailed account of Israelite apostasy (17:7-23). Historically speaking, God had been hugely patient. He had waited 200 years before bringing down the Assyrians as the prophets had predicted.

And still he warned, cajoled and called them to repent at the eleventh hour. Unrecorded in Kings, but noted elsewhere in the Bible, the prophets Amos and Hosea were faithfully hitting their heads against a brick wall in a last attempt to avert the tragedy.

But before we sit in judgment on the recalcitrant people, we should note that the strength of human self-will is as great in us as it was in them. Their determination to dilute their devotion and accommodate some aspects of contemporary culture which conflicted with their faith is repeated in every age. We always take the line of least resistance.

Therefore, as we read this list of spiritually compromising activities, we should look also for contemporary equivalents. They are more likely to be found in the lifestyle sections of Sunday newspapers than in the religious media, and smiling down from neon signs rather than from suggestive pagan shrines. Gods and goddesses can twist themselves into any attractive shape, and they are at their most powerful when they are least recognised.

HARD Question

How can a shadow move backwards?

2 Kings 20:1-11 (Isaiah 38:1-8)

This and Elisha's floating axe-head (6:1-7) are probably the two biblical miracles which most defy any explanation; Joshua's long day (Joshua 10) is easy by comparison.

Miracles by definition are unusual interventions by God in the normal course of events, which speak of his activity to those who have the eyes of faith. If there is a sovereign God who is creator and sustainer of the universe and controller of human destiny, then there is no logical reason why he cannot do anything if he so desires.

However, he has also limited himself to working through, rather than in spite of, the basic structures he created and does not interfere arbitrarily with its processes to rescue people from difficulty or to impress them with his power.

A literal explanation of this miracle requires a sudden reversal of the earth's daily rotation which for a moment would destroy gravity and create a world-shattering jolt; think of the effect of stopping a train dead and immediately reversing it when it is travelling at over 1,000 miles per hour (1,670 kph). To create (and manage the effects of) such a catastrophic incident in order to give one man a sign seems unlike the character of God as revealed in Scripture.

There were only two recorded witnesses of this miracle, therefore it seems most likely that what they saw was for their eyes only. Some mirage or lighting effect is all that is required; shadows may seem to behave oddly when the sun disappears behind or emerges from a cloud, for example.

This in no way belittles God or the event; many people 'see' things which have significance for them but not for others. (The sights and sounds at Jesus' baptism and Saul's conversion seem to have been apprehended differently by the onlookers.)

CROSS CHECK

Josiah's reforms: p 59
Hezekiah: pp 58-9
Judah's kings: p 56
The fall of Jerusalem: pp 59, 187-8

Compromises go before a fall

2 Kings 24-25

Manasseh has a lot to answer for. Despite Josiah's reforms (chs 22-23) and Manasseh's late repentance (2 Chronicles 33:10-17, not reported in 2 Kings), the heart of the nation of Judah has not changed. The prophet Jeremiah, active but not mentioned here, is not having much success.

Manasseh is blamed for the ills (24:3) but his successors were not without fault (24:19,20). By playing with God's laws, they played straight into the hands of their potential oppressors. The entire spirit of the nation had been weakened by decades of compromise.

Judah no longer has a sense of purpose and identity, of mission and status before God. It is just another country, hanging on to its independence as best it can. Churches can get like that too; losing their sense of purpose and identity as God's lights in a dark world, they sink to the level of just another sect or social club.

Judah has lost its grip on God's love by losing its grip on God's law. It is incapable of drawing on God's power and protection when it needs it most. It's not God's fault the Babylonians sack Jerusalem.

KINGS AND PROPHETS – MAKE THE LINK

ISRAEL (N) KINGS	PROPHETS	DATE	JUDAH (S) KINGS	PROPHETS	BIBLE REF
Jeroboam I	*Abijah*	930	**Rehoboam**	*Shemaiah*	1 Ki. 12-14
		913	Abijah		1 Ki. 15
		910	**Asa**	*Azariah*	
Nadab		909		*Hanani*	
Baasha	*Jehu*	908			
Elah		886			1 Ki. 16
Zimri/others		885			
Ahab	*Elijah*	874			1 Ki. 16-22
		872	**Jehoshaphat**	*Micaiah*	1 Ki. 22
				Jehu	
Ahaziah		853			1Ki.22-2 Ki.1
Joram	{*Elisha*	852			2 Ki. 1-8
		848	Jehoram	(*Elijah*	2 Ch.21)
		841	Ahaziah		2 Ki. 8-9
Jehu	{	841	Athaliah		2 Ki. 9-11
		835	Joash	*Jehoiada**	2 Ki. 12
Jehoahaz		814			2 Ki. 13
Jehoash		798			
		796	Amaziah	Anon	2 Ki. 14
Jeroboam II		793			
		792	**Azariah = Uzziah**	*Zechariah**	2 Ki. 15
Zechariah	{Amos	753			
Shallum etc.	{Hosea	752			
		750	Jotham	{Micah	
Pekahiah	{	742		{Isaiah	
Pekah	{	740			
		735	**Ahaz**	{	2 Ki. 16
Hoshea		732		*Oded*	2 Ki. 15,17
FALL OF SAMARIA		722			
		715	**Hezekiah** {		2 Ki. 18-20
		697	**Manasseh**	*Anon*	2 Ki. 21
		642	Amon		
		640	**Josiah**	{Jeremiah	2 Ki. 22-23
		609	Jehoahaz	{Zephaniah	
		609	**Jehoiakim**	{Nahum	2 Ki. 23-24
		598	Jehoiachin	{Jeremiah	2 Ki. 24
		597	**Zedekiah**	{	2 Ki. 24-25
		587	FINAL FALL OF JUDAH		

Notes:

1. *Italic prophets* are mentioned in Scripture but do not have books of their own
2. **Bold kings** are the main ones for the biblical story
3. * = were priests, rather than prophets, but who were also spiritual advisers
4. { = continues through several reigns or designates prophets working at the same time
5. There are further accounts of some kings (mostly of Judah) in 2 Chronicles.
6. Dates are approximate and relate to a king's sole regency. Some kings overlapped in co-regencies (e.g. Hezekiah was co-regent with Ahaz when Samaria fell, 2 Kings 18:9)

The Old Testament story at a glance

Where the Bible books fit the story

Bible readers often find the link between the various books confusing, because the Bible is collected in thematic groups (Pentateuch, history, poetry, prophecy) and the links are not obvious. The confusion becomes greatest in Kings (and Chronicles) because of the relatively narrow time scale and the greater number of books involved.

This simple table provides a refresher outline of the entire Old Testament narrative so that you can see not only where Kings and the prophets relate, but how they also fit in with the rest of the story. A narrative outline of the story can be found in the Introduction on pages 12-15.

APPROXIMATE DATES	PERIOD	***MAIN CHARACTERS***	***BIBLE BOOKS***
Prehistory	Dawn of time	*Adam, Noah*	Genesis 1-10
2000 – 1600 BC	The Patriarchs	*Abraham to Joseph*	Genesis
1300 – 1200 BC	The Exodus	*Moses*	Exodus, Numbers *(Leviticus, Deuteronomy)*
1200 – 1050 BC	Settlement in Canaan	*Joshua, the Judges*	Joshua, Judges, Ruth
1030 – 930 BC	The first kings	*Saul, David, Solomon*	1 & 2 Samuel, 1 Kings, 1 Chronicles *(Psalms, Proverbs Ecclesiastes)*
930 – 722 BC	The divided kingdom (Israel – north; Judah – south)	*Elijah, Elisha,, Amos Isaiah*	1 & 2 Kings, 2 Chronicles, Amos (N), Hosea (N), Isaiah (S), Micah (S), Jonah, ?Joel, *(Deuteronomy)*
722 – 587 BC	Fall of Judah	*Isaiah, Jeremiah*	2 Chronicles, Isaiah, Jeremiah, Lamentations, Nahum, Habakkuk, Zephaniah
(605) 587 – 537 BC	The Exile	*Jeremiah, Ezekiel, Daniel*	Jeremiah, Ezekiel, Daniel,Obadiah, *(Psalms, Wisdom books,Leviticus,?Job)*
537 – 440 BC	The Restoration	*Ezra, Nehemiah*	Ezra, Nehemiah, Esther, Haggai Zechariah, Daniel, Malachi, ?Joel

Note: Italic book titles indicate uncertain dates of authorship or compilation. Many books show signs of later editing.

Express your grief, maintain your faith

The Book of Lamentations

- Is a series of five poems mourning the fall of Jerusalem
- Recognises that the calamity has been caused by Judah's sin
- Describes the state of life among people who remained in the city after others were taken into exile
- Expresses trust in God for the future

Think of some of the TV pictures you have seen of refugees or survivors of a natural disaster or military attack. See children, hungry, tearful and bewildered. Women wailing at the loss of husbands and sons. Older men dazed and confused, wandering around the wreckage searching for belongings, or for food and water.

The architecture and technology may be different, but otherwise that's the scene as you open the book of Lamentations. Indeed, things are so bad that women are prepared to eat their dead children (4:10; cf. Jeremiah 19:9).

Law and order have broken down, children have to work and the sound of gaiety has been silenced (5:8-15). Dead bodies lie unburied in the streets (2:21). Children beg for food, weakened by famine and thirst (4:4,5,9).

The anonymous author of this heart-rending book weeps. These are his people; this is his city (2:11). In common with the prophets, he lays the blame for the tragedy at the feet of the people of Judah who for decades, if not centuries, have refused to heed God's warnings (1:8-10). But he identifies with them, rather than merely railing against them (3:40-51; 4:6).

He has his personal griefs, too. Enemies have hounded him without a cause (3:52). It felt like being imprisoned (3:6-9) and being thrown into a pit from which the Lord eventually rescued him (3:55-60). It is very reminiscent of Jeremiah's recorded experience (Jeremiah 37,38).

What is new to us, perhaps, is that the author feels with and for his people. We tend to distance ourselves from our nation, our church and from those who are far removed from us. We are quick to criticise and slow to empathise. We can live in semi-detachment and rarely feel the pains of others acutely.

Yet there is a 'brotherhood of mankind' from which we can never be detached, whatever the causes of people's sufferings and whatever their spiritual state. It is one of the marks of the Christian to mourn with those who mourn (cf. Romans 12:15).

But in his grief, the author maintains his faith. Here are the unlikely verses which inspired the hymn 'Great is thy faithfulness' (3:22-24). Slap in the middle of tragedy the author affirms God's goodness and is willing to wait for him (3:25-27) because his love is so great (3:31-33).

He can even manage a prayer that God will stir himself as in days of old and rise up on behalf of his stricken people (5:19-22). God, he knows, keeps his covenant, and he grips hold of that truth like a drowning sailor clings to driftwood.

KEY QUOTE

Though he brings grief, he will show compassion, so great is his unfailing love. For he does not willingly bring affliction or grief to the children of men.

Lamentations 3:32,33

Lamentations is cathartic. Use it as an aid to express your own griefs. Use it to help you understand what grief is like. Use it to stir yourself to human sympathy when you read or hear of others' griefs. And use it as a source of hope: God is faithful, and even if we do suffer the effects of our foolish actions, his mercies will still be new every morning.

God offers no concessions

Lamentations 2:20-22; 3:34-51; 4:11-16

A standard marketing ploy is to offer members of a club or organisation certain privileges, usually in the form of discounts. We tend to think of our membership of God's family in similar terms. We expect a concession for life's slings and arrows in return for being faithful to God.

However, while the biblical promise of eternal life through faith in Christ is secure, God offers no discounts on human suffering and does not mitigate his judgment when his own people are in the wrong.

The author of Lamentations seems surprised by the severity of the disaster which has crushed Jerusalem. The suffering of relatively innocent women and children is heart-rending. The author has the faith to believe that it will not go on for ever (3:31-33), and he also sees how everyone is caught up in the avalanche of judgment.

Towards the end of the twentieth century there were several financial disasters in the world which caused ordinary people to suffer. They included the property boom and crash, the mis-selling of personal pensions, and the collapse of Barings Bank. They illustrate how we can be caught up in suffering which is not directly of our making but which results from our involvement in a faulty system.

The faith of the author of Lamentations is vital for when we face such situations. God is good to those who love him (3:25-27); that is, he loves, cares for and supports his people. But that does not always divert the human catastrophes which sweep through a fallen world. Don't take it personally when you suffer with your world, but recognise just how imperfect and open to judgment that world is.

FAST facts

Author: The book is anonymous but traditionally it has been ascribed to Jeremiah because he was said to have written 'laments' (2 Chronicles 35:25) and the style is similar to some of his prophecies. He would have been ideally placed to write it; he remained in Jerusalem after the exiles left, and had constantly predicted the destruction which he said could have been avoided.

Date of composition: Jerusalem finally fell to the Babylonians in 587/6 BC, after several attacks in which exiles were taken spread over the previous 20 years. It was probably written shortly after that final catastrophe.

Structure: The book is carefully composed of five poems. The first four are acrostics (each verse begins with the next letter of the Hebrew alphabet, although the third poem has three verses per letter). The fifth poem has all 22 letters of the Hebrew alphabet but not in order. None of the poems focuses on a particular theme, however; several themes range across them all.

Parallel books:
Jeremiah.
2 Chronicles 36 tells the story of the fall of Jerusalem; parts of Ezekiel look back to Jerusalem from Babylon during the siege and destruction.

Place in Bible:
Comes after Jeremiah and before Ezekiel in the Old Testament

It's good to be peculiar

There used to be a small, independent Christian group in Britain known as 'The Peculiar People'. Today the word 'peculiar' means odd, weird or strange. But originally it meant different, separate or independent. The book of Leviticus presents us with God's call to his people to be separated to him, and spiritually different from others.

It is probably one of the least-read books of the Old Testament simply because its detailed regulations concerning animal sacrifices and its obsession with ritual cleanliness seem irrelevant to Christian spirituality and mission. Christ has abolished all that. Leviticus takes us into an alien culture. However, if we follow the rule that timeless principles underlie now unnecessary customs and that to understand those customs will help us to appreciate who God is and what Christ has done, we can find much of value in this book.

God seems to be fastidious – and, in a way, he is. The slightest sin blights his relationship with his people. Therefore, his people are to be fastidious too. Holiness covers a multitude of scenes and is a whole way of life.

Leviticus gives modern readers the spiritual equivalent of a multi-volt electric shock. The rituals and sacrifices may now be obsolete as a means of meeting with God but our spirituality often seems like paddling in the shallows. Leviticus invites us to be peculiar, and to plunge into the depths.

The Book of Leviticus

- Sets out rules for Israelite sacrifices
- Shows why the sacrifices were needed
- Gives rules for social personal behaviour
- Describes rituals covering everyday needs
- Stresses the holiness of God and his people

KEY QUOTE

You are to be holy to me because I, the LORD, am holy, and I have set you apart from the nations to be my own.

Leviticus 20:26

LEVITICUS

1	Rules for burnt offerings
2	Rules for grain offerings
3	Rules for fellowship offerings
4	Rules for (unintentional) sin offerings
5	Rules for sin and guilt offerings
6	Various offerings
7	The priest's share of offerings
8	Consecration of Aaron
9	God appears to Aaron and his sons
10	Failings among the priests
11	Clean and unclean animals
12	Ceremonies after childbirth
13	Rules about skin diseases
14	Ceremonies for skin diseases
15	Rules about bodily discharges
16	The day of atonement
17	Why blood is important
18	Rules for sexual conduct
19	Miscellaneous rules
20	Punishments for various sins
21,22	Rules for conduct of priests
23	Various feasts
24	Tabernacle offerings; blasphemer stoned
25	The jubilee principle
26	God's view of sin
27	Rules for redemption

Many offerings but never enough

Leviticus 1-7

Most households have a selection of similar but different tools. Milk pans and frying pans are used for different cooking methods. The domestic toolbox probably has several screwdrivers because small plugs and large shelves are fixed differently. So with Israel's offerings. They look similar, but they perform different functions to deal with many spiritual needs.

Burnt offerings (1:1-17; 6:8-13) symbolised a person's (or the nation's) devotion to God. They formed the bulk of Israelite sacrifices.

Cereal offerings (2:1-16; 6:14-23) were a sign of thanksgiving and homage to God, and like a fellowship meal. Salt, when shared, was a sign of bonding; the omission of leaven (yeast) distinguished a loaf from daily bread.

Peace offerings (3:1-17; 7:11-21, 28-38) expressed wholeness and oneness with God. Part was 'waved' before the Lord, perhaps as a physical gesture of 'giving' it to him.

Sin offerings (4:1-5:13) were for unintentional social sins, to recover a right relationship with God. The offences, which seem minor, reinforce the truth that there is no hierarchy of sins.

Guilt offerings (5:14-6:17) were to atone for unintentional sins which directly related to rituals and worship. Apart from those traditions which stress public confession or acts of penitence, there is little provision in Christian spirituality for dealing psychologically and practically with accidental sin.

Saying sorry to God (and to others) is not always enough to remove the feeling of guilt or to appease an offended person. The Old Testament sacrifices were a visible means of expressing sorrow. Today perhaps we would send a bunch of flowers or give to charity, a costly (and prayerful) gesture.

However, there is no regular provision here to atone for deliberate sin, which we know to be wrong but commit all the same. So the writer to the Hebrews says that 'It is impossible for the blood of bulls and goats to take away sins' (10:4). The Old Testament provision falls short of the need, which was dealt with by Christ.

Fat-free diet of perfect animals

Leviticus 1-7

God is perfect, and so the offerings had to be perfect and unblemished (e.g. 4:3); nothing imperfect could enter his presence. This is not denied in the New Testament; the difference is that Christ is said to clothe us in his righteousness to fit us for God's presence (see Romans 3:22; Philippians 3:9).

The offerings were also expensive. The animals came from the herd; they were not rounded up from the wild. The symbolism is of giving something valuable, to one's own real loss. Atonement – being made right with God – is obtained at a price, again as the New Testament emphasises (1 Corinthians 6:20).

And they were personal. On some occasions the worshipper laid hands on them as a sign of identification with the victim. The sins may have been secret, but the penance was public and physical.

The instruction to burn the fat (e.g. 3:17) is puzzling. Some suggest it was for food hygiene reasons (bacteria thrive in warm fat). The reason is probably more symbolic. The fat is the tastiest part and what is best is to be given to God. In modern terms, he deserves our best time and resources, not just our leftovers.

FAST facts

Title:
In Hebrew, 'And he called', from the opening words. In Greek, Leviticus means 'Book of the Levites'. Other Hebrew writings call it 'Book of the priests'.
Authorship:
Traditionally Moses. Several verses refer to him being given the laws, although he is nowhere referred to as the overall compiler.
Date of compilation:
Most of the laws appear to have been codified when the Israelites camped in the Sinai region, c. 1275 BC. (See 7:37,38.) Some scholars suggest later editing took place.
Structure:
The book is in two parts. Chs 1-15 are laws about sacrifices and rituals, chs 17-27 cover mostly behavioural ethics. The 'Day of Atonement' in ch 16 holds the two together. There are stylistic similarities between the two sections.

Holiness is infectious, sin is contagious

Leviticus 11-15

Old Testament Judaism is a highly visible faith. Spiritual principles are 'incarnated' in practical activities to reinforce their importance. Other religions and cultures also had their taboos, so the rules were not simply to make Israel distinctive, but to make the concept of holiness obvious.

They provided a framework of religious discipline by focusing on God in everyday things. The dietary laws and regulations for skin diseases may have had secondary hygienic purposes, but the key to them all is in 11:44: 'I am the LORD your God; consecrate yourselves and be holy, because I am holy.'

Christians need not follow these rules (although there was fierce debate in the early church, culminating in the Council of Acts 15), but they have not always found suitable frameworks for discipline which also remind them of God's pervasive presence.

Ritual uncleanness could be 'caught' by touching unclean things or people (e.g. 11:30). But so too could holiness (6:17). The point is not that these conferred some supernatural stain or purity, but that they showed the effects people have on others. People can 'stain' others by their bad influence or they can be channels of God's grace.

Jesus taught that our inner attitudes can make us 'unclean' in God's sight (Mark 7:1-23). Christians regularly need to pray, 'Cleanse the thoughts of our hearts by the inspiration of your Holy Spirit, that we may perfectly love you and worthily magnify your holy name.' The method may have changed, but the spiritual truth has not.

Unholy smoke!

Leviticus 10

No Bible writer could ever have suggested that 'the ends justify the means'. This incident is one of several in Scripture which deny it. The sin of Nadab and Abihu was threefold:

- They offered unconsecrated ('unholy') coals on their pans, instead of consecrated coals from the altar.
- They did what the high priest alone was supposed to do, thus exceeding their own authority.
- And they did so without consulting the leaders to see if it was permitted, thus usurping the latter's authority.

Therefore they blatantly broke God's rules and were punished accordingly.

The lessons are clear. Firstly, the authority of leadership is to be respected at all times; it is a gift of the Holy Spirit to the church. Today, we tend only to respect leaders when we agree with them, just like Aaron's sons.

Secondly, while the difference between secular and sacred is less clear today, Protestants have a tendency to declare the sacred common. For example, the elements in Holy Communion may be regarded as 'simply ordinary' instead of everyday things set apart for God's use (which is the biblical definition of holiness). Such things are stamped with his label and are to be treated carefully.

A spiritual spring-cleaning day

Leviticus 16

Shakespeare's *Macbeth* is a classic study of the effects of sin on the human heart. Racked with guilt, Macbeth cries vainly,

> 'Will all great Neptune's ocean
> wash this blood
> Clean from my hand? No . . .'

And later, Lady Macbeth goes through her hand-washing routine muttering, 'Out, damned spot, out.'

The Day of Atonement was Israel's spiritual cleansing day. An annual holiday, it celebrated God's caring love and his covenant faithfulness – and atonement was made for the sins of the nation.

It centred around five acts by the high priest. Dressed only in a plain white robe, a sign of his own humility, he sacrificed a bull to atone for his own sins and those of his family and fellow priests.

Then, he killed a goat to atone for the people's sins. He took its blood into the 'Holy of Holies', the inner sanctum of the tabernacle, the place of the intimate presence of God, which he entered each year only on this one occasion. The blood was sprinkled on the ark, and then outside on the people: they were 'at one' with God again.

The second goat was not killed. Instead, the sins of the people were confessed over it, the high priest laid his hands on it, and it was led out into the wilderness, symbolically removing their sins far from them as the 'scapegoat'.

The fourth act was to kill two rams, which were offered as a whole burnt sacrifice for which the high priest wore his coloured garments. This was a joyful celebration of restored fellowship with God. And finally, the remains of the sacrifices were taken out to the tip. The people's spiritual rubbish was thrown out and destroyed for ever. Their sins could accuse them no longer.

Christians will see in the symbolism several parallels to the death and resurrection of Christ; the New Testament writers (especially the author of Hebrews) are not slow to pick them up. The great day provided a remedy for Lady Macbeth's 'damned spot'. But only for a year. Then it had to be repeated. Christ's atonement, by contrast, was 'once and for all' (Hebrews 9:12; 10:10) and human sins are now and for ever removed 'as far as the east is from the west' (Psalm 103:12). This is not the only meaning of Christ's death, but it was a key one for the New Testament writers.

In a society where animals are treated differently, sacrifices may seem obnoxious. But to the Israelites in the culture of 1200 BC they were normal, and became a means God used to reveal his holiness and his forgiveness

CROSS CHECK

Moses' authorship: p 117
Law and grace: pp 370, 376-7
The covenant: pp. 18-21
Priests and Levites: p 230

The Scapegoat, as imagined by William Holeman Hunt

Is God bloodthirsty?

Some ancient religions (as some forms of modern Hinduism) 'fed' the gods, believing that the smell of blood would turn away their anger (so the prophets of Baal slashed their wrists in 1 Kings 18).

That was not the Hebrew view. The refrain that sacrifices were a sweet smell to God (1:17, etc.) is metaphorical; it was the heartfelt action the sacrifice represented that he was pleased with. The Israelites knew that only God could forgive sins; the sacrifices were the God-given symbolic expression of how he forgives and restores his penitent servants. They stressed:

The seriousness of sin. The wages of sin is death (Romans 6:23), the fruit and sign of banishment from the garden of God's presence in Genesis 3. 'Death' is a spiritual condition before it is a physical reality. The blood represents life poured out in death, a symbol of the fate all deserved.

The price is paid. God is 'too pure to look on evil; he cannot tolerate wrong' (Habakkuk 1:13). Retribution, therefore, is the inevitable consequence of wrongdoing. The just penalty for sin has to be paid.

A substitute can atone. The sacrifices introduce us to the idea of 'substitutionary atonement': someone taking the blame in our place, and shedding sacrificial blood to save us.

HARD Question

No access for the disabled?

Leviticus in the New Testament

- Be holy: 1 Peter 1:15
- Called to be priests: 1 Peter 2:9
- Christ does what rituals could not: Hebrews 7:18-28
- Christ is a sin offering: Romans 8:1-4; 2 Corinthians 5:18-21; Hebrews 9:11-21; 10:11,12; 13:11-14
- Christ is a peace offering: Romans 5:1-11; Ephesians 2:13-18; Colossians 1:18-20
- Christ is our High Priest: Hebrews 3:1; 4:14-5:5; 8:1-13

People with disabilities seem to get a raw deal in the Bible. They were forced to beg and were regarded as accursed by God (cf. John 9:1,2). They were also, in Leviticus, barred from the priesthood (21:16-23).

This must be balanced against the law that disabled people are not to be abused (19:14); the elderly, along with widows and orphans, are always offered respect in Scripture (19:32).

The Mosaic law discriminates positively in favour of the disadvantaged. The bar on disabled priests is to make a theological point. They are not lesser people, but they cannot be up-front in worship leadership because of the highly visual and symbolic nature of that worship. Everything had to be visually 'unblemished' because it illustrated God's perfection.

Today, physical disability is still a legitimate bar to certain occupations where full faculties (from colour vision to physical endurance) are essential. Christian ministry is now rightly open to people with disabilities. The role and purpose of ministry has changed; the Levitical rule applied to a different role and symbolism in the past.

Pay up and shut up, as a golden rule

Leviticus 19

It's like a gold nugget gleaming in a pan of brown sand and pebbles. 'Love your neighbour as yourself' (v 18) leaps out of a page of often obscure legislation. Jesus' commandment merely echoed Moses' teaching centuries before.

Leviticus shows how this 'golden rule' can be applied to varied human conditions. Rumour-mongering and gossip is forbidden (v 16); so is harbouring inner hatred (v 17).

Bills are to be paid on time; we are not to fiddle the books nor alter the scales; people are not to be conned by small print (vv 13,35). Here, too, is the early social security legislation (vv 9-10) which ensured the survival of Jesus' ancestor Ruth (Ruth 2:2,3).

Many of these laws have the refrain: 'I am [illegible] Lord.' They do not simply make good social sense. Rather, they reflect God's nature. Being good neighbours is one way of honouring God in our daily lives. To be uncharitable is to deny our faith and harm our witness.

Faithfulness pays spiritual dividends

Leviticus 26

The 'prosperity gospel' gets short shrift from Jesus, who advocated voluntary poverty (Luke 12:33). The Bible has no place for a mechanistic God who gives wealth in return for obedience, although the view that wealth was a sign of God's blessing was popular at the time.

Leviticus promises blessings to the nation as a whole in return for obedience. The promise is not to individuals. The Bible treats 'God's people' as a 'corporate body'. We together will experience God's presence and gifting (not always in material ways) if together we walk in his ways.

Gap year for all

Leviticus 25

At the dawn of the new millennium, the jubilee principle has captured people's imaginations. There have been petitions and campaigns to cancel Third World debts owed to the richer West.

No one knows if the principle was ever applied fully in ancient Israel. But it enshrines basic values and expresses a deep compassion. It teaches:

- Conservation (v 17). Leaving fields fallow for a year was until recently a time-honoured practice. Some would say that it is still important, despite the advances of agricultural science. It illustrates that the land is lent to us, and is not to be misused selfishly.
- Property rights (v 10). Later landowners were criticised for 'adding field to field' and creating an underclass of 'have nots' (Isaiah 5:8; Micah 2:2). In Israelite law, property was leasehold, never freehold (vv 23,24). Empire building was a sin against God because it robbed his people of their basic needs.
- A fresh start (v 54). Every generation was allowed to make its own way not enslaved by the debts and inadequacies of a previous generation. It helped them out of the rut.

Redemption of slaves or land could be achieved before jubilee year. But if an owner complained that it was unfair to lose his property just because of a turn in the calendar, he was reminded that it was unfair to have the slave or property in the first place.

Politicians and financiers today decry this 'unworkable' principle. The Bible's concern is that we do not pay lip service to people's rights, but that we enforce them even if it costs us. The Israelites were not allowed to shunt people around government departments and leave them empty-handed.

HARD Question

Sex is dirty and bad – or is it?

The Bible provides us with one of the ancient world's great celebrations of physical sex, in the Song of Songs. Yet here in Leviticus we seem to have a different picture.

Semen discharges and menstrual flows make people 'unclean', as does even childbirth which biblically is the applauded outcome of intercourse (12:1-8; 15:16-24). However, these rules are not meant to relegate sex to a taboo. They stress (with other laws) that all of life is to be hallowed and purified.

There are several detailed rules about lawful and unlawful sexual unions, which put homosexual and bestial liaisons in the same context as hetero-sexual unions with close relatives (ch 18; 20:10-21). They are there for two reasons.

Some of them relate to marital faithfulness, which is a major commandment (Exodus 20:14). This is viewed in Scripture as a picture of God's covenant faithfulness to us. God is faithful to us, so we are to be faithful to our partners. Sexuality is seen in the context of stable whole-family relationships.

Other laws relate to the fact that sexual experiment and promiscuity was rife in biblical times as it is now, and was sometimes associated with pagan religious practice. The Israelites were called to be different and expressed by a structured code of sexual ethics.

Our task today is to decipher which of these many rules relate to the fundamental principles of sexuality – and which are therefore of abiding relevance – and which are cultural rules relevant only to the past.

For today

- God is holy, so we are to be holy also
- Worship is to be given with care and reverence
- God wants to hallow ordinary things
- God has provided a means to restore our broken relationship with him

The names they called God

Readers of the Pentateuch (Genesis–Deuteronomy) soon become aware that God is given several different names. This is one reason for the 'source' theory of authorship; it is assumed that writers would use only one name for God.

However, we often use different names for the same people, in different contexts or for variety: title (the president); formal (Mr); semi-formal (Christian and surname); informal (Christian name); familiar (nick-name). The Bible writers use different names for God, sometimes to stress some aspect of his character.

Yahweh (Jehovah)
Written in Hebrew as YHWH (there are no vowels in the original) and usually rendered in English versions as LORD this is the holy name revealed to Moses (Exodus 3:14). It may have been known earlier (Genesis 4:26) although this could also be a case of a later writer explaining what was happening in his own terms.The range of its meaning is uncertain. It is to be rendered 'I am who I am' (stressing God's continued, unchanging character) or 'I will be what I will be' (seeing God as the sovereign leader of the Israelites). It stresses in either case his complete independence; he was neither shaped nor influenced by anyone.

The Jews refuse to use this, the only 'personal' name for God, and normally substitute Adonai. This was why Jesus was accused of blasphemy in John 8:58; he applied the name to himself.

Adonai
Means 'My Lord', and has the idea of sovereign ruler or owner.

El, Elohim
The most common Old Testament name, used over 2,500 times. It means 'The strong one' on whom everything depends. The word is also used for other gods. It was often combined with other words to make composite names.

El Shaddai
Means 'The most high God', and was the name (or character) revealed to Abraham (Genesis 17:1).

Descriptive names

The King James Version spelt these out, but most English translations now give only the meaning.

Yahweh-Jireh: The LORD provides (Genesis 22:13,14)
Yahweh-Rophi:The LORD who heals you (Exodus 15:26)
Yahweh-Nissi: The LORD is my banner (Exodus 17:15)
Yahweh-Shalom: The LORD is my peace (Judges 6:24)
Yahweh-Sabaoth: The LORD of hosts (1 Samuel 1:3; used 80 times in Jeremiah alone)
Yahweh-Roi: The LORD is my shepherd (Psalm 23:1)
Yahweh-Tsidkenu: The LORD is our righteousness (Jeremiah 23:6; 33:16)
Yahweh-Shammah: The LORD is there (Ezekiel 48:35)

Israelite festivals and holidays

The Israelite Calendar

The Israelite calendar is offset from ours by approximately two weeks.

Grain harvest						
10	11	12	1	2	3	4
Tebet	Shebat	Adar	Nisan	Iyyar	Sivan	Tammuz
January	February	March	April	May	June	
July	August	September	October	November	December	
4	5	6	7	8	9	10
Tammuz	Abib	Elul	Tishri	Marchesvan	Kislev	Tebet
Firstfruits		Olives		Plough and plant		

Passover: Abib 14
- Celebrates exodus
- Household meal with symbolic actions
- Exodus 12:1-14; Leviticus 23:5
- Numbers 9:1-14

Unleavened Bread: Abib 15-20
- Recalls exodus
- Bread baked without yeast for the week
- Religious assemblies at start and finish
- Exodus 12:15-20; Leviticus 23:6-8; Numbers 28:17-25

Firstfruits: Abib 16
- Offering of first barley sheaves
- Leviticus 23:9-14

Weeks (Pentecost): Sivan 6
- 50 days after Passover Sabbath
- Celebrates grain harvest
- Joyful time
- Exodus 23:16; Leviticus 23:15-21; Numbers 28:26-31

Trumpets: Tishri 1
- Celebrates giving of the Sabbath
- Extra day of rest
- Leviticus 23:23-25; Numbers 29:7-11

Day of Atonement:Tishri 10
- Solemn ceremonies for national sin
- Only day of the year when high priest entered Holy of Holies
- Leviticus 16; 23:26-32; Numbers 29:7-11

Tabernacles: Tishri 15-21
- Recalled the desert wanderings
- People camped out in brushwood shelters
- Celebrates final ingathering of harvest
- Leviticus 23:33-43; Numbers 29:12-34

Sacred Assembly: Tishri 22
- Concludes Tabernacles
- Leviticus 23:36; Numbers 29:35-38

Purim: Adar 14,15
- Inaugurated in fifth century BC to celebrate Esther's 'victory'
- The book of Esther

Hanukkah: Kislev 25
- Celebrates cleansing of temple by Maccabees in second century BC
- John 10:22

A signpost for seekers

Luke's Gospel

- Has a special emphasis on Jesus' birth and resurrection
- Has a special concern for women and for the poor
- Contains some of Jesus' best-known parables (such as the Prodigal Son) and encounters (such as with Zacchaeus)
- Is part of a carefully-researched two-part history leading on to the Acts of the Apostles

If Matthew is the Gospel for the Jews, and Mark is the Gospel for the hurrying person, Luke is the seeker's Gospel. Written in stylish language, it is carefully researched and easy to read.

Luke, who was a doctor and a travelling companion of St Paul, has several special interests. He includes, not unnaturally, some helpful details about Jesus' healings. He also shows how Jesus regarded women and the poor with special compassion at a time when they were usually seen as second-class citizens or outcasts.

At the other end of the scale, he has strong warnings for the rich. His chief concern, however, is to show that Jesus is the Saviour of the world, sent by God to rescue people from the kingdom of Satan and darkness.

Luke alone tells the familiar parables of the Prodigal Son and the Good Samaritan; he alone records the joyful conversion of the corrupt tax inspector Zacchaeus. And only Luke gives us real insight into Jesus' birth, and records the encounter of two ordinary people with the risen Jesus on the Emmaus road. It all makes the book user-friendly and faith-inspiring.

LUKE

1	Two expectant mothers
2	Jesus' birth and boyhood
3	Ministry of John the Baptist
4	Start of Jesus' ministry
5	First disciples, healings and arguments
6	Sermon on the plain
7	John commended; Jesus anointed
8	Parable of sower; Gadarene demoniac
9	Peter's confession; transfiguration
10	Mission of the 72; the good Samaritan
11	How to pray; woes to the Pharisees
12	Teaching about riches and watchfulness
13	Problem of suffering; the narrow way
14	Lessons from a banquet
15	Parables about the lost
16	Parables of the manager, and the rich man
17	Teaching about sin, and second coming
18	Parables of widow, tax collector; rich ruler
19	Zacchaeus; entry into Jerusalem
20	Parable of tenants; disputes
21	Signs before Jesus' return
22	The last supper; Jesus' arrest
23	Jesus' trials, crucifixion
24	Resurrection stories

'The son said to him, "Father, I have sinned against heaven and against you. I am no longer worthy to be called your son." But the father said to his servants, "Quick! Bring the best robe and put it on him . . . For this son of mine was dead and is alive again; he was lost and is found." So they began to celebrate.'

Luke 15:21-24

God's magnificent manifesto

Luke 1:46-55, 67-79

Matthew's Gospel launches Jesus' ministry with the revolutionary teaching of the Sermon on the Mount. Luke launches Jesus' life with an equally revolutionary sound of music.

The two poems here (Mary's is more of a song, Zechariah's more of a prophecy) speak theological volumes. They lay down the themes to which Luke will return time and again.

In both cases the praise is directed to God, not simply for what he has done for Mary and Zechariah personally. That is the nature of true worship: lifting us from the immediate to the eternal, from the personal to the corporate.

Mary's song, called the Magnificat, in some ways resembles that of Hannah in 1 Samuel 2:1-10. Both their sons were to be special servants of God, but Hannah was married and unhappily childless.

Mary's 'humility' was genuine in terms of her human poverty as well as her attitude of heart. She could offer only the poor person's traditional sacrifice (2:24; cf. Leviticus 12:8) and for some while she lived as a homeless refugee (2:7; cf. Matthew 2:14).

But her God is not only holy, he is also merciful (v 50), an implicit acknowledgement that Mary considers herself tainted by original sin.

God's holiness and righteousness are expressed by the way he turns the tables on the rich and powerful (vv 51-54), a constant Lucan theme. This is a prophetic declaration of righteousness which may have its spiritual dimension in terms of personal salvation, but which is far wider-reaching.

To that Zechariah also turns, in the prophecy known as the Benedictus. He sees his son's birth as a stage in God's purposes not just for himself and his wife, but for the nation. He focuses on forgiveness (v 77) but as a Jew this was never separated from God's wider purposes (v 74).

Christians cannot separate the spiritual and personal message from the wider context of God's plan for the world. John the Baptist called for a radical change in lifestyle, and neither he nor his cousin Jesus were afraid to confront the authorities with their unrighteousness. The Christian gospel is both personal and corporate.

Author: Luke is never named but emerges as the only likely author of Acts, the companion volume to the Gospel. Luke accompanied Paul on some of his journeys and was with him near the end of his life, as was Mark. He was a doctor and probably a Gentile (or perhaps a non-Palestinian Jew). According to one source he died aged 84 in Boetia.

Readers: Luke and Acts are addressed to 'Theophilus', meaning 'One who loves God' but is probably a real person's name. He may have been Luke's sponsor and friend in Antioch in Syria where Luke may have been based. The readers were probably Gentiles as Luke explains many Palestinian and Jewish terms.

Date of composition: Acts was probably completed in the mid 60s AD as the fall of Jerusalem and the deaths of Peter and Paul are not mentioned, so the Gospel must be earlier. It reproduces much of Mark (which must therefore have been written first) but it is possible that the two of them could have compared notes in Rome, cf. 2 Timothy 4:11. From inferences in the text Luke may have been edited after the fall of Jerusalem.

Sources: Mark (re-written more elegantly) and some material common to Matthew. Luke also relates some unique material clearly drawn from various sources and conversations.

Hark the herald angels sing!

The nativity stories are full of angels. Zechariah hears one announcing John's conception. One tells Mary she will be the mother of the Messiah. And then, when Jesus is born, the heavenly choir serenades the shepherds in the fields. As far as Luke is concerned, they then go quiet until after the death of Jesus when two angels greet the women at the tomb.

Although these incidents are not unique in the Bible, angels are usually seen only at strategic points in its story. Often dismissed by sceptics along with fairies and UFOs, the parallel world of non-physical creatures associated with God is accepted by Bible writers, but they give no encouragement to speculate about it beyond the bare essentials.

Who are the angels?

They are defined as 'ministering spirits' in Hebrews 1:14. Their task is to serve God by serving his people. When you consider the psalmist's assertion that human beings are created 'a little lower than the angels' (Psalm 8:5), their servant role is all the more remarkable. Angels are God's backroom staff, the school dinner ladies and the motorbike couriers of the spiritual realm.

Some problems arise for interpreters in that the word literally means 'messenger' and can be used of human beings as well as of spiritual beings. When the evil queen Jezebel issued a death threat to Elijah, she sent it via an 'angel', a (human) messenger (1 Kings 19:2). That has led some commentators to suggest that the 'angel' who fed Elijah, for example (1 Kings 19:5,6) was a kindly resident of the locality. The phrase 'being an angel' is often attributed to a kindly person, even now.

We are not told what they look like. At times, they shine with the radiance of God's glory, which is hardly surprising since they come from his presence. They lit up the night sky for the shepherds (Luke 2:9) and on resurrection morning they were dressed in lightning (Luke 24:4). At other times, though, they look just like us. Abraham apparently didn't recognise his heavenly visitors until after they had gone (Genesis 18:1; Hebrews 13:2).

What do angels do?

They have numerous roles in Scripture. Among them are:

- Messengers who bring specific instructions from God to individuals (Matthew 1:20)
- Teachers who explain important visions (Daniel 9:21,22)
- Protectors who guard God's people against spiritual and physical danger (2 Kings 6:17; Psalm 34:7; 91:11)
- Providers who supply urgent needs (Jesus in the desert was helped by angels, Luke 4:11)
- Rescuers of God's people from impossible situations (Peter in jail, Acts 12:8-10)
- 'Soldiers' who execute God's judgment when Christ returns (Matthew 16:27; Revelation 8:2)

The list raises the common question: do we have 'guardian angels'? Jesus seems to imply the possibility in Matthew 18:10, and the 'angels' of the churches (Revelation 2-3) could suggest that there are corporate guardians too. But these are the only references, and are too thin to support a firm doctrine.

Do people see angels today?

There are many stories in circulation, at least some of which should be treated with caution. Not everything the mind sees is 'real'; the imagination is a largely uncharted but extremely powerful human gift.

However, there are too many such stories to dismiss all of them, and if angels were operational in biblical times there is no reason to suppose that they have retired now; this is still 'the day of the Lord' and angels function in his eternal presence.

And so Air Chief Marshal Dowding recalled Second World War fighter crews seeing 'another figure' in the cockpit of a stricken plane when the pilot had been killed. People have reported strangers turning up unbidden to rescue them from some crisis, only to disappear instantly when the problem was fixed. Angels of mercy, certainly, and whatever the 'explanation', God is to be praised.

One intriguing sighting was at a Christian Bible week in the late 1980s in the UK, when people reported hearing angels singing in the tent after a meeting had finished. The local newspaper that week reported an unusual number of 'sightings' of 'UFOs'. Discussion groups might spend an interesting evening considering whether such 'sightings' stem from people's sensitivity to the spirit world interpreted in terms of scientific mythology!

How should we regard angels?
People who see angels are sometimes overcome with awe (which is a more accurate word than 'fear'). This is because they burn with the purity and holiness of God. But nowhere does the Bible suggest that we need be afraid of them; just the opposite, in fact, for they come to aid us.

However, neither should we venerate or worship them, even if we do acknowledge and appreciate them. When John fell at the feet of his heavenly guide, he was sharply rebuked because 'I am a fellow servant with you'. In that sense, they're on our level. Some early Christian cults included angel worship in their repertoire, probably as a hangover from some pagan cults, and Paul expressly forbade it (Colossians 2:18).

Indeed, the angels themselves worship God (Revelation 5:11,12) and hold him in great awe (Psalm 89:7). Their task is to point to God, not to themselves. Therefore, if people today encounter what they consider to be angels, their thanks and praise should be directed to God. Without belittling their experience, what has happened to them is simply that God has intervened in a situation and on this occasion has done so through an angel, when on another occasion he might use some other means. The intervention of an angel does not mark out the person encountering them as any more special or holy than someone who experiences God's help in another, more hidden way.

Did some of the angels fall?
There are hints in the Bible (and only hints) that Satan and the demons are fallen angels. The impression is given that Satan, through pride, rebelled against God (see Isaiah 14:12-17, although this probably has the double-edge of much prophecy and refers also to a historical figure or nation).

The fact that Satan can disguise himself as an angel of light (2 Corinthians 11:14) may lend some weight to this, as does the fact that he also occupies the spiritual realm. But such events lie hidden in the deep mysteries of eternity, and there is no suggestion that what may have happened in the past can be repeated now; angels from the realms of glory are incorruptible and trustworthy servants.

For the devil (Satan): pp. 166, 172, 192, 307
For demons, see: pp. 104, 289

Old folks wait and see

Luke 1-3

Old people often look back on the past with sentimentality and to the future with dread. In Luke, they look back with gratitude and forward with hope. True to his concern for people, Luke singles out bit-part players and gives them special attention.

First on the scene is Zechariah, the ageing and childless priest, who is literally dumbstruck when he sees a vision in the temple (1:5-25). It was the greatest day of his life, because priests normally burned incense there only once in a lifetime. But he fluffed the challenge to believe the angel without question.

His 'punishment' was more of a sign, however, because when he at last spoke after John's birth the neighbours' tongues began to wag also (1:60): what sort of child is this? His prayer for a child was answered, but at personal cost and in God's own way; a theme which Luke will impress on us again.

Then there is Simeon, the elderly man approaching death who believed he would see the Messiah before dying (2:21-36). But he too, having recognised the infant Jesus and rejoiced, focuses on cost with an ominous warning to Mary (2:35).

Finally, Anna enters (2:36-38), a saintly old eccentric who probably had more of a reputation as a nuisance than as a prophet among the temple guards. Who takes any notice of a bent, toothless old babushka muttering in a public square? Luke does; because God does.

All three have a virtue in common: they were waiting on and for God. Luke reminds us that God has kept his promise. Patience has been rewarded. The Messiah is coming. The long night of waiting is over.

Date of events:
about 4 BC to AD 33

Location:
Palestine

Place in Bible:
The third of the three 'Synoptic Gospels'in the New Testament, following Mark. Comes before John

Story leads on to:
The account of the early church in the Acts of the Apostles, which was written by the same author

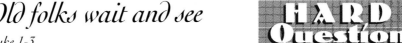

Do we have to believe in the virgin birth?

In order to be a practising Christian assured of one's acceptance by God, one does not have to believe in the virgin birth (which properly should be called the virginal conception) any more than one has to believe that Jesus will physically return to earth at the second coming. But accepting it does help to integrate what otherwise remains a jumble of unconnected doctrines.

Parthenogenesis, as it is called biologically, is known in the animal kingdom. However, the offspring of natural virginal conceptions are always female, because they lack the male 'X' chromosome which can only come from a male. Jesus' birth is a miracle in the sense that it is a supernatural intervention which defies complete natural explanation.

It helps to look at it from the end of the story rather than from the beginning. The apostles realised that Jesus was the unique, pre-existent Son of God, who came to share our existence as someone who was fully human yet also fully divine – a combination which we cannot begin to comprehend.

The virgin birth demonstrates that beautifully. A pre-existent person entered human life in a tangible way, and effected that unique combination of divine and human without violating either. Given that God, all through the biblical record, demonstrates rather than merely states his character and truth, the virgin birth is just the sort of thing God would do.

It has been suggested that the early

church invented the story in order to explain the person of Christ. Against that we can see that his critics believed there was something odd about his birth. They accused him of being illegitimate (e.g. John 8:41; 9:29). He was also described as Mary's son (Mark 6:3; cf. Galatians 4:4) which was normally derogatory.

Luke's Gospel (and Matthew's) were in circulation by the 70s if not before, and there is no record of any eyewitnesses challenging the account. Besides, the earthy apostles were not into 'spiritualising' and their emphasis on truth and honesty (see Acts 5:1-11!) would have rendered fabrication impossible.

Shepherds' pie-in-the-sky

Luke 2:8-20

Shepherds were at the bottom of the social scale in first-century Palestine. Their testimony, like that of women, was not admissible in court. So their story of the angels would have been greeted with derision. (Just as the women's story of the resurrection was not believed in 24:11.)

So this is not just a charming story for the nativity play. This vision has immense theological importance. Luke is showing that the birth of Jesus really is good news for the poor and the despised (cf. 1:52) – and therefore for everyone. The Messiah is not elitist.

Those who are regarded as inferior by others thus not only have their human dignity restored by God, but they emerge as the front runners in his mission to the world. Would you believe a hippy or a hobo who claimed that God had spoken to them?

HARD Question

When did Jesus know who he was?

Luke 2:41-52; 3:21-22

Among the early Christian writings are some apocryphal gospels which contain extravagant accounts of Jesus' early life in which he performed little miracles. They are not accepted as genuine. The first Christians clearly didn't consider that his childhood was either remarkable or, indeed, worth considering. It was his ministry and teaching which counted.

The incident in the temple is the only glimpse we have of his boyhood and it has all the marks of normality. He pursued his own agenda. He was obviously interested in religious matters as he was not far off his own bar mitzvah (coming of age) ceremony. But he didn't give a thought about his parents. It was just the kind of thing a twelve-year-old would do!

The text goes on to say that he grew in wisdom, implying that he did not know or understand everything at once – like any normal human being. He had been told, no doubt, of his unusual birth, but the conscious understanding of his divinity must have dawned gradually. He knew God as his Father at the age of twelve, but he knew him better at the age of thirty.

His baptism may have been an important (but not decisive) moment for his human awareness. The voice from heaven confirmed his calling and status, and launched him on his ministry. (An early heresy called adoptionism suggested that at the baptism God adopted the man Jesus to be his son. This was denied by most of the church.)

The Bible is full of accounts of how God gradually prepared people for their work, and how he revealed himself to them gradually over time. His own Son was not to be an exception to the rule. As a man, he was subjected to all the limitations of being human, and was not given instant maturity.

A testing experience

Luke 4:1-13

Fresh cream cakes in the UK are sometimes advertised with the slogan, 'Naughty but nice' meaning the temptation to indulge isn't such a bad thing because the indulgence is pleasurable. The advertisements naturally say nothing about calories or cholesterol. They are consistent with the post-modern view which makes pleasure an almighty god and personal choice an absolute good.

The temptations which Jesus faced were of a rather different order, but the real temptation would have been to think in that way. His temptations were to pervert God's just purposes by:

- misusing his gifts to meet his own immediate ends (to be self-concerned and indulgent)
- to become famous and to influence people for the sake of fame and power itself
- to take a short cut in order to convince people of his calling and mission.

These were not just silly temptations. Jesus was tired and hungry; they came when he was at his weakest. To get food would have seemed sensible. What human being has not dreamed of exerting influence over others with a presidential signature? And labour-saving devices are always welcomed by hard-pressed people.

Temptations today are strongest when they are related to pride and power, to consumption and convenience. We are rarely tempted to do what we believe strongly is wrong; but *are* tempted in areas where the wrongdoing 'doesn't seem too bad' and for which we can make lame excuses.

Jesus looked to Scripture to resist his temptations. This challenges us to know the Scriptures well in order to remain on the straight and narrow, because the devil quoted the Bible – out of context and with a subtle twist.

HARD Question

Is there really a devil?

Jesus certainly thought so, and Satan (the name means 'the accuser') is referred to many times in the Gospels and epistles. Christians consider him a fallen angel who rebelled against God before the world's creation and cast out of God's presence as a result (Isaiah 14:12-14 and Luke 10:18).

Among the activities ascribed to the devil are deception, temptation, destruction, hindering mission and hurting God's people. He is implacably opposed to God, but although powerful, is not equal to God. The belief that two equal and opposite spiritual forces battle in the world, popular in some 'new age' teachings and the ancient Persian religion of Zoroastrianism is not Christian.

Jesus' incarnation was the first step to 'casting him out' of his position as 'god of this world' (2 Corinthians 4:4). His final destruction is predicted in Revelation 20:7-10. Meanwhile his power is limited by God (Job 1:12).

However, he is not to be despised or underestimated. Jude v 9 says that the soldier-angel Michael refuses to slander Satan, suggesting that his original status was high and still respected even if he has forfeited all right to return to it.

This problem can be approached in two ways. First: if God is personal, and created personal human beings, he could also have created personal spiritual beings (angels), some of whom 'fell' from grace.

A second approach is to read the newspapers. Evil rampages through history; systems run amok; hatred is infectious; violence and cruelty are endemic; greed is insatiable. The good that people do is negated by the crass inhumanity of others. It's not hard to believe that behind the forces of evil in the world there is a malicious evil spirit.

Following Jesus is a very fishy business

Luke 5:1-11, 27-31; 6:12-16

Fishing was not an easy occupation in first-century Galilee. The inland lake was unpredictable and subject to sudden and violent squalls. Boats had no engines, of course, and could be lost. The best catches were to be had at dusk, night and dawn, when the fish were closer to the surface than during the hot day, so it was an anti-social job. And it was plain hard work. There was no refrigeration and no fast transport to take the fish to the large centres of population. But it was a job, and to give it up to tramp the countryside with an unknown preacher and healer must have taken courage. Matthew (Levi) also must have felt this when he left his difficult but lucrative occupation of fishing into people's pockets.

We are not told if the Zebedee brothers, and Peter and Andrew, made other arrangements for their business while they were away. Very likely there were others in the families who continued it. After the death of Jesus, Peter had no difficulty in going back to Galilee and getting out his boat (John 21:1-6).

The twelve did not disappear off the face of the earth into some secretive cult. They did not cut off from their family and friends. Peter's mother-in-law was cared for (4:38,39); Jesus had his friends in Bethany. His later statement encouraging 'hatred' of family (14:26) was about spiritual priorities, not about callous abandonment.

What the first disciples did opt for was insecurity and the unknown instead of the secure and the known. That is the bottom line of discipleship. It involves personal sacrifice and a change of lifestyle and priorities.

Generosity may earn high interest

Luke 6:17-49

When Hudson Taylor, the nineteenth-century pioneer missionary to China, was a medical student in London he was almost penniless. One night he visited a destitute family desperate for medical help and food. In his pocket he had one large-denomination coin, which was all he had to pay for his own food and lodgings. He willingly would have given them half if he had the change.

After a great struggle, he gave them the coin and went home with nothing except a sense of peace and joy. The next morning an even larger bank note arrived anonymously in his post!

Christian biographies report similar stories of people entrusting to God all their worldly possessions and travelling light to serve him. They lend, expecting to lose it (v 35) and give without question (v 38). Jesus said, 'It is more blessed to give than to receive' (Acts 20:35) and Luke's 'sermon on the plain' (v 17) stresses the priority of inner attitudes focused on God, as does the Sermon on the Mount (Matthew 5-7). The related promises will be fulfilled one way or another, but it is often beyond us to foresee just how.

Jesus promises that when we are thoughtlessly generous (Paul's word ''hilariously' in 2 Corinthians 9:7, is tamely translated as 'God loves a cheerful giver') God will ensure that we won't lose out on what we really need.

But we should not give to get back more! Indeed, Jesus does not specify what it is we will get back. Hudson Taylor did make a material profit, but the returns are more often like the others he also received: the spiritual peace and joy of being drawn closer to God in utter dependence upon him.

God deserves a bit of luxury from us

Luke 7:36-8:3

Cosmetics were a relative luxury in first-century Palestine, although basic oils and perfumes for the body were necessary in the hot climate. Clearly in this case, an expensive imported ointment was carried, as such things often were, in a vial hung around the woman's neck.

Her action was the equivalent of pouring an entire bottle of expensive designer perfume from an exclusive Paris shop into one bath, when it might have lasted for months in normal use. Access to Jesus' feet was simple, as guests reclined on their elbows on low cushions. Letting her hair down in public was the sign of a loose or vulgar woman, if not a prostitute.

Luke is interested in the action solely as an expression of gratitude, love and worship (the other Gospels contain comment on a parallel act as a potential waste of money; see box), and he contrasts it with the inhospitable attitude of the host. The value of the woman's gift is that she has not used it for herself; she has given it to God as a 'thank-you' for what he has done for her.

That is an important message for the church today. There is a valid ministry in giving extravagantly to God. The great cathedrals are not necessarily a waste of money, and sharing a hard-earned fortune is not stupid, when both are done for the right motive and not to earn a plaque on a wall. (Jesus condemns those who try to judge others' motives.)

The value is to the givers. It may be a public action, but it is a private spiritual transaction between themselves and their Lord, which God appreciates and receives graciously.

Copy-cat actions or copyist's error?

The other Gospels have a similar incident in a different context, where the woman is identified as Mary of Bethany, who was never reputed to be a 'sinful woman' (Matthew 26:6-13; Mark 14:3-9; John 12:1-8). This woman is anonymous, although often identified as Mary Magdalene (cf. Luke 8:2).

Here, the house belongs to Simon the Pharisee; Matthew says it was Simon the leper; John implies it was in Bethany, but that may not mean at Lazarus' house even though Martha is doing the catering.

The problem is not easily settled, but there is no logical reason why similar incidents should not have occurred on more than one occasion (there is a similar problem over Jesus' cleansing of the temple). The differences in the accounts seem too marked to be the variations one would find from different reporters' angles on the same incident.

As the scope for acts of generous kindness to a person were limited in a culture which by Western standards was extremely basic, it might even be surprising if it happened only twice.

Death has lost its sting for ever

Luke 7:11-17; 8:40-56

The Gospels record only three incidents of Jesus raising the dead. The widow's son is unique to Luke; Jairus' daughter is in all three Synoptic Gospels, and the raising of Lazarus is recorded only by John. To Luke, it is the people that are significant.

- The widow was in great need, and the raising of her son was an act of compassion. There were no social services to provide for her, and the dying-out of one's family line was regarded as a disgrace and a sign of God's cursing.
- Jairus' daughter was a girl; a second-class citizen, far less 'important' than a boy would be. On the way to her Jesus healed an old and ceremonially

'unclean' woman who no one would touch; Jesus is bringing life to the untouchables and the disregarded.

Some commentators have suggested that neither of these corpses was truly dead (Jesus said the girl was 'sleeping'). But the fact that the dead are not raised among us because death is irreversible does not mean that Jesus himself could not do it. These incidents show Jesus as the Lord of life. He, the Creator of life, came to conquer death in his own resurrection, and these miracles anticipate that.

Jesus sets high standards for recruits

Luke 9

Energetic companies sometimes advertise themselves as those who work harder than their competitors.

Jesus' disciples are not to be competitive over achievements and status (vv 46-50), but they do face a stiff challenge to work harder and go further than anyone in a non-Christian frame of mind would normally consider possible or desirable.

This chapter stresses sacrificial commitment. The twelve are to travel light on their mission (vv 3,4; cf. 58). The poor cannot receive the gospel as good news from people who roll up in stretch limos. The disciples have to take on the principle of incarnation which Jesus had embraced.

His call to everyone to 'take up the cross daily' (23-26) is the offer of a one-way ticket. There's no return to the old ways of life (vv 24,25). Paradoxically, we will lose our spiritual well-being (and by extension our general well-being) by clinging to the old life of self-interest.

That is hard. It is to resist the spiritual and emotional equivalent of the physical survival instinct which fights for life when faced with the prospect of death. Committing oneself to Christ is not the same as choosing between equally valid options of joining a golf club or a squash club. It's more like choosing to work for a pittance in a Third World country rather than stay at home and grow fat.

The recently bereaved man (vv 59,60) and the one who wanted to say goodbye (vv 61,62) may have been approaching discipleship equivocally. Jews were always respectful of the dead and supportive of families. Jesus would not have been harsh and callous. He simply stressed that his mission takes priority over everything, however valid.

Most of us want to have our cake and eat it, which isn't possible in Christian discipleship. Later, Luke repeats the challenge, unique in the Gospels, to count the cost before following Jesus (14:25-35). This evangelist is not out to con people into the kingdom in order to increase his tally of souls 'saved'.

How to deal with doubt

Luke 7:18-35 (cf. 3:1-20)

Neither John nor his cousin Jesus fitted preconceived moulds. Here, John appears to suffer from half of the problem that the critics had. He can't make Jesus out, either.

In prison, John questions his belief that Jesus is the promised Messiah. Jesus' response, quoting from Isaiah 35:5,6 and 61:1 should have answered John's doubts without making an overt claim to messiahship, which Jesus usually refused to do. Ironically he went on to commend John after John's messengers had left.

But John had expected the Messiah to come as a judge (3:17) and Jesus was not living up to that expectation. He is not condemned for his doubts, because he explored them seriously and sought an answer to dispel them with an open mind; he wanted to believe.

The Pharisees did not want to believe, and therefore looked for reasons to confirm their doubts. The test of any spiritual quest and doubt is: Do I really want a positive answer, and what will I do if I get it?

Mission is top of God's agenda

Luke 10:1-24

There are over 6,500 languages spoken in the world, many belonging to small tribal groups. Only about 300 language groups have a complete Bible, and some 2,000 have part of the Bible although not necessarily a whole New Testament.

Whenever a new Bible or Testament is published, a fresh group of people rejoice. They can discover Christ and his teaching for themselves and grow in their faith, without having to depend on outside teachers.

In that sense, the harvest is still very ripe, and the labourers woefully few. Nearer to home, there are many 'people groups' or sub-cultures who may have access to the Bible, but who have never 'heard' the Christian gospel in their own cultural thought forms and categories.

The commission of Jesus to take his message by word and deed into all the world is treated by Matthew as Jesus' final will and testament (Matthew 28:19). There, however, it is directed to the apostles; here, it is also the task of a much wider group of disciples. Every generation can be 'harvested' and, as the world population is growing, the need for workers becomes more urgent, not less.

In the 1990s there were 24 missionaries for every one million people. More workers are needed, but so too is the faithful witness of Christians in ordinary occupations. Missionaries can be targets of hatred and abuse (v 3). The call to the church is to go and minister; those who offer for the front line need the prayer and financial support of those in the ranks behind.

HARD Question

Who is on the Lord's side?

Luke 9:49,50; cf. 11:23

These two statements appear to contradict each other. One says those who are not enemies are allies; the other says that those who are not allies are enemies.

The people in the first saying work broadly in the name of Christ, but are not part of the church recognised by the inner group of keen disciples. They are people of goodwill who will not hinder the disciples, and whose general concerns will help prepare the disciples' way.

In the Western world the Millennium celebrations and concerns have brought many such people out of the woodwork, rooting for the Christian church and its broad message but not necessarily embracing all the details of Christian discipleship and belief. Jesus does not speculate on their eternal standing before God, and neither should we. They are not against God's general purposes, and we can work alongside them in many ways.

The second saying is in the context of the Beelzebub controversy in which Jesus is accused of doing the devil's work. Here, those who are not for Jesus are those who do not see a difference between Christ and Satan and who are not predisposed to fight evil in the world.

They may not be actively anti-Christian, but they are not supportive of Christian concerns either. They are like passive collaborators in enemy-occupied territory who do not join the resistance; by not fighting the enemy, they are allowing him to flourish. Therefore they are against God.

Crusades banned

Luke 9:51-55

Unique to Luke, this passage condemns a bleak chapter of Christian history. Jesus refuses to endorse any kind of violent crusade against people who refuse to believe his message. Samaritans were traditional enemies, and therefore he is simply practising his own teaching, and loving them.

The New Testament outlaws any kind of retribution against unbelievers, and never allows evangelism by force (or bribery). The days when Israel conquered the Promised Land in God's name had long gone even in Jesus' time; he brought a higher ethic and a harder method. Later, he banned even physical defence of his cause (22:49-51).

Difficult to balance

Luke 10:25-42

The good Samaritan is a model of good conduct admired beyond the Christian community. Luke, the only evangelist to tell the story, sets it in a broader context which alters the normal focus.

Loving one's neighbour is only half of God's requirement. The two great commandments belong together (v 27). Loving one's neighbour is a demonstration, for the Christian, of loving God. How can we love God, who has given us all, if we withhold consideration from a person in need? Religious people are not always good at expressing practical social concern. Loving God is not a private spiritual matter unconnected to the rest of life and God's world.

Loving one's neighbour in a self-sacrificing way becomes realistic when we are motivated by God's self-giving love. However, the Christian life is not solely about serving others, it is also about worshipping and serving God.

But kind and active people in the community are not always good at giving God the honour and drawing on his power. So the story of the good Samaritan is followed by the touching story of Mary and Martha.

Martha had a servant heart. She just wanted help because she was tired. Jesus recognises that; he doesn't scold her for her hard work, but helps her to put it in a broader perspective. She had to learn to *be*, as well as to *do*. She did; later she's the spiritual one while Mary is devastated (John 11:21-27).

Any attempt to prioritise spiritual devotion, evangelistic witness and social concern founders on the New Testament itself. There, all are equally necessary. What God has joined together, no one should put asunder.

Practical guide to Christian commitment

Luke 12

At the halfway stage of the book, Luke has established the fact that the Christian life is no easy option but a demanding commitment. He will remind us of it later, but just now he gathers together material which illustrates how faithfulness and single-mindedness can be worked out in everyday life.

- Speak carefully, not rashly, and depend on God's Spirit to inspire you (12:1-12)
- Focus your attention on God, not on worldly wealth (12:13-34)
- Live as if Jesus was coming back to assess your progress tomorrow (12:35-48)
- Be prepared for conflict and misunderstanding from people close to you (12:49-53)
- Keep your eyes open for the unexpected things God will be doing around you (12:54-59).

This is one of those chapters in the Bible which is worth seeing (and reading) as a whole, and absorbing the big picture before focusing on the details.

Seekers locked out?

HARD Question

Luke 13:22-30

Jesus promised that all who sought God would find him (11:9-13). Therefore those who 'try to enter' (v 24) are clearly not seekers in that sense. They were more likely to be hangers-on, who have enjoyed the stories, admired the healings, but never in fact become disciples. They haven't begun to apply his teaching in the way he intended.

He probably has in mind those who regard a place in the kingdom of God as their natural right. That would apply especially to the religious leaders of his day. In our own time it may apply to people who attach themselves to a nominally Christian way of life and consider that to be their only duty to God, without relating in any personal way to the Lord who is its source and inspiration.

HARD Question

Why do the innocent suffer so much?

Luke 13:1-8

The problem of innocent suffering is perhaps the most common objection to the Christian faith and the chief stumbling-block for people who are genuinely seeking God. How can he be good if he allows awful things to happen?

Jesus addressed the issue twice, here and in John 9:1-12. On both occasions he gave only the negative half of the answer. He showed simply that 'What have I (or others) done to deserve this?' is not a valid question. Personal suffering is not linked to personal sin.

Some suffering is self-inflicted, of course; the prostitute who becomes HIV positive cannot complain to God for reaping a consequence of a prohibited lifestyle. And the Bible is clear that there is no truly innocent person; all have sinned. But there is not a spiritual quid pro quo formula at work.

Jesus accepts that suffering is endemic in a fallen world; nice people suffer accidents and illness. Christians and others are equally vulnerable. In the Old Testament, Jeremiah (12:1-4) complained that God's people often seemed to come off worse.

It was left to later theologians to piece together a more positive response. Jesus himself suffered enormously, and in him God has entered into human experience. So God is not unmoved by our sufferings; he shares them. To the natural question, 'Why then doesn't he put an end to them now?' the Bible would answer that such a state would be heaven, which is promised for some time in the future (Revelation 21:3-5).

C.S. Lewis, in *The Problem of Pain*, wrote compassionately of God's problem in an imperfect world: 'That God can and does, on occasions, modify the behaviour of matter and produce what we call miracles, is part of the Christian faith; but the very conception of a common, and therefore stable, world demands that these occasions should be extremely rare . . . Try to exclude the possibility of suffering, which the order of nature and the existence of free will involve, and you find that you have excluded life itself.'

Stop the world – someone's missing

Luke 15

Most of us have so much clutter in our homes that losing something becomes a major crisis. We know it's there, somewhere. The search becomes intense, frustrating and time-consuming.

God, fortunately, keeps a tidier house and always knows exactly where everyone is. Indeed, John's Gospel promises that he will lose none of those who come to him (John 6:39). But the fact is, some will go walkies anyway; they will abscond from his presence. When that happens, he sends out the search parties and won't rest until they are recovered.

The shepherd who leaves 99 in the fold (a walled enclosure which kept sheep in, but did not keep wolves out) seems stupid. The local hounds might thank him kindly for free packed lunches while he was away. But God, says Jesus, is so passionate about finding the lost, that he'll take any risk (like sending his Son into the world).

That is because the lost are of personal value to him, like the woman's coin. It may have been part of her dowry or head-dress, of sentimental as

CROSS CHECK

Luke the man: p 28
Temptation: pp 72, 175
Demons: p 289
The devil in society: p 104
Giving money: p 79
Suffering: pp 194, 196-7
Life after death: p 76
Holy Communion: p 74

much as monetary value. People, says Jesus, are very precious to God, just as our treasures are to us.

The younger 'prodigal' son is guilty of a wasted life (his 'wild living' was just the expression of a greater failing). But the father looks longingly for him, and as soon as he appears on the horizon makes a fuss of him. He doesn't ask for the money to be repaid. He doesn't sentence the son to seven years' hard labour on the farm. He throws a party and forgets the past.

God is looking for you harder than you're looking for him, Luke is saying. Whoever you are, wherever you are, turn round, and he'll 'find' you and welcome you.

Mind the gulf!

Luke 16:19-31

It would be nice to have a clear understanding of what happens to people when they die, before the final return of Christ and the establishment of the new creation about which the Bible is clearer.

This parable doesn't tell us, despite some writers' attempts to read specific doctrines into it. The rest of the Bible is hazy, too, and Jesus' promise to the penitent thief (23:43) doesn't add very much. It is something about which we cannot usefully speculate.

The real point of this parable is that the Pharisees would not believe the testimony of someone who rose from the dead (v 31); their minds were already made up. And a gulf exists between us and people in the next life based on what they were like here, so their hardness is spiritually fatal.

'Abraham's bosom' was a common Jewish description of the loyal Israelite's life after death. 'Hades' (hell) is a waiting room before judgment, and the 'fire' should not be taken literally; Hades is not a physical place like the earth, so whatever it is like, it is not the same as fire on earth. The raging frustration of unfulfilled hope and desire would be one possible reality behind this vivid metaphor.

This is certainly one of the saddest of Jesus' parables. Not even he could get through to the closed minds of his opponents. His tale warns us that our future destiny depends on present faithfulness, and that one aspect of faithfulness is being open to what God is doing even when it conflicts with our presuppositions. It could be our beliefs which are wrong.

So shady deals are OK, then?

HARD Question

Luke 16:1-15

Most clergy and commentators wish fervently that this parable had not been included in the New Testament! It almost defies explanation – but not quite.

It commends shrewdness, but condemns dishonesty (vv 8,10). The manager has an eye to the future and is acting strategically for the long-term. So should Christians. We can't expect instant success in our ventures and we have to plan and work to a longer time scale.

Therefore we are to use shrewdly what we have for the long term advance of the kingdom (v 9). If we have wealth or influence, we are to use it to build relationships with people through which we can share our faith. There is nothing wrong in buying lunch for someone you want to get to know. Nor is there anything wrong in spending money to make a church building warm and welcoming for visitors.

Then in the long-term, when we all enter heaven and worldly goods are no longer required, there'll be a reception party full of people who got there because our initial shrewdness led them to be introduced to the host.

The parable is complicated by the inclusion of important teaching which is related but not central to it, including vv 10-12 about God being unable to entrust to dishonest people the task of disseminating his truth, and the blunt warning about two masters in v 13. The simple message of the passage is: be shrewd, be honest, and be single-minded.

Ruler gets needled

Luke 18, 19

Whether Jesus was talking about a real needle or more soberly referring to a low gate in the city wall called 'the needle's eye', his teaching was sharp.

Human possessions can get in the way of spiritual discipleship; we have to unload our baggage before we can enjoy the benefits of God's kingdom.

The proximity of this teaching to the story of Zacchaeus (another of Luke's unique insertions) is surely deliberate. For Zacchaeus paid back far more than the Jewish law demanded for voluntary restitution. His act of contrition was also a spontaneous act of generosity. He paid back what the law required for robbery with violence, recognising perhaps that he had violated people's lives, if not their bodies.

His response to Jesus was not simply to do the minimum. It was to demonstrate real love and gratitude to God for being accepted and forgiven. Get the point?

Judgment on the people as a whole

Luke 20:1-19

This parable is spoken against the people and leaders of Israel as a whole. The Bible often deals with groups corporately, which sometimes sounds strange to Western ears used to affirming the inalienable independence of the individual.

The vineyard is Israel and the tenants are generations of leaders. The servants are the prophets who were ignored or persecuted. Eventually the Son of God came, and was to be killed.

Jesus came with credentials which righteous people could recognise. Even the leaders recognised that he had a unique authority and ministry. But they refused to bow to it, and even the crowd which clapped 'Hosanna!' on Palm Sunday (19:38) booed 'Crucify!' on Good Friday (23:21). Ignorant rejection is understandable and forgivable; deliberate rejection is culpable.

Farewell party full of tension

Luke 22

Farewell parties can be sad as well as joyful. In this party, however, only Jesus seems to know that it is his farewell.

Jesus himself looked forward to it eagerly (v 14), a detail which only Luke records as he focuses on

HARD Question

If I prayed more, would God give me what I want?

Luke 18:1-14 (cf. 11:5-13)

No! He gives us what we need, and does not respond to the length of our prayers, nor to desperate bargains. The persistence here is an expression of the woman's utter dependence on 'the Judge', who represents God.

Her prayer is not the take it or leave it kind: 'It would be nice if you did this, please, Lord, but I guess if you don't I'll get by somehow.' The early twentieth-century American Baptist, Harry Emerson Fosdick, wrote in his book *The Meaning of Prayer* that 'many of the speeches addressed to God that we have called our prayers are not real prayers at all. They are not our dominant desires. They do not express the inward set and determination of our lives. What we pray for in the closet is not the thing that daily we are seeking with undiscourageable craving . . . Prayer that is not dominant desire is too weak to achieve anything.'

The widow and the tax collector in the stories were like that. They craved something from God like a starving person craves food. And the tax collector wanted something eternal: God's forgiveness. That is something for which no sincere prayer will ever go unanswered.

theological and pastoral detail and not on the 'words of institution' ('This is my body . . .') which some important early manuscripts omit altogether:

- It was carefully planned (vv 7-13). Jesus' foresight indicates this is to be a significant event; God is arranging the details for specific purposes.
- It was a Passover meal (v 11), which contained deeply symbolic actions re-enacting Israel's exodus from Egypt. Jesus added symbolic words and actions pointing to his own 'exodus' from the world and liberation of his people from the chain of sin and death.
- Luke includes the dispute about greatness (vv 24-30) which appears in different contexts in the other Gospels, but which fits with the footwashing recorded in John 13.

Only Luke mentions the two swords, in the context of Jesus' teaching about dependence on him (vv 35-38). Perhaps the disciples were made anxious by Jesus' melancholic state of mind and his talk about betrayal.

Jesus' curt 'Enough!' (v 38) probably means, 'Enough of that sort of talk! Remember what I said.' He permitted them to carry swords but certainly had no intention of them being used to defend his cause (v 49-51).

We cannot share in the spiritual symbolism of the Communion, which speaks of loving sacrifice, and then march into the world brandishing the weapons of selfish aggression.

Hope restored

Luke 24

News of the outcome of the Battle of Waterloo was eagerly awaited. As the message was being semaphored across southern England, fog came down and blanked out part of the message. All people in London heard was 'Wellington defeated'. Gloom set in – until the fog lifted and the message was repeated: 'Wellington defeated the enemy.'

That mixture of gloom and joy fills the resurrection narrative. The disciples are dispirited, their leader has been defeated. But when they see him again, they realise that he has defeated humankind's worst enemy. He has conquered death, and really is the King of kings.

The couple on the Emmaus road (sometimes considered to be Cleopas and his wife) were not only mourning the death of a friend, but grieving over what he might have achieved. They had also thought he was the Messiah; being wrong on such a thing meant they might never trust their judgment again.

Doubt, too, would have hovered over them; if God had done so much through Jesus, how had God failed now? The wild stories brought back by apparently hysterical women only added to their depression (vv 22-24). And so in their company, Luke invites us to see the phenomena of the resurrection:

- It was unexpected because it was unimaginable. Jesus had predicted it but it was beyond their experience and even their folk lore;
- Jesus became known in the breaking of bread (vv 30,35). Luke labours this. It became an interactive encounter in a familiar setting.

And so it has been for countless Christians since. Dreams are cruelly erased; our world goes to pieces. Hope and faith sink into despair and doubt. Yet God is not defeated, and in some small, unexpected yet familiar way, his presence is restored and life is rekindled. Thus Luke prepares us for an even more amazing story: of how these disciples went on to turn the world upside down (Acts 17:6, NRSV).

For today

- God is deeply concerned for the people we tend to write off or ignore
- Be patient; God keeps his promises in his own time, not ours
- Accept that being a Christian involves insecurity and uncertainty
- Give to God freely, so that his mission can continue unhindered
- If God seeks the lost with passion, so should we
- Jesus is alive; when things collapse, he can bring something new from the rubble

Prophet for the good times

The Book of Malachi

- Encourages continued faithfulness to God's covenant
- Calls for careful and reverent worship and fulfilment of religious duties
- Stresses the importance of stable family life

Malachi's social milieu was not unlike ours: there was peace, relative prosperity and political stability. But life wasn't perfect. Judah was still controlled by the Persians. The golden age of freedom and the rule of God promised by the prophets of old had still not arrived.

So the people had one of two attitudes. The majority were complacent. They grew morally and religiously slack. The nationalist fires had died down, and there was less respect for religious institutions. Attendance at worship declined, traditions were ignored and commandments broken.

The other attitude was of frustration mixed with confusion. Why had 'the day of the Lord' not come? Why were they still in this spiritual no man's land between oppression and salvation? Were the prophets wrong? It was exactly the same issue as that faced by some early Christians as they contemplated the apparently delayed return of Christ (cf. 2 Peter 3:4–10).

Don't lose heart, says Malachi. And don't give up your wholehearted devotion to God. Maintain the spiritual disciplines and live righteously. Be faithful however long you have to wait – which is just what Jesus said in Matthew 24:45–51. Good times are to be enjoyed, and they present us with a golden opportunity for service before the golden age of peace.

I the LORD do not change. So you, O descendants of Jacob, are not destroyed.

Malachi 3:6

AT A GLANCE

MALACHI

1. Careless worship angers God
2. Warning to priests and against divorce
3. Promise of a new prophet and of blessing on the faithful
4. The day of the Lord will come eventually

HARD Question

Can a God of love hate?

Malachi 1:2–5

The word 'hate' is used here in an idiomatic sense, expressing – by modern English standards, overstating – a relative contrast as an absolute antitheses (just as Jesus does in Luke 14:26). Malachi is saying that God elected (loved and chose) Jacob, rather than his elder brother Esau to be the father of God's special people, the Israelites, and the vehicle of his revelation to the world.

Only one could have that privilege, and (in keeping with much of the biblical story) God chose the more unlikely, first using Jacob's selfish trickery, but later teaching him to trust and obey God.

This does not imply that Esau and his descendants were automatically consigned to the spiritual garbage pit. The context is about national history rather than personal salvation. Paul quotes Malachi's words in Romans 9 and asserts that God's choice in such matters is righteous and just.

Esau became the 'father' of the Edomites and the family feud lasted for centuries, for all of which Edom would be punished (v 4). They refused to accept God's choice and live in peace with him. Only then does God's 'hatred' approach ours, when he exercises his righteous judgment.

Respect your calling

Malachi 1:6-2:10

Although addressed to priests of the Jewish sacrificial system, this passage applies to anyone called by God to a task in life. We have a responsibility to live up to it all the time, even when we are not physically doing it. Predatory priests and sex-offending Sunday School teachers are obvious contradictions of callings, but there are more subtle ones too of which we can all be guilty.

We carry the Lord's name wherever we go, and our lives should be infused with awesome obedience, as were those of Levi and Phinehas his grandson (2:5; cf. Numbers 25:10-13). But the priests in Malachi's day were careless. Anything would do for God so long as the work was done. God is however more interested in attitudes and methods than in results.

Poor people give more

Malachi 3

A survey in 1988 showed that better-off Christians in the UK gave less than poorer people to churches and charities. Of those earning over £40,000 only 2 per cent gave one tenth or more; but 29 per cent of those earning £10,000–£20,000 gave a tenth or more.

The custom of giving one tenth (a tithe) in the Old Testament related not to money (coinage was only invented in the eighth century BC), but to produce. It went to support the Levites who had no land of their own. The promise of God's blessing in Malachi relates to covenant obedience of which tithing was one aspect.

In New Testament times the Pharisees had created tithing laws to include even garden herbs (Matthew 23:23), but the apostles simply encouraged generous giving in proportion to one's means (1 Corinthians 16:1,2; 2 Corinthians 9:6–15). We should not reduce tithing to a legalistic routine, but it does look as if some people have gone too far the other way. Giving generously makes us more open to receive God's blessing.

Where am I?

Place in Bible:
The last book of the Old Testament

Parallel books:
Nehemiah probably covers the same period

CROSS CHECK

God's choice and human responsibility: pp 343, 374
Careful worship: p 74
Giving: p 79
'Mixed' marriages: p 131

FAST facts

Author: 'Malachi' is probably a proper name but as it means 'my messenger' the book is often considered to be anonymous. Some ancient Jewish writers thought the author was Ezra.

Date: The subject matter (such as people marrying partners from pagan religions, and the practice of sacrifice in the second temple) fits the fifth century BC (see below). It is often dated during Nehemiah's return to Susa in Persia between his first and second visits to Jerusalem, as 'the governor' (1:8) doesn't sound like him.

Background: Judah (the southern kingdom after the split in 930 BC) was exiled to Babylon in 586 (the period of Jeremiah and Ezekiel). Many Jews returned to Jerusalem in 537 when Persia conquered Babylon and the second temple was completed in 516 (as told in Ezra, Haggai and Zechariah). Other exiles returned later, including Ezra in 458. The walls were rebuilt under Nehemiah's direction in 445.

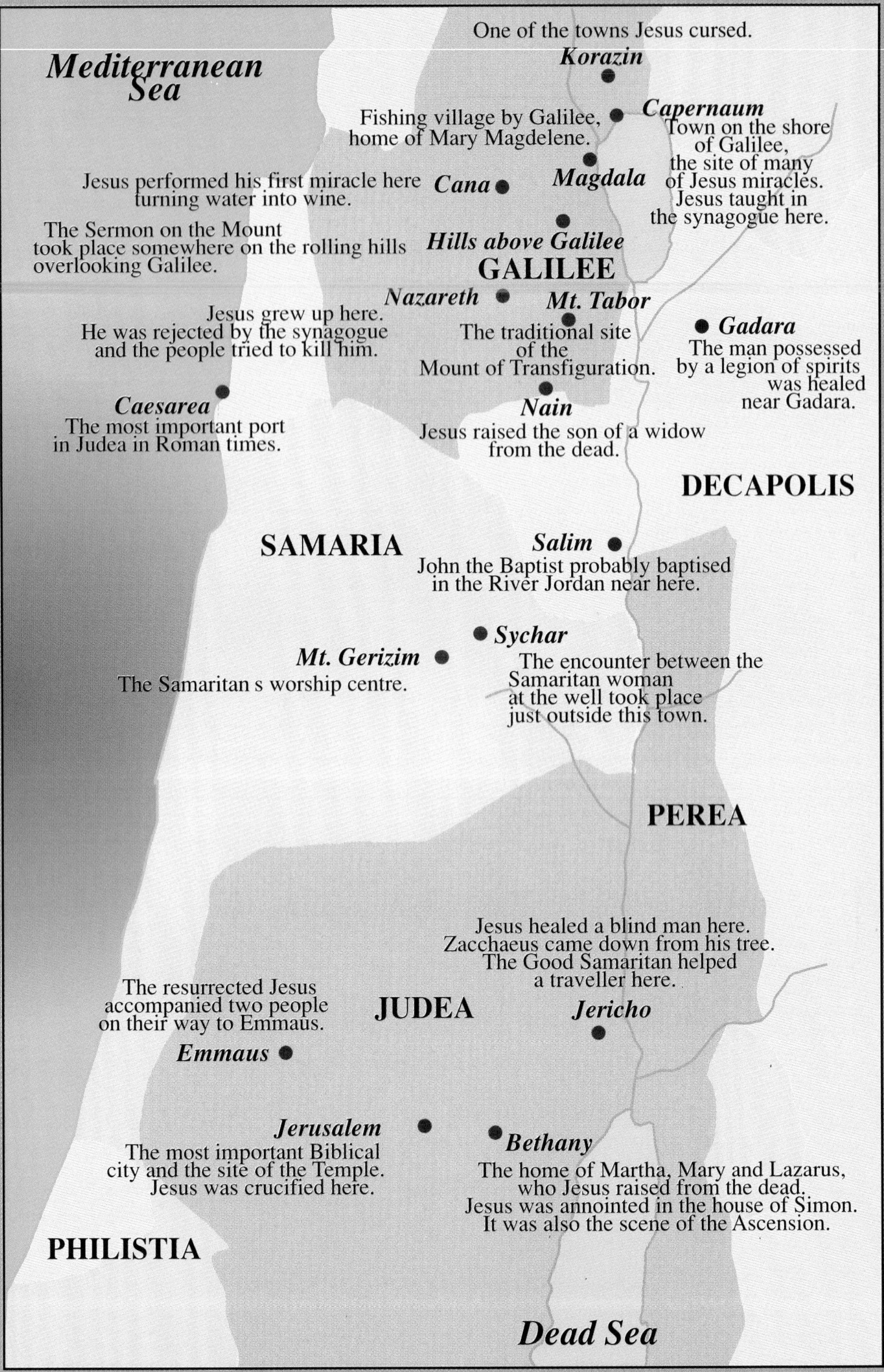

Mediterranean Sea

One of the towns Jesus cursed.
Korazin

Fishing village by Galilee, home of Mary Magdelene.
Magdala

Capernaum
Town on the shore of Galilee, the site of many of Jesus miracles. Jesus taught in the synagogue here.

Jesus performed his first miracle here turning water into wine.
Cana

The Sermon on the Mount took place somewhere on the rolling hills overlooking Galilee.
Hills above Galilee

GALILEE

Nazareth
Jesus grew up here. He was rejected by the synagogue and the people tried to kill him.

Mt. Tabor
The traditional site of the Mount of Transfiguration.

Gadara
The man possessed by a legion of spirits was healed near Gadara.

Caesarea
The most important port in Judea in Roman times.

Nain
Jesus raised the son of a widow from the dead.

DECAPOLIS

SAMARIA

Salim
John the Baptist probably baptised in the River Jordan near here.

Sychar
The encounter between the Samaritan woman at the well took place just outside this town.

Mt. Gerizim
The Samaritan s worship centre.

PEREA

Jesus healed a blind man here. Zacchaeus came down from his tree. The Good Samaritan helped a traveller here.
Jericho

JUDEA

The resurrected Jesus accompanied two people on their way to Emmaus.
Emmaus

Jerusalem
The most important Biblical city and the site of the Temple. Jesus was crucified here.

Bethany
The home of Martha, Mary and Lazarus, who Jesus raised from the dead. Jesus was annointed in the house of Simon. It was also the scene of the Ascension.

PHILISTIA

Dead Sea

Whistle-stop tour of Jesus' life

Mark's Gospel

- Outlines the life of Jesus
- Concentrates on the action
- Presents the facts to show who Jesus is

AT A GLANCE

MARK

1	Jesus' ministry begins
2	Healing the paralysed man; controversies begin
3	Healing the sick; calling the twelve; exorcising the tormented
4	Parables of the kingdom
5	Peace to troubled people and waters
6	Death of John; nature miracles
7	Controversy over what is clean and unclean
8	Food for thought; Peter's confession
9	Transfiguration and hard sayings
10	Teaching about divorce, wealth, greatness
11	Jesus enters Jerusalem
12	Parable of the tenants; marriage; taxes; commandments
13	Signs of the end
14	The last supper; Jesus' arrest and trial
15	Trial before Pilate; Jesus' death
16	The resurrection

Imagine you are a Gentile living in Rome in the middle of the first century. You have been stirred by the preaching of an artisan called Peter and an educated prisoner called Paul. You believe that the Jesus they speak of was indeed the living God in human form, and you have begun to experience his risen presence in your life.

Who was this Jesus? What did he do and say in Palestine? You need to know to increase your understanding of what to believe and how to live as a Christian. But there were no TV news crews to record his teaching. The number of people converted to Christianity is not large compared to the population of the Empire, and as Palestinians rarely travel to Rome there are few eyewitnesses to ask.

You need an official biography. Enter Mark, companion of both Peter and Paul. His Gospel provides a whistle-stop tour of the life and teaching of Jesus, racing from one remarkable event or challenging teaching to another.

It takes only about an hour to read, and was probably the early church's first primer on the life of Christ. It has no frills, no slants. The only assumption is that Jesus was, and is, the Son of God. Mark wants to show us why this is a reasonable assumption. If you just want the facts, Mark is for you.

Faith, not formula

Mark 1:35-39

Having enjoyed the attention of the crowds, Jesus ignores his spin doctors and opts for smaller venues where he is unknown. It takes courage to turn your back on success. But God may call us to do just that to avoid becoming stuck in a spiritual rut.

We cannot rely on winning formulae, but only on God himself. Sometimes the only way to maintain faith is to abandon the formula. Beyond every 'successful' mission are unreached people. God is not a mass producer but a hand-craftsman of disciples who calls his servants to work sensitively and not mechanically.

The large crowd listened to [Jesus] with delight.

Mark 12:37

Healing was partly in the mind

Mark 2:1-12

Human beings are remarkably complex and intricate. Emotions and feelings affect our health, and our health affects how we feel. The exact relationship between body and mind in any given disorder is often impossible to unravel.

Jesus approached the paralysed man as a whole person. He often healed people without referring to their spiritual or mental state, so it is likely that he saw a psychosomatic disorder behind this man's problem.

Indeed, the offer of forgiveness suggests that physical healing could only follow a release from the guilt which appears to have triggered his paralysis. The link between guilt and some physical symptoms is well known to most doctors, and makes prayer an important part of the healing process.

However, Mark is also making two theological points. Although he is not saying that all physical sickness is triggered by sin, he is showing that healing is not complete unless a person receives God's forgiveness as well. Jesus' concern is that people enter into eternal life; to receive an extension of health now is good, but not enough. This challenges our obsession with physical health.

Secondly, Mark underlines Jesus' authority as Son of God, which the onlookers were quick to appreciate (and question). The symbolism is self-evident. Jesus came to set people free from all that binds them.

What we are not told is whether the man offered to repair the hole his friends had made in the householder's roof. If he had left it to the insurance assessors, compensation would have taken about 1,900 years to be paid; 'insurance' did not occur in first-century vocabulary.

Jesus avoids fast lane

Mark 2:18-3:6

Jesus did not repeal the Old Testament law but he did question, re-interpret and even ignore some Jewish customs. Two of the most common tests of Jewish orthodoxy were fasting and Sabbath observance.

Orthodox Jews in the first century fasted once a week, although this was not commanded in the Law of Moses. Jesus also fasted, but for specific reasons. He went without food for six weeks in the desert (Luke 4:2); he spent nights in prayer denying himself sleep; and he encouraged his followers to fast privately (Matthew 6:16-18). He gave fasting a new perspective.

The real value of fasting is not to do it for its own sake – it won't collect bonus points on our spiritual account – nor to use it as a pious reason for dieting. Rather, its chief purpose is to enable us to take time out with God, to remind ourselves of our dependence on him, and to reinforce our belief that God and his purposes are the most important things in life.

Observing the Sabbath (Saturday) was one of the Ten Commandments (Exodus 20:8-11), but this was being observed in such a legalistic way that its true purpose was obscured.

The Sabbath was intended to be time out for people to focus on God; for the Israelites to recall God's character and deeds (Exodus 20:8-11; Deuteronomy 5:12-15). When God took his own Sabbath, he enjoyed what he had created (Genesis 1:31-2:3). The fact that he continued to sustain the universe is used by Jesus as a warning against too narrow an application (John 5:17).

So when Jesus said the Sabbath was made for our benefit (Mark 2:27), he denied the Pharisaic practice that filled it with petty restrictions over what did or did not constitute 'work'. Rather, he implied that it should be a time of re-creation – which the Christian Sunday, the day of resurrection, symbolically recognises.

The day off from money-making, focusing on God and enjoying his creation is important for all of us. It is how we were made to function. Sunday in the West is becoming like any other day, but that need not stop us from slowing down. If enough people did, the world would feel the difference.

HARD Question

Demoniacs or psychotics?

e.g. Mark 3:20-30; 5:1-20

Demons make frequent appearances in Mark's Gospel. The deranged man (ch 5) must have been terrifying. His uncontrollable violence, his super-human strength, his aggression and his wild ravings were not something most people would go out of their way to encounter – although Jesus did. The place was a largely Gentile district which most Jews would avoid even in the best of times.

Today, people like Legion would be kept under sedation until their symptoms could be controlled. They might or might not be given counselling. It is common to regard the Bible's claim that he was demon-possessed as a primitive or unknowing description of psychotic illness. Epilepsy also appears to be ascribed to demon-possession (9:14-29).

Modern cases of 'spiritual abuse' in which people have been subjected to prolonged 'exorcism' and emerge the worse for wear rather than healed has given the idea further bad press. However, the Bible writers – and Jesus – do know how to differentiate between physical, mental or emotional factors and spiritual ones. The paralysed man was not exorcised, but forgiven (2:1-11); another person suffering fits was cured but not exorcised (Luke 14:2).

Scripture is quite certain, however, that personalised evil forces (or spirits) exist:

- Satan is seen as an implacable enemy of God, although not his equal
- God created spiritual beings to inhabit the parallel, unseen world of heaven;
- Some created spirits 'fell' from perfection and now seek to undermine all that is good.

Christians working among some tribespeople have witnessed demonic activity which parallels that described in the New Testament. Shamans who call on the spirits and enter into trances frequently appear to be communing with dark powers which may harm people by spiritual means.

If Jesus was the Son of God and came to 'set the captives free', it is reasonable to suppose that there would be a backlash of evil forces in their death throes during his lifetime. This may explain why there was an apparent burst of violent demonic activity in the Gospels; the incidents become less frequent in Acts and are rarely mentioned in the epistles.

In the West, the tentacles of evil generally entangle people more subtly (see article in Ephesians). That does not make those tentacles any less evil or personal. Satan is regarded in the Bible as a master of disguise (2 Corinthians 11:14), and his purposes are well served by those who deny his existence and thus blind themselves to his activity.

Christians are to avoid two extremes in this matter. One is to look for demons under every bed as if all human ailments can be dealt with by a relatively simple act of prayer and exorcism. The Bible will not permit that view; evil is subtle, human nature is complex and neither is mechanical.

The other is to deny the possibility that satanic forces can cripple, or contribute to the crippling, of some people's hearts and minds. If we are whole people, then spiritual as well as psychological and physical factors should be considered in dealing with all our problems.

Date of events:
about AD 30–33

Location:
Palestine

Place in the Bible:
The second of the four Gospels in the New Testament

Content paralleled by:
Matthew, Luke, and to a lesser extent John

Story leads on to:
The early church in the Acts of the Apostles

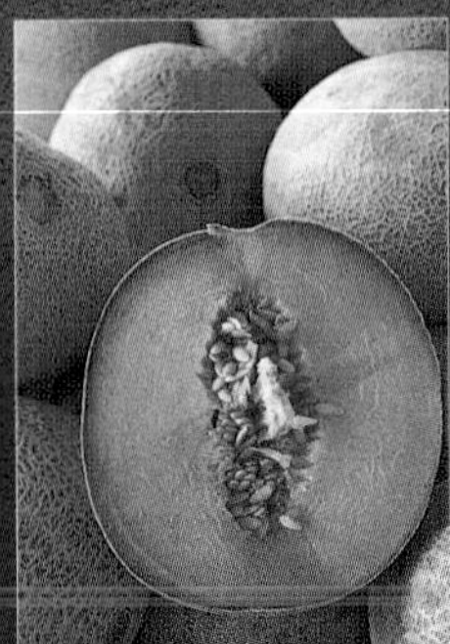

You can't force seeds to grow everywhere

Mark 4:1-34

There are no real-life equivalents of Jack's magic beanstalk, and only a few plants achieve rapid growth, sunflowers among them. Most seeds take a long time to germinate, sprout, flower and fruit.

Jesus' hearers knew that, and their agricultural world provided him with many illustrations of God's work in the world. Here, Mark brings together several related seed-stories.

Seed was broadcast (thrown out by hand) before being covered over, and inevitably some would fall into unproductive soils. That was not the fault of the sower. Stony ground could be covered by soil; the breeze could carry light seed onto the path; and at the time of sowing the dormant weeds would not be in evidence.

However good the seed, and however green the sower's fingers, it cannot grow in the wrong conditions. The farmer in the story has a bad year; three-quarters of his seed fails to grow to maturity.

Christian ministry and service similarly does not come with a guaranteed success rate like some patent marketing formula. The recipients of the 'word' (which surely includes the all-round witness and teaching of Christians, not just the shouting-out of religious formulae) will be varied 'soils' and their response will be unpredictable.

Christians, therefore, have to be prepared for failure. Their faithful sowing is assured of some fruitfulness in time, but they cannot assess their ministry on the basis of the observable results of church growth. That should be a warning to those who see in mega-churches an enviable success which they should mimic. We can indeed learn from how God works in one place, but fruitful ministries do not easily transfer to different 'soils'.

Two other parables develop the image of seed-sowing. The story of the seed growing 'secretly' shows that the farmer can do nothing to promote or hurry growth. Research suggests that people need to 'hear' the Christian message many times before they are ready to respond to it. As it is only God who can nurture the seed, prayer is a vital accompaniment to all Christian witness and evangelism.

But if that makes witness seem impossibly difficult, the parable of the mustard seed suggests that small beginnings can lead to unexpectedly far-reaching results. Few people will be able to chart the growth of the seeds they sow; the parables suggest that we should simply focus on sowing and leave the rest to God.

God trusts you when he seems to be asleep

Mark 4:35-41

Of the few 'nature miracles' that Jesus performed, this is probably the most awesome; it is certainly the most theologically and pastorally poignant. As with all his miracles, it was a teaching medium.

By calming the storm with a word, as God had created the world by a word of command, Jesus was demonstrating his deity, power and authority. He could not simply control nature as some pagan magician might attempt, but he could command it as only God could.

So he slept through the storm. Christians down the ages have joined the apostles in the boat to wring their hands in despair as God seems to sleep through the storms which batter their lives. On this occasion, there was a rather obvious reason. Jesus was not a boatman; the apostles were. They knew how to handle a boat in rough water; so he left them to get on with it without interfering.

God has given his people skills and expects them to use them and not to constantly ask him to bail them out. Human responsibility is itself a gift to be used responsibly. We do not need special guidance or special grace to do what our human nature, already consecrated to God, is capable of doing.

Indeed, the apostles' cry for help was actually rebuked. Afraid that they would all drown, they were blind to the fact that with Jesus in the boat they couldn't: his ministry was not yet over, and certainly would not end in a boating accident.

While following our fallible and often selfish whims may be risky without prayerful checks, using our God-given skills without question or hesitation is a sign of mature faith. When we sail into storms, we need only remember that Jesus is in the boat trusting us to sail on; he has not taken off in the liferaft.

He's only one of us!

Mark 6:1-6

Something perverse in human nature delights in cutting people down to our size. Politicians and pop idols are exposed for their less than perfect private lives as if everyone else were a paragon of virtue. We like to be on a level playing field with the rest of humanity; we reckon we're as good as anyone else (or they're as bad as us), however famous they may be.

That attitude greeted Jesus in Nazareth. His reputation had gone before him, but his home-town acquaintances knew better; he was just the carpenter's boy. He suffered the fate many Christians endure; the greatest opposition and ridicule, often in the early days of Christian witness, comes from people closest to them.

But in the ridicule and rejection, there is an irony. Jesus was ordinary. And perhaps Mark is taking the opportunity to remind his readers that Jesus was no angelic being who looked like a man, but he truly was a man who also was God. His full humanity is used elsewhere to encourage Christians; he understands our frailty from personal experience (cf. Hebrews 4:15).

FAST facts

Author: John Mark. He was a cousin of Paul's companion Barnabas (Colossians 4:10) and his mother Mary was a (probably wealthy) landowner who opened her home to the early Christians (Acts 12:12). It is possible that Mark was the young man of 14:51, acting as night-watchman in the family olive grove which was loaned regularly to Jesus as a retreat centre. Mark was accepted as the author from the early second century when Papias (c. AD 140) said that he had written down Peter's teaching and recollections.

Date of composition: It has generally been supposed that Mark was the first Gospel to be written, largely because most of it is quoted almost verbatim by Matthew and Luke. (A case can be made for the primacy of Matthew, however.) It was probably composed in the early 60s, perhaps shortly before Peter's death (AD 65) or just after it.

Place of writing: Because of Mark's known association with both Peter and Paul (cf. 2 Timothy 4:11) it is generally believed that it was written in Rome where both men were imprisoned.

Intended readership: Mark is a Gentile Gospel (even though Mark himself was a Jew); it explains many Jewish customs and terms for the benefit of readers who would not know them. So the readers were probably Christians who had been converted through the ministry of Peter and Paul on their travels outside Judea.

HARD Question

Was Jesus Mary's only son?

Mark 6:1-6 (cf. 3:31-35)
The description of Jesus as 'the son of Mary' is unusual, even if (as is usually supposed) her husband Joseph had died some time before. Usually, it was a derogatory term, the equivalent of calling someone a bastard.

That in itself may be a small piece of circumstantial evidence to suggest that in his own lifetime people knew that there was something 'odd' about Jesus' birth. Rumours of his illegitimacy were known to circulate (cf. John 8:41; 9:29). This may help to counter suggestions that the virgin birth was invented later by the church.

But what has proved difficult for Christians is to know how to regard his four named brothers and at least two unnamed sisters. There are three possibilities.

1. They were the younger children of Joseph and Mary. This is the natural meaning of the New Testament which regards Jesus as the 'first-born' (Luke 2:7) and says that Joseph did not have sexual relations with Mary until after Jesus' birth (Matthew 1:25).
2. They were the children of Joseph from a former marriage. This is the official view of the Eastern Orthodox Churches and is based largely on the assumption that Joseph was much older than Mary.
3. They were cousins of Jesus. This is the official Roman Catholic view, based on the assumption that Mary wife of Clopas in John 19:25 is also the sister of Jesus' mother (not additional to the sister in the list John gives) and that she was the same Mary of Mark 15:40 who was 'mother of James and Joses'.

Behind suggestions 2 and 3 is the desire to protect the belief that Mary remained a perpetual virgin after Jesus' birth, as was first suggested by Bishop Hilary of Poitiers in the fourth century. While that belief shows a respect to Mary which the New Testament demands (Luke 1:42,43) and which Protestants sadly neglect, it has no biblical or apostolic support.

Furthermore, a basic principle of biblical interpretation is that the plain meaning of any given passage is likely to be correct and the argument of 3 is both convoluted and textually questionable. It does no dishonour to Mary to suggest that the woman who was privileged to bear the Son of God went on to have further children. Indeed, it adds weight to the claim that Jesus was 'normal' in every sense: he grew up in a normal family with true brothers and sisters.

Godliness is more than an actor's mask

Mark 7:1-23
The discussion about Jewish cleansing rituals might have seemed strange to Mark's Gentile readers (hence the parenthetical explanation in vv 4,5) but it makes a point which all Christians need to know.

'Hypocrite' was a term used in Classical Greek to describe actors on stage. They 'became' someone else; their true persona hidden behind a mask and a charade; playing a part.

The risk of religious rituals, however well-intentioned, is that they become a mask which does not express the heart beneath. The cleansing rituals were reminders to Jews that God was pure and that they were to be pure in heart and mind also.

Yet it is precisely the thoughts and intentions of the heart which make a person sinful or 'unclean' in God's sight. Bad actions start with bad thoughts. And bad thoughts come from a heart which is not constantly cleansed by the pure stream of God's Spirit flowing through the believer.

John wasn't cowed by a woman's scorn

Mark 6:14-29

According to the eighteenth-century Irish dramatist William Congreve, hell has no fury 'like a woman scorn'd'. Herodias provides a tragic illustration, putting her into the category of a New Testament equivalent of the Old Testament Jezebel.

The intrigue and feuding within the wider Herodian family is legendary. Here, the Tetrarch of Galilee (Herod Antipas) had been given by the Romans nominal jurisdiction over part of his father Herod the Great's former kingdom. Antipas was not the worst of a bad lot, and among other things he built the city of Tiberias.

However, he divorced his first wife, the daughter of Nabatean king Aretas, in order to marry Herodias, who was already married to his brother Philip. Aretas was angry and declared war, beating Herod's forces soundly. John was angry because Antipas had broken God's law; marriage to a brother's wife was allowed only if he had died, childless.

And Herodias was angry because John was stirring up public opinion against her. Mark, who gives the fullest account of this incident, says she nursed a grudge (v 19).

Mark devotes considerable space to the event of John's death because John the Baptist is a significant figure in the Jesus story. He bridges the Old and New Testaments. A prophet like Elijah, he pointed directly to the Messiah. His ministry was crucial in preparing the way for Jesus.

Matthew records that when Jesus heard the news of John's execution, he went away for a while; he grieved. John was his cousin, after all; presumably they had played together as children. But more than a cousin, he was a colleague in ministry. And Jesus knew that he himself would one day suffer a similar fate.

Today, John rebukes God's people when they fail to speak out against social and public evil, fearing more the opinions and reactions of others than the righteous holiness and judgment of God.

Dog's dinner heals girl

Mark 7:24–37

Jesus is in foreign territory again (he was, more or less, in Mark 5). Mark wants to remind his Gentile readers that Jesus went beyond the borders of Judea.

And Gentiles, according to Jews, were dogs (v 27): despised, unclean, and way beyond God's concern. Jesus is not insulting the woman by implying that she (or Gentiles generally) were indeed dogs; he is using a term familiar to her and which provided her with the perfect cue for a graphic response of faith. She recognises:

- that God rules the whole world
- that he has revealed himself through the Jews
- and that his blessings are meant to spread out from the Jews to the entire human race.

Today, Christianity is not normally associated with nationalism in the way first-century Judaism was. But it can appear to people of other faiths to be identified with Western capitalism and decadence; a warning, perhaps, that the church's prophetic role as a critic of culture has not been fully implemented.

And it is still possible for Christians to be class conscious and parochial, either refusing to take their gospel into the subcultures of their own society and the very different cultures of other countries, or to do so only in their own cultural forms.

When Jesus healed in the Decapolis, east of Galilee, he used a symbol (saliva) which was alleged to have healing properties. He did not need to, but he was not afraid of ministering to people in their own imperfect cultural terms if it helped them to praise God. There is more than one way to celebrate and proclaim the unchanging gospel.

HARD Question

Why did Jesus tell people to shut up?

If you have a message to proclaim or a product to sell, you normally seek publicity for it. You tell the media, you advertise it, and above all you encourage others to talk about it.

Jesus was not short of publicity. Mark is full of examples of how people heard about his teaching and activity, and sought him out (e.g. 1:28,45; 5:19,20). Yet frequently he warned people to whom he had ministered not to tell others who he was or what he had done. German theologian William Wrede argued almost a century ago that these admonitions to keep the 'messianic secret' were invented by the early church in order to explain why Jesus didn't claim directly to be the Messiah. But Jesus' wish for secrecy is better understood in other ways because there are instances where he accepted the ascription of Messiahship, as in Peter's confession (9:29).

Indeed, there is a veil across all Jesus' teaching. The parables were not clear in their meaning to those who would not think seriously about them. Jesus wanted to draw out faith (that is, trust) from people. He did not wish to force them into a grudging, superficial, merely verbal acknowledgement of who he was.

Which is how God operates. He does not thrust himself on unwilling subjects but reveals himself to those who have hearts wishing to seek him and eyes open to see him. The Immortal comes to mortals covered by a veil of mystery; in Paul's terms, we see at best 'through a glass, darkly' (1 Corinthians 13:12 KJV; the correct word, 'mirror', does not tell modern readers that ancient mirrors were rather hazy!).

Jesus did not want to be known as a wonder worker. He did not say to people, 'Come to me and be healed,' but 'Come to me and find rest for your souls' (Matthew 11:28-30). He wanted people to follow him for who he was and what being with him meant to them, not just because of what he could do for them.

Today, some Christians point to signs and wonders' (however defined) as evidence that Jesus is worth following. He is; but not because of his signs and wonders. He is worth following for who he is: the Son of God, Lord, Saviour and Friend. And that can only be seen 'by faith'. Neither evidence nor testimony is enough to produce faith when the heart is not engaged.

Mould spreads

Mark 8:14-21

A mouldy piece of food contaminates other food around it. Yeast, of course, is a benign mould. Usually in the Bible it is used as a symbol of evil. (The parable of the Kingdom growing like a leavened lump in Matthew 13:33 is unusual.)

The teaching of the Pharisees was mouldy, according to Jesus, and could contaminate those who came into contact with it. At the heart of their teaching was pride: self-righteousness which paraded itself as a virtuous example. Close behind it was a distortion of revealed truth based on a blinkered theology.

All human beings are vulnerable to that 'yeast', whatever their specific religious beliefs. Christians are no more exempt than others. But in Christians it is a disastrous witness which sends all the wrong signals and causes people to reject Christian faith just as they did Pharisaic faith.

CROSS CHECK

Where Jesus keeps his secrets: Mark: 1:25,34,44; 3:12; 5:43; 7:36; 8:26,30; 9:9,30; 14:61

Partial solution isn't good enough

Mark 8:22-26

This incident, which is unique to Mark, is also unique among the kinds of healings which Jesus performed. On no other occasion did Jesus heal in two stages. Mark offers no explanation.

Perhaps the man's faith was inadequate. Perhaps he was in too much of a hurry. Or perhaps this was an exceptionally difficult case. Whatever the reason, it still leaves today's reader with plenty to think about.

When Jesus starts something, he does not quit halfway through. He is not satisfied with half measures and he does not give up when the going gets tough. His goal is the renewal of the entire creation. Therefore Christians cannot be content with half measures in their service and discipleship, and can be reassured that God will work thoroughly in all circumstances.

The story also reminds us that it is possible to have a real faith in Christ and yet not 'see' him and his truth clearly. No one can have perfect and infallible knowledge of God's truth or his ways, because he is always bigger than our minds. But people who:

- have an inadequate knowledge of Christian basics; or
- believe on the surface, but have not allowed faith to penetrate to the depths of their experience;

may embrace unorthodox ideas and lifestyles which can bring the gospel into disrepute. If they seek to lead or teach others, then they will be the half-blind leading the blind, and are likely to end up in a spiritual ditch (Luke 6:39).

Master picture for jigsaw puzzlers

Mark 8:27-9:37

The wonder and delicacy of the ecological balance is only slowly dawning on the human race. In Panama, for example, the habitat depends on a fig wasp which germinates fruit trees, which support animals, which spread seeds to propagate more trees. No wasp, no forest.

Just as we cannot often see these links clearly, so Peter, James and John can't yet see how all Jesus' teaching fits together (8:32 and 9:32). But the transfiguration provides them with the big picture into which they could fit Jesus' teaching about his forthcoming death.

It is like a resurrection appearance in advance. It is literally a taste of heaven that Peter understandably wants to prolong; just as anyone would wish to remain for ever in some idyllic holiday spot (9:5).

The brilliance of Jesus' appearance ('No laundry could do anything like it' is C.S. Lewis's way of correctly interpreting the whiteness of his clothes) speaks of his purity and perfection. His conversation reveals he is also superior to both Moses (the bringer of the law) and Elijah (the prototype prophet) both of whom were revered in Judaism.

So Peter's confession (8:29) was spot on, but the Christ has an unexpected role; he is to die and rise again. Therefore, instead of prattling or protesting, they should simply listen to Jesus (9:7). The advice, if taken by successive generations, might have saved the church from a few conflicts.

Brought down to earth with a bump by the failure of the other nine apostles to heal the disturbed boy, they are reminded by Jesus' simple assertion of the primacy of prayer in any ministry (9:29) that they must draw on heaven's power and glory in order to do God's will on earth.

The transfiguration suggests a whole new way of seeing things, in which fresh connections make greater sense. Faith is the ability to live with apparent incompatibilities, trusting that when heaven's windows are opened the light which streams out will reveal a delicate and wonderful balance of otherwise inexplicable events.

For today

- God is concerned with the whole person, and so should we be
- God's rules are meant to increase our enjoyment of his world
- You can't hurry people into faith, so don't try
- Don't keep looking for guidance to do for God what's obvious
- Be bold, be strong, in confronting unrighteousness
- God loves the people you don't
- God isn't satisfied with second best
- Were you there when they crucified my Lord?

Triple jump of faith in Messianic 'parables'

Mark 11

Three acted parables set the scene for the final showdown between Jesus and the religious leaders. In them he does what they want, but in a manner they don't want. He declares himself to be the Messiah – in the triple role of prophet, priest and king – but in a way that threatens the established order.

The triumphal entry was a declaration of kingship. David set Solomon on a donkey (1 Kings 1:33, 34); and Jehu's friends spread cloaks on the ground when he was suddenly anointed king (2 Kings 9:13). The Palestinian equivalent of a ticker-tape welcome was afforded to the Maccabean liberators of Jerusalem 200 years before Christ.

After the latter triumph, Judas Maccabeus 'cleansed' the temple of its pagan altar. Jesus cleansed 'his Father's house' from desecration by the profit of Mammon. He came as a priest to restore true worship.

And the fig tree? This unprecedented action is probably a 'parable' similar to that of the tenants in the next chapter. Israel was occasionally described as a fig by the prophets (Isaiah 28:4; Hosea 9:10). Having rejected Jesus as Messiah, it will be unable to enjoy or bear the fruits of God's purposes. In the declaration, Jesus speaks as a prophet, God's mouthpiece. He also takes the opportunity to teach the disciples about prayer. Aligned fully to the righteous principles and purposes of the conquering King, righteous Priest and inerrant Prophet, they can be assured of answers to prayers for the triumph of God's righteousness in the world.

HARD Question

The end is nigh?

Mark 13

Of all the subjects Jesus spoke on, his promised return has generated the most heat and the least light among some groups of his supporters. Covered by all three Synoptic Gospels this teaching becomes clearer if the most difficult verse (30) is taken as the key to unlock the rest.

He either meant that he expected to return before his contemporaries had died (and was therefore wrong, and also contradicting his own statement that he didn't know when he would return, v 32), or he is not talking in neat historical terms at all.

Many of his predictions were fulfilled in the fall of Jerusalem in AD 70, when the Romans sacked it and destroyed the temple. Not all were fulfilled, however, even if the poetic language of the sky falling in is seen as a graphic picture describing the agony anyone feels when their personal world 'collapses'. He did not return and the dead did not rise (26,27).

The problem disappears if the 'last days' or 'this generation' refers merely to 'the new age of the Spirit' or 'the generation of believers' as a totality. Jesus' death and resurrection, and subsequent sending of the Spirit, inaugurated a completely new era in God's purposes which will be completed at Christ's return. The hardships described here are apparent in almost every period of history.

So 'the end time' is a continuous present. We really don't know when he will come and speculation about whether certain signs are being fulfilled by certain historical events or trends is not only futile but disobedient. Watchfulness does not mean looking for spiritual bill boards; it means driving faithfully and obeying the highway code of holiness which we have already been given.

Murder, mystery and suspense

Mark 14,15

The cross of Christ has become such a familiar symbol, and its meaning of love, sacrifice, atonement, forgiveness and reconciliation so central to faith and worship, that the impact it had on the first disciples is often forgotten.

They did not understand what was happening, or why. And none of the Gospels tell us with any fullness; theological explanation is left to Paul in his letters. Instead, the narrative in each Gospel draws out the horror, tragedy, selfishness, injustice, failure and sheer pain of that bloody, squalid and disgraceful low-point of human history. Mark makes the reader sweat through it. With dramatic irony, he begins with a woman's beautiful act of generosity (14:1-19), and ends with Pilate's shameful submission to public opinion (15:15).

The confused, dumbfounded disciples do not know there will be a resurrection. We cannot blame them for misunderstanding Jesus' predictions. They had nothing to go on, and in their place we probably would have thought and acted no differently.

Crucifixion was one of the world's most horrific forms of slow, torturous execution in which the victim died of exhaustion; every breath was a monumental effort. The narrative intends us to stand at the foot of the cross with Mary and John, with tears in our eyes, and to notice the blood splattered by the executioner on our clothes. We were there when they crucified our Lord.

HARD Question

An unfinished gospel?

Mark 16

The Gospel ends abruptly at verse 8, and although verses 9-16 are attested by some important early manuscripts they are not included in some of the most important ones. It is certain, not least because of the clumsy link between 8 and 9 that they did not form part of the original text.

Why Mark's Gospel ended so abruptly is not clear. There are several possibilities.

- He may have wanted to create a strong, impactful ending.
- He may never have finished it.
- The real end may have just dropped off the end of the hand-written text.

Because it is not original to the text, the longer ending of Mark has to be read with caution. It is a digest of resurrection traditions, and no mainstream church has ever based any doctrine on it which cannot also be properly confirmed from other parts of Scripture.

There is a Christian sect in North America which practises a form of snake charming on the basis of v 18. As Jesus told us not to 'test' God by doing dangerous things, the interpretation of the verse by this group is not truly 'biblical'.

Blasphemy against the Spirit: p 307
Demons in the world: p 104
The purpose of parables: p 309
Jesus' return: p 400

Check out your values

Matthew's Gospel

- Shows how the Old Testament story links with the life and teaching of Jesus
- Focuses especially on Jesus' teaching about 'the kingdom of God'
- Shows that Jesus is the Messiah people were waiting for
- Collects Jesus' ethical teaching into the 'Sermon on the Mount'

The fabled Irish farmer, when asked directions to a distant town, replied that if he was going there, he wouldn't start from here. The same could be said to strangers to the Bible who want to find their way round the story of Jesus. The first book of the New Testament is more of a specialist exposition rather than a general introduction.

However, if you are already familiar with the outline of the Jesus story, then Matthew will enable you to discover its meaning. Matthew is primarily a teaching book rather than a history book, and apart from the beginning and end little of it is in strict date order.

The author wants to show us who Jesus is and why he came. It has been described as a bridge between the Testaments. Matthew wants us to see how Jesus fulfilled Old Testament prophecies and aspirations, and to explain how the kingdom of God relates to the old Jewish customs and way of life.

Matthew also offers some startling challenges. It is far from the caricature of 'Gentle Jesus, meek and mild'. It frequently refers to God's judgment, and the famous 'Sermon on the Mount' offers what one writer has called 'the transvaluation of values'. It stands human wisdom on its head and calls for radical reappraisal of our lives.

Turning the other cheek is not a soft option. So fasten your seat belts and prepare for a bumpy read!

MATTHEW

1 Genealogy and birth of Jesus
2 Persian astrologers visit Jesus
3 John the Baptist and Jesus' baptism
4 Jesus is tempted; begins his ministry
5 Sermon on the Mount: beatitudes and law
6 Sermon on the Mount: prayer and faith
7 Sermon on the Mount: being consistent
8 Many people healed
9 More healings; Matthew called to be a disciple
10 Twelve disciples sent out on a mission
11 John questions Jesus
12 Arguments with the Pharisees
13 Parables of sower, weeds and seeds
14 Feeding the 5,000; walking on water
15 Controversy about cleanliness; Canaanite healed
16 Peter's confession; a call to commitment
17 Jesus' transfiguration; a boy healed
18 Parables of lost sheep, unforgiving servant
19 Teaching about divorce, and wealth
20 Parable of vineyard workers; argument over 'the greatest'
21 Jesus enters Jerusalem, cleanses temple
22 Parable of wedding; arguments with Pharisees
23 'Woes' to the Pharisees
24 Signs of the new age
25 Parables of bridesmaids, talents, sheep and goats
26 Last supper; arrest and trial of Jesus
27 Judas' suicide; Jesus' death and burial
28 Jesus is raised and commissions the eleven

KEY QUOTE

'Do not think that I have come to abolish the Law or the Prophets; I have not come to abolish them but to fulfil them . . . For I tell you that unless your righteousness surpasses that of the Pharisees and the teachers of the law, you will certainly not enter the kingdom of heaven.'

Matthew 5:17,20

Jesus' genes took a long time to make

Matthew 1:1-17

Just when you thought you had left the tedious lists in the dusty corners of the Old Testament, the New Testament opens with – a tedious list of names! But as always, it has a purpose.

If you read classic Russian novels, you will discover the (confusing) habit of giving characters three names: Christian name (Nikolay), patronymic (Petrovitch) and surname (Kirsanov). So in Turgenev's *Fathers and children* this man is sometimes called Nikolay Petrovitch and occasionally just Kirsanov. The patronymic – father's name – links a person to an immediate ancestor, and the surname to a wider family. It locates someone in a known network of relationships.

Matthew is doing that here. He locates Jesus in what to the Jews was a network of important relationships. He traces his ancestors through the line of David to show us his regal status. Some are family names rather than patronymics, too, which explains some of the differences between this and Luke's genealogy.

The genealogy is divided into three sections of fourteen names. Obviously contrived, this is probably to 'show' that God's time for each stage in his purposes has been completed, and the stage is now set for the appearance of the Messiah.

It reminds us that God's purposes led to Jesus through many people. He was not a special creation parachuted to earth from heaven. It also reassures us that all have a place in God's long-term purposes too.

Joseph discovered faith the hard way

Matthew 1:18-25; 2:13-23

Joseph is one of the hidden characters of the New Testament. Apart from the birth narratives, he is mentioned only once again by name (Luke 4:22, and implied in Matthew 13:55 and Mark 6:3). By tradition he was much older than Mary and died during Jesus' childhood.

But he emerges from the narrative as a kind, unflappable sort of man. These few verses show him dealing with huge traumas in an exemplary manner.

Mary's unexpected and inexplicable pregnancy means only one thing to the artisan Joseph: she has been unfaithful. But instead of roaring into a rage, he demonstrates that his love for her is unchanged, and he decides to do what his culture required as quietly as possible.

Then, just as an angel stopped Abraham killing Isaac, a vision stopped Joseph in his tracks. And he simply obeyed, facing the scorn of neighbours and possibly a resulting loss of business. God had broadened his horizons, and Joseph was willing to change his behaviour as a result.

He was also willing to move to a strange place at a time when people were generally not very mobile. He left his immediate family in Galilee to go south, where he stayed for some time, and then obeying another dream moved to a foreign country as a refugee. Joseph was willing to strike out into the unknown in obedience to God, and out of care for his family. He is one of the unsung heroes of faith and a model for Christian obedience.

Where am I?

Date of events:
c.4 BC-AD 33

Location:
Palestine

Place in the Bible:
Matthew is the first of the three 'Synoptic Gospels' telling the story of Jesus. It was placed first possibly because early church writers believed it was the first to have been written, and perhaps also because it is the most Jewish (the first Christians were Jews)

Parallel books:
Mark and Luke, and to a lesser extent John

Story leads on to:
The story of the early church in Acts

Star turn doesn't endorse astrology

Matthew 2:1-12

Although Matthew was written for the Jews, it was not nationalistic. In this, the only reference in the new Testament to the Gentile magi, the author is telling us that Jesus' ministry is to be universal.

For once, however, Matthew does not quote the Old Testament to make his point, despite the fact that Isaiah's 'servant' figure is called to be 'a light to the Gentiles' (Isaiah 42:6) – something which old Simeon sees in Luke's account (Luke 2:32).

The visitors were probably astronomers or priests from Persia, rather than kings as tradition pictures them. In the ancient world, astronomy and astrology were closely linked. There could have been more or less than three; the figure is arrived at solely because of the three kinds of gifts they brought.

The gifts themselves may represent aspects of Jesus' ministry: gold, for a king; frankincense for a priest (representing the prayers of the people); and myrrh for his burial as crucified Saviour.

When in 1998 Pope John Paul II roundly condemned the Italian preoccupation with horoscopes and magic (there were said to be 100,000 clairvoyants in Italy and only 30,000 priests), his critics pointed to this and other biblical passages where astrology appears to be condoned.

Isaiah 44:12-15 scorns astrology and magic, because God's purposes cannot be predicted accurately, let alone influenced. The evil of such practices stems partly from the human desire to control events and to know the future instead of trusting God.

However, this incident reminds us that God starts where people are and speaks in their own language in order to lead them to Jesus. It does not encourage or condone astrology; it says God is bigger than it.

HARD Question

What did they see?

Several suggestions have been offered to explain the 'star of Bethlehem':

- A comet or super-nova (exploding star) is known to have been seen in China in 5 BC, although there are no extant Near Eastern records of it
- There was a bright conjunction of Saturn and Jupiter in 7 BC, an unusual event which only happens about every 140 years, although this would not have moved and is possibly too early
- There was a meteor shower which was not recorded (they are relatively common).

It is of passing interest that the comet appeared against the constellation of Aquila, the eagle, which was the symbol of the Roman Empire. This might have been interpreted as an omen that Roman rule was about to be challenged.

However, there is no conclusive evidence, and indeed there need not be any. The magi interpreted what they saw and others might not have attached the same significance to the event. The 'miracle' is then one of God's guidance through their imperfect knowledge and world-view rather than of a special event.

Matthew's concern is not that a special star heralded the birth of Christ, although it does have the additional symbolic message that the heavens declared God's truth (cf. Psalm 19:1-4). Rather, Matthew is more interested in the fact that Gentiles found Christ and worshipped him.

Matthew sees behind the prosaic

Matthew 2:13-23

Victorian writer Frederick Langridge penned the famous lines:

Two men look out through the same bars:
One sees the mud, and one the stars.

Matthew is one of those people who can see exciting parallels and vivid symbols where others see only cold facts. This passage illustrates it beautifully. However, his lifting of Old Testament quotes, often out of context, would gain him few marks in a modern seminary! It has also led some Christians wrongly to assume that God laid out a pattern for future events and therefore, by extension, he has a precise plan for us to follow also.

That violates biblical concepts of human freedom, and reduces us to actors reading God's script. It also treats all biblical prophecy as if it were pure prediction; some is specifically predictive (see Acts 11:28 for a New Testament example) but frequently it is much broader.

Old Testament prophecy was often fulfilled in more than one way. The reference to the virgin in 1:22 was fulfilled in Isaiah's own experience (7:10-8:4), and the reference to Rachel's children (2:18) comes from a poetic lament concerning the fall of Judah (Jeremiah 31:15). Matthew sees something which had meaning in the past illustrating the present also. He is saying, 'It's just like it was when . . .'

But there are other undeveloped parallels here, too. Moses and the Israelites also came up out of Egypt. Moses, too, survived a cruel king's attempted infanticide. Matthew is saying to those who have ears to hear, 'Jesus is a new Moses.' The parallels would have authenticated the story for a dubious Jewish audience.

As to whether Herod did order the massacre of the innocents (Bethlehem was small and the event would have gone unreported elsewhere) there was no media keeping an eye on the excesses of a cruel tyrant. But as Herod killed three of his own sons when he was afraid of losing his power, this incident is unsurprising.

FAST facts

Author: Matthew is generally identified with the tax collector called by Jesus in 9:9 (known as Levi in the other Gospels). The early church writer Papias said Matthew compiled (which could mean edited or wrote) Jesus' oracles, which could imply he worked on an earlier collection of sayings. As a tax collector Matthew would be fluent in Greek, and his second name Levi could imply a Levite family which would have made him especially familiar with Jewish Scripture and tradition.

Date of composition: Disputed. It is often thought to have been written around AD 80 because it appears to refer to the fall of Jerusalem in AD 70 and it appears to have a developed theology of the church. However, such arguments are not conclusive, and references to the temple can also suggest a date before AD 70.

Place of writing: Uncertain. Its Jewish nature suggests Palestine, but a number of scholars have suggested Antioch in Syria. This was a large city with a strong Jewish population and a thriving church (Paul made it his base). Syria is specifically and unusually referred to in 4:24.

Structure: Matthew is structured carefully, its teaching grouped thematically rather than chronologically. However, scholars do not agree on the exact section divisions. Some consider it to be based around five major sermons, perhaps in Jewish fashion to indicate the 'new' Pentateuch (Law of Moses, the first five books of the Bible).

Content: Only about one third of Matthew is 'new' material. Almost half is paralleled in Mark, and about a fifth is paralleled in Luke.

The secret of happiness

Matthew 5:1-12

It's what everyone wants, many search for, and few find. Happiness is an elusive quality which creeps up on you unawares yet resists every attempt to grasp. And the famous opening of the Sermon on the Mount offers perhaps the most enigmatic recipe for happiness which the world has known. It roots happiness precisely in those areas of life most usually classed as miserable.

The 'Beatitudes' are a commentary on Matthew's messianic declaration that Jesus is 'God with us' who 'will save his people from their sins' (1:21,23). They will find their ultimate fulfilment in the new kingdom of God, which contrasts with the 45 similar beatitudes scattered through the Old Testament (26 of them in the Psalms) which look for fulfilment in physical ways now.

They are not a set of commands which will lead to happiness, but a description of what a Christian is becoming. The word usually translated 'blessed' means 'how blessed by God' although is sometimes rendered 'how happy'. The focus is on God's support and approval, not on human feeling. 'The blessed' are those who are in tune with God's concerns.

Far more than pious sentiments the beatitudes have practical applications in everyday life. If we are to know God's blessing, Jesus is saying, then this is how we must begin to live and think. They are a summary of Christian attitudes, upon which the rest of the New Testament is based and upon which Christian action is built.

No good success

Matthew 5:3

You won't get a job unless you convince an employer that you can do it well. But 'poor in spirit' means acknowledging your own incompetence and relying utterly on God. It describes being at the bottom of the pile.

It is not the two-faced 'humility' of Charles Dickens' Uriah Heep, who in *David Copperfield* declared, 'I'm very 'umble at the present moment, but I've got a little power.' The poor in spirit have no power at all.

God's blessing is granted to those who rely on him and seek first his kingdom rather than their own advancement. That, in his sight, is true success.

Mourning with compassion

Matthew 5:4

Once upon a time piety was clothed in funereal suits and expressed by glum faces. Yet Jesus knew what it was to party and to laugh. It was the Pharisees who paraded piety in dress and manners.

The word 'mourn' means a passionate lament. It describes the groaning sorrow of the newly-bereaved, as when Jesus himself wept over the fate of an unrepentant Jerusalem (Luke 13:34,35; 19:41-44). But it is combined with the compassion which desires to address the problem (Matthew 9:35-38).

So the mourning which is blessed sees the world, and ourselves, through God's eyes. It is not a hopeless grieving over shortcomings, for forgiveness and spiritual power are available, but it is a vision of what the world, and ourselves, could be and alas are not. It is the opposite of complacency.

Animal instinct

Matthew 5:5

Meekness is not, in the Bible, cringing self-deprecation. Rather, the word Jesus uses is that for a trained animal that obeys its handler.

It is another word for holiness. Instead of sailing close to the legal wind, of pushing the barriers as far as we can, the meek set aside their whole life for God, obey his law and willingly stay within the boundaries he has set.

Consequently, they don't throw their weight around, and don't assert their superiority over others by word or deed. Meekness is the opposite of pride and selfishness; it is service, which puts God and others first.

Never satisfied

Matthew 5:6

People who constantly nibble at fast food and snacks lose their appetite for a full meal. Christians whose faith consist of token gestures lose their appetite for God in all his fullness.

Jesus is thinking of a spiritual equivalent of the intense craving of a starving person who has not eaten for days, or the searing thirst of someone stranded in a waterless desert. 'Righteousness' is God-likeness; it is rightness of action and attitude.

The spiritually hungry are not satisfied with second best, with corners cut and cracks papered over. They desire and work for God's honour with the same intensity as the woman in the parable desired justice (Luke 18:1-8) and the blind man called out to Jesus for help (Mark 10:48).

Practical pity

Matthew 5:7

God delights to show mercy (Micah 7:18) which means he doesn't hold our sins against us (Jeremiah 3:12). The merciful person is therefore the opposite of a cynic who bears grudges and believes the worst about others.

To show mercy is to feel pity for someone and then to relieve their need, whoever they are. The classic example is in Jesus' parable of the Good Samaritan (Luke 10:25-31). To do that, we have to lose the natural suspicion of, and aggression towards, others which we may feel, and instead see them as God does.

Pure simplicity

Matthew 5:8

This beatitude is often taken as an injunction against impure, that is lustful, thoughts, but the true meaning is far higher and harder. The pure in heart are those who are simply sincere; they do not do one (good) thing while thinking another (bad) thing.

They do not act from mixed motives. If something needs to be done, they will do it without regard for any personal benefits which may accrue to them or any personal inconvenience which may affect them. The focus is not on what we do but on why we do it. Being pure in heart is the inner application of the fact that through Christ the believer already has access to God. It's the opposite of hypocrisy.

No compromise

Matthew 5:9

Peace-making is often confused with keeping the peace by swallowing words, bowing to demands, or ignoring errors. What Jesus has in mind is more positive. It is the role of reconciler, building on the fact that Christians were once God's enemies (and each others') and are now reconciled to him and to each other (Ephesians 2:14-18; 2 Corinthians 5:18-20).

In every group of Christians, disputes arise over belief and behaviour. The peace-making role is to help both 'sides' move forward to a new understanding and fellowship, as happened in the Council of Jerusalem in Acts 15.

Trouble is inevitable

Matthew 5:10

Perhaps the truest thing that any of Job's 'comforters' said was that we are born to trouble as surely as sparks fly upwards (Job 5:7). Just in case there is any confusion over the term 'blessed' Jesus reminds his disciples that their fate will be as his (cf. John 15:20).

Being a Christian brings unique pressures in a non-Christian world. For some, it is imprisonment simply for worshipping in the Christian way. For many in the 'free' West it is verbal abuse, the pressure to compromise ethically in society, or perhaps dealing with the 'wolves in sheep's clothing' who enter the church (Matthew 7:17). Blessing only comes through buffeting.

Get out of the ghetto!

Matthew 5:13-16

The Beatitudes focus on inner attitudes which are to motivate action, and so Matthew's Gospel encourages Christians out of the ghetto and into the world. The gospel is a call to mission, not to the monastery. So after introspection, he launches into application with the image of 'salt'.

Salt stops the rot. It was used until recent times as a preservative. In science, the law of entropy says that all things tend to disintegrate. History says society tends to do that too. God's will, however, is that society should grow to become his kingdom. His people are to act as salt to prevent human society decaying into anarchy. They do that by their active presence, promoting righteousness at every level.

Salt flavours the meal. Herbs and salt were used to flavour the dishes of vegetables which along with bread comprised the staple diet of people in biblical times. Christian faith makes life 'taste' richer and more appetising because it brings hope in the face of extinction, purpose in the face of meaninglessness, and the gifts of God to enhance the limited abilities of people.

Salt fertilises the ground. This is probably the main application Jesus had in mind. Salt was spread thinly on agricultural land in the ancient world (and at times since, including Europe during the Second World War) as an effective fertiliser. The kingdom of God can only grow when Christians are spread across the whole of society. Many major advances in medicine, education and social reform were made by people who had a broadly Christian world-view.

Protect privacy

Matthew 6:1-6

In current thought, religion is a private matter. Personal beliefs are acceptable so long as they do not intrude into, and determine, public life. Jesus would have had no time for that argument. But he did tell religious people to keep quiet about their devotions.

The Pharisees sometimes arranged to be at the most crowded places when the hour for prayer came. They would stop and pray in public. Jesus is not condemning the prayer, but the showiness. People who parade their faith assertively are more likely to make others feel uncomfortable than they are to attract them to the compassionate God who loves people just as they are.

Nothing but the best is good enough

Matthew 5:17-48

'Love God and do what you will' was St Augustine's often-quoted and misapplied recipe for Christian living. The Beatles' song of the 1960s echoed it: 'All you need is love'.

This could seem to imply that God's law and personal discipline are no longer required subjects for church life. Jesus disagrees. Love is an expression of law-keeping, not an excuse for abandoning it. Love accepts limits and respects other people's freedom and rights. It is not the same as personal licence.

As a result, love is more rigorous, not less, in applying God's law according to the spirit in which it was first given. However, it may seem to be lawless because it will sometimes put the law of love above the secondary customs of people. The Pharisees had tried to 'fence' the law with many additional rules which tied people into a love-less religion.

Jesus is repeating what the Old Testament had constantly stressed: that God desires mercy before sacrifice (Hosea 6:6), social justice before religious observance (Amos 5:5-15) and that nothing but perfection is good enough for him (cf. the unblemished animals for sacrifice, Leviticus 5:15).

This love replaces murderous hatred springing from wounded pride by peace-making (vv 21-26), regards all people as precious and not as objects for personal use (vv 27-30) and is willing to discriminate positively in favour even of those who would otherwise be classed as 'enemies' (vv 38-48).

Father sets out family priorities

Matthew 6, 7

Jesus repeatedly described God as his 'Father'. It was, for a Jew, an unusual title because generally God was regarded as distant. For Jesus, God was the head of a large and loving family, approachable and caring. Here he shows that

- He is the author and sustainer of life (5:45; 6:26)
- He delights in his children and 'rewards' them when they please him (6:4, 6)
- He forgives those who ask him (6:12-15)
- He values people highly (6:26)
- He provides for his people's needs (6:33)
- He can be found by those who really seek him (7:7,8)
- He never inflicts them with bad things but loves to give them good things (7:9-12).

The purpose of Christian living, Matthew reminds us, is to trust God, to build on his righteousness and to adopt his priorities. When we focus on the real meaning and purpose of life and do not allow ourselves to be side-tracked into anxieties about crusts and coats, then we can discover its true riches.

Hence the promise of providing our needs should be read in its broader context. It does not offer Christians an oasis of plenty in a famine zone while others around them are dying.

Rather, Jesus is stressing that focusing on God and giving to others will not diminish our lives. Mutual sharing will ensure that his people always have enough (although not always all that they want). And the act of giving brings with it a measure of personal wholeness – it is one of the highest virtues of humanity – which far outweighs any loss of material goods.

Matthew adds the customary cautions. For Jesus, living faithfully is more important than achievements. We are warned that we cannot enter the kingdom just because we are busy in God's service (7:21-23). The disciple is to be broad-minded (how else could you love your enemy?) yet paradoxically the way of discipleship is very narrow (7:13,14) because it leaves everyday human concerns at the gate.

The power of the word we should obey

Matthew 8:1-9:7

The centurion's statement in 8:8, 'just say the word', has been incorporated into some Christian liturgies. It is a classic expression of absolute trust in Jesus which recognises his power to command all to conform to his will.

Matthew's readers would have known that God created and sustained the world through the word of command (Genesis 1:3; Hebrews 1:3). So here is an unspoken acknowledgement of Jesus' messianic status in a group of several incidents.

Jesus heals the leper by a command: 'Be clean!' (8:3); he stills the storm by speaking to it (8:26); and he expels the demons by a word, 'Go!' (8:32). Finally, Jesus' authority is asserted when he pronounces his forgiveness of the paralysed man's sins, something only God could do (9:2).

Human attitudes to authority are always ambivalent; we resent being told what to do but we also crave 'strong leadership'. Matthew shows that Jesus has true authority that is worthy of our obedience.

There's nothing wrong with tax collectors!

Matthew 9:9-13

The necessary and socially beneficial duty of collecting taxes for the common good gets an even more raw deal in the New Testament than it does today for two reasons.

First, tax collectors were normally local people who worked for the occupying Romans, and in popular eyes that made them traitors to the Jewish cause. The official line was that while rebellion was not encouraged (it could invite harsh reprisals), neither was active collaboration.

Secondly, tax collectors were not paid a salary. Instead they were given a target and any money they raised above it was theirs to keep. So in effect, they became extortioners – and often very rich.

Matthew left that behind him to follow Jesus, but rich lifestyle apart the other eleven left their occupations too. The significance in the narrative is not Matthew's 'reform' but the entrée to his circle of friends (vv 10,11) and the sermon text (vv 12,13) which his conversion gave to Jesus.

The people who Jesus welcomes include those who are rejected by others and all who are acutely aware of their own need. He can give little to people who are self-satisfied; as Augustine said, their hands are full and there is nowhere for him to put his love-gifts of forgiveness and new life.

You're on your own now

Matthew 9:35-10:42

The first time you venture on your own into a new activity which hitherto has always been supervised by someone else – such as driving a car or moving away from home to college – is always accompanied by both excitement and fear. It's exhilarating to do, but what if something goes wrong . . . ?

The twelve must have had similar feelings as Jesus sent them out to do his work without his physical presence. Like a good teacher or parent, he tried to prepare them for all eventualities. This passage seems to have been compiled by Matthew from a number of separate discourses by Jesus (the material is dotted all over Mark and Luke), but no doubt he would have repeated it often anyway.

As Christians set out on their mission, with the added advantage that they are accompanied by the risen Jesus in the power of his Spirit, the points Jesus makes offer inspiration, encouragement and warning:

- The proper motive for mission is compassion, not compulsion (9:36)
- There will be a response to the gospel message when it is proclaimed (9:37)
- More people are always needed actively to share in mission (9:37)
- It can only be engaged in with God's blessing and commission (9:38)
- Mission includes proclamation and practical compassion (10:1,7)
- The place to begin is where you understand the culture and know the people (10:6; Matthew elsewhere is very concerned for the Gentiles; this is not an anti-Gentile tract)
- Depend on God to provide the resources you need (10:8b-010)
- You are not responsible if people reject the message you have explained (10:14)
- Don't leave your commonsense behind (10:16)
- Expect setbacks and opposition, even from people close to you (10:17-36)
- God will enable you to deal with problems when they occur, not before (10:19,20)
- Justice will be seen to be done, and truth will be revealed, when Jesus returns (10:26,27)
- Whatever happens, God hasn't forgotten or forsaken you (10:31,32)
- There's a proper reward in heaven for everyone who shares in God's mission (10:40-42).

True to form, Matthew majors on the problems and spells out the warnings in some detail. God does not call his servants to a picnic; but like a caring Father he's there to see them through the panic.

HARD Question

What is the unforgivable sin?

Matthew 12:22-45

When he was dying on the cross, Jesus forgave his captors and a condemned criminal (Luke 23:34,42,43). Once, he let an adulterer go with merely a charge 'to sin no more' (John 8:11). He understood human weakness and was compassionate towards it.

Yet here he speaks of an unforgivable sin. The statement is made in the context of a dispute about the power with which he exorcised demons and healed people. The Pharisees claimed that Jesus was using the devil's own power (v 24).

He points out the illogicality of that view (Satan would be cutting off his nose to spite his face, vv 25-29) before assuring his hearers that all sins can be forgiven, including blasphemy such as cursing Jesus, except 'blasphemy against the Holy Spirit' (vv 31,32).

Which is what the Pharisees were doing: fully aware that God was doing good things among them (healing the sick), they ascribed that work to the devil. Such a vicious claim could only come from hearts so hardened and wilfully closed that they wanted to destroy God's work.

People who have worshipped the devil (in tribal cultures and in Western occultism) have been converted to Christ and experienced his renewing power. Their past is not held against them; they did not commit the unpardonable sin. Anyone who wants to be forgiven anything can be; the person Jesus is describing would never dream of asking.

Parables in Matthew

Sower (13:1-23): Faithful sowing of kingdom values will lead to a harvest of some kind
Weeds (13:24-30, 36-43): The kingdom grows alongside the negative influences of the world
Mustard, yeast (13:31-33): The kingdom starts small but grows larger and has a big impact
Treasure (13:44,45): The kingdom is priceless and is worth all we've got
***The net (13:47-50)**: God will separate out the different elements at the last judgment
Lost sheep (18:12-14): God searches for those who have lost their way
***Unmerciful servant (18:23-35)**: Offer forgiveness to others as God has offered it to you
***Workers' wages (20:1-16)**: All who respond to God are included in his kingdom on equal terms
***Two sons (21:28-32)**: What you do with God's law is more important than what you say about it
Tenants (21:33-44): The kingdom will be given to new tenants, not the old ones (the Israelites)
Wedding (22:1-14): Israelites who reject the invitation to the kingdom will be replaced by others
***Ten bridesmaids (25:1-13):** Keep yourself ready for the coming king
Talents (25:14-30): Faithfully use the resources which God has given you
***Sheep and goats (25:31-46):** Kingdom people are those who have been faithful in small ways to God.
**Unique to Matthew*

A gentle touch

Matthew 11:25-30

This passage echoes the kind of sentiments more usually expressed in John's Gospel. Its inclusion here reminds us that the differences of the Gospels are complementary rather than contradictory. It was not only John who noted Jesus' more compassionate and 'devotional' sayings.

True to Matthew's rugged realism, however, it does not offer a stress-free Christian life. It simply substitutes one burden for another. The Jews of the time spoke of their duty to carry the 'yoke' of the Mosaic law, but it had become impossible because of the extra requirements they had piled on to it.

A yoke was a bar across the shoulders which would link two working oxen together. It might also be the kind which supported sacks or pails on human shoulders, making them easier to carry. So the intention is that God's 'yoke' aids believers in their life-tasks.

The weary, then, are people who have found the requirements of legalistic religion impossible. Jesus' yoke is easier because it does not consist of many rules, but of simply keeping in step with a loving God. It is not his intention to make life hard for us; it is hard enough already. He desires rather to give us a helping hand, which is the practical comfort to which Christians in all generations can testify.

Thy kingdom has come – in part

Jesus spoke a great deal about 'the kingdom of God'. (Matthew prefers the title 'kingdom of heaven' but his is a reflection of his Jewish readership and interest and means the same thing.)

It is not a geographical territory or human race. Some Christians since the time of Augustine (fifth century AD) have equated the kingdom with the visible, organised church, but most commentators recognise that the meaning is much wider. Even the idea of an international community or fellowship (the 'invisible' church of all believers) explains it less than adequately.

Primarily it is a term which describes God's kingly rule within the entire human sphere. The kingdom 'exists' wherever and whenever God's rule is applied. Hence Christians who are not allowing God to rule in every area of their activity (including work and community sectors) may be operating 'outside' the kingdom, and non-Christians may be operating 'inside' it as they seek, for example, to extend God's rule in terms of natural and social justice.

Therefore it is important to

distinguish the teaching about building the kingdom from the evangelical commission to promote spiritual salvation. The former includes, but is more than, the latter. The ways Jesus speaks of the kingdom helps to unpack this:

- The kingdom is here already. It is especially seen in the physical presence of Jesus (4:17)
- It is not yet in its complete state. That will be achieved when Jesus returns (25:34)
- Meanwhile, we are to help build the kingdom by the way we live in the community (25:40).

In the parables, the kingdom grows secretly; it is an underground movement slowly creeping over the face of the earth (13:32). It is not always easily distinguishable from the surrounding culture and it is mixed up in the corruption and evils of the social milieu (13:24-30; this is one reason why attempts by sects to create 'kingdom communities' separate from the world get no biblical backing).

The concept of the kingdom reminds us that God is concerned for all his creation. The Christian mission is not simply one of spreading personal salvation. The Christian message is not simply about 'me and my God'. In the epistles, Paul writes of Christ's purpose being to reconcile all things to himself – not just individual people, but human systems and the physical creation too.

It is important to God's purposes that all people on earth live within his kingdom rule, respecting righteousness and justice, whether they acknowledge him as king or not. Of course, as Christians seek to extend his rule they will also want to testify to the king's existence and call people to acknowledge his personal rule in their lives as well as in society.

HARD Question

Blind to the Truth?

Matthew 13:10-17, 34-35

'What is the use of a book,' thought the heroine of Alice in Wonderland, 'without pictures or conversations?' Jesus was a master of telling stories which included conversations and evoked pictures. But it was not enough. Some could never get the point.

Ordinary people delighted in them, but the theological experts got nothing out of them, drawing Jesus' sad quotation from Isaiah 6 that they were blind as proverbial bats. However, the quote almost implies that the parables were meant to make them blind, which modern readers find puzzling.

The parables were used to convey profound truths in picture language. Normally they were intended to make only a single point. They are not allegories in which every detail 'means' something. So in interpreting them, we should not press the detail too much.

They were more like paintings than photographs. The experts found them frustrating because the deliberate vagueness left them arguing over the meaning (which was Jesus' intention) and not grappling with concepts in the way they were used to.

The quote from Isaiah 6 is therefore not a prescription – 'I'll make sure you never understand' – but a description of people whose minds are closed to new ideas. They don't want to discover anything about God which doesn't conform to their preconceived formulae; they are incapable of seeing it even if it stares them in the face.

The most dangerous state of mind is a closed mind. Diseased minds can be healed; confused minds clarified; minds in error corrected; uninformed minds educated; narrow minds broadened. God, who is bigger than our minds, would like to enlarge those which are open. But even he cannot penetrate a closed mind. And Christians can be as closed as their critics.

For today

- Trust God even when you don't understand the reasons for his commands
- Worship Jesus as the fulfilment of all that God planned long ago
- Be prepared to have your lifestyle turned on its head
- Look for ways of extending God's kingdom (his rule) in every sector of your daily life
- Don't expect the Christian life to be easy but do expect God's powerful help
- Look for principles in stories and hard sayings; don't press the details
- Take part in proclaiming the gospel and making disciples

HARD Question

Rock solid key holder

Matthew 16:18-20; 18:18

The description of Peter as 'the rock' is grammatically ambiguous and is one issue which lies behind the divisions between Catholic and Protestant churches. It could refer to Peter personally (whose name also means 'rock' or 'stone') or it could refer to his confession with the stress 'but on *this* rock'.

Even if it is more natural to apply it to Peter personally, he was a representative and spokesman of the twelve. Therefore the 'keys of the kingdom' are more likely to apply to the apostles as a whole and to their ministry in the future. Their teaching would form the bedrock of the church and their pronouncements would carry the authority of Jesus himself.

These verses are then part of the 'commissioning' process which goes on throughout Matthew (see especially ch 10, and 28:18-20).

The mandate for absolution (18:18) is in the context of future church life. On the delegated authority of Jesus and on the basis of their bedrock teaching, the apostles can declare that the penitent are forgiven. There is a certainty in the gospel which does not need the physical presence of Jesus to authenticate it.

The tradition of giving accredited ministers the authority to pronounce absolution is an attempt by some branches of the church to establish a spiritual discipline in the area of personal sin and penitence which, because of human fallenness, is wide open to self-deception.

Loaded question about tax returns

Matthew 17:24-27; 22:15-21

The question about the annual half-shekel tax for temple upkeep was less innocent than it sounds. It was a test to see which side he was on.

Not everybody paid the tax. The Sadducees turned their rich noses up at it. And the Essenes in Qumran insisted on making only a once-in-a-lifetime payment to satisfy the strict demands of the Old Testament law.

Jewish opinion about paying taxes to the Roman occupiers ('Caesar') was also divided. Refusniks were secretly admired but also branded as anti-Roman and therefore liable to summary execution. Those who paid up without protest were collaborators equally to be despised. Either way, they had Jesus in a 'no win' situation. Or so they thought.

On each occasion his answer focused on broad principles. There is no obligation to pay religious dues, he says (contra some sects today), but it can be expedient to do so. What's the point of putting people's backs up or being different for its own sake? Perhaps the discovery of the coin in the fish is also meant to illustrate that God provides for his own needs!

In God's purposes for the world, the ruling authorities have the right to receive taxes because they coin the money and make commerce and social intercourse possible. The image of God, the unique humanness with which we are endowed, belongs to God, however, not to the state. Good citizenship is important; honouring God even more so.

What's in it for me?

Matthew 18-20

There may be no such thing as a free lunch but in modern marketing there is always added value; buy two, get one free. So when Jesus points out the draconian cost of discipleship, it's natural to ask what return we can expect for 'taking up the cross' (16:24). Some of the apostles clearly looked for preferential treatment (20:20,21). Jesus suggests that we get nothing out until we put something in.

Compassion (18:1:11; 19:13-15)
Roman fathers could consign new-born babies to the rubbish tip. Jews were more conscientious but children in the ancient world had a hard time. Jesus taught that they were little people worthy of respect and serious attention.

Forgiveness (18:15-35)
If God forgives us completely, then we should forgive each other with no strings attached. We are not to prolong people's sense of guilt and failure.

Faithfulness (19:1-12)
Easy divorce is nothing new; the Pharisees found many ways to extend Moses' permission. God's desire, Jesus says, is faithfulness for better or for worse. Serial monogamy (divorcing one for another) is adultery made legally respectable.

Generosity (19:16-30)
Possessiveness is an arm of selfishness, the opposite of God's will and the root of all sin. The real test of commitment is whether we regard all wealth as 'mine' or 'God's'.

Acceptance (20:1-28)
There is to be no jealousy and no rivalry in God's kingdom, no status seeking. God has no favourites except those who serve others without looking for kickbacks.

So what is the reward? This lifestyle is assured of God's approval (20:26), and compensated by the mutual fellowship and sharing of the like-minded Christian community (19:29). Giving and caring prompts giving and caring; wait for someone else to start and you'll wait for ever. Which could be why the kingdom is so long in coming in all its fullness.

HARD Question

Did Matthew suffer from double vision?

In comparing the accounts of incidents in different Gospels you will see that Matthew sometimes doubles the number of participants: two demoniacs in Gadara (8:28); two blind men outside Jericho (20:30); two donkeys for Jesus to ride on (21:2,7). There are also two other blind men (9:27) not mentioned elsewhere, and two witnesses at Jesus' trial (26:60) where the other Gospels are unspecific.

The donkey could well have had a colt with it. The other writers may have focused on one healing and Matthew wants to tell us there were others at the same time. Or he may have used a different set of notes.

His reference to two witnesses is interesting. Jewish law required two for someone to be convicted. So perhaps, as the healings include statements about Jesus' divine character, Matthew is using a Jewish device to indicate to his readers that the testimonies are reliable: Jesus is Messiah.

Whatever the reason, the veracity of the Gospel record is not at stake. The differences here, as elsewhere, are the sort which two journalists would offer in their accounts of the same event. The Gospel writers are constantly editorialising; they are not offering an objective diary of events.

It gets worse!

Matthew 23

If you thought that the Beatitudes at the start of Jesus' ministry were searching enough, just ponder these 'woes'. In Matthew this is Jesus' last recorded discourse to the crowds. As the Gospel has gone on, the teaching has got tougher. It ends with a powerful warning to people who think they have God taped.

Jesus directs his ire at the Pharisaic system, rather than at individual Pharisees. It intended to do good but ended up doing harm. It twisted God's priorities completely out of any shape. The term 'hypocrite' in this context does not mean 'insincere' but 'inconsistent with God's intentions'. It is possible to be sincerely wrong.

The Pharisees have got the life of faith out of perspective. They see it rather like a two-dimensional Egyptian wall painting. There's no distinction between sizes of objects, so trivia are magnified to mega status.

They have been zealous evangelists, but they've brainwashed rather than liberated their converts spiritually. They are casuists, playing with words to get the best deal for people who want to break their promises. They are fastidious about tithing a pot of garden herbs, but walk by on the other side when they see the poor and the downtrodden crying for help.

Above all, they are concerned about outward appearances. A modern equivalent analogy to the whitewashed tomb would be a gleaming, polished car with a dead engine.

Our smile at their folly may be wiped off our faces when we look in the mirror. The Pharisaic trait is not far from each one of us. We too care more about others' opinions than God's requirements. We too put a spin on theology to get round the hard bits. And we also get our perspectives wrong; read church history and look around modern churches for some alarming examples.

Tragic end for mixed-up kid

Matthew 26:14-16, 23-25, 47-50; 27:1-10

Why does anyone betray or let down their country, family, employer, partner or friend? Usually, their motives are complex, a combination of small things. We will never know why Judas Iscariot felt and acted the way he did. But we can trace possible contributory factors to his confused state of mind:

- He was an outsider, probably the only southerner among the Galilean apostles
- He tended to be crafty and deceitful (he misused the group's funds)
- He may have become disillusioned with Jesus' spiritual mission
- Or, frustrated with waiting, he may have wanted to force Jesus to declare himself Messiah
- He may have thought Jesus was safer in official hands than at the mercy of the mob
- He may have been blinded by his own confusion and acted impulsively
- He was off his guard and susceptible to evil influence.

What is clear is that afterwards, like Peter, he bitterly regretted what he had done. Only Matthew records his return of the money and says specifically that he hung himself, making Judas another of his warnings. The betrayer could have been anyone. No one is immune from temptation. The account is out of chronological order next to Peter's denial. He is contrasting two different responses to similar sins. Peter sought forgiveness, and lived to serve Jesus. Judas didn't even try.

Going out with a bang

Matthew 27, 28

Only Matthew records the earthquakes at the crucifixion and resurrection, and the bizarre account of resurrected saints walking in Jerusalem (27:51-53; 28:2). Before dismissing these as figments of imagination, it is worth noting that the temple mount is on a geological fault which is subject to earth tremors.

In the Bible, earthquakes are seen literally as 'acts of God' and Matthew places these events in the same category as the giving of God's law on Mt Sinai. Further, the Jews expected the dead to be raised at the start of the new age, and Jesus' death and resurrection was seen by the early church as inaugurating just that.

Matthew is also the only Gospel to mention the guards and subsequent bribe. It adds a significant detail to show that simple but erroneous explanations can satisfy public opinion which is not inclined to believe in miracles and prefers not to have its preconceptions challenged by inexplicable events.

The Old Testament in Matthew

(Matthew references in brackets)
Genesis 1:27 (19:4)
Genesis 2:24 (19:5)
Exodus 3:6 (22:32)
Exodus 20:12 (15:4)
Exodus 20:12-16 (19:18,19)
Exodus 20:13 (5:21)
Exodus 20:14 (5:27)
Exodus 21:17 (15:4)
Exodus 21:24 (5:38)
Leviticus 19:18 (5:43; 19:19; 22:39)
Deuteronomy 6:5 (22:37)
Deuteronomy 6:13 (4:10)
Deuteronomy 6:16 (4:7)
Deuteronomy 8:3 (4:4)
Deuteronomy 19:15 (18:16)
Deuteronomy 24:1 (5:31)
Psalm 8:2 (21:16)
Psalm 22:1 (27:46)
Psalm 78:2 (13:35)
Psalm 91:11,12 (4:6)
Psalm 110:1 (22:44)
Psalm 118:22,23 (21:42)
Psalm 118:26 (21:9; 23:39)
Isaiah 6:9,10 (13:14,15)
Isaiah 7:14 (1:23)
Isaiah 9:1,2 (4:16)
Isaiah 13:10 (24:29)
Isaiah 29:13 (15:8,9)
Isaiah 34:4 (24:29)
Isaiah 40:3 (3:3)
Isaiah 42:1-4 (12:18-21)
Isaiah 53:4 (8:17)
Isaiah 56:7 (21:13)
Jeremiah 7:11 (21:13)
Jeremiah 19:1-13 (27:10)
Jeremiah 31:15 (2:18)
Daniel 9:27 (24:15)
Hosea 6:6 (9:13; 12:7)
Hosea 11:1 (2:15)
Micah 5:2 (2:6)
Micah 7:6 (10:35,36)
Zechariah 9:9 (21:5)
Zechariah 13:7 (26:31)
Malachi 3:1 (11:10)

AMONG JESUS' CRITICS WERE:

Sadducees: An upper-class group who looked down on the people. They controlled the Sanhedrin (the supreme Jewish court) during Jesus' lifetime. Most of them were priests (but not all priests were Sadducees). They were theologically woolly; they accepted only the Pentateuch (Genesis–Deuteronomy) and denied the resurrection.

Scribes: Not a party, more a profession earning its keep from writing documents for the illiterate. They also copied out the Scriptures, and studied the law intensely. They assisted in organising synagogue worship and children's education, and were closely associated with the Pharisees.

Pharisees: A group of about 6,000 people in Jesus' time, having originated during the Maccabean period (200-100 BC) as devotees of strict Jewish religious observance. They were very nationalist and anti-Roman, austere and lower middle class.

Priests: They traced their descent from Aaron, Moses' brother and first high priest, and officiated at the temple ceremonies and sacrifices. High priests tended to run in families.

Voice of the silent minority heard at last

Politicians listen to 'public opinion' but often the concerns of ordinary people are not aired strongly enough to challenge those of the powerful lobbyists and vested interests. In our own day the doubts of many about the long-term effects of genetically modified crops, and the detrimental effects of pornography, are shouted down by commercial interests who have made consumer choice the first commandment.

Now and again a voice of the people rises above the babble and articulates in media-friendly terms what many have instinctively felt. Micah was such a person. The condemnation thrown at him (2:6) is in the plural, indicating that his was not a lone voice.

That was probably normal in Old Testament times, although we tend to assume from the narrative that the prophets were, like John the Baptist, individuals 'crying in the wilderness'. In 1 Kings 18:3-15 a whole band of prophets loyal to Yahweh were sheltered by a sympathiser from the evil intents of King Ahab, but it is only Elijah's voice that we hear centuries later.

And in 4:1-3 Micah repeats an oracle which is also in Isaiah, and he has other similarities to both Isaiah and Amos. Perhaps he (or Isaiah) plagiarised; copyright law was not in place in the eighth century BC. It is more likely, however, that here are certain themes, certain turns of phrase, which were current slogans among the resistance, the concerned minority.

God's word is worth repeating, and Micah's similarities with others suggest that there was a vigorous minority reform movement. There were many ordinary people of good will (not least the victims of greed) who were glad that the prophets spoke as they did.

Micah provides us today with an example of someone who was unafraid to speak out against abuses he saw. We should too. Our words may never be quoted in the White House or 10 Downing Street, but if they are true to God's concerns then they will never be lost in the air (cf. Isaiah 55:10,11), and may encourage others to turn up the volume of public opinion.

The Book of Micah

- Highlights social abuses in Israel and Judah
- Forecasts God's judgment on the people's sins
- Promises God's restoration in the future
- Says that the Messiah will come from Bethlehem

MICAH

1 The destruction of Samaria and Jerusalem foretold
2 Evil plans and false prophets
3 God will not speak to the leaders and will punish social evil
4 Judah's exile and restoration foretold
5 The coming Messiah and the siege of Jerusalem foretold
6 God is against Israel because of its social sins
7 Godly people have been swept away but God will forgive

What does the Lord require of you? To act justly and to love mercy and to walk humbly with your God.

Micah 6:8

Never mind the eloquence, feel the effect of the words

Micah 2,3

Some people are just plain embarrassing – especially children. They say the wrong things at the wrong times. They set the cat among the pigeons, rock the boat, raise needless questions or fears. And they do it most when you are trying to keep the peace.

The professional prophets of the eighth century were official religious advisers attached to the temple and some were consulted by kings. They were career diplomats; they knew which side their bread was buttered (3:5). They most certainly did not rock the boat. They said what people wanted to hear at a difficult and sensitive time.

But Micah and others did rock the boat. And he was criticised (as was Amos) for refusing to toe the party line (2:6,7; cf. Amos 7:12,13). He responded by predicting that the regular prophets would lose their cutting edge (if they had not done so already) and the light of their insight would be darkened; they would become incapable of discerning the word of the Lord (3:6,7).

The proof that the professionals were wrong and amateurs like Micah right was found in the fruit of their ministry. It had fuelled rather than foiled social injustice (2:7-11). Their beliefs were held sincerely, no doubt, and were proclaimed powerfully and accepted as plausible. There was no point in arguing, but the sad effects of their work were now clearly visible.

That is why we need to judge policies and statements not only by biblical teachings but also by their practical effects. In our own day, some church leaders have questioned the unbridled market economy by pointing to its harsh effects on the poor and disadvantaged. Their criticism has been dismissed as theologically inept and economically ignorant, but the bitter fruits have not been sweetened nor the poor rescued.

Jesus reminds us that we will be able to tell whether people and policies are from God 'by their fruit' (Matthew 7:16). There is a time to rock the boat, to expose the empty or self-interested rhetoric by unwrapping its fruits. And therefore there is also a responsibility to ensure that we are neither fruitless altogether nor the producers of bitter fruit (cf. Isaiah 5:3).

Place in Bible:
The sixth of the minor prophets at the end of the Old Testament, after Obadiah and Jonah and before Nahum and Habakkuk

Parallel books:
Several passages are similar to Isaiah (e.g. Micah 1:10-16/Isaiah 10:28-30; 4:1-5/2:2-4; 5:2,3/7:14; 5:10-15/2:6-8)

FAST facts

Author: Micah was a countryman who came from Moresheth in south-west Judah (1:1,14). He was less acquainted with court life than Isaiah, but observed the same social abuses.

Date: The prophecies are dated during the reigns of three kings of Judah (the southern kingdom), c. 750-700 BC (1:1). Micah was a contemporary of Isaiah and Amos. Some scholars have dated Micah much later on stylistic grounds. But Micah 3:12 is quoted in Jeremiah 26:18 (which is later) as having been said in the eighth century.

Background: Both Israel (the northern kingdom) and Judah were gripped by social evil and religious compromise. Prophets regularly warned of national oppression and defeat as God's just punishment on their abandonment of his ways. The Assyrians were expanding their influence, and in 722 defeated Israel and destroyed its capital, Samaria. They pressed south to oppress Judah in the time of King Hezekiah (c. 716-686 BC), who was advised by Isaiah, but they did not defeat the invaders.

For today

- Speak up about wrong things within your own circles of influence
- Check that your faith is producing spiritual 'fruit'
- Give rather than grab; share before you stockpile

Stripped to the bone

Micah 3

Most petfoods and some cheap processed meat products include 'mechanically separated' meat in their ingredients. It means that after the main accessible flesh has been taken off whatever soft tissue is left on the carcass is scraped off the bone by a machine.

No doubt butchers in ancient times, lacking such mechanical aids, still had considerable skill in extracting the last edible ounce before throwing the bones to the dogs. Micah, perhaps familiar with the slaughterhouse in his area, uses the image to describe the effect of the political and religious leadership on the ordinary people (3:3).

It is a regular Old Testament theme. Psalm 14:4 speaks of evildoers 'who devour my people as men eat bread' and Zephaniah 3:3 likens corrupt rulers to lions and wolves 'who leave nothing [on the carcass] for morning'.

Micah lists the specific abuses which concern him most:

- Judah has copied Israel instead of learning from its example (1:10-16)
- Ruthless landowners ignore the covenant law and deprive people of their livelihood (2:1,2)
- Debtors and the poor are bled dry by the rich (2:8,9)
- Bribery and corruption oil the machinery of state (3:8-11)
- Idolatry and witchcraft are widely practised (5:12-14).

This is not very different from the game of 'beggar your neighbour' played by people in every generation as they get what they can by any means. It is hated by God yet alarmingly common. It can infect us all, which is why the New Testament antidote is not to live and let live, but to give and share instead of take (Mark 10:18-23).

Prophetic message posted early for the first Christmas

Micah 5

If you complain that Christmas hype starts earlier every year, just remember that the oracle naming the 'little town of Bethlehem' as the Messiah's birthplace was uttered some 700 years before Mary and Joseph arrived to find no room at the inn.

Traditionally used at carol services, this prophecy did not merely look forward; it made sense on the day it was uttered because it looked back to Bethlehem as the birthplace of King David (1 Samuel 16:1,4; 17:12).

Inserted into an oracle about King Hezekiah's current weakness (v 1) the prophet then predicts a future messianic ruler who will be born in David's family line (v 4). David had been promised that a family member would occupy his throne (2 Samuel 7:16).

Great David's greater son did not fulfil this oracle in the way many expected from the Messiah, but he did surpass the model. The fact that Jesus was also born in Bethlehem was one of those deliberate divine coincidences that reinforced the Davidic link and gave Jesus a significance which would be noted by observers centuries later.

Micah saw this 'from a distance' (Hebrews 11:13) as he searched intently for God's purposes (1 Peter 1:10-12). God loves to tie things up. It gives us confidence today that his future plans will tie up what seem at the moment to be the frayed ends of history and the ragged fragments of our personal lives.

Look out behind you!

It's the oldest trick in the book: get an attacker to think there is someone behind them, then counter attack (or run) while their attention is distracted. That isn't far off what Nahum is doing: 2:1 says, in effect, 'Look behind you'. The bullying Assyria is about to be overpowered by Babylonia. The only difference is that Judah can neither join the fight nor run; she just has to watch and wait.

The prophet addresses the Assyrian capital, Nineveh (although whether his words ever got there is unknown) but his chief audience is in Jerusalem which is harassed by the ruthless superpower during the righteous King Josiah's reign. The message is simple: The Lord is a refuge in times of trouble, caring for his own and defeating their enemies (1:7).

Assyria was rightly feared. Although a cultured nation (Nineveh housed a magnificent library) it was also barbaric; bloodthirsty (3:1), ruthless (3:3) and cruel (3:19).

Twice God declares to Nineveh through Nahum, 'I am against you' (2:13; 3:5); he has already dug its grave (1:14). Although addressed to a specific group on a specific occasion, this message has important applications for all time.

It tells us that God is against any form of institutionalised barbarism and cruelty, and will bring his judgment upon it. And it tells us that he is also against those groups or individuals who threaten his people, and that he will judge them also.

When God is against someone, they are in deep trouble. He is one opponent who can never be overthrown and yet whose identity is not always obvious to the assailant. From ruthless business moguls to genocidal dictators, those who assault the poor and defenceless are assaulting God whether or not the victims worship him. People are as responsible to God for their social conduct as they are for their spiritual commitment, and will be judged accordingly.

How God's opposition to them is expressed is a secondary issue. In this case it came through military conquest after many years. The Babylonians sacked Nineveh in 612 BC and brought its whole empire under their control by 605. The Assyrian reign of terror had lasted for over a century and a half.

Standing somewhere behind all oppressors is a caring God who hates what he sees them do. Our part is to trust that he will move against them in his own time and so demonstrate his righteousness. It may be in this life or the next, but it will occur. This is one of the biblical antidotes to stress and anxiety. Justice is assured; rescue is likely; support is offered in the meantime. Only the timing of the end result is uncertain, not the result itself.

NAHUM

Where am I?

Author:
Unknown

Date:
Between the fall of Thebes (663 BC; 3:8-10) and the fall of Nineveh in 612

Place in Bible:
The seventh of the minor prophets in the Old Testament, after Jonah and Micah and before Habakkuk and Zephaniah

Parallel books:
Jonah is also about Nineveh. Nahum probably lived about the same time as Zephaniah and Jeremiah

The LORD is good, a refuge in times of trouble

Nahum 1:7

Action man model

The Book of Nehemiah

- Describes how Nehemiah came to Jerusalem
- Recounts how he organised the rebuilding of the ruined walls
- Shows how he dealt prayerfully and practically with opponents
- Describes the people's fresh commitment to God
- Brings us to the end of the Old Testament narrative

Some great leaders are remembered for what they did rather than for who they were. That is not so with Nehemiah. The book named after him – drawing largely on his personal diaries – provides Bible readers with a rich character study.

Nehemiah was the quintessential spiritual leader. He earned his living as a servant, doing what he was told, rising to a position of considerable responsibility as cup-bearer (wine taster and poison tester) for the king of Persia.

Then he suddenly faced a call to a career change. Hearing that the walls of Jerusalem were still ruined almost a century after the first return of the exiles, he acts, combining prayer and practical management skill with considerable determination and drive.

With his feet firmly on the ground, his eyes and ears alert to danger and opportunity, his hands willing to get dirty alongside his co-workers, and his body prepared to work round the clock, Nehemiah had his heart based permanently in heaven.

As a result, an ancient problem was resolved within a few weeks and the whole nation experienced a spiritual revival. Nehemiah the civic leader was the perfect balance for Ezra the religious leader whom Nehemiah brought in to take the people on where he was unqualified to lead. His job done, he stepped back and supported Ezra who took over the controls.

Nehemiah is a character. He is determined (his rough justice in 13:25 would have him up on assault charges today!), resourceful, prayerful, and humble at the same time. He sounds self-righteous, but that underlines both his humanity and his single-mindedness. He is a model for anyone to follow, whatever their calling.

'We will not neglect the house of our God.'

Nehemiah 10:39

NEHEMIAH

1	Nehemiah prays for Jerusalem
2	Nehemiah returns to Jerusalem
3	List of wall builders
4	The wall building opposed
5	Nehemiah corrects social injustice
6	Walls completed despite further opposition
7	List of exiles who returned to Jerusalem
8	New Year assembly to hear Ezra read the Law
9	Public confession of sin
10	The people agree to obey God's law
11	List of people chosen to live in Jerusalem
12	Dedication service for the new walls
13	Further social and religious reforms

Spontaneous prayer springs from continuous trust

A French Carmelite monk in the seventeenth century, known as Brother Lawrence, resolved on entering the cloister 'to live in the continual presence of the Lord and if possible never to forget him'.

Starting his daily tasks in the kitchen, he would pray, 'O my God, since Thou art with me, and I must now, in obedience to Thy commands, apply my mind to these outward things, I beseech Thee to grant me the grace to continue in Thy Presence; and to this end do Thou prosper me with Thy assistance, receive all my works, and possess all my affections.'

Brother Lawrence might have had Nehemiah as his example. Never does the book mention a set time of prayer (unlike another exile, see Daniel 6:10) although he does have a special period of prayer in 1:4. But instead we have examples of spontaneous 'arrow' prayers as he goes about his work of managing a civil engineering project.

His method, and his underlying theology, provide a timeless example which all can follow:

- He was concerned for God's honour (e.g. 1:9). Jerusalem was God's special city and its chaos reflected badly on God
- He was convinced of God's sovereignty (e.g. 2:20; 6:16). The task was great (no one had managed to do it in a hundred years); only God could enable it to be completed now
- He was conscious of God's grace (e.g. 5:19; 13:14). His prayers may sound self-righteous, even implying 'salvation by works', but within his pre-Christian understanding of God Nehemiah acknowledged that he had no personal merit to claim God's love; his work was an example of his devotion, which recognised his need of grace
- He was content to leave judgment to God (e.g. 6:14). Having taken commonsense steps to protect himself (6:10-13) Nehemiah did not take God's law into his own hands but left vengeance to the eternal Judge.

In his classic book on prayer, O. Hallesby wrote: 'prayer is opening the door of our life to Jesus', defining 'life as the whole of who we are and what we do. Nehemiah did the Old Testament equivalent of that and was thus able to practise the presence of God everywhere.

'Blue hat' gets the job completed

Nehemiah 2-5

Edward de Bono, the twentieth-century guru of creative thinking, labels different approaches to a problem by giving them coloured 'hats': white for essential information, black for objections, yellow for optimism, red for hunches, green for alternatives, and blue for managing the whole process.

Nehemiah is definitely a 'blue hat'. He finds out the relevant data (2:11-16) and presents his plans to the workers (2:17-20). Then he organises them so that each team knows what to do and where they fit into the whole.

When the black hat (objection and opposition) is thrown into the ring, he combines yellow (optimism) and green (alternatives) to devise a practical solution (ch 4)!

Nehemiah was also a good people manager. At the height of the work, he was with the labourers experiencing the same hardships (4:21-23). He cared about their welfare and in the midst of a hectic project he also instituted a programme of radical social reform (ch 5).

The skill of managing projects (and people) is as valid in the church as in commerce. Church projects might have a different motivation, but the mechanics of executing them are similar. There is nothing spiritual about leaving business skill at the vestry door when the church council meets.

Nehemiah combined spirituality, creativity, pastoral care, practicality and personal involvement. He succeeded where others had either not tried, or failed. We can hardly overlook the implications for local church life.

Where am I?

Date of events:
Nehemiah returned to Jerusalem in 445 BC. He was recalled to Babylon and returned again to Jerusalem in 433 (5:14; 13:6)

Location:
Mostly Jerusalem (ch 1 is Babylon)

Place in Bible:
After Ezra, before Esther in the Old Testament

Story follows:
that of Ezra, who also appears in this book

Bible books it relates to:
Esther (dated shortly before Nehemiah); Malachi (possibly a contemporary)

For today

- Practise the presence of God always
- Make all decisions and activities of daily life a matter for prayer
- Don't consider management skills and common sense to be 'unspiritual'

New Year's resolution

Nehemiah 8-10

Big religious conventions are not a recent phenomenon. This one meets on and off for a month (cf. 8:2; 9:1) marking the Jewish New Year (8:2) with something like the Methodist 'Covenant Service': a new start with God on the basis of his word.

The people were hungry for God's truth. They seem not to have been taught much or well in the past. They listened attentively (8:3,13), prayerfully (8:6) and thoughtfully (8:8), and came back for more.

Ezra and the Levites explained things carefully. Simple, clear teaching is like tasty food; it whets the appetite. Clarity is a gift that not all have, however, and those who possess it, need to be set apart to hone it because tasty food takes time to prepare (cf. 7:1; 13:10,11).

Having listened, the people took action first by celebrating the feast of Booths (8:13-17) and then by sorting out their sins (ch 9). It is easy to put off response to God's word to the point where the initial challenge has faded and the need does not seem so great. The Judeans did not make that mistake; nor should we.

Bounds beaten but laws broken

Nehemiah 12-13

There was appropriate rejoicing and worship as the city once again publically testified to the divine Rock who was its ultimate guardian. Again we see the harmony of Nehemiah the civic leader and Ezra the religious leader as both share equally in the ceremony. At that time, any attempt to separate church and state would have divided what God had joined.

We no longer live in such a 'theocracy' but the God-honouring style of civic life established by Nehemiah is less an option than an obligation for any society that wishes its Christian foundations to remain firm.

But Nehemiah discovers that the lure of wealth once again leads God's people to bend and break the rules. He addresses 'cronyism', lack of support for church ministers, Sabbath trading and the continuing problem of intermarriage.

His prayers (13:14,22,29,31) can be echoed by anyone. He did what he could but he was not entirely successful. God remembers and blesses our acts of faithfulness however much they seem to be mere drops in the ocean (cf. Matthew 25:40).

Author: Probably the same as for 1-2 Chronicles and Ezra. There are similarities in style and content, including the interest in lists of names. The book contains a number of first-person records by Nehemiah, but it also contains third-person reports from unnamed sources.

Date of compilation: Probably in the late 400s BC. (See Fast Facts — Ezra.)

Background information: The Judean exiles, deported to Babylon by Nebuchadnezzar between 605 and 587 BC, began to return to Jerusalem in 537. A second return was led by Ezra in 457. The temple had been rebuilt and was dedicated in 516.

Rebels without a pause

It might better have been called 'The Book of Warnings'. On several occasions the fractious Israelites oppose Moses and complain. Even his brother and sister oppose him.

Each time the rebels are punished by a divinely-appointed event, reinforcing Moses' authority and leadership, and reminding the people that God is holy and just; a theme of the book. His holiness is demonstrated in the detailed instructions for religious rituals, stressing the need for God's people to be pure and to deal with him carefully.

His justice and care for the Israelites is seen in the way in which he defends their cause against the Moabites in the strange tale of Balaam. The pagan priest's curses are turned into divinely-inspired blessings.

The Israelites had expected to go straight from Egypt into Canaan, a journey taking a few weeks at the most. Numbers tells the sad story of their refusal to trust God after the spies sent into Canaan brought back a report of 'giants in the land'. As a result, they were sentenced to 40 years solitary confinement in the desert until all who had left Egypt had died.

All, that is, except for Joshua and Caleb, the two scouts who produced a minority report saying that Canaan was accessible with God's help. They eventually took the Israelites across the Jordan as the story continues in Deuteronomy and Joshua.

Numbers makes for sober reading. Any generation can embark on new projects with the same buoyant enthusiasm reflected in the first census which prepared the Israelites for conquest. But the temptation to begin to rely on human wisdom, to forget God's absolute holiness and to neglect the spiritual disciplines, returns every time. Numbers is a warning not to make the same mistakes as the Israelites.

NUMBERS

Key:

Narrative:	CAPITALS
Lists and censuses	Light
Religious instructions	**Bold**
Partition of the land	*Italics*

1 First census
2 Camp arrangements
3 Priests and Levites
4 Levites by family
5 **Laws of purity**
6 Nazirite vows
7 Tally of offerings
8 DEDICATION OF LEVITES
9 The Passover
10 JOURNEY FROM SINAI
11 FIRE AND QUAIL FROM GOD
12 MIRIAM AND AARON REBEL
13 SPIES GO TO CAANAN
14 REACTION TO SPIES' REPORT
15 **Various offerings**
16 KORAH'S REBELLION
17 AARON'S STAFF BUDS
18 **Laws for priests and Levites**
19 **Laws for cleansing**
20 WATER FROM THE ROCK
21 BATTLES ON THE JOURNEY
22 BALAAM'S DONKEY
23 BALAAM'S ORACLES
24 BALAAM'S ORACLES
25 IDOLATRY IN MOAB
26 Second census
27 INHERITANCE DEBATE; JOSHUA'S APPOINTMENT
28 **Daily offerings**
29 **Various feasts**
30 **Various vows**
31 BATTLE WITH MIDIANITES
32 TRIBAL DISPUTE OVER LAND
33 LOG OF ISRAELITES' JOURNEY
34 *Boundaries of Canaan*
35 *Levitical towns*
36 *Inheritance rules*

The Book of Numbers

- Tells the story of the Israelites in the desert
- Lists the Israelites who came out of Egypt
- Shows how Canaan is to be divided
- Gives instructions for Israel's religious life

HARD Question

How many?

The total number of men aged over 20 in the censuses comes to over 600,000 (2:32; cf. 26:51, and Exodus 12:37; 38:26). The records in different passages are consistent.

But when we add the Levites, the women and under-20s there must have been a total population of well over two million. Jacob's family was just 70-strong when it entered Egypt (Exodus 1:5).

This seems high. In the first half of the twentieth century (before the wave of Jewish immigration after 1948) the entire land of Palestine supported only one million people.

Other tribes in the area were much smaller (according to the remains which have been unearthed), yet the Israelites' fear of entering Canaan was that they were fewer than the existing residents (see Deuteronomy 7:7). And the logistics of providing so many with food and drink in the desert (cf. 11:21) would test any nation today.

In favour of the high numbers is the consistency of the record, and the fact that the Israelites had large and healthy families (Exodus 1:7-20). 'Exponential' population growth (as in the sequence 2-4-8-16) could explain rapid growth in a few generations.

Against them is the number of first-born sons (22,273 in 3:42) suggesting an average family of over 50 children! Scholars are unsure how to interpret both 'firstborn' and the Hebrew for 'thousand'. Also, oddly, the figures 100, 800 and 900 never appear.

So there may be quirks in Hebrew counting which we do not understand. But whatever the truth, the impression remains that the Israelites were being bonded into a single orderly unit. The rabble of fugitive slaves was becoming a force to be reckoned with.

The censuses make sense

Numbers 1-4, 7, 26

No one reads the phone book for pleasure, and therefore the temptation to skip the lists in Numbers is strong. Yet they serve a purpose and have a positive message for today.

The censuses were taken as a record of the Israelites' military strength (1:3; 26:2). So they offer a picture of a united federation of 12 tribes preparing for combined operations.

Entry into Canaan was going to be costly; they would have to fight even though they saw the land as God's gift. Unity and co-operation were essential for success.

They also give us a snapshot of the relative strengths of Israel's tribes. Judah, for example, with 74,600 men over 20 years is more than twice the size of Manasseh with its 32,200. Later in Israel's history we will see inter-tribal conflict, and Judah (with the smaller Benjamin) eventually separating from the other ten.

The list of offerings for the Tent of Meeting (ch 7) reads like an accountant's stock list. But how exciting it is! Little Manasseh gives exactly the same to God's 'church' as mighty Judah!

The tribes are seen as equal before God. Judah cannot be closer or more valuable to God because it is bigger, and Manasseh can't be of less value to God because it's smaller. This is an exact parallel to Paul's teaching about the body of Christ in 1 Corinthians 12:14-27.

Ministers of God are a tribe apart

Numbers 3, 4, 18, 35

Ministers of God are needed to perform sacred rituals on behalf of his people, and to keep the tribes mindful of God's laws. Numbers illustrates how this principle was built into Israel's earliest history. It distinguishes between priests and Levites (the distinction became blurred later).

- Priests are the direct male descendants of Aaron, Moses' brother (3:3) and offer all sacrifices
- Levites are the male descendants of Levi, the third son of Jacob and Leah (Genesis 29:34), who look after the Tent and later lead in music and prayer.

Numbers concentrates on the Levites. They had shown their zeal for the Lord by killing the idolaters who had worshipped the golden calf (Exodus 32:26-29). From that point on they were earmarked for special service to God.

The Levites are divided into three branches named after Levi's three sons; they each have different functions, described in chapter 4.

The Kohathites look after and carry the Tent of Meeting's furnishings; the Gershonites carry the Tent's curtains (its walls and roof); and the Merarites carry the framework. They may do other things as directed by the priests (4:27f).

They were not to be given a specific region in Canaan, but had 48 towns scattered among all the tribes (35:7f). The Levites would be living reminders of spiritual values in every part of the new nation.

Although they would have their own fields for food production, they were also to be supported by the gifts (tithes) of the people, which they themselves had to tithe (give away one tenth; 18:21-32). Throughout Scripture, ministers are not a law unto themselves but are subject to the same disciplines as all of God's people.

We should therefore remember their human fallibility, not expecting perfection from them and praying that God will protect them from falling prey to the temptations which assault them.

Nazirites take a vow

Numbers 6

Nazirites, the equivalent of monks and nuns, could take special vows of consecration to God, either for life or for a specific period. They consumed no grape products; they did not cut their hair; and they were forbidden to touch any dead body. They had to offer the costliest sin offerings – lambs – and not the cheaper pigeons (6:14f; cf. Leviticus 5:7-10).

Among the biblical Nazirites Samson is the most famous (Judges 13:4f). Samuel and John the Baptist may have been life-long Nazirites, and the temporary vow which Paul took (Acts 18:18; cf. 21:23) may also have been Nazirite.

Such vows seem an anachronism today, but that may be because we despise any form of formal spiritual discipline. Yet we applaud such dedication in sportspeople, who compete only for fading medals (1 Corinthians 9:24-27). Perhaps we need to receive that spirit.

The LORD bless you and keep you; the LORD make his face shine upon you and be gracious to you; the LORD turn his face towards you and give you peace.

Numbers 6:24-26

Date of events:
c. 1280–1240 BC
Location:
Sinai Desert (Arabia)
Story follows:
Exodus
Story leads onto:
tail end of Deuteronomy, then Joshua
Book overlaps with:
Leviticus, Deuteronomy
Key people:
Moses and the Israelites; the Moabites; Balaam
Place in Bible:
After Leviticus, before Deuteronomy, in the Old Testament

Mutiny despite the bounty

Numbers 11-16

The manna – the coriander-flavoured flakes which sustained the Israelites – was still falling (11:16). Canaan, their destination, was rich and productive (ch 13). Some leaders were even 'baptised in the Spirit' (11:23-30).

But a series of complaints and personality clashes taxed the patience of both God and Moses. The complaints were of three types.

- Frustration with desert life (ch 11)
- Fear of defeat in Canaan (ch 14)
- Jealousy of Moses by other leaders (chs 12,16).

The divine response was a series of unusual events. The author of Numbers shows that these were warning signs from God. Whatever we make of them, their message is that God does not take complaints lightly.

There were two outbreaks of 'fire from the LORD' (11:1-3; 16:35). The first reads like a lightning strike affecting only a small number of offenders, but the others knew what it meant.

The second only affected the offenders. No explanation is offered; perhaps the fire they were using set light to the men and their tents. But always in the Bible, fire is a sign of God's holiness. It came after Korah and his associates were swallowed into the ground. The area had mud flats in which a hard crust covers a sticky bog. The crust can, and perhaps did, crack and the mud suck down whoever or whatever was on it. The 'underworld' is itself a symbol of death and separation from God.

Miriam's 'leprosy' (12:10-15) cannot have been true leprosy because it did not exist here at this time, and it does not come and go suddenly. Her condition was probably psoriasis, a flaking skin condition. The guilt-ridden Miriam would quickly interpret it as a sign of God's displeasure.

The final punishment was the exclusion from Canaan of all the Israelites who had left Egypt, except Joshua and Caleb, (14:39-45) and the premature death by disease of the ten faithless spies. It is a classic biblical example of how a whole group can suffer for the wrong attitudes of some.

The author is stressing that God's laws are to be obeyed and his leaders respected. It is a timely message in an age which idolises personal choice and freedom, and delights in faulting church leaders. We may not suffer God's displeasure in such an obvious way, but we cannot expect churches to prosper when criticism is rife.

FAST facts

Title of book: 'Numbers' comes from the Greek translation and refers to the lists. The Hebrew title is 'In the wilderness', from its opening words.

Structure: The storyline is interspersed with census and ceremonial details. There are three main groups of events: at Sinai (ch. 1-8); at Kadesh Barnea (chs 9-20); on the plains of Moab (chs 21-36). The other material may belong to these periods or be inserted to maintain a theological theme of God's holiness.

Author: Traditionally, Moses: clearly some material comes from a later editor. In 12:3 and 15:22f Moses is referred to in the third person. There are acknowledged quotations from other documents: the Book of the Wars (21:14f); an Amorite song (21:27-30); and Balaam's oracles (23-24).

Final date of composition: Probably in this form by the time of the early kings (c.1000 BC).

Moses' patience snaps at last

Numbers 20:1-13

Moses sounds like an exasperated parent of a demanding child, smacking and giving in at the same time: 'Oh, all right then – have it!'

Early in the journey, he had struck the rock at Sinai and tapped into an underground aquifer (Exodus 17:1-7). Now at Kadesh, near the end of the journey, he is told to speak to the rock, but he strikes it as well.

God's reaction, to bar Moses from Canaan, seems harsh. But Moses' words are revealing: 'Must we bring you water out of this rock?' Although renowned for his humility (12:3), he is not now acting as God's servant but as his deputy, as he decides on the method he will use to bring about God's will.

The balance of doing God's will in God's way is always difficult to achieve. Moses was not alone in failing, and the example is a salutary one for Christians eager to see 'results'; ends do not justify means.

He may also have assumed that because God acted in one way in an identical situation before, he would do the same second time around. It would be more true biblically – and in experience – to say that God rarely works in the same way twice. He shows his holiness – his supremacy – by varying his methods and seeking his people's trust (cf. Deuteronomy 32:51).

Aaron's rod for budding clergy

Numbers 17

No clear explanation can account for a stick which bears fruit overnight. But its meaning is clear. It is a visual demonstration that Aaron's priestly line (and the Levites he also represented) are to be Israel's ministers – and no one else. The rod is stored as a permanent reminder of the fact.

In other words, the call to ministry is God's. People, however well-intentioned or qualified, cannot effectively exercise ministry unless they have that calling. In Numbers it is recognised by checking parentage; in our time by careful selection procedures. Paul makes the point in Romans 10:15.

Clean up the act

Numbers 5, 15, 19, 28-30

Just as washing is central to personal hygiene, so the Israelites found spiritual purity in cleansing rituals.

In chapter 19 holy water is made by adding the ashes of a wholly-burnt red (the colour of blood) heifer to ordinary water. This was sprinkled on an 'unclean' person, especially one who had touched a corpse.

Moral purity was achieved in more costly ways. The unfaithful wife (5:16-28) drank specially-prepared water and was cursed. Unintended sin was cleansed by sacrifice (15:22-29), and Sabbath-breakers were killed (15:32-36).

The concern over corpses reflects the awareness that death is (in the Old Testament mind) the ultimate separation from God, and therefore distasteful, even if natural. Hebrews 9:13f speaks of the blood of Christ achieving permanently what the heifer's ashes could achieve only temporarily.

Quaint – or objectionable – as these sanctions sound today, they remind readers that nothing is excluded from God's concerns. Holiness is more than abstinance from sins, it is positive dedication of everything to God.

A general view of Makhtesh Ramon, near the centre of the Negev desert.

Numbers in the New Testament

John 3:14 – the bronze snake
John 6:30-33 – the manna
1 Corinthians 10:1-10 – desert wanderings
Hebrews 3:7-4:5 – rebellions in the desert
Hebrews 9:13f – the heifer's ashes
2 Peter 2:13-16 – Balaam
Jude v. 5 – rebellion in the desert
Jude v. 11 – Korah and Balaam

Snake charm

Numbers 21:4-9

This unusual form of 'healing' is often dismissed as a piece of tribal fetishism. But the snake (which may have been pure copper, more red than bronze, the colour of atonement) was a focus for faith.

To look up at the image (which was beyond reach) was a sacramental act. The worshipper said, in effect, 'I trust the God I cannot touch to achieve by his chosen means that which I cannot do.' It provided John with a picture of Jesus' death on the cross, the effect of which cannot be understood and only accepted by faith (John 3:14f).

Prophet obeys donkey

Numbers 21-25

The story of Balaam stretches many people's credulity. But as commentator Gordon Wenham writes, 'The charming naiveté of these stories disguises a brilliance of literary composition and a profundity of theological reflection. The narrative is at once both very funny and deadly serious.'

Balaam is also known from an inscription in the Jordan valley dating from about 700 BC. He is said to have brought messages from a number of gods. He did not worship God (Yahweh) but knew of him. His insistence in speaking only what Yahweh says may have been more of a ploy to extract the highest possible fee from Barak rather than a sign of faith or reverence.

This incident is an example of a person being captivated by God's Spirit and speaking spontaneously words from God which they have not previously thought. It is the 'prophetic gift' seen in action.

But Balaam is a foreigner and an unbeliever in the technical sense. So the fact that God communicates through him (as well as to him) is significant. Yahweh is not a tribal god but the supreme Lord; so Israel can take heart, and the other nations take heed. In the Bible, God never demands that people from different cultures and beliefs change their mindset before he will speak to them. Pagan astrologers were the first non-Jews to realise who Jesus was (Matthew 2:1-12).

There is a still greater irony, and message, remaining. Where Balaam failed, the Moabite women succeeded. Spiritual curses could not weaken Israel, but old-fashioned immorality could (ch 25). 'If you think you are standing firm, be careful that you don't fall!' (1 Corinthians 10:12); Numbers ends where it began, with warnings.

CROSS CHECK

Moses' authorship of the Pentateuch: p 117
Laws for ceremonial purity: pp 262-3
Feasts and sacrifices: p 267
The Tent of Meeting: p 114-5
The exodus: p 108-10
The entry into Canaan: pp 224-6

FAST facts

Israel's Enemies

Arad (Hormah): A fortified town about 30km (18 miles) north-east of Beersheba in southern Judah. A large fortress was built there in David's time (about 1000 BC).

Amorites: A Canaanite tribe living on both sides of the River Jordan. They had ruled in Babylonia during the time of the Patriarchs (c. 2000-1750 BC). When the Israel-ites approached Canaan they controlled the area east of the Jordan. Under Solomon's rule (c. 950 BC) they became slaves to the Israelites (1 Kings 9:20).

Edom: The descendants of Esau, Jacob's brother, and the land they occupied to the south of the Dead Sea (Genesis 36). They often clashed with the Judeans during the period of the kings (1000-600 BC). During the Maccabean period (c. 150 BC) Edom was annexed by the Jews. Herod's family had Edomite roots.

Moab: The descendants of the son conceived by Lot and his daughter (Genesis 19:30-38) and the area they occupied to the east of the Dead Sea. It became a strong and prosperous nation. Ruth, the ancestor of David (and hence of Jesus) came from Moab. There was tension between Judah and Moab for most of the period of the kings (1000-600 BC).

Did the donkey talk?

The account of Balaam is presented as a story to be read, enjoyed and learned from. It is not presented as a fly-on-the-wall documentary. If we accept that it has a historical basis, four things can be said.

First, animal divination – fortune-telling by observing animals – was standard equipment in the Mesopotamian magician's bag of tricks. So the donkey's obtuseness was a natural way in which God could communicate to Balaam in terms he readily understood.

Secondly, people and animals do develop a relationship which includes an intuitive two-way communication. The Bible pictures a close relationship between humans and the animal kingdom both before the fall of Adam and Eve (Genesis 2:19f) and after the new creation (Isaiah 11:6-9). It would be surprising if that is not sometimes foreshadowed now, seeing that other aspects of it are. (The Holy Spirit is a foreshadowing of what will be fulfilled later, in Ephesians 1:14.)

Thirdly, most people use the image of 'something spoke to me' very loosely. A beautiful sunset, an ugly rubbish tip, a work of art can all 'speak' to us. Balaam could be waking up to what God is saying through the donkey's action: 'It was as if he said . . .'

Finally, if God diversified language (Genesis 11:1-9), there is no logical reason (apart from scepticism) as to why he should not do the unusual thing which a literal reading of 22:28 suggests!

The point of the story is that Balaam was as obstinate as the donkey, and that God broke through his pride to achieve his purposes. The story is a commentary on the first commandment: 'You shall have no other gods before me' (Exodus 20:3).

Balaam being thrown off his donkey (here illustrated by Rembrandt) caught the popular imagination!

Fair shares for all

Numbers 27, 32, 34-36

Discussions about the inheritance of the daughters of Zelophehad (27,36) show that the Old Testament story is not simply a saga of battles over land rights. It recognises people's need to have a place in which their family roots can sink deeply.

Women were not normally entitled to own land. The exception is made when the family would otherwise become extinct and its descendants disinherited (27).

And a law is enacted to prevent stronger tribes from gaining more land at the expense of weaker ones by intermarriage (36). Later prophets condemned those who extended their estates by dispossessing the poor (Isaiah 5:8).

For today

- God is supreme over all nations and defends his people
- God is holy and requires careful worship and devotion from his people
- Hardship is not a reason to question God but an opportunity to trust him
- Leaders are to obey God fully in every detail of their lives
- Each person is to be faithful to their own calling and not copy others' ministries

Don't fret if your enemies gloat

Place in Bible:

The fourth of the minor prophets at the end of the Old Testament, after Amos and before Jonah

Charles Blair was the pastor of a large church in Denver, Colorado. As a result of his presumption, which he wrongly viewed as faith, he was convicted of charges of financial fraud in some major expansion programmes. During the trial, he and his wife found it increasingly difficult to face other people because of the shame they felt and the criticism they received. Once, when a commercial researcher called innocently at the door, Blair's wife just burst into tears.

It always feels worse if, when you have been hit by some circumstantial blow (whether deserved or not), others have a good laugh or gossip at your expense. It depresses you further and makes it harder to hope for recovery. You just want to crawl away and die.

That is the situation in Obadiah. Judah has been attacked and decimated. Edom (also called Esau after its founder) is gloating (cf. Psalm 137:7). But the tables will be turned, Obadiah promises. Judah will be restored and Edom will be destroyed.

No one is quite sure when Obadiah worked. Jewish scholars placed him at the time of King Jehoram (c. 850 BC) making Obadiah a contemporary of Elisha (2 Kings 2-9). However, verses 11-14 are so like the Babylonian destruction of Jerusalem in 587 BC that many scholars date Obadiah shortly after it. In that case the prophet is a contemporary of Jeremiah (and verses 1-9 are very similar to Jeremiah 49:7-22).

Whatever the date, Obadiah is saying that God will one day make Judah's (and our) opponents laugh on the other side of their faces. But that doesn't satisfy our desire for immediate vengeance. It is, however, the standard message of the biblical prophets who recognised that God's timescale is different from ours. God hears our cry, sees the gloating enemy, and does not forget it. In discomfort and even in disgrace, God does not abandon us. He forgives, restores and promises that those who laugh now will mourn later.

While awaiting sentence, Charles Blair began spending more time alone with God. The message he received was, 'You caught my vision and then galloped ahead without learning how I wished to bring it about . . . You've made mistakes – that's human nature. I've forgiven you – that's my nature.'

Judah had often deserved Edom's attacks. But God, unlike her enemies, never laughed at her discomfort but wept silently with her.

Edom: The country lay between the Dead Sea and the Gulf of Aqabah. The people were descendants of Esau, Jacob's brother who was tricked out of his birthright. The family feud continued for generations and Edom often oppressed Israel and Judah, including refusing permission for the migrating Israelites to pass through the land (Numbers 20:14-21). Israel was ordered to stay on good terms with Edom, however (Deuteronomy 23:7,8). The compliment was not returned, and sometimes Edom, sometimes Israel (or Judah) was on top. Ironically, the Herodian kings of the New Testament were descended from the Edomites.

Other views: Obadiah is not alone in denouncing Edom. See also Jeremiah 49:7-22; Lamentations 4:21,22; Ezekiel 25:12-14; Joel 3:19; Amos 9:11,12.

Refiner's fire makes Christians glow

1 Peter 1:6-9; 4:12-19

From needles under the fingernails to hot pokers on sensitive body parts, human beings have devised 101 clever ways of inflicting pain on each other often for no good reason except to dominate and control.

In AD 64 the emperor Nero thought up another one. He rounded up Christians (who he wrongly accused of having started the great fire of Rome; rumour had it that he started it himself) and skewered them alive on long poles. Coating them in tar, he set fire to them as human beacons to illuminate his palace gardens at night and provide char-grilled kebabs for the crows the next day.

Peter probably wrote this letter before that happened, but he could see it coming. Almost since the day of Pentecost the apostles and their converts had been arrested by authorities or lynched by angry mobs. Suffering was not a new experience, but it was starting to get institutionalised. (The worst period was in the late 80s, under the emperor Domitian.)

Such things seem far from the sanitised modern West, disturbed only by media reports of lone sex offenders, serial killers and overseas war lords with unpronounceable names. Yet all through history Christians have been persecuted (sometimes by each other). In our own time there have been attacks on churches in some Asian countries and much personal brutality to Christians in both Asia and Africa.

It could never happen here, we think. But Christians can be pilloried in the press, obstructed at work, ridiculed at home. That does happen here. In applying the whole letter, and especially the sections on suffering, we should recognise that while all suffering is terrible, we should keep it in perspective because we haven't yet had to pay the ultimate price for our faith; and accept all kinds of suffering as opportunities for our faith to be refined.

Peter is thinking of gold being heated to melt off the impurities (1:7). Sometimes, suffering reduces our life to the basics. The wrappers get burned off. What's left underneath? Is it something durable that can outlast the comforts of life? Or is our 'faith' dependent on those comforts for its existence?

When we focus on what is permanent, rather than on what is transient, our faith will take on a fresh spiritual glow and we and the world will be better for it. And you don't need to suffer to let that happen.

1 PETER

1	Suffering refines faith so purify yourselves
2:1-12	The church is God's people with a mission
2:13-25	Follow the example of Jesus; don't retaliate
3	Live in harmony in family and church
4	The end is near; serve God in your suffering
5	Care for each other and stay alert

The first letter of Peter:

- Encourages Christians to keep the faith during persecution
- Urges them to be holy and regard suffering as 'refining'
- Describes how Christians are God's people with a mission
- Tells us to adopt loving attitudes to each other

KEY QUOTE

I urge you, as aliens and strangers in the world, to abstain from sinful desires, which war against your soul.
1 Peter 2:11

Eternal life is set in physical stone

1 Peter 2:1-10

Natural stone – textured and coloured sandstone, polished marble – is attractive and naturally strong. Peter could see some spectacular stone buildings in Rome, like the Coliseum.

Although church buildings did not yet exist, the building analogy illustrated the nature of the church: it is to be beautiful and strong.

Its strength comes from the 'cornerstone', a large foundation block which defines the angle and takes the stress. Jesus defines our faith and supports our life. Without him there would be no church, because he was its Saviour, not just its teacher. People who are not built onto this foundation will sooner or later fall, for no alternative structure can stand for ever.

The stones built on the foundation combine to form a functional and attractive structure. The 'priesthood' of believers, called to sacrifice themselves in whole-life worship of God, are adorned with the beauties of God's own holiness. Think about the picture next time you see a church building.

Aliens told to r… worldly abducti…

1 Peter 2:11-17; cf. 1:13-22; 5:6-9

As the approach of the year 2000 caused global anxiety, an American survey found that the happiest people were those who believed that they had been abducted by aliens and were to join a space ship at the stroke of midnight.

Aliens have captured the public imagination and bred fear and fascination and express our unconscious awareness of the forces of darkness. But Peter doesn't have that kind of alien in mind in 2:11 although he expects Christians to behave like them. Aliens are different and Christians are different because they have been 'born again' (1:3,23) yet they are still integrated into ordinary society.

Aliens have a special mission; and so do Christians: to capture the world (for Christ, 2:10; cf. 3:15). During that mission, aliens run the risk of being abducted themselves or even turned from their cause; so Christians must control themselves and stay true to their real identity (1:13-21), remain alert and resist the devil (5:8,9).

And aliens stick together; they are a close-knit force. And so are Christians (2:9,10). Sadly, that seems to be where the analogy sometimes breaks down.

FAST facts

Author: There has been no serious doubt that 1 Peter was written by the apostle Peter although the literary Greek seems too good for a Galilean fisherman. Silas (5:12) who was also associated with Paul was an educated Roman Jew (Acts 15:22; 16:37) and no doubt polished up the Greek as Peter dictated – a usual scribal custom.

Date: Likely to be between AD 60 and 67 (Peter was probably martyred in 67).

Place of writing: Peter says he is in 'Babylon' (5:13). There were two places with that name. One was a military garrison in Egypt and the other a small town in Mesopotamia. Neither seems likely. Later in the first century 'Babylon' was a code name for Rome; maybe Peter coined it. As he apparently died in Rome, it is assumed that is where he meant he was, and where he wrote this.

Readers: It is addressed to Christians across Asia Minor (1:1). Although this was Paul's church-planting patch, Peter may also have visited it. He had certainly met people from it (cf. Acts 2:9-11).

HARD Question

Do the dead get another chance?

1 Peter 3:18-22; 4:6

This passage is often taken to mean that upon dying Jesus went into the abode of the dead to tell humans waiting there the good news of his saving sacrifice and to give those who lived before him a chance to believe.

However, a more natural interpretation is that he proclaimed his triumph to the evil spirits, and began the process by which eventually 'every knee shall bow' before him whether they are 'saved' or not. (Philippians 2:10 refers explicitly to those 'under the earth', again meaning the demons in hell (cf. Jude 6) rather than the dead who would be raised.)

The eternal destiny of those who lived before Christ, therefore, is not addressed here. It is only a problem to us because we are trapped in time. The New Testament says that salvation is possible only by God's grace through the death and resurrection of Christ (cf. John 14:6; Acts 4:12).

Historical time, and even personal awareness of the facts, are not involved. Old Testament believers 'saw from a distance' that God would deal with their sin problem (Hebrews 11:13). They were justified by faith just as Christians are even though Jesus had not yet come (Romans 4).

God looks for trust in his remedy, not knowledge of it – although such knowledge enlightens faith and is to be shared with those who have not heard it. Nowhere does the New Testament promise a 'second chance'. One lifetime is enough in which to trust God, however imperfectly.

Serve the relations

1 Peter 2:13-3:12; 5:1-4

If everyone lived as Peter tells us, there would be no audience for the TV soaps that thrive on family feuds. Peter's use of 'submission' here must not be interpreted as 'subservience'. Neither he nor Paul would have had a problem with the modern stress on partnership within marriage.

But they were concerned within their own cultural context about the break-up of relationships and poor witness caused by Christian women who neglected their families for fashion. The 'service' of one's family is a model of service in the church (3:9; 5:3,5). It has more give than take, even when it's not appreciated.

Self-employment unspiritual

1 Peter 4:1-11

Charles Williams wrote *Many Dimensions*, a complex and deeply symbolic novel about a stone from King Solomon's crown which had mysterious powers. It could be divided without losing its mass and the new stones were used selfishly by their owners.

The original stone came to Chloe, a judge's secretary. She had to decide whether to use it at her own behest to gratify someone else's desires, or to let it have its way with her. She chose the latter. By resigning herself to it, rather than controlling it, she became the means of bringing all the stones together again, so preventing their further misuse.

Williams is suggesting that God's gifts are for God's use. Peter is saying that here: 'our' gifts are not ours; they are 'God's grace' (v 10). They are expressions of his presence for him to work through, not tools for us to 'minister' with as we decide we would like. Only so is God praised and truly honoured (v 11).

God's gifts are not for self-employment – they are at his disposal alone – and for use only as your heart tells you he wishes. Wilfulness never pleases God.

For today

- Use difficulties as an opportunity to grow in faith
- Are you cemented into 'God's building' or crumbling off it?
- Don't copy the world, try to change it
- Let love rule your relationships, even if it means backing down

No one invented Christianity

According to psychologist Sigmund Freud, religion is a dangerous illusion of a sick mind. Other psychologists, including Freud's pupil Carl Jung, took a more moderate approach, recognising that psychology is not qualified to pronounce on the existence of God.

Peter knew nothing of ids, egos and libidos but he did know that people would attempt to dismiss the faith as an illusion. So he reminds his readers that it isn't an invention but a revelation. He saw some of it himself, notably on the Mount of Transfiguration (1:16-18) and in his personal encounters with the risen Lord (Mark 16:7, Luke 24:34; John 21; 1 Corinthians 15:5); Christianity for us as for Peter, is based on objective facts. Scriptures relate prophecies of Christ which have been fulfilled; that could never be humanly engineered (1:19-21).

Some later writers, like Paul, were less easily understood and therefore more easily misinterpreted (3:14-16)! The false teachers of chapter 2 probably offered something more plausible to the mind and attractive to the flesh (cf. 2:1); such always have, and still do.

The Scriptures provide a strong argument against Judeo-Christianity being a human invention, precisely because they are so wide-ranging in styles, time and concern. The unity of the message is all the more remarkable for the diversity of the writings composed of over 40 authors during a period of more than 1,000 years. Compared with the biblical faith, pagan and false religions were obvious human inventions.

When doubts occur, read the Bible narratives and see how God has woven a compelling message about himself, revealed to and through a long series of people who never knew each other.

2 PETER

1 **Stand firm in the faith and trust the Scriptures**
2 **False teachers will be destroyed**
3 **Look forward to the return of Jesus**

Make every effort to add to your faith goodness . . . knowledge . . . self-control . . . perseverance . . . godliness . . . brotherly kindness; and . . . love. *2 Peter 1:5-7*

Place in Bible:
The letters of Peter are towards the end of the New Testament, after James and before the letters of John and Revelation

FAST facts

Author: Supposedly the second by the apostle Peter (1:1; 3:1). However, outside the Bible there are known letters written under pseudonyms and many scholars dispute Peter's authorship. The difference in style and language to 1 Peter might be a result of using different secretaries. It counters the false teaching of gnosticism (sometimes held to be later than Peter) which Paul also countered in Colossians. Peter's polemic is also similar to Jude's (one probably borrowed from the other). However, no obvious alternative authors have been suggested and there is no reason for doubting its authenticity.

Place in canon: 2 Peter is referred to by the early church fathers less than any other New Testament book – although there are more references to it than to any other writings not included in the 'canon' of Scripture, and some early writers seem to allude to it without naming it. At the reformation Luther accepted it (he rejected James) and so did Calvin, but noted that its style was unlike 1 Peter.

Love your revolting brother

Spartacus led an uprising of some 90,000 slaves less than a century before this letter was written. The rebellion was put down, with thousands of slaves being crucified, but fear of a repeat was never far from Roman minds.

Onesimus had run away from Philemon having stolen from him (v 18); for that, he could be executed. But he had been converted to Christ, and Paul seeks a seemingly impossible reconciliation between slave and master.

Forgiveness is never easy. It is doubly hard when there is a cultural barrier to clear. Attitudes take longer to change than constitutions. Think how difficult it has been to achieve genuine racial harmony in South Africa and the southern states of America.

Paul's great gospel theme was reconciliation between God and people, resulting in a new humanity united in Christ (cf. Ephesians 2:11–22). He approaches Philemon sensitively, with humour (verse 11 is a play on Onesimus' name which means 'useful'), implying that because Paul could use the slave in ministry, Philemon should be able to receive him back.

This short, personal letter challenges us to forgive without reservation, and to rebuild damaged relationships. We are one in Christ, and we are to live out that truth as a demonstration of the gospel.

Why didn't Paul outlaw slavery?

HARD Question

Slavery was institutionalised in the Roman Empire. A few slaves rose to positions of power but most suffered degradation. There was a growing unease about slavery among a minority of intellectuals in the second half of the first century when Paul wrote.

Paul did effectively abolish it within the church. Slave trading was 'contrary to sound doctrine' (1 Timothy 1:10,11). Masters were equals with slaves in Christ (Galatians 3:28) and were to treat and pay them fairly (Ephesians 6:9; Colossians 4:1). Then, obedience of slaves wasn't a problem (Ephesians 6:5-8). Thoughtful service was part of Christian witness to unbelieving masters (1 Timothy 6:1,2). Paul aims to undermine an evil from within.

To advocate abolition at this time would not have served the cause of the gospel well, aligning the young church with a political minority, and obscuring its message as it struggled for a hearing.

The slave trade was finally abolished largely through the efforts of a Christian, William Wilberforce. His example and that of the Old Testament prophets remains. God's love embraces all human activities including the social, economic and political, because they impinge on human life about which he cares deeply in all its aspects.

Where am I?

Place in Bible:
After the pastoral letters (Timothy and Titus) and before Hebrews in the New Testament

Date and place of writing: This letter was written at the same time as Colossians. Paul mentions Onesimus in Colossians 4:9 as one of the group accompanying the letter, and Archippus is mentioned in both (Colossians 4:17; Philemon v. 2). The letter is usually dated about AD 60-61, being written while Paul was under house arrest in Rome.

Thank-you notelet packed with treasure

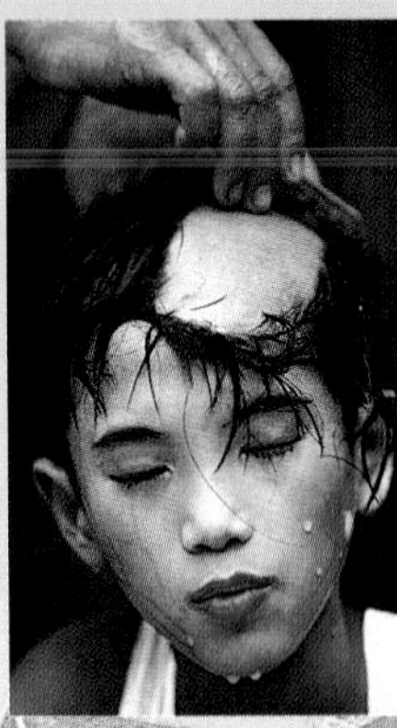

The Letter to the Philippians

- Shows how Paul's imprisonment has not silenced his witness
- Includes a famous hymn describing Jesus' humility and ministry
- Encourages readers to press on in the Christian life

It's always good to get a letter from friends who thank us for a gift, update us on their news and share a few matters of mutual concern. Philippians is such a letter. There is no crisis in the church (although there is the ever-present danger posed by zealous Judaisers, 3:1-11), so Paul's mood as he writes is relaxed.

Philippians introduces us to another side of Paul's character. In letters such as 1 Corinthians and Galatians we see him stern and authoritative. Here we see him warm and pastoral, a friend rather than just a leader.

He writes to thank them for their gifts. He is in prison (or under house arrest), and although he doesn't say so directly, without their support he would suffer (cf. 4:12); Romans did not see the need to feed prisoners (unless it was to the lions).

The letter is a treasure chest of truth about Jesus and of practical advice about Christian living. Eloquent and quotable, it lifts both heart and mind, and informs our actions.

AT A GLANCE

PHILIPPIANS

1	The gospel isn't chained even if Paul is
2:1-18	Follow the example of Jesus' humility
2:19-30	Personal notes about Timothy and Epaphroditus
3	Press on and don't rest on your laurels
4	The secrets of peace and contentment

Death is a door to something better

Philippians 1

When the Buddha died in 483 BC, his alleged last words were: 'Decay is inherent in all living things.' When Jesus died 500 years later, his last words were, 'Today you will be with me in paradise' and 'Father into your hands I commit my spirit' (Luke 23:43,46). Buddhism is a pessimistic doubt, but Christianity is a hope-filled *faith*: it looks forward to the as yet unseen reversal of death.

Paul contemplates the end of his life. He doesn't know if he will leave prison alive. But he doesn't mind either way (vv 20-26). He has been here before; facing death was no new experience. He had been almost killed by a stoning (Acts 14:19), and 'despaired for life' during intense suffering (2 Corinthians 1:8,9).

He knows that death is a doorway to God's presence (cf. 3:10). He can face it; he does not fear it; he can even choose it (1:20-24). But he does not court it. Paul is not close to suicide; he has Christ to live for, even in the apparent hopelessness of imprisonment.

People today do fear death; there seems so much to lose, with no certainty of anything to follow. But if we have something else (and better) to look forward to, the pressure and stress is removed from this life. We have nothing to lose, and much to gain, so we do not need to grasp all we can (whether possessions or experiences) now.

Date and place of writing: There is no doubt that Paul is the author, and that he is writing from prison (ch 1). But which prison is debated. The two main choices are Caesarea and Rome (some have also suggested Ephesus although there is no recorded imprisonment there in Acts). Most commentators opt for Rome, making this one of four 'prison epistles' from there (with Ephesians, Colossians and Philemon).

Origin of the church: Paul had planted a church in Philippi after seeing a vision of a man from Macedonia. His stay was relatively brief and ended after a riot following the exorcism of a fortune-teller. Her employers stood to lose a small fortune after she lost her powers, so they rioted. Paul and Silas were imprisoned but released after an earthquake, and then left the city (Acts 16:8-40)

CROSS CHECK

The person of Christ: pp 205, 213
Attitudes to the past: p 350
Death and eternal life: p 216
Disputes in the church: p 398

Humble pie nourishes spiritual growth

Philippians 2

Uriah Heep, a character in Charles Dickens' *David Copperfield*, exclaims 'When I was a young boy, I ate 'umble pie with an appetite. I'm very 'umble to the present moment, but I have a little power.' For most of us this is the limit of humility; we will take a back seat as long as we still have a little power.

Humility is not high on our agenda. There are numerous training videos and practical manuals on how to get your own way, win more customers, make more money, avoid being a dogsbody or an also-ran. Humility is seen as the sort of idea to leave for the monastery or retirement home.

Writing three decades after the crucifixion, Paul knew that life in Roman society was nasty, brutish and short. Babies were abandoned on the street. Public life was riddled with intrigue. Humility? Count others better than yourself? That was the quickest way to go to the wall. You needed a little power. But Jesus, he says, laid aside his power (v 7); and servants, in Paul's day, had no power.

That is what makes Christian living so radically different – and difficult. We have to let go of self-interest. Humility is the opposite of pride; it does the servant's job, as Jesus did at the last supper (John 13:1-17). We prefer, like the disciples, to do only that which enhances our image and status.

Humility sets aside personal interest and puts others' interests first. It welcomes their strengths and encourages their gifts. When Basil Hume, until 1999 leader of Britain's Roman Catholics, was a teacher he realised and always kept in mind that every child had at least one gift that was better than his own. Thinking like that is one practical way of developing humility. Everyone is unique; humility values them all and does not consider them to be rivals or threats.

Humility is essential for growth in purity and holiness (cf. v 15). The word comes from the Latin *humus* – that vital organic material which makes soil fertile. When we lay aside self-interest and put others first, whether they are colleagues or customers, relatives or friends, then the ground is being prepared for a crop of spiritual fruit.

Keeping hold of a little power is a quick way of sterilising the soil and neutralising the witness of the church.

But one thing I do: Forgetting what is behind and straining towards what is ahead, I press on towards the goal . . .

Philippians 3:13, 14

Location:

Philippi was a leading city in northern Greece (Macedonia). It was a Roman colony and home to many retired army officers

Place in Bible:

After Ephesians and before Colossians among Paul's letters in the New Testament

All members to lose their status

Philippians 2:5-11

Politicians rarely retire gracefully. The stories of China and the Soviet Union especially are littered with ageing leaders who clung to power and refused to step down.

In what may have been an early Christian hymn, Paul says that Jesus was just the opposite. He did not seek power, but he laid aside his majesty in order to share our humanity, because human salvation was more important to him than divine status (v 6).

Paul stresses that Jesus was fully God (v 6), but precisely what he meant by Jesus 'emptying' himself ('made himself nothing', v 7) caused considerable theological disputes in the past.

He does not mean that Jesus ceased to be God, but that Jesus accepted the limitations of humanity which necessarily restricted the way in which his deity could be displayed and exercised. He could not, for example, be everywhere at once.

Especially it means that he emptied out his whole life in death, as Paul goes on to stress (v 8), perhaps borrowing the phrase from Isaiah 53:12. In Jesus' crucifixion we see the true extent of his self-sacrifice. That God should allow himself to be killed is the ultimate way of 'making himself nothing'.

The example of Jesus sets a high standard. He himself taught that we too should lay aside claims to human status (cf. Matthew 23:8-12). There is to be no clinging to power in the church. Our identity and status comes from being 'in' Christ alone, to whom we are joined in one 'body'.

Paul cites the self-giving life of Epaphroditus who 'almost died for the work of Christ' as an example of what that could mean in practice (vv 25-30). Like Jesus, he did not cling to his life, and was willing to lose it. This is what it means to 'bow the knee' to Jesus and confess him Lord (vv 10,11).

Bury your past, don't praise it

Philippians 3

'I come to bury Caesar, not to praise him,' Mark Antony said in his famous speech in Shakespeare's *Julius Caesar*. Paul might have said that he came to bury the past, not to praise it. He had a brilliant pedigree by Jewish standards (vv 4-6) and he also had an impressive CV by Christian standards (cf. 2 Corinthians 11:16-33).

But he threw his medals in the bin, tore up his certificates and smeared his own reputation. The word he uses for rubbish (v 8) is the one we would use for dung or dog-food; the unusable residue of a feast. Only Christ is worth having, he claims.

This is a challenge to change. We can praise Christ for what he has done in and through us in the past (and sometimes we need to look back to remind ourselves of his power), but we cannot serve him by browsing in the photo album. Paul is like a fanatical athlete, always aiming for a higher jump, a faster time. What we have done can be bettered. Look for the opportunities and take them.

Secondly, it is a reminder of forgiveness. If some people live on past achievements, others are bowed by past traumas. The memory of past sins (of which Paul had many, 1 Timothy 1:15) can drain our confidence, make us feel useless. But the past has gone, the new has come (2 Corinthians 5:17). Sin is never held against us, and need not hold us back. That aspect of our past *is* buried with Christ (Romans 6:4); don't let the devil dig it up.

The secret of peace

Philippians 4:2-7

In 1973, an argument in the Afghan royal family became a war that lasted over two decades and is known as Russia's 'Vietnam'. Disputes can escalate.

There has been an argument in Philippi between two women. Paul doesn't want it to escalate; disputes cannot further the gospel and can fragment the church. He tells them to sort it out and asks others to become peacemakers (cf. Matthew 5:9).

In Colossians 3:15 Paul says that God's peace is to 'rule' us. He uses the word for the umpire at the Greek games: peace is to referee our churches. So when a dispute arises,

- if it is about doctrine, search the Scriptures together;
- if it is about behaviour, check if it is of primary (moral) or secondary (cultural) importance;
- if it is about church practice, pray further, listen to each other, and submit to leaders.

We can only do this if we have personal peace. Disputes will continue to simmer when people lack inner peace. Paul declares that peace is a gift from God but we can do two things in order to receive it.

First, we should rejoice together (v 4). Disputes or personal circumstances should not stop us praising God for who he is and what he has done. Praise lifts us up into his eternal presence and tunes us into his eternal purposes. Then, second, we are to trust him prayerfully (v 6), especially when something is perplexing or disturbing us.

The resulting peace is more lasting than vodka or valium. And it is neither the glazed-eye resignation of a cult devotee nor the trance-like oblivion of someone high on drugs.

The peace which passes understanding is an assurance that God is bigger than our problems, and an inner strength to see us through them as we trust him. The word 'guard' (v 7) means a garrison or fortress. The solid wall of God's peace protects us from anxiety while the referee of God's peace arbitrates in our relationships.

Get your thinking straight

Philippians 4:8-9

It used to be called 'the power of positive thinking' but now it's called 'neuro-linguistic programming' (NLP). This latest technique, popular in business circles, helps people to re-order their thinking patterns to maximise their creativity and productivity.

Paul says that Christians are to re-order their thinking patterns too. (In 12:2 he says this re-ordering is one of the Holy Spirit's tasks in us; here he reminds us that it requires our active co-operation.) Our transformed mind is to have a positive, Christ-centred world view (cf. 2 Corinthians 10:5).

Our thinking and decision-making must be governed by our knowledge of the existence, sovereignty and world-embracing purposes of God. His righteousness, justice, loveliness and love, holiness and truth mould our ideas.

So, Paul says, crowd out sinful, negative and untrue thoughts by pure and positive ones. When an angry, lustful or negative thought arrives, capture it with its Christ-centred opposite. The more we feed our minds on good things, the fewer negative ones will occur to us.

This may determine our viewing and reading, or the company we keep. We are not called to join an exclusive sect (cf. John 17:15), but there is no virtue in exposing ourselves unnecessarily to influences which compete with the Spirit's renewing work.

For today

- Don't let fear of death obscure your view of life
- Look for the virtues and value of others
- Don't live in the past; build on it and move on from it
- Gorge your mind on luxury thoughts of God and goodness

Down-to-earth advice for godly living

The Book of Proverbs

- Contains hundreds of pithy sayings about daily life
- Says that wisdom is more valuable than wealth
- Gives practical advice about relationships and conversation
- Exposes the short-sighted attitudes of 'the fool'

The book of Proverbs is blunt, earthy and practical. It belongs to the genre of 'wisdom' literature which was common in the ancient world. It is not a book from which to cull theology but it is a book to show how theology can be applied.

Commentator Derek Kidner writes, 'It is a book which seldom takes you to church . . . Its function in Scripture is to put godliness into working clothes; to name business and society as spheres in which we are to acquit ourselves with credit to our Lord, and in which we are to look for his training.'

Although rooted in the culture and lifestyle of an ancient world, much of its wisdom can be extrapolated into modern life. The advice to have honest scales (in which 'the LORD delights', 11:1) is fundamental to social order in any age, and the statement that getting drunk is unwise (20:1) has always been rued by those who ignore it.

The book originates from the sayings of a class of 'wise men' in ancient Israel, from the time of Solomon onwards. They seem to have been given a status close to that of the priests and prophets as guides of God's people (cf. Jeremiah 18:18). Other cultures had them too, but we know little of how they operated.

This is a book to be read in short sections, and meditated upon. It is perfectly possible to dip into it at random and gain some insight, encouragement or warning – a practice which is inadvisable for any other Bible book.

AT A GLANCE

PROVERBS

The book of Proverbs is a haphazard collection of sayings and there is rarely a theme to any of its chapters. The book consists of several separate collections of sayings, and these are:

1-9	The value of wisdom
10:1-22: 16	The proverbs of Solomon
22:17-24:34	Two collections of 'Sayings of the wise men'
25-29	Proverbs of Solomon collected by Hezekiah
30	The sayings of Agur
31:1-9	The sayings of King Lemuel
31:10-31	An alphabetical celebration of the ideal wife

Trust in the LORD with all your heart and lean not on your own understanding; in all your ways acknowledge him, and he will make your paths straight.

Proverbs 3:5,6

Better than winning the lottery

e.g. Proverbs 8

Today, wisdom is not often praised as a virtue, but that is partly because we have other ways of describing it. Knowing what is the right thing to do; avoiding mistakes we might regret; keeping our eyes open; seeing all sides of a situation; not being driven by foolish desires.

Wisdom is the mind controlling the heart, the heart informing the mind, and both subjected to the law and leading of God. As a result, compassion, thoughtfulness and generosity are displayed in social relationships, and blind impulse gives way to far-sighted consideration.

Throughout the book wisdom is lauded as something to be treasured. It produces better returns than monetary wealth (3:13,14), and is more attractive than a bride's garland (1:8,9); it is the supreme principle of successful living. Get wisdom and you get a lot else thrown in.

Living by wisdom is living God's way, in harmony with the rules and constraints which he built into creation. With it, we can avoid the pitfalls of sin (2:9-11), look forward to a rewarding life (3:1,2) and enjoy protection from needless danger (4:6).

The author of the first section seems so carried away by his theme that he personifies wisdom, elevating it almost to divine status, but being a Jew, he cannot be suggesting that there is a real divinity named Wisdom.

Christians can see the imagery as a pale foreshadowing of the New Testament image of Jesus as the divine 'Word' (Logos) in John 1:1. But it would be stretching the Old Testament too far to suggest that Wisdom in Proverbs 8 is an exact portrayal of the Second Person of the Trinity.

Instead, he is using a poetic image to convey a truth. In human affairs, wisdom is supreme; everything worthwhile in life depends on it, just as life itself depends on God. But the ability to live wisely as God intended does not come naturally; it has to be sought and learned, just as God waits for us to turn to him and does not force himself upon us.

The Word made flesh is the source of our wisdom which is mediated through the Holy Spirit (1 Corinthians 2:6-10; John 16:7,8,13). And the New Testament agrees that to become a human trait, wisdom needs first to be received as a divine gift (James 1:5). The fact that it restrains the excesses we rather enjoy may be one reason why we don't seek it with the same urgency as did the authors of Proverbs.

Author/compiler: The book contains several collections. Named authors are Solomon, 10:1; and Agur (30:1) and Lemuel (31:1) both of whom are otherwise unknown. Hezekiah is credited with another collection of Solomon's sayings (25:1). Who finally grouped them is unknown.

Date of compilation: Solomon is credited in 1Kings 4:32 with having devised 3,000 proverbs and assuming that those ascribed to him here are genuine, then much of the book dates from the time around 950 BC. Hezekiah lived 250 years later (c. 715-686 BC) so his collection must be from that period. It would seem likely, especially in view of Jeremiah's comment (18:18) that the book was substantially completed well before the time of the exile.

Parallels in other cultures: Just as other Near Eastern cultures had law codes which bear some similarity to parts of Israel's, so they also had 'wise men' and 'proverbs'. The Queen of Sheba trekked from Yemen to Israel because of Solomon's undisputed supremacy in the art of wisdom (1 Kings 10:1). Collections of proverbs and wise sayings are known to have existed in Egypt and Babylonia even before Solomon's time.

Where am I?

Place in Bible:
After Psalms and before Ecclesiastes in the Old Testament

Belongs with:
Job, Ecclesiastes, and the Song of Songs as 'Wisdom literature'. Also has affinities with Ecclesiasticus in the Apocrypha

Period of history:
Relates to the monarchy from Solomon onwards

Be kind, be careful

Most Western people tend to be cautious when it comes to giving money or sharing possessions. Finding the balance between being generous or foolhardy on the one hand, and selfish or uncaring on the other, is not easy.

Proverbs suggests two principles to inform our actions. One is to help the poor. Under no circumstances are we to take advantage of them (22:22). To pour scorn on them is to insult our Maker (17:5) while being kind to the poor is like lending to God (19:17).

This is echoed in Jesus' parable of the sheep and the goats (Matthew 25:31-46) in which acts of kindness to others are in fact done to God.

It is unwise to withhold good from those who deserve it (3:27), but wisdom requires more than just being nice to nice people. 'If your enemy is hungry, feed him' (25:21,22) was directly quoted by Paul in Romans 12:20 and alluded to by Jesus in Luke 6:27-30. If nothing else, it makes black deeds even worse, which is the meaning of 'heaping coals of fire on their heads'.

The second principle is that while love may be blind, wisdom isn't. Proverbs draws the line of generosity at standing surety for someone else or 'you will surely suffer' (11:15). It even urges the person who has already underwritten a deal to free themselves from it even if it humiliates them to do so (6:1-5).

It is worth asking why. Human nature probably relaxes when it knows that it is not ultimately responsible for a debt or agreement. It is easy to default after a while. Wisdom acts responsibly, but it encourages responsibility in others, too.

Be a good neighbour, turn down the noise

Few of us have been tempted to remove our neighbour's boundary stone (22:28), although some may have been embroiled in disputes with neighbours over hedges or access lanes. But this quaint injunction from a culture in which property was only marked on the ground (there were no written deeds) introduces a principle which all can follow.

It is simply a practical way of saying, 'love your neighbour as yourself in deed as well as in word'. Making life awkward for someone is wrong, but we might not realise that it is unwise unless we are told. Consideration for others promotes good community relations that can do so much to make a person's life more enjoyable and secure even if their circumstances are difficult.

Wisdom, therefore, is not just about keeping the law. It is also about promoting *shalom,* well-being, within the community. That includes not being a noisy neighbour, although the author seems to despair of lifting the eternal curse on people living in close proximity (27:14)!

It is foolish to get revenge on a neighbour for one offence by committing another (24:28,29); it just breeds more bad feeling. Relations with neighbours are to be cultivated for practical reasons, too; they may be the nearest people on hand when we're in trouble (27:10).

People today desire community, lasting relationships within which they feel comfortable, respected and cared for. Proverbs says that community begins when I start to care for and respect others.

God be in our understanding

Proverbs assumes the spiritual dimension. Scattered through the book are reminders that 'the fear [i.e. respect for and worship of] the LORD is the beginning of wisdom' (1:7). Faith is like a fountain keeping our life fresh and productive (14:27).

With the prophets, Proverbs asserts that sacrifice without faith is detestable to a God who looks for inner truth rather than outward conformity (15:8, 26). Therefore we should confess our sins in order to find mercy (28:13) and accept God's 'discipline' as a means of spiritual growth (3:11). Only then will we be sure of receiving his guidance through the maze of life (3:5; 19:21).

Work hard whatever the reward you get

The so-called Protestant work ethic, for all its bad press, has some scriptural foundations, not least because aspects of it are commonsense. The person who uses his resources eats; the dreamer is courting trouble (12:11).

The encouragement to meditate upon an ants' nest whenever one gets the itch to ease up (6:6-11) reminds us that poverty creeps up on us quickly and no one owes us a living. Those who can enjoy free lunches are a tiny minority who run the risk of pride.

Proverbs is not content with stating the obvious. Wisdom comes from the willingness to make, and be content with, an honest living even if its standard is relatively low. A little with peace of mind is better than a fortune wrapped up in trouble, and simple food with a little love is better than luxury embittered by hatred (15:16,17).

Nor is there any point in wearing ourselves out with making a million; there is more to life, Proverbs reminds us, than a fat bank balance (23:4; cf. Jesus' similar teaching in Luke 12:15). Pleasure-lovers should be aware that money goes faster than it comes (21:17) and that indulgence can damage your health (21:25).

This worldly wisdom, paralleled in any modern self-help book, is consistent with the Bible's concern for the whole of human life. Believers can be as foolish as anyone. Besides, work is one of God's gifts to humankind and part of his perfect purpose.

To work honestly and live soberly is an element of living 'in the fear of the LORD'. It's what we were made for; we should not spiritualise it away.

Friends are for life

Close friends were greatly valued in ancient times but are comparatively rare today. In a more mobile society, we have instead many acquaintances, but that is not the same thing.

Friends have one great advantage over family – they often retain a greater 'distance' from us that results in more respect but does not diminish their ability to criticise or rebuke us. We can be open and honest with each other without being rude or abusive.

Real friends, according to Proverbs, love at all times (17:17) and not just when it suits them. They will stick closer than a good brother (18:24), which has sometimes been compared with Jesus' declaration that his followers are his friends (John 15:15).

That kind of friendship cannot be bought (cf. 19:6). The wise person listens carefully when a friend says something which hurts; they take no notice of the flattery of an admirer (27:6). The humorist Spike Milligan once said, 'Money can't buy friends but you get a better class of enemy.'

Hold your tongue!

According to researchers, politicians and actors (among others) talk so much that they give themselves bad breath. Proverbs suggests that wisdom bites its tongue for deeper reasons.

A person who speaks rashly 'comes to ruin' socially if not materially (13:3), so listen before you give others the benefit of your opinion (18:13). Rash words can cause as much damage as an unsheathed sword, whereas the considered comments of a wise person are like a healing balm (12:18).

Many of our words are a waste of breath; but while the fool 'gushes folly' (15:2) a timely word is good (15:23). Pleasant words are as sweet to the ear and heart as honey to the taste-buds (16:24).

The wise person is patient and thus calms a quarrel (15:18). Wisdom is even-tempered (17:27) offering gentle responses to 'turn away wrath' (15:1).

Lying is the height of folly and detested by God (12:22). Honesty is 'like a kiss on the lips' (24:26). Gossip betrays confidences (11:13) and breaks up relationships (16:28); we never know the damage it may cause. Foolish talk is self-indulgent and arrogant; it is just plain sin (10:19).

Usually we talk too much either because we are nervous or because we want to impress. Proverbs, in common with the rest of the Bible, suggests that as our confidence is in God there is no need to ingratiate ourselves with others. Wise people therefore avoid those who talk too much (20:19).

Family discipline is no laughing matter

The author of Proverbs seems at times to descend to the level of a comedian devoid of any sense of political correctness. He asserts that a nagging wife is as irritating as a dripping tap (19:13), and that a man is better off camping on the flat roof than living under it with a bad-tempered spouse (21:9).

He is not a chauvinistic dinosaur whose extinction is long overdue. He did live in a predominantly (but not exclusively) patriarchal society, but such observations still contain pearls of wisdom. A close family relationship is ruined if one partner berates or dominates the other. We may let our hair down too much at home.

Similarly, the model for a 'godly wife' in chapter 31 (which does not presuppose an idle husband sitting in the pub while she does all the hard work) carries a clear reminder that domestic bliss is only achieved with effort. What we put into home-making adds to the enjoyment of family life.

Proverbs' teaching on parenting stresses discipline and assumes physical punishment of children (as has every generation except those born since the Second World War). However, the suggestion that 'he who spares the rod spoils the child' (13:24) simply reminds us that discipline of some kind is vital (cf. 22:6). The lawlessness portrayed in William Golding's *Lord of the Flies* becomes normal when children are allowed to run wild.

Children won't thank the author for suggesting that wise sons listen to their fathers (13:1) until they become fathers themselves, but the point needs making. The fool who despises his mother (15:20) is callously rubbishing her former nurture and is contributing to the breakdown of community.

Family life is a fine thread and easily frayed, if not snapped. Proverbs suggests that everyone, from the youngest to the oldest, has a part to play in holding together the basic social unit created by God for the welfare of the whole human race.

HARD Question

Can life be so cut and dried!

Proverbs contains the sort of platitudes for which Job's 'comforters' were rightly rebuked (see section on Job and feature on suffering). It suggests, for example, that the righteous will prosper and the wicked will be destroyed (e.g. 10:6).

The serious Bible reader has to ask why such statements are included here if they are denied (at least indirectly) elsewhere. They seem to fuel the charge that the Bible contradicts itself. The start of an answer is that God promises to correct injustice at the last day, when the wicked will indeed be destroyed. At that level, there is no contradiction, just a time lapse between promise and fulfilment.

That is not altogether satisfactory, because the Old Testament statements relate specifically to this life. While the writers had a limited concept of an afterlife, they did believe in a God of justice. They therefore projected his justice into their current experience.

Behind these claims is an inalienable principle – doing right is best in the long term for personal and social welfare, bringing a sense of well-being and encouraging (although not guaranteeing) kindness from others.

Examples of righteousness may promote respect and trust in society. Upright people may be given greater responsibility, for the benefit of all (cf. Jesus' parable about the honest managers in Luke 19:11-26). Conversely, people's sins may find them out and the perpetrators suffer emotionally, physically, socially or spiritually as a result.

The assertions in Proverbs are one side of the biblical coin. They are not meant to convey the whole truth. They embody a general principle, not a universal law. Proverbs acknowledges that wickedness may earn itself a fat (although deceptive) reward (11:18).

HARD Question

Is everything already decided?

If we only had Proverbs, we might conclude that life is already mapped out for us by God. Human creativity exists only to fulfil a pre-determined plan. 'Many are the plans in a man's heart, but it is the LORD'S purpose that prevails' (19:21). Even the lottery is divinely rigged: 'The lot is cast into the lap, but its every decision is from the LORD' (16:33).

This is close to the fatalism which is reflected today in some aspects of Islam. That is partly because the Old Testament writers are very conscious of God's intimate involvement with human life.

But behind the assertion of guidance is the assumption of commitment, clearly stated in 3:5,6. It is those who seek God's honour and ask for his assistance in all their ways who are assured of his guiding and protecting presence, even when to human eyes chance and necessity seem to reign.

God is so perfect in understanding and powerful in his providential activity that he can weave even the activities of those who ignore him into his purposes for his people (cf. Romans 8:28). And, of course, people without faith may also recognise and acknowledge his general care which is meant to draw them more fully to himself. Proverbs is reminding us that God is a loving Father.

For today

- Knowing how to do the right thing will be better for you than knowing how to get rich
- Don't be mean; look for ways of helping others
- Work at your friendships because people need people
- There's no such thing as a free lunch – so don't expect to live without working
- Don't gossip about people and don't slant the facts; be truthful in everything

Poetry scales heights and plumbs depths

Crisp, graphic language – which is the common thread of all poetry – captures mood and emotion more vividly than mere prose. 'My heart pounds, my strength fails me; even the light has gone from my eyes' is far more evocative than 'everything has gone wrong at once'. We can identify with the feelings even if the circumstances are unknown.

Similarly, many spiritual experiences and theological truths cannot be captured fully in prosaic definitions or formulae. 'The voice of the LORD is over the waters; the God of glory thunders' (29:3) evokes a 'picture' of God's majesty by linking him to the awesome power of nature seen in a storm. 'God is more powerful than anything else' is tame, even if true.

That is the genius of Psalms. All human experience is here, from ecstatic joy to despairing pain. And, to many modern readers' surprise, there are complaints and even imprecations – curses – scattered among the 150 poems.

Old Testament believers knew how to bare their souls to God. They reckoned that a covenant-keeping God could cope with their exasperation, for they knew he could not allow his people to suffer oppression for ever.

Many psalms relate to specific historical events. A few can be traced, and others can be described in general terms. Frequently they concern the nation's fortunes rather than the individual's. Understanding them can help us enter into the writer's concerns.

Today's readers need to approach the psalms carefully. Do not look for neat theological formulae. We are meant to feel, rather than analyse, the outpourings of praise or pain. They are to be read meditatively. Ask first, what is the writer trying to express? And then, what insight does he have into God or the human condition which we can learn from, or meditate on?

PSALMS

1 The godly are blessed
2 The Lord is king of kings
3 God protects me against my enemies
4 Please hear my prayer
5 The wicked cannot be trusted, but God can
6 Heal me, for I am struggling
7 Rise up against my enemies, Lord
8 God has honoured mankind
9 The Lord reigns for ever: lift me up, Lord
10 Why do you hide when there's trouble, Lord?
11 The Lord is righteous
12 Protect us from the wicked, Lord
13 Where has God gone?
14 Foolish people ignore the Lord
15 Only those who honour you can enter your house
16 I put my trust in the Lord
17 I keep myself righteous, and the Lord protects me
18 The Lord is a rock, and he rescues me
19 God's truth is supreme
20 A prayer that God may bless us
21 The king rejoices in God
22 Why have you forsaken me?
23 The Lord is my shepherd
24 Everything belongs to God who is great
25 I trust you Lord; please guide me
26 I've kept your word; please help me
27 I need not be afraid
28 Hear us and save us, O Lord
29 The Lord is enthroned for ever
30 The Lord turns sorrow into joy
31 I trust you Lord despite my problems
32 God forgives our sins
33 Praise God for all he does
34 The Lord delivered me from all my fears

35 A prayer against the wicked
36 Your love cannot be measured, Lord
37 Don't fret over the wicked; trust the Lord
38 The cry of someone in pain
39 My life is short but God is my hope
40 The Lord is my rescuer
41 Protect the weak, as God does
42 I long for the Lord who seems far away
43 I'm depressed but I'll trust God
44 You did much in the past; do it again, Lord
45 The king's praise on his wedding day
46 God is our refuge
47 The Lord is king
48 The city of God is secure
49 Don't trust in riches
50 A meditation on worship
51 Save me from my sin, O Lord
52 God will bring the wicked to ruin
53 People have turned from God
54 A prayer for protection
55 A prayer for help when friends betray you
56 A prayer for support in dangerous times
57 People are out to get me
58 May God sort out the world's mess
59 Protect me against my enemies
60 A prayer for national deliverance
61 I want to find you again, Lord
62 God is stronger than my enemies
63 I'm thirsty for you in troubled times
64 A prayer for protection from conspirators
65 Praise for answered prayer
66 Praise God for all he has done
67 A prayer for God's blessing
68 A song of praise for a procession
69 An urgent prayer for protection
70 Come quickly, Lord! I need you
71 An old person's prayer for continued help
72 God save the king
73 I will serve God even when wickedness seems to pay
74 Come and protect us against the mockers, Lord
75 God will keep us secure
76 God is our great protector
77 A meditation on God's help in trouble
78 A call to remember the lessons of history
79 A cry for help against invaders
80 Restore us again, O Lord
81 Remember the warnings of the past
82 A call for justice
83 May our enemies be crushed
84 I love your house, O Lord
85 Restore our fortunes, Lord
86 I'm fragile and I need your help
87 Glorious things are spoken of Zion
88 A cry for help from the pits
89 A lament for the loss of national identity
90 God is holy and we are lamentably sinful
91 We are safe in God's shelter
92 Acts of God make me glad
93 The Lord reigns!
94 The Lord will destroy the wicked
95 'The Venite' – a call to worship
96 Let everyone praise the Lord
97 The Lord is awesome
98 'The Cantate Domino' – sing to the Lord a new song
99 The Lord is King
100 The Lord is faithful
101I will be faithful to you, Lord
102 Aprayer for God's help when under pressure
103 A song of thanksgiving
104 A celebration of God's creation
105 Thanksgiving for God's covenant with Abraham and Moses
106 God's faithfulness despite the people's rebellion
107 Thanksgiving for God's faithfulness
108 A prayer for help against God's enemies
109 The prayer of one falsely accused
110 The role of the King-Priest (Messiah)
111 Praise for God's steadfastness
112 The blessedness of following God
113 Praise for the Lord's love for the lowly
114 A celebration of the exodus
115 God is the helper of his people
116 I love the Lord for he rescued me
117 The shortest psalm – a chorus of
118 Thanksgiving for God's deliverance
119 The longest psalm – a meditation on God's word
120 A call for God's help
121 A pilgrim's song
122 Pray for the peace of Jerusalem
123 A prayer of humility
124 Praise for deliverance
125 The Lord surrounds his people
126 Praise on returning from exile in Babylon
127 Put God at the centre of your family
128 Blessed is the man who trusts God
129 May God's opponents wither like a leaf
130 God forgives those who wait for him
131 An ordinary person's trust in the Lord
132 A prayer for the king
133 A celebration of unity
134 A response in a worship service
135 The Lord is greater than all
136 His love endures for ever
137 A lament of the exiles in Babylon
138 Thanksgiving for God's help
139 I am fully open to you, Lord
140 Rescue me from evil men
141 Don't let me fall into the snares of the wicked
142 I am in desperate need
143 Help, Lord, my enemies are chasing me
144 A king's prayer for victory
145 The Lord is gracious and compassionate
146 Trust the Lord and no one else
147 Praise God for his support
148 Let everything praise the Lord
149 Praise God for his salvation
150 Hallelujah! Praise the Lord!

The Book of Psalms:

- Contains 150 Hebrew poems from varying periods of history
- Expresses praise to God for his greatness and deliverance
- Cries to God for help in times of trouble and oppression
- Recounts the acts of God in the history of Israel

Prophetic edge gives wider meaning

Psalm 2

When we turn to examine what the prophets of the Bible wrote (or said) we see that their words were not always understood in the way we interpret them today, nor in the way some New Testament writers quote them. Some of the psalms also have this 'prophetic' element which was at least partially hidden from the writers (cf. 1 Peter 1:10-12).

This is one such. Verse 7 was used at Jesus' baptism and the letter to the Hebrews begins by quoting it (1:5). Verse 8 is echoed in Jesus' 'great commission' and verse 9 is picked up in the vision of Christ's cosmic rule (Revelation 12:5; 19:15). The first Christians saw it as clearly messianic in their prayer in Acts 4:25,26.

At one level, therefore, we can say that in hindsight the whole Bible points towards Jesus. But it would be wrong to take this psalm, and others like it, simply as poetic forecasts. It meant something to the author at the time also, which is where all biblical interpretation should start.

It rejoices in typical Middle-Eastern terms at the king's relationship to God as his son, and the king's relationship to subservient nations as their 'father'. When church and state are separated, as they mostly are today, it is hard to think of kings as divine appointments, but they did in Old Testament times, which is what the psalm celebrates.

Today's readers can apply the worship and praise in two ways. We can use its prophetic imagery to reflect on the greatness of Jesus. Also, we can use it to reflect on our own relationship with God as his children, privileged to serve as his fellow workers and ambassadors in the world (1 Corinthians 3:9; 2 Corinthians 5:20).

FAST facts

Structure: The Psalter is divided into five books: 1-41; 42-72; 73-89; 90-106; 107-150. While each section has a similar upbeat conclusion (with such words as 'Blessed be the God of Israel') there is no thematic or chronological thread holding any of the books together.

Authors: David is credited with 73 of them. He was still remembered as a musician (1 Samuel 16:14,15) and a poet (2 Samuel 1:17-18) 300 years later (Amos 6:5). A few are attributed to named people (such as Moses, 90), some to a school of musicians (the sons of Korah, as in 87), some are anonymous (such as 'the prayer of an afflicted man', 102).

Style of poetry: Hebrew poetry is unlike the traditional Western style of rhythmic syllables. It is almost blank verse with the 'poetic' element is in the imagery and association of ideas. The commonest style is 'parallelism', in which an idea is repeated in another way in the second line. This is subject to numerous variations such as line two magnifies an aspect of line one.

Musical notation: We do not know what the tunes were, nor how they were transmitted. Some of the headings include musical instructions: 'with stringed instruments' (67) is obvious but 'A *miktam*' (16) 'A *maskil*' (32) are unknown musical terms. Translators can only guess that 'To Lilies' (45) means 'to the tune "Lilies"'. We should not assume that Gregorian plainsong or similar classical settings of the psalms, beautiful and uplifting though they may be, resemble the way that David and the sons of Korah sung them.

Date of compilation: The books were probably put together over a long period, and may have changed shape before being taken into the canon of Scripture perhaps in the third century BC.

Prayer makes sense in real life drama

Psalm 3 (cf. 2 Samuel 15)

Over a dozen of the psalms attributed to David are also linked in their title to specific incidents in his life. Others were clearly linked to events too, but we are not told what they were.

Where possible, it is helpful to read the psalm alongside the historical passage to which it refers. We can learn much from the author's reaction to a specific event with which we can identify to an extent.

This psalm recalls one of the most poignant times in David's life. Having been a fugitive from Saul for so long, he has now become a fugitive from his own son. Absalom has growing support, and David is aware that he is not himself blameless. He is reaping something of the violence he has shown (note his acceptance of Shimei's rebuke in 2 Samuel 16:7-10).

But he has learned from the past, too. Although the trouble and stress is something he could do without in his middle years, the former giant-killer has not forgotten that God can be trusted in a way which banishes the worst excesses of human anxiety: sleeplessness (vv 5,6).

Many people can identify with the mixed feelings expressed here. Things go wrong which hurt, but which are also linked to our past decisions and deeds. David encourages us to accept the situation and to trust God to see us through it.

He does not tell God exactly how to rectify it, however. The sad outcome – Absalom's death – was not what David desired. That happened after the psalm was written; David had to be willing to accept any outcome, which perhaps was the hardest thing of all.

A little angel

Psalm 8

Generally speaking, human beings have too small a picture of God and too big a picture of themselves. This psalm corrects the balance in a context of wonder and praise.

The greatness of God is a common theme in the book of Psalms which often cites the acts of God as evidence for it. Just occasionally, as here, an author looks around at the incredible size and magnificence of the physical creation and praises the Creator who must be even more wonderful.

Compared to the majesty of God, humankind is a miracle. So small and frail, yet given such status and responsibility. This is the true perspective of worship. It does not belittle human ability and life; rather it celebrates it in the context of a great God who has declared himself to love all creatures great and small.

Such an attitude prevents idolatry and self-centredness, but also avoids any sense of worthlessness and lack of human purpose. It is sorely needed today as on the one hand people exert themselves over others and on the other despair of finding meaning and significance for their lives.

For great is the LORD and most worthy of praise; he is to be feared above all gods . . . Splendour and majesty are before him; strength and glory are in his sanctuary.

Psalm 96:4,6

A big fool

Psalm 14

The psalms are not gathered in any thematic order, but this one, coming hard on the heels of Psalm 8, helps to keep the biblical view of human nature in balance. People may be special, but they are also sinful.

The essence of sin in Scripture is turning one's back on God, rather than the specific acts which may then result. Hence someone living a 'good life' can still be regarded as sinful. That helps to explain why this psalm declares that no one does good (v 3); as Jesus pointed out to the rich young man, 'no one is good – except God alone' (Mark 10:18).

We can never match up to God's standards of holiness and perfection. And the overtly sinful, the people who do take advantage of others, cause distress; their victims can take some comfort in knowing that the Lord is ready to support them (v 6).

The psalm concludes with a common theme in Psalms, that of God's justice. The authors often recognise that all is not well with the world, but they never lose their faith that God is a righteous Judge. So here, David prays for justice, as can anyone who, like him, observes the inequity of life with alarm.

Its speech never ends

Psalm 19

The poetry here uses the Hebrew method of parallelism in a different way: having extolled the wonders of creation as a vehicle of God's revelation, it parallels that by extolling his everlasting truth as also a vehicle of revelation. Both are unending, stable and to be praised.

The 'voice' of creation (v 2) is probably intended to be figurative rather than a hint at some mystical communication between its elements. It 'speaks' to us in wordless praise of the magnificence and eternity of the Creator.

So too does his word, which makes specific what is only implicit in creation. Enshrined in Scripture, God's truth is bottomless in its depth, endless in its scope. Delving into it is described here as more than a pleasure; David is almost ecstatic about it. His attitude makes much of our perfunctory Bible reading look rather shabby.

God is all you need

Psalm 23

Life tends to be complicated. For example, there are very few blanket insurance policies which cover every need and eventuality. You have to take out separate policies for your house, car, holiday, health, income and life.

Just as we shop around for specific insurance cover and appliances for specific needs, we tend to shop in the spiritual marketplace for a variety of personal needs: we look to meetings, techniques or people to provide for us. This famous psalm suggests that it is God who will provide all that we want or need, and we should look first to him.

- He is my shepherd (v 1): his guidance and provision is unique to and adequate for each person
- He provides peace and rest in the midst of hassles (v 2)
- He reveals what is right and wrong (v 3)
- His powerful presence can conquer loneliness, fear and death (v 4)
- He resources us to serve him from his rich treasury (v 5)
- He gives emotional as well as practical support (v 6).

Do the righteous really prosper?

e.g. Psalm 37

A number of psalms suggest that the person who honours God will prosper, while the 'wicked' will wither. In this one, 'the wicked will perish' (v 20) while the righteous are never 'forsaken' (v 25) and 'will enjoy plenty' (v 19) in times of famine.

It raises the question of whether God does in fact promise that his people will never suffer poverty or famine. Other psalms may seem to suggest further that they will actually prosper materially more than others, and verse 4 here is often taken as a 'promise' of good things.

The book of Job deals with the inequities of life, and this psalm does not ignore them. The righteous may only have 'a little' in comparison to the wealth of the wicked (v 16) and they are not exempt from participation in 'the times of disaster' (v 19).

Some of those who promulgate the so-called 'prosperity gospel' today may seek to justify their own wealth in terms of their godliness and prayers of faith, which is a form of pride. Despite their assertions, the Bible does not offer simple equations that right living makes us rich, or even comfortable.

The dynamics are more complex. The Bible does promise that God 'will supply all our needs' (Philippians 4:19), but that is in a very specific context. Paul is commenting on sacrificial giving; he is saying, in effect, that God will ensure we do not lose out when we show such extreme love to others.

There was a strong bond of fellowship in the early church that ensured that those who were short were helped by those who had plenty; God supplied needs through close community ties. When Jesus spoke of God giving us 'all these things' (food and clothes, Matthew 6:33) the stress is on keeping worship and money-making in proportion. It is not a slot-machine promise: do this, get that.

We should also remember that the psalms were written in a pre-Christian context in which the simple equation was made, with which Job and others struggled as they awaited further revelation. The psalms are primarily statements of personal faith and trust, rather than statements of universal laws.

Drink is the answer

Psalm 42

There can be many causes of depression. Sometimes it stems from inner, unresolved conflict; an obsessive and unattainable desire; or anger and resentment against someone. At other times it may arise from a sense of guilt. It can also have physical causes such as tiredness or hormonal imbalance.

The psalmist does not know why he feels low, and sometimes neither do we. He handles his feelings by hoping in God because he knows that one day he will praise him again (v 5) – hope can shorten depression. He also remembers happy, pleasant things (v 7) and keeps his Bible and hymnbook open (v 8).

But above all he feels thirsty – for God himself, not just for what God can do (v 2). He's as desperate for a drink from God's eternal stream of life (cf. John 4:14) as an alcoholic suffering withdrawal or a dying traveller in a desert struggling towards an oasis.

It's not often we thirst for God like that. And it's a pity when we do it is only at times of crisis. The stream is on tap all the time.

Cling to the past

Psalm 44

This is written at a time of military defeat. We can probably identify at least with the sense of heaviness and hopelessness that arises when some Christian scheme flounders, perhaps at the hands of unbelievers. We can follow the psalmist's example in dealing with it.

- **He recalls the past achievements of God (vv 1-3).** History is written for our learning; life was not always like this, and God has acted powerfully in the past. The problem has not arisen because God is impotent.
- **He reflects on the present absence of God (vv 4-16).** The psalmist meditates on God's unchanging greatness (vv 4-8) then pours out his heart in sorrow because God didn't intervene to prevent the disaster (vv 9-16).
- **He returns with a prayerful approach to God (vv 17-26).** He protests the nation's innocence: this was not deserved (vv 17-22). Sometimes we grub around for hidden sins when God is simply testing our faith. So then the psalmist hammers at heaven's door (vv 23-26).

God keeps his covenant and will never forget his promises. He is also unchanging. What he has done before he can and often will do (in perhaps different ways) in the future.

Still life

Psalm 46

The world is regularly shaken by disasters: famines in Africa, typhoons in the Far East, tornadoes in North America. And there is always the lurking fear of war or terrorist attack. And in our own lives, nature may be calm, but the human world around us is chaotic. It's all there in verses 2 and 3. But there is a place of stability: the abode of God (vv 4-07). For the writer, this was symbolised by the strong hill-city of Jerusalem watered by the figurative river of God's spiritual life. Today we may need to devise other symbols but the truth remains: God is always a refuge and a helper (v 1).

When the winds blow or the earth heaves – physically or metaphorically – the last thing to do is panic. The first thing to do is be still and recall that God is greater (vv 8-10). Then we won't need to panic.

Sin's greatest victim

Psalm 51

This well-known psalm, often used devotionally by people convicted by guilt, is David's own lament after the shabby affair with Bathsheba and his unprincipled contract killing of her husband Uriah (2 Samuel 11,12).

David exhibits all the standard symptoms of guilt. He feels dirty (v 2), he cannot forget it (v 3), his whole life seems tainted by it (v 5), he feels rotten inside (v 6), tired and lethargic (v 8).

But he also recognises that he has done something worse than rape and murder. He has offended God by breaking God's law and following his own desires (vv 3,4). That is true of the least sin to the greatest. God hurts because any sin is a slap in his face by a selfish person.

David does the sensible thing and asks for mercy (v 1), cleansing (v 7) and renewal (vv 10-12). This is not an easy substitute for apologising to others and making human amends. Confession to God opens us to receive the divine strength necessary to make those apologies and amends.

God's forgiveness, which of course cost him dearly (in the death of his Son) then opens the way to a renewed vision and service (vv 13-19). Sin is serious, but it is not the end.

I want to fly away from this!

Psalm 55

Et tu, Brute? Shakespeare's dying Caesar, surprise and bewilderment on his face, suffers the ultimate blow: betrayal by his friend Brutus. Betrayal is sickening, devastating, to the person betrayed. It drains them of energy and the will to live. David, in this psalm lamenting his betrayal by an anonymous friend in a court conspiracy, wants only to fly away.

Despite the classical song and some Bible translations, David says '. . . for wings *like* a dove' (v 6). He has probably seen one fluttering gently away from the palace roof. The dove suits his melancholy more than an eagle, whose strong wings would provide the obvious image of someone's desire to rise above trouble. David wants peace and calmness, too.

Pause over David's emotion here, and recall that this is sadly a common experience. David clings to God and trusts his justice (vv 22,23), but not without a real struggle. Try to feel what he feels. It is easier than we think to become a Brutus or a Judas when the pressure is on. To cause misery to someone who has been faithful to us is not only cruel, it is wicked.

They've destroyed my church

Psalm 74

Before the Russian Revolution, there were about 1,000 monasteries within the thriving Orthodox Church. The number was reduced rapidly to just 17 until the reforms of the late 1980s. Just as things were improving there, however, many Protestant churches were closed in Ethiopia as part of a secularisation programme.

The tide of church fortune ebbs and flows through history. Sometimes Christians can only stand by and watch as forces outside their control restrict or even destroy church life and activity. Here, the psalmist laments the official vandalism which destroyed the temple (vv 4-9) before Judah's exile to Babylon.

But he can still praise God as King, Saviour and Creator (vv 12-17). God never changes, and to recall those aspects of his character helps us to keep life in perspective even when we are persecuted. On that basis, we can pray for deliverance (vv 18-23).

Persecuted Christians are often drawn closer to God by their experience. But it is never easy. It still goes on today in some countries, and prayer for the suffering church is always needed.

Who's got a big mouth?

Psalm 81

Persian kings used to perform an odd custom for their honoured guests: they would stuff the visitors' mouths with sweets or even jewels. Today in Indonesia, and other Eastern countries, wedding couples feed each other at the banquet with their fingers. Such customs lend new meaning to the strange offer in verse 10b.

It means that God will abundantly bless those who are open to him. It acts as a transition between the praise of verses 1-9 and the warnings of verses 11-15. The theme of sweet gifts returns in verse 16.

Used at Israelite festivals, this psalm reminds us that praise and sober reflection go together. Look at the potential blessings, the author says, and note that we can easily miss them.

God keeps his promises, in time

Psalm 89

This is an uplifting song of praise for God's covenant with David, which breaks into a lament that the impossible seems to have happened: God appears to have broken his side of the bargain (vv 38-43). That cannot be (vv 30-37), but once again we are taken into the angst of the human situation.

This psalm is full of intense symbolism that needs to be 'seen' rather than studied. For example, 'the council of the holy ones' (v 7) is not meant to imply a heavenly court such as the Greek myths portrayed, with furious debates and arguments over how to rule the earth. Nor is it meant to imply some secondary order of spiritual beings to whom such rule is delegated.

But it does support what the Bible elsewhere also implies, that in heaven God is worshipped and respected by unearthly beings. The picture is that of a God who is head of a community, not one who dwells in splendid isolation.

The writer's frustration is increased by his awareness that human life is very fragile (vv 47,48). He doesn't have much time left. He could be snuffed out at any minute. God's timescale seems too long for humans to bear. It is a common feeling, which reminds readers of all generations that we can only make sense of life if we see it, good and bad, in the light of eternity.

Snake charmer's tempting misquote

Psalm 91

In Jolo, West Virginia, there is a church in which members dance with deadly rattlesnakes and dice with death. They base their belief on Mark 16:17,18 (which echoes vv 9-13 in this psalm). Some have been bitten (as a punishment for sins or as a witness to unbelievers that the snakes are real, they say); a few have died.

Satan – the deadliest serpent of all – used verses 11 and 12 to tempt Jesus to jump off a high-rise building (Matthew 4:5-7). Jesus' refusal shows that the promise here is not a command. God may give supernatural protection in emergencies (as in Acts 28:1-6); he does not call us to play games with him and with the natural order.

The warm comfort of Psalm 91 may be despised as a sign of emotional weakness and dependence but the psalmist is only being realistic. We *are* weak, and we face many hazards. By contrast, God is strong, loving and supportive of his people in their weakness and through the hazards. This is a statement of God's character, to give us courage to step out faithfully in his service.

You've spoiled it!

Psalm 94

It happens mostly to young children, but it can happen to adults too. You are about to complete something, or achieve something, when it gets spoiled. It may be by accident, or by deliberate vandalism. And the spoiler dances off, laughing gleefully (v 3).

Verbal violence is more common than physical violence in the offices, shops and businesses of the Western world. Pride and prejudice have always been part of the ungodly person's armoury (v 4), and characters are assassinated even if bodies are not (v 6).

People oppose Christian faith and work by desire (they consider themselves superior, v 4), by dogma (they attack our heritage of belief and practice, v 5) and by default (they don't care, v 7).

God does not stand by helplessly, the psalmist assures us. He knows what they do (v 11) and he can use their wrong to enable us to grow (v 12). He promises to rescue us from their excesses (v 13) because he cares about us (v 14). Ultimately, we know that they will receive their just deserts (v 23). This is a psalm to use as a calming-down devotion when people screw us up.

A glimpse of glory

Psalm 96

Words can lose their value when they are used carelessly or without due regard for their meaning. Many modern worship songs use the word 'glory' yet many people would be hard pressed to define what it means.

It is used four times in this psalm, in three different ways. God's glory surrounds him (v 6); it is part of his character. It is to be ascribed to him (vv 7,8) as a sign of honour and devotion, and it is to be proclaimed to others as something to be noticed and acknowledged (v 3).

The Hebrew word has at least six nuances. It can be understood as something weighty (that is, significant), or something substantial (as in 'abundance'; a person has substantial wealth). Then it can mean wealth (as richness), dignity (as excellence and goodness), and the nobility of a king. When 'given' to someone it means honour or respect, actively expressed.

Biblically, God's glory is seen visibly on such occasions as the dedication of the tabernacle (Exodus 40:34-38), Isaiah's vision of heaven (Isaiah 6:1-5), and Jesus' transfiguration (Mark 9:2-8). But usually it is hidden except from the eyes of faith. Medit-ating on this psalm may help to restore the vision, and lift our hearts to join with feeling in the festal shout (v 10).

For today

Psalms for today

The psalms are not uniform and give rise to varied thoughts. But it can be helpful to group together their insights into prayer:

- Prayer begins with adoration; 'I have seen you in the sanctuary . . .' (63:2); 'I seek . . . to gaze upon the beauty of the LORD' (27:4)
- Prayer requires a quiet heart: 'Be still before the LORD and wait patiently for him' (37:7)
- Prayer inspires holiness: 'Who may stand in his holy place? He who has clean hands and a pure heart' (24:3,4)
- Unholiness demands confession: 'Against you, you only, have I sinned . . . Surely I was sinful from birth' (51:4,5)
- Prayer rejoices in forgiveness: 'He does not treat us as our sins deserve' (103:10)
- It includes thanksgiving for God's many blessings: 'Praise the LORD O my soul, and forget not all his benefits' (103:2)
- Yet in the psalms, prayer rarely includes supplication except for God's assistance: 'Rescue me, O LORD, from evil men' (140:1)

All Christian life is here

Psalm 103

This classic psalm is a masterpiece of poetic language and spiritual insight. Often used as a vehicle for thanksgiving, it reminds us of:

- God's complete forgiveness (vv 3,12)
- God's power and strength given to us (vv 4,5)
- God's drawing the curtain on past mistakes (v 9)
- His regard for our weakness (vv 13-16)
- His promise to remain with us (vv 17,18).

The New Testament depicts God as a caring Father who gives good gifts to his children (e.g. Luke 11:5-13). This psalm anticipates that, and reminds us that Old Testament saints had real glimpses of it too.

HARD Question

Can it be right to curse our enemies?

Psalm 109 (cf. Psalm 69)

Jesus told his followers to break the vicious cycle of evil and violence. 'Love your enemies, do good to those who hate you,' he said in the context of the 'golden rule' of doing to others what we would like them to do to us (Luke 6:27-31).

Often disregarded as impractical or rejected as impossible, his command is widely recognised as the ideal for all human conduct. Vengeance only escalates violence and human society disintegrates as a result.

At the personal level at least, the dream can become reality when the power and love of Christ are deployed. Whether the example is followed by others as the soft answer turns away wrath, or whether it encourages further attack, is unpredictable.

But all this was in the future when the psalmist wrote his intemperate curses. We cannot accuse him of being un-Christian, because he was pre-Christian. As we read through the Bible we are accompanying men and women of God on a centuries-long journey of discovery as God's character and purposes slowly unfold.

Looking back, we can see consistencies and connections. The often difficult and always delicate task of biblical interpretation is to distinguish between those statements made from limited cultural and spiritual viewpoints and those which encapsulate eternal and unchanging truths.

However these so-called 'imprecatory' psalms have more value than merely illustrating how far we have come in our understanding of how to deal with wrong. We should surely have been far more concerned if the psalmist had shrugged off evil with the glazed smile of someone high on drugs or indoctrinated by a cult.

We can never be indifferent to evil and wrong. It is an affront to God and to humanity created in his image. The psalmist expresses that righteous sense of outrage and indignation which every person should feel.

There is nothing wrong with the emotion of anger directed at evil. Often, it is precisely that anger which, rightly channelled, becomes the source of judicial or social reform. If we don't feel angry, then we must ask if we are not in some way morally deficient.

The psalmist prays that the perpetrators of evil will have a taste of their own medicine, and feel for themselves what they have done. Such is the perversion of human nature that the robber may feel no remorse until he is himself robbed. Today, we would pray for a re-sensitising of their conscience. He also calls down destruction on his enemies because he is convinced that God is just. He is, and the Bible assures us that justice will be seen to be done at the last judgment, if not before. With the psalmists we can cry out to God for justice, and also ask, 'Why does it take so long?'

What we cannot do is remain indifferent. These psalms have a place in Scripture. They remind us that God is angered by evil, too. But they do not give us licence to take the law into our own hands. The bombing of abortion clinics by extreme Christian groups may find some analogies in the Old Testament but is ruled out by the New.

What a relief!

Psalm 116

This joyful psalm was used in the 1662 Prayer Book for thanksgiving after childbirth, which in those days was hazardous. The Jews used it to give thanks for the exodus.

We don't know the circumstances behind it, but the author felt strangled (v 3), crushed (v 10), disillusioned (v 11), and chained (v 16). He had been ready to throw in the towel.

But God does not give up his servants to death easily (which is what v 15 means); their *life* is guarded. After the ordeal, the psalmist re-dedicates himself to God (vv 2, 12-14). You can feel his relief. The psalm helps us remember God's gracious rescues which then inspire us for service.

Treasure is for using, not hoarding

Psalm 119

The whole Bible was finally translated into the Maasai language by the early 1990s. At the dedication service for it, the Bishop of Arusha in Tanzania said, 'In the past we were enemies, fighting each other. The Maasai were well-known for their fierceness. But thanks to the Bible, we have a new way. Not the way of tribalism and rivalry, but of co-operation and understanding.'

The civilising effect of the Bible on whole cultures is well documented; its renewing effect on individuals is the subject of a steady stream of testimonies from around the world. It is, as the New Testament declares, 'sharp and powerful' (Hebrews 4:12). God speaks through it in a unique way.

The 'Bible' celebrated in this long and carefully-constructed psalm (each section begins with the next letter of the Hebrew alphabet) was smaller than the one now available in the West. The law of the Lord referred to is the Torah, the Law of Moses.

Yet this alone was sufficient to make the reader wise (e.g. v 98), to give insight (v 99) and understanding (v 100). It shed sufficient light on pilgrims' paths (v 105) to keep them from going astray (v 9). For the author, it was sweet as honey and far more nourishing (e.g. v 103) and contained the secret of happiness (v 111). Not many contemporary Bible readers can truly say that. Perhaps that is why some 2,500 tribes in the world still do not have even a Gospel to read in their own language; we have forgotten its value. Yet with so many versions available in English alone, the accessibility of its spiritual treasures places a burden of responsibility and mission on the shoulders of the church.

Help is never far away from us

Psalm 121

This is one of many 'songs of ascents' which would have been used by pilgrims going up (literally) to Jerusalem for one of the three annual pilgrim festivals (Passover; Pentecost or Firstfruits; and Tabernacles, Booths or Harvest).

The path was rugged and steep, like the path of life and the way of truth (cf. Matthew 7:13,14). Feet could slip, especially as tiredness set in (v 3). Heat-stroke and dehydration were a daytime hazard while wild animals and bandits prowled in the moonlight (v 6).

The author needs assistance, and scans the horizon for it. But none is apparent; he is thrown onto the Lord, whose presence is guaranteed (v 5). The message is that we should constantly and consciously trust God; then we will see the way forward.

A celebration of family support

Psalm 127

It is probably untrue to say that families were any more stable or happy in biblical times than they are today. The Bible gives many examples of feuds which sometimes ended in murder.

However, while they fought hard, they did so in larger packs. The family was wider and more cohesive. When there was a split in one part, both parts survived and looked after their members. The family was a mini-tribe, hence the obsession with numbers (v 5) which were also crucial as parents grew older and needed support.

We must read this psalm in that cultural context. This is a celebration of wider family support. It recognises that every family needs more than human wisdom, family tradition and parenting manuals to survive. It needs a spiritual foundation also (v 1), which accepts each person as a gift from God to the others (v 3).

Is the Internet God?

Psalm 139

The question, 'Is the Internet God?' was actually posed publicly by a British clergyman who was impressed by its apparent access to all knowledge that exists.

It isn't, because even if every last piece of data on everything was available on the Internet, the system still wouldn't know each person intimately. It wouldn't know all the incidents which have happened in each of our lives and which have contributed to making us the people we are.

That knowledge extends way beyond our social security number and list of achievements on our CV. It is and always will be 'too wonderful' to contemplate or comprehend (v 6). But that is how God knows us, and this powerful psalm takes us into mind-blowing mysteries.

God's perception is total (vv 1-6). He knows our thoughts, motives, ambitions, desires, weaknesses, strengths, achievements, failures, secrets, hopes, fears, anxieties and longings – including those we prefer not to admit even to ourselves.

Therefore there is no point in hiding them from God. Indeed, he wants to watch over all we do actively, not as an observer but as a participant. He is not a coach on the touch-line but a player-manager on the field (v 5).

God's presence is global (vv 7-12). There are times when Christians can be especially conscious of his presence, and other times when he seems a million miles away. But the promise is that, whatever our feelings, he never moves from our side:

- He is present in the depths (v 8). The shadowy underworld, which is all the Old Testament knew of life after death, symbolises for us the caverns of despair and the valleys of disappointment.
- He is present in the distance (v 9). The Israelites struggled for centuries to understand that God was not a local deity confined to barracks in Jerusalem. He went where they went; and he was waiting for them when they arrived. Distance, for us, may be simply leaving home or starting a new job, away from the familiar and the friendly.
- He is present in the darkness (vv 11,12). In the Bible, darkness often represents those places from which God is excluded: the Monday morning world of bad tempers, poor relationships and dubious practices. He does not scurry from them like a rat from a sinking ship.

God's plans are fulfilled (vv 13-18). Genetic make-up and life experience are woven together by God to create a unique individual capable of praising and serving him. That does not make us perfect, but it makes us important.

His plans embrace our weaknesses and they are worked out in ways which do no violence to our genuine freedom to which, as the New Testament shows, the call to submit to regeneration by Christ appeals. The future is always present to him, so he is not a dictator but a planner with the best will in the world.

God's patience is long (vv 19-24). Unlike the psalmist, who thinks such an all-knowing and all-powerful God should act swiftly to sort out the wicked, God is prepared to give them more rope, either to hang themselves or to rein in their excesses. Impatience is not to be confused with zeal for the Lord. His plans may include the very people we want out of the way. We don't know, but he does. Which is where we came in.

The stones cry out!

Psalm 148

When Jesus was asked to quieten the exuberant disciples escorting him into Jerusalem on a carpet of cloaks and under an archway of palm leaves, he replied that if they kept quiet, the stones underfoot would cry out (Luke 19:39,40).

He was speaking figuratively, of course, and so is the psalmist when he calls on all creation to praise God. He is not doing what children (or children's stories) may do: projecting human characteristics onto non-human creation.

But to his eye of faith they do 'praise' him by revealing something of his character. The lightning demonstrates God's power, the mountains show forth his everlasting stability, the flowers display his beauty and the animals testify to his generous provision.

Jesus used nature like this too (Matthew 6:26-30). We should look around us for messages from God. Praise is more than singing to God; it is also showing him to others.

Bring on the orchestra!

Psalm 150

Few churches have the human resources to create an orchestra to accompany worship, although probably many have the potential for a small ensemble. The traditional organ may spoil us because of its rich mimicry of so many instruments, and so stifle the musical contribution to worship which others could bring.

In biblical times, they had no organs (despite the King James' Version translation of one ancient wind instrument) but they did have a variety of stringed, wind and percussion instruments. Quite what they were and how they sounded remains a matter of conjecture, but the psalmist gives us a brief listing here.

The trumpet may have been an animal horn, although there were silver trumpets used in the temple too. The harp and lyre were probably similar, one (the kinnor, harp in NIV) may have had ten strings, and the other fewer. They would have been plucked. The flute was probably a pipe, and similar to a recorder. Tambourines and cymbals have probably been similar in every culture.

Worship is, or should be, more than just joining in something which others do. It can and should be a corporate activity in which everyone participates as fully as they are able.

As it was, is now, and ever shall be: The Lord reigns!

The Book of Revelation:

- Is full of symbols and pictures of spiritual truths
- Contains letters of challenge to seven churches
- Explains God's sovereignty in human history
- Describes how evil is being conquered
- Shows what heaven will be like and who will be there

The book of Revelation is a mystery. Even its own explanations leave most readers none the wiser (1:20; 10:7; 17:7). It has been subjected to extravagant interpretations, and almost every commentator disagrees on details or the broad meaning.

Sadly, it has also been divisive. Christians who are united in their belief in the inspiration and authority of Scripture have fallen out over this book and the issues it raises. So you should always keep three things in mind as you read:

1. Revelation was written to encourage. The original readers faced persecution. They needed to know why this was, what God was doing, and when Jesus would return. They needed hope in a depressing situation.

The vision tells them that God is in charge of the world and its history. Evil will be judged and punished in God's own time, but Christians must expect to suffer meanwhile. Those who are faithful will receive their reward in heaven. Keep this big picture in mind.

2. Revelation is an 'apocalyptic' book. Its style unlike any other biblical literature with similarities only to Daniel 7-12 and occasional passages in Ezekiel and Zechariah. Steeped in symbolism, and explaining its imagery only by more imagery it is intended to be read figuratively, not literally or even allegorically: 'This approximates to that *idea*' rather than 'this equals that *event*'.

It is an abstract painting to ponder, not an exact photographic image. The Gnostics in the first and second centuries claimed access to spiritual secrets, and they were heretics. Revelation does not unlock secrets, it describes what lies behind them, namely the clash of redemptive and destructive spiritual forces that ultimately shapes Christian and world history. We climb (painfully at times) towards heaven in faith, not by sight. Let this book broaden the horizons of your struggles.

3. Revelation is probably a series of overlapping, rather than consecutive, visions. Most modern commentators tell us that it is not a chronological count-down of 'the last days'. It does end with a picture of heaven, but it shows pictures of heaven throughout. It seems to be several separate visions *which paint the same picture in a different way.*

This suggests that the whole book is applicable to the whole of history, not to one specific period near 'the end' nor just to the Roman Empire in AD 95. In other words, it is about our time too. The 'last days' stretch between Christ's first and second advents.

This is the approach we have taken here. The expanded 'At a Glance' feature provides a basic interpretation of the main themes of each chapter. (Other analyses and interpretations are summarised in boxes.)

You will see that each section begins or ends with a vision of heaven to emphasise that 'The Lord reigns'. Commentator Michael Wilcock writes, 'We do not need Christ to tell us that the world is full of trouble. But we do need his explanation of history if its troubles are not to be meaningless.' Revelation should be read alongside other Bible passages on suffering and God's sovereignty in history.

REVELATION

Part one: The church in every age
(see article on chapters 2,3)
1 John's vision of Jesus in eternal glory
2 Letters to Ephesus, Smyrna, Pergamum, Thyatira
3 Letters to Sardis, Philadelphia and Laodicea

Part two: Pictures of the church's suffering in every age
4 Worship of the whole church in 'the heavenly places', and God's eternal unchanging nature
5 Jesus opens the scroll: the book of human destiny, showing God's purposes for history unfolding; the unlocking represents his help being made available (which stops John's tears)
6 Six seals opened (see article); four horsemen released; the church is to keep going through the range of life's struggles
7 The full complement of believers gathered in heaven (See article on the 144,000)

Part three: Pictures of the world's troubles in every age
8-9 The seventh seal opened, six trumpets blown; God hears his people's prayers and brings 'plagues' as warnings to the world
10 John receives a scroll of the gospel, which is sweet to him but bitter to those who do not accept it
11 John measures the 'temple', the church, which is partially restricted by the world's constraints; sees two witnesses (the church triumphant despite Satan's attacks); the seventh trumpet announces the glories of heaven

Part four: Pictures of the church's enemies in every age
12 Signs (symbols) of a pregnant woman (Israel) and her child (Jesus) facing a dragon (Satan); the war in heaven is already decided: Jesus defeated Satan on the cross, so Satan attacks the church
13 Vision of a beast from the sea (representing corrupt human institutions) and one from the earth (representing false religion) (See article on '666')
14 A picture of heaven and the 'harvest' of believers after the fall of 'Babylon' (the entire godless human endeavour) (See article on the 144,000)

Part five: Pictures of God's judgment on oppressors in every age
15 Vision of heaven and God's judgments being prepared
16 Seven judgments poured on the earth; God demonstrates his holiness and justice in real punishments afflicting creation and society, but people do not repent; believers are kept safe during the troubles
17 The 'whore of Babylon' persecutes the church; the seven hills represent (all) secular bastions (built on hills in ancient times) which lust for domination over all people
18 The secular state of Babylon falls and is destroyed

Part six: Pictures of heaven as it was, is and ever shall be
19 The Lord reigns in heaven; Jesus destroys the forces of evil
20 God restricts the scope of Satan, who is ultimately destroyed; the dead are raised to be judged (see article on the 'millennium')
21 The new creation is revealed
22 Epilogue: final messages to readers.

KEY QUOTE

'I am the Living One; I was dead, and behold I am alive for ever and ever! And I hold the keys of death and Hades.'
Revelation 1:18

Author: Accepted as John the apostle from earliest times, but later doubted because the very poor Greek is totally unlike that of John's Gospel and letters. No credible alternative has been suggested, however.

Date and historical situation: The early church writer Irenaeus said it was written during the persecution of Christians by the emperor Domitian and this is generally accepted. This dates the book about AD 95. Christianity was not regarded as a legitimate religion, and believers were killed, or had property confiscated, or were exiled, on charges of 'atheism'.

Do the numbers always add up?

You can prove anything with statistics. Numbers are meaningless unless they are interpreted and applied, taking note of the contexts in which the figures have been gathered or occur.

Revelation, like all apocalyptic literature, makes use of numbers. But as the whole book is figurative, the numbers should be treated like other signs and symbols. Discovering what they mean is complicated by our Western obsession with mathematical precision.

But a first-century Jew did not use numbers as we do; precision was the last thought in John's mind as he struggled to write down his mind-blowing visions. Three numbers recur regularly.

Four. A square has four corners. A four-square argument is complete, irrefutable. We have four compass points; four seasons, and four dimensions if you include time with space as relativity demands. In every case, we use the figure to denote more than a number: it means 'the whole thing'.

Revelation depicts four living creatures (4:6-8; cf. Ezekiel 1:5-14). They are all-seeing, all-knowing, mobile, swift, powerful and strong. But so is God! John is 'visualising' an expression of God's character, his glory and worth. Some commentators take the creatures to represent all of creation which praises God just by being there.

Seven. Revelation is full of sevens. There are seven churches, seven seals, seven trumpets, seven bowls (and some commentators see other sections broken into sevens too).

In the Old Testament there were seven days of creation; the seventh year (and the seventh seventh year, the forty-ninth) were 'sabbaticals'. Many rituals were sevenfold: seven sprinklings of blood in sin offerings (Leviticus 4:6) and of oil in purification ceremonies (Leviticus 14:15,16); seven lambs were sacrificed in the 'Feast of weeks' (Leviticus 23:18); transgressors were warned of sevenfold retribution (Leviticus 26:18,21). There were seven lampstands in the temple (and here in chapters 2 and 3).

In the New Testament Peter offered to forgive an errant brother seven times; Jesus said it had to be seventy-sevens: there was to be no end to it. So again, the figure is a picture of completeness. The seven troubles mean 'everything that people experience', and the seven judgments, 'all that is needed and required by justice'. Michael Wilcock goes further to suggest that seven represents the *essence* or nature of things, as well as the full extent of them.

Twelve (twenty-four). There were twelve tribes of Israel – the chosen people of God – and twelve apostles of Jesus (and when one committed suicide, the number was made up, Acts 1:12-26), who were the founders of the new 'people of God' (cf. Ephesians 2:19,20; 1 Peter 2:9). They are brought together in 21:12-14 as the foundations of the 'new Jerusalem'.

So if twelve plus twelve is a picture of God's people, the twenty-four elders on thrones (4:4) may represent the whole worshipping community. Some apply this to the church on earth which is raised *now* to 'the heavenly places' (Ephesians 1:3), to distinguish the picture from that of the final resting place of the innumerable saints (7:9).

This does not exclude a literal interpretation. But if we prefer the literal identification, we should also note the greater things the symbolism suggests.

Date:

Late first century AD.

Location:

The book was written on Patmos, an island (probably a prison camp) in the Aegean off the coast of modern Turkey

Place in Bible:

The last book of the New Testament

HOW SOME COMMENTATORS DIVIDE REVELATION INTO OVERLAPPING VISIONS

Hendriksen: 'Seven parallel sections'	Wilcock 'Eight scenes'	Garrow 'Six instalments for worship'
1. Christ and the lampstands 1:1-3:22	1. Church and the world – 7 letters: 1:9-3:22	1. 1:1-3:22
2. Heaven and the seals 4:1-7:14	2. The suffering church – 7 seals: 4:1-8:1	2. 4:1-8:1
3. The seven trumpets 8:1-11:19	3. 7 trumpets: 8:2-11:18	3. 8:2-11:18
4. The dragon 12:1-14:20	4. The drama of history 11:19-15:4	4. 11:19-15:4
5. Seven bowls 15:1-16:21	5. Punishment for the world – 7 bowls: 15:5-16:21	5. 15:5-19:10
6. The fall of 'Babyon' 17:1-19-21	6. Babylon the whore – 7 words: 17:1-19:10	6. 19:11-22:19
7. The great consummation 20:1-22:21	7. The drama behind history – 7 visions: 19:11-21:8	
	8. Jerusalem the bride – 7 revelations: 21:9-22:19	

Sources:
William Hendriksen, *More than Conquerors*, Tyndale Press, 1962
Michael Wilcock, *I saw Heaven Opened*, IVP, 1975
Alan Garrow, *Revelation*, Routledge, 1997

Front-line tactics

Revelation 2,3

What does God think about the church? Sometimes we are too close to the action to be able to see our situation clearly. The seven churches of Asia (John the Apostle was closely associated with Ephesus and may have been a kind of 'bishop' or senior elder) are typical of churches in every generation. Jesus gives us a kind of SWOT test (Strengths, Weaknesses, Opportunities, Threats) still seen in many fellowships.

The strengths include hard work and perseverance (2:3,13,19; 3:4). Some people are dealing well with false teachers (2:6) and although life is hard, are being faithful (2:10; 3:4). Despite material poverty and deprivation, they have become spiritually rich (2:9) and God is pleased. Our faithfulness may not seem to achieve a lot, but it does not go unnoticed or unrewarded.

But one church's strength is another's weakness. Several are not resisting false teachers (2:14,15,20; the Nicolaitans are probably a group preaching excessive 'freedom' of behaviour). In a similarly tolerant age, we often forget the spiritual dangers of unorthodox teachings; an enemy within can undermine witness and fellowship.

Other weakensses include having cooled in love (2:4) and enthusiasm for the gospel (3:15) and trading off a reputation not matched by reality.

The opportunities include an open door for witness (3:8), something churches today generally face, and God's gracious offer to let us 'wake up' before it is too late (3:2,3). Difficulties provide an oportunity to prove the reality of our faith and the truth of God's love and support (2:10).

The threats are obvious: suffering, false teachers, complacency and pride. So is the application: check out your own church against this. And if you notice only strengths, ask what you are doing to implement them.

Other ways to view Revelation

Commentator Leon Morris lists four ways to approach it. The Preterist view – describing past events, at or near the time of writing. The Historicist view – a panorama of history between the first and second advents of Christ. The Futurist view – describing the 'end days' immediately before Christ's return.

The Idealist (Poetic) view – encouraging faithfulness by describing God's triumph in figurative terms.

For today

- Do a spiritual health check on your church
- Keep heaven in your sights
- Don't waste time trying to figure out what God only knows: trust him and serve him

The cry of the saints is heard at last

Revelation 6

The four horsemen of the apocalypse have ridden daily across the plains of history to plague the common people; 'man is born to trouble as the sparks fly upwards' (Job 5:7). Or, as evangelist Billy Graham wrote in a book based on this passage, 'A kind of madness has gripped the world'.

The white horse, occasionally taken to mean Jesus (it does in 19:11, but that is a different vision), is an ideological conqueror who captures people's minds with lies. Graham calls him 'the deceiver'. Others suggest he represents the delusively attractive 'spirit' of military conquest, driving people into poverty or misery.

The red horse brings conflict onto the streets with knives and guns, and into ordinary people's lives through the bullying violence of impersonal institutions. The black horse is the familiar spectre of famine in a world which has food enough but not the will to share it without profit. And the pale horse haunts us all by breathing disease into our environment.

No wonder all the saints cry, 'How long?' Who hasn't, at some time or another? We are caught up in the sufferings of the world (and later in Revelation these are equated with retribution for the world's godless living, from which we also suffer innocently).

So the sixth seal offers hope and encouragement. The end will come. We are not caught in an endless cycle of suffering, but we will be released and justice will be done (even if after our death). God hears prayer, though the answer may not be immediate.

HARD Question

Does heaven have limited seating and is it a long service?

Revelation 7; 14:1-5

Jehovah's Witnesses claim that heaven has only 144,000 places (and most of those are now taken). The rest of us must be content with a new earth. This is a travesty of both these passages and the rest of the Bible's teaching about life after death.

The 144,000 is a perfect number (see article above on the number '12'): 12,000 from each of the twelve tribes of Israel. It simply means 'all those who are being saved', and is there to reassure the original (largely, it seems, Jewish Christian) readers that no one would be missing. In the same context is a picture of 'a great multitude' which is the Gentile and Jewish church together. Both groups are in heaven.

Jesus told his followers, 'I am going to my Father's house to prepare a place for you' (John 14:1-3) and although spoken to the apostles there is no suggestion that anything different was planned for the rest of us. Revelation assures us that there will be a seat with your name on it if you belong to Jesus.

There will also probably be a job sheet in your pigeon hole! The picture of heaven includes worship and praise, song and statement. But don't assume this means that heaven is an endless church service. In the Bible, 'worship' is much more than saying or singing praise. It is the surrender of our lives, the service of our hands and the sacrifice of our gifts.

If God intended work to be a fulfilling means of serving him (which overall it is no longer in this fallen and disordered world) and created us with a wide range of talents and abilities, is it reasonable to suppose that heaven will be any less than what ideal human existence was intended to be? Surely it will be more, better, greater. We will praise God with our whole selves, in the fullness of our renewed and restored personalities; and what more God will give us to do we wait to see.

What is the 'mark of the beast' and its 'number'?

Revelation 13,14

This provides wonderful scope for fertile imaginations! Bar codes have been one of the alleged manifestations; some add up to 666 and you can't trade without them: *ergo,* they match the descriptions of 13:16-18.

We can make that equation so long as we recognise industrial and technological sophistication it as *a* mark of the beast and not the mark. There will be many manifestations of what these symbols stand for. Some commentators suggest that the 666 refers to the emperor Nero (but you have to use a variant spelling to get the figures).

Six is 'incompleteness'. It describes evil capturing the world and manipulating people for ungodly ends. This puts Christians under pressure. In the workplace they may be forced into ethical compromise. The beast puts profit before people, the cause before concern. Look for subtle 'marks of the beast' around you, and ignore the brazen images of some religious novels.

Millennium fever

Revelation 20

As AD 2000 drew near, fears of massive disruption by the 'millennium bug' grew and cults predicted a variety of cataclysms. Some were associated with this passage.

There are three views about the '1,000 years'. Pre-millennialists believe Christ will come and reign on earth in peace for 1,000 years before the new creation; post-millennialists hold that he will return after a period of peace; amillennialists think the 1,000 years represent his on-going reign begun after his resurrection and continuing now.

This cube-of-ten era, mentioned nowhere else in Scripture, has generated much discusion. Whatever our view, we can rejoice that Christ reigns now over an imperfect world and will reign eternally over a new creation. We don't need to know when, only to be ready to enter fully into his promised future.

Home at last

Revelation 20-22

When British church leader David Watson was dying of cancer, he said one evening to his wife, 'I'm very tired; let's go home.' Later that night he died. John message to struggling believers is: home is round the corner; keep going.

Heaven is the presence of God, if you have followed him in this life you belong there. The new 'Jerusalem', 1,500 miles each way, with walls 200 feet thick illustrates its perfection and also that it has room for all God's saints and all sources of joy and contentment. By contrast, hell is revealed as imperfect. In God's absence thirst for power is never slaked, lust for pleasure is never consummated, desire is never satisfied, people who care nothing for God's righteousness continue their spiritual cannibalism.

The Bible reveals little about either. Heaven will be a surprise, like a special present; trials will be forgotten, heartaches will disappear and weaknesses will be erased. Such a hope can encourage us in all circumstances.

Suffering: p 194
The devil: pp 166, 192, 271, 307
Jesus' return: pp 364, 400

Biblical interpretation: p.10
Book of Revelation: pp 358-63
Jesus' teaching on his return: pp 364, 394, 397, 398
'Millennium': p 363

What on earth is going to happen?

The New Testament as a whole teaches that Jesus will return to earth. Paul's friends in Thessalonica were confused about it. Christians down the ages continued to be confused about it! Here are some principles to guide your reading of Scripture and understanding of the teaching of Jesus and Paul.

Jesus will return

At the last supper, Jesus promised to return and take his disciples to be with him for ever in heaven (John 14:3). At the ascension, they were given a similar reassurance (Acts 1:11). During his ministry, he spoke about 'the Son of Man coming in clouds with great power and glory' and will gather his people to be with him (Mark 13:26).

The picture painted by Jesus and Paul was of a massive, cataclysmic event (e.g. 1 Thessalonians 4:16). Everyone would see him come, and his return would herald the end of the world as we know it. The return of Christ, the last judgment and the 'new creation' are all parts of the same final act of history.

The time is unknown

Both Jesus and Paul warned against speculating about the timing. No one knows when it will be, he said – not even Jesus (Mark 13:32). However, they do stress that it will be unexpected, like a thief in the night (Luke 12:39f; 1 Thessalonians 5:2). Some of Jesus' stories tell of people who were not ready (the five foolish bridesmaids, Matthew 25:1-13). So when we read about 'the signs of the times' we need to resist the temptation to produce a timetable based on them. They are not given for that purpose.

Signs before the end

Paul spoke of the 'man of lawlessness' being revealed and about suffering in 'the last days' (2 Thessalonians 2:1-12). Jesus gave the impression of things going from bad to worse with persecution, warfare, and all kinds of almost unbearable suffering (Mark 13:12-19).

However, Jesus also tells his listeners that it will all happen in their generation (Mark 13:30). Rather than give a specific account of a few months or years before Christ's return, the New Testament declares that we are already in 'the last days'. These cover the period between Christ's first and second comings. Every war, famine and 'false prophet' reminds us that the forces of evil oppose Christ and that he is preparing one day to destroy them.

Even the 'signs in the heavens' can be seen in that way. Today some cults interpret comets as portents of doom. Eclipses of the sun are still seen by tribespeople as threats, reminding them that there are powers greater than themselves. The scientific view has robbed many of that sense of awe which Jesus takes for granted. These 'signs' are like the rainbow in Genesis 9:12-16; natural events endowed with spiritual significance.

So what do we do?

The purpose of the teaching is not to fuel speculation but to forewarn disciples that life will not be easy. Woven in with the promises of joy and blessing for his followers are warnings that at the same time they must expect to suffer just as he did. The teaching also:

- assures us that evil will be punished and justice done
- promises that all who trust in Christ will enter into eternal life with him in heaven
- advises Christians to live every day as if Jesus was about to return, by keeping completely faithful to him
- says we may endure suffering now but there is something much better to come
- advises to keep the good things of this world in perspective: they will pass away.

The world's most effective mailshot

The letter to the Romans is unique among Paul's writings. It is a theological treatise, and not a trouble-shooting letter. It is not a summary of all his beliefs, however; there's not much on the church, the divinity of Christ or the second coming. Instead, Romans focuses on the atonement, telling us how sinful people can be reconciled to God through faith in Jesus Christ.

Paul explains this in terms familiar to first-century Jews, but which Christians today find difficult. Yet Romans can lay claim to being the most effective mailshot in history. Paul sent it to introduce himself and his message; it has transformed people's lives, churches and societies ever since.

In AD 386, a north African lecturing on rhetoric in Milan was struggling with temptation. When he read Romans 13:13,14, 'a clear and constant light infused into my heart; the darkness of all former doubts was driven away'. St Augustine became the major formative influence on Western systematic theology.

In 1515, an Augustinian monk was struggling with a sense of guilt. After working though Romans, 'I grasped that the justice of God is that righteousness by which through grace and sheer mercy God justifies us through faith. Thereupon I felt myself to be reborn and to have gone through open doors into paradise.' Martin Luther went on to inspire the Reformation return to biblical Christianity.

In 1738, an Anglican priest was struggling with doubt. He went reluctantly to a meeting where Luther's preface to Romans was being read. 'While he was describing the change which God works in the heart through faith in Christ, I felt my heart strangely warmed. I felt I did trust in Christ, Christ alone, for salvation; and an assurance was given me, that he had taken away my sins.' John Wesley went on to lead the evangelical revival and to found Methodism.

And in 1918, a Swiss pastor wrote his own exposition of Romans 'with a joyful sense of discovery'. Karl Barth went on to recall liberal theology back towards orthodox biblical roots.

You will not find the letter easy. Resist the temptation to begin at chapter 12, however, but meditate on the argument in 1-11 first. You may discover enriching but humbling truths to illuminate your faith in a fresh way.

AT A GLANCE

ROMANS

1	Introduction; Paul's desire to visit Rome
1	What people are like and how God feels
2	God judges all people fairly; Jews don't get special treatment
3	All have sinned; all can be saved through faith in Christ
4	Abraham's example of faith
5	How we have peace with God; Jesus is a 'second Adam' to repair the damage
6	Our lives should reflect our status
7	The struggle between what we are and what we should be
8	No condemnation: Jesus frees us from sin and death; Christ gives us victory over all adversity now and always
9,10	God's continued concern for the Jews
11	A remnant of Israel is saved; Gentiles are grafted into 'the vine'
12	How to respond to the gospel; renewal of life and relationships
13	The Christian's community relationships
14	Respect each other's differences and weaknesses
15	Paul's news and hopes
16	Final greetings and commendations

The Letter to the Romans:

- Shows that all people have fallen short of God's standards
- Claims that the death of Jesus has made 'atonement' between God and humankind
- Says that the Old Testament way to God was provisional and not completely effective
- Challenges us to receive the benefits of Christ's death by faith
- Encourages us to apply the reconciliation we have with God to our relationships with others

HARD Question

Has God lost his rag?

Romans 1:18-32

In this devastating catalogue of human perversity, Paul says three times: 'God gave them over . . .' (vv 24,26,28). It is his way of describing the start of God's 'wrath' (v 18).

Parents cannot watch while their children defy them wilfully or adopt potentially harmful behaviour patterns. And God cannot sit by and watch people sin without any sort of reaction.

God could stamp out the bad behaviour by destroying its perpetrators at once. Or he could make long-term provision for justice to be done, just deserts to be received, and opportunity for offenders to see their errors and to return to him like the prodigal son of Luke 15. He chose the latter, much to the dismay of victims of injustice and much to the relief of repentant prodigals.

Meanwhile, God's 'wrath' is not a red-faced temper tantrum. He expresses his displeasure simply by leaving us to stew in our own juices. Having given us freedom, he allows us to reap the bitter fruits of misusing it. As C. S. Lewis once wrote, 'They enjoy forever the horrible freedom they have demanded, and are therefore self-enslaved.' Which is what the Bible means by 'hell'.

Sensual pleasure is subject to the law of diminishing returns: it doesn't satisfy unless it is repeated with greater intensity. Fulfilment and pleasure are as fleeting as the wind. The wind of God's 'wrath' blows away our hopes and dreams. God made us to relate to himself, in whom alone lasting pleasure is to be found.

Everyone has a God-shaped hole in their heart

Romans 1:18-23

The real problem for atheists is that they can look at a beautiful sunset or a new-born baby and they have no one to say thank you to. There are times when almost every human being is aware of 'the transcendent', when an intimation of God, of something or someone beyond them, rings in the heart like an echo from a distant mountain.

On only two occasions does Paul acknowledge this universal hunger for God (here and in Acts 17:27) yet the thought is never far from the Bible's surface. True atheists were even rarer in ancient times than today and the point hardly needed to be made.

It does explain to a more sceptical age why religion, with art, is one of the distinctive marks of *homo sapiens*. As Augustine wrote, 'Thou hast created us for thyself, and our heart knows no rest, until it reposes in thee.'

Paul, and other Bible writers, show that not all religions lead to God, and many sublimations of the religious urge are nothing less than perversions of our God-given humanity (cf. vv 22,23). Nonetheless, there is a right way to fulfil the universal hunger for God.

KEY QUOTE

I am not ashamed of the gospel, because it is the power of God for the salvation of everyone who believes . . . in the gospel a righteousness from God is revealed, a righteousness that is by faith from first to last, just as it is written:

Everyone gets the same deal

Romans 2:1-3:8

Very soon in this letter, Paul will be telling us that no one can be saved (made right with God) by what they do, but only by faith. Yet here he seems to contradict that and imply that the Gentiles can get into the kingdom on the basis of good works (2:10).

However, the term 'good' here means that which is in accordance with God's law (2:13). The Gentiles did not have that law as it was revealed to Moses, but they did (and do) have an inherent awareness of God's requirements in their consciences (2:14,15). God will judge them on the basis of how they have responded to it.

While this may help us to understand how God deals with those who have never heard of Christ, the chief point Paul is making is that neither Jew nor Gentile is better off than the other when they face God to account for their lives (2:11,16).

The Jews do have the advantage that God's law has been revealed to them more fully (3:1,2). On the basis of 'from everyone who has been given much, much will be demanded' (Luke 12:48), they are responsible to live out the spirit of the law and not rely only on following its letter (2:25-29).

Christians who assume that observing such rites as baptism and communion they are fulfilling their obligations to God, may fall into the same category, and suffer the same condemnation.

Don't be a hypocrite!

Romans 2:1-24

Paul was a contemporary of Seneca, the Stoic moralist whose most famous pupil was the cruel Roman emperor Nero who almost certainly executed Paul. Seneca exposed hypocrisy, exalted morals, encouraged human equality and practised stern self-discipline, but turned a blind eye when Nero murdered his own mother. Contemporary examples of such double-think are not hard to find.

Paul possibly had such a good but imperfect person in mind when he wrote vv 1,19-22. Paul argues that before God good and bad in a person are not balanced out. Bad is bad, and we're all weighed down by it.

Hypocrisy is especially dangerous because it breeds complacency (vv 3-5). When we seem to be getting away with something, we forget that we will still be called to account for it. God may be withholding his judgment for the time being, but that is to give us the opportunity to turn from our sin.

Paul is reiterating Jesus' teaching that God sees and judges the heart.

Don't single out sex

Promiscuous heterosexual and homosexual behaviour is used here as an example of how far people fly from God's purposes. This needs to be kept in biblical perspective. Sexual deviation from a stable, lifelong heterosexual relationship formalised by marriage is an example of breaking barriers erected for our good. When sexuality deviates from its primary purpose of child-bearing, elevating its pleasure above cementing a lifelong union, unstable relationships may ensue. Sexual expression outside marriage does not ennoble, it enslaves. However, Paul places sexual deviation in the same context as other things which are *equally* harmful. Envy, strife, deceit, gossip, slander and pride, although not life-threatening are biblically declared as serious as sexual deviation. All sin destroys relationships, whatever name it goes under.

FAST facts

Author: Paul the apostle (1:1). No doubt has been expressed about the claim.

Place of composition: Probably Corinth or nearby (several Corinthians are mentioned in ch 16).

Date of composition: During Paul's third missionary journey, probably early in AD 57.

Purpose of writing: To introduce himself and his message to a church he has never visited. It was intended to be presented before his arrival en route for Spain. Paul is not dealing with known problems or questions in the church.

Structure: Romans is a carefully-worked treatise on the work of Christ and how we may benefit from it (chs 1-11). It pays special attention to the respective status before God of Jews and Gentiles. Chapters 12-16 apply the doctrine in the practical terms of Christian relationships.

Date of letter:
About AD 57

Place in Bible:
The first of the collection of Paul's letters, following Acts and before 1 Corinthians in the New Testament

Place in Paul's writings:
Written after Galatians, Thessalonians and Corinthians, before the others

Events it relates to:
Paul's eventual visit to Rome as a prisoner c. AD 60, recorded at the end of Acts

Where the church in Rome came from

The church probably began as a result of Roman Jews being converted on the day of Pentecost (Acts 2:10,11) and taking the gospel home with them. Other Christians would have travelled to the capital, and shared their faith as they did so.

There was a large Jewish community in Rome which was expelled several times. In AD 19 the emperor Tiberius threw them out after a scandal in which a wealthy Roman was persuaded to convert to Judaism and to make a substantial donation to the Jerusalem temple, only for the money to be embezzled.

An expulsion during the reign of Claudius (41-54) is referred to in Acts 18:2. The later writer Suetonius states it was caused by riots 'in the name of Chrestos', often taken to mean 'Christ'. They would have been similar to the riots stirred up by the Jews in Thessalonica and Berea (Acts 17:5-15), but there can be no certainty of this.

Despite the ejections, the Jews seem to have returned quickly, and at least nine synagogues are known to have existed there during the first century. The church would have contained a substantial proportion of Jews and proselytes along with some Gentiles from non-Jewish backgrounds. This may explain why Paul writes about Jewish issues in Romans.

Jerome, writing c. 380, says Peter founded the church and was there for 25 years. That creates problems, because traditionally Peter was martyred in Rome, along with Paul, under Nero about AD 64-65. Twenty years before that he was in Palestine (Galatians 2:7). 1 Peter is addressed from Rome to churches in Asia Minor, so he must have travelled there at some time too. Another writer, Irenaeus, says the first bishop was Titus.

All we know for certain is that there was a flourishing church by the time Paul wrote, and it was already producing leaders of the calibre of Aquila and Priscilla (Acts 18:2,18-26; Romans 16:3,4). From Paul's letter to the Philippians (4:22), probably written from Rome, it appears that some of the imperial staff had become Christians.

We are all in the same boat

Romans 3:9-31

What was so devastating about the sinking of the *Titanic* was that the ship contained the great and the good as well as some of the corrupt and perverted. When it started to sink, whichever category you were in you were doomed. That is the fate of human-kind in its natural, sinful state, says Paul.

It would be easy to match his list of 'sinners' in vv 9-18 with all sorts of people whom we love to hate. But he won't allow us to. There is no difference: all have sinned (vv 22,23).

The Bible defines sin as 'falling short of God's standard' (v 23); in other words, we're not as good as he is, however hard we try. So there can be no comparing ourselves with others; 'If those terrible people are Christians and going to heaven, then I'm sure I'll have no problem getting in!'

And, just as we're in the same boat that's sinking, we're also sent the same lifeboat to rescue us, because there is only one – Christ (v 24). So there can be no boasting about how we earned our passage to heaven (v 27). We'll all arrive there in the same condition: human beings saved from drowning spiritually, clothed only in the righteousness of Christ.

Unearned credit keeps bankrupt solvent

Romans 4

Imagine your bank balance is in the red and you owe money you cannot pay. You have received a bankruptcy notice and are about to lose everything. Then in the post, you receive a cheque from the creditor to whom you owe so much. It is enough to pay the debt.

Relief would be mingled with disbelief as you stared at it. This is not just a generous gift from a well-wisher, this is from the person you should be paying.

That is the metaphor which Paul uses, and illustrates it from the story of Abraham. The patriarch founded the nation of Israel and in some respects was even more important than Moses. True Israelites could trace their descent from Abraham. The covenant between God and his people was given first to Abraham.

However, says Paul, Abraham did not get into God's good books by his own efforts. It was Abraham's faith, trusting in God's unbelievable promise (cf. Genesis 15:6), which put him into a right relationship with God. And that came before Abraham performed the rite of circumcision which was the sign of covenant obedience (Romans 4:10,11). So faith, not the act of obedience, made him 'right' before God.

For Abraham, then, being counted 'righteous' was a gift, not a wage (vv 4,5). And as it was with him, so it is with us, says Paul. God himself credits to our spiritual account the righteousness we need to pay God the debt of obedience we owe him. Either we accept it gratefully, or we go to the wall. There's no way we can ever earn that amount of spiritual credit.

Abraham's faith was 'against all hope' (v 18) but didn't weaken or waver (vv 19,20). His was no academic faith. It was intensely personal, absolutely trusting, and without a shred of factual evidence to base it on. Our faith does have evidence of the life, teaching, death and resurrection of Jesus behind it.

Abraham's example of total trust in the promise of God and in the God of the promise makes our often half-hearted commitment seem poverty-stricken by comparison. He was rich in faith because he was helpless in fact. No wonder Paul treats his faith as a model for us. Only when we are conscious of our spiritual helplessness will our faith become dynamic:

Nothing in my hand I bring,
Simply to thy cross I cling.

And only then shall we be right with God.

The war is over

Romans 5:1-11

The New Testament word for peace is *eirene*, from which we get the word irenic which means peace-making. It includes the fuller Hebrew understanding of *shalom* as wholeness, too. Paul combines those meanings in this passage. We have been like 'enemies' to God (so note that he has practised what Jesus preached, and continued to love us and show mercy to us) but now the war is over; Jesus' death on the cross has brought hostilities to an end. No more war, and a fresh oneness with God: peace!

But now that peace is established, Paul says that it is to be experienced in the hassles of life (vv 3-5). Peace with God equips us to face the turmoils of life, but it does not eradicate them. Paul is under no illusion; heaven is not yet established on earth. God's peace will endure, however; we have been pronounced right with God and therefore we will be spared the condemnation of God's judgment on our former life when we face him on the last day (vv 9-10).

In explaining this, Paul draws a stunning contrast (vv 6,7). We might possibly sacrifice ourselves for a famous person: Jesus sacrificed himself for his enemies. Compared to God, we were no-hopers. But he gave his Son for us nonetheless, before which fact we can only bow in amazement and respond with love and gratitude.

Could you repeat that?

Romans 5:12-21

Not perhaps surprisingly, in this passage, Paul stumbles over himself in his excitement, starting one thought and moving on to another before he's finished the first. His points are:

- The sin of Adam brought death (separation from God's life) to the human race (v 12)
- The Law of Moses provided a provisional (but imperfect) way of escape (vv 13,14)
- Just as Adam brought us down, so Jesus (the 'Second Adam') picked us up (vv 15-19)
- The Law of Moses only magnified the extent of sin by defining it more closely (vv 20,21).

The contrast couldn't be greater

Romans 6:1-7:6

For Paul, the difference between a Christian and a non-Christian was like that between chalk and cheese, black and white, life and death. The person who is justified by faith in Christ has come alive to God. It's parallel to Jesus' teaching about being 'born again' (John 3) or the son who was 'lost' and 'dead' but who was 'found' and 'alive' (Luke 15).

It is not always easy to identify with that picture, if we have come from a standard modern background characterised neither by non-Christian religious activity nor by overtly anti-social behaviour.

But it may become clearer as Paul uses the picture in a different way. If we're alive with the risen Christ, he says, then we're dead to the past non-Christian way of life. It is buried, gone for ever. It was characterised by 'sin', an attitude which shunted God out, or to the margins, of our lives.

So, if God's grace is shown because Jesus has taken away our sin and forgiven us, why don't we go on sinning so that we can enjoy more of God's love? (Some people do outrageous things in order to attract attention because they crave love.)

You shouldn't, Paul says, because the past has been killed off (vv 11-14). If Christ's life is in us, it should show by our behaviour. But if the old law is abolished, we're not bound by it any more so why can't we do what we like?

You can't, says Paul, because although we're not saved by keeping the old law, the basic moral law of the universe is still a valid expression of how God wants us to live. Christ's standards are higher than the world's.

So, whatever our background, we are 'different' because we have the life of God dwelling within us. The contrast may not be so much in a 'before and after' snapshot of our own lives (although we should be able to trace some growth) as in the fact that we are in touch with God in a way others are not. Therefore our task is to ensure that we let the divine life leak – or, rather, gush – out in practice.

HARD Question

What effect does baptism have?

Romans 6:1-4

Paul seems to imply that it is baptism itself which effects our 'burial' with Christ, putting an end to the old life and inaugurating the new.

As with many signs in the Bible, the meaning lies between two extremes. Baptism isn't simply a visual aid nor is it automatically effective in creating a spiritual transformation. Such symbols are powerful in being channels of God's life; they become dynamic when the people witnessing them exercise the faith which they signify.

Immersion speaks of being buried and raised, sprinkling or pouring speaks of being cleansed and renewed. Either way of using water in baptism seems valid. When faith and the action are combined, the action reinforces the faith and the faith gives spiritual and emotional meaning to the action. Luther, in times of doubt, often reflected back on his own (infant) baptism as a powerful reminder that he had indeed been buried with Christ.

The church is full of hypocrites – official

Romans 7:7-25

The critics are right; the church is full of hypocrites and that is why many liturgies include a confession at the beginning. It is not that the compilers or worshippers are unsure of salvation, but because they are conscious that they often fail God. We may have 'bathed' but we still get our feet dirty (John 13:10).

Christian sin is of course a scandal. Bishop John Ryle, in his classic book *Holiness*, wrote, 'far more harm is done by unholy and inconsistent Christians than we are aware of. [They] are among Satan's best allies . . . They cause the chariot wheels of the Gospel to drive heavily. They supply the children of this world with a never-ending excuse for remaining as they are.'

It is some comfort to find that Paul struggled with the same problem (vv 18,19). The law has shown how he falls short of God's requirements (vv 7-13). Having put his faith in Christ, he still fails. He aims at perfection, but still ends up far short of it (vv 14-25).

Some commentators suggest this must be referring to his pre-conversion life, because Paul writes so much of victory over sin elsewhere. In fact, he is being a realist, not a defeatist. There is some victory in our moral struggle, but it is not yet complete.

Paul does not excuse failings, but explains why they occur. He is human, and a prisoner of his humanity (v 23). Until the new creation is complete, his human limitations and weaknesses will always be a source of struggle and occasional failure. Therefore, when we do fail, we can be sure that God understands. Which reminds us how much we depend on God's grace. Ultimately self-sufficiency is self-destructive.

Do Christians have split personalities?

Paul writes of the 'sinful nature' (literally 'flesh') and the indwelling Spirit of God in terms which sound as if the Christian has two distinct and opposite sides to their character, like the yin and yang principles of Eastern religion.

It may be helpful to substitute the term 'natural humanity' for 'sinful nature'. It means the self-interested human personality, with its natural weaknesses and its perverse bias towards self and away from God. When a person becomes a Christian, the Holy Spirit begins to repair the tarnished 'image of God', to scrape away the rust and to polish us so that we can start to reflect God more perfectly.

It is rather like restoring an 'old master' painting. It takes time and it's not completed even by the time we die. The picture remains both old (tarnished) and new (under restoration) at the same time.

Therefore, in this life we are rather like the two-faced subject of Robert Louis Stevenson's classic story *Dr Jekyll and Mr Hyde* who confessed: 'Of the two natures that contended in the field of my consciousness, even if I could rightly be said to be either, it was only because I was radically both.'

The old 'humanity' cannot please or serve God (8:8) and has been crucified with Christ (6:6). Our new existence in Christ through the Spirit (8:9,10) has made us alive to God and exerts a new gravitational pull away from that of our sinful humanity and towards God (8:4,5,11,37).

Paul is a Hebrew, and he believes in the unity and integrity of the human personality. He does not subscribe to the Greek-inspired idea that people are made up of separate components. (That is why life after death is always seen in the Bible as resurrection of the body – the whole person – and never as the immortality of the soul or part of the person.) We do not have split personalities; we are damaged articles undergoing repair.

THE THREE TENSES OF SALVATION

PAST	PRESENT	FUTURE
We were saved	We are being saved	We will be saved
Christ's death opened the way to God	The Holy Spirit infuses us with 'eternal life'	God the Father will transform us in heaven

Cast-iron guarantee

Romans 8

There is nothing more crippling than uncertainty. Did I lock up? Will she turn up? Will I be late? Throughout Romans Paul seems to have a sub-agenda. He wants to deepen his readers' assurance that because of the death and resurrection of Jesus they have no need to worry about the future.

So chapter 8 begins on an even stronger note than chapter 5. We have peace with God (5:1) despite the persisting struggles (chs 6-7), and therefore we are safe for eternity (8:1). The death sentence has been lifted; we have been pronounced 'not guilty'; we cannot be retried and the case against us cannot be re-opened.

God has ensured that his lawful and just requirements concerning our past have been met fully by what Christ has done. We are free (vv 3,4). Our human frailty may cause us to doubt it, so Paul goes on to explain that despite appearances to the contrary we are now under new management (v 9).

Therefore, we are the heirs – the rightful possessors – of the riches of God's kingdom (v 17) and no one can rob us of them (vv 38,39). So we are obliged to live up to our new status (v12a; Paul is so anxious to stress the death of the old nature that he doesn't complete this sentence until chapter 12!).

One evidence of our new standing before God is how we turn to him in prayer, as to a caring parent who can help, guide and support (8:15). If we don't always feel this, one way to become more aware of our heavenly Father's care is simply to relate to him as if it was true, to take it on trust. We will then discover that it is true as we see him at work in and through the daily struggles we bring to him.

CROSS CHECK

Predestination: pp 101, 374
Covenant: pp 18-21
God and other religions: pp 216, 218
Old and new nature: pp 133-5
Body of Christ: p 00 (1 Cor)

Everyone's groaning for something better!

Romans 8:18-27

The Jews thought of the period before the reign of the Messiah as 'the birth pangs', and it is likely that Paul has that image in mind. Childbirth is generally not easy; it is strenuous and painful. So, too, is the period between Christ's first and second comings to earth.

- Creation groans (v 22). It creaks and shudders through our misuse of it and through its natural weaknesses. The Bible sometimes personifies creation like this (cf. Psalm 19:1-4), not because it is a 'god' (the contemporary personification of Mother Earth or Gaia has no biblical basis), but because it is an expression of God's character, in which he is present and with which he is involved.
- Christians groan (v 23). The spiritual conflict can be wearing, and we long for a more perfect life and clearer knowledge of God. We know we could and should be better in all sorts of ways, but we can't quite make it and we may find this frustrating.
- The Spirit groans (v 26). The deep aspirations of God can't be put into human words. This teaching, not repeated by Paul elsewhere, reassures us that the whole Trinity is on our side, willing us on, as it were. It also suggests that our deep wordless prayers (whether expressed as longings or in a 'spiritual' language of 'tongues') may be prompted by the Spirit himself. So when we pray, we should ask him to show us what is on God's mind, rather than simply telling him what is on ours.

God still remembers the Jews

Romans 9-11

Jewish–Christian relations have never been good. At times Christians have wrongly persecuted Jews or verbally assaulted them for crucifying Christ. Recently insensitive evangelism has combined with a renewed Jewish cultural awareness to provoke some bitter disputes.

Paul moves on from his main thesis in Romans to deal with the issue of where the Jews stand as a nation in God's purposes now that Jesus the Messiah has come and has been accepted by only a minority of them.

His argument boils down to the following:

- Israel is God's original 'vine', his chosen people, within whose ranks divine selection operates (9:1-9). The Gentiles are branches grafted onto it and are not a separate plant (11:11-24). Jesus never renounced Judaism or his Jewish mission as such. The two are made one (cf. Ephesians 2:11-22).
- God has no favourites, and is global in his concerns (9:10-29). All who call on him through Christ from any culture will however be saved (ch 10).
- Israelites forfeit the right to enter God's kingdom in the same way as anyone else, if they do not accept the gift of justification by faith (9:30-33).
- God ensures that a proportion of Israelites will be included among those who ultimately come to Christ (11:1-10).
- All Israelites who could be included will be included (11:25-32). It is unlikely that this difficult passage is suggesting that there will be a mass conversion of the entire Jewish race (would that include all those who have died before it happens?) nor that Jews will be included in the kingdom just because they are Jews (which contradicts Paul's teaching about justification by faith). Paul's point is that all Jews saved henceforth will be saved by grace as sinners, just like non-Jews, for the glory of God.

This section contains two encouragements. It reminds us that God does not forget those whom he called long ago and does not grow tired of people or forget us, either. Also, it suggests that Christians should pray for Jews as God's originally chosen people, without whom there would have been no Jesus and no Christian faith.

God requires our co-operation

Romans 10:5-15

When the young William Carey was voicing concern for the unconverted people of other countries in the eighteenth century, he was told by his church leaders that if God wished to convert the heathen, he would do so without human assistance. It was assumed the 'heathen' had already rejected God. Carey was branded a 'miserable enthusiast' for saying anything different!

Carey's concern was that people had never had an opportunity to believe. He wrote a paper quoting Romans 10:12-15, which led to the formation of the Baptist Missionary Society. He himself became a pioneer missionary to India.

The logic is clear. Someone either brought us the gospel or established a church through which we heard it. We therefore have a responsibility to take it to others. Christianity is a missionary religion, not because Paul was a missionary but because Jesus commanded us all to be such (Matthew 28:19,20).

For today

- Understand you are just as sinful as those you judge are really bad
- Religious activities won't bring you closer to God
- Accept Christ's forgiveness and new life as a gift not as an earned right
- Once you accept Christ, nothing can shake you out of his caring hand, even if you suffer
- Give yourself entirely to Christ to say thank you for his love
- Be active in the church; serve and receive from people you might not even like very much

HARD Question

God's choice or mine?

Romans 8-11

A major argument in the Christian church has remained largely unresolved over the past century, between 'Calvinists' and 'Arminians'. The former stress God's sovereign election or calling of people who become Christians, the latter the absolute freedom of the human will in choosing whether or not to have faith in Christ.

The words *predestination* and *election* (they mean much the same thing) take us into the realms of mystery where we must tread carefully. Our belief-statements may approximate to the truth, but they are still the equivalent of a child's eye view of an adult world.

God is perfectly just, therefore we cannot give the impression that he is not and that he refuses to give a person an opportunity to trust him. He is also greater than our minds and we cannot reduce his purposes to neat formulae which reflect our own viewpoint.

The New Testament is clear that no one can turn to Christ unless there is first a prior movement of God towards them. That is seen in two ways: first, in the coming of Christ into the world to bring us to God, and then in the working of God's Spirit in our lives to give us a desire to know him. This was Jesus' teaching, not just Paul's (see John 6:44,65; 16:8,9).

Paul says we were dead to God, and needed him to 'resurrect' us (Ephesians 2:4-6). So, 'faith' is not a 'work', something we 'do' in order to merit salvation. Biblically, faith is humble submission to what God has done on our behalf. Once we receive his gift, the covenant-keeping God keeps his word and preserves us for eternity (John 6:37-40; Romans 8:34-39).

So God takes the initiative. The problem then becomes: Does he predestine only some to life and thereby consign others to hell without giving them a choice? And if we are predestined, how can we actually exercise free will in responding? Does it not make us puppets on God's string?

Paul argues in Romans 9:10-29 (and elsewhere) that no one whatsoever deserves to be saved. If a person isn't saved they can't complain; if a person is, they can only wonder at the privilege. We cannot say God is being unfair (see in Luke 20:9-18).

The Bible also says each person has freedom of choice, although that facility is itself damaged and distorted by the fall. In many respects it is in 'bondage'; and there are some things it cannot achieve. Jesus declared that 'many are invited, but few are chosen' (Matthew 22:14), implying that God's calling is for all who wish to respond.

So how effectual is his calling? Does it always achieve what it aims for, that is, a response of faith? Paul writes as if it does (Romans 8:28, 30; 9:23-25). And this takes us back into the ultimate mystery: the Bible teaches that we can only believe if God awakens us, but that we do have the responsibility of responding freely: choose this day who you will serve (Joshua 24:15).

C. S. Lewis, in the different context of questioning the death of his beloved wife, Joy, wrote, 'When I lay these questions before God, I get no answer. But a rather special sort of "No answer". It is not the locked door; it is more like a silent, certainly not uncompassionate, gaze. As though he shook his head, not in refusal but waiving the question. Like, "Peace, child, you do not understand." '

That was the response Job received to his questions. Until we have the opportunity to question God directly, we are advised to live with the apparently opposite things being integrated into God's good purposes by means we cannot fathom.

New way of doing church revealed

Romans 12

Paul now turns to the outworking of the gospel in our relationships. His thought can be focused as follows:

- Commitment (vv 1,2) Our whole life is to be God's to change and to use. Attitudes as well as actions are involved in the call for a renewed mind.
- Humility (v 3) Individualism is the creed, and sin, of Western society and is foreign to the Scriptures. We need others because we are not self-sufficient.
- Unity (vv 4,5) We were created to live in love and harmony with others. If we trust the 'head' then we are part of his body, the church. Within it, we serve and worship together.
- Responsibility (vv 6-8) The body of Christ has no spare parts. Each has a function and a service to perform. (Why, then, are churches always so short of helpers for essential tasks?)
- Corporate concern (vv 9-16) Unity plus responsibility equals loving concern and mutual support in God's equation.
- Holiness (vv 17-21) Evil is not to be paid back, but overcome by goodness of thought, word and deed. The world judges God by the outward conduct of his people.

Interestingly the initial letters of these points spell 'CHURCH' and may provide a useful test for your church's life.

Leaders deserve respect

Romans 13

It's a hard life, being a president or prime minister, especially when people believe that laws were made to be broken. Paul says that human authority is a divine institution, not a necessary evil, and should be respected.

God does not expect us to live chaotically. Those who rule do so as his vice-regents (whether they acknowledge God or not). By obeying authority we are serving God and preserving the social stability. The Bible does not specify any one type of government structure, but focuses on whether government is just and righteous.

Human authority at its best protects our basic freedoms and restrains those who do evil. Sin is lawlessness (1 John 3:4); even breaking small laws supports the anarchic tendency of the 'old nature' in each of us. Abiding the law is a good spiritual discipline.

But human authority can never become absolute. Peter refused to obey rulers who countered God's clear commands (Acts 4:18-20). Law makers are not above God's law. Augustine quotes a pirate asked by Alexander the Great what he meant by taking possession of the sea. The pirate replied, 'What do you mean by taking possession of the whole earth? Because I do it with a petty ship I am called a robber, but you, who do it with a great fleet, are called an emperor.' Good point!

Freedom is inconsistent

Romans 14,15

Paul achieves a balanced attitude which few of us manage. He refuses to let other people's scruples determine how he will live. He is his own man. Yet at the same time he's prepared to respect those scruples out of love for the people who think differently from himself. This makes a virtue out of correct inconsistency. He tells us:

- To respect each other (vv 1-4,14,15,19-21)
- To sort out what's appropriate for ourselves (vv 5-8)
- Not to judge what others do (vv 9-13,22-23)
- Not to be bludgeoned by others into conforming (vv 16-18).

Paul allows his respect for others actually to limit what he does in their presence. He does not strut his freedom or superiority; he keeps quiet. He is deliberately inconsistent in his behaviour, because he is consistently putting others first. This is a key to harmonious fellowship in the church.

Long words with deep meanings

Almost every religion in the world is concerned with one central question: how can a person be made right with God? Even optimistic people recognise that there is a gulf of scale, if not of character, to be bridged.

The Bible consistently reveals that God is perfect, and we are not: perfection and imperfection, holiness and unholiness are incompatible. The relationship between God and his people is damaged. We can only observe him from afar; we cannot enter his personal presence.

Paul addresses this issue in Romans (also in Galatians and Ephesians), using a number of technical terms. They are metaphors, and are not to be taken crudely. They each point to a truth which is bigger than the picture, and only when all are taken together do we glimpse the whole picture, which is still too big for our finite minds to take in.

Righteousness
This means God's just, fair and perfect character and dealings with his creation. It is the main quality human beings lack. Jesus was the righteous Son of God, the second person of the Holy Trinity, here to restore to us the righteousness we need if we are to enter God's presence (Romans 5:17-19).

Atonement
Literally 'at-one-ment', being made one or reunited with God, the purpose of Christ's death on the cross. He gave us 'peace with God' (Romans 5:1) through his atoning death as the 'lamb of sacrifice' (3:25). He suffered for our sinfulness to bring us back to God.

Reconciliation
Often considered to be the principle which holds together all the other concepts surrounding the death of Christ, this idea is similar in meaning to atonement but with the stress on the effect, whereas atonement stresses the means. We are like former enemies reconciled to God (Romans 5:10,11).

Redemption
Slaves could gain their freedom if they paid redemption money to their owner. The Bible speaks of human beings being slaves to sin. Christ 'paid the price' of our freedom (Romans 3:24).

Justification
This legal term speaks of God's verdict of 'not guilty' on the repentant sinner who puts faith in Christ. In Old Testament practice, to 'justify' was more than just to acquit; it was to say the accused was 'in the right' – hence, 'righteous'. Justification is God declaring that we are 'in the right' because of what Christ has done on our behalf. Sin is no longer a barrier; it is forgiven and forgotten. Christ has removed it; the charge is dropped (Romans 3:21-4:25).

Substitute
Several of these metaphors carry the idea of one who takes the place of another. It was pictured in the Old Testament sacrifices; the lamb died in the place of the sinner. There is also the idea of our substitute being our representative, acting on our behalf.

Representative
Paul deals with this when he compares Christ with Adam (Romans 5:12-21). Adam was the representative of the human race by divine appointment who failed the test and brought us into disgrace; Christ was the appointed

representative of the human race who passed the test and restored our righteousness. Just as we are tarred with Adam's sin by being born human, we are clothed with Jesus' righteousness when we are spiritually born again.

Grace
This, the central concept in Paul's explanation of Christ's death and resurrection, means God's riches freely given to the undeserving. The Father was under no obligation to send his Son into the world to die for us; he did so because he loved us, and Christ went to the cross out of love for us. We cannot earn a restored relationship with God, we can only receive it on the basis of what Christ has done. It is a gift, not a wage; a privilege not a right.

Faith
For Paul, this is the means by which we receive God's gracious gift of eternal life through Christ. We receive it on trust that it will achieve what God says it will. In the New Testament faith means more than believing notions; it means relying on someone or something – staking your life on them. Faith is trusting Christ to forgive us and to give us eternal life.

'In Christ'
When we put our faith or trust in Christ, there is a sense in which the circle is closed and we are 'one' with God once more. Paul frequently writes about being 'in' Christ as if we are made one with him, not in the 'New Age' sense of becoming part of the divine, but in the biblical sense of being incorporated into his body (which is the church) and thus into a personal relationship with head of it. Because we are in Christ, we are 'covered' by or 'clothed in' his righteousness. God sees us no longer as alienated sinners, but as beloved children.

Adoption
An image drawn from the Roman practice of adopting grown youths and making them heirs of their estate. Paul says God has adopted us into his family and given us all the privileges of being his natural children (Romans 8:14-17).

Sanctification
This is the process of growing more like Christ. The person who has trusted Christ embarks on a Christian life in which the old nature is constantly put off and the new constantly put on. Transformation into Christ's likeness is not a once-for-all event but a lifelong process, only completed when we are totally renewed in heaven. Hence many of Paul's letters (including Romans) stress the need to actively apply the faith, and remain vigilant lest sin creeps in (Romans 12:1,2; 13:14).

The terms for today
The essence of Pauline teaching is that God acted in Christ on our behalf. That takes away the stress and uncertainty which otherwise dogs the steps of anyone wishing to be in a right relationship with God. We are assured that that the covenant-keeping God of both Testaments will save eternally people who are sinful but penitent and who trust themselves to Jesus Christ.

Paul's concepts are sufficient to tax the minds of the finest scholars, yet simple enough to be grasped by anyone: 'Christ died for our sins.' We may not understand all the notions, but we can keep hold of this one fact.

But when we do, the Bible challenges us to respond with grateful hearts which are expressed in obedient and God-centred living in every part of our personality and within every part of our society. The wonder of his salvation is such that it is to lift our spirits, thrill our hearts, inform our minds, and direct our paths.

The Book of Ruth

- Is a touching human story of faithfulness, love and decency
- Tells how Ruth, a Moabite, came to Israel and became an ancestor of David (and Jesus)
- Shows how God works in people's lives despite suffering, and that he is in control of events

Faith restored

RUTH

1	Naomi and her daughters-in-law are widowed; Naomi and Ruth return to Bethlehem
2	Ruth gleans in Boaz's field and is protected by him
3	Ruth tells Boaz he is her relative and asks for marriage according to the custom
4	Boaz gives a closer relative the opportunity; when that is refused, he marries Ruth.

Even in the darkest of places and times there is usually some trace of decency and faith. The book of Ruth, set in the lawless period of the judges, is like a candle-flame of hope glimmering in the darkness of despair.

It begins with what seems to be a majestic act of self-sacrifice. Ruth opts to emigrate to her mother-in-law's homeland when common sense suggests she would be better off in her own country.

Relations between Moab and Israel were constantly strained. During the judges period the Moabite king Eglon had oppressed Israel for 18 years (Judges 3). So Ruth could not be sure of a welcome in a country which in any case was hostile to foreigners for religious reasons.

Yet faith in God and love for Naomi overcame personal considerations. Ruth does not know that all will work out well in the end, and neither do we when faith and love demand unusual and sacrificial actions. The story reminds us that God does not let down those who trust him.

But Ruth is also a treatise on God's providence. It illustrates superbly his provision for his people and his sovereignty over their affairs. This superbly-written and carefully-constructed story shows that God has not left his people.

He is not mentioned much, but he does not need to be. People may suffer heartache, grief, and hardship, but he is directing their steps through the hazards even though they are at best

May the LORD repay you for what you have done. May you be richly rewarded by the LORD, the God of Israel, under whose wings you have come to take refuge.

Ruth 2:12

only dimly aware of the fact. God is like a director hovering behind the camera, placing the actors in the right places at the right times. His providence extends over a long time scale and across territories.

Boaz also reflects God's character. He is described as a 'kinsman-redeemer' (2:20). It was the custom – indeed, the law – that the nearest relative should take as an additional wife the widow of his close relation to provide for her and to maintain the family line.

So he becomes a picture of God for hard-pressed believers. Boaz is not tarred with the brush of selfish indulgence we have seen in Judges. Indeed, he is touched by Ruth's willingness to have him as he seems old enough to be her father (3:10). For them relationships are matters of trust and honour, of faithfulness more than feeling.

Throughout Scripture God is seen as a redeemer, bringing his people out of spiritual poverty and slavery and giving them new life and hope. He is faithful, doing what is right and keeping his covenant. And he is kind. This story reminded oppressed people at the time of the judges that the God of the Exodus had not forsaken them; his character had not changed.

Boaz's selfless willingness to take Ruth (when a closer relative refused) and at the same time to abide by the strict conditions of the law provides a colourful illustration of the New Testament picture of God's redemption through Jesus Christ. We too are without eternal hope; we too are dependent on mercy and grace. Christ fulfilled the law and revealed his love on the cross.

Ruth restores our faith in human nature, giving us two great examples to follow. It also rekindles our faith in God. He sticks around in the worst of times, works for our good over long periods of time, and remains faithful to his own character.

Date of events:

During the judges' period: c. 1150-1050 BC.

Location:

Moab, then Bethlehem.

Place in Bible:

After Judges, before 1 Samuel in the Old Testament

Story parallel to:

the book of Judges.

For today

- Faithfulness to God and love for others is more vital than personal comfort
- Trust God to guide your steps when you can't see the future

Author: Unknown. Jewish tradition suggests Samuel, but even if the story dates from his time, a later editor explicitly refers back to 'ancient customs' (4:1-12) and links Ruth with king David (4:8-22) who we know did not take office until some time after Samuel's death.

Date of writing: During the early monarchy (c. 1000-950 BC; cf. 4:22).

Purpose: It is such a good story that the author could have any (or none) of several purposes in mind.As the narrative emphasises God's sovereignty, it is possible that the book was written to encourage hard-pressed believers, or to remind die-hards of the global extent of God's purposes.

Real lives and frank confessions

The Book of 1 Samuel

- Tells the story of Samuel, the last of Israel's judges
- Explains why Israel asked for and received a king
- Describes how Saul was appointed king, and how he fell from grace
- Recounts the rise of David from shepherd boy to monarch

The books of Samuel (originally one document) bring today's reader into familiar territory. They are stories about people, and enable us to see them as flesh and blood, fallible and real, as well as to reflect on their actions.

We join the narrative at the end of the judges' period. The story of decline, oppression, rescue and recovery continues. Samuel, the last of the judges and a prophet, pilots Israel's tribal confederacy into calmer waters. In his old age, the elders ask him to appoint a king.

This is a watershed event in the Bible. Samuel, after much soul-searching, appoints Saul. But as the prophet warned, Saul abuses his power, becomes mentally unstable, and falls from grace. David is secretly anointed as heir apparent.

Saul becomes paranoid (and jealous) of the young giant-killer and David spends the next decade an outlaw on the run, becoming a role model for future Robin Hoods. Eventually, when Saul dies, David is accepted as king.

Later to be hailed as the model for the Messiah, David nonetheless has feet of clay. Apart from his celebrated affair with Bathsheba and contract killing of her husband, he has a shambolic home life and for a while is forced into exile by his rebellious son Absalom.

But for all that, he loves God, and gives the nation a solid foundation on which his son Solomon built a never-to-be-repeated 'golden age' of prosperity and peace (which is recounted in 1 Kings).

It is an absorbing story, written as a prophetic overview of a formative part of Israel's development. Behind the exposed lives we see a righteous God who remains reliable and who continues to be his people's rescuer.

AT A GLANCE

1 SAMUEL

1	Samuel is born to the childless Hannah
2	Hannah's song of praise
3	Samuel called by God
4	Ark captured by Philistines
5-6	Ark returned to Israel
7	Israel gathers at Mizpah
8	Israelites ask for a king
9-11	Saul found and anointed king
12	Samuel's charge to Israel
13	Saul misuses his power
14	Philistines defeated by Jonathan
15	God rejects Saul as king
16	David secretly anointed
17	David kills Goliath
18-19	Saul attempts to kill David
20	David's friendship with Jonathan
21-23	David on the run
24	David refuses to kill Saul
25	David and Abigail
26	David again refuses to kill Saul
27	David takes refuge in Philistia
28	Saul consults a medium
29-30	David defeats the Amalekites
31	Saul and Jonathan die

(Outline of 2 Samuel on p 389)

KEY QUOTE

Does the LORD delight in burnt offerings and sacrifices as much as in obeying the voice of the LORD? To obey is better than sacrifice, and to heed is better than the fat of rams

1 Samuel 15:22

Long wait then model mum gives up child

1 Samuel 1-2

A thousand of our years are like a mere day to God, says Psalm 90:4, and when you're waiting for God to do something it can certainly feel like it. We are still in the judges period when each person makes up their own rules as they go along (Judges 21:24,25), and there is corruption at the heart of Israel's religious life (1 Samuel 2:12-36).

To deal with it, God once again sends a baby. Those who long for change can't see it happening yet. Stories like this are meant to encourage us to believe that God is not asleep but has everything in hand when we get frustrated with his apparent inaction.

From Hannah's point of view her wait is long and painful, but is eventually rewarded with an answer to prayer. Her response (2:1-10) is one of the Bible's classic hymns of praise and is echoed by Mary in Luke 1:46-55.

The 'sacrifice' of her child (1:22-28) is therefore all the more remarkable. In her family-centred society, being childless was interpreted as God's curse, not least because it spelled the end of the family line.

Like Mary anointing Jesus with precious ointment (John 12:1-8) and Abraham preparing to sacrifice Isaac (Genesis 22), Hannah hands back to God what she holds most dear. Unlike Abraham, she didn't get him back (although she did keep in touch, 2:19).

Modern parents might look askance at offering the three-year-old for adoption, but they could learn something too. Hannah is not possessive. Samuel is not 'her' child, to be clasped and used like a doll to boost her own ego, to feed her own desire for reciprocated love, or even simply to provide her with a reason to live.

Samuel is a child of promise, with his own destiny already determined by the loving God who has answered her prayer. Children do not 'belong' exclusively to their parents. They are unique people with a place in God's plans. Hannah is a model parent, not a heartless one who mistakes her own emotional needs for maternal love.

Where am I?

Date of events:
c. 1100-1000 BC

Location:
Palestine

Place in Bible:
After Ruth, before 1 Kings in the Old Testament

Story follows:
Judges

Story leads to:
1 Kings, 2 Chronicles

Parallel book:
1 Chronicles (for David's story)

FAST facts

Title: They take their name from the first main character to appear in the story.

Structure and purpose: These two books were kept as one until the fifteenth century. The history is selective (a 20-year gap is recorded in a single verse, 7:2) with the specific purpose of tracing the spiritual development of Israel's monarchy up to the reign of good King David. There are clear sections, and the book begins and ends with a hymn of praise to a sovereign God who cares for his people.

Author: Unknown. Samuel died well before David and his association with the books is as an actor and not as a writer. Several theories concerning the source documents used by the final compiler have been propounded over the past 200 years, each of them seriously questioned by succeeding generations of scholars. One writer has observed that all that can be known for certain about their compilation could be contained within a small leaflet.

Date of composition: It must be after the time of David (he dies shortly after the end of 2 Samuel) and therefore after 950 BC, perhaps during the time of Solomon. Some comment-ators have suggested that it was compiled during the period of Josiah's revival when the book of Deuteronomy was rediscovered (2 Kings 22), placing it between 640 and 609 BC.

Life's a journey, faith's a leap

1 Samuel 3

It can be helpful to picture the Christian life as a journey. Each person's path is different, even though there are common features, because our personalities, perceptions and circumstances are different.

Christians are not called to be clones. We become 'like' Jesus, not each other, as he works on our unique personhood so that it reflects his presence and God-centred nature. We grow in faith, as Samuel did (2:26), who took his responsibility to God and the 'church' seriously (3:1), yet 'did not yet know the Lord' (v 7).

How can someone believe and serve and yet not know the Lord? It does not mean that he was 'not saved' or that he was living a double life. To God, our spiritual journey begins at (or before) human birth, not at the 'new birth'. Somewhere along the way, there is an awakening (and for most people, more than one) when we discover God in a new way, see certain beliefs more clearly, and step forward in faith.

It is like human growth. Although the first adult tooth might be a significant step forward in a child's development, there are many other developments not noted as the child grows; they are only seen in retrospect. Samuel's experience suggests that it may not be appropriate to demand too much in terms of faith or experience before giving people certain tasks in the church. It is often through executing them that people come to 'know the Lord' in fresh ways.

Ark sinks its captors

1 Samuel 4-7

In the film *Raiders of the Lost Ark*, myths surrounding Israel's covenant box are combined with modern technology to create a spectacular display of tricks as explorers unearth it. These chapters do not imply that there was magic in the box; they can be understood in terms of religious guilt and divine sovereignty.

The Israelites wrongly took the symbol of God's presence into battle like a lucky charm (4:3). Its loss demoralised them (4:21,22); when tribal deities were taken, the tribe was deemed to have lost its god's support. But the ark was never intended to be thought of like that.

The Philistines were then apparently jinxed (ch 5). Their god was bowled over by Israel's and their people fell sick. (What with is unclear; bubonic plague was not known in the area until much later.) Interpreting this as Yahweh's punishment they set about reverently returning the ark. If the cows (6:7-10) turned back to their calves (as would be natural) the Philistines would conclude that the disasters were a coincidence. They walked on, so God was clearly looking after his box.

We are back in the thought forms of Leviticus. The artefacts of religion are holy. They are not to be treated like ordinary things given for a religious purpose; they belong to God, and are wholly his. Thus to touch them is to come close to God. That such a belief could degenerate into superstition is obvious. But it could also create genuine awe and reverence for God which our more utilitarian culture has singularly lost.

God dethroned as Saul is crowned

1 Samuel 8-10

There is a form of Christian spirituality which suggests that God has one plan or purpose for each individual. If we fail to find it or to follow it, then we can never be within God's will and thus never receive his full blessing. This passage suggests that reality is more complex.

God intended Israel to be exemplary in its social organisation as well as in its spiritual orientation. It was a theocracy, a unique nation with God as its King and no distinction between church and state. The people's request for a leader who combined the roles of chief executive, Lord Chief Justice and Commander-in-Chief of the armed forces was natural but wrong. It implied that they considered God's guidance and jurisdiction through the priests insufficient.

Having made the decision, they were not ejected from God's plans. Samuel is told to give them what they asked. God accommodates himself to their faithless request, after a due warning about the human consequences. He even leads Samuel carefully to Saul. God did not want a king, but he chose one for them.

It is a classic example of his grace. God is not inflexible. He works with human situations in order to achieve his unchanging purposes; he does not impose a rigid scheme. That does not excuse us for taking wrong or unwise courses of action. It does reassure us that having made such decisions in the past we are not excluded from God's activity in the present.

Saul wanted to be someone different

1 Samuel 9-16

King Saul had everything going for him: good looks, great talent and God's approval. Yet he ended his life as a mentally unstable tyrant. David's lament for him has passed into common speech as a sad indictment of fallen heroes: 'How the mighty have fallen' (2 Samuel 1:19). We can trace in his early life some of the factors which contributed to his complex character and decline.

- He was naturally shy and retiring (10:22) and self-conscious, perhaps feeling inferior, about his humble origins (9:21). This seems more than natural modesty. He did not pray as Solomon did for divine inspiration in the face of a seemingly impossible task (cf. 1 Kings 3:6-9); he seems to have been overwhelmed by it.
- He was a better 'number two' than a 'number one'. He needed a lot of exact instructions from Samuel (e.g. 10:1-8). His venture into the underworld (ch 28) showed how unsure he was of his own judgment. He was probably indecisive.
- Yet he tended to be impulsive without regard for the consequences. When he stepped wrongly onto holy ground (13:1-15) the punishment probably demoralised him and clouded his judgment still further.
- He was harsh and arbitrary with people (14:24), the mark of an insensitive despot. He led by fear rather than by winning respect. His willingness to kill his own son would hardly have endeared him to the rank and file who, more decent by far, saved Jonathan's life.
- He was afraid of people (15:24) so he gave in to their demands without arguing his case.
- His self-interest alienated him from God's Spirit and opened him to bad influences, 16:14. ('An evil spirit from the LORD' means 'under God's permissive control'; the Israelites saw all events, good and bad, as under God's control.)

In all this, Saul is revealed as a weak man trying to appear tough. Perhaps if he had accepted the limitations of his own personality, and learned to live with them instead of covering them with a false macho image, he would still have been a successful military leader and would have become a successful human being too.

Instead, he fell into manic depression and even murder (18:10,11; 22:17-19), leaving the sobering lesson that it is better to accept our limitations and allow God to use us through them, than to seek to become what we are not leaving a trail of wreckage behind us.

Philistines were not so bad

The term 'Philistine' is reserved today for someone who is uncouth or uncultured. In biblical times the Philistines were tough warriors but they were not barbaric animals. They had migrated to the south-west of Palestine from the Aegean area. They were skilled metal workers and soon had a monopoly of iron forging (1 Samuel 13:19-23). They set up strategic garrisons in five centres (Gaza, Ashkelon, Ashdod, Ekron and Gath). They appear to have adopted the Canaanite language and were happy to absorb Canaanite gods as well; their three main deities were Dagon, Ashtoreth and Baalzebul.

Hard knocks form rounded character

1 Samuel 17-19

Some people become sharp and angular when pelted by life's hard missiles. Others, like David, are rounded by them and their corners are rubbed off. Once again, a Bible author is giving us a potted biography that reveals the familiar pattern of God's dealings with those who he calls to his service.

David began in obscurity where he learnt survival and faithfulness in the harsh realities of an unsympathetic world (17:14,15,34-37). His secret anointing was perhaps not fully understood by either his family or himself (ch 16). It was followed by minor service in Saul's court which may explain why Saul knows him in 16:14-23 but not in 17:55, unless the chronology is reversed for the sake of giving us an earlier summary.

He is then elevated quietly to high office (18:5), succeeds, but becomes the object of Saul's jealousy and is ousted from his job, surviving several assassination attempts.

Many Christians in such a situation would ask why God behaved so badly towards them. The author is telling us that it is Saul who is behaving badly and that God is protecting David from him. The heir apparent is a victim of human injustice, not of divine caprice. It was that knowledge that enabled David to survive his outlaw years, and it will enable us to survive the wilderness periods when God's call seems to have been forgotten by God himself.

Samuel: a case study

The biblical record never identifies a single blemish in Samuel. He is an example of a godly leader. As one writer put it, 'He knew how to get on with men, because he knew how to get on with God.'

- He was dedicated to God as a child (1:28)
- He was specifically called to God's service (ch 3)
- He trained under an experienced but imperfect leader (2:11,26)
- People confirmed his gifts (3:19-20)
- He was faithful in routine matters (7:2, 15-17)
- He was unselfish and obedient to God (ch 8)
- He was a man of integrity (12:3,4)
- He was a man of prayer (12:19,23)
- He was not afraid to confront wrongdoing (ch 15)
- He cared for Saul even when the king sinned (15:35-16:1)
- He protected young David (19:18)
- He was a mentor to other leaders (19:14-20)

True friends are closer than brothers

1 Samuel 20-23

Friendship is difficult to handle. In our intensely self-centred and suspicious culture, we trust few people fully and close relationships outside of partnerships invite sneers or allegations of sexual impropriety.

It is one facet of human life in which the ancients, even the Victorians, outscore us. Close friendship and the affection which goes with it was accepted as normal and healthy and did not require sexual expression. The book of Proverbs extols its virtues (e.g. 27:10).

In the twelfth century AD, Aeldred, Abbot of Rievaulx Abbey in Yorkshire, described friendship as 'a foretaste of heaven where no one hides his thoughts or disguises his affection'. David and Jonathan were friends like that.

Crown prince Jonathan, heir to the throne (14:49) was a strong, brave man (14:1). After David's giant-killing episode, they became such firm friends that Jonathan gave David the emblems of his authority (18:1-4).

In the unenviable choice between his father and his friend, Jonathan supported David against the patent injustice of Saul (19:1,4) and in an episode full of cloak-and-dagger secrecy warned David to flee (ch 20). Although parted, their bond remained secure (23:15-18) which must have been dangerous for Jonathan.

Theirs is not the only biblical example of friendship, but it is one of the most detailed. It leaves modern casual acquaintances standing. There can be no Christian fellowship without friendship; if we desire closer Christian community, it will have to start with personal friendship.

Unselfish David lets his rival win

1 Samuel 24,26

Imagine a Wimbledon tennis final in which the top seed and reigning champion faces a lower-ranked player. The favourite is carrying an injury and can't move quickly. The underdog, instead of punishing them mercilessly and carrying off the coveted trophy, plays soft shots which the champion can return in such a way that they retain their title.

Twice David was offered what some saw as a God-given chance to carry off the kingship of Israel. Saul was within a single shot of death, but David deliberately played into the net and allowed him to keep his title. His supporters must have thought he was mad; they had urged him to bury Saul for good.

There are few more selfless acts in Scripture than this, apart from Christ's death. David has one over-powering belief: when it's time for him to be king, God will give him the kingship; he cannot and will not take it by any means, even when it apparently looks like a gift.

A possessive and acquisitive society such as ours finds this hard to understand. We may admire him from a distance but find his example hard to follow. Advertisers shout at us to buy now and pay later. Management manuals urge us to apply for and grab top jobs as soon as we can; we may never have another chance if we stay where we are.

David would turn in his grave. He knew all about competitiveness, but he abandoned it in deference to God. He spoke often of 'waiting for the Lord' (Psalm 27:14). He knew that God would sort out the ends so long as God was left to choose the means as well. Today, we live in another world, and consequently we are the only people who can change it.

Fair shares

1 Samuel 30:21-25

The phrase 'share and share alike', more often rendered 'fair shares for all' owes its origins not to Karl Marx, but to David in this passage. It sets an important principle of fairness which reflects God's justice and righteousness. It is picked up by Jesus in his parable about the vineyard workers receiving equal pay for differing tasks (Matthew 20:1-16).

It tells us that different kinds of service for God are equally important. The helper or administrator is no less important or effective as an apostle or an evangelist. God looks for faithfulness where we look for measurable results. In the parable of the talents (Matthew 25:14-30) people were judged not by their differing gifts but by the way each used their gifts.

David had looked at life through God's eyes. The back-room team deserves as much recognition as the rest.

Let off the hook

1 Samuel 29-30 (cf. 27)

This would have been David's trickiest ethical dilemma of all, a real Catch-22 situation in which he could only lose. Having sheltered with the Philistines, pretending to attack the Israelites, but in fact destroying outlying Philistine settlements (ch 27), he was about to be pitched against Saul. To refuse would endanger his life; to agree would make him an enemy and destroyer of his own people.

He was let off the hook by nervous Philistine commanders and went to hound the nomadic Amalekites. The author is reminding us that when, like David, we are forced by circumstance (and not by our own foolishness) into 'impossible' situations, God will provide some form of escape route (cf. 1 Corinthians 10:13). He did not have to contrive it; it was there for him to accept.

HARD Question

Can we ever consult the dead?

1 Samuel 28

For all his faults, Saul had previously obeyed the Law of Moses (Exodus 22:18; Leviticus 19:26,31; 20:27) by expelling all spiritist mediums from Israel (vv 3,9). Now he consults one.

The only other biblical example of someone asking for a visit from the dead is in a parable, and the request is turned down (Luke 16:19-31). Biblical resurrections (such as of Jairus' daughter, the widow of Nain's son and Jesus' friend Lazarus) are true restorations to life, not messages from across the abyss.

Jesus' own resurrection is a foretaste of the new life of heaven, similar to yet different from this one. In his transfiguration (Mark 9:2-8) Jesus talks with (the dead) Moses and Elijah in their resurrected form, because a window is opened into heaven and Jesus temporarily returns to (and so radiates) the glory he had laid aside for his incarnation. It was a unique experience of a unique being.

But if the Bible prohibits attempted consultations with the dead, we are left with the problem of interpreting what happened here. Theoretically, God can do anything, yet he always abides by the laws he has set himself. (He is just, so can never act unjustly, for example.) Even miracles seem only to modify the 'laws' of nature (which are temporary arrangements for this life only) rather than to flout them. The most extreme of Jesus' miracles, walking on water, is not quite so crazy given the natural surface tension of water which supports insects.

That leaves us with three possibilities. One, an evil spirit which usually controlled the medium was taken over by God's Spirit to impersonate Samuel. Secondly, both Saul and the woman saw a vision of Samuel and heard the words which came from God.

Or thirdly, and most likely, the woman used her powers of telepathy to 'see' Samuel in Saul's mind. He was, after all, in a heightened state of emotion, desperately 'willing' the prophet to return. God would then have given the woman God's words which only repeated what Saul already knew, apart from the prophecy of his death.

The medium's surprise (v 12) suggests that she did not expect to see Samuel, which is an ironic comment on the side concerning her normal (and therefore deceptive) 'messages' and 'manifestations' of people's loved ones.

On biblical grounds, Christians have always avoided seeking the dead. They are promised the continuous presence of the Holy Spirit of God, who is all-knowing (which the dead are not). He is promised in the New Testament as a guide and teacher, and may even on occasions reveal the future (John 16:13; cf. Acts 11:27-30; 21:10-14).

However, we are not promised that we shall know everything about the future, and we are not promised complete understanding about our current circumstances. We are called to walk by faith and to exercise responsibly the free choices God gives us on the basis of what we already know of him. Mature faith does not act like a child who every five minutes goes back to its mother and says, 'What shall I do now?'

Clash of honour

1 Samuel 31-2 Samuel 1

Saul's consultation with the medium (ch 28) was the ultimate tragedy in his life. He was a broken man, desperate for the advice he had spurned in the past. His prophesied death was just a matter of time (28:19). He must have entered the battle already morally defeated.

Taken at face value the two accounts of his death appear contradictory but they can be reconciled. Suicide was dishonourable in Israel, but so too was having one's body mutilated or finished off by opponents. Greater honour was to be had through death on the battlefield. Saul chose suicide as the lesser of two evils.

The Amalekite had a different code and was sadly unaware of David's higher ideals which had twice prevented him from killing Saul (chs 24,26). To the Amalekite, there was honour in putting someone out of their misery.

Everyone knew Saul was a bad lot and that David was destined to succeed him, so a little embroidery on the scene he had witnessed would be to his advantage: David would honour him. He was mistaken.

David's time on the run might almost be over, but his sensitive heart and God-centred mind could only look back on Saul's life with sadness. There was nothing to rejoice about. Saul had behaved stupidly, but he was also God's chosen king, not without talent and dignity, and therefore to be respected in both life and death.

Jonathan, too, was dead: the friend who had saved David's life. Had he lived, the dynamic between them would have been intriguing, because Jonathan was Saul's choice as heir although David had been anointed in advance by Samuel. It would have tested their friendship, but could have been a superb partnership. As it is, David has only his memories, and rightly he weeps, inviting us through the psalm to share in his feelings.

Civil war sets trend for the future

2 Samuel 2-5

With Saul gone, readers are probably expecting the story to move on to a happy reign and national harmony. Instead, it's a messy mix of success and failure. As it was in the beginning, so it was to continue until its end.

- Ambitious Abner knows David is destined to be king (3:9), but takes a chance and declares Saul's son as a puppet ruler; Abner pulls the strings.
- The normal method for settling differences by a contest of champions (2:12-16; cf. 1 Samuel 17:4-11) was indecisive.
- Abner wisely prevented further bloodshed but left a running sore; he had killed Joab's brother (2:17-32).
- The dispute lasted several years (3:1).
- Abner, when his male pride was offended, changed sides (3:6-12)
- David insisted on getting Michal back, destroying her new home and marriage, even though technically she was still his wife (3:13-16; cf. 1 Samuel 25:44).
- Joab reneges on the peace agreement, to David's dismay (3:22-39).
- Ish-Bosheth is killed, again to David's dismay (ch 4; just who is in charge?).
- David becomes king.

The author shows that David had to work hard to achieve what God had promised. So do we; our call is to be strong and brave (2:7). He is also showing us a recurring trend. David's life will be marked by feuds and follies, some of his own making. God's kingdom is attained only with a struggle against the world, flesh and devil – and ourselves (cf. Matthew 11:12).

AT A GLANCE

2 SAMUEL

1	**David grieves for Saul and Jonathan**
2-4	**Civil war breaks out**
5	**David is king of all Israel**
6	**The ark returned to Jerusalem**
7	**God assures David of his love**
8	**David's battles**
9	**David's kindness to Mephibosheth**
10	**David subdues the Ammonites**
11	**David's adultery with Bathsheba**
12	**Nathan's rebuke**
13	**Family feud**
14-15	**Absalom's rebellion**
16-17	**David on the run again**
18	**Death of Absalom**
19	**David's return to Jerusalem**
20	**Sheba's rebellion**
21	**Saul's final resting place**
22	**David sings God's praise**
23	**David's prayer, and helpers**
24	**David holds a census**

(N.B. The story of David from Saul's death onwards is repeated in 1 Chronicles, with variations)

Worship ranges from awe to zeal

2 Samuel 6 (cf. 1 Chronicles 13,15,16)
Christians differ sharply over ways to worship God. Today, styles vary from the formality and ritual of the Orthodox Churches to the free and spontaneous style of the Pentecostal and 'New' churches. Such differences are not restricted to specific human cultures, but often range across them.

This passage focuses on what is appropriate in worship for all traditions. It begins with David overstepping the mark. He is so excited that he ignores the biblical rules. The ark, the symbol of God's presence, was not meant to be carried on a cart but slung between poles and borne on the shoulders of the priests.

When 'holiness' slays Uzzah, David shows anger at God, but he is angry with himself and afraid of God (v 9). He was too familiar with God. Next time he acknowledges God's holiness in an appropriate manner (v 18), visibly declaring that the Lord is mighty and 'other'.

Worship of any style needs a sense of awe and reverence which befits our approaching a holy God, otherwise it becomes 'me-centred' and vacuous.

David then does what his wife thinks is the very antithesis of awe and reverence: he strips off his king's uniform and dances fervently 'before the LORD' (v 22). What Michal cannot see is that this is no showy act of worship for people to admire, nor a self-oriented demeaning of spiritual 'freedom'.

This is an act of humility. David is oblivious to the people and to what they expect. If 'freedom' is exalted as a virtue in itself, then 'charismatic' worship becomes as showy as 'ritualistic' worship can be and equally empty. Worship is not self-expression; it is God-devotion. Humility may be expressed in many ways, but worship is incomplete without it.

Finally, David's action reminds us (as does the whole Old Testament) that worship is a whole-person activity. He worships with body, mind, heart and spirit. Omit any part of the personality, and worship is at once impoverished.

There's a limit to what you should do

2 Samuel 7 (cf. 1 Chronicles 17)
We expect our politicians to control the economy (promoting wealth), protect lifestyle (make us happy), combat crime (give us security), promote morality (reduce crime), preserve the environment (improve health), subsidise health care and transport (so we can do what we like), ensure full employment (so we can earn), and educate our children (because we're too busy). No wonder they can never live up to their election promises!

In reality, they are human with limited talents and resources. David was king of a far less complex society than ours and soon discovered that he could not do everything, either. He wants to build a temple to God in his newly established capital. But God says no: it's not your job.

In this superb passage of reassurance, God stresses his love and care for David and his family but the time is not right for the temple. The nation is not yet at peace, and the person is not right, because he has blood on his hands (cf. 1 Chronicles 22:7-10).

David accepts the limitations graciously. He expresses what St Paul calls 'contentment' with his circumstances (Philippians 4:12). We are thereby warned not to over-reach ourselves (as Saul had done). We are also warned by Nathan's mistake, too; the prophet had to learn that even good ideas are not always in accord with God's will.

Friendship renewed

2 Samuel 9
When close friends or relatives die, you don't forget them. Life has to go on, but the memories remain and there are times when you wish you could do something with or for them again. It is one of those small indications that we

naturally feel that death is not the end, but an intruder into life.

Jonathan had been wrenched from David, first by his father Saul and then by death in battle. David longed for his friend, and the best way to express his feelings was to help Jonathan's family. Mephibosheth had been injured when his nurse had dropped him as a baby (4:4). Physical handicap was often viewed as a curse in ancient Israel, despite the commands to care for the vulnerable (including widows and orphans). When David took him under his wing he was doing Mephibosheth a great favour and treating him with dignity.

The benefit was probably two-way. David may have gained emotional comfort from giving in this way, and as Mephibosheth was a potential rival it was also a demonstration of trust. Later, David thought the young man had betrayed him, but it was the servant Ziba who was the traitor (cf. 16:1-4; 19:24-30). We may not know very well the bereaved relatives of our friends, but they often appreciate such gestures of support.

He killed for sex

2 Samuel 11,12

The story of David and Bathsheba is well-known. The facts are:

- David was becoming complacent (11:1);
- He thought he could do anything (11:3,4; 12:7-9);
- He tried to cover one sin by committing another (11:6-17).

Beneath the surface of this tragic story in which the author does not spare David's blushes, many lessons can be drawn.

The cover-up drew in people: Joab who acted as executioner and the courtiers who escorted Bathsheba and acted as couriers. Their loyalty to David forced them to do wrong things. Joab had to adopt unwise military tactics which might have incurred further casualties (11:20-24). In any cover-up, the ripples spread out.

Uriah died as an innocent man, sacrificed by the callousness of another. It is this, rather than the adultery, which is the greater sin. All human life is precious, and no one has the right to take another's life needlessly. The author implies that Bathsheba loved Uriah (11:26); she was hurt by David's action too. To kill is the ultimate act of selfishness, the antithesis of Christ laying down his life for others.

The story shows just how blind our selfish desires can make us. And David is (generally) a good man! Psalm 51 records his repentance, and Psalm 14:3 may reflect his greater understanding of human nature as a result: 'There is no-one who does good, not even one.'

The postscript should not be overlooked. Bathsheba became the mother of Solomon, a king of peace and builder of the temple. Out of the tragedy some good emerged, by God's grace and not of David's doing.

CROSS CHECK

Bibical wars and killing: p 227
David's life: pp 49-50
Solomon's life: pp 51, 54, 243-5

David's Achilles' heel revealed at home

2 Samuel 13

David had six wives before he recovered Michal and before his affair with Bathsheba, and many children by them (3:2-5; 5:14-16). His household was therefore bound to have a high level of rivalry and divided loyalties.

Marriage between half-brothers and sisters was not allowed (Leviticus 18:9; 20:17) but Tamar was desperate enough to suggest anything (v 13). To lose her virginity before marriage was to be shamed in her culture, and to lose it through rape in any culture is a cause of intense emotional stress. She had been violated in a deeply personal way and could never be the same again.

The dynamics here are intriguing. Amnon was David's eldest son, and technically heir (although the principle of dynasty had not yet been established). But Absalom was David's favourite (cf. v 39) perhaps because he has something of his father's initiative and daring.

Absalom takes Tamar under his wing and his restraint probably fooled David (v 22) into thinking that vengeance was not on his mind, especially after David had expressed his own fury towards Amnon (v 21).

We cannot make judgements on David's family life from these cameos (and there are more feuds to come). Nathan had warned him that they would be a feature of his life as a punishment for his adultery (12:11,12) but there were no doubt many human factors contributing to them.

The author's purpose in recording them seems to be twofold. First, he is showing us how Solomon came to rise to pre-eminence even though he was one of the youngest in the family. The second is to remind us that David was flawed and suffered the same as countless other parents of wayward children.

He may have been a model king, but he did not have a fairy-tale home life. Leaders in many walks of life suffer from similar Achilles' heels. If nothing else, they may keep people looking to God, like Paul's 'thorn in the flesh' (2 Corinthians 12:7-10).

Hearts bleed as King David flees again

2 Samuel 15-20

David may have sown the wind with Bathsheba and reaped the whirlwind in his family as a result, but the author of 2 Samuel shows that there is a lot of love for the ageing king as he flees for his life once again.

Absalom's rebellion has a powerful but small fighting force, although his careful cultivation of public opinion (15:1-12) has all the marks of modern spin-doctoring. David did welcome people to his palace to judge their causes (e.g. 14:2-5) and Absalom may have used the inevitable delays to imply that David was inaccessible.

Most people are still loyal to David. So, as the family flees, people weep (15:23). The priest's touching offer to take the ark with David is rightly refused. He knew what happened when it went into battle before (1 Samuel 4). His faith that Jerusalem was God's 'home' was unshaken; the city would outlast David, and the ark belonged there.

His grief as history repeats itself is made worse by the defection of one of his closest aides (15:30,31), causing David to put his own double agent in Absalom's camp (15:34-37). The betrayal of Ziba (falsely implicating Mephibosheth, 16:1-4; cf. 19:24-30) rubs salt into the wound.

David even has to run the gauntlet of curses shouted by a cowardly and probably 'odd' character from a safe distance across a narrow ravine (16:5-14). And then he has to deal with Absalom's brutal murder by Joab, David's ruthless but fiercely loyal commander-in-chief (18:1-18). Yet for once, Joab's harshness has its value as he exposes David's inconsolable grieving as utterly selfish (19:1-8).

David's prayer for protection and restoration (Psalm 3) had been answered, and he returned probably more chastened and humbled than ever. The author makes us feel for him as we follow this sad tale. It would be easy to say it served him right, but the Bible will not allow us to.

It shows that sin can lead to tragedy, and that tragedy is always painful, not to be wished on anyone. Human nature can be fickle in its support for leaders. Loyalty and affection for flawed but good people is a vital thread in the fabric of church and society. David deserved the support he received, and so do those in other ages who suffer even from tragedies to which they may have contributed by their own foolish actions.

Pride leads to a fall

2 Samuel 24

There can be at least two reasons for stock-taking. One is to see what resources are available and how they might be deployed. The other is to feed the feel-good factor. David counts his men for the second and unworthy reason. Even Joab the brutal fighter can see the spiritual folly in it.

The point of the account is that no good – and probably some harm – can come from doing what may be right in some situations (a census of fighting men was commanded by God in the book of Numbers) in the wrong place, at the wrong time, and for the wrong reason.

Good ideas need to be examined for spiritual flaws. Some churches prosper by using certain methods of mission or training courses, and everyone gets on the bandwagon as if they are God's standard. But they cannot be transposed into different situations like light bulbs and expected to work at the touch of a switch.

Above all, good ideas need to be examined for pride. We can list all the 'right' activities in church publicity leaflets and bask in the warmth of good feeling, without contributing much in real terms to God's mission. Humility and dependence on him are the foundations for all service. We may feel good when we see him at work; that is a bonus, not a right and should never be an objective.

For today

1 & 2 Samuel

- Don't become possessive over God's material gifts; hand them back and don't be surprised if he takes them
- Don't over-emphasise your 'experiences'
- If you took a wrong turn, trust that God will stay with you on the new path
- Don't try and be what you're not.
- Cherish your friends
- Don't take opportunities to get God's work done in human ways
- Bring awe and zeal into worship, whatever your 'tradition'
- Stay loyal to those who make mistakes and know it

David's wives and their sons

Ahinoam	Ahigail	Maacah	Haggith	Abital	Eglah	Bathsheba	Other wives
Amnon	Kileab (Daniel)	Absalom	Adonijah	Shephatiah	Ithream	Solomon	Ibhar
						Shammua	Elishua
						Shobab	Eliphelet
		Tamar				Nathan	Nogah
							Nepheg
							Japhia
							Elishama
							Eliada
							Eliphelet 2

Other daughters are not named

God's sex appeal

The Song of Songs

- Is an explicit celebration of human love and sexuality
- Is a poem written like an exchange of love letters
- Has been used as an illustration of the relationship between Christ and his church

According to press reports, students at the State University of New York are lectured by sado-masochists and have courses in homosexuality in the animal kingdom. Their colleagues at the University of Minnesota can attend a newly-endowed Centre for Gay, Lesbian, Bisexual and Transgender Studies, and students in Iowa University can take a certificate course in sexuality.

From tabloid newspapers to street-side billboards, from daytime broadcasts to workplace innuendo, sex is definitely 'in your face' at the turn of the millennium. Sex sells anything, and having largely been divorced from lasting relationships it has become a commodity in its own right.

Readers unfamiliar with the Bible may be surprised to discover that, as Ecclesiastes 1:9 puts it, there is nothing new under the sun. There's plenty of sex in the Bible, too. Apart from Samson and Delilah and David and Bathsheba, not to mention Abraham and his concubine and Solomon with his 1,000-strong harem, there is this little book, often called The Song of Solomon, which is as explicit as a top-shelf magazine.

It has not been an easy book for religious people to come to terms with. It has been the subject of numerous debates and attempts to interpret it as an allegory or a religious drama. Certainly Paul uses the sexual relationship as a picture of God's intimate relationship with his church (Ephesians 5:25-33), and Jesus seems to be echoing 5:2 in Revelation 3:20. But helpful as that might be, there is no indication that this is the Song's main intention.

And there is no reason why it should have been. The Hebrews did not separate body and soul, matter and spirit. From the opening pages of Genesis sex is seen as a gift for the human race and a natural part of God's created order. Adam and Eve's covering of themselves does not imply that sex itself is dirty but that pure innocence has been lost.

The Bible does decree that this most powerful and treacherous of gifts should be channelled carefully and controlled vigorously. The stoning of adulterers was not a verdict on sex as such, but on the destruction of relationships by casual sex. Sexual activity in God's purpose finds its proper place in the context of two people sharing their entire lives, not just part of them.

With those caveats, Scripture gives us this celebration of physical love. It is an echo from the Garden of Eden: 'And God saw all that he had made, and it was very good' (Genesis 1:31). The book is its own commentary: wonder at sex, enjoy it in its place, but don't stir it up until the place and time are appropriate (2:7).

KEY QUOTE

Many waters cannot quench love; rivers cannot wash it away. If one were to give all the wealth of his house for love, it would be utterly scorned.

Song of Songs 8:7

Love is patient, not stud-fast

In his commentary in the Anchor Bible series published in 1977, M.H. Pope listed a *selection* of studies on the Song of Songs. It covered 55 pages and included over 1,000 titles. This is not an easy book!

The chief problem is identifying the speaker in each section and at what point the speaker changes. Versions such as the NIV and GNB offer headings to try to remedy this, but helpful as they are, such schemes are not universally agreed.

The book focuses on the woman ('The Beloved') and evokes a tenderness of sexual attraction that is far removed from the performance-related obsessions of a post-Viagra age. The man ('The Lover') reciprocates; he is not a stud. He admires his partner, desires her, and is patient with her. He also seems to have other interests in life; he's not always on her doorstep.

The third 'speaker' is a group ('Friends', NIV; 'Women', GNB). It is like the chorus of a Greek or medieval play, part commentator and part cheer-leader. It is there to guide, not to pry; these are not peeping toms but almost angelic guardians of a precious relationship.

Two practical observations arise from this book. One, it reminds us of the intensity of sexuality. It is no wonder that something so intense can become an obsession. It reminds us of the urgent need to discipline our instincts and to create a moral framework for their appropriate expression. Unbridled sex is a Pandora's box unleashing powerful and destructive forces.

Secondly, it reminds us that sexuality can masquerade as spirituality. That is why many pagan religions (including those encountered by the ancient Israelites in Canaan and by the Christians in Corinth) featured cult prostitution. Intercourse with the priest (or priestess) was a means of achieving union with the god.

That should caution us against allowing sex to become an idol. It also challenges our spirituality. Our desire for God is rarely so intense as our desire for a partner. And that is a sad mark of the Fall, for our partners are mortal and temporary, but God is eternal and permanent.

Place in Bible:
Comes after Ecclesiastes as the last of the wisdom and poetry books, and before Isaiah and the major prophets in the Old Testament

FAST facts

Author: Usually considered to be Solomon because of numerous references to him, but no external proof has been found.

Date: Mid-tenth century BC if written by Solomon; otherwise unknown.

Identity of the 'Beloved': The woman has been variously identified as the Queen of Sheba and, more probably, the daughter of an Egyptian Pharaoh (cf. 1 Kings 9:16,24). However, this remains conjecture; and remember, Solomon had 300 wives and 700 concubines!

Use of the book: In later Judaism, the Song of Songs was traditionally read at Passover time, possibly to present a contrast of tender love with the horrors of the deaths and traumas involved in Israel's flight from Egypt.

Rapid growth despite lack of follow-up

Paul's letters to the Thessalonians

- Rejoice at the church members' growth
- Give practical advice on Christian living
- Encourage Christians to work responsibly in the world
- Deal with misunderstandings about the return of Christ
- Defend Paul's own conduct and motives

Mass evangelists who jet into a city, conduct a campaign, and jet out again, are often accused of leaving their 'converts' high and dry, with no on-going support.

Paul, on his visit to Thessalonica, may not have intended to do this but in the end had little option. He was there for just three weeks before opposition forced him to make a hasty exit.

His new converts had no trained ministers to teach and support them. They had no New Testament to learn from, and no Christian books to read. They had no established church traditions to latch onto. They didn't even have a telephone over which to get quick advice from the apostle.

Yet they not only survived, but grew spiritually in double quick time. They became examples for others to follow. The letters to the Thessalonians provide today's Christians with important encouragement: When God begins to work in someone's life, he is able to continue it even if no human support is available.

That does not excuse any lack of pastoral follow-up. Paul was anxious to provide it: the letters are one means he used; visits from his associate Timothy were another.

Despite their growth in numbers and vitality, like any other fledgling church they had their problems. Not surprisingly, they had to endure on-going opposition which raised doubts about Paul and his motives in some minds.

Others, captivated by the thought that Christ had promised to return, assumed that he was coming soon and packed in their jobs to wait for him. They present us with one of the first examples of the trend repeated later by 'millennium cults'. Beliefs about Christ's return often excite as much passion now as they did then.

Thessalonians provides some simple guidelines for today. Unfortunately, because they are simple and incomplete, they have been the source of as much speculation in the centuries since Paul wrote them as was the apostle's original verbal teaching to the church. What follows seeks to return to the original simplicity.

Note: references are abbreviated thus:
I.2:20 = 1 Thessalonians, chapter two, verse twenty
II.3:6 = 2 Thessalonians, chapter three, verse six, and so on

1 THESSALONIANS

1:1-10	Thanks for their response
2:1-16	The Apostle's example of ministry
2:17-3:13	Paul's concern for news
4:1-12	How to live for God
4:13-5:11	The second coming of Jesus
5:12-28	How to keep going

2 THESSALONIANS

1:1-12	Keep going – Jesus is coming
2:1-12	Beware the lawless person
2:13-3:5	Keep the faith
3:6-18	Work hard

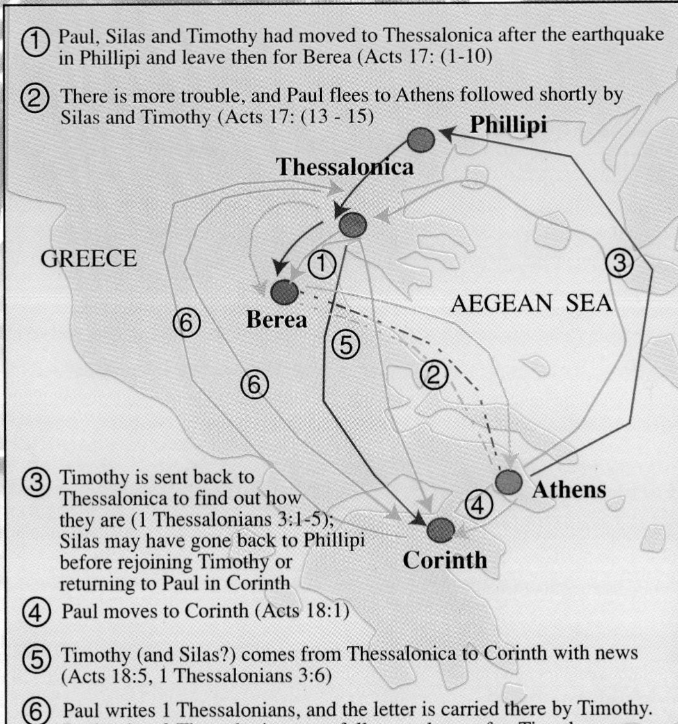
① Paul, Silas and Timothy had moved to Thessalonica after the earthquake in Phillipi and leave then for Berea (Acts 17: (1-10)
② There is more trouble, and Paul flees to Athens followed shortly by Silas and Timothy (Acts 17: (13 - 15)
Phillipi
Thessalonica
GREECE
Berea
AEGEAN SEA
Athens
Corinth
③ Timothy is sent back to Thessalonica to find out how they are (1 Thessalonians 3:1-5); Silas may have gone back to Phillipi before rejoining Timothy or returning to Paul in Corinth
④ Paul moves to Corinth (Acts 18:1)
⑤ Timothy (and Silas?) comes from Thessalonica to Corinth with news (Acts 18:5, 1 Thessalonians 3:6)
⑥ Paul writes 1 Thessalonians, and the letter is carried there by Timothy. Paul writes 2 Thessalonians as a follow-up letter after Timothy returns with more news.

Paul's travels to Thessalonica.

Paul and his various companions travelled frequently to Thessalonica. This map will guide you through their several journeys.

'I couldn't stand it any longer!'

1 Thessalonians 1:2f; 2:17–3:13
2 Thessalonians 1:3f, 11f; 2:13-17

Paul was a man of intense emotional passion who had a deep personal care for other people. His prayers and his longings set a high standard of pastoral care and give a powerful example of what 'fellowship' should mean.

Like a proud parent, he cannot stop talking and boasting about the Christians in Thessalonica. They are his 'glory and joy' (I.2:20), and an example all should follow. But neither can he stop worrying about them! (I.3:1).

As he boasts and frets, so he also prays. He punctuates his letters with prayer. He thanks God always for them (I.1:2; II.1:3; 2:13). He blesses them with longings for more growth (I.3:12f; 5:23f; II.2:16f) and intercedes that they may persevere (II.1:11f).

Good mentor that he is, he also encourages them to greater things. He commends them for imitating his conduct and becoming an example to others (I.1:6-8), and their love for one another (II.1:3).

Finally, he shows that fellowship is two-way. He asks them to pray for him (I.5:25; II.3:1-5). Paul is not a 'Big Brother' checking up on them; he is just their brother, and they are partners with him in the gospel. He treats them as adult friends and leaves yet another example for leaders to follow.

Share the gospel

1 Thessalonians 1:1-10

Becoming a Christian for Paul's first readers was much more than affirming a formula.

- They welcomed the message with joy (1:6b)
- They turned from their old way of living (1:9)
- They modelled themselves on the apostles (1:6a)
- They took the message to others (1:7f).

Thessalonians reminds present-day readers that evangelism is less dependent on specific activities or even on gifted individuals as on the living witness of God's people corporately.

Don't listen to critics before checking facts

1 Thessalonians 2:1-6; 5:12f

A concerted smear campaign was launched against the absent apostle Paul in Thessalonica. It aimed to undermine his credibility and to unsettle the new Christians. Paul's response provides a template for dealing with criticism.

The critics, who were probably the same people who had hounded him out of town, alleged that his visit was a failure (2:1). This may have been because it had resulted in a relatively small response, or more likely because he was accused of having conned the believers.

The accusers said that he had got his facts wrong, and that the church's beliefs were therefore mistaken. They suggested that he was like any pagan preacher peddling a form of cult prostitution (which is what 'impure motives' implies, 2:3).

They also condemned his methods as trickery, using the word normally associated with a fisherman luring his catch with a bait. They alleged that Paul was just out for his own profit.

Paul denied the charges by appealing to the evidence of his visit which the readers could still remember. The apostle's endurance of opposition was enough to show them he was genuine; no trickster would put his life on the line (2:2).

His preaching had been straight and neither flattering nor profit-seeking, he said (2:4). In fact, he and his colleagues had taken jobs in order to earn a living during their stay (2:6-9). As for their sexual conduct, there had been no question of even an indiscretion, let alone an affair. They had exemplary lives (2:10-12).

Persecution was a hazard of being a Christian, he said, pointing to the universal experience of it; preachers and church members were all in the same boat (2:13-16). He also reminded his readers that leaders are to be respected (5:12f).

Paul's message is twofold. The first is implicit, for leaders: keep everything above board and do nothing which can be misconstrued. The second is for church members: check critics' accusations against the facts, and beware of the spin they put on the facts.

May [the Lord] strengthen your hearts so that you will be blameless and holy . . .

1 Thessalonians 3:13

No work, no food

1 Thessalonians 4:11f; 5:14;
2 Thessalonians 3:6-15

Some church members had packed in their jobs. Probably most expected Jesus to return at any minute and they wanted to be ready. Perhaps some saw the close fellowship of the church as an opportunity to take it easy and sponge off others.

That was adding to the pressures on the church, fuelling resentment, and was just plain wrong.

Paul appeals to his own example to shame the lazy-bones. He had worked hard and sponged off no one. In fact, he said, 'Anyone who will not work shall not eat' (II.3:10). In effect, such people should be excommunicated, he said.

This does not of course say anything about people who are unemployed or on inadequate wages. Paul's teaching is in the context of people who have skills and refuse, rather than are unable, to use them.

The first Christians had no doubt that the poor and unemployed should be supported and helped. There is every biblical reason to do so today, whatever state support is available.

Fasten your faith belts and hope!

1 Thessalonians 4:13-5:11;
2 Thessalonians 1:5-10

There is usually a difference between a letter and an academic thesis even if both are written by the same person and deal with the same subject. The letter picks out highlights in the context of an on-going conversation; the thesis explores the theme systematically.

These books are letters, not a thesis. That needs to be remembered especially when Paul's teaching about the return of Christ is read.

Paul makes six points about Christ's return. They are all related, but he does not offer a complete 'Dictionary of the last times'. Rather, he is answering questions which have been put to him, or which he knows are a matter of debate within the church in Thessalonica:

- Has Jesus returned already? (No; II.2:1-3)
- Have those who had died already missed the party? (No; I.4:13-18)
- When will Jesus come back? (Don't know; I.5:1-3)
- What will happen to those who are persecuting us? (They'll get their just desserts, II.1:5-10.)

He does not stop at explaining things. He goes on to encourage his readers to apply them.

Those who mourn can look forward in hope to sharing in the kingdom with their loved ones (I.4:18). The uncertain timing of Jesus' return leaves no room for complacency. Christians are to be holy people all the time (I.4:4-11).

In other words, Paul's teaching on the second coming is not primarily for the mind but for the heart. This life [illegible] nasty, brutish and short, but God's world needs God's people to demonstrate hope where there is despair, faithfulness where there is deceit, and goodness where there is evil.

Today, our culture sees little, if any, hope beyond this life. Hence all our hopes and dreams, expectations and ambitions are focused on this life and their fulfilment seen in terms of measurable wealth and well-being, status and success. Christians [illegible] easily sucked into this way of thinking and thus lose sight of God's great eternal purposes. To remember heaven is to forget the stress of an acquisitive world.

For today

- Nurture new Christians – give them time
- Let your life speak as loud as your words
- Don't listen to rumours – check the facts
- Don't get hung up on details about Christ's return
- Live as if Christ is coming today – he might!
- Live responsibly as a good witness
- Care for each other in practical, loving ways

HARD Question

Did Paul change his mind about Jesus' return in his lifetime?

Thessalonians, two of Paul's earliest letters, seem to imply that Jesus would return soon – within most people's lifetimes. Paul writes of 'we who are still alive' at Christ's coming (I.4:15).

However, a decade later in his letter to the Philippians, Paul's hope lay much more in his imminent death. He wrote of his desire to 'depart and be with Christ' and of pressing on for the prize of his heavenly calling (Philippians 1:23; 3:14).

But in the same letter he did also write of eagerly awaiting the Saviour who would come from heaven and transform Christians' bodies and lives to be like Jesus (Philippians 3:20f).

So the answer would seem to be 'yes and no'. Paul's comments to the Thessalonians were in answer to their queries, and so as he dealt with them i was natural for Paul to associate with the hope that Jesus was coming soon. After all, he did believe that it could happen at any time.

But ten years is a long time in Christian ministry, especially when it is characterised by the range of experiences Paul had. He was more than once close to death. It would be surprising if his teaching did not mellow with time.

To mellow in one's beliefs is not the same as to deny what has been believed before. It is to see one's earlier beliefs in a broader context. The fact that Pau holds both the hope of Christ's return and the hope of dying to be with Chris together in Philippians suggests that is exactly what happened.

Throughout his life he seems to have lived as if every minute was his last. He never lost sight of the eternal dimension within which this earthly life fits. That is the practical thrust of the New Testament teaching abou Christ's return. By remaining aware o the eternal context, we can live more loosely to the concerns of this world.

FAST facts

Author: Paul the Apostle. His authorship has been questioned but is generally accepted. More questions have been raised over the second letter because of differences of phrasing and emphasis, but these can be explained by the different circumstances he was addressing.

Co-authors: Silas, a long-standing companion of Paul's and Timothy (see page 403) .

Place of writing: Corinth (see map with the order of events on page 395).

Date of writing: AD 51/52; about six months separates the two letters. The date can be fixed with some accuracy because Paul was in Corinth when Gallio was proconsul of Achaia (Acts 18:12). An inscription in Delphi can date this at 52/53, and proconsuls only held office for a year. Paul was in Corinth for approximately 18 months.

Reasons for writing: News has reached Paul about questions and wrong emphases in this young church, which he seeks to correct. He also wants to 'follow up' the new converts who he had to leave suddenly.

Readers: Christians in Thessalonica. They are from both Jewish and Gentile (non-Jewish) backgrounds, and there may well have been more non-Jews than Jews (I.1:9 and Acts 17:4).

CROSS CHECK

Paul's life, a summary: p 34-5, 40
Principles of biblical interpretation: pp 9-10
Return of Christ: p 364
Work in the Bible: p 65

Guidelines for Christian living

1 Thessalonians 4:1-10; 5:14-24

This is a brief manual for Christian living. It is incomplete because Paul has already given it verbally (4:1f) and here he is stressing only what the Thessalonians need to give further attention to. Which is what most people need to give attention to.

On the subject of personal conduct he warns against unbridled lust and encourages marital faithfulness (4:3-8). The former was common and the latter rare in his first readers' society.

Perhaps some church members were still struggling and failing. Being different is not easy and new habits take time to learn. There is none of the righteous indignation here which he unleashes against the Corinthians. Instead, he stresses the social dimension of immorality. It destroys relationships within the church.

As history repeats itself and people come to Christ from non-Christian lifestyles, his firm but non-judgmental approach sets a pastorally sensitive example.

Social conduct seems to be his chief concern. Brotherly love exists and he encourages it further (4:9f). He describes what it looks like in 5:14f: patient, kind, supportive and encouraging.

As for spiritual conduct, Christ, not circumstance, is to dominate Christians' thoughts and feelings (5:16-18). The Thessalonians faced potentially depressing battles with their opponents, yet even then they were to rejoice and give thanks. Christ is bigger than our problems.

They are also encouraged to keep the charismatic balance. The gifts of the Spirit are not to be despised, but neither are they to be received and exercised uncritically (5:19f).

HARD Question

Who is the 'man of lawlessness'?

2 Thessalonians 2:1-12

This passage is like a cryptic crossword clue, made impossible to solve by the fact that no one knows how many letters the answer has!

Paul had already spoken about this to the Thessalonians (v 5) and therefore we are listening in to only part of a conversation and we do not know what was said before.

Reports of Jesus having already come again are false (vv 2,3). It will be obvious when he does (1:10; cf. I.4:16). Before then, Paul anticipates the arrival of 'the man of lawlessness' who is totally opposed to, and claims to be, God (v 4). He will operate under the auspices and with the deceptive power of Satan (vv 9-11). However, he will only be revealed at an unspecified 'rebellion' (vv 3,6,8). He is currently restrained by an unidentified power (vv 6,7) and is doomed to destruction by Jesus (vv 3,8).

Paul adds that the secret power of lawlessness is already at work (v 7). The Greek word for 'secret' implies something which cannot be understood by humankind. Therefore Paul is not writing in a code to which his readers had a key, but about broad principles personified in one cruel leader.

The restraining power is probably the principle of law and order (as in Romans 13:1-7), which in Paul's day was upheld by the Roman Empire, and in varying degrees by governments ever since.

In our own world, we can see the forces of lawlessness like rough waves beating against a sea wall. It is not hard to imagine that one day the wall will crumble, and the tide of lawlessness sweep away the people sheltered behind it.

That seems to be Paul's plain meaning. Meanwhile, the waves sometimes splash over the wall. Paul therefore calls his readers to be vigilant in living and faithful in witness.

Manuals for troubleshooters

The Pastoral Letters:
- Describe the qualities required for church leaders and officers
- Tell apostolic delegates how to deal with certain problems
- Warn against false teachers who are in it for money and status
- Stress the reliability of God and the Scriptures he inspired

If you read only Acts, you might think that the early church was one big happy family (once they had sorted out a bit of racial tension, Acts 6:1-8; 15:1-6). Generous sharing, daily praying, hundreds being converted, miracles of healing and deliverance, with only the odd arrest to hinder the flow of the Spirit at revival level.

Well, it wasn't like that all the time; Acts is like a newspaper, it focuses on 'news': the unusual rather than the normal. And it certainly didn't last. The sensual excesses of Corinth (Paul's letters to them spare no blushes) highlighted the fact that the church was made up of human beings who, by biblical definition, are prone to more errors than a crashing computer.

And so by the mid 60s the first generation of Christians was being superseded by the next, and familiar problems were sprouting everywhere like weeds after a shower. The three 'pastoral letters' (two to Timothy and one to Titus) are manuals for the pair of troubleshooters to use as they sort out problems in Ephesus (Timothy) and Crete (Titus).

In laying down the law, Paul has given us a timeless set of guidelines for church leadership. He expects leaders to have exemplary lives and orthodox beliefs; and he expects his own colleagues to labour tirelessly and sacrificially. Along the way he gives some valuable truths memorably expressed about God and the Scriptures.

They apply especially to anyone in Christian leadership today. But they also give church members an insight into what to pray and look for, as they call people to various responsibilities (not just the pastorate). In church life, manual workers must have similar spiritual qualifications to managers.

1 TIMOTHY

1 Instructions about false teachers; Paul's testimony to God's love
2 How worship is to be conducted
3 Qualifications for church leaders
4 Take a positive stand for truth and against falsehood
5 How to treat the needy, ministers and slaves
6 How to handle money; final instructions

Don't get sidetracked

1 Timothy 1,4,6

The human mind has a huge capacity for learning and remembering. Most of us use only a fraction of it, yet the world is an infinite source of information. However, what can be known is far greater than anyone can take in.

Theology – the knowledge of God revealed through the Scriptures, interpreted by successive generations of believers and applied to our lives by the Spirit – is no exception to the rule. There is always more to discover and more than one mind can take in.

Paul encouraged his readers to learn the Scriptures and the 'sound – that is healthy, right-minded doctrine

Set an example for the believers in speech, in life, in love, in faith and in purity.

1 Timothy 4:12

–(cf. 1 Timothy 4:6, 5:7, 6:3; 2 Timothy 3:14) but warns against fruitless speculation which leads us away from the gospel.

The false teachers in Ephesus had done just that. Some commentators have associated them with later heresies and thus questioned Paul's authorship. But there are hints of similar problems elsewhere (Colossae, for example). The details are vague which makes them widely applicable:

- Excessive interest in legends (1:4) about biblical or other 'saints'
- Fascination by genealogies (1:4), for theological reasons (as Mormons today) or personal status (Jews tracing their descent from Abraham)
- Delight in controversies (1:4,6); arguing for the fun or kudos of it rather than from a desire to grow in faith
- Unhealthy interest in the occult (4:1-2); Christians have caused more harm by witch hunts than was caused by the original unapproved practices
- Insistence on a legalistic lifestyle regarded as 'super-spiritual' (4:3).

The net effect is 'envy, strife, malicious talk, evil suspicions and constant friction' (6:4,5). All this destroys fellowship. We are to be wise and not do the devil's work.

Broaden your prayers

1 Timothy 2

Intercessory prayer is probably more difficult than any other sort of prayer. In church services, if it is included at all, it tends to focus on known needs of members or the local community.

Paul sets a wide agenda for prayer and worship. Jesus is the sustainer of all things (Colossians 1:17) and all society is his concern. He wants the world to be ordered according to his righteous laws and for us to worship him. So, says Paul, if they are God's concern, they should be ours also.

Which makes the need for prayer diaries greater than ever. We can list the many groups and people within Paul's categories, and give them regular prayer time. Prayer is important for them (in ways we shall never know) and also for us to keep sight of God's vision for the world.

The modest dress prescribed here is probably to prevent the church from becoming a dating agency. We meet to worship, not to attract a mate. If relationships happen, that is a by product of faith, not a purpose of it. Motives should be pure if worship is to be blessed.

The silence of women has been given several interpretations, from a blanket ban on any female input to a local restraint because wordy women dominated the fellowship with their ignorance. (In Ephesus, the female cult of Artemis (Diana) provided a pool of domineering women.) That is a restraint which Paul might wish to lay before some men today!

Means testing for benefits

1 Timothy 5

Giving to charity or to individuals is not always as easy as Jesus' command to give to whoever asks (Matthew 5:42). We naturally feel we should be discriminating, yet may also feel guilty when we are. Paul allows discrimination; in fact, he seems almost harsh.

He throws responsibility back onto the family first. The church should not be seen as a soft touch for those who can't be bothered to care for their own. However, he is writing in a society where the family could be easily contacted and he is probably thinking of church families anyway.

Then he considers the character and lifestyle of the applicant. Some of what he says is contentious today although the situation in Ephesus where many women traded off religion (the cult of Artemis) probably demanded it. His position sug-gests that we should be discerning, indeed discriminating, in our giving. But that is not an excuse for meanness.

Location:
Timothy is in Ephesus
Date:
c. AD 65
Place in Bible:
After 1 and 2 Thessalonians, before 2 Timothy and Titus in the New Testament
Parallel books:
2 Timothy and Titus

HARD Question

Is Paul's style of ministry still relevant?

The structures of church government have evolved over the centuries. New churches which want to 'return' to biblical patterns soon find the need to restructure as they grow. This is right; the New Testament does not lay down strict patterns for church order, only general principles and God does guide us as we seek to apply them in contemporary situations.

By the mid 60s the order had developed which Paul describes here. A group of 'elders' or 'overseers' (literally 'bishops' in Greek, but also sometimes called 'presbyters' as in 4:14, the two terms seemingly being interchangeable) guided the affairs of the church and were responsible for pastoral oversight and teaching.

Deacons, who seem to date back to Acts 6, continued as organisational managers. Their spiritual qualifications, similar to those for elders, indicate that any 'ministry' like coffee-making or cleaning is as 'spiritual' as counselling; all God's work must be done by godly people in God's way.

Although they were to be paid an honorarium (the probable meaning of 5:17) there is no indication that elders were 'full time' – but they may have been – or that they alone could preside at the communion service.

Today we should apply the broad principles. A flexible structure is needed which may change as the Spirit leads. The early church also seems to have had a tiered structure so that local leaders were accountable to and supervised by others – including Paul's apostolic delegates Timothy and Titus – which commonsense says is valuable But what is most important is that the task of preaching and teaching, disciplining and discipling, caring and supporting and maintaining edifying order, actually be well done, everywhere.

Money bags don't give change

1 Timothy 6

Money has a unique power to enslave people, like the ring in Tolkein's *Lord of the Rings* which the miserable Gollum called 'my precious'. Dickens' Ebenezer Scrooge stayed up all Christmas Eve counting it. Paul's often misquoted statement in verse 10 (the word 'love' is often omitted and Paul says *a* root and not *the* root) complements Jesus' teaching in Matthew 6:24 that we cannot serve God and 'Mammon'.

The French theologian Jacques Ellul comments that 'Jesus gives this term [Mammon] a force and precision which it did not have in its milieu. This personification of money . . . reveals something exceptional about money, for Jesus did not usually use deifications and personifications.'

Money is like a colourless, odourless poison which contaminates us without our knowledge. Take away a Christian's money, and you'll soon know whether their faith is real. The biblical basis for handling money is not 'enough' (that is, moderation), but contentment with whatever we have (vv 6-8), something Paul learned through hard experience (Philippians 4:11-13).

Wealth does not change us for the better; it can change us for the worse (v 9). True wealth, Paul reminds us, is to be found in our worship of God and service of others (vv 17,18). Investors in people get better returns than investors in ISAs (v 19).

How to mentor someone different

Timothy is a good example of how personality alone does not define a leader. He did not fit the stereotype and was very unlike Paul. He was timid rather than assertive (2 Timothy 1:6,7; cf. 1 Corinthians 16:10,11 where Paul pre-empts potential rejection of his envoy). He was also young (I Timothy .4:12) and not in the best of health (I Timothy 5:23).

Born in Lystra (Turkey), the son of a mixed Jewish–Gentile marriage (Acts 16:1; 2 Timothy 1:15) Timothy was converted under Paul's ministry (1 Corinthians 4:17; 'my son') and saw the persecution of Paul (2 Timothy 3:11).

Paul recognised his spiritual gifts and took him under his wing, circumcising him in order not to offend the Jews (Acts 16:3). Timothy's call to ministry was confirmed by the church and through prophetic words (I Timothy 4:14; 2 Timothy 1:6).

He accompanied Paul and Silas on the second missionary journey (Acts 16:3) and was present in Corinth (2 Corinthians 1:19) to which he was dispatched (in vain) to deal with their problems. He went with Paul to Jerusalem (Acts 20:4,5) and became apostolic delegate to Ephesus. According to Hebrews 13:23, he was later imprisoned, but we do not know where.

Paul appointed Timothy as his helper to learn on the job. In his letters, Paul is warmly encouraging. Timothy needs his forth-right instructions, but he might buckle if they were given insensitively. Mentors in the church should give others opportunity to learn alongside them, graciously give them responsibility, and remain supportive as their ministry develops.

2 TIMOTHY

1	**Don't be ashamed of Christ even when under pressure**
2	**Remember Jesus, and don't get caught up in quarrels**
3	**Don't be surprised by false teachers, and hold to what you know**
4	**Keep serving even when you don't feel like it; personal instructions**

Location:
Timothy is still in Ephesus; Paul is probably in Rome

Date:
Probably c. AD 67

Place in Bible:
After the letters to Thessalonians and 1 Timothy, before Titus, Philemon and Hebrews in the New Testament

Parallel books:
1 Timothy, Titus

FAST facts

Date and circumstances: The brief biographical notes in 1Timothy and Titus show that Paul was at that time free, but not when he wrote 2 Timothy. He had been in Ephesus (1 Timothy 1:3) and Crete (Titus 1:5) and planned to be in Nicopolis (western Greece, Titus 3:12). When he wrote 2 Timothy he had been in Troas (4:13), Corinth and Miletus (4:20), and now appears to be in prison on trial for his life (1:8; 4:6). This does not fit into the narrative of Acts, which ends about AD 63.
It is assumed that after his house arrest and preliminary trial in Rome (Acts 28:30) he was released and took a fourth journey to the east (not to Spain as he had once planned: see Romans 15:24,28). The date therefore would be c. AD 65 for 1 Timothy and Titus, and c. AD 67 for Titus; Paul was martyred c. AD 67 in Rome.

Keep your head in all situations, endure hardship, do the work of an evangelist, discharge all the duties of your ministry.

2 Timothy 4:5

CROSS CHECK

Women in ministr: p 73
Attitudes to money: p 176

For today

- Focus on the whole of God's truth
- Train others to do your job in the church
- Be content with what you have
- Expect to endure as well as enjoy your Christian life

Record breaker!

2 Timothy 2

Some people will do anything to get in the *Guinness Book of Records*. It just has to be longer, faster, higher, heavier, bigger, more than the last achievement. But we know that to win you have to train, and to train you have to endure. The tension generated by watching is enough for most of us. Endurance is for fanatics.

And certainly not for Christians. Paul would never have been invited onto the platforms of some of today's churches and conventions offering sustained excitement and instant fixes, as the Holy Spirit leads us down the fast lane, headlights blazing. But Bible Christianity is not really like that.

Close to the end of his life and writing from deep personal experience, Paul is offering the younger man hardship and telling him to endure. Paul did write of peace and joy elsewhere, but they were by-products of the endurance test called living faithfully for God.

He gives six illustrations to drive the point home:

- Soldiers on duty are disciplined and forgo pleasures (v 4)
- Athletes in the games train and compete according to strict rules (v 5)
- Farmers plough in toil and reap in sweat (v 6)
- Workers who don't fine-tune their skills get sacked (v 15)
- If you want wholesome food you don't eat from the dog's dish (v 20)
- Servants serve others before they please themselves (vv 24-26).

Contemporary spirituality sometimes owes more to contemporary superficiality than to the contemplation of Scripture. Biblical biographies all include endurance for there is no gain without pain. The pain stops in heaven; 'if we endure we will also reign with him'. That endurance record will never be broken.

Some looks can kill

2 Timothy 3

In 1994 a mother dived into a deep tidal pool in France to save her six-year-old daughter. Sightseers just stared. When someone eventually called the emergency services a helicopter managed to save the child, but not the mother. A tourist videotaped it all and sent it to the local TV station.

That puts a fresh angle on the social violence which Paul addresses in verses 1-9. It isn't simply about guns and knives in schools and on streets. It's about hearts and minds and how we treat people every day. It's about 'lovers of themselves', 'having a form of godliness' – being decent enough people – 'but denying its power' to make a difference in their lives.

In *The Selfish Gene*, written from a rampantly anti-Christian standpoint, Richard Dawkins claims that 'we're survival machines – robots blindly programmed to preserve the selfish molecules known as genes'. He's right in his observation of behaviour, although wrong in his explanation of why we're so selfish. It's a mark of our fallenness, and Christ came to change it.

But in addressing this state of affairs, Paul does not suggest an evangelistic crusade or social education programme; he tells us to look at ourselves in the mirror of Scripture (vv 14-16). Christians are as prone to selfishness as anyone. You don't only do violence to someone when you push them into a pool, but also while you're looking on through your (or someone else's) videocam as they drown. Scripture will show us what is wrong with us and how in practical terms we are to be put right.

Wild passions must be tamed

For one period in human history, about the time of the early kings of Israel, Crete was to the Mediterranean what Britain was once to the world. Minoan civilisation, pottery and customs spread widely; Cretans were great traders and travellers. For a small island, it had great influence.

But by the end of the Old Testament era it was divided into a community of city-states always at each other's throats, until the Romans imposed their law and order in 67 BC. Crete's fierce warriors were sought as mercenaries; they specialised in guerrilla tactics learned in their mountainous terrain.

Paul's assessment of the Cretan church reflects their island mentality: insular and self-assured on the one hand, highly expansive on the other. The quote from Epimenides (1:12) was accepted by the entire empire. No one liked the Cretans; there was more honour among the Mafia.

Titus had an uphill task. He had to re-educate church members into a whole new way of thinking and behaving. Sure, the Holy Spirit would begin to change them, but even he relies on the active co-operation of a person's will. And the will won't do what the heart can't see.

TITUS

1 Make sure church leaders are behaving properly
2 Teach everyone to be self-controlled and godly
3 Stress the kindness and love of God

On the positive side, if Titus could get them to harness their national passion and confidence into speaking truthfully, giving sacrificially and caring compassionately, he would have one powerful task force for the gospel. Churches will always reflect their local communities; Christian faith does not eradicate local culture and characteristics. But it should iron out some of the creases.

The letter to Titus reminds us that any church plant or new Christian needs re-educating without crushing what is good in the local culture. Some churches have resurrected the early Christian practice of a 'catechumenate', an apprenticeship course for new Christians similar to but more rigorous than today's 'basics' courses.

Place in Bible:

The third of the 'pastoral letters' after 1 and 2 Timothy, before Philemon and Hebrews in the New Testament

Author: Paul, to Titus, a Gentile like Timothy. Unlike Timothy he was not compelled to be circumcised before becoming an apostolic delegate (Galatians 2:1-3). Titus was evidently more robust than Timothy and an envoy from Paul to Corinth (see 2 Corinthians 7:6,7,13-15; 8:6,16-21; 12:18). Tradition suggests he became bishop of Crete after Paul's death, and that he was also the brother of Luke (which may explain why he is not mentioned in Acts despite his close association with Paul).

Date and circumstances: The letter to Titus is considered to have been written about the same time as 1 Timothy but before 2 Timothy. It is assumed that Paul made a fourth journey east after his house arrest in Rome. He hopes to meet Titus in Nicopolis (3:12) so may be writing from Corinth on his way there, about AD 65.

When life is grey, God adds colour

The Prophecy of Zechariah

- Has eight visions to encourage the rebuilding of the temple
- Has other visions looking further into the future when God's rule is further revealed
- Is quoted in the New Testament for 'Palm Sunday' and Judas' betrayal

Jerusalem, 15 February 519 BC: You are one of thousands who returned from Babylon about seventeen years ago, with high hopes of starting a new life. You began to rebuild the temple which Nebuchadnezzar had destroyed in 587.

But it's hard being a settler. The local inhabitants have done their best to hinder your progress; you are not welcome, a stranger in your homeland. Life's a plod. It's all monochrome, grey like a winter's day.

Whenever we feel like that, the first thing to suffer is the church. We slip into maintenance mode. We do the essentials to keep the system going, but mission is out of the question. Expansion, development, gets shelved.

And in the time-kept West, where neon signs shout and colour magazines create the false assumption that life is all colourful *pzazz*, the honest truth is that life's still a plod, and the colour is only small patches on a grey backdrop.

Theologian James Houston writes that many people have 'a past blocked by guilt, a future repressed by anxiety . . . so boredom becomes the emotional experience of the present'.

And that's what the former exiles feel in Jerusalem, only instead of modern boredom with plenty, they have ancient drudgery with little. But believers potentially have a different perspective. Houston continues, 'For the Christian, release from past guilt is forgiveness, while future hope and therefore freedom from anxiety make possible the enjoyment of the "now".'

ZECHARIAH

1,2	Visions foretelling the restoration of Jerusalem
3	Vision of Joshua the high priest being commissioned
4	Zerubbabel and Joshua confirmed as leaders who will help restore Jerusalem
5	Visions showing that the evil of Babylon will be defeated
6	Vision of God's Spirit giving Judah rest from oppressors
7	God requires justice, not just fasts and prayers
8	Promise of future glory for Jerusalem
9	Prophecy of the coming king 'riding on a donkey'
10	Prophecy of the restoration of Judah
11	Vision of bad shepherds
12	Jerusalem will stand when its enemies fall
13	Unworthy leaders will be struck down
14	Vision of the last days when God comes to reign

Jerusalem, 16 February 519 BC: Enter Zechariah. Last night he had a series of visions (chs 1-8). Now the prophet tells us that God is present, there is hope, and we must build the temple we abandoned so long ago. Now is the day of salvation. And the people did. Within three years the temple was finished.

Martin Luther called this book 'the quintessence of the prophets', because it distils so much of Old Testament teaching. It tells us that God's world is not meant to be seen in monochrome, but only God himself can provide the

'Not by might nor by power, but by my Spirit,' says the LORD Almighty.

Zechariah 4:6

colour it needs. Developing, growing, expanding are all part of normal church life. So look at it through Zechariah's prism, and see your church life painted in God's colours.

God groans with his people's suffering

Zechariah 1

The groans of God's oppressed people are heard frequently in the Bible, although only here is the emotion ascribed to an angel (v 12). It is a graphic reminder that all heaven identifies with their suffering.

The context is unusual. Judah is not crushed by an enemy (although occupied by Persia) but by circumstance (see introduction). The peace of the Near Eastern world means that lowly Judah (the myrtle) is taxed by Persia but is of no interest, military or otherwise to nations which might resource the rebuilding in return for co-operation.

Myrtle emits its sweet fragrance only when bruised. The paradox of Scripture is that God's power is often seen only when his people are helpless. We see answers to prayer when we know we have no strength of our own, and our groaning is heartfelt.

Small things need greater protection

Zechariah 2-4

Fire is the most impenetrable barrier known. Walls can be broken down, water can be crossed, but fire stops everything. God's chariots of fire protected Elisha (2 Kings 6:17). His protection is absolute; nothing can penetrate his 'wall of fire' (2:5).

God's ultimate purpose at all times is the renewal of his people's worship. Nothing can stop that. Life is a voyage; God's concern is to get us to port and not always to flatten the waves. However, while he steers we are safe.

But Judah is such a small craft and the beginnings of the temple seem so insignificant. How can she survive such an epic journey? Here is the Bible's equivalent of the Chinese proverb that the longest journey begins with a single step. The 'day of small things' is not to be despised (4:10); God's Spirit is greater than human ingenuity (4:6). Our weakness is his opportunity.

So long, that is, as we are committed wholly to his way (3:6,7). Joshua, snatched from the fires of exile (3:2), must be spiritually renewed (the symbolism of the fresh clothes, 3:3-5). As high priest, he represents the entire people. Don't expect God to bless even the small things you have in hand unless you are first clothed in his righteousness and truth.

For today

- Look for God in daily life and discover his colour among the greys
- Don't look down on small beginnings but build on them
- Pray for all leaders, and don't look for personal gain from your responsibilities

God's judgments are considered

Zechariah 5-8

The scroll of chapter 5 shows that God's judgments are written in advance and are not spur-of-the-moment tantrums And they are recorded in advance for all to read and perhaps to avoid, if they bother to listen. If you ever wondered why there are so many threats in the Old Testament, this is the reason: if you read the scroll and respond, then they will not happen.

Although evangelism should have a positive message, this provides one incentive for doing it: the world is under God's threat of destruction, and we are responsible to work with him to help others escape ruin.

Evil will be banished eventually (the basket of chapter 5 is taken to Babylon, the place of destruction). But human responsibility remains in the equation. God rescues people for them to live by his rules (8:14-17). Look back on his rescues in your life, and seek to be faithful in all your ways now. His blessing in your life depends on it.

Where am I?

Location:
Jerusalem
Date:
519-518 BC (chs 1-8); the rest later
Place in Bible:
One of the twelve minor prophets in the Old Testament, before Malachi and after Haggai
Parallel books:
Zechariah was a colleague of Haggai; the events of Ezra 5,6 coincide with chapters 1-8

You just never know

Zechariah 9,11

Things sometimes turn out differently from what we expect. People in New Testament times regarded chapter 9 as messianic and so recalled this passage when Jesus rode into Jerusalem on the first 'Palm Sunday' (9:9; alluded to in Matthew 21:5; John 12:15).

But Jesus was not what they or Zechariah expected. And although chapter 11 seemed to be messianic also, no one foresaw that verse 13 would have its fulfilment in the dire work of Judas Iscariot (Matthew 26:14,15; 27:3-10).

There are many promises in the Bible, but we can never be certain exactly how any of them will be fulfilled. The prophets who predicted the coming of Christ and his kingdom were in the same boat with us at this point (1 Peter 1:10-12). Faith looks for God to be at work, as he has promised to be, but never tells him how or when to do his job.

Shepherds have a difficult job

Zechariah 10-13

Sheep are short-sighted and follow the crowd. To liken God's people to sheep sounds insulting to modern ears. But in rural Palestine it was appropriate and the biblical image focuses not on the sheep but the shepherd.

Shepherds represent both political and spiritual leaders. Bad shepherds scatter the flock (10:2,3) or even consume (profit from) them (11:15-17). The identity of the three shepherds (11:8) is not known and commentator Joyce Baldwin says at least 40 different interpretations have been offered, making this passage 'probably the most enigmatic in the whole Bible'.

Conor Cruse O'Brien, former Irish politician, once wrote that most rulers 'are narrow-minded, self-centred, mentally indolent, pompous, and pretentious creatures of the past. They've got enough for themselves, they cling to power, live in relative comfort and immense dignity, chiefly engaged in the defence of their own conceit while millions of humans are leading lives of want, limitation, humiliation and toil'.

By contrast, the good shepherd cares. Judah, however, given a final chance to follow him, rejects him (11:4-10); the good shepherd's narrow way is deemed too hard. When he is struck down, the sheep suffer (13:7-9; cf. John 10). No wonder we are told to pray for our leaders (1 Timothy 2:1-4); their task is riddled with temptation and trouble.

FAST facts

Author: Zechariah is named several times in chapters 1-8. The son of a priest, he probably returned to Jerusalem as a child in 536 BC. Chapters 9-14 contain no references to an author and are of a different style. Some conservative and most critical scholars consider this section to be, with Malachi, a collection of anonymous prophecies added to the end of the Old Testament. But Zechariah, blessed with typical prophetic foresight, could have writen this section later in his life, .

Date: Chapters 1-8 are dated specifically between February 519 and December 518. Chapters 9-14 are undated.

Structure and genre: The two sections (1-8,9-14) are carefully constructed literary units based on a 'chiasmus', in which the contents can be 'tabulated' in the form of an X (part 1 relates to part 4, and 2 to 3). The content and style of 9-14 are 'apocalyptic' (as in parts of Daniel, and most of Revelation) in which symbolism is employed to express ideas in broad terms rather than making exact detailed predictions and God's final triumph is the overall theme.

The meek shall inherit the city

When you stand back from the biblical narrative and see the progress from creation in Genesis to the new creation in Revelation, one thing stands out. It does not end as it began. The heaven of Revelation is not a revitalised Garden of Eden, but a city whose streets are paved with gold.

When human beings first went their own way and were excluded from God's presence in Eden, Cain, the son of Adam, built a city (Genesis 4:15-17). It was a walled enclosure for self-defence and self-sufficiency. It symbolised human attempts to live without God.

Jerusalem became the new symbol of God's presence among his people. David made it 'the city of God' and it housed the temple. The new Jerusalem of heaven illustrates God's gracious love. He takes what fallible people have attempted to create, and remoulds it to reflect his perfect character.

Nothing in the Bible suggests that God intended the rural habitat of Eden to be the only expression of human community. He called people to 'subdue the earth', that is, to make something of it. We are endowed with genuine creativity, with minds to explore and invent. With them, we have built cities.

Paul says in Colossians 1 that Christ the Creator is also the redeemer of all things. Nothing that we have attempted to create is entirely wasted, but is transformed by God. The impurity and imperfection is taken out, and we are left with the shining new creation; God fashioned it, but we contributed to it.

Zephaniah looks forward to the renewed Jerusalem. For him the vision would have begun as a physical, literal rebuilding of Zion, but his prophetic eye sees beyond that. The remnant of Israel did do wrong and 3:13 envisages a perfect end when people worship God truly.

The Christian is thrust by verses 9-20 into the scene of Revelation 7 and 21, where the meek truly inherit the new heavens and earth (cf. Matthew 5:5). Just now, they inhabit Cain's cities, bringing God's rule into the institutions and customs which exist, being salt and light in the dark streets. The renewal process has begun.

Zephaniah is not the last book of the Old Testament but by virtue of its name is the last book covered in this volume. Its reminder of renewal and its call to meekness (obedience to and trust in God) is an appropriate place to end. It sums up the message of all that has gone before.

ZEPHANIAH

1. **Judah will be destroyed for harbouring false religion**
2. **The nations will be judged on the 'Day of the Lord'**
3. **Jerusalem will be restored and renewed**

Location: Jerusalem

Date: Late 7th century BC

Place in Bible: The ninth of the twelve minor prophets, between Habakkuk and Haggai in the Old Testament

Parallel books: Jeremiah, Nahum

FAST facts

Author: Nothing is known of Zephaniah apart from what he says in 1:1. He was descended from the royal family and may possibly have been a priest or court prophet.

Date and background: After Israel (the ten northern tribes) were destroyed by Assyria in 722 BC, Judah (the two southern tribes) came under prophetic scrutiny because they too tolerated false religion and social injustice. There was reform under Hezekiah (c. 715-686) and Josiah (c. 640-609) brought in a fresh return of righteousness (cf. 2 Kings 22,23). Zephaniah probably worked after Josiah's reforms, which had not filtered through the whole land. Judah was attacked by Babylon in 605, and Jerusalem destroyed in 587.

Index